KT-152-898

SOCIAL DIVISIONS

Social Divisions

THIRD EDITION

Edited by

GEOFF PAYNE

Selection and editorial matter © Geoff Payne 2000, 2006 2013
Ch. 1 © Geoff Payne 2013; Ch. 2 © John Scott 2013; Ch. 3 © Pamela Abbott 2013; Ch. 4
© David Mason 2013; Ch. 5 © John A. Vincent and Iain Phillips 2013; Ch. 6 © Stevi Jackson
and Sue Scott 2013; Ch. 7 © Sue Scott and Stevi Jackson 2013; Ch. 8 © Mark Hyde and Rory
Shand 2013; Ch. 9 © Alan Aldridge 2013; Ch. 10 © David McCrone 2013; Ch. 11 © Philip
Stanworth 2013; Ch. 12 © Tim Strangleman 2013; Ch. 13 © Lucinda Platt 2013; Ch. 14 ©
Ruth Graham, Judy Payne, Geoff Payne and Matthew Bond 2013; Ch. 15 © Graham Crow and
Catherine Maclean 2013; Ch. 16 © Robert Holton 2015; Ch. 17 © Steph Lawler 2013; Ch. 18
© Geoff Payne 2013

All rights reserved. No reproduction, copy or transmission of this
publication may be made without written permission.

No portion of this publication may be reproduced, copied or transmitted
save with written permission or in accordance with the provisions of the
Copyright, Designs and Patents Act 1988, or under the terms of any licence
permitting limited copying issued by the Copyright Licensing Agency,
Saffron House, 6-10 Kirby Street, London EC1N 8TS.

Any person who does any unauthorised act in relation to this publication
may be liable to criminal prosecution and civil claims for damages.

The authors have asserted their rights to be identified
as the authors of this work in accordance with the Copyright, Designs
and Patents Act 1988.

First published 2013 by
PALGRAVE MACMILLAN

Palgrave Macmillan in the UK is an imprint of Macmillan Publishers Limited,
registered in England, company number 785998, of Houndmills, Basingstoke,
Hampshire RG21 6XS.

Palgrave Macmillan in the US is a division of St Martin's Press LLC,
175 Fifth Avenue, New York, NY 10010.

Palgrave Macmillan is the global academic imprint of the above companies
and has companies and representatives throughout the world.

Palgrave® and Macmillan® are registered trademarks in the United States,
the United Kingdom, Europe and other countries
ISBN 978-0-230-22821-4   ISBN 978-1-137-36816-4 (eBook)
DOI 10.1007/978-1-137-36816-4

This book is printed on paper suitable for recycling and made from fully
managed and sustained forest sources. Logging, pulping and manufacturing
processes are expected to conform to the environmental regulations of the
country of origin.

A catalogue record for this book is available from the British Library.

A catalog record for this book is available from the Library of Congress.

In memory of
Max Gluckman, Frank Jones and John Rex
who first interested me in social division
and social cohesion

Contents

List of Figures

List of Tables

Notes on the Contributors

Pamela Abbott is an Honorary Professor in the School of Social Sciences at the University of Aberdeen. Her research interests span health and gender. Most recently she has been developing a sociological perspective on quality of life. She carries out research in the EU, the Commonwealth of Independent States and East Africa. Her publications include *An Introduction to Sociology: Feminist Perspectives* (with Claire Wallace, Routledge, 2005).

Alan Aldridge, formerly Reader in the Sociology of Culture at the University of Nottingham, is the author of *Religion in the Contemporary World*, a third edition of which was published in 2013. Other books include *Surveying the Social World* (co-authored with Ken Levine, 2001), *Consumption* (2003) and *The Market* (2005).

Matthew Bond is a Senior Lecturer in Social and Policy Studies at London South Bank University. His current research interests are in the sociology of elites, sociological theory, and social research methods.

Graham Crow is Professor of Sociology and Methodology, Edinburgh; Director of the Scottish DTC; and Deputy Director of the ESRC National Centre for Research Methods. His interests include the sociology of families and communities, sociological theory, comparative sociology and research methods. He is currently writing a book on community studies.

Ruth Graham is a Senior Lecturer in Sociology at Newcastle University. Her research in the field of medical sociology focuses on exploring the meanings and experiences of reproductive loss in contemporary society. Her research findings have been published in, inter alia, *Sociology of Health and Illness*, *Social Science and Medicine*, and *Social and Legal Studies*, and she is co-editor of the journal *Social Theory and Health*.

Robert Holton is Emeritus Professor of Sociology and Fellow of Trinity College, Dublin, and Adjunct Professor of Sociology at Flinders University of South Australia. He is the author of a number of books and articles in social theory, historical sociology, and the study of globalisation. His latest book, *Global Finance*, was published by Routledge in 2012.

Mark Hyde is an Associate Professor in Public Policy and Management at the University of Plymouth. His research on disabled people has been published in several journals, notably *Work, Employment & Society*, and *Disability & Society*. A co-director of 'Pensions Worldwide', he has written several studies of the privatisation of pensions, most recently *Comparing How Various Nations Administer Retirement Income* (Edwin Mellen Press, 2010).

Stevi Jackson is Professor of Women's Studies and Director of the Centre for Women's Studies at the University of York. She is the author of *Childhood and Sexuality* (Blackwell, 1982), *Heterosexuality in Question* (Sage, 1999), *Theorizing Sexuality* (with Sue Scott, Open University Press, 2010) and *Gender and Sexuality: Sociological Approaches* (with Momin Rahman, Polity Press, 2010). She has also co-edited a number of volumes including *Gender: A Sociological Reader* (with Sue Scott, Routledge, 2002) and *East Asian Sexualities* (with Liu Jieyu and Woo Juhyun, Zed Books, 2008).

Steph Lawler is a Reader in Sociology at Newcastle University. She has worked extensively on issues of identity, especially those of class, gender and generation. She is especially interested in the ways in which concerns about identity underwrite contemporary anxieties about social relations, and with the relationship between everyday life and large-scale social relations. She has published widely on identity, inequality and value, and her most recent book is *Identity: Sociological Perspectives* (Polity, 2008).

Catherine Maclean undertook doctoral research which examined social change and migration in remote rural areas through the study of a community in the northwest of Scotland. Having worked as a lecturer at the University of Edinburgh, she now teaches schoolchildren on the Isle of Skye.

David Mason is Emeritus Professor of Sociology at Nottingham Trent University and Visiting Professor in the Department of War Studies at King's College, London. He is currently Treasurer of the European Research Group on Military and Society (ERGOMAS) and is an Academician of the Academy of Social Sciences. His research includes work on labour markets and equal opportunities issues, the recruitment of minority ethnic nurses and diversity in the armed forces. His publications include *Race and Ethnicity in Modern Britain* (2nd edition, Oxford University Press, 2000) and *Explaining Ethnic Differences: Changing Patterns of Disadvantage in Britain* (Policy Press, 2003).

David McCrone is Emeritus Professor of Sociology at the University of Edinburgh. A Fellow of the British Academy, and of the Royal Society of Edinburgh, he coordinated the research programme funded by The Leverhulme

Trust on National Identity (see *National Identity, Nationalism and Constitutional Change*, edited with Frank Bechhofer, Palgrave Macmillan, 2009). He has written on the sociology and politics of Scotland, and the comparative study of nationalism.

Geoff Payne, AcSS, teaches Social Inequalities and Social Research Methods at Newcastle University. He is Emeritus Professor of Sociology, University of Plymouth and a former President of the British Sociological Association. He has published on social mobility, employment, health, community and research methods, for example, *The New Social Mobility* (Policy Press, 2014).

Judy Payne is a former Research Consultant whose work on housing, social class, health and deprivation has been published in *Sociology, British Journal of Sociology, Sociological Research Online* and the *Journal of Social Policy*. Her books include *Researching Health Needs* (Sage, 1999) and *Key Concepts in Social Research* (with G. Payne, Sage, 2014).

Iain Phillips is a final-year PhD candidate at Newcastle University. His ESRC-funded PhD project examines the formation of expectations for first-generation students in higher education. His interests are in the consequences of social and economic change on transitions and social mobility across the life-course with a particular emphasis upon social class.

Lucinda Platt, now Professor of Sociology at LSE, was previously Professor of Sociology at the Institute of Education and Director of the Millennium Cohort Study, a survey of over 19,000 children born in the UK in 2000/2001 who are followed over time. Her main research areas are ethnic minority poverty, pay, social networks and social mobility; ethnicity and identity; and child poverty. She has published widely in these areas, as well as on disability and public law. Her most recent book, *Understanding Inequalities: Stratification and Difference* was published by Polity in 2011.

John Scott is Professor of Sociology and Pro Vice-Chancellor for Research at Plymouth University. He is also Honorary Professor at the University of Copenhagen, Denmark. He has written widely on social stratification, social theory, and methods, most recently publishing *Sociology* (4th edition, with James Fulcher, Oxford University Press, 2011), *Conceptualising the Social World* (Cambridge University Press 2011), *Sociological Theory* (2nd edition, Edward Elgar, 2012), and *What is Social Network Analysis* (Bloomsbury Academic, 2012). A former President of the British Sociological Association, he is a Fellow of the British Academy and has previously taught at Strathclyde University, Leicester University, and Essex University.

Sue Scott, AcSS recently retired from the posts of Pro Vice-Chancellor (Research) and Professor of Sociology at Glasgow Caledonian University. She was previously Dean of the Faculty of Humanities and Social Sciences at Keele University and Postgraduate Dean at Durham University. She was President of the British Sociological Association 2007–2009. Her research interests are in the sociology of gender, sexuality, childhood and risk. Her most recent book, *Theorizing Sexuality* (with Stevi Jackson) was published by Open University Press in 2010. She is currently working on a study of feminist academics' understandings of self and the relationship between biography and academic work.

Rory Shand is a Lecturer in Public Management and Policy, and Deputy Director of the Sustainable Leadership, Governance and Policy Research Group (SLGP) at Plymouth University, where he has recently completed research on the Big Society and environmental NGOs. He has published on housing, sustainability and regeneration in the Thames Gateway and in Germany.

Phil Stanworth has taught in a number of universities, including the University of York, where his teaching and research interests focused on the analysis of power, globalisation and place. His chapter on elites in this volume marks a return to the topic after a long absence, having published 'Elites and Privilege' in P. Abrams and R.K. Brown (eds) *UK Society* (Weidenfeld & Nicolson) in 1984. He retired in 2008.

Tim Strangleman, AcSS, is a Professor of Sociology at the University of Kent, Canterbury where he teaches sociology of work, de-industrialisation, unemployment, social class, and research methods. His publications include *Work Identity at the End of the Line? Privatisation and Culture Change in the UK Railway Industry* (Palgrave Macmillan, 2004) and *Work and Society: Sociological Approaches, Themes and Methods* (with Tracey Warren, Routledge, 2008). Tim has carried out research projects in a wide variety of work-places and industries, and his current interests are in the changing nature of work identity and meaning and the impact of de-industrialisation on communities.

John Vincent trained as a social anthropologist at the University of Sussex. Following professional, political and voluntary association activity related to the condition of old people, he started academic research and publication in social gerontology in the 1980s. More recently, he has specialised in extending his critique of ageism to the anti-ageing movement. His book publications include *Inequality and Old Age* (1995), and *Old Age* (2003). He retired from the position of Associate Professor in the Department of Sociology and Philosophy at the University of Exeter in 2009.

Preface to the Third Edition

This book is about the way society consists, not of a uniform mass of people, but of groups which differ from each other in many ways. The basis of these differences is widely recognised in everyday conversation: we talk about men and women; about those older or younger than ourselves; about others with authority over us at school, work or in politics; or simply about 'people like us'. These categories provide us with a means of making sense of the complexity of human life. By routinely classifying others as belonging to the same group as ourselves, or to a contrasting group, we impose an order on our direct and indirect social interactions with the rest of society. The principles which we use to make sense of our social worlds are the cross-cutting *social divisions* that divide up society.

Even when the first edition of this book was in preparation, the term 'social divisions' was already widely used as a short-hand term for all sorts of social differences, social inequalities and social groupings. Since then, social scientists have made increasing and more specific use of the idea to describe how these structural elements intersect, connect with individual social identities, and frame the social processes in which we play a part and live our collective lives. Each of us possesses a *social identity* made up of a *combination* of positions within the social divisions framework. In different social settings, various social divisions become more or less important.

Most sociologists have come to accept as normal the idea that sociological explanations based exclusively on any single social division (the way much sociology was conducted in the twentieth century) are likely to be less convincing than accounts which try to bring together several divisions. Social class, gender and ethnicity still loom large in our consciousness, but other dimensions have increasingly come to the fore, such as sexualities, religion, and nationalism. The idea of a book about social divisions was to develop this perspective by introducing an analysis of this broader range of social inequalities and hierarchies, and their intersections.

However, *Social Divisions* has not been written as a general introductory book per se, although it is intended to be engaging and accessible to a wide student readership in higher education and beyond. What we have in mind is a text which could equally well be used at both introductory and intermediate stages of most university degree programmes rather than restricting ourselves to the level of work which is typically found at the very start of a sociology course. We have tried to deal with some challenging ideas in a systematic, clear and rigorous way and this, combined with a breadth of topics and extensive bibliography, should mean that students (and even some of our fellow professional sociologists!) will find some new insights in its pages. Many of its examples are taken from Britain, but the ideas and arguments are equally relevant in other contemporary societies. Our hope is that readers in other countries will also be able to use and enjoy this book.

Although there is a coherent perspective running through the book, each of the topic chapters (Chapters 2–17) is intended to be free-standing. The contents have been organised so that, while seeking to develop a coherence of its own, parts of the book can be taken out and used in other contexts. This should be helpful, because there is no uniformity in which parts of sociology are taught at each stage in every university, even if research indicates there are greater similarities between the programmes than are often assumed. The apparent similarities between most current omnibus introductory texts hides a degree of variation in teaching (Bailey 1998). Thus our choice of particular topics is not an attempt to prescribe the content of particular stages of sociology, but to assist those involved with making those choices. The chapters follow a common format, but readers can select those chapters that most interest them; the book is not primarily designed to be read from cover to cover.

The three chapters on class, gender and ethnicity are deliberately longer than the others because these three social divisions have been more extensively researched, and they help to give a purchase on other divisions. Indeed, these three topics are what most sociologists would initially think of as 'social divisions' and, as such, they already have an established place in the curriculum. While recognising the centrality of 'the big three', one of the key purposes of this book is to advocate that the notion of social divisions should be extended to explore the significance of other social divisions.

There is nothing revolutionary about such a view: new topics are always emerging from narrow specialisms to take a more substantial place in the sociological sun. Whereas courses once prioritised the single social division of social class, now room has been found for gender and ethnicity. Feminism, post-modernism, and cultural and social identity are other examples which initially had to struggle for space in the curriculum alongside more traditional topics like classical sociological theory or social stratification. Our expansion of social divisions therefore offers introductions to areas that are of increasing consequence. I hope that not too many readers' 'favourite' topics will prove to have been left out.

Social division, in whatever set of examples is chosen, is something more than just a useful principle around which to assemble a number of reports about major facets of contemporary society. The cumulative effect of reading the chapters is to produce a sense of a strong, coherent perspective, a way of thinking about social conditions and the social order, with social inequalities and power very much to the fore. The contributors did not necessarily start with this in mind nor would they all equally subscribe to the implications of the distinctive approach more explicitly articulated, particularly in the final chapter. The idea that social division represents a distinct sociological standpoint of some significance certainly became clearer to me during the process of developing the book. As editor, I take full responsibility for any shortcomings in representing the overview in Chapter 18.

Social Divisions can thus be seen as working on three levels. At its most basic, it is a collection of individual chapters, each dealing with a topic of major concern in sociology, but not totally dependent on the concluding overview. Second, it has been designed as a source book to support individual interests or a variety of teaching programmes. In addition, it also offers a particular *perspective* – but not a fully-developed *theory* – for making sense of society.

There are three main changes to this new edition. In rewriting their original chapters, the contributors updated their statistical information, so retaining the emphasis on timely data which was a welcome feature of earlier editions. However, a striking finding during this search for current data has been the lack of new sources at the present time. The findings of the 2011 Census are still only partially available as we go to press, and, more significantly, much of the social analysis from a decade ago has not been carried forward. For example, the reports on race by the Policy Studies Institute spanning 1968 to 1997 have not been continued (see Chapter 4). Similarly, new indicators of health inequalities were difficult to find for Chapter 14, so that we cannot show how some of our earlier patterns have since changed. While gender and income have become almost routine features of Office for National Statistics tabulations, social class has virtually disappeared. Until now, this general shift in emphasis has gone largely un-noticed among the academic social science community. As a result, while we can follow some older trends, very recent social changes are hard to document as fully as we would like. This has a particular impact on the chapters dealing with class, ethnicity, religion, and health.

The second change to the new edition is that contributors have, however, incorporated the latest ideas and findings from studies in their field. We hope that this enhances the reputation established by earlier editions of this volume for the depth of its coverage of current research. Third, three major new chapters – on work, globalisation, and social identity – have been added, so giving greater breadth and providing further development of the social divisions approach.

A lot of people have played a part in the success of *Social Divisions*. I originally invited chapters from a team of contributors (now expanded) who would
combine academic credibility and reputation with an active concern for explaining and communicating sociology. I knew that they all could write in a
clear and engaging way, which certainly helped me over the inevitable difficulties that are part of editing a set of newly commissioned and now substantially
updated pieces. They, and the new contributors, are due my thanks for their
good-natured cooperation and willingness to write to specification.

I am also grateful to the publishers and their reviewers for their support
and advice: in particular to Catherine Gray, publisher for Palgrave Macmillan's Higher Education Division, who first suggested that an interesting book
about social divisions could be put together, and to Aleta Bezuidenhout and
her colleagues at Palgrave who have handled this third edition. I would also
like to thank other former and current colleagues who offered comments on
ideas and drafts of this and earlier editions, while my special thanks go to Judy
Payne, whose assistance with the technical aspects of the production of the
typescripts was invaluable, and whose intellectual collaboration and personal
support continue to be a major source of inspiration.

GEOFF PAYNE

Acknowledgements

We are grateful to the copyright holders for permission to reproduce material from the following sources:

The following are reproduced under terms of the Open Government Licence v1.0:

Table 2.2: 2011 Census: Key Statistics KS611EW: r21ewrttableks611ew-ladv1_tcm77-290886. Table 2.3: *Living in Britain*, (ONS 2002a), Table 4.20. Table 2.4: ONS (2010) *Infant and Perinatal mortality by Social and Biological Factors 2009* Table 7. Table 3.1: Department for Education (2012). Table 3.3: Department for Education (2009). Table 3.5: ONS 2012d (see bibliography). Table 3.6: Equal Opportunities Commission (2004). Table 3.7: Cracknell, R. (2012*) Women in Public Life, the Professions and the Boardroom.* SN/SG/5170 House of Commons Library. Table 4.1: 2011 Census: KS201EW Ethnic group, local authorities in England and Wales. Table 4.2: Nomis Table DC6206EW: www.nomisweb.co.uk/census/2011/DC6206EW. Table 4.3: Nomis Table DC6206EW: www.nomisweb.co.uk/census/2011/DC6206EW. Table 5.2: *Family Spending 2010*, ONS (2011). Table 8.3: Whitfield, G. (1997) *The Disability Discrimination Act.* Department of Social Security, Table 2.5. Table 9.1: ONS, Table KS209EW 2011 Census: Religion and Local Authorities England and Wales, 2012. Table 9.2: Census 2001, ONS (2003). Table 9.3: Census 2001, ONS (2003). Table 13.1: DWP (2011), Table 3.5db. Table 13.2: DWP (2011), Table 3.5db. Table 13.4: DWP (2011), Tables 4.3db and 4.5db. Table 14.1: Table 7 ONS (2010), and figure 6.4 ONS (2004e). Table 14.2: ONS (2003a), Table 7.35. Table 14.3: ONS (2011c) General Lifestyle Survey 2009, Table 7.21. Table 14.4: ONS (1998b), Table 8.38. Table 14.5: ONS (2009c). Table 14.6: DoH (1999) Tables HSE 02.1, 02.2, and 02.3, Health-SurveyForEngland/Healthsurveyresults/DH_4001561 http://www.dh.gov.uk/en/Publicationsandstatistics/ PublishedSurvey/. Fig 2.3: Social Trends 39 (2009). Fig 2.4: *Health Statistics Quarterly* 49 2011, 18, Fig 1: ONS. Fig 2.5: Adult Psychiatric Morbidity in England (2009, 32, figure 2E) © 2012, re-used with the permission of the Health and Social Care Information Centre. Fig 3.1: *Labour Force Survey 2007*, ONS. Fig 3.2: Labour Force Survey 2007, ONS. Fig 4.1: 2011 Census: Key Statistics for England and Wales. Fig 4.2: ONS (2006a). Fig 4.3: ONS (2006b). Fig 9.1: Census 2001, ONS (2003).

Fig 9.2: Census 2001, ONS (2003). Fig 12.1: Labour Force Survey, from NOMIS 2011. Fig 12.2: Labour Force Survey, from NOMIS 2011. Fig 13.2: DWP (2011), Tables 3.1tr and 3.2tr. Fig 13.5: DWP (2011), Tables 3.3db and 3.5db.

From other sources:

Table 2.1: Goldthorpe, J. and McKnight, A. (2004) 'The Economic Basis of Social Class', CASE Paper 80 London: LSE. © Centre for Analysis of Social Exclusion, London School of Economics and Political Science, London, UK, Table 1. Table 2.5: Li, Y. and Devine, F. (2011) 'Is Social Mobility Really Declining?', *Sociological Research Online*, 16(3) 4, http://www.socresonline.org.uk/16/3/4.html, 10.5153/sro.2424, Table II. Table 3.2: Russell Haggar, www.earlhamsociologypapers.co.uk/genddata.htm. Table 3.4: http://www.tuc.org.uk/extras/Apprenticeships_and_Gender, TUC. Table 5.1: UN *World Population Ageing* (2002) United Nations Publications. Tables 8.1 and 8.2: Michael Oliver, *The Politics of Disablement*, published 1990, Macmillan are reproduced with permission of Palgrave Macmillan. Table 11.2: Theakston, K. and Fry, G. 'Britain's Administrative Elite: Permanent Secretaries 1900–1986', *Public Administration*. 67, 2, Table 2, Blackwell Publishing Ltd/Wiley and Peter Barberis, *The Elite of the Elite: Permanent Secretaries in the British Higher Civil Service*, Tables 6.2 and 6.4. Fig 2.1: Resolution Foundation (2011) *Growth Without Gain? Report of the Commission on Living Standards*. London, Resolution Foundation. Fig 2.2: Move to England, Your complete guide to immigrating to the UK. Fig 2.6: Russell Haggar, http://www.earlhamsociologypages.co.uk/education%20data.html.

Every effort has been made to trace all copyright holders but if any have been inadvertently overlooked the publisher will be pleased to make the necessary arrangements at the first opportunity.

SECTION I

Introduction

CHAPTER 1

An Introduction to 'Social Divisions'

GEOFF PAYNE

This chapter will provide you with an introduction to the following aspects of social divisions:

- Social divisions are not 'natural' biological categories
- Using a provisional definition: a social division is a substantial social difference between two or more categories of people
- Social divisions consist of material and cultural differences, where one category of people is better placed than another: three major examples are class, gender and ethnicity
- Social division is related to social inequality, social stratification and social differentiation, but is a separate concept
- 'Memberships' of the groups which make up social divisions overlap in many different combinations
- How we experience divisions: individuals, groups and social identity; 'us' and 'them'
- Lesser social differences and major social divisions
- Rules of social interaction and behaviour in division
- Forms of division in contemporary society
- New forms of division under globalisation and social fragmentation
- Social exclusion and social division
- The plan and content of the chapters of the book

Without consciously thinking about it, we perceive other human beings as being male or female, black or white, older or younger, richer or poorer, sick or well, friend or foe. In forming a perception of others, we place them in social pigeonholes, adapting our behaviour and attitude to them in terms of the slots into which we have placed them. In short, it is impossible even to begin to think about people without immediately encountering 'social divisions'.

At first sight, some of the categories we use, such as 'older', 'female', 'healthy' or 'white', might seem to have a natural, biological basis, but they are actually sociological labels. The meaning we bring to these labels depends on the cultural significance we have learned to attach to them during our lives up to this moment. The origins of the definitions we use, the ways in which separations between one category and another have been created and are maintained, the extent of inequalities that exist between groups, how people come to think about their own identity and the consequences of this for future action are all sociological issues. 'Age', 'gender', 'health', 'ethnicity', 'class' and so on are the 'social divisions' that shape society. Their power to influence our lives is sustained through intricate rituals, beliefs, and often taken-for-granted assumptions. If we are to make coherent sense of our own lives – let alone understand what is going on in the rest of our own society and why society as a whole operates as it does – the idea of 'social divisions' is one of the most useful and powerful tools available.

This chapter goes back to basics, deliberately setting out to explain the idea of social divisions in simple terms. This means reflecting on the nature of social life as sociologists see it and our assumptions about contemporary society. The later chapters develop this simple introduction into a more detailed and advanced treatment. The full meaning and some of the implications of a 'social divisions approach' are then brought out in the final chapter of the book.

What are 'social divisions'?

One could almost say that social divisions are so self-evident that we need no formal definition. You do not have to be a professional sociologist to see that society is not only made up of individuals, but that some individuals are very similar to one another, yet different from others. In some cases, the differences between sets of people are sharp, with major contrasts of social conditions and 'life chances' (the chances during a person's lifetime of sharing in society's material and cultural rewards – income, employment, education, health and so on). Social divisions may be marked by visual cues like dress, as in the case of gender and age. Others may share a sense of co-identity through their exclusion at the hands of more advantaged groups, as can be the case with ethnic groups, the disabled, or those with particular sexualities.

However, if we need to explain why some things are social divisions whereas other social differences are not, the picture is suddenly less clear. For instance, a division does not necessarily separate people into two parts: sometimes we need to think of several distinct categories, for example, when noting differences between minority ethnic groups. Social divisions also often overlap, so that an explanation of people's employment positions may mean exploring how far class, gender, ethnicity, age or disability are contributing factors, in different combinations, to what we can observe happening. Some divisions are more obvious and extensive than others. Some of them will seem more important than others, although such evaluations will change with time and also vary from reader to reader. (For alternative distinctions between divisions and differences, see Carling 1991; Anthias 1998, 2001; Braham and Janes 2002; Best 2005.)

Thus it follows that, rather than starting with a full-scale complex definition, it is probably more helpful to explore the dimensions of 'social division' in more detail. This will be done mainly by using concrete examples – class, gender and so on – to indicate what we mean by social divisions. At this stage, a preliminary sketch of the main features of a definition of social divisions will suffice. (Alternatively, readers who would feel happier starting with an abstract definition might like to look at the opening pages of the concluding chapter.)

When we talk about social divisions, we mean those substantial differences between people that run throughout our society. A social division has at least two categories, and often more, each of which has distinctive material and cultural features. In other words, one category is better positioned than the other and has a better share of resources because it has greater power over the way our society is organised. Membership of a category is closely associated with a social identity that arises from a sense of being similar to other members and different from other categories. This affects how people conduct their social interactions. Movement from one category to another is not easy.

However, social divisions are the outcome of previous social interactions, events, decisions and struggles. They are not 'natural' products of physical differences, or inevitable in the form they take, despite a tendency for the media and everyday talk to assume that they arise from some essential 'fact' of life. Although the distinctions between categories are strong and tend to be long-lasting, they are not fixed for all time. They are 'socially constructed' so that, while there are always social divisions, their precise form varies from society to society, and from era to era.

At this point, we can usefully distinguish between social divisions and several similar terms used in sociology. 'Social inequalities' refer to the differences in people's share of resources (not just money, but chances of health, education and so on). Such differences are often graduated over a wide range, rather than clearly defining two or more categories. Social divisions give rise to social inequalities, and so social inequalities are often a marker of the advantages and disadvantages that accrue though membership of particular categories that are socially divided. Thus, while we saw in our earlier definition that social inequality is part of the idea of social division, it is only one part. Social divisions are similarly related to 'social stratification', but stratification is a term better reserved for specialist discussions of class, status and power. In this case, we can regard social stratification as a subset of social divisions, the latter, wider term placing more emphasis on the many types of divisions and their capacity to structure identity and interactions. On the other hand, social division is a more focused and restricted idea than 'social differentiation', a general term used to describe the increasing complexity of specialised roles and relationships that are evident as societies grow in size, utilise new technologies in production, develop more elaborate social institutions and form into new social groupings.

Social division is therefore a 'middle-range' concept that offers a way of thinking about society as intelligible components, based on a set of principles. In the past it was often said that sociologists were only interested in 'social class', to the exclusion of all other divisions. Since the 1980s, gender and ethnicity have become more central to sociological research. Even more recently other divisions, such as sexuality and national identity, have become prominent in the sociological repertoire. This growth of new sociological interests – and its associated tendency for increased competition between sociologists to define 'what sociology is really about' – reflects the way most people's senses of personal identity had begun to draw more strongly on a wider range of social factors or, as some sociologists have argued, on a sense of individual differences (Isin and Wood 1999; Bauman 2001a; Beck and Beck-Gernsheim 2002). This in turn is a product of new ways of life replacing older, more traditional ones associated with former class structures.

In dealing with identity, the emphasis in this book is placed on what is shared by people as a social identity – in the sense of what identifies them and brings them together as a group – rather than on personal identity or individual differentiation. The idea of identity is important but secondary to that of division. It would be possible to develop the discussion of identity much further, but that would go beyond the scope of this book (see Chapter 17).

A characteristic of both these older and more recently prominent social divisions is that everyone in society is involved: we all have a class, an age, an ethnic identity and so on. Each social division is 'universally inclusive': we all sit on one side or the other of each dividing line, in this category or that, whether it seems to matter much to us or not. A person may not at this precise moment be, say, 'ill', but that is only because that person currently occupies the associated mirror image category that goes with it: in this case, 'healthy'. When or if this person becomes ill, her or his currently passive awareness of the social divisions of health is likely to increase.

Social differences are rarely 'separate but equal'. The examples we have introduced show that social divisions divide people into 'better' or 'worse' categories. Divisions result in social inequalities. Those in the 'better' categories have more control over their own lives, usually more money and can generally be seen to lead happier lives. Those occupying the better positions often take their advantages for granted but, nonetheless, social divisions are still all about advantage and disadvantage. They are therefore also about who has the power to create and maintain this situation in which inequalities persist.

It follows from this that the various social divisions often connect and overlap, reinforcing inequalities (although for ease of presentation we shall need to discuss each of the social divisions in its own right and normally one at a time). In any one situation, a particular social division may assume greater importance, but people do not exist in a social world where only class, or only gender, or only ethnicity matters. It is not that there is a single category which is distinctive. All of us have multiple memberships in a number of such groups, so that, depending on one's standpoint, people may be different in one context but similar in another. Personal links with people in one category may sometimes be at odds with one's differences from them owing to membership of some category on another social division.

The particular combination and balance of memberships also matter. For example, to be white, middle class, and male is not only different from being black, working class, and female, but also different from being black, middle class, and male. Furthermore, the relevance of these categories will matter to a greater or lesser degree depending on the social setting in which people find themselves. We cannot simply add one social division to another. In other words, as well as looking at each division separately, we need to consider how the various divisions seem able to work in specific combinations and in a somewhat less coherent way.

One purpose of studying sociology is to discover the nature of these unequal divisions and categories of people that together add up to a society. How have they come about, how do they relate to one another in a structured way and what are the consequences of such social divisions? The idea of social divisions addresses the distinctions between sets of people and also the question that lurks behind such variation: if there are all these differences, why do they continue to operate as they do and what prevents a society (in most cases) from splitting up into warring factions? How do divisions work together as a whole to make up the normally cohesive system we know as 'society'?

Social divisions as a way of thinking about society

A useful starting point for the analysis of the social inequalities and systems of social divisions that make up contemporary society is, paradoxically, the 'individual' rather than 'social groups'. On the face of it, the most obvious division is between you, the reader, as an individual and the rest of humankind. One of the great perceptual paradoxes of life is that humans are simultaneously individual entities and 'social animals'. Each of us is a physically separate being, with an independent consciousness, experiencing in her or his own particular way a physical world populated with other humans, all different from us but largely behaving in ways that are at least partially intelligible to us. Each of us feels unique: one's emotions about, understanding of and reactions to new encounters are the outcome of a discrete set of previous experiences that each person, and that person alone, has accumulated.

Yet at the same time, our day-to-day life is a social one. Our very survival depends on a complex, largely invisible, web of group activities that produce, deliver and regulate the production and consumption of goods and services. We cannot exist in isolation from one another, even after we cease to be infants dependent on our families for support. Just as we pigeonhole other people and adapt our own behaviour towards them, so too do they adapt to us, in a continuing creative process.

It is true, of course, that a very small number of people live as hermits, but such a tiny minority does not challenge our basic observation about our social nature. Even people living as 'single-person households' – a situation that has grown more common in recent years – still have contact with the outside world. Most people who 'live on their own' in fact work or study outside the home, in organisations. They do so in densely populated towns and cities, meeting other people as they buy food and clothes or engage in leisure pursuits, and indirectly connecting with other people by electronic and print media. Even if they live alone, many have family and relatives as a potential support. A feeling of loneliness is not the same as being alone or divorced from society; rather it confirms our social nature. The unfortunate cases where people experience real problems of isolation and too little human contact only prove the point that we prefer and expect to organise our lives on a collective basis of meeting with, and depending on, other people.

In practice, we lead our lives in social groups defined by what we have in common that is different from other groups – belonging to this one but not that one, in this society rather than another. Our personal sense of identity draws on how we routinely interact with the members of our groups: it is a social identity. We share sets of values and attitudes, a 'culture'. We take our cues for action from those who share that culture through membership of 'our' group, or against those who belong to the 'other' groups, with their rival values and beliefs. We are partners in a series of 'imagined communities'.

It is not just being a member that counts: not being a member of another category is just as important. We define who 'we' are in terms of who we are not. Our encounters with 'others' point to their differences from 'us' and help us to identify our own distinctiveness. 'Our team', 'our gang', 'our kind of music', 'our part of the country' make sense in contrast – and sometimes active opposition – to 'others'.

This does not mean that we mix exclusively with members of a particular category or that all social interactions with other people are the same. For instance, despite the mandatory cheerful 'Hello!' at the supermarket checkout (resulting from research finding that customers prefer to be greeted as if they were individuals with a known identity, rather than treated as anonymous punters), our impersonal exchanges with shop assistants are not the same as the intense personal involvement we have with our family. Nor are acquaintances our close friends. Nonetheless, even the most minimal of social transactions are still orderly and governed by learned and regularised conventions. The social divisions that define both the shop assistant and customers (for example in terms of class, gender, age or ethnicity) set 'rules' for how we are allowed, and not allowed, to interact.

To the extent that societal arrangements define and physically separate young from old, men from women, upper class from working class and so on, it is simply more difficult to mix with people who are different from ourselves, even if that is what we want to do. The case of personal and sexual relationships between young adults, where members from different categories of the social divisions of gender and sexuality are meeting, mixing and mating, illustrates how difficult cross-boundary contact can be. Even at this most personal of levels, social interaction is still structured and segregated: mixing is not an open and free process.

We do not have to meet face-to-face with 'others' for rule-driven constraints, inequalities and power to come into play, although these encounters often raise our awareness of our own identity. Equally, in the usual situation where all members of a social category cannot meet or closely interact as a 'social group', the looser 'category' that is formed as part of the process of social division still imposes constraints on our individual actions. It places us inside a social structure. The common bond of a social identity, which is a mechanism for this, is not exclusively dependent on direct interpersonal interaction with other members of the shared category. It may also be a product of a more abstract awareness of similar circumstances, interests and experiences.

For example, when we talk about national identity or sexuality, we are dealing with social divisions that separate large numbers of people, are complex and extend well beyond the individual's direct personal experience. Over and above direct contact, we sense that we also belong to larger, notional categories of people who do not meet together. These 'imagined communities' provide us with identities in terms of which we define ourselves and the right way to act, and how in turn others define us and react to our behaviour (for example, as belonging to a particular age group).

The connections between the large-scale and small-scale interactions between categories work both ways: just as we may experience the grand social divisions through localised contacts, so too do the divisions determine our often unconscious selection of friends and mates, careers and places to live. These are overwhelmingly chosen from people like ourselves, on one or more division (for example, most marriages are between people from the same social class). Whatever our reactions to this fact, it is inescapable that we can most easily select for close relationships those whom we are most likely to meet.

Whether we are talking about encounters within a category, or between two differing categories when people from both sides of the social divide meet, social interaction is rule-bounded. Indeed, not only are interactions rule-bounded, but the rules establish a social inequality between participants, marking out our shared circumstances, or the disparate situations of the members of other categories. Membership of a category offers social advantages or disadvantages vis-à-vis members of a matching category.

These social advantages make membership of some categories more desirable than others. Who would seriously argue that it is less advantageous to be young, fit, white and upper class, than to be old, ill, black and working class? People on the 'right' side of the social division lines take precedence over others, once their identities are known. Social divisions reflect the imbalance of power between categories: they are hierarchical. This is why some forms of social difference are more important than others and warrant the title 'social division'. Of course other kinds of social differences do exist, and can confer a sense of identity without being social divisions.

Thus the social divisions with which this book deals are not the small-scale ones, such as a gang, a family, or a team, nor are all shared consumer lifestyles – like 'surfing' or 'clubbing' – counted as social divisions. Groups may thus be interesting for what they tell about wider processes, without being the core focus in a social division approach. This is not to ignore the fact that when major social divisions such as class or gender are encountered, they are normally experienced through membership of smaller collectivities. Divisions are often encountered indirectly, through participation in, say, a group of co-workers or students, and it is within such groups that we are likely to develop face-to-face relationships and social interactions based on the underlying principles of division. However, this process makes most sense when it is seen as the outcome of the underlying social division.

Social divisions as 'social rules'

Broader and less tangible social divisions share with smaller, more concrete groups the characteristics of recognisable behaviour patterns and sets of attitudes. For the most part, unwritten rules of conduct apply. 'The rich man in his castle, the poor man at his gate' of the Victorian hymn expressed the imperative that the lower orders should 'know their place' and keep to it. A more up-to-date set of rules for proper conduct, this time for older people, is suggested by Jenny Joseph's well-known poem in which the speaker imagines how, in later life, she might defy custom, by dressing in purple and wearing a red hat, buying summer gloves, satin sandals and brandy, while claiming she could not afford butter (Joseph 1987: 229)

In reading this description of how one older woman might think of behaving we can, as sociologists, see by implication the rules about how older women in general are *expected* to act. Older women should not run their sticks along the railings, spit, swear in the street, press alarm bells and so on. The poem is about how one might behave at a different age, not about gender. From a social divisions point of view, however, one might also note that behaviour at different ages will also be influenced by gender.

Similarly, in his fascinating book about life in a northern English city in the early 1960s (only two generations ago), Jackson (1968) combines compassion with sociological insight to describe the details of the routine daily lives of 'ordinary people' working in the mill, getting into grammar school, meeting in the coffee bar or 'the club', watching football from the terraces, or using gossip with family, friends and neighbours to express the right and wrong way of doing things. *Working Class Community* still makes a wonderful read, but it does so now as a social history. It is an account of a world we have lost. It tells us about living with greater certainties and more clearly patterned and predictable life experiences, governed by much sharper sets of social conventions specifying how people were expected to lead their lives. It shows how class and other divisions prescribed people's lives.

As post-modern writers have demonstrated, many such 'rules' have lost their force since the break-up of the old monolithic industrial social classes and their traditional ways. Even those rules and the more subtle ones that have replaced them should not be thought of as fixed, prescriptive, absolute laws of nature. They are there to be bent or broken. This operates at a variety of levels. Feminists have challenged male dominance, gay groups have campaigned for the lowering of the age of consent, patients now ask for second medical opinions, and young children still try to stay up past their bedtimes. As groups and as individuals, people seek to change their social positions in major and minor ways.

That does not mean that rules do not exist, but rather that the codes of conduct around social divisions, although structured and constraining, will not always be encountered in a precise and rigid form. Sometimes they will be implicit and in other instances explicit. Conflicts of interests are sometimes played out in nationwide struggles to mobilise state support for particular pieces of single-issue legislation, and subsequently in the courts. Equally, disputes can arise between two people from different categories whose lives together throw up contradictions in what they believe is 'the right thing' for 'people like us' to do. There is no uniform way to encounter the 'rules' that are intrinsic to social divisions.

Nonetheless, exploring social rules and their infractions helps us to identify boundaries and continuities in social divisions. A focus on social divisions offers an organised way of seeing and thinking about society; a 'perspective' but not exactly a social theory for finding out what is going on and understanding social outcomes. It enables us to describe and explain our social world, starting from the position that society is not a neatly integrated, tidy, consistent and, in particular, simple thing. Nothing in human society is a 'given', fixed for all time or absolute. All social arrangements are worth examining, whether we are seeking explanations as specialists in sociology, or as students of health, welfare or social policy who want to use concepts and methods of sociology to situate our own work. Social divisions are important cleavages in society that affect us all. Social divisions are not just about society at a national or global level, they are about what separates one individual from the next.

Social divisions in a post-modern world?

The relative importance of the various social divisions is then both situationally imposed by those around us and personally selected by ourselves. In the past there have been periods when the social behaviour expected as a result of major social divisions was more clearly defined and conformed to more uniformly. Although individual lives involved unique personal autobiographies, their broad shape was socially determined. Sons followed fathers 'down the Pit'. Daughters became wives and mothers. Old people did not wear purple with red hats.

These certainties (or constraints, depending on how one wishes to see them) are starkly illustrated by photographs of male workers in northern industrial cities, going home from the shipyards or factories in the 1930s and 1940s, at trade union or political meetings, or 'on the terraces'. Their uniformity of social condition is symbolised in their 'uniform'. There is scarcely one that does not wear a flat cap and a 'muffler' (a small scarf worn at the neck because British 'working men' – as distinct from 'white-collar' office workers or American denim-clad 'blue-collar' manual workers – could not wear collars on the weekday work shirts that would get dirty, worn and, in any case, be uncomfortable). Today, what we wear to and from work, or at leisure, is more likely to be an individual statement about how we want people to see us, in terms of more specific personal identities or memberships of other sub-cultural communities.

The older rigidities can be exaggerated. Not all workers lived in northern industrial towns, worked in heavy industry or followed their local football team. The upheaval of the late stages of the Industrial Revolution, two world wars, the Great Depression, massive technological changes in transport, housing and engineering production, the wholesale creation of new types of occupations, together with political and social welfare reforms, make it difficult to talk convincingly about a single period of 'modernity', even in the first half of the twentieth century. It is even more difficult to see a coherent period reaching back to the fifteenth century, as some have implied (Kumar 1978; Hall et al. 1992). Calls to see our world as 'post-modern' are frequently based on an over-simplistic understanding of history.

Nonetheless, there are significant differences between pre-Second World War Britain's economy of mass production and the social arrangements that went with it (see Chapter 2), and contemporary society. In particular, it is generally accepted that, for most people, life in the first half of the twentieth century involved far fewer choices of behaviour. Our own society, with its media access to other cultures and ways of life and its greater separation of workplace, home and leisure, is less prescriptive. With national economies becoming increasingly interconnected in the process of globalisation (Chapter 16), new possibilities have been opened up as our secure, localised little worlds and fixed positions in a traditional labour market have been eroded.

Over a century, the shift from manufacturing production to a services economy destroyed old jobs and created new ones. As a result of this 'occupational transition', the proportion of people working in manual jobs was halved. Most women with young children are now in paid employment. The majority of us stay on in education well past the minimum school-leaving age, because more jobs now require advanced skills. Our experiences are broader and our encounters with different ways of life more common, but we have a greater sense of uncertainty about the future in the face of these new circumstances. The old localised and relatively rigid patterns have declined.

By contrast with earlier eras, the more fragmented society of our own times offers greater opportunities (and for most people, the money) to select from a multitude of styles, groups and identities. We have greater opportunities to construct, from among the partial social identities that social divisions give, the particular version we want. Consumption and lifestyle can be manipulated. In a 'global society', we like to believe that we have a new freedom, that we can 'be what we consume', as we exercise greater choice over what we consume or do, acting out our daydreams through our purchases and fashions.

We can distinguish two processes here. On the one hand, the contemporary world cannot be explained simply as a set of nations or localities, because multinational corporations have established a world economy of production and consumption as part of the boom in world trade since the mid-1960s. This has led to a homogenisation of our cultures and lifestyles. In this sense, we are less divided from each other: we are all consumers of a world economy in which national differences are less important, although of course huge differences in per capita income and life expectancy remain between 'rich' and 'poor' nations.

On the other hand, our patterns of consumption provide ways of introducing new differentiations between ourselves. Within the underlying tendency for multinational corporations' products to be designed for global markets and more of our lives to be 'commodified' into patterns of consumption involving purchases under the influence of marketing, we can manipulate our own consumption to build and signal our identities. Better-off groups can use 'positional' goods as markers to display their distinctiveness. Some writers, such as Saunders (1990) and Dunleavy (1980), have even suggested that new lines of social division can be drawn to mark 'consumption cleavages' between home-owners and renters, between those still dependent on core social welfare services (housing, state schooling, the NHS, welfare benefits) and the rest, and between those who work in the public sector and others.

Any new freedom of action has to be balanced by the recognition that choices operate within frameworks. Those in poorly paid, insecure, unskilled manual jobs cannot easily 'choose' to lead the life of, say, the mobile phone addict or vacation tripper, let alone become cosmopolitan celebrities: these lifestyles cost money. The physically disabled are disabled from having access to vast tracts of the buildings in which consumption lifestyles are acted out. Women cannot simply behave like, and 'pass' as, men. These various social divisions may be complex but they remain powerful discriminators. Globalisation and consumption are important in their own right, but social life is still far from being totally homogenised.

Because we do still live in a fragmented world, our knowledge of others is necessarily incomplete. We may all be members of one 'society', but we live our lives as members of large, imagined categories or groups, with boundaries between them – middle class and working class, men and women, young and old. On the other hand, none of us belongs only to a single category: we belong to a whole series of such identities. While, within limits, we can manipulate these identities according to our particular circumstances of the moment, it is membership of, and identification with, groups that make up social life. Social divisions, then, blur not only because each is not a dichotomy, nor because a post-modern world offers a bedazzling variety of choices, but also because overlapping social divisions shape people's lives into complex combinations.

These combinations mean that a social divisions approach shares some similarities with the idea of 'intersectionality' (discussed in more detail in Chapter 18). We are interested in how divisions interact or 'intersect', and we see sociological explanation as having to draw on more than one social division or 'factor', although how many divisions we identify remains a problem. Intersectionality has been mainly concerned with the intersection of gender and race and so has a more limited applicability, although its current popularity (and somewhat imprecise application) now extends beyond this narrow, if important, field.

The complexity of social divisions

In *The Sociological Imagination* ([1959]1970), C. Wright Mills makes two important distinctions: between 'personal troubles' and 'public issues', and between 'individuals' and 'history'. Mills is making the point that we can interpret what happens to us in life either on a personal basis or as part of a wider social process. For example, to be unemployed is a genuine problem for somebody, whether it is 'their own fault' or not. If we were talking about one unemployed person among a city population of 100,000 all in paid employment, we might look to personal circumstance to understand (and possibly remedy) the individual's misfortune. But in times of high and rapidly rising unemployment, it is not credible to blame each person and expect each one to seek individual remedies. At the time of writing (2013) the ConDem Coalition's deliberately chosen economic policy is predicted to increase unemployment from eight per cent year on year until at least 2016: the blame for this does not lie with the nurses, teachers, social workers, soldiers, street cleaners and others who will be sacked as a result of the government's actions.

Similarly, 'history' is not simply the record of kings and queens, but of social and economic movements and changes. Mills does not want us to forget the individual, but he wants us to see the importance of the social processes that shape each life. He is concerned with systems, but sees systems as being made up of people with differing amounts of power. By addressing the interplay of systems and people, Mills ([1959]1970: 15–17) seeks to avoid the two extremes of a sociology exclusively of individuals and a sociology of social structures where the people are just pre-programmed robots.

The similarities between Mills' sociological perspective and the one outlined so far in this chapter are obvious. If anything, we have stressed the individual and small groups more than Mills did, but that will be balanced by what follows. The contributors to this book start by considering the powerful forces that tend to constrain and influence us, rather than the things that we can directly control ourselves. The emphasis tends to be on the patterned way we are shaped, rather than on the way we can modify our own actions. However, whereas Mills made his point in terms of two dichotomies, with a neat contrast between personal and public and between individual and history – which made them sharper, easy to remember and therefore all the more influential – the idea of social divisions is a little more complicated.

In the first place, we have seen that there are not one or two social divisions, but many. Mills' 'public issues' category turns out to be greatly subdivided. This book deals with 16 major social divisions, but there are others which are discussed as aspects of the major divisions here but could legitimately claim a chapter in a bigger volume: educational qualifications, consumer lifestyle, political affiliation or kinship. The 16 social divisions selected are a personal choice of topics central to the sociological curriculum, not least because they largely determine the patterns of difference in other potential divisions not included here.

For example, at first sight, it may seem surprising that there is no chapter on 'social exclusion'. To be socially excluded sounds, on the face of it, to be something akin to being socially divided off from sets of other people and ways of life. However, when we unpack the notion of social exclusion, we soon discover that it is political shorthand for the consequences of poverty, and the particular New Labour policy approach of the 1990s allegedly designed to provide 'joined-up' administrative solutions (Levitas 1998). In as far as we currently have explanations of exclusion, they are mainly couched in terms of employment, class, ethnicity, disability, gender, community structures and health inequalities (for example, Hills and Stewart 2005). In other words, to explain social exclusion, we must first start with an understanding of the social divisions that produce it and are in turn reinforced by the processes of exclusion. The main topics in each of the chapters are the major social divisions which structure contemporary society, and so there is no chapter devoted to social exclusion.

This means that the picture of a divided society which emerges is a complex one. In practice, we can artificially simplify it by dealing mainly with one division at a time, bringing together ideas and evidence about its particular set of categories from the extensive specialist research carried out by sociologists in each of our selected areas. This enables us to explore each division in some depth and see the richness of its details.

The plan of the book

We can begin to demonstrate these points by looking at the titles of the chapters in this book. They indicate the range of key social divisions, starting in Section II with sociology's 'big three' of social class, gender and ethnicity, and going on in Section III to age, childhood, sexuality and disability. Section IV includes religion, national identity, elites, and work. Each of the chapters discusses the ideas we use to think about these divisions, together with the material, status and even mundane inequalities between the categories.

However, we shall also see that it is not possible to keep each division tidily in its own chapter. On the one hand, class, gender and ethnicity are themes running throughout the book. It is no accident that these three comprise Section I and have longer chapters than the later contributions. On the other hand, the chapters in Section V on poverty, community, and health involve greater consideration of the other social divisions. While social inclusion or social exclusion or rural/urban differences may be important, poverty and community (which underpin them), and health are valid social divisions in their own right as well as 'arenas' in which the consequences of the various social divisions are acted out and come together in people's lives. Some of the ramifications of this are discussed in Section VI, where we elaborate our basic picture by discussing identity, globalisation and the idea of division in more detail.

The social conditions we are trying to analyse have changed considerably, not least in recent decades, a point that John Scott makes strongly in his discussion of class and stratification in Chapter 2. The vocabulary of 'social class' – the idea of upper, middle and working classes – did not emerge until the eighteenth and early nineteenth centuries. Manual workers decreased from over 80 per cent of the workforce before the First World War to less than 45 per cent in the 1990s. Over a similar period, the intermediate classes of professionals, managers and white-collar workers grew and saw their work position radically changed, while what was called 'Society' – the exclusive, expensive social life of a small upper-class set – disappeared in the 1950s.

This does not mean that 'class is dead'. Drawing on an explanation of Weber's original conception of social stratification, Scott (Chapter 2) demonstrates continuing class differentials in material conditions, security of employment, health and life expectancy. Arguing that when most people think about 'class', they are actually referring to status and lifestyle, he presents a distinctive occupations-based account of the three main class groupings – the subordinate (manual, wage-paid) classes, the intermediate (salaried or self-employed) classes and the 'advantaged classes' (capital and property owners, and employers). This shows that, despite social change, the social division of class survives in new forms, even if it has become unfashionable to talk of class. Occupational transition, culture, identity and consumption may blur the picture, but it is the underlying class situations that still determine life chances.

Occupations also loom large in Pamela Abbott's analysis of gender in Chapter 3, which she develops through a discussion of current patterns of work, education and poverty, and how they link with class and ethnicity. Work is pivotal to the position of women, representing both the public domain from which they have been largely excluded – an arena in which the struggle for equal pay and against the 'glass ceiling' is carried on – and in the form of unpaid, domestic work, representing much of the day-by-day oppression of women by men. She demonstrates a variety of gender-based material inequalities, concerning employment and pensions, state benefits, labour market access, 'home life' (in which mothers are the first 'to go without') and the poverty of the lone parent family, as the products of a patriarchal system of social division which, although more oppressive of women, constrains men as well.

The strength of her analysis is the integration of past and present ideologies and conceptions of female roles with contemporary social inequalities. This is exemplified both in terms of the development of sociological ideas, and in the way improving school performance by girls can be re-problematised as the declining performance of boys as a precursor to their youth unemployment. The 'natural' role of women and 'gender segregation' take on a particular significance when seen as related aspects of social division, interacting with ethnicity and class. As Abbott comments in Chapter 3 on this interconnection:

> In the nineteenth century it was mainly middle-class women who were excluded from paid employment, while in the late twentieth century, African-Caribbean women are most likely to experience public patriarchy and Muslim/British women private patriarchy.

Thus, whereas at first sight one might expect gender to be exclusively a social division of two halves, Abbott unpacks much of the complexity of its categories. We have already observed that ethnicity is far more complicated than a simplistic dichotomy and Chapter 4, in which David Mason examines the notion of ethnic identity and demonstrates the differences between ethnic groups and their various experiences of discrimination, can be seen as a natural partner to the chapter on gender. It also draws a deliberate contrast to Scott's account of class: we cannot start from material circumstances, argues Mason, because:

> only in situations of extreme segregation will these kinds of information offer us good clues to people's ethnic status and, even then, few would argue that these characteristics represent the essence of their ethnicity. (Chapter 4)

In other words, while unemployment, earnings, type of work and location are important (and duly documented in Mason's chapter), the real issue lies in the meaning of ethnic identity. This not only requires an appreciation of the historic origins of ideas of 'race' and 'ethnicity' and how they have been adapted in this country, but also how discrimination has played a part in shaping identities. As the Policy Studies Institute (Modood and Berthoud 1997) found, 'black' teenagers define themselves as much in terms of job, education or religion as any physical characteristics – but tend to think of themselves as 'black' when they are in contact with white people. Despite the disadvantaged positions of the minority ethnic groups that he describes, Mason is, on the whole, optimistic about the prospects for ethnic identity to be negotiable and open to change, not least as social conditions evolve and new senses of identity – the black woman, my religion, our specific minority ethnic group – enter the sociological and public consciousness.

This discussion of ethnic identity sets up Section III, because Chapters 5 to 8 present examples of social divisions which may superficially also seem to be physical or biological. In each case an alternative sociological analysis is developed, challenging common-sense assumptions and using the idea of social divisions to explore the social positions of those in the less advantaged categories. In so far as these chapters can also be thought of as equivalent examples of social divisions, readers may choose to follow their own interests by concentrating on particular topics.

Chapter 5 deals with age as a principle of social organisation, in particular with old age. All human societies have used age as a basis for distinguishing groups: we operate with a potentially confusing range of concepts – chronological age, cohort, generation, age group and so on. John Vincent and Iain Phillips draw on history and anthropology to explain how these terms differ, and how demographic changes have set up new tensions between older and younger members of families. The divisions between the two, and among different groups of older people, are demonstrated through sharp contrasts of material circumstances. Together with their concern with gender and class differences among the elderly, this connects directly into current social policy debates over how future pensions are to be financed. The authors also address the social construction of ageism. Their discussion of how our ideas shape our views of older citizens is echoed in Mark Hyde and Rory Shand's treatment of disability (Chapter 8).

There is also a natural link from Chapter 5 to Chapter 6 on childhood, the other end of the age range. Here, too, the idea of 'childhood' is not taken as a given, but systematically explored as a social construction. Earlier research (including that influential in the caring professions) has mostly adopted a psychological development, or preparation for adulthood, model. This has not properly taken into account children's own experiences of being divided off into a subordinate position. Our pre-Industrial Revolution history, when children were more integrated into work, has been forgotten, which adds to our ethnocentric view of children as needing to be protected from 'growing up too fast', and the 'evils of the adult world'. Stevi Jackson and Sue Scott's sociological framework allows an extensive discussion of current issues about child safety, abuse, parental powers and the confusing transition points into 'maturity'. Together with the comparisons of ethnic and class differences in models of childhood, this chapter will be of particular interest to those with a vocational interest in the well-being of children.

The same authors develop a similar analysis in respect of sexuality in Chapter 7. Their first task is to dismantle the idea that heterosexuality is 'natural', 'normal' or universally the same. Sexuality is socially constructed through institutions such as (male-dominated) marriage, and the meanings and feelings that arise in and from social interactions. What is regarded as sexuality and sex depends on the society in which it exists: what is regarded as acceptable or deviant is largely a matter of power relations. Class and ethnic divisions mean there is no single shared 'normality'. Using examples such as sex education, the sex industry and current fashions to think of the 'successful self' in sexual terms, Scott and Jackson argue that normative heterosexuality, rather than being a simple biological process, makes more sense as a form of gender-based control. Instead of seeing sex as 'special area' of human life, it needs to be reintegrated into the mainstream of social life.

The idea of integration, together with access, dominates Chapter 8 on disability. The disabled have unique and particularly intense experiences of deprivation; they are economically disadvantaged, excluded from mainstream social activities and stigmatised. In making a strong case for disability to be seen as a key social division, Mark Hyde and Rory Shand argue that disabled people's social exclusion comes not from their disability, but from the way society interprets it primarily as a medical problem. An alternative social model, and different social arrangements, would release disabled people from the sharp social division they currently encounter. Access to education and jobs would reduce dependency on welfare and 'charity', and offer an escape from the poverty that is so frequently associated with disability. Access to the political process has the potential to bring about change, not least as a mechanism by which to challenge negative stereotyping. Access to places – and many disabled people do not fit the stereotype of being wheelchair-bound – would reduce the physical division between the disabled and not-disabled.

In Section IV, attention shifts from the physical to beliefs and social relationships. Alan Aldridge shows how conventional patterns of religious observance have given way to newer forms of religiosity. His account brings out the way in which beliefs can unite a group (for example a congregation), while being the basis for intense antagonisms towards other faith communities, or reinforcing ethnic differences. One of the strengths of his analysis is the range of religions he covers and the concrete examples he draws from British society in particular. While religions do not sit neatly in a single hierarchy, their capacity to isolate minorities and manoeuvre for position shows how they operate as a social division.

Religion and ethnicity are also bound up with national identities but, as David McCrone shows in Chapter 10, this also needs to be seen in terms of political and historical processes. The physical boundaries of a society may be governed as a single state, but those living there may have a sense of identity with only one part of it. Using contemporary events, he asks under what conditions people call themselves 'British' rather than 'English', 'Welsh' or 'Scots', or even say they are from 'Yorkshire' or 'the Highlands'. These expressions are markers of social division – so much so that they form the basis for political mobilisation – which are less to do with material differences than with cultural symbols and 'imagined communities'. McCrone is therefore less concerned with tangible material differentials across geographical areas than explanations that draw on political ideas. He locates the nationalism issue in the lack of fit between 'nation' and 'state', a problem of no small significance whether illustrated by governance and devolution, or the violence of civil unrest in Northern Ireland, Yugoslavia or other parts of Europe in the latter half of the twentieth century.

This political dimension is also evident in Chapter 11 on elites. Whereas class starts from issues of who owns what and economic power, the idea of the division between 'elites' and 'masses' is based in who has political power and control of the state. Phil Stanworth traces the origins of theories of elites from the early twentieth-century work of Pareto and Mosca through to more recent discussions of democracy, pluralism and political parties. He shows how, as new social formations developed in the middle of the twentieth century, a new generation of writers (Burnham, Mills, Djilas) tried to account for the power accruing to alternative social groups. As well as bringing out the potential political dimension of social divisions, Stanworth's recent research on the educational profiles of contemporary British elites illustrates how recruitment to groups underpins structures of difference and identity.

Whereas elites are located in the political domain, work is normally understood as an economic activity. However, as Tim Strangleman's Chapter 12 explains, work is also about the social relationships between employers and employees, between work groups, and between the members of each team of workers. The tasks which make up work in industrial and post-industrial society require differing skills, which contribute to the creation of occupational identities that in turn play a part in how work is shared out. This has ramifications for access to paid employment, and its corollaries: unpaid work and unemployment. Work is gendered, but is also an activity in which age and ethnicity play significant roles, a point developed through three case studies of particular industries.

Section IV takes up this theme of the interplay of social divisions in human life, shifting the emphasis from single divisions towards the interaction of divisions. The three topics – poverty, community and health – can be treated as divisions in their own right, but are easier to understand as outcomes or processes in which many of the other divisions are also at work. That does not, however, mean that they are less important.

In Chapter 13, Lucinda Platt's account of poverty starts by disentangling the several threads of meaning in discussions about poverty. She points out that, as soon as one moves beyond a 'common-sense' view of what it means to be poor, poverty can be thought of in many ways: as a lack of income, a lack of the necessities that money can buy, or the state of deprivation and isolation that being poor produces. Even these three perspectives can be further differentiated by variations in definition and measurement. For example, what exactly do we mean by 'necessities' and how much 'lack' marks the boundary of a division between tolerable disadvantage and intolerable deprivation? This careful analysis takes us beyond a simple absolute/relative dichotomy, providing the grounds for selecting some measurements and definitions over others, and for seeing how changes over time come into play. The second half of Chapter 13 presents data on the scale of contemporary poverty, which Platt uses to show how other social divisions come into play.

The purpose of Chapter 14, as with the two other chapters in this section, is not simply to show that divisions exist, but to demonstrate the interplay of social divisions and how there can be competing explanations of what people experience in their everyday lives. Health is a topic with a long history of social inequality research, containing an extensive debate about how health and (particularly class-based) inequality are related. Ruth Graham argues that a medical or 'lifestyle' approach fails to address the connections between illness and the poverty, unemployment, bad housing and poor services that make up the daily experience of the more disadvantaged sector of society. She also extends the idea of social division from this structural and material view, considering the divisions between health workers and their clients, and between the ill and the well.

Chapter 15 on community also brings a fresh look at social divisions, rather than treating 'community' as a social division per se. In this sense, like the health chapter, Graham Crow and Catherine Maclean's contribution differs from most of the other chapters, although they too bring out the importance of identity conferred by membership of a community (whether of place, occupation or imagined community of attachment). Studies of place-based communities have richly documented the 'us' and 'them' divisions between incomers and locals over housing and local politics, which mobilise class, ethnic and gender identities. But, as with the other chapters, the authors try to escape conventional wisdom, drawing attention to the normative pressures of 'community', the prevalence of migration, and the significance for identification of the contacts with the outside world. Because community tends to bring together many facets of human life, they are able to show the shift and play of social divisions during the dynamics of daily living.

The final section consists of three chapters which seek to broaden and deepen our treatment of social division. Robert Holton argues that social divisions cannot be understood properly if we think of them as occurring only within the boundaries of one nation. Not only are there differences between countries, but what happens *in* each nation-state is conditioned by the relationships *between* nations. This interaction is not only a matter of contemporary economics, but part of a collective international history of empire, power, and migration. It is both cultural and material. Holton uses this framework to demonstrate the inequalities and hierarchies of the global world today, in particular the way class, gender, and ethnicity play their part in global inequality. In the final section of his chapter he explores explanations of what drives globalisation, such as the global 'network society', and the role of the 'global city'.

Whereas Robert Holton goes global, Steph Lawler expands our notion of division in the opposite direction, by addressing the individual consequences of life in a divided world. She explores the idea of social identity, the key element which links structural divisions to individual awareness and action: identities 'are intrinsically linked with social divisions: they are produced within the crucible of social division and social inequality and carry their traces.' However, identity is not reducible to particular social divisions, and has a complexity that makes it a challenging concept to handle. Following Elias, Goffman and Hall she argues that identity is both an active phenomenon (it has to be performed) and a response to social interactions and categorisations by others. Although identities operate in various ways, they involve identifying and being identified, being evaluated and placed in hierarchical relationships. The undesirable aspects of division, Lawler argues, can only be resisted if we understand how identities are socially produced: 'social divisions, and social inequality, *work on and through identity*, conferring value on some and stripping it from others.' To confront these hierarchies of social inequality, they must be recognised, and the resource differentials they represent have to be redistributed – two rather different things.

Finally, Chapter 18 revisits the core idea of a social division approach. Using the other chapters, it offers a formal definition of social division and addresses the questions of cohesion, continuity and inter-connection that divisions pose.

A contrast is drawn between this and other perspectives from sociological theory. This is a more conceptual chapter and, while there is an element of reprise, no new data on divisions are introduced.

Social divisions begin to make sense once we know what is being divided, how it is divided and what the results of the divisions are for our lives. This collection of essays testifies to the range and quality of contemporary sociological research, demonstrating the relevance of sociology for understanding current social conditions. It also helps us to escape from the narrow confines of small sociological compartments into a broader view. The point of sociological analyses is to promote a better understanding of society and social processes, so that we can operate more effectively. As Albrow (1994: 241) has observed, sociology has no reason to be ashamed in 'staking its claim to enhancing the competence of its students to meet the demands of living and working'.

Discussion Questions

1. Why is 'my gang' not a social division?
2. List the differences between social division, social inequality, social differentiation and social exclusion.
3. How do we become aware of our own social identities?
4. What is it about contemporary society (compared with the 1950s) that makes a social divisions perspective so useful?
5. Write a brief scene from an imaginary novel in which three characters meet: one is white, male, middle class, fit and under 25; one is black, female, working class, unwell and over 50; and the third is chosen by you using the social divisions mentioned in this chapter.

Three Core Social Divisions

CHAPTER 2

Class and Stratification

JOHN SCOTT

This chapter will provide you with a broad critical understanding of the following issues in social class as a source of social division:

■ The difference between everyday and sociological understandings of 'class'
■ The key sociological definitions of class, status and social stratification
■ The relationship between class and inequality
■ The grounding of class relations in matters involving property and employment, and the occupational division of labour
■ The foundations of status in prestige and social honour
■ The role of social mobility in the formation of social class boundaries
■ The ideas of class consciousness and class identity
■ The various class schemas devised by Wright, Goldthorpe and the Office for National Statistics
■ Trends in the size and composition of the principal social classes since the early twentieth century
■ Variations in the life chances associated with social class membership
■ The idea that social inequalities have moved in a 'post-modern' direction
■ The transformation of the 'working class'
■ The growth and expansion of the 'middle classes'
■ The structure of advantage and the propertied classes

Many of us use the language of class in our everyday lives to refer to a social hierarchy in which everyone 'knows their place'. Class is generally seen as referring to matters of 'breeding' and social background, as reflected in attitudes and lifestyles, accents, and ways of dressing. For this reason, class has also come to be seen as outmoded and old-fashioned. Class distinctions are thought to be tied to a world of tradition and subordination that no longer exists, and the language of class is seen as incompatible with contemporary attitudes and values. This view is held by many journalists and social commentators, who see the persistence of class-ridden attitudes and the continued use of the word 'class' itself as evidence that Britain has failed to adopt the more modern – or perhaps 'post-modern' – approach to life found in such apparently classless societies as the US.

On the other hand, sociologists have typically used the word 'class' to describe economic divisions and inequalities, especially those rooted in property and employment relations – a particular kind of social division. This has led them to question whether Britain actually is any more, or any less, of a class society than the US or the countries of Continental Europe and other parts of the world. All these societies are unequal societies – they show vast and continuing differences in income, wealth and property ownership – and so all can be described, in these terms, as class societies. Other differences of culture, attitudes and lifestyle are not ignored, but they are seen as pointing to quite different kinds of social division. In sociological analyses, therefore, the economic relations of class are often contrasted with cultural differences of 'status', which are seen as those more visible 'styles of life' that affect people's standing in the community. What non-sociologists tend to describe in the everyday language of class, sociologists describe in the language of status.

Of course, not all sociologists take this point of view, as there are few things on which sociologists are unanimous. For some, especially in the US, class is seen as a matter of culture and identity, and not a matter of underlying material inequalities. According to these sociologists, cultural change has indeed undermined the power and relevance of the language of class. They hold that 'class is dead', a thing of the past, even though economic and other inequalities may persist (Kingston 2000).

Even if it were true that class is dead and that a new framework of analysis is needed, it would still be necessary to know exactly what is being consigned to a historical grave. Unfortunately, as has already been noted, class does not mean the same thing to everybody. A considerable task of clarification is necessary before it is possible to make an informed judgement on the importance – or lack of importance – of class as a social division.

Linguistic confusion is a recipe for misunderstanding in any field, and sociology is no exception. If progress in sociological understanding is to be made and sociologists are to contribute to public debates, there needs to be some common ground in the language and concepts that are used. We must have concepts that will help in understanding the many inequalities in such areas as resources, health, and education in contemporary societies. This understanding will help us to see how social divisions relate to each other, and, in particular, how these inequalities relate to gender, sexuality, ethnicity, and age. We must also agree about which aspects of these inequalities can legitimately be described and analysed as aspects of 'class' relations. Only then is it possible to investigate whether these class inequalities and class differences are increasing or declining in importance in particular societies. This kind of investigation raises the question of the relationship between the facts of class and their interpretation by commentators and those who experience them in their everyday lives.

It is for this reason that this chapter begins with a conceptual exploration of the terms required to make some sense of this kind of social stratification. This exploration returns to the works of the classical sociologists, not for reasons of 'ancestor worship', but in order to recapture the important distinctions they recognised and that have been lost in many contemporary debates over class and stratification.

Conceptualising class and stratification

Social inequalities are central to any understanding of social stratification, but social stratification itself consists of more than simply inequalities in life chances. The concept of social stratification as a particular form of social division refers to the idea that individuals are distributed among the levels or layers of a social hierarchy because of their economic relations. These layers or 'social strata' are real social groupings, forged together through both their economic relations and their associated social relations and interactions; they are groupings that are able to reproduce themselves over time. Working in similar occupations, marriage, kinship and informal interaction with others all connect individuals together and help to build up boundaries that close strata and divide them from others.

These social strata are not simply statistical categories defined in an unequal distribution of resources, such as the 'top 10 per cent' or 'bottom 30 per cent' of a distribution of income and wealth. Social strata are a kind of social grouping. They are a particular form of what, in Chapter 1, were called the 'categories' that comprise a social division. In this sense, social stratification is a typical social division, but differing from others in that it is solidly based in economic relations.

The inter-connections between social stratification and divisions such as gender, sexuality, ethnicity and age are complex. Social inequalities are invariably structured by all these social divisions: inequalities are gendered, sexualised, racialised and aged. On the one hand, each division has an independent importance in sociological analysis, as do relations of social stratification. Social exclusion and discrimination on the basis of gender and ethnicity, for example, generate inequalities in life chances. On the other hand, this often operates through a process that combines exclusion in one division with exclusion in another, so that these other social divisions can become crucial conditions for the formation of social strata.

This relationship comes out clearly in the other chapters in this book, particularly in the chapters on health and community that deal with how social divisions interact in ordinary life. However, this does not mean that the social inequalities arising from other divisions should simply be equated with stratification. In this chapter, the term 'social strata' is used only to refer to those situations in which the economic and social relations of people tie them into larger, more complex and more permanent structures that take the form of a system of 'social stratification'.

To develop these arguments, I want to return to some distinctions first made by Max Weber ([1914]1968, [1920]1968) in his comparative investigations into economy and society, studies that have been massively influential in contemporary sociology. He identified three distinct aspects or dimensions to the distribution of power within societies. These are class, status, and authority or command. Weber's discussions concentrate on class and status and their relationship to 'party', which has led to a widespread misunderstanding that his three dimensions were class, status and party. However, his third dimension is more accurately understood as 'authority', as I shall shortly show. This misunderstanding is not, however, my main concern here: a more extensive discussion of this particular point can be found in Fulcher and Scott (2012: Ch. 15) and in Scott (1996: Ch. 2). My main concern is to clarify Weber's core ideas on social stratification and the ways in which they can inform our understanding of social divisions.

For Weber, class, status and authority are all aspects of power, each of which has a separate effect on the production of life chances. He defined class relations as those that result from the distribution of property and other resources in capital, product, and labour markets. It is the possession or non-possession of economic resources that gives people a specific capacity or power to acquire income and assets and thereby to enhance their life chances in various ways. Company shares yield an investment income and can be sold at a profit on the stock market, while educational credentials or technical expertise may give people the opportunity to earn a higher income in the labour market. It is the distribution of economic resources that defines the various class situations that individuals can occupy in a society. A class situation exists wherever the distribution of resources is such that a particular category of individuals have similar abilities to secure advantages (and disadvantages) for themselves through the use of their marketable resources. A person's class situation is a causal component in determining both their life chances and the interests that they have in protecting and enhancing these life chances.

In setting out his view of class, Weber quite deliberately sought to build on Marx's work, much of which he took as valid. Marx saw property ownership, especially property in the means of production, as the basis of class relations. For him, it was the ownership or non-ownership of factories, machines, and land that determined people's life chances and shaped their actions. Marx recognised just two principal class situations in contemporary societies – those of capitalists and proletarians. Capitalist class situations rest on the ownership and control of capital. Their occupants include industrial entrepreneurs, bankers, and landowners, as well as those who simply live on an income from company shares. Proletarian class situations involve a lack of ownership and are based on the exercise of labour power as an employee. They include those of people involved in skilled work, manual labour or office work, in other words, people involved in sets of similar types of occupation.

Debates that have taken place largely within Marxism have modified this basic picture of two classes, leading to the recognition of lines of differentiation among both capitalists and proletarians, and the identification of a whole array of 'intermediate' class situations. The proletarian class, being larger, has more obviously been subdivided, and there have been extensive arguments about the relative merits of how this subdivision should be carried out, and which resulting classification scheme of class situations is best. The most important of these debates are around the work of E.O. Wright (1985, 1989, 1997) and are in line with Weber's suggestion that it is necessary to recognise a great variety of class situations in any society. In later sections, I will show how it is possible to build on these ideas to investigate contemporary class divisions.

Differentiating class, 'status' and 'authority'

One of Weber's objections to Marxism was its economic determinism. He pointed out that non-economic factors were important, alongside the economic, in determining life chances and shaping patterns of social stratification. The first of the non-economic factors he discussed was status. He saw divisions of status as originating in the distribution of prestige or social honour within a community. People judge one another as superior or inferior in relation to the values they hold in common and so a person's status is their standing or reputation in the eyes of others. When people act in conformity with these values, they build up a good reputation and a high status in their community. Those who deviate from these values are accorded a lower status and may be excluded from the benefits and advantages given to others.

Most typically, a person's status follows from what Weber called their 'style of life'. This term refers to the ways that people carry out the tasks associated with their occupations and sex/gender roles and the customs and practices they follow as members of ethnic and other social groups. These patterns of behaviour define their particular and distinct styles of life (Chapter 4). Thus, manual workers, women, or ethnic minority groups may have a low status because of the way their style of life is perceived and evaluated. 'Dirty' or routine work may be seen as undesirable or demeaning, a feminine style of life may be valued less highly than a masculine one, or a whole minority culture may be devalued.

What Weber called 'status' corresponds closely to what is often, confusingly, referred to as 'class' in everyday life. A style of life involves specific types of dress and bodily adornment, types and sizes of house, areas of residence, clothing, accent, methods of cooking and eating, and so on. These markers of social identity – symbols of status – are often very important. Much public discussion of 'class' has tended to highlight status and to concentrate on its relatively minor and superficial aspects, disregarding and disguising economic class in its strict sense.

However, a more sophisticated, sociological analysis must recognise that inequalities in life chances reflect the effects of both class and status situations. Status situation, like class situation, is a causal component in life chances. Class situations comprise the property and employment relations through which control over marketable resources is organised, while status situations are the communal relations through which prestige is given to a particular lifestyle. Both situations operate to determine the life chances of individuals. An occupation, for example, involves both specific employment relations in the labour market and a particular level of occupational prestige (Parkin 1971). These two aspects of occupational position operate interdependently in determining life chances and their separate effects can be difficult to disentangle. To claim that class and status should be seen as two separate and distinct dimensions of stratification is not to prejudge their relative importance. This is always an empirical matter. The distinction does, however, allow questions about the salience of class to be formulated with greater clarity than is the case in much discussion of the subject.

Weber's third dimension of stratification is to be found in his discussions of authority and bureaucracy. Authority relations in states and business enterprises, he argued, involve relations of command in which one person is empowered to give orders to another. What Weber had to say on this can best be understood by introducing the concept of a 'command situation' to parallel his concepts of class situation and status situation. A command situation is a causal component in life chances that results from differentials of authority in formal organisations.

Weber's analysis of domination and authority gave him an acute under-standing of the formation of ruling minorities in the top command situations of political, economic and other hierarchies, but, for all his insights, the con-ceptualisation of ruling minorities was one of the least developed parts of his sociology. His insights were independently developed, so far as social stratifi-cation is concerned, by Mosca (1896, 1923) and Pareto ([1916]1963: 1430). Their argument was that the crucial social division in any society is that be-tween a dominant minority and a subordinate majority. In other words, it is al-ways possible to identify two fundamental categories: a small one at the top of society and a large one below it. Mosca and Pareto believed that this is an in-evitable consequence of any social organisation of authority and that authority relations always involve the formation of ruling minorities or what they called 'elites'. While we do not have to adopt their model of a society based on elites and masses, the argument illustrates how the delineation of class situation, status situation, and command situation is the crucial basis for any analysis of the patterns of social inequalities that comprise social stratification. A more detailed discussion of elites and their power can be found in Chapter 11. This chapter concentrates on issues of class and status.

Occupations and social stratification

In distinguishing class, status, and command in contemporary societies, I have already noted that occupations are central to the analysis of class and sta-tus situations. Occupations also lie at the core of structures of command. Occupations are positions in economic and social organisations in which each occupation has a different degree of authority, or lack of authority, over others. In all companies, government agencies, or charities, people in some occupa-tions direct and manage the work of those in other occupations. Any particu-lar occupation also rests on specific marketable skills or resources and has a particular level of occupational prestige. A sociological analysis of the class, status, and command situations of contemporary societies involves, for many purposes, a simple mapping of occupational structures. Investigating social in-equalities involves assessing the relative importance of class, status, and com-mand in the life chances that are associated with particular occupations and groups of occupations.

Sociological research has used a variety of 'class schemes' to explore this. In most of these, occupation is taken as an indicator of class situation in order to study classes as 'employment aggregates' (Crompton 2008: Ch. 4). This work is extremely important – and I make use of it below. It is sometimes held that the usefulness of particular class schemes and their advantages over others are to be judged on purely pragmatic grounds: whichever has the best predictive capacity for dealing with whatever is being studied is to be preferred (Erikson and Goldthorpe 1993; see the criticism in Morris and Scott 1996). However, the implication of my argument is that class schemes must be judged on theoretical as well as empirical grounds, and they must be seen as more or less adequate attempts to offer a coherent and operational concept of class. It is Weber's framework that offers the best basis for this.

A system of social stratification can be treated as a number of separate social strata that are layered one above another. Each social stratum contains people in similar distinctive class, status, and command situations. Each stratum is a social group with boundaries that mark off those inside from those outside. These groups are clusters of social positions, with individuals moving between these social positions and interacting (or 'associating') with each other as they do so. They may modify their own and their children's social position by marriage or by changing jobs ('circulating' within the boundary of their group). Through kinship and close intimate interactions such as leisure-time socialising and club membership, they associate with other people like themselves who make up their social stratum. For these reasons, both occupational mobility and patterns of association must be seen as central to strata formation.

These movements of individuals from one occupation to another and interactions among those engaged in particular occupations define the key boundaries within a system of social stratification. Occupational categories are a part of the same social stratum if there is easy and frequent movement between them. This might involve the lifetime mobility of individuals between different types of occupations (called *intra*-generational mobility), or it might involve occupational movement between generations, for example from father to son (*inter*-generational mobility: see Payne 1989). Equally, it frequently involved intermarriage between those in similar occupations or their interaction with one another in leisure activities. Whenever these relations of circulation and association reinforce one another in such a way as to create regular and established patterns of connection among the people working in a set of occupations, the connected occupations form part of a single stratum.

Occupations fall into the same social stratum when they are connected through chains of frequent and relatively easy circulation and association. They fall into different social strata when they are connected – if at all – only through infrequent circulation and association. Boundaries between social strata exist wherever patterns of circulation and association produce divisions between categories of occupations. In sociological research, individuals are allocated to the occupations that combine together various class, status, and command situations. Rates of mobility and social interaction must be examined in order to uncover how those occupations are clustered together into social strata.

For Marx, occupants of capitalist situations form one distinct social stratum because they 'circulate' freely around the forms of material capital. They are involved in extensive networks of intermarriage, and their children are able to inherit accumulated capital and enjoy the advantaged life chances that this generates. In the same way, Marx saw the occupants of proletarian situations as forming a separate social stratum because they move from one type of work to another similar type and from work to unemployment, they marry other workers, and their children have no choice but to try to enter paid employment.

One perennial topic in studies of stratification has been the question of whether the individual or the family household should be taken as the unit of analysis (Goldthorpe 1983; Abbott and Sapsford 1987; Scott 1994a). This debate has been fired by feminist criticisms of those conventional approaches to stratification that have allocated women to social classes according to the occupational position of their husbands (Stanworth 1984). Proponents of this approach claim that women's class attitudes and behaviour can be adequately 'approximated' by this method (Erikson and Goldthorpe 1993). This pragmatic argument offers little theoretical purchase on class, and its critics have rightly argued that women's work must be considered independently of men's work and must play an equal part in determining positions in a system of social stratification.

When considering the class, status, and command situations of individuals, it is important that each individual is classified on the basis of his or her own occupation. However, this is not the end of the matter. When considering the formation of social strata (rather than just the occupancy of class, status, and command situations), the social relations among members of family households cannot be ignored. Marriage and intimate partnerships connect or divide occupations from one another, and the question of the social stratum to which a person (man or woman) belongs cannot be decided without reference to their various family and domestic relations. Households are formed through marriage or cohabitation and it is within households that the educational and other opportunities that shape occupational mobility are generated. Households are also the bases for the organisation of much free-time interaction. In all these ways, household membership is central to the allocation of individuals to social strata.

Class societies

Class, status, and command operate alongside one another, but their relative importance can vary a great deal. In contemporary capitalist societies, they operate in and through the occupational division of labour and the associated system of property relations. One of the central features of the development of capitalist societies has been the way in which class situations have become, through the occupational system, the fundamental determinants of all other aspects of stratification. Status relations and command relations are, to a considerable extent, consequences, or reflections, of class relations. It was for this reason that Weber thought it appropriate to describe contemporary capitalist societies as 'class societies'. A class society is one in which individuals' class situation is the most important determinant of their life chances. Weber contrasted class societies with 'status societies', where the most important determinants of life chances and the overall pattern of social stratification were status situations. An example of this is traditional feudal and patrimonial societies. Similarly, it is possible to recognise 'command societies', where command situations are of paramount importance. An example of such a society is the former Soviet Union. These distinctions are important for comparative investigations, but they need not concern us here.

In a class society, social strata take the form of what Weber called 'social classes'. A social class is a cluster of households whose members owe their life chances principally to their property ownership or employment relations. It has been argued that the language of 'class' developed in the eighteenth and nineteenth centuries as an attempt to grasp the new social relations that emerged with the increasing salience of class situations in capitalist industrial economies. The language of class was central to the recognition of 'social classes'. By the early nineteenth century, it was widely recognised that capitalist societies contained three social classes – upper, middle, and working.

The final conceptual point that I need to make concerns class consciousness and class identity. We all attempt to interpret and understand the social world in which we live, and a central part of this social understanding is the attempt to interpret the social inequalities that we experience. Where people have life experiences in common, they are likely to develop a shared awareness and outlook on those experiences. Those who occupy the same class, status, or command situation and the members of a social stratum are likely to develop a shared understanding of patterns of social stratification and the boundaries of social strata. This common awareness is most likely to result when people work together, live in the same neighbourhood, and engage in the same leisure activities. It is also influenced by the imagery conveyed in the mass media, although this is often mediated by personal, face-to-face contacts. This consciousness of social stratification (whether strong or weak) forms a central part of overall images of society, those cognitive maps that guide us in our relations with others.

What Marx and Weber called 'class consciousness' is that form of class awareness that develops in social classes and, at its fullest, defines the interests that their members have in maintaining or enhancing their life chances. This shapes their political outlook and may lead them to form what Weber called 'parties' – conflict or interest groups of various kinds that give voice to their interests in political struggles. It is also likely to shape individual political action. Even in the absence of strong, class-based parties, a class consciousness may, for example, result in a close association between social class position and voting.

The formation of a class consciousness is by no means automatic, as the awareness of social stratification may be only weakly developed or may be outweighed by other elements in social experience. One important aspect of investigations into social stratification, therefore, is the extent to which people's social imagery and identity actually does centre on a sense of class membership. This means that we can add to the concepts we have set out so far – principally those of social stratification based on economic relations, the differences between class, status, and command situations, and the way occupations have been used to define strata – the ideas of identity and actions. One thing to have emerged from the debate on the alleged death of class is the fact that economic divisions of class may persist and even deepen, although people may no longer see class identities as ways of defining themselves and may not engage in collective, class-based action.

Mapping classes

I observed earlier that, to understand class fully, clear concepts and a coherent way to operationalise them in research are needed. The ideas just discussed have underpinned, often without being made explicit, the extensive discussion on how the class situations and social classes of contemporary Britain can be mapped into clear and reliable categories. Many different official and unofficial schemes have been proposed, by sociologists and non-sociologists alike. In these schemes, the number of classes and their composition vary quite considerably. In most cases, the theoretical basis of the scheme is not spelled out, and few have been constructed along explicitly Weberian lines. It sometimes seems as if there is a huge gap between stratification theory and empirical research on social stratification, with the latter showing a bewildering variety of class maps. This has led some sociologists to suggest a radical revision of how stratification is conceptualised and measured. The Cambridge approach, for example, sees stratification as involving a continuous scale rather than discrete categories (Prandy 1991; Blackburn and Prandy 1997).

The range of disagreement can be seen quite clearly in the differences between two of the leading class schemes, those of E.O. Wright (1985) and Goldthorpe (1980). Wright's scheme – the most developed of a number he has produced – contains 12 distinct class categories. These categories are defined by ownership and control of property, organisational assets of authority and skills and education. These 12 categories are seen by Wright as a halfway house between the detailed listing of class situations and a briefer listing of real social classes, and they were intended to grasp broad differences in life chances in a large comparative study. Marshall et al. (1988) applied Wright's scheme to British data and showed that the classes ranged from a 'bourgeoisie' of property owners, accounting for 2.0 per cent of the population, to a 'proletariat' containing 42.9 per cent of the population. Between the bourgeoisie and proletariat was a whole range of propertied and non-propertied classes covering those working in various kinds of managerial, supervisory and technical work.

Goldthorpe's scheme was an attempt to move closer to a true social class map, and he allocated class situations to seven separate categories. The extremes of this scheme were a 'service class' containing 25 per cent of the population and a class of non-skilled manual workers containing 22 per cent of the population (Erikson and Goldthorpe 1993). Unlike Wright, Goldthorpe did not incorporate substantial property ownership into his scheme, on the grounds that there were too few large property holders to figure in any national sample survey. Nevertheless, he recognised that, for some purposes, it was sensible to try to distinguish an 'elite' of property owners that would amount to a fraction of one per cent of the population. Goldthorpe has also modified his basic scheme in order to use it in the wide range of different societies that he has investigated in comparative research. This enlarged scheme is less useful for investigations of any one society.

Neither Wright nor Goldthorpe can be taken as having produced a completely accurate map of the class structure of contemporary Britain. Nevertheless, a wealth of secondary evidence suggests that Goldthorpe's basic scheme – modified by the inclusion of his eighth 'elite' category – does provide a remarkably accurate mapping of contemporary social class boundaries.

The older and rival 'official', that is government-produced, schemes, however, have been widely used for a variety of purposes related to the investigation of life chances and lifestyles and are likely to continue in use for some time, if only to make sense of reports of older research. In much of this chapter, these categories will therefore be the ones used. In many studies and especially in official statistics, two alternative sets of 'official' class categories have been used. These are the so-called 'Registrar General's scheme' and the SEG (Socio-Economic Groups) scheme. These are far from having the plausibility of the Goldthorpe scheme (not least because their origins and subsequent changes of detail were not grounded in a systematic sociological analysis), but they are nevertheless useful bases for mapping contemporary differences in life chances and lifestyles. Their particular attraction is that for many years they were the only schemes available to access data collected by the government's large-scale social surveys.

The basic Registrar General's scheme contains five social classes, in which Class III is divided into manual and non-manual sections. In its most developed form, therefore, the Registrar General's classification contains six social classes. This scheme attempts to see class differences in terms of the skill and employment relations of occupations, and it combines this with an assessment of the social standing of the various occupations. The 17-category SEG scheme was more systematically economic in its basis, and in its 'collapsed' version also contains six social classes. These boundaries, however, are drawn at different points and do not correspond to the Registrar General's categories in a one-to-one way. The SEG scheme has sometimes been converted into a 7-category scheme by the subdivision of white-collar workers by their grade. With numerous qualifications, it is possible to summarise the relationship between the various schemes as in Table 2.1.

A significant advance in sociological research techniques was the introduction of a new official social class scheme that extends the Goldthorpe classification and integrates it with the Registrar General's and the SEG schemes. This scheme is the NS-SEC, produced by David Lockwood and David Rose (see Rose and O'Reilly 1998), which allows a far more effective integration of official and sociological research into social class. For the first time, official and sociological maps of class structure have converged and, in the future, it will be possible to make far more accurate comparisons of census and survey data than ever before. The most common version of this scheme is shown in

Table 2.1 Social class schemes

Social classes		Goldthorpe categories	Registrar General categories	SEG categories
Advantaged classes				
	Capitalist class	'elite'		
	Service class	I, II	I	1, 2
Intermediate classes			II, IIIn	3a, 3b
	Petty bourgeoisie	IV		
	White collar workers	III		
	Blue collar elite	V		
Subordinate classes				
	Skilled manual	VI	IIIm	4
	Unskilled manual	VII	IV,V	5, 6

Source: CASE Paper 80 (2004) *The Economic Basis of Social Class*, London: LSE, Table 1. © Centre for Analysis of Social Exclusion.

Table 2.2 The NS-SEC social class classification

			Percentage of working population*
Advantaged classes	1.1	Large employers and higher managerial	2.3
	1.2	Higher professional	9.3
Intermediate classes	2.	Lower managerial and professional	24.4
	3.	Intermediate occupations	14.9
	4.	Small employers	11.0
	5.	Lower supervisory and technical	8.2
Subordinate classes	6.	Semi-routine occupations	16.5
	7.	Routine occupations	13.0

* England and Wales, 2011, aged 16–74 excluding full-time students and other 'never worked'.

Source: adapted from 2011 Census: http://tinyurl.com/lwclclh (accessed 13 August 2013).

Table 2.2, where it can be seen that official estimates see these classes ranging in size from 12 per cent of the British population in the highest class of employers and top professionals to the 33 per cent in the classes of routine and semi-routine workers. It should be noted that, for practical reasons related to sample sizes, the NS-SEC did not attempt to differentiate the 'small capitalist' class from the larger Class 1 of employers, managers and higher professionals in the scheme.

Recent work by Mike Savage and colleagues has used the resources of a BBC on-line survey to construct a scheme of classes which takes account of Pierre Bourdieu's distinction between occupational position (economic capital), patterns of interaction (social capital), and cultural consumption (cultural capital) (Savage et al. 2013). The research suggests the existence of seven classes in contemporary Britain: 'elite', established middle class, technical middle class, new affluent workers, traditional working class, emergent service workers, and 'precariat'. There is more information on this class scheme at http://www.bbc.co.uk/labuk/articles/class/, where you can also find your own (or your parents') location in the class map.

Changing class relations

These class schemes can be used to map the shape and size of classes and how these have evolved over time. Class relations have not stayed the same in British society. The structure of class relations itself is subject to change, and these patterns of change cannot be reflected in a fixed scheme of social classes. Nevertheless, the use of these categories in historical research does give some indication of how class relations have altered. A key element in this is the declining significance of the subordinate classes of manual workers. The subordinate classes amounted to over 80 per cent of the population in 1911, and in 1951 they still accounted for almost three-quarters of the population. By 1981, however, they represented only just over half of the population, and they now make up less than half of the population.

The decline in the number of manual workers, both skilled and unskilled, has been matched by a growth in the number of non-manual workers employed in the new service industries that grew massively over the course of the twentieth century. Between 1911 and 1951, non-manual workers increased from just over 12 per cent to around 25 per cent of the population. By 1991 they had risen to over 55 per cent of the population and have remained at that level.

These figures, like all official statistics, must be treated with caution. However, they do give a general impression of the principal change in the system of social stratification. The key to understanding this change is what Payne (1987b; see also Clark 1940) has described as the 'occupational transition'. This term refers to the shift in occupational structure that occurs with developments in technology and the division of labour. Industrialism involved a shift away from a structure of primary sector occupations (in industries such as agriculture and mining) to one in which secondary sector occupations (those involved in the manufacturing of machinery and consumer goods from the products of the primary sector) play the leading part. Developments in manufacturing technology, however, led to the growth of technical and specialist occupations that require high levels of education and training. These occupations grew at the expense of purely manual work and, at the same time, there was an expansion in the tertiary sector of public service and commercial occupations concerned with distribution, banking and insurance. The occupational transition is a process in which, successively, the primary, secondary and tertiary sectors become the most important bases of occupational differentiation.

The implications of these changes in the occupational division of labour have been widely discussed. For many observers, the changes point to a long-term development from an 'industrial' to a 'post-industrial' society, while others have described it as one aspect of a transition from a 'modern' to a 'post-modern' society. Whatever might be concluded about this, it is clear that the occupational transition has been associated with the development of forms of social structure in the second half of the twentieth century that were radically different from those that existed in the first half. The old pattern of social classes, their boundaries and forms of consciousness have all been transformed. The large, cohesive social classes that existed in the early twentieth century have developed into the more fragmented and divided classes of the new millennium.

These changes in class relations will be discussed later in this chapter, but I would first like to look in some detail at the distribution of life chances across the social classes as they exist today. This will establish a benchmark from which the social changes of the twentieth century can be assessed.

Class and life chances in contemporary society

Figure 2.1 uses broad statistical measures of *income* distribution – a relatively crude approximation to class divisions – to show a clear continuing class differential, despite an increase in real income over the period 1970–2010 for all classes. Although the rise in incomes slowed in 2011–12 due to the international banking crisis and the Coalition Government's economic policy, this basic pattern has continued (Department for Work and Pensions 2012: 21). However, growth has been the greatest for those at the top. Thus, the higher classes (the '90th percentile') have increased their income far more than the lower classes (the 10th or 25th percentile), resulting in a growing class division between top and bottom.

Controlling for household composition, tax and benefits, median weekly household income was about £419 in 2010–11 (*Guardian*, 2012). However at

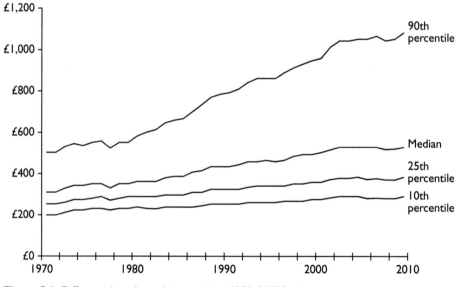

Figure 2.1 Differentials and trends in earnings, 1970–2010*

*GB weekly earnings, full-time male employees, constant 2009 prices, controlled for RPI inflation.

Source: Resolution Foundation (2012) *Gaining from Growth: the final report of the Commission on Living Standards*, London: Resolution Foundation. Available on www.livingstandards.org/our-work/final-report/ (accessed 12.06.2013).

the 90th percentile it was £846, whereas those at the 10th percentile received only £216 per week. The conventional 'poverty line' calculation was equivalent to the 18th income percentile, £261, i.e. 18% of households were living in poverty. (See Chapter 13 for more detail on poverty and low incomes.)

Although the various ways of measuring incomes can be a source of confusion, we can say that by 2011 gross weekly full-time earnings ranged from a median of about £720 for managers, directors and senior officials to £330 for 'elementary' – or 'unskilled manual' – occupations. Figure 2.2 shows how this varies between occupational groupings (another approximation for social class). The middle levels of the scheme do not form a neat and clear-cut hierarchy: skilled trades ('skilled manual workers'), for example, earn slightly more per week than administrative and secretarial ('routine' or 'white collar' non-manual workers).

These differences are reflected in such measures as the ownership of shares and membership in pension schemes. Almost three-quarters of professional men and two-thirds of professional women are in private pension schemes, compared with just under a half of unskilled men and a quarter of unskilled women. The level and continuity of income determines the opportunities that a person has to purchase property and, in addition to inequalities in

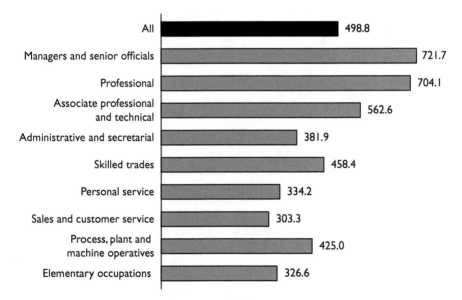

Figure 2.2 Earnings by occupational groups, 2010*

*Median gross weekly earnings, GBP

Source: *Your Complete Guide to Immigrating to the UK.* http://www.move-to-england.com/average-income.html (accessed 1 November 2012); based on Office for National Statistics (2011) *2010 Annual Survey of Hours and Earnings.*

income-generating shares, there are marked inequalities in home ownership. Rates of home ownership are much lower for semi-skilled and unskilled workers than they are for all other classes. The rate for unskilled workers is half that found among professionals.

Unemployment is a life experience that can push people into poverty, and all the evidence shows that unskilled workers are especially likely to become unemployed. The data in Figure 2.3, relating to broadly defined occupational categories, show the significant differences that exist between routine and manual occupations and all others. Rates of unemployment over a period of years have been almost five times as high for unskilled manual workers as they are for professionals and managers, and unskilled workers are also far more likely to remain unemployed for a year or more. It is also notable that the unemployment rates for male workers are almost uniformly higher than those for female workers.

Table 2.3 presents some evidence on how incomes are spent in different groups. It can be seen that certain consumer durables (television, telephone, washing machine, freezer) are owned by almost all households, with central

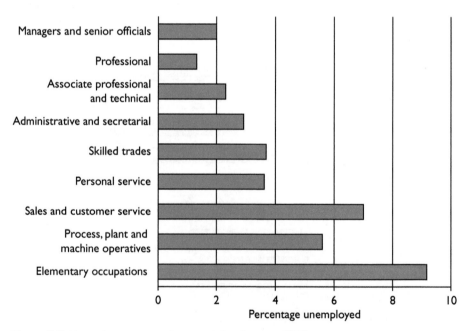

Figure 2.3 Unemployment rates by occupational groups, 2008

Notes
The percentage unemployed is the proportion of all persons in employment in the relevant occupation plus those unemployed who last worked in that occupation.
Data are at Q2 and are not seasonally adjusted. They include only people aged 16 and over.

Source: Office for National Statistics (2009) *Social Trends 39 – Labour Market.*

Table 2.3 Consumer durables, central heating and cars by social class (NS-SEC)

	Large employers and higher managerial	Higher professional	Lower managerial and professional	Intermediate	Small employers and own account	Lower supervisory and technical	Semi-routine	Routine
Percentage of households with:								
Television								
colour	100	98	99	99	99	100	98	99
digital	37	30	35	30	38	41	32	30
Telephone (fixed or mobile)	100	100	100	99	100	100	99	99
Central heating	100	98	95	92	93	92	92	90
Washing machine	99	98	98	95	97	96	95	96
Deep freezer/fridge freezer	97	96	97	96	96	97	96	96
Video recorder	97	94	95	95	93	96	93	93
CD player	98	97	96	94	90	93	87	88
Microwave oven	93	89	89	89	91	94	93	92
Home computer	89	88	80	65	67	64	53	47
Access to internet at home	82	83	70	52	58	51	36	33
DVD player	60	49	43	38	43	48	36	37
Tumble drier	71	63	61	60	63	59	56	56
Dishwasher	59	56	43	28	44	27	19	18
Car or van – more than one	61	50	43	31	54	32	21	24

Source: Office for National Statistics (2002) *Living in Britain*, Table 4.20.

heating, video recorders, CD players, and microwave ovens being almost as common. However, it is the lower classes that are less likely to own these basic goods. Home computers and internet access, by contrast, are far more unequally distributed, as are DVD players, tumble dryers, and dishwashers. Multiple car ownership, which occurs in over half of higher class households, is found among just a quarter of those in routine occupations.

These class inequalities are reflected in inequalities of health, life and death. A clear, although far from perfect, class gradient is apparent in all such data, some of which are documented in Figures 2.4 and 2.5, and Table 2.4. Even a basic thing like length of life is class-related. Although life expectancies improve, the gaps between the classes remain over long periods, so that we do not always need the latest data to see class differentials.

Rates of neonatal and infant mortality vary by class, regardless of how births and deaths are recorded, or whether actual numbers or rates are considered. The proportion of babies with low birth weight, rates of child mortality, and

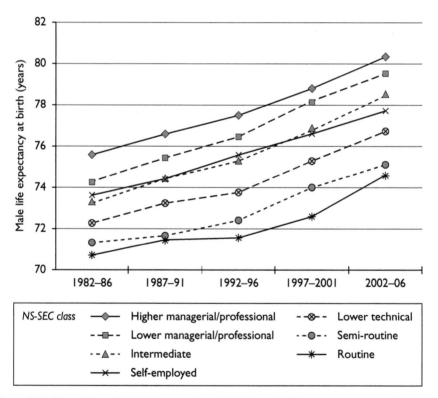

Figure 2.4 Class differentials in life expectancy, England and Wales

Source: Health Statistics Quarterly, 49 (2011), 18, Fig 1: Office for National Statistics. www.ons.gov.uk/ons/rel/hsq/health-statistics-quarterly/spring-2011/index.html (accessed 13 October 2012).

Table 2.4 Infant and perinatal mortality in England and Wales by social class

	Number of births		Deaths per 1000*					
	Live births	Stillbirths	Stillbirths	Perinatal	Neonatal	Post-neonatal	Infant
All	662,475	3,395	5.1	7.4		1.3	4.4
Inside marriage							
All	380,040	1,900	5.0	7.2	2.9	1.2	4.1
1.1 Large employers and higher managerial	3,553	132	3.7	5.4	2.2	1.0	3.3
1.2 Higher professional	5,248	202	3.8	5.6	2.5	0.8	3.2
2 Lower managerial and professional	8,968	362	4.0	6.1	2.6	0.9	3.5
3 Intermediate	2,317	133	5.7	9.1	4.1	1.2	5.3
4 Small employers and own-account workers	5,245	242	4.6	6.5	2.6	1.1	3.7
5 Lower supervisory and technical	3,910	184	4.7	6.6	2.4	0.9	3.2
6 Semi-routine	3,796	271	7.1	10.1	3.9	1.5	5.4
7 Routine	3,247	227	6.9	9.5	3.8	1.8	5.6
Other	1,726	145	8.3	10.9	3.4	2.6	6.0

* Stillbirths and perinatal deaths per 1000 live births and stillbirths. Neonatal, postneonatal and infant deaths per 1000 live births.

Source: Office for National Statistics (2010) Infant and Perinatal Mortality by Social and Biological Factors 2009, Table 7.

life expectancy all show the same class gradient, and these differentials in life chances persist into adulthood. Table 2.4 shows the numbers of births and death rates by NS-SEC class for births inside marriage (about 60% of births). Births outside marriage registered by couples show very similar patterns.

Mental health is also class-related: Figure 2.5 shows that common mental disorders are around two-and-a-half times more common among those with low incomes than they are among those with high incomes. Even the less critical aspects of health such as long-term eye, ear, and tooth problems (see also Chapter 14) show this same class gradient.

In addition to these demographic life chances, class situation appears as a clear determinant of both housing and education. The proportion of those living in overcrowded housing or without central heating shows the familiar gradient. The same pattern is also found in measures of educational achievement. Figure 2.6 shows that the attainment of five or more GCSEs at grades A to C is more than twice as high among children of professional parents as it is among children of parents with routine occupations. Rates of attendance at private schools, where attendance depends on income, are predictably unequal, so also are rates of higher education and the proportion of those leaving school with no formal educational qualifications of any kind. Again, as the

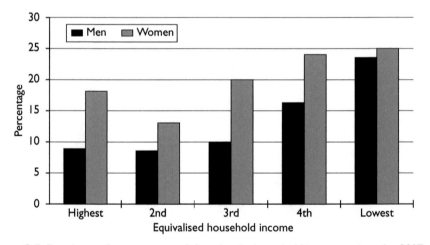

Figure 2.5 Prevalence of common mental disorders by household income and gender, 2007

Notes

Common mental disorders are those which produce emotional distress and interfere with daily life. Data are for adults and are age standardised.

Equivalised household income is household income adjusted to take account of the number of people in the household. Each column shows a quintile (20 per cent of the sample).

Source: Adult Psychiatric Morbidity in England, 32 (2009) (figure 2E), www.ic.nhs.uk/pubs/ (accessed 13 October 2012) © 2012, re-used with the permission of the Health and Social Care Information Centre. All rights reserved.

Royal Society of Arts reports, the gaps between the classes show no sign of diminishing (Perry and Francis 2010).

Inequalities of life chances in education of the kind shown in Figure 2.6 are especially important because these are central to the reproduction of class relations in successive generations. The chances of entering highly-paid occupations are closely related to educational achievement, which is, in turn, related to class origin as measured by occupation. This is the most striking result of research into social mobility (the movement between classes), the consequences of which are shown in Table 2.5 and Figure 2.7. Data from the 2005 General Household Survey, analysed by Li and Devine (2011), show high levels of self-recruitment in each class. In the top left and bottom right corners of Table 2.5, more than one-third of the men born with skilled, semi-skilled or unskilled fathers (classes VI and VII), and of those born into class I professional and management families, stayed in their origin classes. Only a little over 10 per cent moved from bottom to top, or from top to bottom of the class hierarchy. Despite apparently high levels of social mobility in the middle

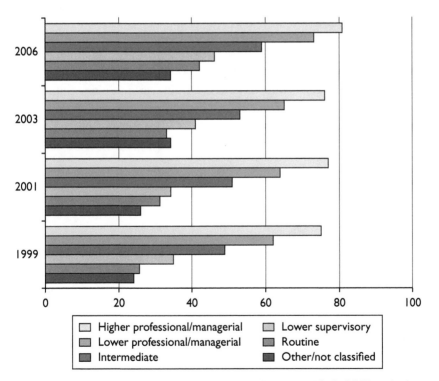

Figure 2.6 Percentages of students aged 16 gaining 5 or more A*–C GCSE grades by parental social class, 1999–2006

Source: Youth Cohort Studies 2008, www.earlhamsociologypages.co.uk/education%20data.html.

Table 2.5 Male social mobility in England and Wales

| Origin | Respondent's adult social class (NS-SEC) | | | | | | | Total | |
	I	II	III	IV	V	VI	VII	Percentage	Number
I	38	29	6	7	6	5	10	100	792
II	24	29	5	12	9	9	12	100	982
III	21	30	4	11	13	8	13	100	158
IV	15	21	3	17	15	14	16	100	487
V	17	23	5	13	15	13	16	100	487
VI	13	20	2	13	16	16	20	100	432
VII	11	20	3	13	16	14	23	100	622

Source: Adapted from Li and Devine (2011) Table II.

of the table, class inequalities in chances of mobility remain strong, and they closely follow the other documented inequalities in material life chances.

Payne and Roberts' (2002) study of trends in social mobility since the 1970s demonstrates that patterns of mobility have altered considerably over that period. Focusing on the advantaged (or service) class, the intermediate class and the working class of the Goldthorpe scheme, they show that about one-third of all men had been upwardly mobile between 1972 and 1997, and only one-sixth had been downwardly mobile. These were long-term trends, although there was some evidence that the increase in upward mobility had fallen somewhat in the years 1992–97. The manual working class is shrinking and becoming more homogeneous, while the service class is becoming larger and more diverse in its composition. The service class, nevertheless, remains highly self-recruiting, with little tendency for the sons of service class men to be downwardly mobile.

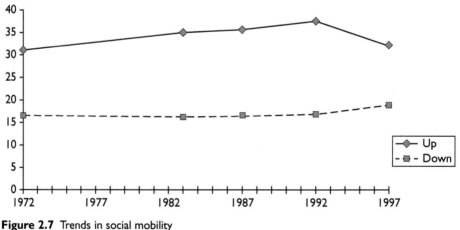

Figure 2.7 Trends in social mobility

Source: Payne and Roberts (2002) Table 2.

These figures on inequalities in life chances are illustrative only – such inequalities are documented more comprehensively for earlier periods in Reid's (1998) summary and in official publications such as *Social Trends* (no longer available), but seem to have received less coverage in recent times. My purpose in using them is to demonstrate that class situation, however this is measured, remains an important determinant of life chances in contemporary Britain. For a number of key measures, there is a clear class gradient and this has to be recognised in any discussion of the relevance of class analysis.

Images of class

Class differences are, however, far less directly reflected in distinct differences of *social status* and so are less directly reflected in sharp differences of attitude and outlook. Class consciousness, at least as conventionally understood, is no longer a central feature of contemporary class relations. The traditional status values that for so long defined the character of British class relations have decayed. This has undermined the everyday use of the language of 'class', which I have shown to rest, in fact, on 'status' differences in accent, dress and social background.

Cannadine (1998) has convincingly shown that the language of stratification in Britain has drawn on three distinct and often contradictory images, which he terms the hierarchical, the triadic, and the dichotomous. People draw on these to varying degrees and according to their social position (Lockwood 1975). They are rhetorical and interpretative devices that allow people to construct an understanding of the complex social structures in which they live. When thinking about the social stratification of their society, people are 'silently and easily shifting from one social vision to another' (Cannadine 1998: 165).

Hierarchical imagery has been dominant in social thought, especially in the form of a status hierarchy focused around traditional distinctions of education, dress, accent, ancestry and other aspects of style of life. This imagery began its long-term decline in the inter-war years, when the tripartite idea of upper class, middle class and working class consolidated its position in the popular mind. However, for many in the working class of subordinate manual workers, this shaded into a dichotomous opposition between 'us' and 'them'.

In the second half of the twentieth century, social imagery became more complex and less clear-cut. The old hierarchical and class divisions continued to decline as traditional and deferential values generally decayed with the decline of empire and the sense of 'greatness' that went with it. The growth of consumerism and the encouragement of a greater diversity in lifestyles fragmented the tripartite and dichotomous images and encouraged the formulation of new hierarchical images in which spending power and consumption were the central elements. Such 'money models' of society established new and highly flexible forms of status division that mask, rather than solidify, underlying differences in economic resources. Class, as defined by Marx and Weber, remains the crucial determinant of life chances and shapes the opportunities that people have for pursuing particular lifestyles, but it is less visible to the people themselves, who tend to define their positions in status terms.

Having sketched the persistence of class differences, it is now possible to look in more detail at each of the classes in turn. This will involve taking a broadly historical perspective, examining the most important social changes that have taken place at the various levels of the system of social classes. Only on this basis is it possible to understand contemporary patterns of stratification and recent debates about them. I will start with the subordinate, manual classes, followed by the intermediate or 'middle' classes, before discussing the 'advantaged' or upper classes.

Subordinate classes

The employment relations that define the social position of the subordinate manual worker are those of the wage labour contract. Manual workers are engaged to work in exchange for a wage that is supposed to compensate them for their labour time. Most typically, this kind of work has been paid on a weekly basis, although large numbers of manual workers are employed on a casual basis for shorter periods, or part-time. The limited autonomy allowed or expected for manual workers is apparent in the fact that their wages are generally calculated on an hourly basis, with employers exercising controls over both the time and pace of their work.

The market situation of the manual worker depends on the physical skills they can bring to the labour market. Those skills that are in the greatest demand are likely to command a higher rate of pay than skills that are less in demand, and a significantly higher rate than unskilled labour. The major source of internal division within this class has tended to be along the lines of skill (see Chapter 12).

The employment relations of manual workers also involve them in distinct work situations. Within the occupational division of labour of the enterprise that employs them, they are in a subordinate position and are subject to managerial authority in all aspects of their work. Manual workers in large organisations, such as car plants, engineering works, chemical plants, local authorities, banks, and so on (and formerly in now declining industries such as shipbuilding and coal mining) are subject to an extensive managerial hierarchy, the top levels of which may be far removed from them socially and physically. Manual workers in smaller organisations, which are typical of light industrial and building work, farm work and domestic service, are employed in smaller work groups and may have closer and more immediate contact with the managers and owners who supervise their work. Cross-cutting these lines of skill division is a secondary line of internal division between those involved in large-scale and those in small-scale work situations.

Similarities in their conditions of employment – their involvement in a wage labour contract and their subordination to managerial authority – form these workers into a distinct class at the economic level. Unless lines of division by skill and work situation become particularly sharp, workers will constitute what Marx referred to as a 'class in-itself'. They will be united by the shared economic conditions of propertylessness and subordinate employment, and the life chances with which these are associated. Where internal divisions become marked and are reflected in differences in life chances – and I have documented some evidence for this in the previous section – it may make more sense to identify a number of different subordinate classes, or subclasses, at the economic level.

The identification of economic class boundaries, however, is merely the first step towards the identification of social class boundaries. It will be recalled that those in various economically-defined class situations form a single social class whenever mobility and association are easy and frequent among them. When a class in-itself is forged into a social class through the relations of mobility and association of its members, it is on the way to becoming what Marx described as a 'class for-itself'. In its fully developed form, a class for-itself not only has a real existence as a clearly bounded social class, but also has a consciousness of its own position and its interests relative to other social classes. The class for-itself is most likely to act politically in pursuit of its collective interests.

For much of the nineteenth century, manual workers formed neither a class in-itself nor a class for-itself. They were, for the most part, employed in relatively small workshops where there were few opportunities for them to develop a consciousness of themselves as members of a single class and solidarity with each other. At the same time, they were greatly divided by differences of skill (Thompson 1968). From around the middle of the nineteenth century, however, the scale of production began to increase and workers were brought together in larger and larger productive settings. The discipline of the factory became the common experience for manual workers (Foster 1974). Within large-scale factory systems of production, the occupational division of labour brought workers with different skills into closer contact with each other, and many forms of craft work underwent a process of de-skilling. Manual workers, while still differentiated by their skills, became more homogeneous in terms of their market and work situations.

This gradual forging of manual workers into a class in-itself was matched by high levels of mobility and association across the lines of skill within the working class during the nineteenth and early twentieth centuries. Manual workers were sharply separated from non-manual workers and were internally unified as a distinct social class. Very few manual workers or children of manual workers entered non-manual work, even at its lowest levels, and there were very few marriages across manual/non-manual lines (Savage and Miles 1994). On the other hand, skilled workers whose jobs disappeared with technological change had little option but to take up unskilled work. Consequently, unskilled workers and their children could sometimes enter semi-skilled work through on-the-job training, especially in times of economic growth and relative prosperity.

These relations of mobility and intermarriage closely linked workers in a particular locality with one another, although they were far less closely linked with similar workers in other localities. As a result, the great industrial towns and inner cities each became distinct, but structurally similar, communities of families dependent on manual work. It was in these conditions that the idea of a 'working class' took root. The proletarian communities were fertile seedbeds for sentiments of class solidarity and the forging of a shared consciousness of class.

By the inter-war years of the twentieth century, this process was well developed. Contemporaries could refer to 'the working class' and everyone would know what this meant. Manual workers themselves embraced the label wholeheartedly and took it as their basic marker of social identity. The social institutions and agencies of the working class community sustained this identity (see Chapter 15). The dense networks of kinship and friendship that tied together neighbourhood and place of work (Young and Willmott 1957) had a more formal expression in the shared leisure-time involvement in pubs and clubs, cinemas and dance halls with which they were associated (Dennis et al. 1956; Jackson 1968), and in participation in trade unions, cooperatives and the Labour Party. Through the first half of the century, the electoral strength of the Labour Party grew in parallel with the crystallisation of these working-class communities. Support for the Labour Party was seen as a natural reflection of the stronger and deeper-rooted local solidarity of a working-class community.

The degree of unity found in the working class until the middle of the twentieth century should not be exaggerated. Skill differences persisted, associated with differences in life chances, and they could often undermine class solidarity. Highly skilled male craft workers – those who had served an apprenticeship or some similar period of training – could generally command higher wages and had greater job security than the semi-skilled and unskilled. Many were also able to exercise a degree of authority at work as the foremen and supervisors of other manual workers. Their relatively high wages and involvement in authority meant that there was a tendency for them to see their interests as distinct from those of unskilled workers (Gray 1981). As an 'aristocracy of labour', they were especially likely to be committed to ideals of self-help, getting on and respectability. One aspect of this respectability was that their wives withdrew from the labour market and took on full-time responsibility for domestic work and family obligations.

In a similar way, the persistence of small-scale production, often in small towns, meant that large numbers of manual workers were isolated from the mainstream of the labour movement. Their work situation encouraged a greater sense of identification with, or at least accommodation to, their employers and managers. Isolated from the supportive institutions of the oppositional subculture, they were more likely to defer to the authority of their employers (Stacey 1960; Newby 1975).

At the other end of the scale, there were large numbers of manual workers who lived in poverty and experienced long periods of unemployment. Casual work, lack of a skill, old age, and illness all made people susceptible to economic downturns that could push them below the poverty line (Booth 1901–2; Rowntree 1901). Poverty was the fate that could all too easily befall any manual working family. Once forced into poverty, their lives were degraded and demoralised and they became the targets of moralising attack by respectable society – manual and non-manual alike – which saw them as the 'rough' and 'undeserving' members of society. The poor were not, however, a distinct social class, they were the lower level of the working class. The rise and fall of families across the poverty line ensured that there was no sharp separation between the poor and the rest of the working class (see Chapter 13).

The mainstream of the proletarian working class, therefore, coexisted with the small-town working class of deferential workers and workers who aspired to improve themselves within the system (Parkin 1971; Bulmer 1975; Lockwood 1975). The lower levels of this working class formed a poor working class that amounted to 30 per cent of the whole population at its peak. The cultural division between the 'rough' and the 'respectable' working class, rooted in real economic differences, became a persistent theme in national politics.

Although there have been great changes, not everything has changed significantly since the middle of the twentieth century. Many of these changes had their roots in the early years of the century, while others are only just beginning to make themselves felt. It is undoubtedly the case, however, that the mid-twentieth century marked a watershed in the history of the working class.

The subordinate classes today

Manual workers, as I have shown, have come to account for a much smaller proportion of the population than was the case a century ago, and the economic boundary between manual and non-manual work has become less sharp and less salient. Changing technology has transformed much manual work. It has led to the collapse of whole industries and, through the resulting migration of workers in search of employment, it undermined the stable working-class communities with which they were associated, and and led to their eventual disappearance. The sociologists who first commented on these changes tended to see this as a process of 'embourgeoisement': a process in which manual workers, and society as a whole, were becoming more 'middle class' in character and outlook and, as a result, were abandoning old patterns of class solidarity and class politics (Zweig 1961; Klein 1965). These claims involved a serious overstatement of their case and many of the changes that were occurring were misinterpreted. They did, nevertheless, highlight the quite critical changes in class structure that were taking place.

Manual workers were not becoming middle class, but many of them were becoming far better-off than earlier generations. The 1950s and 1960s saw a real growth in manual worker incomes, and the general improvement in economic conditions allowed many more people to buy domestic consumer goods that were, in the past, available only to the privileged, or were simply not available at all. 'Affluent' workers were able to buy houses, washing machines, cars, and televisions, and they were able to furnish their homes in more comfortable ways than before.

This partial homogenisation of standards of consumption between manual and non-manual workers (apparent in Table 2.3) was not matched, however, by changes in their property and employment relations or their life chances more generally. The conditions of work for manual workers remained inferior even to those of routine non-manual workers. Their work was dreary and monotonous, it was not a source of intrinsic satisfaction, they had less security of employment, inferior pension and holiday provision, and few opportunities for promotion. They often had to move long distances to obtain this work. These conditions were tolerated only because of the size of the pay packet – the higher their pay, the greater their willingness to tolerate their inferior working conditions (Goldthorpe et al. 1969; see also Lockwood 1960; Goldthorpe and Lockwood 1963; Goldthorpe 1964; Devine 1992a).

Most importantly, consumer goods were acquired because of the opportunities that they opened up, not because they were the status symbols of a middle-class lifestyle. It is still worth making the obvious point that people buy washing machines to wash clothes, televisions to provide entertainment, and cars to provide them with mobility. These things are not accumulated simply in order to make a claim to higher status. Indeed, status divisions, like class divisions, remain sharp. Manual workers do not regularly and frequently entertain non-manual workers at home, nor do they engage in many common forms of leisure-time associations with them. They have, in fact, been forced to become more 'home-centred', more concerned with the life chances and lifestyle of their own family, as they no longer have extensive working-class communities to support them in times of need.

'Affluence' is a cyclical phenomenon, not a permanent state, and it is a matter of relative differences. Times of economic downturn involve reduced living standards, although levels of consumption remained much higher than in the past for most people in the post-2008 recession. For a significant minority, however, poverty conditions have persisted (Townsend 1979). For some commentators, the minority who remained in poverty during the post-war period have been seen as indicating the emergence of an 'underclass' which is separate from the social class of subordinate manual workers (Murray 1984). The evidence does not support this claim.

In the first place, poverty is associated with other social divisions, particularly gender, age and ill health, as we see in Chapters 3, 5 and 14. Equally, as in the past, poverty remains an ever-present possibility for all manual workers, and its incidence is generally beyond their individual control. The collapse of a firm or an industry in an area of high unemployment can throw workers at all levels of skill into protracted periods of poverty. On the other hand, those living in poverty are not necessarily condemned to a life of poverty. Many are able to obtain employment or better-paid work after a period of poverty, and there is, overall, a substantial turnover among those in poverty (Morris 1995). Those who do persist in poverty are predominantly the aged and the infirm, whose families and friends often do not themselves live far enough above the poverty line to help them out. Poverty is a real and important problem in contemporary society – an inevitable consequence of the way that it operates – but the poor do not form an underclass that exists separately from the rest of the class of subordinate manual workers (Scott 1994b). Poverty is not a class situation per se, although aspects of it can be considered to arise from many poor people's lack of opportunities to sell their labour in the market (Payne et al. 1996). These issues are discussed further in Chapter 13.

Changes in consumption and spending have largely concerned the extent to which a class of subordinate manual workers can be regarded as forming a class for-itself. Their market and work situations, and their associated life chances, remain distinct from those of other workers. Patterns of mobility and association still form them into a distinct social class, but these ties are neither so strong nor so intense as they were in the past. There is not the institutional support for the degree of class solidarity and cohesion that characterised the period before the Second World War and persisted into the 1950s.

Instead of a class consciousness rooted in common cultural and political traditions and participation in the labour movement, manual workers today are more likely to see their society, and their own position within it, in terms of a more open and flexible 'money model' of society that stresses relative spending power rather than political power. A focus on consumption and spending has made traditional class and status distinctions less relevant and has replaced them with new distinctions rooted in differences in consumption. To the extent that manual workers see the language of class as relevant – and most will use it if given some encouragement by a researcher – they do not regard it as the sole, or even the most relevant, way of describing themselves (Savage et al. 2001; Payne and Grew 2005).

People are likely to report themselves as being members of a large class that contains virtually the whole of society, with only the very rich and the very poor falling outside it. Within the main class, they make distinctions on the basis of the income and standards of living that they believe people to have achieved. Their knowledge of the true extent of income differences, however, is generally poor, and the correspondence between real conditions and perceived conditions is slight. Most manual workers feel that those who are better off than themselves are not that much better off, and so they look for only relatively modest improvements in their economic situation. They see the less well off as being not much worse off than themselves, often tending to be unsympathetic towards welfare payments. For some, this central class is described as a 'middle class', while for others it is a 'working class'. For yet others – perhaps a growing number – it is a sign of 'classlessness': if almost everybody is in a single class, then 'class' distinctions are no longer relevant (Savage 2000).

Subordinate manual workers, therefore, no longer live class in the same way as their counterparts did in the working-class communities of the past. This makes it more difficult to use the term 'working class' to describe them. They are a more fragmented social class than before. The differences between 'rough' and 'respectable', skilled and unskilled, proletarian and 'deferential' have become more visible and, at the same time, submerged in a larger and diverse pool of social identities. Despite the inferior life chances that were documented earlier in this chapter, manual workers have neither the solidarity nor the consciousness that is needed to sustain a strong commitment to collective class action. This declining sense of class identity is one of the most important factors underlying the decline in the traditional Labour vote since the 1940s. If a greater percentage of manual workers now support Labour than at any other time in the post-war period, this is evidence, not of a resurgence of class consciousness, but of the transformation of the Labour Party itself. New Labour's commitment to the 'classless' society required the party to mobilise the support of those who saw themselves in the large central class through pursuing the politics of the centre. When this failed to deliver promised benefits, support declined because the party could no longer rely on traditional class solidarity and identity.

Intermediate classes

Just as the subordinate classes can be thought of as either a single block or subdivided, the middle classes cover a range of positions. The three main segments of the intermediate classes comprise those who are employed in professional, managerial, administrative and technical occupations; those who are self-employed; and those with small-scale property. The employment relations of middle-class workers are distinguished from those of subordinate workers by the much greater autonomy and involvement in authority that their work situations involve and, for those at the more senior levels, by the possession of a longer-term 'service' contract of employment rather than a time-based labour contract. They are contracted to employ their skills in the service of an employer – generally a large-scale organisation – and they have a great deal of autonomy and discretion as to when and how they provide these services (Goldthorpe 1980). They are paid on a monthly, salaried basis, with significant additional benefits over and above their basic salary.

Self-employed workers, such as lawyers, accountants, doctors and many business consultants, whether working alone or in partnership, exchange their professional services for a fee paid by their clients. By virtue of their self-employment, they also have considerable discretion and autonomy over the conditions under which they work, with leeway in determining the level of their own fees. Small-scale property owners involved in the running of manufacturing or service businesses may, legally, be employees of their own businesses or self-employed. In practice, however, it is their property that defines the petty bourgeoisie's market situation and allows them to earn an income.

These differences in market situations have meant that the intermediate classes have never had quite the degree of economic homogeneity achieved by subordinate manual workers. Nevertheless, at the inception of the tripartite class grouping in the nineteenth century, there was an economic gulf between the two classes. The intermediate classes were more closely linked to each other than they were to those who stood below them in the economic structure. This was matched by the sharpness of the social imagery that, for most of the nineteenth century, separated the 'middle class' – often called the 'middle classes' – from the mass of society.

The middle classes were the leading elements in the towns and cities, occupying positions of power in local councils and running a whole array of church, civic, charitable and other voluntary associations (Morris 1990). Around the formal associations were formed extensive networks of interlocking committee memberships, informal meetings and leisure activities. Their economic circumstances and lifestyle sustained a cultural and political individualism that precluded any collective action except that in pursuit of sectional professional privileges and business interests. Individuals were to help themselves and not expect the state to act on their behalf, although this self-help often involved the mobilisation of the informal social networks that abounded within the middle classes. In small towns across the country, this pattern persisted into the 1950s (Stacey 1960).

Internal differences within the intermediate classes did, however, sharpen towards the end of the nineteenth century. The numbers of doctors, lawyers and teachers grew only slowly in the years leading up to the First World War, as did the numbers of small property owners. However, there was rapid and substantial growth in the number of managerial and clerical workers: there were nearly three times as many clerks in 1911 as there were in 1880. Clerks accounted for 0.8 per cent of all male employees in 1851, but by 1911 they accounted for 5.7 per cent. By 1951, they constituted 10.5 per cent.

While these clerks did not have the long-term service contract and the autonomy enjoyed by the old middle class, they did enjoy conditions of employment that were far superior to those of subordinate manual workers. They were generally recruited through the interpersonal connections ('social capital') that they or their families could mobilise, and their promotion depended on their maintaining good personal relations and loyalty to their employers (Lockwood [1958]1989). These employment conditions secured them clear advantages in income and status over manual workers. The numbers of shop assistants, commercial travellers and technicians were expanding similarly. However, all these workers remained at some distance from the established middle classes and tended to be defined as 'lower middle class' (Crossick 1977).

The continued growth in the numbers of clerical and managerial workers in the twentieth century further increased the diversity of the 'middle classes'. The increasing scale of management in large business enterprises produced a growing 'service class' of managers who became increasingly sharply separated from the equally large number of clerical workers whose working conditions were being transformed. No longer dependent on the mobilisation of personal contacts, clerks became more dependent on the educational qualifications they could secure. The expansion of management was also associated with a mechanisation of office work, which progressively devalued the skills that these qualifications signified. Office work became more routine and, in many respects, more 'manual' than 'mental' in character (Braverman 1974). Promotion opportunities for clerks declined, while the work itself became more feminised (Holcombe 1973; Anderson 1976). By 1951, over half of all clerks were female. The women who entered clerical work were often the wives or daughters of manual workers, further reducing the significance of the boundary between clerical work and manual work. Clerks were no longer as unambiguously 'middle class' as they had been in the nineteenth century, while the middle classes had become more exclusively professional and managerial in character.

The transformation of the middle classes, therefore, began much earlier than the changes experienced by subordinate manual workers. Nevertheless, the middle of the twentieth century does mark an important point of transition for the intermediate classes also. Economic competition meant that small businesses came under greater pressure from the large enterprises (in which the vast array of managers were employed), and consequently the position of the petty bourgeoisie was much weakened. Small business owners also had high levels of self-recruitment, and correspondingly lower rates of mobility in and out of other intermediate class situations (Scase and Goffee 1982). The growth of large-scale enterprise also transformed the position of many managerial and professional workers, forcing them to convert from self-employed to employed positions (Johnson 1972). Those in service locations became more diverse. Particularly significant was the growth of the public sector and the 'semi-professionals' employed within it (teachers, social workers, nurses and so on). The vast growth of financial services in the 1980s led to an expansion in the numbers of non-traditional service workers in insurance, pensions and estate agency. At all levels, then, the intermediate classes have been tied to bureaucratised conditions of employment.

The class cohesion of the middle classes was always rather low. They formed a clearly bounded social class in relation to the working class, but they were internally divided by the relative difficulty of moving from propertied to employed and self-employed positions. Savage et al. (1992) have argued that this separation became more marked in the second half of the twentieth century, and that the managerial, professional and propertied sections of the intermediate classes are now sharply distinct from each other. The intermediate layers of the class structure have, like its subordinate levels, become more fragmented. This fragmentation at the intermediate levels has been along the lines of organisational assets, educational assets and property assets.

As a result, traditional middle-class individualism and civic power have weakened (Stacey et al. 1975). Workers in the vast managerial bureaucracies – especially those in the public sector – are more likely to consider collective action in pursuit of their interests. In place of the individualism of the old middle classes, the collectivism of the new middle classes has emerged.

The term 'middle class', however, may be less useful as a designation for those in these intermediate employment and property relations. The term 'middle class' as a self-description, as I have already shown, is as likely to be used by manual workers as it is by non-manual workers. Large bureaucracies, with their extensive professional and managerial hierarchies based on entry by educational qualification, technical competence, measured performance and competitive promotion, form the bases of intermediate class situations. This encourages their occupants towards the social imagery of an ostensibly open and 'classless' society. Intermediate class situations still exist and their members still enjoy life chances that divide them from subordinate manual and routine non-manual workers, but their self-perception – even when it employs the phrase 'middle class' – is not one that emphasises either their traditional status or a solidaristic class identity.

Advantaged classes

The advantaged classes comprise people who are involved in property and employment relations that give them ownership and/or control over large amounts of capital. Whether in the form of land, buildings, machinery or financial securities, property is the key to their power. In some cases, this involves the direct personal ownership of substantial property. This might be as the exclusive or part-ownership of a large integrated block of capital (such as a landed estate or large business enterprise) or it might be the holding of diversified portfolio investments in a large number of different types of capital. In other cases, the class situation might involve an employment relation that defines a position of control over these kinds of assets. The chief executives of large enterprises, their part-time directors and the investment managers of large financial enterprises are all able to use their control over capital to secure, directly or indirectly, significant advantages for themselves. This view of a class determined by their ownership or control of property contrasts with that of elites who occupy positions of political power (see Chapter 11).

For much of the nineteenth century, there was a sharp separation between land and manufacturing as sources of class advantage. Landowners – closely linked to the financial sector – saw themselves and were seen by others as forming an 'upper class', rooted in the aristocracy and, more narrowly, in the peerage. Landed wealth was the source of the biggest fortunes (Rubinstein 1981), and it was the landowning upper class that dominated the political machinery of the state (Guttsman 1963). Manufacturing capitalists, often provincial in their origins, became an increasingly significant category of wealth, but they were barely distinguished by their contemporaries from the vast mass of the middle classes. The social imagery of upper, middle and working class made manufacturing capitalists virtually invisible as a class. Towards the end of the nineteenth century, land and industry came closer together. Peers and other landowners, who were experiencing a fall in the returns on their estates, became more willing to invest in industrial enterprises and sit on the boards of the large business enterprises that were formed from the 1880s onwards in banking, insurance and railways, as well as in manufacturing. A 'lord on the board' was an important marker of stability and probity in a more complex business environment. Through these connections, and through mobility and intermarriage, manufacturing capitalists came grudgingly to be accepted as part of the upper class (Thompson 1963; Stone and Stone 1984; Scott 1991).

At the turn of the twentieth century, the advantaged class numbered just under 40,000 people, approximately 0.1 per cent of the population. Its position in society was confirmed more by its status than by any widespread recognition of its economic resources. The popularity of the royal family was central to this because, as major landowners, they were core members of the class. Victoria, Edward VII, George V, and George VI were well integrated into the advantaged class and, through the ceremony and glamour that was attached to royalty, they ensured that the social class as a whole received a high level of public approval and at least overt deference. The cement that held together the increasingly diverse upper class as a distinct status group was the round of 'Society' activities: dances, dinners, parties and salons held by the aristocracy and other prominent families in their London and country homes (Weiner 1981; Rubinstein 1993; McKibbin 1998).

As it became less exclusively aristocratic, Society became more ostentatious and more focused around glamour and frippery. The relaxation of traditional standards helped to weld the diverse elements of the upper class together, but in the long run Society was incapable of preventing the disintegration of the class in the face of this diversity. The institutions of Society became more open to sheer wealth and less able to impose a single lifestyle on all its members. This is clear in the informal social networks that were rooted in kinship and friendship, and sustained through attendance at public schools and prestigious Oxford and Cambridge colleges. These networks were important bonds of solidarity for the male members of this upper class, who could rely on the mobilisation of the social capital of their 'old boy networks'. As the twentieth century progressed, these networks became weaker. They could no longer guarantee success for landowning families, although they were still highly successful in the social placement of the sons of the aristocracy, and they could not meet the needs of those who were closer to the margins of the class. Advantaged class situations were becoming ever more business-based in character and less exclusively landed. In parliament and government, public schools and old universities, and the top levels of the military and civil service, the upper class was beginning to lose its distinctiveness and its cohesion (see Chapter 11).

By the early 1950s, 'Society' had virtually ceased to operate in its traditional form, its demise having been hastened by wartime conditions. The advantaged classes could no longer really be defined as an 'upper class'. Instead, they formed a diversity of overlapping cliques and sets, an 'upper circle' rather than an 'upper class'. These cliques were diverse. Some followed traditional country pursuits, some were involved in the media and entertainment, some were members of a 'jet set', and others simply kept to themselves and made their money

This decay in the traditional status of the upper class – the death of the upper class – was the counterpart of the growing economic complexity of property and its management. The middle decades of the twentieth century saw a transition from the direct personal ownership of land and business that had prevailed in the nineteenth century to more indirect and impersonal forms of corporate ownership. The number of large personal shareholdings in major companies declined and there was a corresponding growth in the proportion of shares that were owned by financial enterprises such as insurance companies, banks and pension funds (Scott 1997). In this situation, it was the directors and top executives who controlled the capital embodied in these enterprises.

These directors and executives were recruited disproportionately from those who were, individually, property owners, although new channels of mobility to advantaged class situations had been opened up. Wealthy families had diversified their assets by taking stakes in a large number of enterprises and entrusting the management of these assets to the growing financial enterprises. At the same time, they were able to ensure their continuing control over the assets that generated their wealth by taking top board and management positions in them. Whether as rentiers, who depended passively on the management of their capital by others, or as active finance capitalists and finance executives, the propertied were able to secure a continuation of their advantaged life chances. Indeed, the demise of Society made their privileges far less visible and therefore less open to attack than in the past (Scott 1997: Ch. 8).

This trend has been described as a 'managerial reorganisation' of the capitalist class (Mills 1956). Business enterprises have become ever more closely tied together through the interweaving shareholdings and interlocking directorships of the big financial investors. The directors and executives of these enterprises are overwhelmingly drawn from a propertied background, although with a growing influx from management and the professions, and their children are, thereby, able to become the propertied inheritors of the next generation. The capitalist class of today combines personal wealth with top-level participation in corporate management.

Conclusion

I have tried to show that a Weberian approach to social stratification – especially the distinction between class and status – makes possible an understanding of both the contemporary contours of class division and the long-term processes that have brought them about. There has been a move away from a stable tripartite system of social classes (upper, middle, and working) to a more fragmented class structure in which the advantaged, intermediate, and subordinate levels are no longer so directly defined in status terms. It was the close association of class and status from the 1880s to the 1950s, underpinned by the economic conditions of the period, that allowed the formation of a stable system of social classes. In these circumstances, the members of the various classes readily accepted this in their own social imagery, class consciousness, and political action.

Economic change and the demographic changes that have gone along with it have destroyed this structure. These changes have long roots, but they have been especially marked since the 1950s. Class divisions still exist, but they are no longer so easily mapped into a tripartite imagery of social classes. There is still a sharp gradient of life chances, as shown in the evidence on health, mortality, housing, and education presented in this chapter, but it is no longer so obvious exactly where the real social boundaries are to be drawn on this gradient. Boundaries are fuzzier, less distinct. Indeed, it is not clear whether it is more useful to focus on the broadly defined advantaged, intermediate and subordinate classes or their internal divisions along the lines of their property and employment relations.

In this sense, class as a social division is a complex one that does not divide society neatly or conspicuously into two, three, or even half a dozen categories. It is also true that, certainly compared to the past, many more individuals can move between classes during their lifetimes (Payne 1992). As will be seen in Chapters 3 and 4, other social divisions such as gender and ethnicity have become increasingly important to the sense of identity. However, the 'fuzziness' of class boundaries and the increased complexity in the structure of subdivisions do not necessarily invalidate the idea of social divisions.

The new complexity of multiple class situations should not disguise this fact. It would be wrong to mistake contemporary society's increased individual capacities to manipulate the cultural trappings of identity as meaning that class no longer matters. No amount of personal choice to 'mix and match' consumption behaviour or symbolic life goals will remove the underlying economic constraints inherent in class situations. The fact that we encounter so much political rhetoric about 'classlessness', the importance of individual choice or the latest fashion in 'achievement', does not mean that class has disappeared.

It is not necessary for everybody to believe in the existence of class or constantly think of themselves in terms of class identity for class to be a social division. The system of class situations is not dependent on people's awareness of it or their faith in it. Differences in health and mortality, for example, exist as material facts, independently of what people may, or may not, think about them. Social divisions do not always lead systematically to a sense of distinctive group identities, or to action with others on the basis of such shared personal social identities.

Despite lacking in visibility, and however imperfectly measured in the existing social classifications, class divisions remain central to social life in contemporary Britain. Of course, we recognise that in contemporary society, people are less likely spontaneously to describe their own experiences in the language of class. They search for more direct and specific determinants of their life chances to put alongside their recognition of class, and they recognise the independent parts played by age, gender, and ethnicity. We do not live in a 'classless' society, although we do live in a society whose members no longer spontaneously and unambiguously use the language of class as the obvious, taken-for-granted way of describing social inequalities. Class is not dead, but perhaps the monolithic social imagery of class has, indeed, had its day.

Discussion Questions

1. To what extent do people today identify themselves as members of a particular social class? Has class consciousness declined in the face of a growing consciousness of gender, ethnicity and other sources of social division? Draw on evidence from other chapters in this book to consider this question.

2. Is it still appropriate to see the working class as the source and basis of radical political action aimed at changing the structure of inequality? To what extent has the transformation of the working class and the declining salience of working-class identity undermined the basis of radical political commitments? Are there new sources of opposition to class inequalities?

3. Does the growing significance of consumption and consumerism point to a new source of social division distinct from that of class relations based in production? To what extent is consumption independent of production? Have the consumer identities promoted through advertising become more important than traditional class identities?

4. Can we still see modern societies as dominated by a propertied, capitalist class? What kind of evidence is needed to assess the continuing inequality in property ownership? Is there evidence that such a class also dominates the state as a 'ruling class', as depicted in Marxist theory?

FURTHER READING

The most comprehensive overview of data on class differences is Reid, I. *Class in Britain* (London: Polity Press, 1998), although now a little dated. More detail can be found in the various editions of *Social Trends* and other publications (now available online). Payne, G. *Mobility and Change in Modern Society* (London: Macmillan – now Basingstoke: Palgrave Macmillan, 1987) is an excellent summary of the debates and trends in social mobility, while McKibbin, R. *Class and Cultures: England 1918–1951* (Oxford: Oxford University Press, 1998) is a social history of earlier class differences that adds some life to the statistical bones. A useful balanced summary of the theoretical debates can be found in Crompton, R. *Class and Stratification* (Cambridge: Polity Press, 2008, 3rd edn), while empirical material is well covered in Roberts, K. *Class in Modern Britain* (Basingstoke: Palgrave Macmillan, 2011, 2nd edn). A useful overview that pays particular attention to more recent changes in lifestyle and outlook is Savage, M. *Class Analysis and Social Transformation* (Buckingham: Open University Press, 2000).

CHAPTER 3

Gender

PAMELA ABBOTT

This chapter will provide you with a broad critical understanding of the following issues in gender as a source of social division:

- The social construction of gender
- Changing gender relationships in western societies
- Social as opposed to biological explanations for gender inequalities
- Gendered power relationships
- Gender differences and inequalities in education
- Gendered patterns of inequalities in paid employment
- Gender and poverty across the life-course

Given the central position of gender within sociology in the second decade of the twenty-first century, it is easy to forget that it is only since the 1970s that the discipline has attached greater importance to the distinctive positions of women and men. Assumptions about gender and gender differences are now seen as embedded in the structures and institutions of British and other societies, in our way of thinking and talking, our beliefs and attitudes, and in employment, education, politics, the family and leisure. In identifying gender as an important social division, sociologists are going beyond arguing that men and women have *different* roles in society and are typically found performing different jobs. We are concerned with *explaining* the division – to provide theoretical accounts based on the idea that these differences are structural, that they are predominantly social in origin, and that men as a category have more power than women as a category. While there are considerable differences in the various theoretical accounts (see the discussion on 'patriarchy' below), men are seen as being able to use their power to control resources, maintain their position of dominance vis-à-vis women and so are able to exploit women. However, although men are thus in a position of advantage, they are also structurally constrained by ideas of masculinity and what is expected as the correct way for a 'man' to behave.

Underlying gender divisions, there continues to be a (generally unspoken) view that the sexual division of labour and the inequalities between men and women are natural and immutable. This is reflected, not only in the assumption that women should be responsible for domestic labour and child care, but also in the occupational roles that are available to women, or indeed those from which women continue to be excluded. There continues to be a view that women are naturally good at caring, service work, secretarial work and so on, and an expectation that when men do this work they will do it differently from women. The assumed natural basis for women being able to perform these occupational roles is also used to justify the low pay of female occupations compared with male occupations, whether they are routine, non-manual or professional. Inequalities between men and women persist across the life-course, from girls and young women being denied the freedoms enjoyed by their brothers, through inequalities in the labour market, to the poverty and dependency on the state for income and care that many older women experience (Chapters 5 and 13).

Gender identity is fundamentally ascribed at birth and structures all our experiences and the expectations that others have of us. The first, or at least the second, comment made on delivery of a baby is its gender. This is marked in the hospital by the colour of band that is placed on the baby's wrist. In UK hospitals, boys have a blue band and girls a pink band. From that point on, they are regarded as fundamentally different – as boys or girls. This ascription of gender at birth is reflected by the clothing in which they are subsequently dressed, which in turn is the fundamental basis of our cues for social interaction and those expectations which are dependent on the assumed gender of the person with whom we are interacting.

Sociologists have challenged the view that gender divisions can be explained by biological differences between men and women. They argue that biology is an inadequate explanation, and that we must look to social, cultural and structural reasons for the differential access that men and women have to power, wealth and privilege in modern industrial societies. Smith (1979) has argued that there is a distinct female life experience which is a reflection of the essentialist notions of what it is to be male or female. The notions of what constitutes femininity and masculinity are used as the basis for interacting with girls/women and boys/men, both in terms of expectations and the behaviour that is encouraged or discouraged and punished. Boys/men are expected to be domineering, aggressive, noisy and active, whereas girls/women are expected to be caring, quiet and less assertive. These very characteristics are those that are seen to differentiate men and women in terms of employment. Characteristics associated with men are those that are said to be necessary for management positions within non-manual occupations and skilled positions within the manual classification. By contrast, the 'natural' qualities of girls/ women are seen to suit them for occupations which are accorded lower status and lower economic remuneration, such as nursing, teaching, or employment as care workers, waitresses, domestic workers, and so on (see Chapter 12).

This division between men and women now seems so obvious that it is easy to forget that, until the 1970s, sociologists rarely considered gender divisions to be significant, focusing mainly on class and status differences. Indeed, it is possible to go beyond mere criticism of sociology for ignoring the importance of gender divisions and to argue that women were often ignored. Most socio- logical research focused on boys and men. Women were not even included in many samples and, when they were, gender was not seen as a significant vari- able for analysis. Even when differences between men and women were noted, these were usually seen as 'natural', the outcome of biological differences. As Hartman (1978) indicated, sociology was at best sex-blind, and at worst sexist.

Changes in gender relations?

This chapter argues that gender inequalities persist as a significant social divi- sion and illustrates this by focusing on three areas: education, work, and social exclusion. The ascriptive principle of gender – our genders are something that we are born with – continues systematically to disadvantage women and to deny them freedom and equality with men. In other words, structural con- straints continue to limit the opportunities available to women in a masculine culture. At the same time, although men benefit from this relationship, the same masculine culture also imposes constraints on men.

This not to deny recent changes in men's and women's roles, as the latter have moved from the private sphere of the home into the public sphere of work and wider social involvement. However, there continue to be different expectations of the roles of men and women. In particular, there is continuing evidence that women's entry into the public sphere actually increases their burden. They are expected to take on more roles – worker as well as domestic labourer and mother – whereas men's major role remains that of breadwinner. A Eurobarometer poll (1997) found that nearly 50 per cent of men but only 30 per cent of women thought that 'the jobs that need to be done to keep a home running such as shopping, cooking and cleaning' were shared equally between themselves and their husband, wife or partner.

As women move into the public sphere, control by men in the home is re- placed by control in the workplace or by the state (Abbot and Ackers 1997). This is exemplified in the role of office wife/secretary (Pringle 1988), mother/ primary school teacher (Burgess 1990) and wife/mother/tart/female flight at- tendant (Tyler 1997). In other words, the servicing work that women have traditionally undertaken for men in the private sphere becomes part of the work they are expected to perform in the public sphere. Men employed in the same jobs are not expected to undertake this work. So, secretaries are expected to perform wifely duties for their male bosses, primary school teachers have to 'mother' their classes of children, and flight attendants are seen as being there to 'serve' the needs of male passengers. Women are expected to relate to men in the public sphere in the same way as they do in the private sphere.

This is not to suggest that women are passive victims. Women do struggle to resist male power and this is evidenced by the considerable gains that women have made since the 1980s, not least in western societies. Gender relations have been transformed: girls are now doing as well, if not better, in the educational system than boys. Women (including married or cohabiting women) are increasingly in paid employment, with some women challenging men for the 'top' jobs. Women are no longer largely confined to the domestic sphere – they are part of the 'public sphere' of paid employment and politics.

One reaction to this has been a concern that male dominance – masculinity – is being challenged. Many working-class boys are now taking on masculine identities in situations where the usual transition for boys is from work to (un)employment whereas they see their male relatives without paid employment and their mothers as the breadwinner, often engaged in low-paid service work. In this situation, some of the most powerful 'truths' about gender – that men are breadwinners and women are housewives and mothers and economically dependent on men – have been exploded. In the face of this uncertainty about what it is to be a man, there are now a variety of masculinities rather than one hegemonic understanding.

Many areas with high levels of social deprivation have witnessed the construction of an exaggerated masculinity, whereby to 'be a man' is to engage in activities such as binge drinking, joy-riding, burglary, and arson. Even in less harsh circumstances, boys/men still value forms of maleness which involve the routine harassment of girls and women, homophobia and a rejection of 'female' characteristics (Mac an Ghail 1994). Boys continue to take on masculine identities within which they see themselves as dominant, more powerful than, and controllers of, women. In particular, working-class lads remain 'sometimes/always sexist, homophobic and often explicitly racist' (Dixon 1996). Middle-class boys adopt the role of intellectual masculinity – an apparently effortless success (Power et al. 1998). The culture of masculinity also perpetuates a kind of domineering manhood – the definition of masculinity that boys take on has femininity as the subordinate term. Boys therefore 'need' to dominate girls in order to demonstrate that they are 'real men'.

An alternative position has suggested that women are increasingly rejecting their 'natural' roles as wives and mothers. This is seen as an important factor in explaining male unemployment, the rise in crime and divorce rates and the lower educational achievement of some young men. However, feminist sociologists have argued that these New Right and 'Christian sociologists' – Murray, Marsland, Cox, Dennis – were doing no more than simply blaming women for social problems (Abbott and Wallace 1992).

Although the initial focus of much feminist sociological work was gender divisions, writers have also come to recognise the importance of divisions amongst women (and men) based on race, ethnicity, age, social class and sexuality (Phizacklea 1983; Crompton and Mann 1986; Arber and Ginn 1991). As Guillaumin (1995: 17, 19) has pointed out:

> women, blacks and other dominated social groups are not categories existing of and by themselves ... they are constituted in the context of social relation and dependence and the process of sexualisation and racialisation ... functions so as to allocate humans within specific social categories and positions.

More recently, it has been argued that differences between men and women are no longer as great as they were. Young women are doing as well, if not better, than young men in the formal education system, and women are competing on more equal terms with men in the labour market. However 'in Europe inequalities between women and men remain substantial in a large number of areas', not least in employment and public policy (Eurobarometer 1997: 3; Wallace et al. 2004).

Feminist sociologists have pointed out that these inequalities apply within academic circles as well as outside. The work of nineteenth- and early twentieth-century female sociologists, in particular that which recognised the centrality of gender analysis, has been erased from the sociological cannon (Lengermann and Niebragge-Brantley 1998). Who now has regard for Harriet Martineau, the first translator of Comte; Marianne Weber, a sociologist in her own right but reduced to the status of Max Weber's wife; Jane Adams and the other Chicago sociologists who published in the *American Journal of Sociology*, but who came to be regarded as 'social workers'; or Beatrice Webb, whose own contributions became merged with her husband's as 'The Webbs'? These are examples of the way in which the power of men in privileged positions can be used to determine what is to count as important and significant knowledge, while in the process the work of women is discounted. This process has been called the construction of a 'man-made world' – knowledge produced by women has been ignored, marginalised or erased from history (Abbott et al. 2005).

Nineteenth- and early twentieth-century sociologists accepted biological explanations for gender division. More accurately, perhaps, in the terms of

Sydie's (1994) book title, *Natural Women, Cultured Men,* they attributed female behaviour to women's physical characteristics, and saw men as dealing
in logic, reason, intellect, and so on. Contemporary sociologists have generally
sought to replace this gendered explanation by sociological explanations. An
important starting point for this was the distinction between sex, meaning biological differences (anatomical and hormonal), and gender, meaning socially
constructed expectations and behaviour.

> Gender refers to the varied and complex arrangements between men and
> women encompassing the organisation of reproduction, the sexual divi-
> sion of labour, cultural definitions of femininity and masculinity. (Bradley
> 1996: 203)

Beck (1992) calls this the 'omnidimensionality' of the inequality between men
and women.

Gender is a social category – a lived relationship between men and women
– which structures every aspect of our daily lives. It is both cultural and material. Men are able to control women, not only by marginalising them in
discourse, but also by the exercise of political, economic, social and physical
power. Furthermore, gender is a 'script' – we have to learn how to 'do gender',
that is, behave in gender-appropriate ways. All gender behaviour is an act, a
performance. As Jan Morris (1974: 140) has said about her own transition
from male to female, 'There seems to be no aspect of existence, no moment
of the day, no contact, no arrangement, no response, which is not different for
men and women.'

Explaining gender divisions

I have already pointed out that gender divisions have traditionally been seen
as natural, inevitable and therefore immutable. This acceptance that different
roles, associated statuses and access to scarce resources are based on natural
differences went unquestioned, not only by the founding male sociologists,
but in academic sociology until the 1960s. Whilst some sociological work did
explicitly accept the biological argument, most omitted a gender analysis –
assuming either that men and women experienced the social world in the
same way, or that gender differences were natural and/or of no interest or importance. As Simone de Beauvoir ([1949]1972: 16) has pointed out, women
have been defined as 'other':

> She is defined and differentiated with reference to men and not he with
> reference to her. She is the incidental, the inessential, as opposed to the es-
> sential. He is the subject, he is the Absolute. She is the Other.

However, in the 1960s and 1970s, female sociologists began to argue that the sociological imagination was a male one – it did not speak to the experiences of women. Despite its claim to neutrality, sociology had a male bias. Smith (1979) argued that this was because women's concerns and experiences were not seen as authentic but subjective, whilst men's were seen as the basis for the production of 'true' knowledge. Consequently, sociological knowledge portrayed women through the eyes of men and male-made theories.

In this way, sociology, along with other disciplines such as biology and anthropology, was implicated in maintaining the subordination of women by providing a scientific justification for it. Mainstream sociological theories underpin and justify the subordination and exploitation of women by claiming to be factual. They have framed what is considered to be the subject matter of sociology – what should be studied, how studies should be undertaken, what questions it is important to seek to answer, what variables are significant and inform the conceptualisation and interpretation of the research findings. Feminist sociologists have, therefore, argued that it is necessary to re-conceptualise sociology, not just to add women, but to develop adequate theories for explaining the exploitation and subordination of women – ones which will enable us to make sense of women's and men's positions in contemporary society.

Kuhn (1970) has argued that theories are only replaced when more adequate theories have been developed. They are not rejected just because they have been shown to be inadequate, but because other theories can explain more adequately than the existing ones. Whilst feminists in the 1960s and 1970s wished to demonstrate the inadequacies of existing sociological theories, carry out empirical research in areas of interest to women and argue for the inclusion of gender as a variable in research, they also began to develop theories to explain gender divisions. There was not a single feminist theory, but a number of theories that challenged mainstream theoretical explanations for gender divisions and the exploitation and subordination of women.

Thus, on the one hand, feminist sociologists were united in their rejection of mainstream theories, being concerned with explaining how a male monopoly of knowledge and positions of power is exercised, how social relations are structured around gender and how women can challenge man's privileged position. On the other hand, differences began to develop. The feminist theories developed in the 1960s and 1970s had been 'totalising' theories that saw oppressive power as located in the structure of society, such as the capitalist economic system. However, there was a division between 'realist' feminists who argued that gender divisions had an existence in society beyond the lives of individuals who made them up, and those who argued from a 'social constructivist' position that gender relations were bound up in our personal beliefs and how these were acted out in our day-to-day interactions with other people. The early feminist theories were mainly concerned with theorising gender divisions, but since the mid-1980s the need to recognise that race, class, age, disability and sexuality also structured the experiences of women has been increasingly acknowledged (Abbott et al. 2005; Chapters 2 and 14 in this volume).

More recently, feminists' accounts influenced by post-modernism and post-structuralism have been concerned with explanations of the operation of power through institutional arrangements and how social control is exercised through agencies that discipline the body. Post-modernism has been particularly problematic for feminists. On the one hand, feminist sociologists' critique of mainstream sociology has been seen as an important element of the development of post-modernism within sociology. However, the post-modernist claims that there is no valid or verifiable knowledge and that knowledge is about control not liberation are problematic for feminists who are trying to uncover the systematic disadvantage of women and produce the knowledge that will enable them to liberate themselves. Whilst recognising that it is important to ask how we think about male power, it is also necessary to recognise the reality of the exercising of male power, which is a constant force within society, and its impacts on women's lives. Male power has a real existence outside of the 'discourse' of theoretical discussion, for example in rape, domestic violence and sexual harassment.

Feminists are more ambivalent about the post-modernist claim that society and social relations are too complex to be understood through totalising theories. Some (for example, Walby 1990) maintain that it is possible to have a theoretical explanation for the subordination and exploitation of women, whereas others (for example, Doyal 1995) argue that, despite differences, there are shared commonalities in women's experiences. Barrett and Phillips (1992), among others, argue that it is no longer possible (if it ever was) to have universal theories, and that the concern must be with explaining, understanding and theorising the local and the particular – the world as experienced by women and men in their everyday lives.

Gender and power

The key concept developed by feminists to describe male power was 'patriarchy'. This term, originally meaning 'rule of the fathers', was used in a specific sense in social anthropology to describe a kinship system in which males had dominant positions with respect to their female relatives. It was then adapted by feminists to mean any kind of male domination of women – at the level of society or within households. Although intended as an explanation of the multiple disadvantages experienced by women, patriarchy in this second, looser sense has been a problematic term. It is such an all-encompassing, general idea that it does not enable us to identify the causal elements that make up the patterns of gender divisions. Power relationships between men and women vary both historically and geographically, so to describe these just as 'patriarchy' is too universalistic and abstract. It also rules out the possibility of a society in which men and women are equal.

Furthermore, the term has been used in a variety of ways. The main difference is between 'realist' and 'social constructivist' explanations. The former sees patriarchy as embedded in economic structures (for example, the labour market, the family) – the ideology of patriarchy justifying inequalities rather than giving rise to them. For example, Hartman (1978: 11) uses the term to refer to male control of the female labour force:

> The material base upon which patriarchy rests lies most fundamentally in men's control over women's labour power. Men maintain this control by excluding women from access to essential productive resources (in capitalist societies for example, jobs that pay living wages) and by restricting women's sexuality.

However there are a variety of realist explanations. Firestone (1974) sees the material base of patriarchy as being men's control of reproduction, while Delphy (1984) places it in the domestic mode of production, that is, the ways in which the structure of the family means that women provide domestic services for husbands and children.

In contrast, social constructivists see patriarchal control as emanating from men's aggression and use of sexual power in rape, domestic violence and sexual harassment, which are all designed to keep women in their place. Men's superordinate position is maintained by an ideology which values men's 'natural' characteristics – aggression and competitiveness – over those of women – cooperation and caring. Radical feminists see men as dominating and controlling women in their day-to-day relationships, whereas realist feminists (Marxists, materialists and dual systems) see patriarchy as a system that dominates women.

The most developed analysis of patriarchy from a realist perspective is that of Sylvia Walby (1990: 20) who defines it as 'a system of social structures and practices in which men dominate, oppress and exploit women'. She suggests that it exists in six structures: paid work, domestic labour, sexuality, the state, violence, and culture. Walby rejects the view of patriarchy as unchanging, and argues that the system is integrated with capitalism and is dynamic. In particular, she points to the move from private patriarchy in the nineteenth century, when women were controlled within the private sphere, to public patriarchy since the twentieth century, by which women are controlled within paid employment and by the state. However, many feminists argue that even this more dynamic version of patriarchy is inadequate to take account of the complex power relationships between men and women and between women and women.

Influenced by Foucault, post-modernist feminists have replaced the idea of patriarchy – top-down power – with an interest in analysing gendered power and the way in which power is embedded in everyday practices and relationships at every level of society. This involves exploring how 'discourses' create particular forms of control and surveillance. 'Discourses' are groups of statements (which can change over time) which provide a language for talking about, and representing knowledge or 'truth' about, a topic. Discourses exist as dominant ways of framing what we believe, and men and women use them in their day-to-day lives every time they think or talk about each other. As a result, gender relationships are routinely re-affirmed and re-constructed in a way that enables male power to be perpetuated.

Discourses of masculinity and femininity powerfully control and regulate female behaviour, for example, controlling the lives of young women as they try to avoid being seen as a 'slag' or 'easy lay' (Halson 1991; Lees 1993). Young men are similarly controlled as they strive to become seen as 'real men' (Mac an Ghail 1994). The difficulty with this approach is that we are left with analysing local narratives of a particular context, such as young black women in school, and the view that, if discourses are changed, men's domination of women will cease. It is possible, however, to recognise the importance of the deconstruction of women and men as categories and develop more adequate understandings of how different men and different women are placed within the dynamics of gender inequalities.

Thus, Holland et al. (1998) have argued that it is important to recognise that there are layers of power within which gender power is experienced and each layer must be analysed. They suggest that power is:

- Institutionalised and hierarchical.
- Embedded in and represented in language, ideas, beliefs, norms, values and so on; for instance, the belief that boys are 'naturally better at science than girls'.
- Embedded in and represented in agency and action; women's freedom to go out at night is curtailed by fear of rape and violent attack from men.
- Embedded in 'embodied practices'; that is, lived gender/how we do gender, also reproduces power relationships.
- Historically specific and subject to change.

Holland et al. (1998: 11) argue that, whilst individual men may lack power, Britain is still a male-dominated society, but point out that this controls men as well as women:

Individual men may reject, resist or ignore the demands and constraints of dominant masculinity. Yet in their first sexual relationship, they and their partners continue to be aware of, and subject to, the exercise of its surveillance power articulated through the male peer group and the efficacy of sexual reputation and both young men and young women live by these rules or take the personal and social consequences of social transgressions.

Holland et al. suggest that men have more access to power than women and are both oppressors and oppressed. Hegemonic masculinity controls men and there are powerful pressures on men to conform. Women do resist male power, for example by challenging male dominance, by resistance and by celebrating rather than conforming to male expectations of behaviour. However, their overall conclusion is summed up by the title of their book, *The Male in the Head*. As Bartkey (1990: 72), says: 'in contemporary patriarchal culture, a pan-optical male connoisseur resides within the consciousness of most women; they stand perpetually before his gaze and under his judgement'.

Nevertheless, gender cannot be adequately represented solely as a single hierarchical division between men and women. As Lees (1993) points out, relationships between men and women and structured gender relationships are changing – they are not static, but gender remains as an important dimension of stratification. The structures of opportunities available to men and women remain unequal, but not fixed. Women do have 'agency' (self-determination and choice), but this agency is constrained by structures – unequal and controlled access to opportunities. There are also divisions between men and between women in their access to opportunity structures based on race, social class, age, sexuality and geographical location (as other chapters in this book show). The next section develops the ways in which young men negotiate their masculine identity in the face of changing labour market opportunities which mean that 'real men's jobs' (Willis 1977) no longer exist for the lads.

Gender and education

The educational process is central to an understanding of contemporary manifestations of gender. It is through the schooling process that identities are developed, and it is on the basis of educational outcomes that subsequent access to employment opportunities is determined. One might even argue that educational experience and qualifications are so important as to almost constitute a social division in their own right. Education therefore merits consideration in some detail.

Initially, sociologists were mainly concerned with understanding why girls did not achieve as well as boys at school and in the education system more broadly. However, by the 1990s, this lower performance had disappeared. The question was reversed: why were young women achieving *better* results than young, particularly working-class, men in public examinations. Indeed, there was widespread concern about underachieving boys, which amounted to a 'moral panic'.

At the time of writing, this is still seen as one of the most disturbing problems facing the education system. Media headlines continue to express anxiety about girls outclassing boys, especially each summer when the results of public examinations are published. In an interview with Sky News, David Willetts, Conservative Minister for Universities, talked about 'the gulf in educational achievement between men and women' as being 'a major challenge for society' because it would result in 'changes in the pattern of household living' (*The Telegraph* 2011). Local education authorities continue to express concern about the underachievement of boys and how to develop strategies to reverse the increasing tendency for them to become disaffected with schooling. However, whilst girls are outperforming boys, more boys than girls tend to score at the extremes, gaining either very good or very poor results in examinations. It is important to keep these differences in perspective. Sociologists are also aware that race (Chapter 4) and social class (Chapter 2) interact in complex ways with gender in terms of educational achievement, both having greater impact on educational achievement than gender itself.

The main changes that have taken place since the mid-1980s in the relative achievement of boys and girls come in the late secondary and post-compulsory school years. Up to the 1960s, girls outperformed boys in the primary and early secondary years, before boys caught up with and outperformed them in public examinations at 16+. Since the early 1980s, girls now also outperform boys in GCSE examinations at 16+ and in A levels and Highers in Scotland at 18+ (see Table 3.1). In the same period, there has been a considerable improvement in the proportions of young men and women gaining educational qualifications. In 1983, 26 per cent of boys gained five or more GCSEs grade A–C. By 2010/11, this had risen to 72 per cent, while in the same period, girls' performance improved from 27 to 84 per cent.

Similarly, the proportion of young people passing A levels has increased dramatically since the mid-1980s, with girls' performance improving at a faster rate than boys. In 1983/4, more boys than girls achieved three or more A level passes; 11 per cent compared to 9.5 per cent. By 2002/03, 34 per cent of boys were gaining two or more passes, but 43 per cent of girls.

Table 3.1 Examination results of school pupils by gender, 2010/11

Two or more A levels[1]		Five or more GCSEs[2]		Grade A* to C including Maths and English	
Males	Females	Males	Females	Males	Females
93.9	94.2	72	84	54.6	61.9

Notes

1 Pupils aged 17–19 at end of school year in England, Wales and Northern Ireland as percentage of 18-year-old population. For Scotland, figures relate to pupils in years S5/S6 gaining three or more SCE Higher passes as a percentage of the 17-year-old population.

2 Pupils aged 16 at end of school year as percentage of 15-year-old population at start of school year. Scottish pupils are in year S4.

Source: Department for Education (2012). For further details, see The Guardian Datablog (2011).

There are also differences in the subjects that boys and girls choose to study after the age of 16. (English, Science and Mathematics are compulsory to GCSE level.) 'Boys' subjects' are computer studies, mathematics, physics and technology, while 'girls' subjects' are humanities, arts, social studies and languages (see Table 3.2). This broad pattern of girls specialising in arts subjects and boys in science and technology is even more marked in their choices of higher education (Abbott et al. 2005). However, the subjects that are seen as appropriate for one gender or the other can change over time. Until comparatively recently, chemistry and medicine were seen as boys' subjects, whereas, by 2013, they were gender-neutral in terms of the proportion of girls and boys choosing to study them.

It is often assumed that subject choice is determined by the natural differences in the academic ability of boys and girls, with boys being better at mathematics, science and engineering than girls. There is no marked difference in performance between boys and girls in the primary and early secondary stages, except for English where girls markedly outperform boys (see Table 3.3). Subsequently, girls who choose to take boys' subjects do as well as boys. In the past, boys outperformed girls in science and mathematics at 16+ examinations and A level, but by the 1990s, girls achieved the same level of performance as boys in these subjects (Office for National Statistics 1999, 2004b).

At university, proportionately more women than men complete their undergraduate programme and are awarded a degree. However, more men get first class and third class degrees than women. Slightly more men than women go on to study for higher degrees by research, but roughly the same numbers take postgraduate taught degrees. Twice as many women as men study for a postgraduate teaching qualification. In considering the increase in the proportion of women taking higher education qualifications, we need to remember that a number of female-dominated professions have upgraded their required

Table 3.2 Girls' and boys' subjects

GCSE		A Level		Degree	
Boys	*Girls*	*Boys*	*Girls*	*Boys*	*Girls*
Single Sciences	Home Economics	Computing	Performing Arts	Computing	Subjects allied to
Design &	Social Studies	Physics	Sociology	Science	Medicine
Technology	Art & Design	Science subjects	Psychology	Engineering	Social Studies
Business Studies	English Literature	Mathematics	Art & Design	Physical Science	Languages
Geography	Drama	Business Studies	Communications	Architecture,	
PE	Media/Film/TV	Political Studies	English	Building &	
	Religiuos Studies	Technology	French	Planning	
			Drama	Mathematics	
			Spanish		
			Law		
			Critical Thinking		
			German		

Source: Department for Education and Science (2007); www.earlhamsociologypapers.co.uk/genddata.htm.

Table 3.3 Percentage of pupils reaching or exceeding expected standards, 2009

		Boys	Girls
Key stage 1	Reading	80.5	88.5
	Writing	75.3	86.7
	Mathematics	87.9	91.1
	Science	87.2	90.6
Key stage 2	English	75.8	85.0
	Mathematics	79.8	80.3
	Science	84.0	86.0
Key stage 3	English	73.0	86.0
	Mathematics	79.0	81.0
	Science	79.0	82.0

Source: Office for National Statistics (2011) Social Trends, 41: Education and Training (ST41) Table 3.

qualifications to higher education levels. These include nursing and other professions allied to medicine, social work, school teaching, child-care work and much secretarial work. To make valid comparisons it would be necessary to calculate the proportion of men and women training for these occupations in the past as well as those taking higher education qualifications.

Further education and vocational training is also gendered. Young women tend to study social sciences, subjects aligned to medicine or the creative arts, with hairdressing, secretarial studies and health and social care almost exclusively 'women's subjects'. Men are more likely to study mathematics, agriculture, engineering and technology. The proportion of young women and young men participating in youth vocational training is roughly the same. However, young men are more likely to be working towards a higher-level qualification and to be paid a wage, while young women are more likely to be on youth training because they could not find a job or gain the college course of their choice. A slightly higher proportion of Advanced Modern Apprenticeships are held by men (58.6 per cent). Conversely, women hold 53 per cent of Foundation Modern Apprenticeships. Modern apprenticeships are also gendered, with nearly 100 per cent of apprenticeships in the motor industry, construction and electrical installation engineering going to young men. Young women predominate in hairdressing, health and social care and business administration. There is also a 21 per cent gender pay gap in favour of men. This is mainly because the occupations in which men predominate have higher pay (Table 3.4).

Given that the changes in the relative performance of boys and girls in the education system are relatively recent, sociological explanations are only just beginning to be developed and empirical evidence is limited. Researchers

Table 3.4 Modern apprenticeships (L2 and L3) by gender, sector and pay, 2007/08

Sector	% women	% men	Average pay (per week) 2007
Automotive trades	0	100	£170
Construction	1	99	£174
Electro-technical	1	99	£210
Engineering	3	97	£189
Retail	69	31	£168
Business administration	81	19	£168
Hairdressing	92	8	£100
Health and social care	92	8	£157
Child care	97	3	£142

Source: TUC and YWCA (2010), Table 3.

have pointed to two key questions: why are boys underachieving in the education system and why has the performance of girls improved so dramatically since the 1980s? Those who focus on the former question tend to assume that boys are disadvantaged in the education system – that schools are failing boys. They argue that schools are not 'boy-friendly' and need to become so. In other words, it is suggested that in meeting the earlier criticisms that schools were not 'girl-friendly', the changes have gone too far and it is now boys who are disadvantaged. The move towards coursework for public examinations, since reversed, was said to favour girls. Another is the feminisation of teaching, with a majority of primary and secondary school teachers being female, and the consequent lack of role models for boys – although the majority of secondary school heads are male, as are academics in higher education.

However, concern about the underachievement of boys and young men at school is not new. Cohen (1998) traces commentary on the poor performance of boys back as far as John Locke's treatise, *Some Thoughts Concerning Education* ([1693]1989). The Taunton Commission (1868) also found that girls outperformed boys in reading, spelling, geography and history; in arithmetic, algebra and Euclid, girls did better than boys when they had been prepared for the same examinations. Cohen (1998) also quotes a government report of 1923 which expressed concern about girls outperforming boys (*The Teaching of English*, Board of Education). She points out that boys' underachievement is explained by factors external to them, for example the education system, whereas their success is seen to be intrinsic – high ability is seen as natural for boys. Conversely, girls' success is explained by extrinsic factors, or low status internal characteristics such as neatness and conformity. Failure in girls is seen as natural – girls are seen as 'naturally less able' than boys.

Those who focus on the second question of why girls' performance has improved tend to assume that, in the past, schools failed girls and they underachieved, whilst now girls' achievement is more in line with their potential. They point out that in the 1950s and 1960s, the pass grade for the 11+ examination was set higher for girls than for boys, in order to ensure that more of the slower developing boys were able to pass. So-called 'selective secondary education', supposedly based on ability as objectively measured in the 11+, was covertly selective in a fundamentally sexist way that made a mockery of the notion that selection was based on merit and that grammar schools therefore provided a route to upward social mobility for working-class children. The move to comprehensive secondary schooling removed this barrier. However, there is no evidence that schools themselves have become more girl-friendly. Indeed, they argue that, while there has been some reduction in the bias against girls, girls are still at a disadvantage in schools. For example, in terms of teaching, 45 per cent of secondary school teachers are male but 69 per cent of senior posts are held by men (National Association of Head Teachers 2008).

Indeed, some researchers have argued that schools in fact continue to be boy-friendly, in that boys continue to dominate the classroom and teachers do little to challenge this (Skelton 1993; Jackson and Salisbury 1996). Lees (1993) argues that mixed comprehensive education has increased sexism in schools, and teachers rarely challenge the sexual harassment that girls experience. There is evidence that teachers continue to believe, or at least work on the assumption, that boys are more academically able than girls. Textbooks and other teaching material continue to divide men and women into stereotypical sex roles. It follows that explanations for the rapid improvement in the educational performance of girls in public examinations, and the slower rate of boys, must be sought in factors outside the school, for example the decline in manual jobs for boys and the increasing labour market opportunities for women. In other words, we should ask why girls do as well as they do in the education system, given that they still underestimate, and have less confidence in, their ability compared with boys, get less teacher time and have to tolerate the disruptive behaviour of boys in the classroom.

Among answers to this question are several based on notions of the masculine role. On the one hand, teaching staff are more tolerant of disruptive behaviour, poor performance and lack of effort by boys than girls. Because more boys are disruptive in the classroom than girls, they lose more time and are more likely than girls to be permanently excluded from school. On the other hand, parents control their sons less than their daughters, meaning that boys are less likely to do homework. Furthermore, boys think that they can 'muck around' in the early years in secondary school and catch up later, but they fail to do so. This is especially the case in their inability to catch up with and complete coursework for GCSEs (Abbott et al. 2005).

It is also important to ask which boys underachieve and, indeed, which girls do well. There is considerable overlap in the performance of boys and girls in school. Whilst many boys underachieve at school, many others do very well. Underachievement of boys is a strongly classed and racial phenomenon (see Chapters 2 and 4). For young men and women, social class is the major determinant of success (or otherwise) in school examinations. While there are differences between schools' examination results, the best predictor of a state school's position in a league table is the LEA's position on the index of deprivation (Department of Communities and Local Government 2011).

The decline in masculine jobs, as contemporary society moves ever more to an economy based on the services sector, means that working-class young men, living in areas of high unemployment with no tradition of education, see few prospects for their future. This results in the 'new lad' culture, in which young men attempt to construct a positive self-image and draw attention to themselves by laddish behaviour and aggressive macho posturing. For many, the instrumental orientation to school, a limited compliance in order to get a job, no longer holds. In many deprived estates, especially in the north of England, the response to lack of opportunity has been a rejection of schooling.

In other words, the key issue is not that these young men may be achieving less well at school than their fathers did, but that the unskilled and semi-skilled jobs that their fathers took when leaving school no longer exist. To the extent that there are employment opportunities in these areas, they require credentials that these young men have failed to acquire, or are seen as cissy jobs – not jobs for real men. Rather than making the transition to 'adult man' in terms of full-time paid employment, marriage and fatherhood, they become dependent on welfare benefits and 'fiddly' jobs (cash in hand employment taken whilst registered as unemployed). The restructuring of the labour market means that there are more jobs available for educationally low-achieving young women, who also have the 'option' of becoming lone mothers. In public debates, when concern is expressed about teenage lone mothers, the pathway to this status is rarely directly related to underachievement in education.

Given all the arguments for why boys underachieve, it is important to remember that boys' performance has actually *improved* in recent years. After all, while some boys may be underachieving, overall their levels of education and achievement have markedly improved since the 1980s. In the same period, girls have improved their performance at a faster rate than boys, and it is the improvement in girls' performance that needs to be explained. One explanation is that the gap between the educational achievement of working-class and middle-class boys has widened, while the gap in performance between girls of different socio-economic backgrounds has not. The reason for this is that the traditional working-class culture has decayed while the women's movement has widened the aspirations of young women in general, so that the majority now expect to have paid work as well as being wives and mothers. There are more employment opportunities for girls than in the past. Many occupations to which girls from all backgrounds aspire require post-16 educational credentials at least equivalent to A levels, and more often higher education qualifications. Nursing and social work, for example, are now graduate professions and administrative positions in 'business' also often require higher educational credentials. The occupations to which boys from manual backgrounds often aspire, such as skilled and craft occupations, do not require the same level of educational credentials. In addition, many of the employment opportunities in heavy manufacturing industries that existed in the past have almost disappeared.

Furthermore, it is important to recognise that not all girls conform to the demands of the school system or succeed in it. In the same ways that schooling is an important element in boys learning appropriate masculinity, so the majority of girls take on an appropriate feminine identity. School is centrally important to the process by which girls take on a complex identity that is feminised, racialised and located within a class system. Lees (1993) has suggested four approaches that girls adopt in secondary school:

1. The pro-school, academic orientation of white girls from middle-class backgrounds who aspire to academic success and an occupational career.
2. The anti-school, pro-work orientation typical of some African-Caribbean girls who reject the racist attitudes of the school system, but are nevertheless committed to academic success and an occupational career.
3. The pro-school, anti-work orientation of some working-class girls who reject the discipline and academic elements of school, but see school as a place to have contact with friends.
4. The anti-school, anti-work orientation of some working-class girls who want to leave school at the earliest opportunity and see their future major roles as wife and mother.

Girls' orientations are crucially mediated by class and race, which inform their expectations for their future careers. While most young women expect to combine motherhood and marriage with paid employment, it is only academic girls, mainly from middle-class backgrounds, and some African-Caribbean girls, who expect careers. Mirza (2003) found that African-Caribbean girls anticipated a career, but that Irish girls saw their future as home-makers, child carers and part-time workers. Working-class girls anticipate having part-time employment that fits in with their domestic responsibilities. As we shall see, schoolgirls' anticipations of 'work' are often misplaced.

Gender, 'work' and domestic labour

One of the major contributions of feminist sociology in the area of work was to redefine the term itself. In 'malestream' sociology, 'work' was used to mean paid employment, with priority given to full-time, lifelong employment and the (male) breadwinner role. Feminists have challenged this, pointing to both the domestic labour and emotional work that women undertake, saying that this too is real work. Glucksman (1995: 68) has indicated that work refers to all 'activity necessary for the production and reproduction of economic structures irrespective of how and when it is carried out'. By opening up the black box of the family, feminists have been able to demonstrate not only the persistence of the gendered inequality of power in the private sphere, but also the long hours of unpaid work that women undertake in the home, doing the bulk of caring for the household, children and other dependent relatives, in addition to their paid employment – working the 'double shift'.

In looking at gender and work globally, Seager (1997) indicates that time diaries show that both men and women do more total work than conventional measures suggest. However, while most of men's work is paid, most of women's is not. Women and girls have the major responsibility for domestic labour. She concludes that not only do women work more than men, but they also perform a greater variety of tasks and have less rest. Similarly, in Britain, women do more unpaid work than men, and, while men do more paid work than women, they also have more leisure time than women (Office for National Statistics 2004b). The one feature that is universal is that women do the bulk of domestic and child-care work, even when they have paid employment (Ferrant 2009; Lewis 2009). In 1995, the monetary value of unpaid work in Britain was estimated to be between £341 and £739 billion. The lower value exceeded the value of the UK manufacturing sector, and the higher value was equivalent to 120 per cent of the GDP (Murgatroyd and Neuburger 1997). In 2005 it was estimated that the value of unpaid domestic work was equivalent to 37 per cent of the European GDP (Giannelli et al. 2010). It was estimated to be around 35 per cent of GDP in the UK.

When men become unemployed, some take on more responsibility for domestic labour, but most tasks remained gendered. Cooking the main meal and thorough cleaning remain exclusively female tasks, while washing the clothes and ironing are done predominantly by women, as is shopping and handling the household budget. The predominant male tasks are mowing the lawn, doing household repairs and taking out the rubbish. The *British Social Attitude Survey* (Park et al. 2002) found that women were more likely to claim the main responsibility for tasks than men, who were likely to describe tasks as shared with their partners. Even allowing for this, the only domestic task done mainly by men (80 per cent men/65 per cent women) in households headed by a married or cohabiting couple was making small repairs about the home. The only other task not seen as mainly the responsibility of women was shopping for groceries, where nearly half of men and women indicated that it was a shared task, although nearly half the women said they were mainly responsible (49 per cent). Women were mainly responsible for doing the laundry (75/81), looking after sick family members (46/62), household cleaning (55/65) and preparing meals (55/62). Less than 10 per cent of men said they were mainly responsible for any task except household repairs (Office for National Statistics 2004b). As Delphy and Leonard (1992) point out, men do household work, but few are obliged to do family work.

Women also continue to take the major responsibility for looking after children, especially young children (Lewis 2009; Wallace and Abbott 2011). Fathers do, however, take on some responsibility for child care. Half of the men interviewed in a survey in the UK in the early 1990s said that they would take on more responsibility for child care if they had the time. Clift and Fielding (1991) found that, the nearer the wife's earnings were to a breadwinner's, the more equally domestic labour and child care were shared. In 2007, 60 per cent of mothers with dependent children said that they did more than their fair share of the housework, whereas about 35 per cent of fathers said that they did less than their fair share (author's calculation from *European Quality of Life Survey* data). Despite an increasing view that women, including those with dependent children, should have paid employment they are still expected to prioritise their domestic roles. Women expect, and are generally expected, to take time out of the labour market when they have children (or considerably to reduce the hours of paid work they undertake) and, as their children grow older, to take paid employment that fits in with child-care responsibilities (Lewis 2009).

In Sweden, where both part-time paid work and child-care leave are equally available to wives and husbands, mothers are much more likely to take maternity leave and/or part-time employment than to withdraw from the labour market (Lewis 2009). Women are still seen primarily in their roles as wives and mothers, and domestic responsibilities are expected to be given priority. The Eurobarometer survey (1997) found that 60 per cent of women, but only 30 per cent of men, said that they were prepared to give up their job to look after children, and about 55 per cent of women (and 30 per cent of men) said that they would be prepared to give up paid employment to look after a dependent relative.

Despite married women's increased participation in employment, there is little evidence that men have taken on significantly more responsibility for domestic labour and child care. The traditional domestic bargain – that women take on responsibility for child care and domestic labour and men the bread-winner role – is still the predominant ideal, even if not every family is able to live up to this. Women continue to be seen not only as the main performers of domestic labour, but the ones principally responsible for ensuring that it is carried out. This means that women are trapped in a cycle of dependency – they are not expected to be a breadwinner and are often not trained for an occupation that provides a breadwinner's wage. Taking time out of the labour market to have children further reduces a woman's economic potential and her opportunities for career advancement and promotion. Women continue to be dependent on men for part of their livelihood (Lewis 2009; Wallace 2010). As Joshi (1990: 52) notes:

> The traditional domestic bargain does not work to the advantage of all women. It involves loss of earnings, future earning potential and pension rights. It can involve social obligations, loss of autonomy and self and social esteem and, perhaps most importantly, loss of security.

Gender and the labour market

Despite the 'traditional domestic bargain', there has been a steady increase in women's participation in the labour market in Britain, especially since the Second World War. The most dramatic increase has been in married women in paid, especially part-time, employment outside the home. The majority of women (including married women) are in paid employment for the majority of the years that they are of employment age. The time that married women take out of employment for child care has also reduced significantly. The employment pattern for women in Britain was, until the 1980s, an M-shaped curve, rising as more women came onto the labour market in their late teens and then falling as the vast majority of married women took a break from paid employment whilst they had young children. The curve then rose as they returned to work when their children became more independent, before dipping again as women withdrew from the labour market as they neared 60. Now it is more of an 'inverted U', the same as for men – the majority of women, including those who have children, do not take a break from paid employment.

At the same time that the participation rate for women in the labour market (albeit mainly in part-time jobs) has been going up, it has been declining for men. In 2009, 76 per cent of men were economically active compared to 69 per cent of women. The comparable figures for 1971 were 92 per cent for men and 56 per cent for women (Hicks and Thomas 2009). In 2009, women made up 47 per cent of the labour force, although 41 per cent worked part-time and only 11 per cent of male workers worked part-time. In 1971, for example, just over half of women aged 25–44 years (the period during which women are most likely to take a break) were economically active (in paid employment or seeking work); by 2003, over three-quarters of women in this age group were economically active. In comparison, 98 per cent of men aged 45–54 years were economically active in 1971, but by 2003, this had fallen to 92 per cent. This change occured partly because of an increase in the number of men, especially in their fifties and sixties, on long-term sick leave, taking early retirement or being made redundant and unable to gain further employment and partly because of the increase in female employment. It is predicted that the gender gap in economic activity will continue to narrow. The economic activity rate for women may indeed be an underestimate because it does not take undeclared homework into account.

The reasons for non-employment also vary by gender. The main reason in 2003 for women being economically inactive was that they were engaged in non-remunerated work; 45 per cent looking after a family or home. The main reasons for men were that they were in full-time education or training (28 per cent), or that they were long-term sick (38 per cent). Only 6 per cent of men were looking after a family or home (Office for National Statistics 2004b). Non-employment is, of course, also connected to other factors, such as level of qualification, disability and ethnicity. However, even here, gender interacts with other social divisions. Thus, differences in unemployment rates among women from different ethnic groups and women with different levels of educational qualifications are also marked (see Chapter 4; Abbott and Tyler 1995; Iganski and Payne 1996; Iganski et al. 2001).

The majority of married women, even those with young children, are economically active: in 2007, 62.8 per cent of married or cohabiting women whose youngest child was under five years and 77.6 per cent of those whose youngest child was 10–15 years were in or seeking paid work. This compares with 73.3 per cent of all women in or seeking paid work (Figure 3.1). However, the majority of employed married or cohabiting mothers work part time – although the proportion of those in full-time employment increases as the youngest child gets older, from 40 per cent for those whose youngest child is under five years old, to just over half (53.3 per cent) for those whose youngest child is 11–15 years old. Married or cohabiting women with no children are twice as likely to be in full-time as part-time employment (52 per cent compared with 25 per cent).

Lone mothers are less likely to be in paid employment than partnered mothers (Figure 3.2). They are also less likely than partnered mothers to work short part-time hours. Lone mothers are also more likely to be employed as their children grow older, 40.7 per cent of those with children under five are economically active, compared with 68.1 per cent of those whose youngest

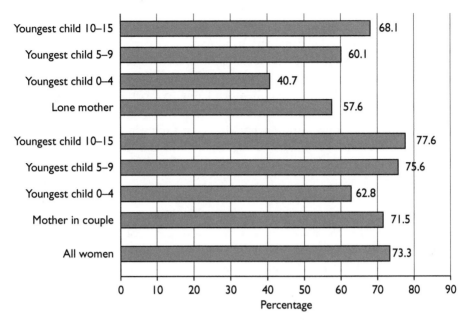

Figure 3.1 Employment rates of women and mothers in UK, 2007

Source: Office for National Statistics (2007) *Labour Force Survey 2007*, London: ONS.

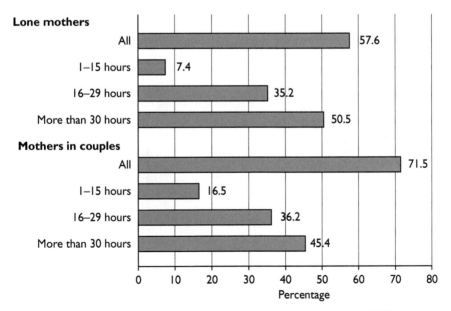

Figure 3.2 Working hours of employed single and coupled and mothers, UK, 2007

Source: Office for National Statistics (2007) *Labour Force Survey 2007*, London: ONS.

child is aged 10–15 years (Figure 3.1). The proportion working full-time also increases as children get older – from less than one-third of those in employment with children under five years to a marginally higher proportion working full-time for those whose youngest child is aged 11–15 years (35 per cent working full-time and 32 per cent part-time). Single, divorced and widowed women with no children are much more likely to work full-time than part-time (46 per cent compared with 21 per cent). In contrast, being married or having a child has no impact whatsoever on men's labour market activity (Abbott and Ackers 1997). Indeed, in the UK, men with children are likely to work even longer hours than other men (Abbott and Wallace 2011; Wallace and Abbott 2011).

Gender also affects the kind of paid employment available, with women more likely than men to be in non-manual occupations. However, as Table 3.5 shows, men are more likely to be employed in the more 'desirable' (higher status and higher remuneration) occupations as managers and professionals, and women are more likely to be in lower paid and less attractive routine, non-manual work and caring professions (Abbott et al. 2005). Similarly, within the manual category, men are more likely to be categorised in skilled occupations than women. Despite over 30 years of equal opportunities legislation, there is still clear evidence that the 'glass ceiling' (a barrier to women's upward mobility into the higher level positions) and the 'glass wall' (a barrier to women entering occupations defined as male) still act as obstacles (European Commission 2010).

We have seen that the choices that young men and women make – which subjects to study in formal education (especially post-16 years) and the training

Table 3.5 Employment by occupation, 2011[1]

Occupational group	Percentage of working population		Percentage of women in occupation
	Female	Male	
Managers and senior officials	12.1	19.2	35.2
Professional	12.7	13.8	44.4
Associate professionals and technical	16.9	13.7	51.6
Administrative and secretarial	17.8	4.9	75.8
Skilled trades	1.8	18.0	0.8
Personal services	15.7	2.9	82.3
Sales and customer services	10.1	5.0	63.5
Elementary	11.2	11.8	45.1
Process, plant and machine operatives	1.6	10.5	11.7
All occupations[2] (000s)	13,461	15,545	46.4

Notes
1 UK employees and self-employed aged 16 years and over.
2 Includes those not stating an occupation.
Source: Office for National Statistics (2012d).

schemes that they enter – remain gender stereotyped. Education influences the job choices that are made on leaving formal education, despite the changes in the relative educational success of young men and women. Occupations are still heavily gendered, especially manual occupations in the declining industrial sectors of manufacturing. In 2003, 20 per cent of men were employed in manufacturing, compared with 7 per cent of women; in construction, the figures were 8 per cent of men, compared with 1 per cent of women. Women were mainly employed in 'other services' (42 per cent of all employed women compared with 20 per cent of employed men) and distribution, hotel, catering and repairs (26 per cent of all employed women, compared with 22 per cent of employed men) (Office for National Statistics 2004e: Table 4.13).

The largest employment category for women remains clerical and secretarial work, although the percentage of women employed doing this kind of work has declined from 29 per cent in 1991, to 17.2 per cent in 2011. The single largest employment category for men is managerial and senior officials (19.2 per cent), followed by skilled trades, with 18 per cent of men engaged in this category. Employers clearly have a view of what is appropriate work for women and women generally share this view (Chaney 1981; Yeandle 1984; Beechy and Perkins 1986) – attitudes that seem to have persisted into the twenty-first century. Many 'female' occupations, clearly regarded as using women's 'natural abilities', are in the private sphere: caring for young children, nursing, preparing and serving food and in general securing the needs of others – 'emotional labour'. Thus, there is continuing evidence that women find it difficult to obtain employment in traditional male occupations and that men continue to be reluctant to move into traditional female ones (Table 3.6).

Table 3.6 Occupational segregation – selected occupations, 2003

Female occupations	% women	Male occupations	% women	Neutral occupations	% women
Sales assistants	73	Taxi driver	8	Solicitors, lawyers,	
Waiters and waitresses		Security guard	12	judges and	
Cleaners and domestics	73	Software		coroners	42
Retail cashiers and checkout		professionals	14	Shelf fillers	48
operators	79	ICT managers	16	Chefs and cooks	49
General office assistants and		Police officers	22	Secondary	
clerks	82	Marketing and		teachers	55
Primary and nursery teachers	83	sales managers	25		
Care assistants and home		IT technicians	32		
carers	86	Medical			
Hairdressers and barbers	88	practitioners	39		
Nurses	89				
Receptionists	96				

Source: Equal Opportunities Commission (2004).

There is evidence, for example, that it is still virtually impossible for young women to get training places in the traditional male craft and related occupations, while those who do succeed then experience discrimination and sexual harassment (see Table 3.4; TUC and YWCA 2010). In terms of entry to middle management, women are less likely to be promoted than men, and are often promoted to positions that do not give them the experiences seen as necessary for further promotion. Examples include women police officers being promoted within the Domestic Violence Unit, women managers in the NHS running health centres rather than positions in the central NHS administration, and female teachers promoted to pastoral posts rather than the management of resources (Abbott et al. 2005). Savage (1992) found that female bank managers were generally employed in specialist units where they used specific expertise and were rarely promoted to managerial jobs involving the exercise of client control and/or authority. In her study of women engineers, Devine (1992b) found that they were promoted to managerial positions where they managed women rather than men.

In addition, men are often seen to have the skills and competence necessary for senior managerial positions, whereas women are perceived to have the characteristics necessary for the caring roles. There is some evidence that women may choose the types of positions in which specific expertise dominates because these jobs enable them to cope with the conflicting demands of family life and 'organisation' (Evetts 1994). Crompton and Le Feuvre (1996) found female pharmacists in jobs in which expertise or professional technique were predominant, because they were more flexible than those in which the main function was exercise of organisational power.

The glass ceiling exists at a number of different levels, not just as a barrier to women entering top jobs. Organisations are dominated by masculinities, and femininities are subordinated. There is a denial of emotional life in organisations (Pringle 1988). Women often feel uncomfortable in the masculine environment and sexual harassment is one way in which men subordinate and control women in the workplace. It is one of the tactics used by men in restricting and resisting moves towards sexual equality in organisations (Cockburn 1991).

While there is clear evidence that the glass ceiling remains, some cracks may be beginning to appear. It is true that there are now more female head teachers, vice chancellors, women professors and managers, but they remained in the minority in the first decade of the twenty-first century (Table 3.7). Only 19 per cent of university professors are female, 15 per cent of senior police officers, 12 per cent of senior officers in the armed forces and 22 per cent of MPs. Only 9 per cent of supreme court judges are female and in total only 22.3 per cent of judicial appointments in 2010 were female. The private sector

Table 3.7 Women in top positions

	% women
MPs (2012)	22
Cabinet (2012)	22
Government (2012)	17
Members of Scottish Parliament	35
Members of the Welsh Assembly	40
Members of the Northern Ireland Assembly	19
Leader/Deputy leader local councils, England (2010)	21
Boards of public bodies (2011–12)	36
Senior Civil Service (2011)	35
Justice of the Supreme Court (2011)	9
All judges (2011)	22
GPs (2010)	45
Consultants (2010)	31
Secondary school head teachers (2010)	37
University professors (2009–10)	19
Officers in the Armed Forces (2010)	12
Police Officer chief superintendent and above (2011)	15
FTSE 100 companies directors (2012)	15

Source: Cracknell (2012).

is no better, with only 15 per cent of directorships of FTSE 100 companies held by women (Chapter 11).

Despite the implementation of the 1970 Equal Pay Act, in 1975 women still earned less than men. The gender pay gap in 2009, for example, between male full-time and female part-time workers was 40 per cent, a figure that has barely changed since 1975 (Hicks and Thomas 2009). The gap between men's and women's pay increases with age, and this is partly because men's average pay does not peak until they are in their fifties, whereas pay for women peaks in their thirties. Younger women are better qualified than older ones, which is part of the explanation for this. Differences in pay are partly accounted for by differences in labour market positions and partly by hours worked, but there is a gender pay gap at every qualification level. The gender pay gap in hourly earnings is 22.5 per cent taking account of full- and part-time work, excluding overtime, and 12.8 per cent for full-time employees (Hicks and Thomas 2009). However, the weekly gap is larger because, on average, women engage in paid employment for fewer hours a week than men. The majority of women work fewer than 45 hours a week and 44 per cent work fewer than 31 hours, whereas 33 per cent of men work over 45 hours a week and only 11 per cent work less than 31 hours (Office for National Statistics 2004e: Table 4.17). Even when women are in full-time employment, they work, on average, for fewer hours than men – 40.7 hours compared with 45.8 hours a week. This is partly because men are more likely to work overtime than women, and partly because of differences in basic hours of work in predominantly male and female occupations.

Even when they are in similar jobs, women earn less than men – the 'gender premium'. Surveys of the earnings of lecturers in higher education, for example, have found that the gender pay gap is much the same as the national average figure (see also Equal Opportunities Commission 2003). However, the gender pay gap is much lower in the public than the private sector (Trades Union Congress 2012). The gap for full-time employees in the public sector is 9.2 per cent compared with 18.4 per cent in the private sector, and for part-time employees the gap is 36.3 per cent in the public sector and 42.8 per cent in the private sector. Thus, despite formal access to employment in Britain for women since the Second World War, the Equal Pay Act 1970 and the Equal Opportunities Act 1975, women have not achieved equality with men in the labour market.

The labour market remains vertically and horizontally segregated, with women occupying the lower strata, less well-paid levels within all strata and concentrated in particular industrial sectors. Women are less likely to be promoted than men and are concentrated in jobs that have fewer opportunities for career progression than men. Even in female professions such as social work, nursing and primary school teaching, men are proportionately more likely to be promoted than women. Routine non-manual, service and manual occupations are more clearly and specifically gendered than professional and managerial ones.

As with professional and managerial occupations, the movement of women into an area of employment tends to result in a decline in its status and relative remuneration. This process is clearly evident in the history of clerical work (Lockwood 1958). It is not self-evident, however, that any less skill is involved now than was the case in the past, even if the skills required may be different. This contrasts with the ways in which male printers in the newspaper industry have retained high status and remuneration despite the move from traditional to digital typesetting.

As Diane Perrons (2009, 147) has argued, pointing not only to the increasing number of women in the labour market but also the range and levels of occupations they have entered:

> gender imbalances remain with respect to the scale and form of employment and in remuneration. In many ways the organisation of the workforce and the domestic division of labour retain the imprint of a male breadwinner society which presents a challenge to gender equality within employment and society more generally.

Explanations of women's labour market participation

Feminist sociologists argue that the major factor explaining the segregated labour market is structural (Crompton and Le Feuvre 1996). However, Hakim (1991, 1995) has argued that, in exploring the patterns of women's participation in the labour market, insufficient account has been taken of their orientation to paid employment and work commitment. She gives estimates for three main groups of women:

1. The home-centred – 15–30 per cent of women, who prefer not to work and whose main priority is children and family.
2. The adapters – 40–80 per cent of women, who comprise a diverse group including women who want to combine work and family and those who want to have paid employment but are not committed to a career.
3. The work-centred – 10–30 per cent of women who are mainly childless and whose main priority is paid employment.

Hakim suggests that there are also two extreme groups of women: those who are childless from choice and those who see motherhood and domesticity as their destiny. Professional managerial women are, Hakim argues, a minority who cannot provide the basis for a general theory of women's employment choices. She develops what she calls a 'preference theory', arguing that women can now choose whether to have an employment career or not. She argues that the majority of women who combine domesticity with employment (the adapters, or 'the uncommitted') seek part-time work even when it is concentrated in the lower grades and is less well-paid than other work. Contrary to feminist sociologists who have argued that women's employment patterns are the outcome of structural factors and the exclusionary tactics used by men, Hakim argues that many women positively choose low-paid, low-status, part-time work that fits in with their domestic and familial roles, which they themselves see as the priority. Tam (1997) found that female part-time employees are generally satisfied with their employment, although younger and well-qualified ones are less so.

However, Crompton and Le Feuvre (1996), arguing on the basis of their study of women in banking and pharmacy employment in both Britain and France, conclude that there is little empirical evidence to support the view that there are different categories of women as far as work commitment is concerned. They suggest that there is no evidence, even when these professional women work part-time, to suggest that they are not committed to their paid employment. Martin and Roberts (1984) found that social and domestic circumstances had a considerable influence on the way women thought about work. Some, for example, found it difficult to cope with paid work and domestic responsibilities. However, the type of work and employment situations also affected women's orientations to work. Contrary to popular opinion, they found that the majority of women, including married women, were highly dependent financially on their wages from work, and the majority of women were fully committed to work, but this varied over the life cycle. The most highly committed were childless women older than 30 years (see also Hakim 2003; McRae 2003a, b).

Further support for this argument is provided by the findings from a study of 1182 part-time female workers in Australia (Walsh 1999). Walsh argues that female part-time workers are not homogeneous in terms of their characteristics or orientations, and that they work part-time for a variety of reasons. Whilst a majority of women in her sample were content with their current situations, a substantial majority wanted to return to full-time work in the future. She questions Hakim's view that the majority of female employees are not committed to a career and suggests that female employees' commitment to the labour market varied over the life-course. Women are expected, however, to cope with the 'double shift', and this influences their ability to demonstrate total loyalty to the job in same way as men can. They have to juggle their responsibilities to their families and their employers in ways that men rarely have to do. Furthermore, working in paid employment part-time does not prove a lack of commitment to that employment or to a career.

In order to understand women's position in the labour market, and their experiences of paid employment, we need to understand the ways in which patriarchy and capitalism work together to subordinate and exploit women. The essence of patriarchy is that women should be subordinated to men and serve their needs, including their sexual needs, whereas capitalism as an economic system can only function with a flexible, cheap labour force. It is in the interest of patriarchal relations to keep women in the domestic sphere and in capitalism's to employ them in the labour force. In terms of employment, this has meant a move from strategies designed to exclude women from paid employment to segregationalist and subordinating strategies. Women's participation in the labour force and the segmentation of the labour market into separate jobs for women and men are not only determined by the economic forces of supply and demand for labour. They are also driven by family and sexual ideologies. The search for profit in the capitalist system of production is not incompatible with the power of men to exploit women and to define skills (Phillips and Taylor 1980; Walby 1986).

The relationship between capitalism and patriarchy is a dynamic and changing one, and it impacts differently on different groups of women. In the nineteenth century, it was mainly middle-class women who were excluded from paid employment, whilst in the early twenty-first century, African-Caribbean women are most likely to experience public patriarchy and British Muslim women private patriarchy (see also Chapter 4). Patriarchy and capitalism have competing interests but reach an accommodation. Thus men (as husbands) clearly benefit from the additional income generated by their wife's paid employment – especially as research suggests that women retain the major responsibility for child care and domestic labour. Conversely, employers have been able to create jobs that use the assumed 'natural' skills of women, justifying the low wages the women are paid. Men benefit from the servicing and emotional labour that women provide in the public sphere as well as enjoying and controlling women's sexuality. Employers are able to sell goods and services by exploiting women's sexuality.

Finally, it is essential to remember that women choose to combine their commitments to both unremunerated (and often undervalued) work with paid employment. The choices they make, and their orientation to both, are the outcome of the socially constructed expectations of women's roles and women's responsibilities. For example, highly qualified women in managerial and professional occupations can pay for quality child care and domestic help and thereby avoid the criticisms often directed at working mothers or wives of neglecting their children and husbands.

Gender, poverty and the family

Until comparatively recently it was assumed that the economic well-being of all the members of a household could be determined by the income level of the household. However, feminists have pointed to the importance of considering the economic circumstances of each member of a family. Pahl (1985) and Graham (1987) found that household resources are not necessarily shared, and that some women in households with average and above-average incomes have little or no access to these resources. In her work on money management in marriage, Pahl (1983) found that, whereas joint or male management of finances was the norm in households with average and above-average incomes, in low-income households it was the women who were expected to manage the household's resources. In couple households, men's income accounted for two-thirds of total family income. The (assumed) social and economic dependency of women on men means that women are more vulnerable to poverty than men (for an extended discussion, see Chapter 13).

Sociologists have pointed to the feminisation of poverty since the 1980s, although women have always been more vulnerable than men. While similar proportions of men and women live in households with incomes below 60 per cent of the median income (22 and 25 per cent respectively), it is women who usually bear the brunt of poverty when they live in poor households. They are the ones who 'do without', and have to manage the scarce financial resources. Middleton et al. (1997) have pointed to the sacrifices that many mothers make: 'often' or 'sometimes' going without clothes and shoes, holidays and entertainment in order to provide things for their children. Lone mothers on income support are more likely than other mothers to go without each item and go without more of the items. These mothers are 14 times more likely to go without food than mothers in two-parent families that are not on income support. Glendinning and Miller (1992: 60) have suggested that:

> women bear the burden of managing poverty on a day to day basis whether they live alone or with a partner, on benefits or low earnings, it is usually women who are responsible for making ends meet and for managing the debts which result when they don't ... As more women and men lose their jobs, as benefits are cut or decline in value, women are increasingly caught in a daily struggle to feed and clothe their families ... usually at considerable personal sacrifice.

Women are also more likely than men to feel poor, to be on income support and to lack two or more socially perceived necessities (Equal Opportunities Commission 2003). Women's vulnerability to poverty is the outcome of their restricted roles in the private sphere and the weak position they hold in the labour market. Women earn less than men (as we have seen above), have breaks in employment to care for children and elderly relatives and not only live, on average, longer than men but also, given the tendency of women to marry men older themselves, outlive their partners. Women are especially vulnerable to experiencing poverty when they are caring for children and in old age.

Since the 1980s there has been a widening division between 'work rich' and 'work poor' households. Married or cohabiting women in paid employment generally have a partner who is also in employment. The wives or partners of unemployed men rarely have paid employment because the benefits system is a disincentive to do so. There is then an increasing gulf between households in employment (and young pensioner households with occupational and/or personal pensions) and those dependent on welfare benefits. Furthermore, in a substantial proportion of two-earner households, women's earnings contribute to keeping the family out of poverty. Households with a male breadwinner and a female home-maker have a four to six times higher risk of being in the bottom income quintile than those in households where both partners have paid employment.

The groups of women who are most vulnerable to poverty are lone-parent mothers, women caring for children who are married to men in low-paid jobs or who are unemployed, and women in later life. In 2003, 40 per cent of one-parent households (9 out of 10 female-headed) were in the bottom fifth of the income distribution and 33 per cent in the next fifth. Those households in the bottom two-fifths are heavily dependent on state benefits in cash and kind.

There has been a dramatic increase in the number of one-parent families since the 1960s. In 1961, 2 per cent of households comprised a lone parent with a dependent child or children. By 2012 this had risen to 24 per cent. This is mainly because of the increase in the divorce rate. The main route to lone parenthood is divorce – 72 per cent of one-parent families are headed by a divorcee, whereas only 18 per cent are the result of the birth of a child outside a relationship. Despite the introduction of the Child Support Agency to force the absent parent to pay towards the cost of child support, the normal consequence of divorce is that the absent parent is financially better off and the parent with custody is less well off than before the separation. Children are generally looked after by their mothers when parents separate or divorce: the assumption that children should be cared for by their mother is deeply embedded in cultural and legal attitudes and values, and only about 9 per cent of one-parent households are headed by a father.

Poverty and older women

Older women are especially vulnerable to poverty. Women make up the majority of those aged 65 years and over, and the proportion of older women to men increases with age (see Chapter 5). While around three-quarters of men over 65 live with someone, only around a half of women do so (Winquist 2002). Fifty-five per cent of women expect their husband or partner will provide for them in retirement (Caine 1997) but women outlive their partners by about ten years on average. Two-thirds of all people aged over 75 years and three-quarters of those over 85 years are women. Older women are much more likely to live in single-person households than older men: 44 per cent of women (35 per cent of these being widows) do so compared with 22 per cent of men. While 65 per cent of men aged 75–84 years and 41 per cent of those aged over 85 live as a married or cohabiting couple, only 30 per cent of women aged 75–84 and 19 per cent of those over 85 do so.

Retirement from paid employment for both men and women means reduced economic and other resources for the households in which they live. The average income of women over 65 years living alone is 51 per cent of that of people below 65 years, while for men living alone it is 62 per cent.

Forty-four per cent of British women aged over 65 years live in households with incomes below 60 per cent of median income, compared to 33 per cent of men – one of the largest gender gaps in the EU (Winquist 2002). Women are less likely than men to have an occupational private pension. Over two-thirds of men over 65 years have an occupational private pension, compared with 43 per cent of women (including widows receiving occupational pension income from a deceased spouse's pension). Only 28 per cent of married women over 65 years receive an occupational pension compared with 74 per cent of men. The average private pension income of all women over 65 years is 53 per cent that of men and for married women it is only 37 per cent. Even when women do have an occupational pension, its final value will be considerably reduced by the time they reach very old age (Arber and Ginn in Office for National Statistics 2004e). When they die, men's occupational pensions often cease, or their widows only receive a considerably reduced pension, and, again, the 'real value' declines with increasing age.

Married or cohabiting women are also less likely than men to have a state pension in their own right. Many older women did not have paid employment in the past and therefore have no entitlement to a state pension, whilst others chose to pay the married women's contributions (an option that was abolished in 1976) and forfeited their entitlement to a state pension in their own right. Many married or cohabiting women who have been in paid employment will often have worked too few hours a week over extended periods to pay NI contributions, and therefore have no entitlement to a pension, or have a reduced pension, when they retire. Four-fifths of the 2 million employees who had weekly earnings below the NI lower earnings limit (McKnight et al. 1998) and 3.1 million of the 3.5 million pensioners who did not qualify for a basic pension were women (Baroness Hollis of Higham's statement in the House of Commons: *The Times*, 1997).

Women in old age, then, are more likely than older men to be dependent on means-tested state benefits and less likely than men to have an employer's or private pension. Even when they do, it will be considerably smaller because women on average earn less than men. Three-quarters of pensioners on income support are women (1.5 million women: *The Times*, 1997) and many more women than men live on incomes just above the poverty line. Three in five older women rely on their own meagre income (see Chapter 5).

Whilst sociologists and others frequently talk about 'the third age' – a period of relative affluence and good health after retirement which is enjoyed by pensioners in countries like Britain – this is not the case for all. Women are much less likely than men to enjoy this third age for a number of reasons. They are less likely to have the economic resources, they are more likely to have to care for dependent relatives (including their male partner) and domestic labour does not cease on retirement, and older women are more likely to have chronic health or disability problems. Furthermore, older women are more likely than men to live into the fourth age of increased dependence and have to live on a low income – including those who may have lived in a relatively affluent household when their partners were alive.

When New Labour came to power in 1997, it made tackling poverty and inequality a major concern. However, it focused on social exclusion, raising educational standards and in particular on getting people into employment – tackling the causes of poverty, rather than compensating people for its effects. This core approach recognised that poverty is part of wider social exclusion, a more inclusive term that takes in health, housing, employment and so on. However, it is less concerned with the dynamic processes by which individuals and communities come to be disadvantaged or questions about the role of social institutions, including the welfare state, in generating these problems. New Labour's terminology was essentially an attempt to signal an inter-departmental collaborative style of seeing social exclusion.

However, the policies were not based on consideration of the differences between men and women in terms of their role in the community or the family – they were 'gender-blind'. Single parents (mainly women) were encouraged to take paid employment with child care and wage subsidies provided to make this possible. This took no account of the difficulties of being a lone-parent mother and combining this with paid employment. Policies designed to encourage community participation took no account of the different ways in which men and women involve themselves in the community. While women tend to play a greater role, it is generally on an informal basis, helping neighbours and other members of the community. When men become involved in the community, it is normally in formal organisations. Agencies working with communities are more likely to work with organisations and therefore men are likely to be over-represented in consultation and empowerment exercises, thus marginalising women. Since 2010 the ConDem Coalition has promoted a policy of reducing the welfare state in favour of the 'Big Society' which is intended to solve our social problems. While it is still too early at the time of writing (2013) to assess the results of their programme, their approach to gender echoes much of New Labour's stance.

Conclusion

In this chapter, I have examined gender divisions in modern Britain – the persistence of inequalities between men and women. Despite equal opportunities and equal pay at work legislation, there has been little improvement in the overall situation of women vis-à-vis men in paid employment. The majority of women continue to be dependent on men because legal changes do not change relationships between men and women in the private sphere, where women are expected to provide care for children and other dependent relatives. Nor do they provide help for women in carrying out the informal care for which they are perceived as being responsible. Whilst the welfare state has challenged patriarchal power – for example, by assisting women to leave men who beat them up – it has replaced private patriarchy with public patriarchy.

Gender is a key aspect of social division and classification in modern industrial societies. It is not just that there are differences between men and women, but that the inequalities are built into the structures of society. Gender is a fundamental way in which every aspect of our lives is organised. It is the key category through which we make sense of our social and natural world and our experiences of that world. There are inequalities in the distribution of wealth, power and privilege between men and women. Gender inequalities are ordered and consistent in type, although in the longer term there are changes. Gendered relationships exist outside of the ways in which we categorise men and women, although the categories affect the ways in which gendered relationships evolve.

Nevertheless, gender as a concept is a social construct that is used to define, explain and justify inequalities and, as such, is unstable and contestable. The structured inequalities and the socially constructed discourses of gender work together to perpetuate gender inequalities in hierarchies. Everyday struggles to change and resist the discourses of gender take place within the context of the pre-existing structural relationships which, on the whole, give men more power, more ability to control and more access to scarce resources than women. Historically, women have resisted men's power and fought to gain equality, and men have resisted the attempts of women to improve their situation vis-à-vis men.

Despite the gains of women over the last two centuries in terms of achievement of the right to vote, laws against rape, laws to protect women from domestic violence, equal opportunities and equal pay legislation, women on the whole continue to be subordinate to men within contemporary industrial societies. However, we should not lose sight of the fragmentary nature of social stratification and social divisions within contemporary societies. Men and women's experiences are structured not only by gender, but also by class, ethnicity, age, sexuality and so on. At the same time, gender remains an important and fascinating element of social division in its own right.

Discussion Questions

Public institutions including universities and colleges have a duty to promote gender equality. This means that, where inequalities exist, they will have a duty to take positive action to eliminate them. Write a briefing paper for the head of your institution, setting out:

1. The reasons why the institution should audit programmes for gender representation across the institution.

2. The partners with which the institution would need to work if it were to develop positive actions to reduce gender imbalances.

3. The research that would need to be undertaken in order to develop positive action recommendations.

FURTHER READING

Abbott, P., Wallace, C. and Tyler, M. *An Introduction to Sociology: Feminist Perspectives* (London: Routledge, 2005) offers a broad introduction to gender inequalities in contemporary Britain and feminist explanations for them. Bradley, H. *Fractured Identities: Changing Patterns of Inequality* (Cambridge: Polity, 1996) gives a comprehensive introduction to past and current theories of stratification and inequalities, with a major focus on gender. A more specialist edited collection, dealing with gender inequalities and ageing, is Arber, S. and Ginn, J. (eds) *Connecting Gender and Ageing: A Sociological Approach* (Buckingham: Open University Press, 1995). A selection of articles that considers and analyses the debates about the changing outcomes of education, as based on gender, can be found in Epstein, D., Elwood, J., Hey, V. and Maw, J. *Failing Boys? Issues in Gender and Achievement* (Buckingham: Open University Press, 1998) and Skelton, C. and Beck, F. (eds) *Investigating Gender: Contemporary Perspectives in Education* (Buckingham: Open University Press, 2001). The Equality and Human Rights Commission website (www.equalityhumanrights.com) provides a range of up-to-date briefing papers on gender, while relevant statistical information can be accessed via the government website.

CHAPTER 4

Ethnicity

DAVID MASON

This chapter will provide you with a broad critical understanding of the following issues in ethnicity as a source of social division:

- The origins of the concept of ethnicity
- The relationship of ethnicity to other concepts such as class and race
- The relational character of ethnicity
- British conceptions of ethnicity
- Problems of measuring ethnic difference and disadvantage
- Problems of categorisation and identity
- The broad demographic profile of minority ethnic groups in Britain
- Patterns of ethnic advantage and disadvantage in the British labour market
- Discrimination
- The dynamics of ethnic divisions in Britain
- Changing ethnic identities
- The intellectual and political challenges of recognising diversity and change while measuring disadvantage and tracking social divisions

As outlined in Chapter 2, the analysis of class divisions has traditionally been concerned first with mapping and explaining the causes of underlying material inequalities, and then investigating their implications for people's conceptions of themselves and how this affects their relations with others. In other words, people's identities, and their relationship to others' identities, are usually second-order questions in the study of class (but see Payne and Grew 2005 for alternative approaches). Ethnicity, by contrast, presents us with a different problem. Ethnic differences are not constituted by material inequalities, even if they may frequently be marked by them. We cannot know people's ethnicity by seeking information about their occupations, income, wealth, or housing circumstances. Only in situations of extreme segregation will these kinds of information offer us good clues to people's ethnic status and, even then, few would argue that these characteristics represent the essence of their ethnicity in the way that is common in class analysis. Thus, if we are to understand the implications of ethnic differences for social divisions, we must ask some rather different questions.

Specifically, we must start by considering what constitutes ethnic difference. Then we need to map the patterning of that difference in the societies that we are studying. Only then can we proceed to ask what, if any, patterns of material inequalities are to be observed among the groups concerned. In other words, when we begin to consider ethnic differences we may find that these divisions are manifested in ways other than simple material inequality.

Some conceptual ground-clearing

Thus far we have spoken of ethnic differences as if the concept of ethnicity were unproblematic and uncontested. Unfortunately this is far from being the case. Before we can proceed, therefore, we need to consider what we mean by the term. As in the case of social class, we rapidly discover that 'ethnicity' is used in a variety of different ways and has been subject to a range of different theorisations. Moreover, the term is not one confined to sociological discourse but is widely used in lay debate and policy formulation in ways that considerably complicate our task in this chapter. Not only that, but the concept is related in complex ways to other commonly used terms such as 'race' and 'minority'. Indeed, in order to understand the origins and character of the concept of ethnicity it is necessary briefly to consider its relationship to the concept of race.

The first thing to say about both the terms 'race' and 'ethnicity' is that they are distinctively modern. They are products of what Kumar (1978) has called 'the great transformation' of European societies, and particularly of their global expansion, from the late fifteenth century onwards. As Europeans explored other parts of the world, they came into contact with human societies which had unfamiliar patterns of social organisation and were populated by persons whose physical appearance was noticeably different from their own. Europeans' encounters with other societies rapidly turned to conquest and annexation, while they adapted the ancient institution of slavery to the new requirements of colonial expansion and capitalist production (Davis 1984). Against this background, it was not only the striking differences between themselves and those whom they met and conquered, but also apparent European superiority that seemed to require explanation. The result was the emergence of a distinctive way of thinking about and explaining human variation – race.

The modern concept of race emerged between the end of the eighteenth and the middle of the nineteenth centuries (see the discussions in Banton 1967, 1977, 1987, 1988; Stepan 1982). By the middle of the nineteenth century, race 'science' was characterising human diversity in terms of divisions between fixed, separate and hierarchically ranked races, rooted in biological difference and a product of divergent ancestries. The differences between them were seen not merely as markers of current status but as determinants of their past history and future potential. As the nineteenth century ended, this view, expressed increasingly in terms of 'Social Darwinism', was being harnessed to the justification of conquest and war as the age of high imperialism dawned in wake of the 1885 Congress of Berlin (Mason 2000: 7).

By the end of the Second World War, as the horrors of the Holocaust were revealed, race science was becoming discredited. At the same time, the emerging science of genetics was undermining notions of biological fixity. The result was the gradual disappearance of the concept of race from natural science debates (Banton and Harwood 1975; Montague 1964, 1974). Nevertheless, biological notions persisted in popular conceptions of human variation. Consequently even those, such as sociologists, who were convinced by the evidence that races in the biological sense did not exist, found themselves having to confront the persistence of the term. However uneasily, sociologists found themselves continuing to use the concept on the basis that social actors treated race as real and organised their lives in terms of it (cf. van den Berghe 1967). From the 1980s writers such as Miles (1982, 1993) challenged this usage, arguing that it served to legitimise an ideological category, naturalising divisions that were really the outcome of exploitation and oppression. As result, sociological writing began increasingly to substitute the problematic of 'racism' for that of 'race' (see, for example, Solomos and Back 1996).

In what follows, I shall not use the term 'race' except where this is unavoidable in referring to the work of others. Nevertheless, if we are to understand the status of the concept of ethnicity – the focus of this chapter – it is necessary to grasp the extent to which it emerged, and continues to appear, in dialogue with that of race. This is so, despite the fact that the concept of ethnicity represents an attempt to replace the emphasis on physical difference with a stress on cultural variation. Moreover, the concept of ethnicity entered sociological and policy discourse partly as a reaction to the perceived inadequacies of race. It is frequently seen as more legitimate because it avoids biological determinism and appeals, at least in part, to people's self-definitions.

Despite this, the terms 'race' and 'ethnicity' are widely used interchangeably in both policy and academic discourses, as well as in everyday speech. Thus, we have policies to counter the 'racial' harassment of 'ethnic minorities' while the term 'race' has been enshrined in law itself – in the title and content of the various pieces of 'Race Relations' legislation that have sought to eliminate discriminatory practices in the UK. Moreover, even in places where one might anticipate a little more conceptual rigour – such as undergraduate textbooks in sociology – the terms are frequently used interchangeably, even when an attempt is made conceptually to distinguish them (see the discussion in Mason 1996).

In many ways this is a peculiarly British phenomenon. In the United States, where the concept of race is perhaps even more entrenched in the national consciousness, and in political and administrative life, there is nevertheless a well-established understanding that the concepts are not identical. There are all sorts of intellectual problems with the way the distinction is made in the US, but at least it is made. In continental Europe, apart from a few far-right political movements, the concept of race is scarcely encountered at all, other than when incorporated into the term 'racism' which is used generally as a term of disapproval for particular political attitudes and movements.

I suggest that the widespread interchangeability of the concepts of race and ethnicity in Britain is intimately bound up with the colonial roots of Britain's post-Second World War immigration experience. Fallacious biological beliefs about human differences, which periodically reappear in public debate, were galvanised by the distinctive visibility of those who came to be seen as quintessential 'immigrants' (see the discussion in Mason 1994). Indeed, as Modood (2003) and others have suggested, the racialisation of ethnic difference is key to understanding some of the ways in which British conceptions of ethnic diversity have developed.

Matters are complicated further because, as a result of the range of theoretical traditions from which ethnicity can be approached, there is no universally accepted definition of the term. It is probably true to say that, if pressed for a definition, most academics and policy makers would stress some sort of cultural distinctiveness as the mark of an ethnic grouping. For example, M.G. Smith defined an ethnic unit as 'a population whose members believe that in some sense they share common descent and a common cultural heritage or tradition, and who are so regarded by others' (1986: 192).

Nevertheless, there are among sociologists considerable differences of view about the negotiability of ethnicity. How much freedom do social actors have to define themselves and their relationships to others? To what extent can people choose their ethnicity? For some there is a primordial element to ethnicity that explains the fervour of commitments to particular cultural identities. For others, ethnicity is little more than a symbolic resource to be used instrumentally (see the discussions in Jenkins 1986b, 1997; Mason 1986; Yinger 1986: 26–31, 1994).

One influential approach places emphasis on the processes by which ethnic boundaries are drawn. Whether and how social boundaries are erected is an empirical question and not one that can be simply read off from the existence of cultural difference (see the discussion in Jenkins 1997, also Barth 1969; Wallman 1986). In this view, ethnicity is situational. Whether or not members of a group celebrate cultural markers to distinguish themselves from others depends, in part, on such matters as their immediate objectives – including political and economic ones. This perspective also allows us to recognise that people may have different identities in different situations. Thus it is possible to be simultaneously English, British, and European, stressing these identities more or less strongly in different aspects of daily life (Chapter 10). Similarly, the same person might self-identify as Gujarati, Indian, Hindu, East African Asian, or British depending the situation, immediate objectives, and the responses and behaviour of others.

The responses of others are important, of course, because they too are making identity choices, and constructing and maintaining their own boundaries. In other words, as well as being potentially situational, ethnicity is also, and fundamentally, relational. As a result no-one's identity choices are unconstrained. This point has particular importance in a British context because nowhere are these constraints more significant than in relation to public policy and its capacity to frame and shape the opportunity structures in which people play out their lives. In this context, a key role is taken by the processes by which ethnic difference is defined and measured.

In Britain, in much popular and official parlance, the term 'ethnic' is used to refer only to those who are thought to differ from some assumed indigenous norm of 'Britishness' (Chapter 10). It is frequently used as a synonym for those who are considered to be culturally different. Talk of an 'ethnic look' in the world of fashion is only one, relatively trivial, example of the way white British people are apt to see ethnicity as an attribute only of others – something that distinguishes 'them' from 'us'. This is exemplified by the way in which in Britain the term 'ethnic' is frequently qualified with the word 'minority'. We almost never hear mention of an ethnic *majority*.

Matters are, however, more complicated still. Not every group having a distinctive culture and constituting a minority in the British population is normally included in the designation. Instead, in order to qualify for designation as an ethnic minority, a category of people must exhibit a degree of 'difference' that is regarded as significant. In practice, a mixture of skin colour and distinctive culture is the criterion that is usually thought to mark off 'ethnic minorities' from the 'majority' population in Britain. At the same time, 'ethnic minorities' are frequently seen to have more in common with one another than with the 'majority'. The term thus often seems to de-emphasise *diversity among* minority ethnic groups while exaggerating *differences from* the white population. Even those who argue that 'ethnic minorities' are united by a common experience of racism often fail to be sufficiently alert to the diverse ways in which racism may impact upon different communities or, within them, upon men and women (Field 1987; Modood 1988, 1990, 1992; Yuval-Davis and Anthias 1989; Anthias and Yuval-Davis 1992; Mason 2003c; Mirza 2003).

Ethnic differences in Britain: some problems of measurement

We have seen that the terms 'ethnic minority' and, by extension, 'ethnicity' have a particular resonance in Britain. Despite the fact that Britain's population is one forged from successive historical migrations, the term characteristically refers to people descended from the populations of the countries of the former British Empire – the so-called New Commonwealth. Indeed, it is interesting to note that, until recently, the term 'immigration' was automatically associated in popular parlance with the immigration to Britain of people whose origins lay in these countries. Since 2000, migrations from the new EU states of Eastern Europe and growing numbers of asylum seekers entering the UK have undermined this connection to a significant extent. This does not, however, prevent the burgeoning public concern about these new migrations from spilling over into renewed hostility to long-settled British citizens of minority ethnic descent.

A key reason for this lies in the rapid growth of the immigrant population in the years following the end of the Second World War. At that time, the British Empire was still largely intact. It provided a ready source of potential labour for the UK until the period of immigration control was initiated with the passing of the Commonwealth Immigrants Act in 1962. (For a discussion of the history of immigration control to Britain, see Layton-Henry 1992 and Mason 2000.)

A severe labour shortage developed in post-war Britain because of a number of factors. In part, this shortage was a result of the need to engage in post-war reconstruction. At the same time, British industry was becoming increasingly large-scale and capital intensive, with a growing demand for skilled workers. In addition, new employment opportunities were opening up in the rapidly developing service industries and in a public sector which was expanding as a result of the welfare state established by the post-war Labour government. Increasingly, British workers, and in particular those of the first generation to receive secondary education, had access to avenues of upward social mobility as they took up newly created and more desirable occupations. This process left a pool of hard-to-fill unskilled and routine semi-skilled jobs at the lower levels of the labour market. These were often dirty, poorly paid and involved unsocial hours like night shift working. Many were found in declining industries where cheap labour was an alternative to capital investment or collapse (see Fevre 1984; Duffield 1985). Given Britain's labour shortage in a period when women had been encouraged to leave the labour market and raise families, these vacancies could best be filled by substantial immigration.

From an early stage, then, Britain's new minority ethnic citizens found themselves differentiated from the rest of the population, first by their socio-economic situation and later by their immigration status. These characteristics established the conditions in which there were early attempts to measure the size and growth of the minority ethnic population. However, over time the sources of data about Britain's ethnic diversity have developed and altered in the light of changing policy concerns, changing political priorities (both within government and outside) and changing patterns of political contestation, including the demands of minority ethnic communities themselves. The same is true of the categories by which members of the population are differentiated. As a consequence, tracking changes over time is extremely difficult.

Early discussions of Britain's growing ethnic diversity were framed within debates about immigration. As a result, early official estimates of the size of the minority ethnic population were based on the place of birth of those born outside the UK, in the 'New Commonwealth'. The term New Commonwealth was a euphemism for the countries of the former British Empire populated by people whose skin colour was not white. The New Commonwealth was thus distinguished from the Old Commonwealth of countries which were thought of as having predominantly white populations. The term 'New' was justified largely on the grounds that these countries attained independence after the Second World War, in contrast to Australia, Canada and New Zealand which had been granted effective self-government much earlier. The convolutions entailed in this usage are well-illustrated by the fact that, when Pakistan left the Commonwealth in 1972, it was necessary to revise the term to 'New Commonwealth and Pakistan'. This was often rendered as 'NCWP'.

Counting those born in the New Commonwealth made some statistical sense in the early days of immigration but it became increasingly unsatisfactory as a growing proportion of the New Commonwealth-descended population were being born in Britain. The initial solution was to count those living in households where the 'head of household' had been born in the New Commonwealth. Yet again, this could only ever be a temporary solution until the children of initial migrants began to establish their own households. Nevertheless, until data from the 1991 Census became available, estimates of this kind based on the Censuses of 1971 and 1981 were the main sources for both official and academic purposes.

The 1991 Census asked respondents for the first time to classify themselves in ethnic terms. The Census categories were also adopted by the Commission for Racial Equality as those that it recommended for ethnic monitoring purposes. This increasing standardisation offered the future benefits of comparability between data sources and over time. As we shall see, however, these features were not without their problems when faced with the realities of changing ethnic identities.

The following schema was the one finally adopted in 1991:

White
Black – Caribbean
Black – African
Black – Other (please specify)
Indian
Pakistani
Bangladeshi
Chinese
Any other ethnic group (please describe)

In the 2001 Census, respondents were required to select one section from A to E and then tick the appropriate box to indicate their ethnic group.

A : White
- British
- Irish
- Any other White background (please write in)

B : Mixed
- White and Black Caribbean
- White and Black African
- White and Asian
- Any other Mixed background (please write in)

C : Asian or Asian British
- Indian
- Pakistani
- Bangladeshi
- Any other Asian background (please write in)

D : Black or Black British
- Caribbean
- African
- Any other Black background (please write in)

E : Chinese or other ethnic group
- Chinese
- Any other (please write in)

The categorisation was further elaborated in the 2011 Census with 'British' being subdivided into nationalities and 'Gypsy or Irish Traveller' being added; 'Chinese' relocated into the Asian box; and 'Arab' was added as a new category. The ongoing additions of new categories were a response to a number of emergent problems: the difficulty many minority ethnic citizens found in locating a category that adequately matched their own self-identity; the absence of opportunities to affirm differentiated white identities; and the failure to keep pace with the rapid increase in the numbers of people wishing to record 'mixed' origins or 'hybrid' identities. The 2001 Census also introduced a question on religion that, it was hoped, would allow further, fine-tuned, disaggregation of the population.

Nevertheless, it remains the case that, underlying the 2001 and 2011 Census questions, there is still a sense that the most significant ethnic differences are those associated with the conventional British conceptualisation of 'ethnic minorities' described above; one that is, above all, racialised. The result is that, increasingly sophisticated attempts to disaggregate the minority population notwithstanding, there is still a tendency to conceptualise this population as relatively unchanging, both in terms of its boundaries and perceptions of associated problems. In other words, despite successive refinements of the categories, the underlying logic of the Census question remains unchanged. For a fuller discussion of some of the key problems of measurement see Mason (2003a).

In addition to figures derived from the Census, there have been some other sources of data. The most important, and widely used, are the periodic surveys conducted by the Policy Studies Institute (PSI) (formerly Political and Economic Planning) (Daniel 1968; Smith 1974; Brown 1984; Modood et al. 1997), and the results of the annual Labour Force Survey conducted by the Office for National Statistics. Both have utilised self-classification measures of ethnicity. However, there are technical differences, not only between one another but also with those used in the Census (the Labour Force Survey being brought closer in line to the latter only in 2011), so that comparisons are fraught with difficulty, particularly where they involve attempts to measure change over time.

In the rest of this chapter much of the discussion relies upon the data from the Census and other analyses by the Office for National Statistics. Comparisons are made with other and earlier sources where appropriate but, since 1997, there has been no repetition of the hitherto periodic, and highly influential and comprehensive, PSI studies. As a result, new and accessible sources of data are limited; a fact reflected in the continued reliance in parts of this discussion on some older data sources.

Minority ethnic groups in Britain

Table 4.1 reproduces results from the 2011 Census showing that nearly 8 million people of 'non-white' minority ethnic origin were resident in England and Wales; 14 per cent of the population. As we know from the 2001 Census, there were relatively fewer people of minority ethnic origin in Wales, Scotland and Northern Ireland than in England.

Table 4.1 Population of England and Wales by ethnic group, 2011 Census

Ethnic group	Total population		Non-white population
	Numbers	Percentages	Percentages
White	48,151,715	86.0	–
British	45,134,686	80.5	–
Irish	531,087	0.9	–
Gypsy or Irish Traveller	57,680	0.1	–
Other White	2,485,942	4.4	–
Mixed or multiple ethnic group	1,224,400	2.2	15.6
White and Black Caribbean	426,715	0.8	5.4
White and Black African	165,974	0.3	2.1
White and Asian	341,727	0.6	4.3
Other mixed	289,984	0.5	3.7
Asian or Asian British	4,213,531	7.5	53.6
Indian	1,412,958	2.5	18.0
Pakistani	1,124,511	2.0	14.3
Bangladeshi	447,201	0.8	5.7
Chinese	393,141	0.7	5.0
Other Asian	835,720	1.5	10.6
Black African/Caribbean/Black British	1,864,890	3.3	23.7
Caribbean	594,825	1.1	7.6
African	989,628	1.8	12.6
Other Black	280,437	0.5	3.6
Other ethnic group	563,696	1.0	7.2
Arab	230,600	0.4	2.9
Any other ethnic group	333,096	0.6	4.2
Totals			
All non-white ethnic groups	7,866,517	14.0	100
Total population	56,075,912	100	–

Source: 2011 Census: KS201EW Ethnic group, local authorities in England and Wales, March 2012, www.data4nr.net/resources/population/1564 (accessed 13 August 2013).

Figure 4.1 shows that the 2011 population had an uneven geographical spread, concentrated as it was not just in England but also overwhelmingly resident in the most densely populated urban areas. The minority ethnic groups made up about 40 per cent of the population of London, 17 per cent of the West Midlands, around 10 per cent of Yorkshire and the Humber, the East Midlands, the North West, and the East and South East of England, and only about 5 per cent in each of the South West and North East regions of England, and Wales. The largest proportions of both Black Africans and Black Caribbeans (58 per cent) were resident in London, as were about half of Bangladeshis. Other minority groups were more dispersed with around 20 per cent living

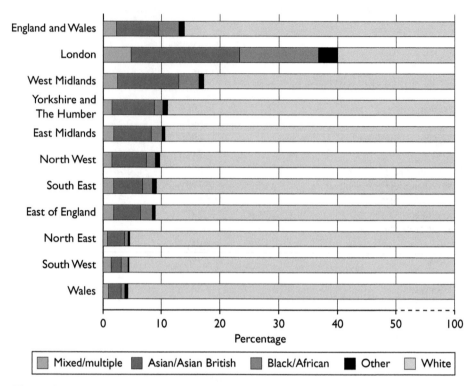

Figure 4.1 Regional distribution of minority ethnic population, 2011

Source: 2011 Census: KS201EW Ethnic group, local authorities in England and Wales, March 2012.
www.data4nr.net/resources/population (accessed 13 August 2013).

in each of London, the West Midlands, and Yorkshire and the Humber, and 16 per cent in the North West.

There has been a tendency, over a lengthy period, for the minority ethnic population to become more spatially concentrated (cf. Brown 1984: 59; Owen 1992: 9–10, 2003). It is important to note that the distribution of individual ethnic groups varies widely within this overall pattern. For at least some groups, this concentration in areas of initial settlement has important implications for their economic and other opportunities (see Mason 2003b).

As we have seen, ethnic differences are not, in themselves, constituted by material inequalities. However, to the extent that ethnicity is a source of social division it would be surprising if ethnic differences were not associated with such inequalities. Indeed, access to economic resources is usually a key to people's ability to control other aspects of their lives, and, for most of Britain's citizens, income from employment represents the major economic resource for day-to-day living. As a result, it is appropriate, in the next part of the discussion, to focus on labour market placement.

Research from the 1960s through into the 1980s (Daniel, 1968; Smith 1974; Brown 1984) consistently showed that people from minority ethnic groups were clustered in particular industries and occupations, over-represented in semi-skilled and unskilled jobs, and frequently excluded altogether from the labour market. More recent evidence reveals both continuity and change from earlier periods. We should remember, however, that material inequalities have other dimensions (some, but not all, directly related to control of economic resources). They include housing status and access to health and healthcare. For an introduction to these issues see Mason (2000; 2003c) and Modood et al. (1997).

Employment, unemployment and poverty

Successive studies (Smith 1974, 1981; Brown 1984; Jones 1993; Owen 1993; Mason 2003b) have revealed that persons of ethnic minority origin are at a consistently higher risk of unemployment than are white people. There is evidence that unemployment among people from minority ethnic groups is 'hyper-cyclical' (Jones 1993: 112; Berthoud, 2000). In other words, it rises faster than white unemployment in times of recession and falls more rapidly when the economy recovers. Over an extended period, however, we can say that the rate of unemployment among minority ethnic men has tended to be roughly double the rate for white men. Figure 4.2 presents data from the Annual Population Survey for 2004 which show that unemployment rates for minority ethnic groups were generally higher than those for white people, for both men and women. However, among men, Indians were closer than other minority ethnic groups to the various white groups.

We should, however, note that there are marked variations in the experience of different groups, and of men and women, in the UK in 2012. The data set out in Figure 4.2 pre-date the onset of the recession in 2008. After then, of course, unemployment rose among all ethnic groups, with little sign that earlier patterns of hyper-cyclicality had significantly changed. At 17.5 per cent men from Black Caribbean and Black African groups had the highest unemployment rates; more than twice the 8 per cent figure recorded for White British and White Irish men in 2012. Men from Pakistani, Bangladeshi, Chinese and Mixed groups had unemployment rates of between 11 and 13.7 per cent. Pakistani and Bangladeshi women had the highest unemployment rates at 22 per cent. The next highest female rates were among women from the Black African or Black African ethnic groups. At around 15 per cent, these rates were two-and-a-half times the rates for White British and White Irish women (Office for National Statistics 2013). These *differentials* remain broadly comparable over long periods despite changes to abolish absolute rates.

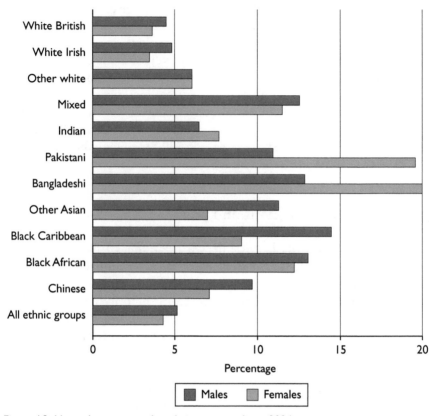

Figure 4.2 Unemployment rate by ethnic group and sex, 2004
Source: Office for National Statistics (2006b).

Nowhere are the patterns starker than among young people, who represent
a larger proportion of minority ethnic groups than of white groups. Analysis of
Labour Force Survey data by the Institute for Public Policy Research (IPPR)
(2010) indicates that, as in previous recessions, ethnic minorities had been
disproportionately affected by the rise in unemployment. At the beginning
of 2010, youth unemployment was at its highest level for 15 years. Among
young people of minority ethnic descent, the recession appeared to have had
greatest impact among Black and Black British young people, whose rates had
risen to over 48 per cent, and among those of mixed race, over 35 per cent
of whom were unemployed in November 2009. Youth unemployment had increased least among the Asian and Asian British groups, although it remained
high at 31.2 per cent. By contrast, rates among white young people stood at
20.4 per cent. These data reflect relatively longstanding patterns (compare
Jones 1993: 113, Owen 1993: 7 and Modood et al. 1997: 88–93). Moreover,

the true position may also be masked by the higher post-compulsory educational participation of minority ethnic young people (Modood 2003).

There are also regional variations in unemployment rates, with a number of important areas of minority ethnic residence in the North and Midlands of England exhibiting high levels of unemployment. At the risk of oversimplifying, we can note that, while levels of minority ethnic unemployment are consistently higher than the white rate, these differences are larger outside Greater London. In these areas, even groups such as African Asians are likely to experience higher unemployment than white people (Jones 1993: 113–14; Owen 1993; Modood 1997a: 88–93; Institute for Public Policy Research 2010). Having said this, it is not clear that geographical distribution itself can be held to account for differences between white and minority unemployment rates (see Fieldhouse and Gould 1998).

A long series of studies, dating back to the 1960s, has shown that in general terms members of minority ethnic groups have been employed in less skilled jobs, at lower job levels than whites and that they have been concentrated in particular industrial sectors (Daniel 1968; Smith 1974; Brown 1984). More recent data, such as Jones' (1993) re-analysis of the Labour Force Surveys for 1988, 1989 and 1990, the fourth PSI survey (Modood 1997b), Iganski et al. (2001) and analyses by the Office for National Statistics (2006a), however, indicate that the position is becoming more complex as the experience of members of different groups has diverged.

Table 4.2 suggests that, by the first decade of this century, many male members of some minority ethnic groups had begun to experience employment patterns increasingly similar to those of white men. This was true of men in the Indian, Mixed, and 'Other' categories, with Indian and Chinese men approximating or exceeding the proportions of white workers in each of the top two categories. However, these figures concealed important variations because, although Indian and Chinese men were more likely to be professional workers than white men, they were considerably less likely to be represented among senior managers in *large* enterprises. Among those of Afro-Caribbean, Bangladeshi and Pakistani descent, there was much less evidence of progress in the top categories (although there was some convergence in the technical and routine administrative categories). Bangladeshi men in particular, two-thirds of whom were in manual occupations, remained concentrated in the lower echelons of the labour market.

Table 4.3 presents comparable data for women. It shows that women of all groups except the Chinese were less likely than men to be in the top category and the largest concentrations were to be found in the 'associate professional and technical', and 'administrative and secretarial' non-manual categories, followed by 'personal services' and sales and customer services'.

Table 4.2 Ethnic group men in paid work, aged 16–74, 2011 Census

Occupational group	White	Mixed	Indian	Pakistani	Bangladeshi	Chinese	Black Carib/African	Other
Managers and senior officials	18.3	15.6	20.7	14.0	14.3	10.9	11.3	20.4
Professionals	13.6	14.3	20.3	11.3	8.3	21.3	12.8	18.3
Associate professional and technical	13.3	16.4	10.1	7.4	5.7	9.5	14.0	14.6
Administrative and secretarial	5.2	6.8	7.5	6.1	5.5	4.9	8.4	6.4
Skilled trades	19.6	13.6	9.9	9.2	24.3	26.1	13.6	9.3
Personal services	2.0	3.0	1.3	1.6	1.3	1.0	4.6	2.5
Sales and customer service	3.7	7.1	7.9	10.3	9.6	4.7	6.3	8.3
Process and plant operatives	12.6	9.1	12.2	25.0	8.3	3.1	11.9	8.3
Elementary occupations	11.5	14.1	10.1	15.2	22.9	9.6	17.3	11.8
Totals								
Non-manual	50.4	53.1	58.6	38.8	33.8	46.6	46.5	59.7
Manual	49.6	46.9	41.4	61.2	66.2	53.4	53.4	40.3

Table 4.3 Ethnic group women in paid work, aged 16–74, 2011 Census

Occupational group	White	Mixed	Indian	Pakistani	Bangladeshi	Chinese	Black Carib/African	Other
Managers and senior officials	11.2	10.7	11.5	8.6	5.9	13.9	8.1	9.2
Professionals	9.9	11.8	12.9	12.8	11.4	14.9	9.6	11.8
Associate professional and technical	14.0	17.6	11.9	10.9	10.5	16.4	20.0	20.6
Administrative and secretarial	22.8	20.4	21.7	20.0	22.4	14.4	23.2	17.1
Skilled trades	2.4	1.8	1.7	1.3	2.2	8.1	2.1	2.4
Personal services	12.8	11.9	6.0	11.4	12.2	4.1	15.2	11.8
Sales and customer service	11.9	13.0	14.6	18.8	21.8	12.8	9.9	11.3
Process and plant operatives	3.0	2.2	8.6	5.7	3.9	1.9	1.9	3.3
Elementary occupations	12.0	10.6	10.9	10.5	9.6	13.4	9.9	12.6
Totals								
Non-manual	57.9	60.5	58.0	52.3	50.2	59.6	60.9	58.7
Manual	42.1	39.5	42.0	47.7	49.8	40.4	39.1	41.3

This finding broadly matches that of the 1982 Policy Studies Institute survey (Brown 1984) and Jones' (1993) re-analysis of Labour Force Survey data. Both of these studies offered a similar explanation: women are already disadvantaged in the labour market relative to men and, as a result, there is limited scope for an additional disadvantage arising from ethnicity (Jones 1993: 71). Despite detailed variations between groups, therefore, there is some evidence that 'gender divisions in the labour market may be stronger and more deeply rooted than differences due to race and ethnicity' (Modood 1997c: 104; see also Iganski and Payne 1996).

So far as distribution between employment sectors is concerned, there is evidence both of continuity with, and some changes in, previously established patterns of concentration. That concentration to some degree reflected patterns of residence and demand for labour at the time of initial settlement. However, major economy-wide changes in the 1980s associated with the decline in manufacturing employment and the growth of the service sector led to significant changes for members of all groups. It might be thought, given their concentration in semi-skilled and unskilled manual occupations, that the descendants of New Commonwealth migrants to Britain would have fared rather badly in these transformations. In fact, the evidence suggests that, continued disadvantage and exclusion notwithstanding, minority ethnic groups were not disproportionately negatively affected (Iganski and Payne 1999).

Data from the Labour Force Survey (Jones 1993) and Annual Population Survey (Office for National Statistics 2006a) suggest that, since the 1990s, the largest proportion of all groups, including white employees, have been found in distribution, hotels, catering, and repairs. Within this broad pattern, people of South Asian origin are rather more likely than white people to be employed in retail distribution, while those of Chinese and Bangladeshi origin are markedly more likely than white people to work in hotels and catering. Pakistani men were particularly likely to be found in the transport and communication sectors (23 per cent) by 2004. By the same date, half of Black Caribbean (54 per cent) and Black African women (52 per cent) worked in the public administration, education or health sector. Indeed there remains a marked concentration of women of all groups in the service sector, reflecting the continuing general pattern of segregation of women in employment (Jones, 1993: 66–8; cf. Rees, 1992).

Some caution has to be exercised in interpreting the data that are available. Apparently similar proportions in the same occupational category may conceal important differences in status, in the kinds of enterprise or in the working conditions enjoyed by members of different groups. Thus it appears that even successful members of minority ethnic groups may have greater difficulty in accessing high status positions in major companies. This in turn may help to explain the enthusiasm of minority ethnic students for the professions where there are opportunities for the establishment of independent practices. A good example is law, where minority ethnic groups have been increasingly over-represented among students registering with the Law Society while remaining under-represented in large firms of solicitors and in the higher reaches of the legal profession (Home Office 1998: 37–8; for a fuller discussion of this issue see Mason 2003a).

It is sometimes argued that self-employment, not just in the professions, represents an escape route from disadvantage and discrimination in employment, and that this accounts for its prevalence among minority ethnic groups. This characterisation may, however, owe as much to popular stereotypes – notably the corner shop – as to real evidence of high levels of minority ethnic self-employment. The 2004 Annual Population Survey revealed some important changes over time in the levels of self-employment among different ethnic groups with Pakistanis, Chinese and White Irish people increasingly standing out as groups for whom self-employment was likely to be significantly higher than other groups.

The evidence suggests a variety of experiences, with widespread disadvantage coexisting with significant upward mobility for some. Modood's analysis and Census data appear to show an increasing similarity of experience between white people and at least some minority ethnic groups (Owen 1993; Modood 1997b). The growth of a middle class of professional and managerial workers in some ethnic communities, and the entry of these groups into the service sector, has led some to suggest that there is under way a convergence in the class structures of minority ethnic groups towards that of the white population (Iganski and Payne 1996, 1999). Moreover, some evidence has also suggested that these patterns of upward occupational mobility have been matched by a diminution in earnings differentials (Leslie et al. 1998: 489; 503–4). However, the patterns are complex and need to be approached with caution. (For a more detailed examination of the evidence on upward occupational mobility, see Mason 2003a.)

The first point to note is that there are significant differences between members of different ethnic groups. We have seen that those of Caribbean, Pakistani and Bangladeshi descent, in particular, tend to occupy the lowest positions in the labour market, and also experience the highest levels of unemployment. Indeed patterns of complete exclusion from the labour market must be taken into account when considering the successes of those in work. The same is true for the differences between the experiences of women and men.

We should also remember that upward mobility is not incompatible with continued occupational segregation, or with continuing discrimination. We know, for example, that there may be important differences of level within broad occupational categories, such as those between senior and middle management. (Compare the experience of women in this regard: Cockburn 1991, and see Chapter 3.) Members of all minority ethnic groups remain under-represented among managers of large companies. The kinds of enterprises in which people work may also have significant implications for their opportunities and earnings. These may even be reinforced by patterns of self-employment if their result is to increase opportunities for advancement by other members of the same groups. This suggests that there may be significant patterns of ethnic segregation in the labour market.

Finally, we should reiterate the extent to which experience in the field of employment is in some ways the key to overall life chances. The labour market situation of minority ethnic groups has had knock-on effects in other fields, such as health and housing. In this regard, a key piece of evidence about material inequalities that must be considered is that relating to household incomes and standards of living.

The fourth PSI survey (Modood et al. 1997) attempted for the first time to produce an analysis of the household incomes of minority ethnic groups. This is important because the household is commonly used as the unit of analysis in studying living standards and economic well-being. As we have seen, there is some evidence that patterns of upward occupational mobility are beginning to be matched by changes in individual earnings. It is a plausible assumption that individual earnings differences would be likely to feed through into household differences, but the manner in which this takes place is complex. Among relevant factors influencing outcomes will be relative household size, the number of wage earners, the number of dependants and the availability of sources of income other than earnings.

The analysis undertaken for the PSI reveals that the outcomes are complex and influenced by a range of factors. It also shows that, while some of the patterns revealed by analyses of employment continue to hold, there are other patterns that differ. Among key findings, we should note the extent of poverty (defined as incomes below half the national average) among Pakistani and Bangladeshi households. As Berthoud put it:

> Name any group whose poverty causes national concern – pensioners, disabled people, one-parent families, the unemployed – Pakistanis and Bangladeshis are poorer. (1997: 180)

The data also show that only Chinese households had incomes close to those of whites. Caribbean, Indian and African Asian households were all more likely than whites to experience poverty and less likely to have large family incomes (see also Chapter 13). These results lead to an important qualification to the evidence on upward occupational mobility. When household incomes are taken into account, African Asians and Indians fare less well than those of Chinese descent, while Caribbeans are much better placed than Pakistanis and Bangladeshis (Berthoud 1997: 180). These data thus provide further reasons to be cautious in assessing the significance of occupational mobility and the relative labour market placement of groups.

Explaining ethnic disadvantage – discrimination

A variety of explanations for the disadvantage suffered by members of minority ethnic groups in the labour market have been reviewed by the various studies conducted under the auspices of the PSI or its predecessor Political and Economic Planning (Daniel 1968; Smith 1974; Brown 1984; Jones 1993; Modood et al. 1997; see also the discussion in Mason 2003a). All have shown that, when matters such as language competence, skill levels and qualifications are controlled for, there remains a residue which is not explained by such factors. This residue is commonly called an 'ethnic penalty' (Heath and Yi Cheung 2006). The existence of ethnic penalties, in itself, does not provide conclusive proof of employment discrimination. However, it is difficult to avoid the conclusion that it plays a significant part in the labour market placement of minority ethnic groups.

In this context, it is interesting to note that the fourth PSI survey found that a large majority of all respondents believed that discrimination was widespread. Indeed white respondents were the most likely to hold such a belief (Modood 1997b: 129–35). More recently, a survey by Business in the Community (2010) found that, despite having a strong work ethic and high career aspirations, many members of minority ethnic groups do not aspire to careers in the professions because of an expectation that they will suffer discrimination.

These beliefs are consistent with the findings of an overwhelming body of research evidence which has exposed direct, and apparently intentional, discrimination in employment selection decisions (Daniel 1968; Hubbock and Carter 1980; National Association of Citizens Advice Bureaux 1984). A common investigation method has been to submit job applications from candidates matched in every way except ethnic origin. Using this method, Brown and Gay revealed continuing systematic discrimination, despite the many years of race relations legislation. They found that white applicants were more than 30 per cent more likely to be treated favourably than those of minority ethnic origin. Moreover, when compared with the results of studies dating back to the early 1970s, the researchers found no evidence of a diminution in the level of racial discrimination, and concluded that a major reason was the fact that employers were very unlikely to be caught in the act of discriminating (Brown and Gay 1985).

Later research by Noon (1993) involved sending matched speculative employment inquiries to personnel managers at the top one hundred UK companies in *The Times 100 index*. The letters were signed by fictitious applicants called Evans and Patel. They were presented as MBA students who were about to qualify and who already had relevant experience. The research compared both the frequency of responses sent to the two applicants and their quality in terms of the assistance and encouragement offered. It found that, overall, companies were more helpful and encouraging to white candidates. Moreover, the author concluded that, even in companies that were ostensibly sensitive to equal opportunities issues, discrimination was taking place on a routine basis.

Research commissioned by the Department for Work and Pensions has indicated that discriminatory decision-making has persisted in the employment selection process (Wood et al. 2009). The authors sent carefully matched applications (in terms of such features as qualifications and experience) in response to a selection of advertised jobs across a range of employment sectors. The applications were differentiated only in terms of the applicants' names, chosen to be characteristically associated with particular ethnic origins. The authors found net discrimination of 29 per cent in favour of white names over equivalent applications from minority ethnic candidates. In terms of success rates, this meant that 74 per cent more applications had to be sent from minority ethnic candidates to achieve a comparable level of success to that secured for white candidates. In the absence of more recent research, this is strongly suggestive of continuing direct discrimination in the employment selection process.

An equally serious problem is posed by indirect discrimination, where selection criteria are applied equally to everyone but where they are such that they disproportionately affect members of particular groups. A good example is occupationally unnecessary dress requirements that members of some groups cannot comply with for religious or other reasons. Indirect discrimination may be deliberate, but it may also frequently be unintentional and unrecognised. Jenkins (1986a) argued that many selection decisions are based not on whether candidates have the right qualifications for the job but on whether they are thought to be likely to 'fit in' to the workplace without causing any trouble. Such judgements are applied equally to everyone, but become discriminatory when they are consciously or unconsciously informed by managers' stereotypes of minority ethnic groups.

Jenkins' research and other studies (Jewson et al. 1990) revealed that negative stereotypes were widespread among managers responsible for recruitment decisions. Even ostensibly positive stereotypes can be disadvantageous. For example, Gray et al. (1993) found that employers' characterisations of Asian women workers as loyal, hardworking and uncomplaining could work against them in a situation where the qualities demanded of employees were increasingly those of flexibility, ability to exercise initiative, and readiness to carry responsibility and acquire new skills. These examples reveal how easy it is for the taken-for-granted routines of everyday working life to disadvantage minority ethnic groups unintentionally. Of course they also make it easy to hide intentional discrimination as the unplanned and accidental results of impersonal forces.

Ethnic inequalities in Britain: changing social divisions and identities

In the preceding sections we have reviewed some of the evidence of material inequalities among Britain's varied ethnic communities that has been revealed through official and other data sources. These material inequalities are changing in often complex and subtle ways. Any generalisations about the patterning of divisions based on those inequalities are fraught with difficulty, not least because of changes in official categorisation and measurement practices. As we saw, the 2001 and 2011 Censuses disaggregated a number of formerly used ethnic categories. These revised categories have also been adopted in other official data sources. As a result, patterns have been revealed that may variously reflect actual change, previously unrecognised complexities or some combination. A good example is provided by the disaggregation of the 'White' category.

We saw above that many recent analyses have identified patterns of upward occupational mobility among some minority ethnic groups that suggest a convergence with the white population. When, however, the white category is disaggregated, a more complex picture is revealed. Figure 4.3 shows the distribution of people in professional and managerial occupations in Great Britain as measured by the 2004 Annual Population Survey (Office for National Statistics 2006b). It reveals a pattern which complicates earlier analyses suggesting convergence. Measured in these terms, the greatest convergence is found between those from the Indian and Chinese groups with the White Irish and other non-British White groups. By contrast, White British people had relatively smaller percentages of people working in professional occupations, with only the Black and Mixed groups, Bangladeshis and Pakistanis exhibiting lower rates.

It is not clear whether this pattern is a new phenomenon or merely one previously concealed by the use of an undifferentiated 'white' category. However, it certainly complicates our understanding of patterns of ethnic disadvantage in Britain, challenging a number of previous over-simplifications, including

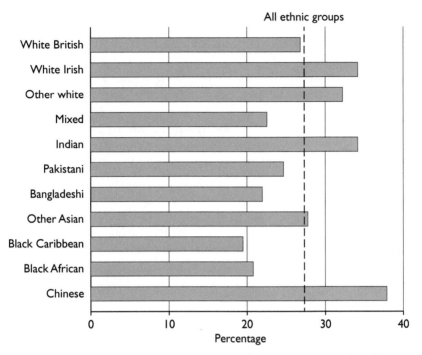

Figure 4.3 People in employment in managerial or professional occupations by ethnic group, 2004

Source: Office for National Statistics (2006a).

those relating to unambiguous 'white' advantage. In this connection, we may note that the civil disturbances that took place in a number of towns in the north of England in 2001, and in many major cities in 2011, revealed, all too clearly, the potential consequences of unchallenged deprivation (see the discussions in Mason 2003c). They also illustrated how, in many deprived areas, the 'white' population frequently also experiences exclusion, albeit differently mediated and labelled.

As the riots in Oldham, Burnley and Bradford of 2001 showed, deprivation can all too easily fuel damaging inter-ethnic conflict, particularly when it is exploited by far-right political parties. They point to the dangers of conceiving ethnic difference in a way that fails to recognise the diversity of the 'white' population or to see that aspects of its experience may be shared with those who are ostensibly ethnically different. These instances of civil unrest reinforce the need, in particular, to make greater efforts to understand the interactions between class and ethnicity as well, of course, as the relationship of both to gender. The success of 'other White groups', in particular, may well be a reflection of a key feature of the recent immigration history of the UK. There is clear evidence that a substantial proportion of economic migrants since 2000 have come from Europe, the Old Commonwealth and the US to take up highly skilled positions in an economy suffering chronic skills shortages.

A further innovation in the 2001 Census was the introduction, in mainland Britain, of a question on religion. This revealed evidence for some previously suspected patterns that may have significant implications for the ethnic landscape of twenty-first century Britain. The data show that Muslims represented the second largest religious group and made up more than half of those who affirmed a non-Christian religion. They exhibited the highest rates of social disadvantage across a range of aspects of social life, including unemployment, education and health, with Muslim women faring worse than men (*The Guardian* 2004a). Muslims also had the largest households, the youngest age profiles and the largest proportions of their populations born outside the UK. We have already noted the high levels of disadvantage to be identified among Bangladeshis and Pakistanis. It is, therefore, no surprise to note that Muslims accounted for 92 per cent of members of these groups. There are, however, also significant Muslim minorities among both the Indian and Black African populations, a fact that may be relevant to some of the polarities of experience to be identified in these groups.

Material inequalities, manifested primarily in labour market placement and household incomes, are overlain by a complex of advantages and disadvantages in a variety of other aspects of social life (see the discussions in Mason 2003c). As Scott (Chapter 2) observes, it is not just the direct differences in income, wealth or power that define social class divisions. It is the location of people in class situations that shapes their life chances, even to the extent of setting the length of life and probable cause of death (Chapter 14). Shared social experiences generally follow from a structured sharing of material circumstances.

As we noted at the outset, however, the understanding of social divisions cannot rest simply with the mapping of material differences. In addition to the question of whether we can discern social categories on the basis of 'objective' structural characteristics there is also the question of whether the people so discerned think of themselves as constituting a group and act in terms of this perception. This brings us back to the question of identity, a concept that, as we have seen, is central to ethnicity.

Ethnicity is a matter both of self-identity ('we' statements) and of categorisation ('they' statements). Moreover, identity and categorisation do not proceed entirely independently of one another. In most societies, some groups and individuals have a greater capacity than others to define the terms under which categorisations are made. As a consequence, self-identification takes place in contexts where others' categorisations to some extent constrain the choices that can realistically be made. In other words, if others do not accept one's identity choices it may be difficult, if not impossible, to act out the implications of those choices (Chapter 17).

These kinds of constraints may take the form of subtle social cues and messages that restrict behaviour. They may, however, take much more concrete forms. An example of some importance in modern Britain has been the operation of immigration law. From the outset, the increasing restrictions on inward migration that followed the introduction of the 1962 Commonwealth Immigrants Act targeted potential migrants whose skin colour was not white. Indeed the very term 'immigrant' has often been a synonym for 'person of minority ethnic descent'. A continuing source of grievance in many minority ethnic communities has been the way in which they, their relatives and often their legitimate visitors and business contacts, are more likely than their white counterparts to have the legitimacy of their residence questioned, or to experience difficulties at passport control when entering the country (Mason 2000: 123–4). Once again, the subtle message received by many of Britain's minority ethnic residents is that they are second-class citizens.

Such messages are only reinforced by the nature of press coverage of scares about illegal migration and allegedly bogus asylum seekers (Gabriel 1998: 97–128). Press coverage of this kind both reflects and feeds popular concerns and, in turn, exerts pressure on politicians to act. Such pressures are characteristically most acute in the run-up to elections. Thus, the campaigns for both the 2005 and 2010 general elections saw attempts by the two major political parties in Britain (Conservative and Labour) to present themselves as the most likely to 'get tough on immigration' whilst retaining its benefits and acting fairly and humanely. The resultant debates frequently conflated – perhaps intentionally – the issues of how to deal with claims for asylum and illegal entrants with that of whether or not additional controls were required on legal immigration. Much of the discussion failed to take cognisance of the actual profile of immigration into Britain and, instead, seemed to draw on popular fears and confusions by stressing the need for quotas based on skill shortages and for checks on health status.

There is not space here to dissect these political discourses adequately. It is clear, however, that they carry messages that equate 'immigration' with a threat of alien swamping and the potential overwhelming of public resources. In the process, they help to reinforce long-standing messages about the relationship of migrant and minority ethnic status. As a result, they implicitly challenge the citizenship claims of the long-settled descendants of earlier migrants. Paradoxically, therefore, even as the diversity of ethnic identities becomes ever more apparent, so these political discourses help once again to reinforce a simplistic division between undifferentiated ethnic majorities and minorities.

We noted above that the 2001 Census had revealed evidence of significant deprivation among Muslims. It is no accident, perhaps, that 2001 saw the participation of significant numbers of Muslim young men in urban disturbances in cities in the north of England with significant Muslim populations. Although this was not an entirely novel phenomenon, it fuelled an already emerging process of demonisation, in terms of which young Muslim males began to replace young black men as the object of white fears. These processes had already been given some momentum by the 1991 Gulf War and the Salman Rushdie affair (see the discussion in Mason, 2000: 113, 141–2). They were to be given even greater impetus by the events of 11 September 2001, the London bombings of 2005, and the wars in Iraq and Afghanistan. There is also some evidence that, in the context of a continuing popular tendency to be unable to differentiate their 'Asian' fellow citizens, members of other communities have been caught up in hostility to Muslims.

A particularly interesting feature of the debate surrounding the 2001 disturbances was the emergence of a concern, in government and other policy circles, about the threats to community cohesion posed by the alleged increasing segregation of different ethnic communities in some British cities. In particular, claims began to emerge that this segregation was the result of the conscious choices of Muslim communities in particular, and that these choices impacted negatively on the opportunities open to other groups – notably the white working class. In point of fact, there is little evidence that community segregation was as marked as some of the more alarmist commentary suggested. More importantly, a number of analyses have shown that, where it exists, residential concentration on ethnic lines (with knock-on effects for school populations, patterns of socialising and employment) is more likely to be a product of the ordinary operation of the housing market than of ethnically-informed self-segregation. (See Harrison (2003) on housing and Finney and Simpson (2009) on more general claims about segregation.)

One of the consequences of these developments – as well as changes in the activities of the police and security services in the context of the so-called 'war on terror' – has been an increasing sense among British Muslims that they are not trusted, and that their Islamic faith is incompatible with British citizenship and identity. Nevertheless, it is interesting to note that, notwithstanding their concerns about not being respected by their fellow citizens and government, a significant proportion of those interviewed in successive pieces of research have expressed a commitment to a British identity alongside a Muslim one (see, for example, *The Guardian* 2004b).

Of course, a variety of different characteristics go to make up the identity of all citizens, including, crucially, gender. Like everyone else, Britain's minority ethnic citizens call on a wide variety of cultural and other characteristics in defining their identities. In order to explore this issue, the fourth PSI survey adopted the strategy of asking respondents to rank a range of characteristics which they might use to describe themselves to strangers. These included na-tionality, skin colour, country of origin, age, job, education, height, colour of hair or eyes, level of income and father's job. In other words, the list contained a range of more or less visible personal characteristics and attributes, only some of which are conventionally associated with ethnicity. Characteristics of-ten used in the measurement of social class, such as job and education, scored highly among all minority ethnic groups. In addition, religion was of great sig-nificance, especially among members of the Asian groups. Put another way, it is clear that, in constructing their identities, the respondents in the PSI survey utilised a range of physical, positional and lifestyle characteristics in combina-tions which both varied between groups and also exhibited considerable simi-larities (Modood 1997a: 290–338). This should, perhaps, warn us that it is dangerous to assume that, wherever putative ethnic differences are ostensibly present, they necessarily always have causal priority.

Nevertheless, there was also evidence that people make identity choices in the recognition that others categorise them in a way that may constrain those choices. A number of PSI respondents of Asian descent, for example, indicated that they were inclined to think of themselves as 'black' in situations where they were in contact with white people. Among the reasons given was the belief that this was how they were defined by whites – in other words, they felt their choices were constrained (Modood 1997a: 295–6). All too often, then, the everyday experiences of many members of Britain's minority ethnic communities convey subtle messages about what constitutes 'Britishness' that exercise exclusionary pressures and limit their identity choices (Chapter 17).

Having said this, it would equally be a mistake to believe that identities are static or that Britain's minority ethnic citizens are simply passive victims in the face of economic exclusion and racist attitudes and behaviour. There are myriad examples, ranging from self-help community organisations through various forms of political mobilisation, of Britain's minority citizens chal-lenging their exclusion. More subtly, there is considerable evidence of a pro-cess of continuous change in the ways the identities of all of Britain's varied citizens are constructed and negotiated. Modood has attempted to capture the ways in which, for second and third generation members of minority ethnic groups in Britain, subtle and complex changes in patterns of ethnic identification have occurred. His analysis suggests that there is no straight-forward relationship between 'the cultural content of an ethnicity and strate-gies of ethnic self-definition' (Modood 1997a: 337). The result is a shift from what Modood calls 'behavioural difference' to an emphasis on 'associational identity':

for many the strength of their ethnic identity was owed to a group pride in response to perceptions of racial exclusion and ethnic stereotyping by the white majority. The consequent sense of rejection and insecurity was instrumental in assertions of ethnic identities, often in forms susceptible to forging new anti-racist solidarities (such as 'black') and hyphenated (such as British-Pakistani) or even multiple identities. (Modood 1997a: 337)

Modood is at pains to argue that the resultant identifications are not weaker than those of the first generation, but differently constructed. They are much less taken-for-granted (based on shared cultural values) and more consciously chosen, publicly celebrated and debated, and part of a contested arena of identity politics. As a result, they are potentially fluid and may change with political and other circumstances. In the process, they may either revive old cultural practices or generate new ones (Modood 1997a: 337).

We should also note that, just as the disaggregation of the 'white' ethnic category offers the potential to reveal hitherto unacknowledged patterns of advantage and disadvantage, so there are processes afoot which are increasingly challenging many of the things we take for granted about white British ethnic, and for that matter national, identities. One does not need to subscribe to the 'break-up of Britain' thesis (Nairn 1981) to recognise that the process of devolution has led to a reinvigoration of long-standing national identities among both the Scots and the Welsh. Hand in hand with devolution is a persistent regional agenda, at both national and EU levels, which has the potential to reawaken regional identities which have long appeared dormant.

An interesting by-product of these developments has been the way in which Englishness as an identity has been increasingly problematised (Chapter 10; McCrone and Kiely 2000). As the dominant national group in Britain, it was not necessary until recently for most English people to reflect upon the relationship between English and British identities. With the increasing assertiveness of other national identities within Britain, however, the English have been forced to confront the question of what exactly marks them off (Paxman 1999). These processes parallel and interact with the changing identities of minority ethnic citizens, offering yet wider scope for hybrid identities that may challenge still further what used to be an apparently unproblematic national category.

It is appropriate, at this point, to note that much work in sociology has argued that, in the modern world, all identities are more fluid, provisional and multifaceted than some traditional characterisations of cultural difference would suggest (see also Chapter 17). We may identify two broad' bodies of literature from which these kinds of arguments have developed. The first is a feminist critique, and the second is writing in the post-modern and post-structuralist schools of thought.

One of the earliest challenges came from feminist scholars and activists who, from the early 1980s onwards, began to challenge the idea that women constituted a single, undifferentiated category sharing a common set of interests. Some of these criticisms came from black feminists who contested what they saw as the dominance of white middle-class perspectives, and argued that patriarchal oppression was mediated by racism in ways that made the experiences and opportunities of black and white women quite different. Other writers in the feminist tradition have challenged the essentialisation of ethnic difference, arguing that ethnicity is gendered in ways that differentiate the experience of men and women but which are also constitutive of ethnic difference (Anthias and Yuval-Davis 1992: 113–15; Mirza 2003).

A second source for the recognition of the provisionality and negotiability of identity is to be found in post-modernist and post-structuralist writing. According to this view, old-style, modernist explanations of the social world in terms of large-scale and relatively stable social categories (such as class) do not do justice to the complexity of individuals' everyday experiences. Instead, it is argued that the pace of change in the post-modern world creates conditions in which individuals are increasingly free to make multiple identity choices that match the purposes (or even the whims) of the moment (Rattansi and Westwood 1994; Bradley 1989: 21–7). It will be apparent from what I said above about the relationship between choice and constraint that I am sceptical about the more extreme versions of this kind of perspective. Nevertheless, there is some evidence that Britain's young minority ethnic citizens do perceive a wider range of identity options than some of the more rigid characterisations of ethnic difference may suggest.

Understanding social divisions, difference and diversity

It is difficult to deny the power of accounts that recognise the dynamism of ethnic identity in modern Britain. They are, after all, consistent with the conception of ethnicity (discussed above) that recognises the significance of the boundary process. Moreover they also challenge the simplistic victimology that has all-too-frequently characterised discussions of ethnic inequalities in Britain. On the other hand, they present a potential problem. When we take these insights together with the evidence about increasing social mobility, it is all too easy to make the mistake of assuming that social divisions based on ethnicity are, if not a thing of the past, at least on the way to solution. As the evidence above demonstrates, however, measured by material inequalities and differences of treatment, this is still far from being the case.

The difficulty arises not simply because of a debate about the meaning of the evidence, or even the pace of change. There is a more fundamental difficulty arising from the clash of modernist and post-modernist perspectives. As the example of traditional class analysis shows, concern with social divisions based on material inequalities is firmly located within a modernist world view. From whatever theoretical perspective it is approached, there is an implicit acceptance that social divisions are problematic. This may be because they are thought to undermine some minimum common standard – expressed in such notions as equality or human rights. Alternatively, it may be because they are perceived to threaten social cohesion, either by undermining shared value systems (anomie) or by encouraging political dissent. Thus, whether inequalities are to be challenged or justified, there is a common belief that solutions are available in the form of political and social action.

By contrast, for post-modernist writers the old meta-narratives underpinning these traditional approaches are no longer tenable in a world characterised by diversity, fluidity and fragmentation. Abandoning faith in such certainties, post-modernism is more likely to move to a celebration of difference rather than to detect in it signs of social decay. In its extreme forms, post-modernism represents a celebration of choice and the triumph of style. Even in its less triumphalist guise, however, it identifies in the diverse identity options open to individuals in the modern world, the opportunity to challenge the stereotyping and categorisation that is all-too-often characteristic of the behaviour of 'ethnic majorities' (Jenkins 1997: 29–30). It thus celebrates rather than problematises difference. At the same time, it challenges the essentialisation of the ethnic categories that are central to the process of measuring and tracking social inequalities, conventionally defined.

The difficulty with this is that, while it may be easy to agree that ethnic diversity in modern Britain should be viewed positively – as something contributing to the richness of the lives of all citizens – all too often difference has been seen as problematic. Indeed, as we have seen, even when it gives rise to positive assertions of identity, 'difference' has frequently been a product of exclusionary processes and practices. Is there a solution to this apparent impasse? Modood has suggested that the way forward lies with a conception of equality that recognises: 'the right to have one's "difference" recognised and supported in both the public and the private spheres' (1997a: 358). It implies, he argues, common rights and responsibilities and, in the end, a renewal of concepts of Britishness within which currently negative views of difference are framed. We need, he argues:

> to develop a more plural approach to racial disadvantage, and to formulate an explicit ideal of multicultural citizenship appropriate to Britain in the next decade and beyond (1997a: 359).

But herein lies the dilemma. Without the capacity to measure the patterning of material inequalities and differences of treatment among Britain's minority ethnic groups, how will it be possible to know whether there has been progress in reducing disadvantage? Such measurement must, by definition, use some set of categories in terms of which data can be collected. However sensitive to people's self-definitions we seek to be, any category system runs the risk of failing to capture the richness and complexity of people's identity choices. Indeed, it may itself even help to constrain those choices. There is a danger, then, that we may reproduce the very divisions we seek to problematise.

I have tried to show in this chapter that there are very real social divisions in modern Britain which arise from ethnic difference. They are, however, neither static nor unchallenged. Moreover, they interact in complex ways with sources of social differentiation based on class and gender to the extent that not only are their effects difficult to disentangle but that they may be thought of as mutually constitutive.

Discussion Questions

All British citizens regularly encounter occasions on which they are required to complete ethnic monitoring questionnaires. They all, therefore, frequently have to make decisions about 'which box to tick'. This chapter has argued that the categories they are offered result from a mix of historical accident and changing policy preoccupations. They do not always keep pace with the real-world dynamics of ethnic divisions and identities. Thus claims and attributions of ethnicity involve a complex process in which people's choices are constrained, provisional and contested. In light of this:

1. What do you consider to be your ethnic identity?
2. What leads you to this choice?
3. To what extent do you think your answer provides a satisfactory representation of the 'real you'? What are your reasons for your answers?

FURTHER READING

Mason, D. *Race and Ethnicity in Modern Britain* (Oxford: Oxford University Press, 2000, 2nd edn) is a comprehensive introduction to race and ethnicity in modern Britain, linking conceptual and theoretical debates to detailed empirical evidence of ethnic stratification in a range of areas of social life. Pilkington, A. *Racial Disadvantage and Ethnic Diversity in Britain* (Basingstoke: Palgrave, 2002) offers another wide-ranging introductory overview of key debates and research on 'race' and ethnicity in contemporary Britain. Mason, D. (ed.) *Explaining Ethnic Differences* (Bristol: Policy Press, 2003) is a volume comprising contributions from a number of key experts in the field, and offers a more advanced and detailed discussion of several of the themes of this chapter, as well as providing analyses of patterns of changing ethnic disadvantage in a wider range of aspects of life in modern Britain. Bloch, A. and Solomos, J. (eds) *Race and Ethnicity in the 21st Century* (Basingstoke: Palgrave Macmillan, 2009) is written by leading experts in the field, and gives a wide-ranging and up-to-date review of many of the issues touched on in this chapter. At a more advanced level, Gallagher, C. and Twin, F. (eds) *Retheorizing Race and Whiteness in the 21st Century* (Abingdon: Routledge, 2013) is a collection situating 'whiteness' and white identity in class, gender and national terms. The political dimension is further explored in Pero, D. and Solomos, J. (eds) *Migrant Politics and Mobilisation* (Abingdon: Routledge, 2013). Solomos, J. and Back, L. *Racism in Society* (Basingstoke: Macmillan, 1996) is an accessible introduction to some of the key debates surrounding racism in modern societies. Jenkins, R. *Rethinking Ethnicity* (London: Sage, 1997) is a key and accessible resource for anyone seeking to understand the concept of ethnicity.

Social Divisions: the apparently physical

CHAPTER 5

Age and Old Age

JOHN A. VINCENT AND IAIN PHILLIPS

This chapter will provide you with a broad critical understanding of the following issues in age and old age as sources of social division:

- Age as a universal marker of social distinction
- The different ways in which age is institutionalised in different societies
- The social construction of age
- Intergenerational relationships
- The terminology of age, generation and cohort, and the contrast of life cycle and life-course
- Patterns of age stratification
- The history of the life-course – pre-modern, modern and post-modern western life-courses
- Life-course and social change; consequences for old age of changing patterns of employment and family relationships
- Population ageing
- The social conditions of older people and the material inequalities in old age
- The generation equity debate
- Ageism and bodily ageing
- The 'double jeopardy' of age and gender
- Age as a distinctive social division

Age has been used in all societies as a way of differentiating people. Anthropological studies suggest that age is one of the few genuinely universal social criteria, forming a significant part of the social structures by which collective life is ordered. However, this fact in itself, although directing us to look towards issues of age, does not take us very far. Understanding age as social division requires us to understand the wide variations in:

- the degree to which age is used as a mechanism for social differentiation;
- which age criteria are used;
- the significance attached to these criteria.

The treatment of all three factors is extremely varied. Societies range from those in which age is not particularly important to those in which it is the key structural principle; from those in which old age is highly valued to those in which it is of very low status. Further, what is thought to constitute 'old age' varies not only cross-culturally but even within our own society. Our first step needs to be an exploration of the idea of age divisions, and how age has been 'used' in organising human society.

In more egalitarian types of society, the social categories of age and gender do not take on the rigidity and determining quality that these criteria do in many other societies. For example, the Mbuti, as described by Turnball (1984), illustrate the highly flexible character of small-scale societies that live by foraging and have low social differentiation. Many accounts of foraging societies characterise their members as living opportunistic lives in the natural environment, gathering and hunting a wide-ranging diet (Lee and De Vore 1968). These people live together in small bands in which, although differences between men and women and old and young are acknowledged, all voices make some contribution to communal decision-making.

On the other hand, in societies in which access to inherited property is crucial for economic well-being, age and gender criteria are frequently quite rigid and strongly sanctioned (Vincent 1995). The idea of the patriarchal extended family, as found for example in parts of rural India, contains the notion of patriarchy as not only the domination by male members of the household over the females (see Chapter 3), but also of the older (particularly the senior generation) over the younger. All household structures have the potential for problems or conflicts. Thus the power and authority of the older over the younger and the duty and obedience owed by the younger to the older may create frustrations in some circumstances. Waiting for the old man to retire so that the younger generation can take control of the land and make their mark on the world is observed in many cultures through literature (Hardy 1902, 1975; Synge 1911; Naipul 1964) and ethnography (Arensberg and Kimbell 1940, on rural Ireland). From the opposite point of view, the older generation may feel a lack of filial piety on the part of children who have left to work in distant towns.

These frustrations of rural family farmers have parallels in modern Britain, in the emotions of elderly people and their families when making decisions about continued independent living in the face of increasing frailty. What are the right amounts of duty owed and reasonable expectations anticipated from one generation to another? Society's general norms can seldom be applied unambiguously to the complexities of individual circumstance.

The aspect of age that is significant to a society may be the accumulation of years, but in many societies without formal or bureaucratic recording of age, people are not interested in and do not know their chronological age in a precise way. People may measure the passing of the years by reference to personal, social and historical events – when they had their first child, when the pogrom took place or when the great flood happened. In these ways, people know who is older or younger and may be differentiated into age strata even without an exact counting of the years.

In the UK, people's ages are usually described in terms of calendar age – the numbers of years that have elapsed since birth. One may be described as being 'aged 21' between 7665 days and 8030 days (give or take the odd leap year) after one's birth. This is because we use the Gregorian calendar, which has become a worldwide standard. But there are other ways of measuring dates and times – the Jewish and the Islamic systems to mention but two. Age can be both a verb (to age; to grow older) and a noun (how old one is; the age of consent). Ageing is a process that is continuous. Thus, strictly, age as an attribute requires an additional set of criteria to demarcate people into groups. Society recognises that a group of people, defined by chronological age or through collectively reaching a certain stage in their lives, should occupy certain social roles and be entitled to certain privileges or duties.

In many societies the transitions from one 'age' to another are marked by ritual; ceremonies such as initiation rites, which publicly mark the change from one social role to another. Some age categories may be given or obtain a special significance. In modern society, many legal rights are defined by age. For example, the age at which you can legitimately buy alcohol or tobacco, drive a car, have sex, leave home, marry, join the army, vote, serve as a juror or be expected to retire as a judge are legally defined. Hence 'old age' is associated with those aged 65 years and over, because historically this was the pensionable age for men in the UK. Similarly, in the UK, centenarians are regarded as special and until the telegraph system became obsolete, were acknowledged 'on behalf of the nation' with a telegram from the monarch.

It is important to note that the boundaries of age categories are not fixed by any objective criteria or by biological absolutes: they are social constructions. A recent European Social Survey reported national differences in the perceived start of 'old age', ranging from 55 in Turkey to 68 in Greece (AgeUK 2011). The age categories introduced by demographers or legislators for their own convenience, such as the recent raising of the state pension age (SPA) in a number of European countries including the UK, are just as much social constructions as any reported sense of common identity among teenagers, pensioners or 'the over forties'. People will move in and out of age strata as they add years to their life. Because of historical social change, the age at which individuals born at different times acquired these age-based rights and duties may be different. The experience of a generation, or the common experience of those born at a particular time, can form part of developing age-based social structures.

Age and stratification: age groups, chronological age, age classes

Given the wide variation in the way in which age is used as a social criterion, it is important to be clear about the conceptual basis of the categories with which we describe age-based divisions in society. We may first talk of 'age strata' or 'age classes', that is, *groups of people of the same age who, by virtue of this characteristic, have distinct sets of life chances and similar social rights and duties*, much like, but not identical to, social classes (see Chapter 2). The roles and norms that society allocates to age groups create barriers and opportunities. This can be seen to give people of similar age common interests as against those of people of other chronological ages. A weak view of 'age strata' would be that the people in each stratum simply happened to be in the same chronological age band; a strong view would be that they are people who have common interests that conflict with those of other age strata (see, for example, the discussion of childhood in Chapter 9).

The idea of age strata is sometimes mixed up with 'generation' and 'cohort'. 'Generation' refers to the fact of *reproduction* that each family experiences as a sequence of people passing through life. The idea of generations is used to refer to position within the family. Thus, today's children will be tomorrow's parents and will subsequently take their turn as grandparents. The idea of 'generation' can rather more usefully be used to refer to position within the family. Confusion between this and age is easily made when the image of the nation or the society as a family is used, such that those over 60 can be referred to as the 'older generation'. Generation and age are not synonymous – grandparenthood and retirement do not occur together; nephews and nieces may be older than their aunts or uncles. Further, 'the 60s generation' refers to people who were young during a particular period of history, that is, a 'cohort' (or 'historical generation': Edmunds and Turner 2002).

Demographic or birth cohorts are groupings of people born at the same time. Just as age since birth is a continuous variable, so dates of birth can be allocated into cohort categories only by the use of culturally constructed systems of classification. Birth cohorts may be socially recognised in a strongly structured way, as when a set of people are given a shared identity early in their lives, perhaps by all being initiated into adulthood together in the same ritual. They then carry that common identity through the rest of their days. In anthropology, these groups are called 'age sets'. Societies structured around age sets often have a static set of age grades (or collective social roles such as 'warrior' or 'elder') into which successive age sets pass (Bernardi 1985).

Members of a birth cohort age simultaneously and consequently have many historical experiences in common. Rapid change in society means that people with similar dates of birth may well have distinct sets of experience. The experience of military service differentiates cohorts in Britain and also provides contrasting experiences in different European and North American societies. Those who did national service in Britain or were drafted in the US carry the mark of this experience throughout their lives. The experiences of the cohort of 'immigrant' minority ethnic groups are quite different from that of the cohort made up of their children (Chapter 4). Common experience may even give rise to a label, such as 'baby-boomers' or 'Thatcher's children'. In contemporary society, there are forms of voluntary organisation based on cohorts. Graduation groups from American schools or colleges identify themselves by their 'year' and keep in touch and hold reunions long after they have graduated.

Cohorts whose formative years have given them similar attitudes, values or perceptions may thus form an identifiable group (Mannheim 1997). Their shared experiences may lead to a distinctive sense of identity and even expression of common interests. For example, people in Britain who were children in the First World War were starting families in the Great Depression of the 1930s, went through the Second World War in prime middle age and reached retirement when the long post-war economic boom was coming to an end. They developed a distinctive range of political beliefs and behaviours during an era which saw the height of state-led social democratic politics, nationalised industries and trade unionism (Westergaard 1995; Vincent 2001, 2003; Davis 2009). Similarly, it has been argued that the cohort born in the post-war baby boom, who experienced the changes in social conventions of the 1960s and the collective sense of liberation at that time, together with the transformation of the occupation structure and opportunities created by an expanding service class from the early 1970s to mid-1990s (Payne and Roberts 2002), consequently has a degree of common identity (Edmunds and Turner 2002).

One social repercussion of this differing cohort experience is sometimes referred to as a 'generation gap'. This term is misleading because there is a difference between 'being in' a generational category and 'identifying' with it and undertaking collective and social action as a result (Ryder 1965; Braun-gart and Braungart 1986). A number of authors suggest that there is more variation within a generation than is to be found between them when look-ing at diversity of lifestyles and opportunities in old age (Gilleard and Higgs 2000; Smith and Gerstorf 2004). Nonetheless, these cohort differences are not merely cultural: they also fundamentally affect people's chances of social mobility and material success. Chauvel (1999) has shown how the increased social mobility and relative affluence at a young age of those entering the labour market in the 1950s and 1960s contrasts with poorer economic pros-pects, and longer dependence on parents for those who set out on their adult life in the 1980s and 1990s.

The 'life cycle' is a common-sense term used to describe the typical se-quence of age categories in a society. It is most frequently understood in terms of the normative sequence of age statuses which repeat themselves with each generation; a continually turning wheel. Thus, all members of society are thought to age by following typical sequences of roles, for example from child, to adolescent, spouse, parent, grandparent and then ancestor. Sociologists, however, prefer the term 'life-course' because, whereas 'life cycle' presents a static image of an unchanging society, 'life-course' creates an image of a process that reflects the flow of time and the sequencing of cohorts as well as generations. Life-courses happen to people in historical time and in particular places, so they reflect the fact that 'life cycles' change over time and place. Life-courses vary not only between different social groups, for example across genders or ethnic groups, but significantly they also vary historically. Demo-graphic considerations and other changes in family structure will mean that the experience of parenthood, and other intergenerational social relations, will change. The current life-course will now, more typically, include the experi-ence of being grandparents in middle age and a great-grandparent in later life (Bengston 1996).

The life-courses of different cohorts also interact in a complex and dy-namic pattern. The cohort born in the years 1920–30 have had opportunities achieved by the struggles, often through trade unions and the Liberal and Labour Parties, of the preceding generations who started the movement down the road to universal retirement pensions. The success of those struggles ena-bled them to retire with greater security than their parents. Subsequently, they have been affected by the increasing proclivity of their children to separate and divorce. Thus they may find themselves adjusting their previously held expectations of grandparent/grandchild relationships (from loss of contact to quasi-parental responsibilities). In other words, the experiences of that cohort have been determined in part by the action of the immediately preceding and succeeding cohorts.

Age strata and cohorts are two separate bases on which social life is patterned. There are difficult methodological problems when trying to study old age and inequality in working out which phenomena are the result of becoming a certain age and which result from being a member of a particular cohort (Hardy 1997). Thus, for any particular moment in time, those who are old appear to have certain characteristics. However, when viewed critically, these characteristics may not be due to advancing years per se but to cultural conventions that define differences between age strata or cohort experiences of specific historical circumstances. As will be seen in Chapter 14, explaining the health of older people is not just a question of the physiology of ageing, but may well involve looking at particular dietary, housing or occupational experiences earlier in their lives or specific historical circumstances with health consequences.

The changing historical pattern of life-courses

In the centuries leading up to the radical social changes of the eighteenth century, life-courses in Europe and America were structured around certain basic social realities. The most important of these were uncertainties about longevity. Demographic characteristics of the time included high rates of infant mortality, death in childbirth and epidemics of fatal infectious diseases. On the whole, living standards and nutritional levels militated against living in a healthy condition to a ripe old age. There was not the close association between death and old age that exists in contemporary society; death could, and did, strike at any time. The demographic patterns were different, and poverty and the poorhouse existed alongside kinship and community obligations (Phillipson et al. 2001; Thane 2003). We need to be careful not to exaggerate the position of respect and care provided for elderly people in these earlier extended families in a romanticised image of a traditional past, as a lost golden age.

The agrarian basis of much of society and the relatively lower levels of geographical and social mobility meant that life-course transitions could be marked by public rituals in the local community, not strictly tied to a bureaucratised, national, legal framework. Baptism, confirmation, marriage, funerals of parents or spouse and the birth of one's children were ritualised transitions that placed people appropriately and publicly into their life-course positions. Old age was not identified with a particular chronological age but implicit in relationships vis-à-vis children and other relatives, control of property or whether an individual could perform the tasks or work expected of them (Grillis 1987; Cole 1992; Thane 2002, 2003).

Three major changes since the eighteenth century have been industrialisation, urbanisation and the development of the nation-state (Chapter 6), and along with these have come characteristic ways of thinking and behaving. Kohli's (1986) threefold life-course pattern identified pre-work, characterised by education and training and other forms of socialisation; work, as the dominant life-course stage; and post-work, usually characterised by loss of income and status. The key life stage in 'modern' society was that of work. It was through employment that people gained their principal income and achieved status. The pre-work and post-work stages were, as a corollary, of less status and income. Thane (2003) suggests that our current perceptions of old age come as a result of both cultural and material developments which have been mutually reinforcing. As retirement became a more established stage of life, older people became marginal workers and this gave rise to the view of the elderly as redundant and dependent. Before the wider implementation of pensions, poor relief systems still encouraged older people to work and were based upon a form of 'means-testing' to supplement, but not replace, incomes earned through employment.

Retirement and pensions were originally the prerogatives of the military, professional and administrative classes. In eighteenth-century Britain some of the first systematic pensions for public servants were provided as a means of removing those who were thought to have aged past their usefulness from public service in an acceptable manner. This contrasts with France where such pensions were a mark of being held in esteem and being rewarded for public service (Raphael 1964; Bourdelais 1998). For the majority, however, there was little choice but to work and earn for as long as possible.

In the late nineteenth and early twentieth centuries came the experience of a common mass of retired working people. Although an improvement on a situation where people had to either work or depend on charity or endure the rigours of the workhouse, this retired population generally had a lower standard of living than the working population. Almost universally, a person's rights to a pension still derive from their work history. Occupational pensions for clerical and white-collar occupations became more common during the first half of the twentieth century. The introduction of state pensions in the postwar years meant that retirement from manual and blue-collar employment increased significantly from the 1940s onwards (Johnson 1994; Thane 2002, 2003). With state pensions came the fixed threshold between old age and the post-work stage, linked to a chronological and bureaucratic marker. This 'retirement age' (made possible by national systems for birth and death registration introduced under the Births and Deaths Registration Act of 1836), replaced a more flexible approach based upon continued good health and functional ability within work and other activities (Thane 2003).

From the 1970s to early 1990s in the UK, the average effective retirement age dropped and there were more instances of early retirement, particularly for men (Banks and Smith 2006; Organisation for Economic Co-operation and Development 2011b). This was driven by a combination of state and occupational pensions, technological change and generous packages in the face of redundancies and company downsizing due to economic restructuring. More recently however, this trend has been reversed, with an increased number of older workers staying on. This is linked to a 'moral panic' over the impact of an ageing population and fears of a mass employee exodus resulting in insufficient numbers of people in work to pay for the increasing state pension costs (Organisation for Economic Co-operation and Development 2004; Pensions Commission 2004; 2006). At the same time as occupational pension schemes have been closed to new employees, existing employees have been shifted from 'defined benefits' schemes linked to final working salary to 'defined contribution', where pension payments are dependent on the level (and timeframes) of contributions made by employees, as well as stock market performance (Minns 2006).

The meaning of old age and the idea of retirement clearly has a social history. Kohli's threefold life-course pattern of pre-work, work and post-work may well represent a short historical interlude. Rapidly changing contemporary patterns of work, employment and lifestyles suggest greater diversity in the final stages of the life-course. Some have asked whether 'it's time to retire retirement' (Dychtwald et al. 2004) while others suggest that older workers should make way for the young unemployed. The nature of work and provision for those who, voluntarily or otherwise, do not have it will affect the condition of old age. Certainly the differentiation between a 'third age' of active retirement and a 'fourth age' of illness and decline is increasingly made.

The interconnection of age and social change

Over the past 200 years, life-course patterns in the West do appear to be more regulated by age than in the past, but certain writers have started to suggest that this age-determined life-course is now starting to break down (Grillis 1987; Hareven 1994). Elderly people are now able to choose from a wide diversity of lifestyles. Featherstone and Hepworth (1989), writing from a postmodernist perspective, suggest that the life-course is becoming de-structured. Common social patterns determined by chronological age are becoming less critical to people's life experiences. In many parts of today's world, political instability and forced migration have added to the unpredictability of the life-course. Mass expulsions and genocide may be as old as state society, but modern society has an unparalleled technical and organisational ability with which to execute them.

Two key areas where this apparent breakdown of established life-course patterns, and therefore a weakening of the social division of age, has been particularly remarked on are the fields of employment and the family. With regard to the first, the former threefold pattern of school, work and retirement that framed employment has been undermined. There have been significant changes in retirement – early retirement has dramatically expanded, depriving the age of 65 (for men) of its watershed character (Kohli et al. 1992). During the 1990s across most of Europe the effective retirement age had dropped and Guillemard (1989, 1990) suggests that, not only was the age of retirement dropping, but there was a loosening of the life-course grid. Early retirement was more popular with firms, workers and the state, but could also be seen as a response to the particular conditions of the labour market, the growth in unemployment and the structure of incentives in particular pension systems.

More recently in the UK, many state policies have been directed at raising the retirement age, and labour force participation amongst people in their fifties is rising. In 2004 the average age of withdrawal from the labour market was 63.8 for men, and 61.2 for women. In 2010, these had increased to 64.6 for men and 62.3 for women. Labour Force Survey data suggest that in 2002 50.7 per cent of men aged 60–64 were retired from economic activity. This figure had dropped to 20.4 by 2011. For women in the same 60–64 age category, in 2002 80.1 per cent were in retirement, compared to 51.8 per cent in 2011 (Office for National Statistics 2012b). At the other end of the age range, education has been extended. A comparatively small section of the population leave school at 16 while fewer still start their work careers from such a young age (Chapters 3 and 9).

Decreasing labour market stability and rapidly changing employment patterns introduce increased uncertainty and decreased standardisation of the work career components of the life-course. Patterns of migration, employment and early retirement interact, as do periods of unemployment, retraining and extended periods of education, to create complex life careers. Because welfare structures across Europe still depend substantially on insurance contributions and a work record, high levels of unemployment and disrupted careers will have lasting effects into old age for young, casualised entrants to the labour market (Laczko and Phillipson 1991; Hugman 1994; Giarchi 1996).

In the face of mounting challenges to state provision, many countries have been examining and revising their pensions systems. Alongside the raising of retirement and state pensionable ages there has been an increased reliance on private and occupational pensions (World Bank 1994; Blackburn 2002; Pensions Commission 2006; Organisation for Economic Co-operation and Development 2011b). The 1990s saw the growth of a fragmented society in which some have been able to use market position (earnings-related pensions and property-related windfalls) to secure good (that is, not much reduced) material conditions while others have missed out. Those who miss out are those with poor market opportunities. However, growing dependence in many countries, including the UK, on pensions which depend on the value of stock markets adds a further layer of uncertainty (Minns 2006; Price and Ginn 2006). In the Credit Crisis caused by international banks, the ; Organisation for Economic Co-operation and Development 2011b (2009) estimated that private pension funds lost 23 per cent of their value in 2008 alone; a total of around $5.4 trillion.

The second area of life-course modification lies in the family. Patterns of married life and cohabitation are changing. This is often portrayed as consisting of more couples living together instead of marrying, and more divorce among those who do marry. It is also the case that the family of orientation (the family in which we were born) is no longer automatically followed by a single, formalised family of procreation (the family we set up on marriage and in which we raise our own children): this transition takes place increasingly later in peoples' lives.

However, whereas it is clear that divorce rates have increased substantially, it would be simplistic to look on this as the sole cause of family dissolution and changes in the form of the family. In 1891, a woman in mid-life would have had a 20 per cent chance of being a widow, while a woman of the same age in 1991 a 5 per cent chance of having become a widow, a figure declining to 4 per cent one and two decades later (Office of Population Censuses and Surveys 1993, 2003; Office for National Statistics 2011d, Fig 4b). The chances of women aged 50–54 being divorced in 1891 were so small they were not recorded in the census, but since 1991 over 10 per cent of women of this age were divorcees, with a peak in 2001 of 15.6 per cent (ibid; Office for National Statistics 2010a). Although early widowhood has declined, widowhood in old age has become normal and has been predominately feminised. Women will experience an average of nine years' widowhood. On the other hand, male widowers are more likely to remarry.

The problems of adjustment/bereavement after a long marriage are not to be underestimated. Davidson (2001) discusses domestic and caring relationships through the language of older widows. The widows described themselves as 'selfish'. The gendered nature of selfishness as articulated by widows seemed to express both a desire, but some difficulty, in distancing themselves from normative lifestyles. Davidson suggests that selfishness to the widows meant doing what they wanted, when they wanted and not having to consider the needs of a partner. Several said the primary reason for not wishing to form a new partnership, particularly marriage, was that they had become so selfish. They had been prepared and, for most of them, happy to look after the man they had married when they were young and lived with for a number of decades, but they were not prepared to 'take on' another man (Davidson 1998).

One solution to these issues for people of late-middle age is 'living together apart', that is, an intimate relationship involving frequent companionship, sharing leisure, holidays and lifestyle but with each partner retaining their own domicile (Gierveld et al. 2001; Arber 2006). This increasingly popular phenomenon is also linked to the value of property,

It is also important to consider recent trends and changes in the life-course of the younger generations, and their impacts and implications for those approaching old age. In 2008 in the UK 2.8 million men and women aged between 20 and 34 lived with their parents (Office for National Statistics 2009c), a growing trend that can be traced back 30 years (Office for National Statistics 2009a). Young adults themselves state that continued living with their parents is linked to financial constraints and not being able to afford to move out (38 per cent), as well as a decided lack of affordable housing (44 per cent) (Office for National Statistics 2009c). These lengthening periods of dependency not only impact upon their parents' ability to take early retirement, but also their intentions towards downsizing from the family home or simply saving and making preparations for withdrawal from the labour market (Berlin et al. 2010; Furstenberg 2010; Osgood and Siennick 2012).

Whereas many policy initiatives and much research are actually oriented towards 'strengthening the family', the dissolution of family units and kinship networks comes from several causes, such as greater geographical mobility and changing life expectancy. Rural–urban migration and the ageing of the countryside population are worldwide phenomena (Sen 1994). The social barriers erected by the cultural assimilation of migrants also disrupts intergenerational expectations of old age and the final part of the life-course (Askham et al. 1993; Blakemore and Boneham 1994; Chapter 4).

Changing demography

Changing patterns of longevity mean that spouses live together for longer and the majority of married life is no longer spent rearing children. One of the successes of modern society has been the improvements in the health and increased life expectancy of people. Thus, in contrast to what 'post-modernist' writers have seen as a decline in stability of family work and lifestyle patterns, a certain demographic standardisation has taken place. People are now more likely to live a full span and die in their eighties. The age of death and length of life is becoming more standard; although more people are living to older ages, the maximum life span does not seem to have increased.

Although recently some demographers have challenged this view, and some bio-gerontologists are claiming breakthroughs in scientific knowledge which will extend the life span, the life span for those currently alive has strongly-determined biological limits. Further, medical advances mean that fewer couples are childless because of infertility, while the extent to which more women in the UK are choosing childlessness as a lifestyle is the subject of conflicting evidence. The expanded technical ability to control family size has meant that it is standardising at one or two children, most typically born to parents in their twenties, and with extended periods of family life in a post-child-rearing stage (Jackson 1998).

The world's population has started to age as a result of the successful diminution of premature mortality and decline in the average numbers of babies born to each mother. The developed world experienced the earliest decline in fertility, with countries like France, Sweden and the UK leading the way. Late-industrialising countries, for example Japan and Italy, have experienced rapid post-war declines in fertility and are amongst the most rapidly ageing populations at the beginning of the twenty-first century. The pace of demographic ageing is increasing fastest in the developing world. It is most noticeable in countries like China where fertility has successfully been checked within a relatively short time span. Projections suggest that by 2025 China alone will contain more over-60-year-olds than the whole of Europe. The median age of the world's population increased from 23.5 years in 1950 to 29.4 years in 2011. By 2050, the median age is projected to reach 37.8 years (United Nations 2011b).

In 2010, UK life expectancy for females at birth was 82.4 years, compared with 78.3 years for males (United Nations 2011b). British life expectancy continued to rise in the last decades of the twentieth century and into the new millennium, but for different reasons to the large increases achieved in the first half of that century. In 1901, life expectancy stood at 49 for women and 45 for men. It was the decline in infant mortality which largely drove the earlier increase in life expectancy, particularly associated with control of infectious disease through public health measures. Between 1981 and 2002, life expectancy for those aged 65 increased by three years for men and two years for women. This may reflect changes in health-promotion practices and the decline in heavy industries and improved health and safety at work (Arber 2006; Walker and Foster 2006). Projections from the Government Actuary's Department in 2013 suggest that life expectancies for those at retirement age will increase by around a further three years by 2020 (Government Actuary's Department 2013). Cancer and heart disease remain the major causes of death in old age, but deaths due to smoking-related illnesses are on the wane (Chapter 14).

The social conditions of older people

Demographically, economically and culturally, old age is experienced differently by different people. Difference in life expectancy means that old age

Table 5.1 Historical and projected changes in the age composition of the UK population

	Age	1950	1975	2000	2025	2050
Age groups	0–14	22.3	23.3	19.0	15.2	15.0
(percentage)	15–59	62.1	57.0	60.4	55.4	51.1
	60+	15.5	19.6	20.6	29.4	34.0
Median age (years)		34.6	33.9	37.7	44.5	47.4
Sex ratio	0–14	74.3	69.8	76.4	83.9	83.8
(men per 100 women)	15–59	71.9	63.4	71.2	79.1	80.0
	60+	56.5	39.3	46.4	58.2	62.6

Source: United Nations (2002).

has typically been a feminine stage of life (but projecting forward it may well become less feminised than in the past: see Table 5.1). Women also tend to marry men older than themselves, so that women are not only more likely to be widowed, they are also more likely to live on their own. The General Lifestyle Survey (Office for National Statistics 2010e) suggests that 60 per cent of women aged 75 and over live alone, while only 34 per cent of men at that age do so (also Chapter 3). In the 85-and-over age group, about twice as many women as men are in residential care: 12 per cent of men and 23 per cent of women (Arber and Ginn 2004). This is linked to the gendered differences in marital status as the widowed and never married are far more likely to live in care homes, and at present these are disproportionately women. Those married or in a relationship largely rely on their partner for care, or for children to provide 'care "at a distance"' (Arber 2006: 58). However, the changing social landscape in terms of increased life expectancy for males, as well as the impacts of divorce, remarriage and step-parenting in reconstituted families, may well impact on the availability and dynamics of carers (Arber and Ginn 1995; de Jong Gierveld 2003; Arber 2006).

Material deprivation in old age is of central importance. Age helps to explain the distribution of 'poverty' (Chapter 13), and lack of income is the means by which social divisions can be seen to open up. Poverty in old age interacts with former social class and gender: the interplay of social divisions is striking. We therefore need to discuss income and pensions as indicators of poverty, and the way these have changed in recent decades. In practice, making such comparisons is not straightforward because we need to know who are dependent on pensions and whether we are to count people or households.

The United Nations Development Programme has estimated that only 20 per cent of people aged 60 and over in the world can be regarded as having income security. Retirement pensions are available to only a small proportion of the world's older people. Only 30 per cent of people aged 60 and over worldwide are eligible for any form of pension and most of these live in more developed countries. Pensions are most frequently the prerogative of those who work for government or the formal sector of the economy; even in many quite highly developed countries, the rural population has little or no cover (Help Age International 1999).

In the UK, material deprivation in all areas of society is structured by gender, class and ethnicity, but these differences become exaggerated in later life. This is related in particular to the structure of the labour market. As incomes in later life tend to be dependent on pension rights achieved through contributions from salary and saving and investments made from income during working life, those who received the best material rewards in their working lives do best in old age. Those who found difficulty entering the labour market at all and who achieved poor rewards from their labour tend also in their old age to be among the most materially deprived section of the British population.

While the value of the *state* pension declined relative to average earnings since 1979, in recent years average pensioner income has risen because of improving occupational pensions (Office for National Statistics 2010c; Department for Work and Pensions 2011b). Under the 1997–2010 Labour Government there were increases in means-tested state benefits, many of which formed part of what the government called 'pension credit'. For pensioner couples in 2009/10, the average net income per week (before housing costs) was £388 compared with £287 for single pensioners (Department for Work and Pensions 2011b). At the time of writing (2013), changes by the ConDem Coalition to pension calculations and the 'Granny Tax' seem likely to reduce the purchasing power of state pensions.

However, these figures do not show the disparity of income between households, and how this has widened since the mid-1990s. In the period 2007–10, the top 20 per cent of pensioner couples with the highest incomes had average incomes (£776 per week) that were 3.7 times higher than the bottom 20 per cent of the income distribution (£205 per week) (Department for Work and Pensions 2011a). For single pensioners, the median among the top 20 per cent (£367 per week) was 3.1 times higher than those at the bottom 20 per cent (£118 per week). The rate of growth between 1998 and 2010 was roughly the same across all pensioner couples (between 29 and 28 per cent), but it has to be remembered that such a *rate* of growth equals a much greater return for those with higher incomes to begin with compared to those already struggling on less.

Walker and Foster (2006: 44) argue that social class 'is a critical factor influencing how people experience old age and, in particular, the quality of lives they lead'. However, as a person's social class is conventionally linked to their occupational position and role (for example, managerial, non-manual, manual), old age and retirement does not *in itself* reproduce the earlier class-based divisions once the centrality of occupation is removed (Estes et al. 2003). How-ever, employment still 'remains one of the most important ways of acquiring material resources across the adult life course' (Walker and Foster 2006: 45). The increasing reliance and drive towards private and occupational pensions noted above has had a profound impact upon continuing income differentials into old age. Among those over the age of 65, 90 per cent of males who were professionals or managers in large organisations had a private or occupational pension. This compares to less than 60 per cent of males who had been em-ployed in unskilled manual occupations (see Ginn and Arber 2001; Summer-field and Babb 2004). Furthermore, experiences of episodic unemployment, job insecurity and part-time work within an increasingly flexible economy all impact upon both state and non-state pension contributions, which further affect those at the bottom of the occupational scale. It is also necessary to consider the impact of increased home ownership. Those pensioners who have bought their property and paid off the mortgage, or 'downsized' into smaller properties (again, generally those from higher social classes) experience lower housing costs compared to those who are still required to pay rent on their accommodation (Office for National Statistics 2010c).

On average, pensioners who have retired more recently tend to have higher incomes than older pensioners because they are likely to receive more occu-pational pension and earnings. Therefore 'cohort' effects need to be taken into account, with the rapid rise in occupational pensions in the 1950s and 1960s. In 2009/10 couples aged 75 or over had an average net income after housing costs of £403 a week compared with £421 for those aged under 75 (Depart-ment for Work and Pensions 2011a). Across all pensioners in 2009/10, state benefits accounted for 42 per cent of income; occupational pensions made up 25 per cent, earnings 20 per cent, investment income 8 per cent, and personal pensions 4 per cent. Since 1998–99, the average income from occupational pensions has seen a growth of 38 per cent, compared to a 29 per cent growth in real terms of the average benefit amount. This has further widened the gap between those depending predominately on the state pension and those also in receipt of occupational or personal pensions (ibid.). Income in the form of earnings is predominantly limited to the more recently retired, and is also linked to employment opportunities, with 35 per cent reporting earnings as a source of income. It should also be remembered that, within younger pen-sioner couples, there is also the greater chance that one member will be below state pension age, at least for a period.

The poorest pensioners tend to be older people who live on their own and who are dependent on state benefits. In 2011, for those who have worked, exit from employment is typically at 64.6 for men and 62.3 for women (Office for National Statistics 2012c). This means that men average 17.6 years and women 20.1 years of life after leaving paid employment (ibid.). Women are more likely to work part-time and tend not to have the same benefits from occupational pensions as men. Women were often excluded from occupational schemes during their early history. The General Lifestyle Survey (Office for National Statistics 2010b) suggests a reasonable equalising in terms of occupational and personal pensions between full-time employed men and women. However, while 73 per cent of full-time employed women have some form of occupational or personal pension, only around 51 per cent for those employed part-time do so. Again, the impact of social class is evident even within part-time employment as 79 per cent of managerial and professional employed women have either an occupational or personal pension, compared with only 38 per cent of those in routine or manual employment. There is a great deal of ignorance amongst many sections of the population about their pension entitlements. Small occupational pensions tend to bring women only up to the point where they become ineligible for income support so that many do not really gain benefit from having paid into such schemes.

It might be argued that expenditure is a better guide to the material standards that older people can achieve. Certainly, expenditure is clearly greatly influenced by age (Table 5.2). Middle age groups spend more than young

Table 5.2 Average weekly household expenditure (£) by age of head of household, 2010

	Under 30	30–49	50–64	65–74	75 and over	All households
Housing (net), fuel and power	91.7	68.4	52.0	47.5	42.9	60.4
Household goods and services	22.1	35.2	39.6	24.7	18.9	31.4
Food and non-alcoholic drinks	39.1	59.7	59.4	49.7	37.7	53.2
Alcohol, tobacco and narcotics	9.9	13.6	14.0	10.4	5.5	11.8
Clothing and footwear	21.5	31.2	25.4	15.1	7.7	23.4
Health	1.7	4.3	6.5	6.4	5.2	5.0
Education	25.9	12.0	10.2	0.4	1.0	10.0
Transport	57.0	80.5	76.9	49.0	20.2	64.9
Communication	13.7	15.7	13.7	9.7	7.0	13.0
Recreation and culture	40.6	65.5	72.0	54.9	27.5	58.1
Restaurants and hotels	39.4	49.1	44.4	27.1	14.1	39.2
Miscellaneous goods and services	31.8	44.2	36.6	28.7	22.4	35.9
Other expenditure items	54.0	93.7	67.7	41.6	30.5	67.3
All expenditure groups	448.4	573.1	518.6	365.2	240.0	473.6

Source: Office for National Statistics (2011) *Family Spending 2010.*

people and much more than older people. Older people spend substantially less on housing and travel, but spend about as much – and a much greater proportion of their income – on fuel and power.

These figures document a growing substantial material inequality (and by implication social division) between older people and the general population, and a growing differentiation among older people themselves. However, older people's subjective feeling about their standard of living is influenced by a range of things over and above simply how much they can afford to spend. They have, for example, a variety of reference groups against which to compare their own living standards. Older people's memory of the past includes memories of the conditions in which older people lived in the middle part of the last century. They are also aware of the former standard of living they were able to achieve before retirement. They may also compare themselves favourably, or otherwise, with other retirees, as well as with those enjoying the current general living conditions of society as a whole. Thus, just as there is no clear single common experience of material deprivation among contemporary older people, so there is also no common interpretative framework by which older people feel a collective sense of their standard of living (Gilleard and Higgs 2000; Smith and Gerstorf 2004).

Social policy issues: everybody needs pensions

The most obvious change shown in Table 5.1 was the increased number of people over 75. The extent to which the prolongation of life results in a consequent extended period of physical frailty, greater dependency and need for new services, or merely moves later the onset of the 'fourth age', is controversial (Victor 1991; AgeUK 2009). It is in the interests of certain sections of society, such as the financial elites seeking to expand their profit-making potential in the fields of pensions and insurance or the professional groups whose members provide care for the elderly, that such concerns become widespread (Vincent 1996). It is clear that the issue has been taken up as a threatening 'social problem', to the extent of warranting reports from the World Bank, the OECD and even the CIA. How will care for these very old people be delivered and how can a society, with relatively fewer of its members being of working age, afford to pay for it? This reaction has the character of a 'moral panic', where a small-scale issue is amplified by the media and those with other agendas into appearing to be a much bigger problem than it really should be.

This is not to deny that there are real problems to do with the social conditions in which many older people live, and the way society needs to provide for them. However, this is a problem of wealth distribution, not demography. Where economic growth is progressively produced by an economy that requires a smaller and smaller labour force, with time to adapt and plan, no country is facing a crisis of elder care. Nor is it true to represent 'older people' as being 'a problem', as if they were a single homogeneous category. There are substantial differences in the way in which pensions systems are organised in different countries. Pensions have become an important political issue in that they form a key point in the debate on the role of the state in the redistribution of wealth, the provision of welfare and managing a framework for economic activity. Should the state provide pensions for all? Should it merely look after the most vulnerable, whether economically or through infirmity? Should the state administer pensions schemes or should that be left to the private sector?

What is at stake here can be called 'generational equity'. It has been argued that the younger age groups are being disadvantaged by paying for the pensions of the current generation of older people, but, because of demographic changes, they cannot themselves necessarily expect to receive an equivalent pension from the succeeding generation (Johnson et al. 1989; Johnson 1995; Price and Ginn 2006). Despite the way it is frequently presented, this problem is not merely, or at all, a demographic issue. The issue is in essence one of re-distribution and the role of the state in evening out unacceptable inequalities of wealth and power. In other words, it is a question of how government deals with the factors that generate a significant part of the social division based on age. If we take a wider view of redistribution than who pays and who benefits from various forms of taxation, we can also take into account issues associated with exploitation and non-financial contributions to society's well-being.

In these terms, the debate centres on rights and claims to a share of society's current and future economic output. After all, nursing care cannot be stored or saved up to bring out when needed later in life. 'Care' exists only at a single moment, so that if there is currently not enough to go round, it has to be rationed (allocated) through some mechanism, whether this happens through a market to the highest bidder, by allocation to the most needy, offered first to those who fought to defend their country or some other process. We need to see age as a division in a wider context, but a balanced one. Why do we hear more about the future cost of state pensions or healthcare than, for example, the long-term cost to future generations of disposing of nuclear waste or the vast floating North Pacific Garbage Patch which has been estimated to be at least the size of the US and made up of discarded human rubbish and debris?

The extent to which there will be an economic difficulty in meeting the need for satisfactory pensions in the future must be related to the future productivity of the workforce and the extent to which declining rates of economic participation among older people continue. The assumption is frequently made that the older population is economically unproductive. Patterns of work and the reasons for non-participation in the labour market have varied considerably over time, but older people have not always withdrawn from work. In Britain in 1881, according to Johnson (1985), 73 per cent of the male population of 65 and over were in employment, but by 1981 the percentage had shrunk to less than 11 per cent. In 2011, this figure had increased again to 23.3 per cent for those aged 65–69, and 6.5 for per cent those 70 years of age and over (Office for National Statistics 2012b). These major changes in the distribution of work have not occurred because the population has become physically less (or more) able and therefore less (or more) employable. Non-employed does not mean non-productive; it may mean productive potential is being lost or that useful work is not recorded or recognised as such. Most countries across the world have taken steps to increase the official age of retirement, but many social commentators identify the way in which retirement is in practice used by governments and employers as a way to manage the supply of labour.

Ageism and the cultural construction of old age

There is a debate between critical gerontologists who wish to examine the position of old people as part of an unequal society and cultural sociologists who give priority to understanding the diversity of old-age phenomena in a post-modern world. Cultural gerontologists draw on themes of post-modernism which emphasise that modern affluence for at least some pensioners creates new cultural agendas based on consumer choice. Examples of such work are Gilleard and Higgs (2000) and Blaikie (1999). These writers are correct in drawing attention to the importance of cultural phenomena in understanding contemporary old age. They are, however, sometimes in danger of neglecting the empirical evidence that older people in Britain remain consistently amongst the poorest in the community and most remain excluded from the benefits of consumer society. Older people not only suffer from increased chances of a materially deprived lifestyle but are also subject to the experience of 'ageism':

> Ageism is about acting on stereotypes about chronological age which prevent (older) people from having control over their lives and participating fully and purposefully in society. (Age Equality Action Group, 1991, quoted in Meade 1995)

Because old age tends to be culturally devalued, getting older is regarded by most people as a kind of inevitable tragedy, although some people do develop cultural resources with which to resist these ascriptions. A number of writers have been suggested the emergence of two categories of older age: 'the third age of leisure and personal fulfilment, and the fourth age of decline and decrepitude' (Blaikie 1999:13; see also Laslett 1987, 1991). One commercial company that is particularly symbolic of this 'third age' is Saga, which offers a range of holiday, financial and insurance products exclusively for over-50s. It also runs Saga Zone, an online social networking website for the over-50s, and Saga Connections, a dedicated over-50s online dating service. Jenny Joseph's poem, quoted in Chapter 1, has itself become a focus for older women who have taken the image as a symbol around which they can form social groups. The women in the 'Red Hat Society' meet together to expand their own and other people's cultural horizons. They wear red hats and purple dresses as a badge of membership. Those who have not yet attained sufficiently mature years but wish to attend are required to wear violet instead. There are even local groups of older adults who choose to label themselves as 'the wrinklies' and political activists who call themselves 'grey panthers' in ways reminiscent of other oppressed groups using the stigmata of their identity as a badge of pride.

The cultural construction of femininity and sexuality has its impact on older people. Sociologists of gender have shown how patriarchy involves male control of female bodies, not just for their labour value, but also reproductive sexual functions, and how it impacts on the aesthetics of femininity. These aspects of patriarchy have been challenged by women's groups and other social movements. Three stages of the feminist movement have been identified, coinciding firstly with campaigns on civic status, property rights and the vote, secondly on work and career opportunities, and thirdly on femininity, personal appearance identity and sexuality. It has been argued by de Beauvoir ([1949]1972) and others that there is a 'double jeopardy' of age and gender. For women who are also older, the risks of marginalisation and deprivation are significantly greater. Their experience of multiple divisions is not simply one plus the other. Their experience of being old and being a woman needs to be understood as an experience which is unique and has its own problems and possibilities. It does not contrast simply with younger women or older men, but, in de Beauvoir's term, constitutes a 'third sex'. A woman's gender status changes post-menopause with the loss of reproductive function.

De Beauvoir and others argue that a woman's status derives from presenting a 'desirable' appearance and the perceived reproductive value of her body. The enormous market in anti-ageing products (in excess of £3 billion annually) is indicative of the anxiety about lack of attractiveness linked with age. Sexuality in old age is suppressed and gender-specific. Large age differences between spouses or lovers attract social unease, but the opprobrium for an overtly sexually-active older woman is the greater – indeed so much so that she cannot be named. While there are words in various English dialects for an older man (sugar daddy) with a young woman (trophy wife), there are none for an older woman with a younger man (toy boy). Positive images of older women are desexualised. They are associated with 'matronly figures' and caring social roles:

> Sexuality in old age is a subject which is enveloped with secrecy and half-knowledge, and referred to in society in general with embarrassment and by joking allusions, that is if it is not dismissed altogether, the old so patently being 'past it'. (Pickard 1995: 268)

The areas of gender, old age and sex indicate vividly the constraints that age imposes on behaviour.

Ageism, like racism or sexism, refers to both prejudice and discrimination; the first being an attitude, the second a behaviour. Comfort (1977, quoted in Meade 1995) suggests that ageism is based on fear, folklore and hang-ups and, like racism, needs to be met by information, contradiction and, when necessary, confrontation. Negative stereotypes of people based on their age may refer to different age groups; both young and old can be stereotyped. The negative image of old age is extremely prevalent and, indeed, getting older often seems to carry no positive connotations at all. A quick browse through any shop selling birthday cards will indicate the disgust with which ageing is widely held.

A European Social Survey suggested that age discrimination is the most widely experienced form of discrimination across Europe: 35 per cent of people had experienced unfair treatment because of their age, compared to 25 per cent based upon their gender, and 17 per cent due to their ethnicity (AgeUK 2011; see also AgeUK 2009). In 2006 the Employment Equality (Age) Regulations were introduced into UK law. In principle this was aimed at securing the legal rights of older workers and improving their treatment within the workplace. However, the legislation still included a Default Retirement Age clause which allowed employers to force people from their workplace. Any attempt by an employer to force an employee to leave their occupation on the basis of their gender, ethnicity or sexuality would have resulted in legal sanctions on the grounds of unfair dismissal, but the inclusion of this clause meant that just by reaching a specific birthday there was sufficient grounds for someone to lose their job, albeit with six months' notice (DirectGov 2012a). In October 2011 the Default Retirement Age was abolished as grounds for compulsory retirement (Department for Business, Skills & Innovation 2011), but further legal disputation followed. This was a precursor for the raising of the state pension age from 65 for men and 60 for women, to 66 for both in 2020, and then to 67 in 2026 under the Pensions Act 2011 (DirectGov 2012b).

Nevertheless, it is common for young job applicants to find themselves passed over for older, supposedly more mature applicants and for older people looking for work to find that potential employers prefer younger, supposedly more lively, people. It may be feared that training older workers will not be cost-effective, or that they will be more prone to illness and absence. Reverse discrimination also takes place, whereby older workers are offered dead-end jobs that employers assume would not be attractive to younger people looking to further themselves (Shah and Kleiner 2005; Roscigno 2007; AgeUK 2009).

Bytheway (1995) suggests that simple definitions of ageism are inadequate for two reasons. First, they should not be based on parallels with sexism and racism because each is a unique phenomenon. Second, he points out that it should not be presumed that old people exist as a group. Older people are as varied as the rest of the population and labelling them with a single category is itself part of the problem. Separating out older people for special consideration (even for special study, as in the field of social gerontology or this chapter) implies a 'them' and 'us' situation. It is to take the social division of age as a given.

However, old age can also be an opportunity for liberation from social constraints. In social terms, this could mean liberation from the constraints of middle age and burdensome social obligations. In terms of the world of work, this would mean the end of wage slavery with retirement and the opportunities of the third age. However, such liberation also depends on solving issues of poverty that still afflict many older people. In terms of the constraints of family life, the meaning of the empty nest phase of life, despite the negative imagery implicit in the term, might be construed positively. Car stickers proclaiming 'recycled teenager – spending the kids' inheritance' suggest at least the potential for liberation in a post-child-rearing period of life.

One of the exciting prospects for the newly developing period of extended retirement associated with the third age is that it offers the prospect of new forms of social relationships. Will the Sixties generation, now growing old, also seek liberation from the cultural constraints of ageism? There are many ideas for new forms of social relationships and institutional arrangements in old age. People do not necessarily get more conservative as they get older, and the young are not automatically the radicals. It may be that future old age will be a time for rebellion and attempts to change the social order. Some writers, such as Betty Friedan (1993), have suggested that groups of women living in various forms of domestic arrangements, perhaps with a man, could provide support, care and physical relationships more effectively than lone widowhood. For some, these possibilities represent a nightmare, for others a challenge.

Age as a social division

Age is a distinctive social division, if only because we anticipate moving from one side of the division(s) to the other, thus ultimately having direct experience of it in more than one form as we follow our life-courses. As we have seen, life-courses are social because they have general and observable patterns, shaped by norms and values (for example those associated with the life-course), which are part of the structure of society. They are also given characteristic forms by historical patterns of social change. This means that, while the life-course is the normatively expected transition of stages in the process of social ageing, those of us currently at different ages will not experience the life-course in the same way. The life-course is both an individual and a social process of ageing.

Life is periodicised through age strata sequences: the teenagers of today will become the pensioners of tomorrow. It is structured by the sequence of generations: today's children are tomorrow's great-grandparents. It is further structured by history, in that the life-course of each succeeding cohort takes its form from the historical events through which it lives. The idea of the life-course, in addition to these social and historical aspects, has a psychological dimension, in that individuals will develop and change personality in response to life experience.

Therefore, when we seek to understand social inequality and stratification, we must consider the life-course as a social process, rather than a static social divide between age groups. The systematic differences in material circumstances and life chances of people of different ages do not arise because, when people's hair gets greyer, they slip into a prepared social box labelled 'old, poor and useless'. Rather, in the struggle for a decent standard of living and a modicum of social esteem, the life-courses of some people offer them greater chances of success than others. Some people collectively reach old age in times and circumstances in which their personal history and changing social circumstances lead to a relative lack of social and economic power; it is this that constitutes the real basis of social division.

Discussion Questions

1. Look at the birthday cards you sent to someone 10 years younger and 30 years older than yourself. How do they differ from the ones you got at your last birthday? What kinds of people sent them, what kinds of written messages do they include, what kinds of images are portrayed? What does this tell you about attitudes to age and getting older?

2. Talk to a relative, neighbour or friend who is over 70 years of age. Ask them (politely and respectfully, without being intrusive) what is the single most important thing that has happened to them in their life. What would their life be like now if that 'most important' event had not happened? Does this tell us anything about the social significance of the life-course?

3. Make a list of all the things you are allowed to do and those you are not allowed to do when you are 18 years of age. How would this differ for someone who is 85 years of age? What conclusions would you draw from this comparison?

FURTHER READING

A good starting point for the sociology of old age is Estes, C., Biggs, S. and Phillipson, C. *Social Theory, Social Policy and Ageing: a Critical Introduction* (Maidenhead: Open University Press, 2003), while Vincent, J.A. *Old Age* (London: Routledge, 2003) and Vincent J.A., Phillipson C.R. and M. Downs *The Future of Old Age* (London: Sage, 2006) sets out contemporary conflicts, struggles and issues using a global perspective. Blaikie, A. *Ageing and Popular Culture* (Cambridge, Cambridge University Press, 1999), Gilleard, C. and Higgs, P. *Cultures of Ageing* (New York: Prentice Hall, 2000) and more recently Fairclough, C. (ed.) *Ageing Bodies* (Walnut Creek, CA: AltaMira Press, 2003) offer important cultural insights. Wilson, G. *Understanding Old Age* (London: Sage, 2000), focusing on globalisation, and Grubium, J. and Holstein, J. *Ageing and Everyday Life* (Oxford: Blackwell, 2000), on social constructions, also have distinctive useful approaches. An overview of current ways of understanding old age can be found in Phillipson, C. *Reconstructing Old Age* (London: Sage, 1998). An excellent anthropology of the cultural process of ageing, which looks at both children and older people, is Hockey, J. and James, A. *Growing Up and Growing Old* (London: Sage, 1993), while Arber, S. and Ginn, J. (eds) *Connecting Gender and Ageing* (Buckingham: Open University Press, 1995) is a valuable source for a thorough empirical examination of the relationship between the two social divisions of age and gender. AgeUK produce a consolidated summary of general statistical information which is updated on a monthly basis and available online: http://www.ageuk.org.uk/professional-resources-home/.

CHAPTER 6

Childhood

STEVI JACKSON AND SUE SCOTT

This chapter will provide you with a broad critical understanding of the following issues in childhood as a source of social division:

- The social construction of childhood
- Changes in childhood and the conception of the child over time
- Conceptions of the innocent and demonic child
- Child-rearing as a reflexive project
- The tensions between protecting children and allowing them autonomy
- The social division between adults and children
- Social divisions between children
- Risk anxiety surrounding children and childhood
- Differing conceptions of children's rights

Childhood is the only form of social subordination that is still romanticised as a state of freedom. This may seem a startling assertion, given that this is not how childhood is usually thought about in everyday life. Generally, childhood is seen as a natural state, as a stage of biological immaturity during which children are both prepared for and protected from the 'real', adult world. It is supposed to be a carefree time, a time for play rather than work, a time without the burdens of adult worries and responsibilities. Yet childhood is also, and perhaps self-evidently, a social status, one of subordination to adults. Childhood is defined, in part, by exclusion from adult rights of citizenship and also by dependence on adults. Children spend most of their lives either within families or within institutions catering for their supposed 'needs'. In all these settings, they live under adult authority.

Traditionally, social scientists have conceptualised childhood primarily within the socialisation paradigm, in which children were seen as adults-in-waiting, whose experiences were only worth investigating in so far as they shaped adult attributes or life chances (Thorne 1987). Since the 1980s, sociologists have challenged such adult-centred approaches (Thorne 1987, 1993;

James and Prout 1990; Leonard 1990; Waskler 1991; Mayall 1994; Wyness 2005), but developmental perspectives remain prominent in everyday thinking and professional and public discourse. It is still taken for granted that the process of maturing from child to adolescent to adult unfolds as a series of naturally occurring stages, that there is a 'right age' at which children should develop certain competences and acquire particular freedoms and responsibilities. These assumptions are so pervasive that it is difficult to think outside them, they are so widely accepted that they have become unquestioned 'truths'. Childhood is thought of as a linear trajectory towards the future and children as themselves representing the future. It is not only the future of society as a whole that is the issue, but the propensity of parents to live vicariously through their children, to treat them as carriers of their own hopes and dreams (Beck and Beck-Gernsheim 1995).

Contemporary sociological approaches suggest that, rather than viewing children as future adults in the making, we should focus on children's own lives and activities. This entails a shift away from the idea of a child as 'becoming' an adult to the 'being child', conceptualised as an active social agent (James et al. 1998). While such perspectives are essential in challenging adult-centred views, we should not forget that children's lives are largely bounded by adult surveillance. There is no free and autonomous realm of childhood outside the social relations in which childhood in general, and particular individual childhoods, are forged. In this chapter, we are concerned with the construction and maintenance of the social division between children and adults and therefore treat childhood and adulthood as social constructs rather than natural, given stages of life.

The lives of children are, of course, shaped by divisions of gender, class, ethnicity, (dis)ability and so on. Since these divisions are discussed in detail in other chapters, here we are concerned with the division between children and adults as a fundamental social division in its own right. We begin by discussing the social construction of childhood, drawing attention to its cultural and historical variability and identifying specific features of late modern childhood. Two issues are explored in some detail: relations of power and dependence between adults and children, and the risk anxiety associated with childhood and children. We conclude by drawing attention to differences among children, locating childhood within wider social divisions.

Childhood as socially constructed

In arguing that childhood is socially constructed rather than being intrinsic to the state of being a child, we suggest that the construction of childhood needs to be understood at a number of different levels: the structural, the discursive and the situated. Childhood is institutionalised through the family, education and the state, resulting in dependence on adults and exclusion from full participation in adult society. At the level of discourse, childhood has been constituted as an object of the scientific gaze through such disciplines as psychology, social work and education, which have claimed expertise in monitoring, categorising and managing childhood and children. These expert knowledges have in turn shaped common-sense thinking, so that we are all assumed to 'know' what a child is and to be able to comment on what constitutes a 'proper' childhood. The meaning of childhood is also negotiated through everyday situated interaction, where children themselves enter into the picture as active social agents. However, children's participation in constructing their own everyday world takes place within the constraints set by their subordinate location in relation to adults.

Anthropological and historical evidence suggests that current ideas of childhood and practices of child-rearing are culturally and historically specific. Childhood is not the same the world over. There are vast differences between the cosseted and protected lives of many children in wealthy (post-)industrial nations and the harsh realities facing street children in, say, India or Brazil. Yet 'western' ideas about childhood profoundly affect the ways in which children in poorer countries are represented in the global media. They are almost universally depicted as helpless victims deserving of our sympathy and patronage – an image exploited in charity fund-raising campaigns (Wells 2009). The autonomy and resilience of these children, their ability to look after themselves, is rarely acknowledged, or where it is noted, it is seen as either a tragedy or a threat, evidence of children deprived of the childhood they should have had. This is not to deny the harsh reality of such children's lives, nor the exploitation and suffering they experience, but rather to point out that our ideas of a 'proper childhood' may be entirely inappropriate to the social, cultural and economic contexts in which such children live (Punch 1998). In societies based on subsistence technologies, children are more fully integrated into adult life, whether or not they play an active part in the economy, and generally develop adult competences earlier than is common in the modern West (Turnbull 1966; Fortes 1970; Draper 1976; Punch 1998; Lancy 2008 – but see also Chapter 5).

In European societies, ideas about children and childhood have changed markedly over the centuries. In drawing attention to these changes, the historian Ariès (1962) suggested that there was no concept of childhood in medieval Europe, that once past infancy children were simply treated as miniature adults. They were dressed like adults, took an active part in adult work and recreation and were held fully responsible for their actions. However, Ariès has been much criticised for over-simplifying or even distorting the past of childhood (see Heywood 2001). He certainly overstated his case. While children in medieval times were treated far more like adults than they are today, it is clear that they were not regarded as exactly the same as adults. In particular, Ariès' own evidence indicates that children were seen as social subordinates within a patriarchal and feudal social order, that they were very much under the authority of the head of the household in which they lived and worked. Moreover, childhood was regarded as a stage that prepared the young for later responsibilities, a period of moral and practical training for later life (Shahar 1990). Yet medieval childhood was not childhood as we know it today. Archard (1993) suggests that, while there has probably always been a concept of childhood, the current conception is a modern invention (see also Heywood 2001). The way childhood is actually lived has also changed over time.

In medieval and early modern times (up to the early eighteenth century), infancy, childhood and youth were socially recognised as stages of life preceding adulthood, but these stages did not have the same meaning as they have today (Gillis 1974). Infancy was the period before a child attained the 'age of reason', which for most medieval thinkers was at the age of 7, the age at which they could be betrothed, or, in the case of boys, begin training for the priesthood (Shahar 1990). Even before they reached this age, however, children could be expected to work, to make a contribution to household subsistence, though this would depend on their parents' circumstances and status. Although children could be tried and sometimes executed for crimes, from age 7, the age of full criminal responsibility corresponded with the beginning of youth, at 12 for girls and 14 for boys. These were also the ages at which it was legally permissible to marry, although early marriage was in fact very rare. During youth, it was common for children of all classes to leave the parental home to enter service or apprenticeships in another household, thus becoming more independent of their parents but remaining under the authority of their employer or patron. The end of youth and the beginning of adulthood was ill-defined, but was usually taken to occur on marriage and the establishment of an independent marital household, which for women, who could not hold property once married, meant becoming dependent on their husbands.

In general children were far more integrated into adult working and social life than they are today. For those privileged enough to receive any formal education, there was no notion of age-grading or reading material tailored to children's needs. Boys (and only boys) could go to university at age 11 or 12, and only in the seventeenth century was the age of university entrance raised to 15. By this time, it had become less common for the sons of the bourgeois and landed classes to be sent into service and more usual for them to be formally educated – trends that affected girls of these classes a century later (Pinchbeck and Hewitt 1969). Age-grading in schools was gradually being introduced, books to educate and entertain children began to be published and children began to be dressed differently from adults.

The inception of modern childhood was, however, apparent only among the privileged classes. The bourgeoisie, in particular, became concerned for the moral welfare of children. It has been argued that the dominant image of the child at this time was that of the 'demonic child' tainted by original sin (Skolnick 1973), whose spiritual well-being was best safeguarded by breaking his or her will. The idea of the 'innocent child' did not appear until the end of the eighteenth century and did not gain wide credence until its Victorian sentimentalisation in the nineteenth century. By this time, modern ideas of childhood were beginning to affect working-class children (Heywood 2001).

Once industrialisation separated the worlds of work and home, working children became more visible and increasingly offensive to the bourgeois ideal of childhood. As the nineteenth century wore on, children's work was gradually limited, while their lives came under more surveillance from philanthropists, educators and legislators. As older family or craft-based forms of training became obsolete, schools came to be seen as the most efficient context in which to impart knowledge. As children were excluded from work, it was seen as necessary to keep them occupied and contained. Elementary education became compulsory in 1870. Moral welfare, especially that of girls, also became a major issue and the age of heterosexual consent for girls was raised to 16 in 1882. Childhood was thus prolonged and increasingly seen as a stage of life requiring particular forms of regulation, protection and guidance:

> The modern child has become the focus of innumerable projects that purport to safeguard it from physical, sexual and moral danger, to ensure its 'normal development', to actively promote certain capacities or attributes such as intelligence, educability and emotional stability. (Rose 1989: 121)

This trend has continued and is particularly evident in the developmental paradigm and its institutionalisation in school age-grading. The result is that children are held to be incapable of doing what, in fact, they are not permitted to do (Thorne 1987). This learned incapacity in turn justifies their exclusion from the adult world.

The late modern conception of childhood entails an imputation of 'specialness' to children (as particularly cherished beings) and childhood (as a cherished state of being). There is a strong cultural emphasis on marking the boundary between childhood and adulthood (Jackson 1982), on maintaining childhood as a protected state and children as a protected species. Childhood is now frequently being constructed as a precious realm under siege from those who would rob children of their childhoods, and as being subverted from within by children who refuse to remain childlike. Anything which threatens to destabilise the boundary between childhood and adulthood provokes anxiety about childhood itself:

> To have to stand and wait as the charm, malleability, innocence and curiosity óf children are degraded and then transmogrified into the lesser features of pseudo-adulthood is painful and embarrassing and, above all, sad. (Postman 1994: xiii)

Here Postman is expressing a widely aired concern that children are growing up too quickly without experiencing childhood to the full. Childhood is seen as being at risk from pressures towards early maturity, conspicuous consumption and precocious sexuality, highlighting a fundamental contradiction in discourses around children and childhood: childhood is regarded as a natural state and yet also as perpetually at risk. This contradiction and the constant vigilance required in order to protect, preserve and manage childhood should lead us to question whether childhood is as natural as it seems.

The boundaries we construct between childhood and adulthood are clearly products of history and change over time. Modern legal systems institutionalise childhood by setting an age of majority at which a person becomes a legal subject responsible for their own affairs and able to exercise citizenship rights. The UN Convention on the Rights of the Child defines a child as anyone under the age of 18 unless, under the laws of his or her country, the age of majority comes sooner. Even with such legalistic dividing lines, there are still areas of ambiguity. Within any one country there may be various markers of adult status, so that one ceases to be a child for some purposes while remaining one for others. For example, the right to vote and the right to marry without parental consent may be acquired at different times. In both the US and the UK, a young person can hold a driving licence, marry and fight for his or her country while still being below voting age – in the words of the Barry McGuire song from 1966, 'old enough to kill but not for voting'. Indeed in some states of the US it would be possible to marry (with parental consent) 6 to 8 years before being able legally to purchase alcohol. In the UK the age of consent is now 16 for both heterosexual and homosexual sex (see Chapter 7).

Despite the cultural emphasis on the distinction between childhood and adulthood, we lack a clear rite of passage marking the boundary. The prolongation of childhood and uncertainty about where it ends has created adolescence as a peculiarly problematic liminal stage of life. Young people in their teens are excluded from many adult activities while being expected to behave like adults in other respects. However, when they do behave like adults, for example in relation to sexual activity, it can cause an outcry in defence of the need for the retention of childhood innocence. It is hardly surprising that young people are often confused and resentful. Adolescence itself, along with many of the problems associated with it, is a product of a specific, modern, western construction of childhood.

Power and dependence

As we have noted, children in western societies have historically lost their role as economic actors. Children's exclusion from work has been seen as a mark of social progress, so that forcing children to work is now seen as intrinsically problematic. Children's exclusion from work has become a mark of social progress, differentiating us from Third World nations where child labour is still common, and from an exploitative past, when children laboured in mines and mills. Yet 'freeing' children from economic exploitation has rendered them economically powerless, increasing their dependence on adults, specifically their parents. Economic dependence is now a defining feature of childhood, one that marks children as subordinates in a society where the capacity to earn – and thus to spend and consume – is central to the construction of identity.

Economic dependence has long been a marker of subordinate social status and power. For women, gaining economic independence, the right to earn and the right to control their own income was seen as a key step towards emancipation (Chapter 3). Yet, as women have gained financial independence, children have lost it (and, ironically, mothers' extra earnings often go into maintaining children's dependence). The gradual raising of the minimum school-leaving age from 12 to 14, to 15 and finally to 16 has prolonged economic dependence. Little over a generation ago, most young people left school and entered the labour market at 15. Indeed, until the 1940s, most did so at the age of 14.

More recently, changes in the benefit structure have meant that those who leave school early have no entitlement until they reach 18. For the more privileged ones who go on to higher education, the demise of student grants and their replacement by loans has lengthened the period of dependence on parental support until young people reach their early twenties. At the same time, a higher proportion of young people have been entering higher education. Hence, although the legal age of majority was reduced from 21 to 18 in 1971, for many young people the period of dependence has since increased.

Paradoxically, as economic dependence has increased, so children have come to be targeted as consumers. Indeed, the pressure to consume is often seen as a pressure towards precocious maturity (Postman 1994). While the emphasis on the child as consumer has no doubt intensified in recent years, there has long been a trend in this direction. As soon as children became sin-gled out as a special category of being, this created a market niche for products designed specifically for them – toys, games, books, clothes, and wallpaper and furniture for their rooms. Those targeting parents and children have drawn heavily on developmental psychology to fragment the market for children's goods and create categories such as 'the toddler' (Cook 2000a, b). Children's very separateness from the adult world thus serves to include them in the adult economy as consumers.

Children do not, however, consume in quite the same way as adults: chil-dren's consumption is dependent, adult-mediated consumption (Leonard 1990). Children have things bought for them and exercise consumer choice only if their parents permit it. Gifts of money and pocket money are given at adults' discretion and adults may seek to influence how these sums are spent. Young children in particular are constrained to consume only what their par-ents buy for them. They can wheedle, cajole, shout and scream to get what they want, and they may sometimes succeed, but ultimately it is adults who hold the purse strings. Older children may be permitted more latitude in dis-posing of their own pocket money but only if, in their parents' eyes, they exercise this discretion responsibly. However, despite widespread discussion of and concern about the impact of the market on children, relatively little re-search has been done on children's own consumption practices in the context of their everyday lives (Martens et al. 2004).

The ability to earn their own money through paper rounds, weekend or holiday jobs can be attractive to children in enabling them to have an income which is not dependent on the goodwill of adults (Morrow 1994). Children may also work, paid or unpaid, in the home (Brannen 1995) or a family busi-ness (Song 1996). Paid work is often seen as bad for children, as exploitative, but this is not necessarily the case and depends on the context in which such work is undertaken. It can also benefit children in terms of both their auton-omy and preparing them for adult life (see Bourdillon et al. 2010). However, whether or not children are allowed to undertake any paid work or receive payment for tasks in the home will depend on whether parents view this posi-tively as preparation for economic independence. On the other hand, parents may see such economic activity as a slur on their ability to provide adequately for their offspring, or as interfering with more legitimate childhood activities, such as homework or recreation. Giving and withholding money, and indeed permission to earn outside the home, is one means by which parents seek to control their children.

Parents not only exercise power over children through controlling them, but also seek to mould and shape their children. This is a facet of the responsibil-ity placed on parents to raise children 'properly'. This responsibility extends beyond caring and providing for children, because parents are also held re-sponsible for their children's well-being and conduct. Not only are parents expected to govern and regulate their children's current lives, but their futures as well. Child-rearing can thus be seen as a reflexive project:

> A child can no longer be accepted as it is, with physical idiosyncracies, perhaps even flaws. Rather it becomes the target of a diversity of efforts. All possible flaws must be corrected ... all possible talents must be stimu-lated ... Countless guides to education and upbringing appear on the book and magazine market. As different as each one is, at bottom they all have a similar message: the success of the child is defined as the private duty of the parents/the mother. And the duty reads the same everywhere: the parents must do everything to give the child 'the best start in life'. (Beck-Gernsheim 1996: 143)

Of course, the resources available to parents for this project vary according to not only the income (Chapter 2) but also the knowledge and social net-works (what Bourdieu (1984) has termed 'cultural capital') available to them. The ways the project is executed will reflect parents' own priorities for their children, their ideas about what is appropriate according to their children's gender, the neighbourhood in which they live and the cultural milieu they in-habit. Nonetheless, the assumption that children are what their parents make them is widespread. Modern families are often described as child-centred and certainly children's needs may be given a high priority, but these needs are de-fined for them by adults. Children's own autonomous desires frequently take second place to their parents' view of what is best for them.

It has been suggested that parental power is no longer as absolute as it once was, that child-rearing is now 'policed' by a host of experts and state agencies (Donzelot 1978) and that, with the rise of the 'psy' professions, child devel-opment has become subject to increasing surveillance (Rose 1989). 'Expert' advice not only informs parents' practices, but bureaucratises child-rearing and increases anxieties about 'doing it properly'. While this constrains parents, it does not necessarily increase children's autonomy within families. Children are neither citizens nor full legal subjects and thus live, in a very real sense, under their parents' jurisdiction. Any other agencies that deal with them, from schools and clubs to care facilities, are seen as acting in loco parentis. Parents themselves retain a great deal of latitude to rear their children as they wish, set acceptable standards of behaviour and decide how they should be edu-cated and disciplined. Think, for example, of the ways in which debates about choice of schooling for children are framed in terms of parents' rights rather than children's rights. If others interfere with parents' practices or choices, it is seen as an infringement of their rights and an assault on family privacy. Public regulation is seen as justifiable only where parents are deemed to have abused their power or not exercised it effectively enough – where children are 'at risk' or 'out of control'.

Holding property in one's bodily person is a fundamental aspect of citizen's rights in modern democratic societies. However, this right is not extended to children. Adults, and parents in particular, exercise an exceptional degree of control over the bodies of children (Hood-Williams 1990). Children's bodies are routinely regulated by adult decisions about what and when they should eat, what clothes they can wear on what occasions, admonitions about bodily movement and deportment, and restrictions on their mobility – all of which would only be experienced by adults under extreme conditions of institution-alisation, in prisons, residential care or the military (Goffman 1961). It is quite acceptable for known adults to pat children's heads, tickle them, throw them in the air, tidy their hair and clothing and even pick them up and move them bodily – behaviour that would only be acceptable between adults in the most intimate of relationships, and then only with consent. It is interesting that one of the greatest anxieties surrounding children today is that they might be mo-lested, and they are taught, in order to protect themselves, that their bodies are sacrosanct. Yet those same bodies are routinely interfered with and contained in the name of hygiene, tidiness and discipline, and also, ironically, to ensure their safety.

Children are not always willing to be bounded either by definitions of them as dependent and lacking in adult competences or by attempts to curtail their activities. Moreover, the powerlessness of children does not go unchallenged by the wider, adult society. At the same time as we have seen increasing sur-veillance of children in the name of protection or control, we have also wit-nessed a growth in the movement for children's rights, enshrined in docu-ments such as the 1989 UN Convention on the Rights of the Child. At first sight, this would seem to signal a shift towards recognising children as auto-nomous beings, but this is not always the case. The discourse of children's rights coexists with vestiges of the nineteenth-century 'child-saving' discourse in which children were seen as unfortunates to be rescued from a variety of so-cial ills ranging from poverty to immorality (Wells 2009). The UN Convention itself veers between protecting children and recognising them as autonomous beings. Some of the rights conferred by the UN Convention include children into basic internationally recognised human rights such as freedom of associa-tion, freedom of expression and the right to privacy. Other provisions of the Convention exclude children from adult activities or responsibilities such as work and armed conflict. Still other rights are specific to children, such as the right to education and freedom from abuse and neglect. On the other hand, the rights conferred on parents by the Convention can, in practice, undermine all these rights.

The confusion evident in the different forms of rights enshrined in the UN Convention derives from a widespread ambivalence about the forms of rights children should be granted. Children's rights can be framed from two opposing perspectives: in terms of rights to autonomy, control over their own lives and independent status as citizens or in terms of rights to protection and freedom from adult risks and responsibilities. The former conceptualisation of rights challenges the subordinate status of children, the latter rarely does. The UN Convention attempts to balance these opposing views, to expand children's autonomy without undermining adult authority. Hence, children's continued exclusion from citizenship is tacitly reinforced.

However, even rights that offer protection rather than independence can improve children's lives and potentially temper the near-absolute authority that parents wield over them. Within the UN Convention, parental rights are not absolute and legislation within Britain and elsewhere can override parental authority in the interests of the child. For example, state agencies can now intervene to protect children against parents who abuse or neglect them. In such cases a higher – adult – authority is called on to decide what is in 'the best interests of the child' (the guiding principle behind the Convention).

Risk, risk anxiety and the construction of childhood

The tension between protecting children from harm and fostering their autonomy also underpins many of the anxieties expressed about children and childhood in late modern society. Social theorists such as Giddens (1990, 1991) and Beck (1992) have suggested that we live in a climate of heightened risk awareness, engendered by an increasing lack of trust in both the project of modernity and expert knowledges. While anxieties about children and childhood – a product of the modern idea of the child as an innocent in need of protection – date back to the nineteenth century, the conditions of late modernity may have exacerbated them. The anxieties specific to childhood are part of a general sense that the social world itself is becoming less stable and predictable, coupled with nostalgia for an imagined past in which children played safely throughout a carefree innocent childhood.

Risk anxiety helps to construct childhood and maintain its boundaries – the specific risks from which children must be protected serve to define the characteristics of childhood and the 'nature' of children themselves. Threats to children's well-being are seen as coming from all-pervasive, global social 'ills', such as the 'pernicious' consequences of sex and violence in the media, and the unforeseen (but constantly anticipated) danger from a specific 'monstrous' individual – the shadowy figure of the paedophile who haunts the popular imagination. For example, in May 2008 a controversy arose over a photographic exhibition, in a gallery in Sydney, which included a picture of a naked 12-year-old girl, raising fears that such images 'might be used by paedophiles for their sexual titillation' (Simpson 2011: 291).

Sex itself is seen as inimical to the well-being of children, as polluting their innocence. Since the year 2000 there has been increasing public concern about the sexualisation of children, in particular the sexualisation of girls, although the gendered dimension is not always explicit. In 2003, a British tabloid newspaper ran a campaign against 'sexy' underwear, such as thongs and padded bras to pre-teen girls (see Renold 2005). In 2007 the controversy re-emerged around two events. First the National Union of Teachers in the UK called for regulation of the 'inappropriate sexualisation of pre-pubescent children', citing such examples as supermarkets selling pole-dancing kits and lace lingerie for children (the former may well have been an invention born of anxiety). Second, the American Psychological Association (2007) published a report on the dangers of early sexualisation for young girls. Media reportage, in tones of shock and horror, played up the sexualisation of children who 'ought' to be innocent.

More recently the British government commissioned two reviews on sexualisation. One was for the Home Office, focusing on young people (Papadopoulos 2010); the other, on children, was for the Department for Education, authored by the Chief Executive of the Mothers' Union (Bailey 2011). Both called for greater protection of children and young people from sexualisation, constructing sexualisation, first, as a threat to 'healthy' sexual development and, second, as a threat to the very essence of childhood, summed up by the title of the Bailey report: 'Letting Children be Children'.

While there are, of course, grounds for concern about the ways in which women (and girls) are represented in much of the sexual imagery available today, presenting the problem as one of 'lost childhood innocence' misses the point. In the first place, innocence has often been sexualised, as in soft porn images of childlike women. For example, as Emma Renold (2005) points out, the same newspaper that spearheaded the 2003 campaign against sexy underwear for girls features pictures of semi-nude models using props and poses resonant of childhood innocence. Furthermore, the effort to keep children ignorant of sex prevents them from being able to make adequate sense of the sexual representations which they will nevertheless inevitably see around them. Adult anxieties around these issues can serve to render children less safe by potentially depriving them of the knowledge they need to interpret the sexual mores of the world in which they must make the transition to adulthood (see Jackson and Scott 2010).

Beck (1992, 1998), one of the major theorists of the 'risk society', associates risk anxiety with the individualisation and de-traditionalisation characteristic of modernity. Individualisation entails the almost constant reflexive monitoring of risk that pervades our sense of how to manage ourselves and the world. Risks may be produced by social conditions, but we are expected to assess and manage them as individuals. De-traditionalisation has produced a less predictable world, in which we are faced with many options and no easy solutions (Beck 1998). Where childhood is concerned, de-traditionalisation engenders anxieties about the loss of stable families embedded within secure communities (Chapter 15). The everyday world of childhood no longer seems so safe and predictable. At the same time, individualisation renders each parent uniquely responsible for their children and encourages them to invest in their children's childhood as part of their own life project (Beck and Beck-Gernsheim 1995; Beck-Gernsheim 1996). Parents must not only guard against immediate threats to their children's well-being but must also plan for any event that might disrupt their development towards physically and psychologically healthy adulthood. Hence the developmental paradigm, so central to modern constructions of childhood, may heighten risk anxiety.

It is these individualised parental hopes and fears for their children that are mobilised in wider, publicly aired concerns about children and childhood. Increasing anxiety about risk has been superimposed on an older 'protective discourse' (Thomson and Scott 1991), within which children are located as vulnerable innocents to be shielded from the dangers of the wider social (implicitly adult) world. The fusion of risk anxiety with protectiveness engenders a preoccupation with prevention (Scott and Freeman 1995; Green 1997), a need for constant vigilance in order to anticipate and guard against potential threats to children's well-being. Concern for children's safety is of a different order from concerns about adult safety. Risks to children are represented as inherently more grave than risks to adults. This is most marked in extreme circumstances, as in the media reaction to the shooting of 16 children in the Scottish town of Dunblane in March 1996.

Children most often come under public scrutiny when they are perceived as being in danger (as victims of adult abuse or neglect) or as a danger to others (as delinquents and vandals: Thorne 1987). Often such concerns can be seen to reflect risk anxiety as much as actual danger; for example heightened awareness of sexual and fatal risk from strangers in the UK, despite the lack of evidence that risk to children comes primarily from this quarter. While there has been an increase in recorded crimes of violence against children, three-quarters of the perpetrators are parents and other relatives. The children most at risk of being murdered are infants under the age of one – hardly those most exposed to 'stranger danger' – while children aged 5–15 are, of all members of society, the least likely to be victims of homicide. Since 2004/5 the largest number of children (under 16) to have been killed by a stranger in any given year is 9 and in some years the figure is as low as 1or 2. Parents remain the most likely killers of their children. For example, they accounted for 76 per cent of all child murders in 2009/10 (Home Office 2012). This has been a relatively stable pattern for decades, yet danger to children from strangers is popularly perceived as widespread and growing.

It would, however, be unwise to interpret this apparent gap between parental worries and statistical probabilities as indicative of ignorance or stupidity. We cannot assume, in the absence of reliable research, that parents fail to assess risks 'realistically'. Parents may know the statistical probability of their child being sexually assaulted or murdered by a stranger to be slight, but the fact that it happens at all might be enough to make them fear for their own. This point has been borne out in our own research. Parents cannot even be sure that their children are safe from others at home, since electronic media render them open to contact from 'strangers' via the internet and exposure to 'unsuitable' material through television, video and computer games (Buckingham 2000).

Risk anxiety has material effects. Parental fears can limit children's lives and experiences in a range of ways, thus increasing their dependence on adults. For example, whereas 80 per cent of seven- and eight-year-olds in the UK went to school on their own in 1971, only nine per cent were doing so in 1990 (Hillman et al. 1990). This trend has persisted: in 2008 86 per cent of children aged 7–10 were accompanied to school by an adult (Office for National Statistics 2010d). This is indicative of the continuing decrease in opportunities for children to develop autonomy and self-reliance. This in turn produces yet another set of publicly aired risk anxieties relating to children's health and life experience.

It is hardly surprising, given the tensions between protecting children and permitting their autonomy, that parents should look to 'experts' for a set of rules which, having external authority, may lend a sense of certainty to the decisions taken by parents. In Britain, the National Society for the Prevention of Cruelty to Children offers guidelines on the age at which children are competent to do certain things. For example, eight-year-olds are too young to go to school alone and seven-year-olds are too young for unaccompanied visits to the shops (National Society for the Prevention of Cruelty to Children 2010). Such guidelines tend to bureaucratise decisions in relation to children, producing standardised responses without regard to the social context or life experience of individual children. They are couched within a developmental linear model that serves to delineate the boundaries of children's lives, thus creating a self-fulfilling prophecy – children cannot be competent to do things which they have never been allowed to do (Thorne 1987). Thus keeping children 'safe' can entail keeping them childlike and dependent.

The degree of anxiety generated by risks to children is associated with a particular construction of childhood as an age of innocence and vulnerability. Yet the idea of the innocent child has never entirely subsumed an alternative, older view of the child as sinful and unruly (Skolnick 1980; Jackson 1990). Children are often characterised in everyday talk as little devils in one breath and little angels in the next. However, it is common for parents to see their own children primarily as innocent and vulnerable, as opposed to other children who are potentially threatening (Valentine 1996). Whereas the dead children of Dunblane, as innocent angels, symbolically became all our children (Scott and Watson-Brown 1997), those children whose actions belie the notion of innocence are characterised as truly demonic. This is particularly the case with children who kill other children. Not only are they demonised in the media at the time of the crime, but their actions remain in the public memory, which renders their whole lives open to scrutiny. Two British cases are good examples of this.

When, in 1993, the British toddler James Bulger was murdered by two older boys, idealised images of childhood were de-stabilised (Jenks 1996); hence the efforts made to distance the boy killers from 'normal' children through depictions of them as evil beyond comprehension. The British media continue to find opportunities to remind us of these crimes. There was renewed media coverage in 2001 when the two killers were released (under assumed names) at the age of 18. In 2010, one of them, John Venables, was convicted of downloading child pornography. It is unlikely that this would have been newsworthy had it not been for his history. As it was, this provided another opportunity for the media to remind us of his past and to debate whether it should have been taken into account in the later sentencing.

The demonisation of child killers parallels the media representation of women such as Myra Hindley and Rosemary West. Women and children who kill are deemed monstrous, doubly transgressive – in having murdered, they have also acted against their feminine or childlike 'nature'. In the case of children, the 'evil child' can never be seen to grow up into a normal adult, especially if she is a girl. This is illustrated clearly in the case of Mary Bell. In May 1998, considerable controversy was generated in the UK by the publication of a book about Bell who, over 30 years earlier when she was 13, had killed two small children. Bell was retrospectively re-demonised as both a child who killed and a woman profiting from her crime by accepting payment for her story. Her depiction as monstrous was highly gendered. 'Her extraordinarily pretty, heart-shaped face looked out beneath headlines, as it looks out again now: a beautiful icon of evil' (*Observer*, 3 May 1998: 3).

Here our attention was drawn to the appearance of feminine, childish innocence and the 'truth' of the evil beneath the surface. We were reminded of
the lack of remorse shown by Mary Bell at her trial (and by implication since),
in contrast with her co-accused who was acquitted and described as 'normal'
in her tearful appearance in court, as 'just a little girl'. Mary Bell, however,
was clearly not a proper 'little girl'. Throughout the trial, she was 'tearless and
defiant, bandying words with the prosecution' (*Observer*, 3 May 1998: 3). Her
cleverness and her refusal to be cowed by the full weight of adult power represented by the court underline her exclusion from normal childhood and her
status as a monstrosity. In 2009 Bell hit the headlines again when she became
a grandmother. A perfectly routine life event was transformed into something
extraordinary and taken as an opportunity to demonise her once again.

Differences among children

Since our primary focus has been on the institution of childhood and the
social division between childhood and adulthood, we have made only passing
references to differences of class, gender, ethnicity and age (Chapters 2–5).
Clearly, children are not socially homogeneous. One aspect of the social construction of childhood and the distinctions drawn between children and adults
is that 'the child' becomes an abstraction representing a universal and often
idealised childhood. It is this universal child that figures in media representations of tragedies affecting children, such as the Dunblane shooting, and
which, as a symbolic representation of all our children, evokes an emotional
response (Scott and Watson-Brown 1997). In other contexts, this universalis-
ing of childhood serves to conceal or pathologise social divisions among children. If children's differing experiences of childhood are noticed at all, it is
within a developmental paradigm that assumes a fixed set of stages that all
children pass through, or within a discourse that marks out 'deviant', 'problem' or 'deprived' children from the ideal, 'normal' child. This normal child is,
unsurprisingly, defined from a white, middle-class perspective that, even in its
most liberal, caring variants, has the effect of branding working-class or black
children as 'other' (Lawler 1999). It is these children who are likely to be seen
as not proper children, cast either in the mould of the demonic child or the
child deprived of a childhood.

   This is not to deny that middle-class children enjoy all manner of privileges that working-class children lack. The point is that setting up middle-
class childhood as the norm results in it being viewed uncritically as a more
positive version of childhood. It also tends to represent the difference of working-class childhoods as the product of cultural deficit or lack, so diverting

attention away from the material inequalities that underpin both working-class and middle-class childhoods. Where ethnic differences are concerned, taking white, middle-class childhood as the norm too easily gives rise to racist stereotypes of dysfunctional black families and neighbourhoods or a glib multiculturalism that celebrates diversity while denying racism.

Arguably the greatest social division affecting children is poverty, both between rich and poor areas of the world and within relatively affluent countries such as the UK. It is important to point out, however, that children are poor because adults are poor and children are, as we have shown, highly dependent on adults economically (Chapter 13). Children are extremely vulnerable to the effects of poverty – malnutrition, disease and so on. Adults with children are generally worse off than equivalent adults without children because of the economic costs entailed in having children. Children are dependent on parental altruism and, while the evidence suggests that mothers generally display such altruism (see the discussion of poverty in Chapters 3, 13 and 14), fathers frequently do not and thus poor households may be financially better off without men (Graham 1987). However, because children are considered to be the personal responsibility, or even the property, of their parents, there is rarely adequate social support for children.

Thus the issue of poverty can be taken as an illustration of children's dependence. While, as a result of their dependence, children are particularly vulnerable to poverty, the ways in which concerns about this are expressed clearly illustrate and reinforce the issues that we have raised in this chapter. More concern is expressed about child poverty than about the situation of women in general or older people (Chapters 3 and 5) – both groups in which poverty levels are high globally. This is, we suggest, because images of 'innocents' are more appealing – quite literally in the context of charity campaigns. Poor children are the antithesis of idealised images of childhood and can easily be appropriated into a story that constructs them as deprived of a 'proper' childhood and thus of particular concern and interest (Lawler 1999).

The central argument of this chapter is that the division between childhood and adulthood, despite not having received as much sociological attention as divisions like class, gender and so on, should, nevertheless, be seen as one of the key lines of stratification along which societies are organised. It follows from this that, for children as for adults, the actualities of their everyday lives are shaped by their location in relation to all the other divisions discussed in this book. It is important therefore that the adult/child division is not simply reproduced by a reading of the other chapters as if they pertained only to adults.

Discussion Questions

1. Look at the UN Convention on the Rights of the Child, available at www. unicef.org.uk/Documents/Publication-pdfs/UNCRC_PRESS200910web.pdf and also on the UNHCR website, www.unhcr.org. Which rights are framed in terms of children's autonomy and which in terms of the protection of children? Are there tensions between these differing conceptualisations of rights?

2. Interview someone over 50 about their experiences of being a child and compare this with your own childhood and with discussions in the media about what it is safe for children to do now.

FURTHER READING

A now classic account of how knowledge of children is deeply adult-centred can be found in Thorne, B. 'Re-Visioning Women and Social Change: Where are the Children?' (*Gender and Society*, 1: 85–109, 1987). Jenks, C. *Childhood* (Routledge: London, 1996, 2006) in the Key Ideas series offers an introduction to sociological ways of thinking about childhood from a social constructionist perspective. The collection edited by James, A. and Prout, A. (eds) *Constructing and Reconstructing Childhood* (Basingstoke: Falmer Press, 1990) provides an emphasis on cultural and historical differences. Mayall, B. *Towards a Sociology for Childhood* (Open University Press: Buckingham, 2002) argues that feminist theory and practice are useful for understanding childhood and that we should start from children's own accounts to show how the organisation of social relations provides an explanation for their social position. A good overview of historical perspectives and debates is provided in Heywood, C. *A History of Childhood* (Cambridge: Polity, 2001); for information on children and childhood in cross-cultural perspective, see Wells, K. *Childhood in a Global Perspective* (Cambridge: Polity, 2009) and Lancy, D. *The Anthropology of Childhood: Cherubs, Chattels and Changelings* (Cambridge: Cambridge University Press, 2008).

CHAPTER 7

Sexuality

Sue Scott and Stevi Jackson

This chapter will provide you with a broad critical understanding of the following issues in sexuality as a source of social division:

- What is meant by essentialism and why it is challenged by social theorists
- The idea of the social construction of sexuality
- Definitions of gender, sexuality and institutionalised heterosexuality
- Social divisions of gender in relation to sexuality
- The institutionalisation of heterosexuality
- The privileging of heterosexuality in relation to other sexualities
- Gender differences in heterosexual practices
- The heterosexual and gendered assumptions underpinning sex education
- Psychoanalytical approaches to sexuality
- The interactionist approach to sexuality
- Foucault's approach to sexuality
- Feminist, lesbian, gay and queer contributions to understanding sexuality
- Issues associated with lesbian and gay rights
- The commodification of sexuality

The social ordering of sexuality gives rise to two forms of social division and inequality. On the one hand, within modern western societies, heterosexuality is institutionalised as the 'normal' form of human sexuality, and this is reflected in various ways from the legal regulation of marriage and the provisions of the social security system in many countries to the content of popular culture and everyday social practices. This privileging of heterosexuality serves to marginalise lesbian and gay sexualities, gives rise to both formal and informal discrimination against lesbians and gay men and sometimes to more brutal forms of oppression. On the other hand, heterosexuality is itself, by definition, differentiated by gender. Being heterosexual does not have the same consequences for men and women – indeed historically it has evolved as an institution that is closely bound up with the perpetuation of male dominance and female subordination, as was argued in Chapter 3.

While there are apparently two distinct forms of inequality here – between heterosexuals and non-heterosexuals and between men and women – they are interrelated. A sociological understanding of both forms of inequality requires that we pay critical attention to the taken-for-granted character of the heterosexual norm. This chapter will therefore draw on sociological analysis of heterosexuality as institution and practice. We will begin by introducing some basic concepts, defining key terms such as gender, sexuality and institutionalised heterosexuality. We will then explore sociological challenges to biological determinism, explaining why sociologists see sexuality as socially constructed and how we might conceptualise the sexual as fully social, rather than 'natural' or individual. Having explained the concepts and theories underpinning sociological approaches to sexuality, we will examine some of the research that has accumulated on both heterosexual relations and the forms of social exclusion experienced by lesbians and gay men. We will argue that, despite changes in sexual mores towards less restrictive and more egalitarian ideals, inequalities associated with sexuality persist.

Sexuality, gender and institutionalised heterosexuality

Sexuality cannot be understood without consistently paying attention to its intersection with gender. The concepts of gender and sexuality both take 'sex', a highly ambiguous term, as a point of reference. In the English language, the word 'sex' can denote either the distinction between male and female (as 'two sexes') or sex as an erotic activity (to 'have sex'). Similarly, 'sexual' can refer to the different activities or attributes of men and women, as in phrases such as 'the sexual division of labour', or it can refer to the erotic sphere of life, for example 'sexual fantasies'. Moreover the term 'sex' can be used – more commonly in French, but sometimes in English – to name sexual organs which are simultaneously erogenous zones and body parts that distinguish male from female.

This linguistic confusion is no mere accident, but tells us something about the male-dominated and heterosexist culture in which we live (Wilton 1996). It is commonly assumed that being born with a particular set of genitals (sex organs) defines one as being of a particular sex (female or male), which means that one will normally become 'properly' feminine or masculine (the appropriate gender) and will desire and engage in erotic activity with 'the other sex', with someone possessing a different set of sex organs from one's own. This circular and deterministic reasoning has served to justify women's subordination as a 'natural' outcome of sex differences and define heterosexuality as the only fully 'natural' and legitimate form of sexuality. As sociologists, we should challenge the taken-for-granted assumptions underlying this way of thinking.

A first step is to separate out the three terms 'sex', 'gender' and 'sexuality'. Sociologists and feminists usually distinguish between them, but there is by no means a consensus on how each of these three terms should be used. Hence we need to define the sense in which they are being used in this chapter. The term 'gender' was originally adopted by feminist sociologists to emphasise the social shaping of femininity and masculinity, to challenge the idea that relations between women and men were ordained by nature. In the past, it was common to make a distinction between 'sex' as the biological differences between male and female and 'gender' as the cultural distinction between femininity and masculinity along with the social division between women and men (Oakley 1972). This is no longer acceptable, because it has become increasingly apparent that our understanding of the anatomically sexed body is itself socially constructed. Scientific understandings of sex difference have been shaped by cultural ideas about gender and the everyday recognition of others as men and women is a social act requiring us to decode cultural signifiers of gender (see for example Butler 1990; Delphy 1993). This realisation also helps to resolve the ambiguity of the word 'sex', which is still often used – even by some sociologists – to denote both the male–female distinction and intimate erotic activity.

Here we will use the term 'gender' to cover all aspects of what it means to be a woman or a man and to refer to the social division and cultural distinction between women and men. The word 'sex' is then reserved for describing erotic activity. The term 'sexuality' is generally broader in meaning, encompassing erotic desires and identities, as well as practices. In this sense, the concept of 'sexuality' remains somewhat fluid, in part because what is deemed erotic, and hence sexual in this sense, is not fixed. What is erotic to one person might be disgusting to a second and immoral to a third. In using this rather slippery term, we wish to convey the idea that sexuality is not limited to 'sex acts', but involves our sexual feelings and relationships, the ways in which we are, or are not, defined as sexual by others, as well as the ways in which we define ourselves.

While gender and sexuality are analytically distinct, they are empirically interrelated. When we label ourselves and others as heterosexual, lesbian, gay or bisexual, we define sexuality by the gender of those we desire. Masculinity and femininity are validated, in part, through conventional heterosexuality, hence the idea that lesbians are not 'real women' and gay men are not 'real men'. Conversely, those who flout conventions of femininity and masculinity are often assumed to be lesbian or gay. Sexual desires and practices are also gendered and heterosexual relationships, in particular, are governed by all manner of gendered expectations from the double standard of morality to the sequences of acts that occur within any given sexual encounter. The normative status of heterosexuality is pivotal to the social ordering of both gender and sexuality.

The term 'institutionalised heterosexuality' refers to all social practices and forms of social regulation through which 'normal' sexuality is equated with heterosexuality (Seidman 2009). Heterosexuality is a social institution. It is definitive of another key social institution – marriage – and is the norm against which other forms of sexuality are judged and policed. Not only does it involve the marginalisation of alternative sexualities, but it governs social expectations about relations between women and men in both the private and public spheres of life. Heterosexuality is so taken for granted, even by sociologists, that we often overlook its importance. We think within what has been called 'the heterosexual imaginary', which masks the operation of heterosexuality as an institution (Ingraham 1996: 169). Moreover, heterosexuality is legitimated by the concealment of its social character, through its definition as simply 'natural'. This brings us to the most important contribution that sociology has made to the study of sexuality: the demystification of its apparent naturalness.

The critique of essentialism

Since the 1970s, sociologists and feminists have challenged 'essentialist' modes of thinking that view sexuality as an innate, universal fact of human nature. Within western culture there has been a long history of religiously-based essentialism within which some sexual practices were defined as natural, in the sense of God-given, and others as 'against nature' and hence a transgression of God's law. In modern societies, however, it is biological essentialism that predominates, although the moral categorisation deriving from its older, religious form has by no means disappeared. It is now common to find human sexuality reduced to hormones, genes and the urge to pass on our genetic inheritance to the next generation. This perspective remains popular in lay and scientific circles, even though sexual activity is now increasingly thought of as recreation rather than procreation.

Sociologists have identified a number of problems with essentialism. In the first place, it rests on something unknowable, a hypothesised 'natural' sexuality somehow uncontaminated by cultural influences. Human beings do not exist outside society and culture; we each become sexual within specific social contexts. The forms of sexuality we are familiar with today are the product of a particular society at a particular point in its history. Even within our own society, experiences of both gender and sexuality are highly variable. Since gender and sexuality intersect with other social divisions, such as those based on class, ethnicity, age and community (Chapters 2, 4, 5 and 15), we each live our sexuality from different locations within society and our individual biographies affect our sexual preferences and practices in complex ways. When we turn to historical and anthropological evidence we find even greater diversity.

Erotic conventions change over time and vary from one society to another. We know, for example, that in medieval Western Europe women were regarded as beings possessed by insatiable carnal lust, while in the Victorian era they were seen as almost asexual. This might be explained by differing degrees of repression of some innate female sexuality, but this is not a very satisfactory explanation. The idea of differential repression cannot account for the complexity and variety found in different cultures. In our own society, the 'missionary position' (man on top and woman supine) has, until recently, been considered the most 'normal' and 'natural' way to engage in heterosexual intercourse. Yet people in other societies did not always agree (hence the term 'missionary position'). According to the anthropologist Malinowski (1929: 284), the Trobriand Islanders 'despise the European position and consider it unpractical and improper' – mainly because it restricts women's movements and deprives them of pleasure. Early anthropologists documented a wide variety of sexual practices within different cultures, demonstrating that what counts as erotic varies from one society to another (Ford and Beach 1952). More recent anthropological work has questioned the very definition of the sexual, suggesting that what is sexual is by no means self-evident. Consider, for example, a young man sucking an older man's penis. Is this a sexual act? Is it, more specifically, a homosexual act? In some Highland New Guinea societies, this act is ritualised as part of the passage to manhood; ingesting the semen of an adult man is essential if a boy is to become a man. In this context, it is an act with more immediate significance for gender than sexuality, although it also prepares the initiate for heterosexual adulthood (Herdt 1981; Meigs 1990).

Given that there is no natural, universal human sexuality, we cannot simply peel back the layers of social and cultural influences and find some core, 'natural' sexuality. The idea that there is an essential human sexuality that is then moulded, modified and repressed runs counter to anthropological and historical evidence. It also misleads us into thinking of the social regulation of sexuality as a negative force and hence does not allow for the social construction of sexuality. The social and cultural shaping of sexuality happens not simply through prohibiting, restricting or repressing sexual practices but, more tellingly, through permitting, promoting and organising particular forms of eroticism. In other words, we learn not only what not to do, but what we should be doing sexually, how we should do it and in what order we should perform the actions which make up a sexual encounter. This is why there are so many cross-cultural variations in what is seen as erotic and in the range and form of acts deemed 'normally' sexual.

The essentialist paradigm does not address the social divisions arising from sexuality. It cannot account for differences in masculine and feminine sexuality except in terms of 'natural' differences or differential repression. Either women and men are innately different and nothing can change this, or women's sexuality is seen as more repressed than that of men. The latter view takes current definitions of male sexuality as the benchmark of unrepressed sexuality, in other words, what sexuality should be like, and does not allow for any other possibilities for either women or men. It also equates normality with heterosexuality. Since the essentialist paradigm ultimately reduces sexuality to reproduction, only heterosexual sex can be fully 'natural'. Hence its implications are heterosexist as well as sexist.

The social construction of sexuality

In countering essentialism, sociologists have suggested that sexuality is socially constructed. 'Social constructionism' is not a single unified perspective, however, and has been informed by three main strands of theory: psychoanalysis, interactionism and forms of post-structuralist and post-modernist thinking influenced by the work of Foucault (1981) and, especially in recent times, 'queer theory' (see Seidman 1996).

Psychoanalysis originated with the work of Freud in the early twentieth century. Freud saw the human psyche as being shaped by the repression of the libido – an inborn sexual energy. According to Freud, infants are born bisexual (neither male nor female, heterosexual or homosexual), with their sexual desires focused on their mothers. It is only through castration anxiety that, as small children, they become differentiated as boys and girls. The realisation that girls lack a penis leads the boy to fear that his father will castrate him for daring to desire his mother. He represses that desire through identification with his father, but remains sexually oriented to women. The girl, seeing herself as already castrated, blames her mother for this fate, despises her for sharing it and turns her attention to her father. She abandons active clitoral sexuality and later adapts herself to passive, vaginal sexuality directed, in adulthood, towards a father-substitute (see Freud 1977). Read literally, this account remains essentialist in that it presupposes an innate sexuality and assumes that anatomy is destiny, even if that destiny is mediated through familial relationships. More recent readings of Freud, influenced by the work of Lacan (1977), suggest that it is through entry into language and culture that we become sexed subjects, and it is the symbolic phallus, rather than the 'real' penis through which this is ordered. Yet the problematic phallocentricity of Freud persists, as does the assumption of an infantile sexuality later repressed by cultural forces.

The interactionist approach, deriving from the work of Gagnon and Simon (1974), is fundamentally opposed to psychoanalysis. Gagnon and Simon argue that there is no such thing as an innate sexuality that can be repressed. What is sexual depends on what is defined as such. It is through learning 'sexual scripts' – the sexual meanings and conventions circulating through social interaction – that we are able to make sense of acts, emotions and sensations as sexual and locate ourselves within potentially sexual scenarios. Since children in western cultures are denied access to adult sexual knowledge, they acquire a gendered identity before they see themselves as sexual actors. Gender then becomes the lens through which they later make sense of sexual knowledge and practices and construct a sense of themselves as sexual. Here, differences between male and female sexuality have nothing to do with genitals and everything to do with the social construction of gender and the scripting of sexuality in gendered terms (for example, assumptions about active male sexuality and passive female sexuality). From this perspective, one's sexuality is not something fixed in childhood but evolves through interaction with others in social settings. Sexual scripts themselves are modified through interaction and subject to historical change (see Simon 1996: Gagnon 2004; Jackson and Scott 2010).

Foucault (1981) also challenges the notion of repression, in this case through historical analysis of shifting sexual discourses – discourses being the language and frameworks of understanding through which we categorise, order and explain the world around us. He contests the idea that the Victorian era was one of repression, arguing that it produced a 'discursive explosion' around sexuality. It was in this period that 'sexuality' as we understand it was brought into being, constituted as an object of discourse, in which diverse sexualities were classified, catalogued and elaborated. These discourses made it possible to distinguish between normal and perverse sexualities, to think of sexuality as an attribute of our inner selves. Acts once considered as carnal sins (to which all were susceptible) came to define the essential character of those who engaged in them. For example, where committing an act of sodomy was once a crime, but one which any sinful man might commit, that act was now seen as definitive of a particular sort of person: it became possible to be a homosexual.

Feminist sociologists have also made major contributions to the study of sexuality. Feminism is not a single theoretical perspective and feminists have drawn on and contributed to all three theoretical traditions outlined above. What feminism has added is a concern with the intersection between sexuality and gender divisions, with the ways in which the current ordering of sexual relations, especially heterosexual relations, is implicated in the maintenance of male domination (see Jackson 1999, 2005; Jackson and Scott 2010). Radical gay and lesbian and, more recently, 'queer' theorists have shared feminists' interest in social constructionism. Queer theory, which has been influential in recent years, sometimes utilises psychoanalytic concepts but is more centrally preoccupied with developing Foucault's ideas on the historical contingency of sexual identities and destabilising the binary distinction between heterosexuality and homosexuality (see Halperin 1995; Seidman 1996, 1997).

These perspectives offer differing ideas about how sexuality is socially constructed and also about what is being socially constructed, whether it be our individual desires, the cultural meanings of the erotic, the distinctions between normative and perverse sexualities or male-dominated sexual practices. Existing theories often concentrate on only some aspects of the social construction of sexuality while ignoring or downplaying others. We would argue that, in order to understand sexuality as fully social, we need to understand how it is constituted at four levels (see Jackson 1999):

1. At the level of social structure and social institutions, through the institutionalisation of heterosexuality and through gender hierarchy.
2. At the level of everyday social and sexual practices.
3. At the level of meaning, through the discourses circulating within our culture as well as the meanings emerging from, and negotiated within, everyday interaction.
4. At the level of our individual subjectivities, through the social shaping of our sexual desires, responses and emotions.

A sexualised culture?

Part of the problem we have in thinking about sexuality is the way in which it is singled out as a 'special' area of life, as uniquely personal and private yet frequently provoking heated and disproportionate public controversy (Hawkes 1996). Think, for example, of the number of politicians whose careers have been threatened by sexual indiscretions that had little or no bearing on their capacity to perform their public functions. The American sexual radical feminist Rubin (1984: 278–9), has called this 'the fallacy of misplaced scale' whereby sexual acts have come to be 'burdened with an excess of significance'. Rubin associates this with 'sex negativity', with a culture that has long regarded sexuality as a dangerous, socially disruptive force. Certainly, its sex-negative manifestations are dramatic, when we realise that a single act of anal sex carried the death penalty in England until 1861, men could be imprisoned simply for being homosexual until 1967, and in many states of the US sodomy (whether heterosexual or homosexual) still carries a prison sentence.

Yet the fallacy of misplaced scale is not only evident among moral puritans but also among those espousing the cause of sexual liberation. Sex is not only uniquely tabooed, but also uniquely valorised as a route to personal fulfilment and even social revolution. The writings of sexual radicals that were popular in the 1960s saw sexual repression as fundamental to the bourgeois social order (Reich 1951; Marcuse 1964, 1972). Hence free sexual expression came to be seen as a means of undermining capitalism. Later libertarian writers do not make such grand claims for the disruptive power of sexuality, but still argue that transgressive sexual practices destabilise the status quo (see Rubin 1984; Halperin 1995). More generally, sexuality is marketed as a means to personal fulfilment in what Stephen Heath (1982: 3) calls 'the sexual fix', which, far from being a form of liberation, represents 'a new mode of conformity'. For example, numerous sex manuals and magazines now tell us that sexual fulfilment is virtually a precondition for a full and happy life (see also Jackson and Scott 2004, 2010).

Contemporary sexual mores are confused, contradictory and contested. We inhabit a culture saturated with representations of sexuality, yet who may talk about it, where and with whom is still circumscribed. Sexuality has become an ingredient of most forms of entertainment and is used to sell everything from cars to chocolate, but it is rarely treated simply as a routine aspect of everyday life. Its very specialness as an area of human experience makes sexuality a problematic public issue and a troublesome aspect of our personal relationships. Young people today grow up in a culture in which they are constantly exposed to sexual imagery and innuendo, yet recent research tells us that they still find it difficult to access appropriate information and articulate their sexual wants and desires within intimate relationships (Tolman 2002; Allen 2005; Fine and McClelland 2006).

That sexuality is still regarded as problematic in many western societies, including Britain, is illustrated by the issue of sex education. Here, the idea of sex as a 'special' area of life meets the conceptualisation of children as a special category of people (see Chapter 6), so that anything which links childhood and sexuality is potentially highly controversial. Sex education has been a topic of public debate for decades. What is at issue is its form, content and timing: when young people should receive it, what they should be allowed to know and how this knowledge should be imparted. It is not, however, simply access to knowledge that causes concern, but what young people do with that knowledge: whether or not it promotes 'promiscuity', whether it might 'cause' or 'prevent' teenage pregnancy (Pilcher 2005). The debate is framed by a tension between public health (the desire to promote 'safer' sex and prevent early pregnancy) and public morality (the concern to maintain 'family' values). In this context, there is little concern with sexual pleasure; at best, sexual activity is an inevitability whose ill-effects should be ameliorated. In practice, school sex education remains didactic, focused on imparting biological and practical information, with little emphasis on the complexities of young people's sexual lives (Allen 2005, 2011; Fine and McClelland 2006).

The form and content of sex education is one of the means through which male-defined heterosexuality is institutionalised as the only 'normal' form of sexuality. Priority is given to reproductive sexuality, in that the most important 'facts' to be imparted concern the link between sex and conception. In this context, relationships are an issue – rights (to say 'no') and responsibilities may be included, along with the emotional entanglements of sexual relationships. Yet the sex that happens in these relationships is skirted round and skipped over. Sexual pleasure, and in particular women's pleasure, is rarely discussed. Heterosexual penetrative sex is, in the main, taken for granted as defining what sex is, so that activities designed to 'turn women on' – if discussed at all – are defined as 'foreplay'. Where gay or lesbian sex is addressed, it is at best treated with liberal tolerance. Discussions of issues of sexual pleasure and alternative sexualities are hedged around with all manner of anxieties, in particular teachers' worries about imputations of corruption, causing offence to more conservative parents or provoking a media furore. Teachers and pupils also lack a common language with which to talk openly about sexuality. The constraints on those entrusted with imparting sex education result in what has been called 'defensive teaching' (Trudell 1993), with teachers staying on safe ground as far as possible and seeking to control the agenda, to guard against pupils who might raise difficult issues (Buston et al. 2001). By default, if not by design, heterosexuality dominates the sex education curriculum, the underlying assumption being that young people will grow up to be heterosexuals. While it may be possible, in a classroom context, to challenge the most coercive aspects of heterosexuality, it is rarely possible to challenge the conventional sexual script in which foreplay leads on to 'real sex' (vaginal penetration) which ends when he 'comes'.

Heterosexuality as a gendered sexual practice

The prioritisation of male sexual needs has long been challenged by feminist writers. Feminists seized on the sexological work of Masters and Johnson (1966), which demonstrated that all female orgasms, however produced, are clitorally centred, in order to demystify the 'myth of the vaginal orgasm'. This created the possibility of de-centring so-called 'sexual intercourse', of treating it as one sexual act among many possibilities rather than the predictable end point of a sexual encounter. Information on women's sexual response is now widespread in women's magazines and such writings tend to assume that women possess active sexual desires and have a right to sexual pleasure. If one drew on these magazines as the only source of data, it would appear that equality in sexual relations had been achieved. However, sociological research reveals a different picture. The first UK National Survey of Sexual Attitudes and Lifestyles (Wellings et al. 1994) found that vaginal intercourse was far more common than any other form of sexual activity and that non-penetrative sex which did not culminate in intercourse was in the main found among the young, who were avoiding 'going all the way'. The consequences of the double standard were also evident in the data, with 24.4 per cent of men reporting 10 or more sexual partners in total, compared with 6.8 per cent of women. Data emerging from the second National Survey suggest that this gap is narrowing, with 34.6 per cent of men and 19.4 per cent of women reporting 10 or more lifetime sexual partners (Johnson et al. 2001). The results of the third UK national survey were published in the *Lancet* in November 2013.

An extensive qualitative study of young people's sexuality conducted in Britain, the Women, Risk and AIDS Project (Holland et al. 1990, 1991, 1998; Thomson and Scott 1991), revealed that young heterosexual women found sexual pleasure both difficult to discuss and hard to attain, and that many of them felt pressurised, by men, into having sex. Almost all the young women and men in the study accepted the conventional equation between sex and penetration. They disciplined their own bodies and pleasures to suit men in ways in which their partners were unlikely even to be aware of. In so doing, they conceded to men's definitions of what was pleasurable and acceptable, finding 'fulfilment primarily in the relationship, in giving pleasure' (Holland et al. 1994: 31). More recent studies have found little change (Tolman 2002; Powell 2010). The ethic of service to men is, of course, not confined to erotic encounters and underlines the importance of placing heterosexual sex in the wider context of gender relations. This is not to say that young women simply passively accede to unpleasurable sex. Many do develop strategies of resistance, but their success is constrained both by the assumptions of the majority of their sexual partners and the generally unquestioned norms of heterosexuality.

There is no comparable data on older heterosexuals, but what does emerge from the few studies that have addressed this issue suggest that these patterns are not confined to the young and inexperienced. Research seems to suggest that sex is experienced positively in the early stages of a relationship, that when couples are 'in love', desire masks any lack of care or competence. In longer-term relationships, women begin to feel uncared for and experience men's sexual demands as unwelcome, objectifying and coercive (Duncombe and Marsden 1996; Langford 1999). Duncombe and Marsden found that women in long-term heterosexual relationships complained of being pressured into sex that was mechanical and preceded by only perfunctory foreplay. Men in this study were more likely to complain about their partner's lack of interest in sex and of therefore being deprived of their conjugal rights. As one man said:

> It would be no skin off her nose ... Sometimes I just want her to let me put it in and do it ... She's broken the contract. Sex is part of marriage. (Duncombe and Marsden 1996: 230)

Langford (1999) also found that women in long-term relationships expressed deep dissatisfaction with routinised sex in which emotional intimacy was lacking. For some, sex appeared to have become simply a chore that was no more enjoyable than housework, and in which they had become objects for men's use. The use of Viagra among older couples has been found to increase pressure on women to provide sex on demand, particularly as men do not always consult their wives before taking the little blue pill and then expect to 'get on with it', often with minimal foreplay. In one study, a 48-year-old woman said of the perceived power of the drug:

> this made sex inevitable. Sometimes there was no discussion about whether ... the sex act was going to take place, so it would be ... 'I've taken the pill, OK, let's go'. (Potts et al. 2003: 709).

A 65-year-old woman tells a similar story:

> Sometimes we go to bed and I think I'll go to sleep and then I realize ... he's sort of trying to get me to want sex, and it'll be a while and then I'll say 'have you taken the pill?' He'll say 'of course I've taken the pill, you know, what did you think'? And I'll say 'well I had no idea ... I've asked you not to take it unless we discuss it'. He said 'well I don't have to get your permission to take it'. (Potts et al. 2003: 707)

Underpinning these accounts is the widespread belief that men are driven by unstoppable sexual urges that must be satisfied – an idea that is also used to explain rape. These data support the feminist claim that sexual violence is an extension of 'normal' heterosexual sexual practice (Kelly 1988; Gavey 2005, Kimmel 2009), that our culture supports coercive sex and sexual violence. All the evidence available suggests that there is nothing particularly unusual about the rapist – he is a very average man. In a US study of convicted rapists, Scully (1990) characterises rape as a high reward, low risk crime, in that men gain a great deal of pleasure from it and run a very low risk of being convicted. In the UK, despite some improvements in the ways in which the police treat rape victims, there had been a dramatic fall in the proportion of rapists brought to justice in the 1980s and 1990s (Kelly et al. 2005). Since an alleged rapist (like any other defendant) is presumed innocent until proven guilty, the courts effectively treat the victim as guilty (of having 'provoked' rape or 'consented' to it) until proven otherwise. Although there has been legislation limiting the intrusive questioning of rape victims, British courts still scrutinise their sexual histories and reputations. Defence lawyers still use any evidence of autonomous female sexuality to discredit a woman's testimony, and still routinely imply that, if she is less than completely chaste, she must have deserved it (see Brown et al. 1993; Lees 1997; McMillan 2007). These problems have become particularly evident in recent years in the context of date rape (Gavey 2005; Kimmel 2009).

We live in a society that constructs a form of male sexuality which can readily turn predatory and then fails to call the predator to account. This is why feminists have argued that rape is a product and expression of male domination (Jackson 1999). It is the starkest possible illustration of the inequality and oppression scripted into heterosexual practices.

Heterosexuality as institution

The linchpin of institutionalised heterosexuality is marriage – or at least heterosexual coupledom. Some sociologists, notably Giddens (1992), argue that this emphasis is declining, that we are living in the era of the 'pure relationship', which is freely chosen and conditional for its continuation on both partners defining it as successful. While marriages may be less stable and enduring than was once the case, there is little evidence of the population abandoning the ideal of heterosexual monogamy – even if the reality is now more commonly serial monogamy. The vast majority of the population still marry at least once.

As an institution, heterosexuality is not just about sex, it is as much about who washes the sheets as what goes on between them (van Every 1996). As we have seen, women are still expected to service their husbands sexually and this is bound up with the other services they provide, such as housework and child care. Historically, men acquired rights in women's bodies, property and labour through marriage. This is why, until 1990, a British man could not be accused of raping his wife: if he did so, he was simply exercising his conjugal rights. It was and is sex (the act of consummation) that confirms the existence of marriage.

The assumption that everyone is or should be living in a heterosexual union with a male breadwinner has also underpinned the welfare state and structured the labour market. While many of the resultant gender inequalities are slowly being eroded (Chapter 3), the presumption of heterosexuality itself remains firmly in place although many rights have now, in the UK at least, been conferred upon those living in lesbian or gay partnerships. As recently as a few decades ago lesbian and gay sexualities were seen as 'threats to family values'. The best example of this is the infamous clause 28 of the Local Government Act 1988, which barred local authorities from 'promoting' homosexuality as a 'pretended family relationship', especially in schools (Weeks 1991; Cooper 1995). Since the beginning of the twenty-first century there have been major changes to legal and civil rights in the UK and many other countries. In Britain same-sex couples gained rights to adoption in 2002 and the Civil Partnerships Act, which came into effect in 2005, granted most of the rights associated with marriage to lesbian and gay couples, albeit at the price of conforming to conventional standards of monogamous coupledom (Jackson and Scott 2004). Despite opposition from parts of the Conservative Party, the Marriage (Same-Sex Couples) Bill made progress through Parliament during 2013, but the legislation still exempts the Anglican Church. Civil partnership, a legal relationship for same-sex couples, was introduced in 2004, giving the same legal treatment as marriage on inheritance, pensions rights and next of kin. Such rights now exist in a number of western countries, but they are by no means universal and there are many parts of the world in which lesbians and gay men are still persecuted by the state.

The lesbian feminist writer Rich (1980) first coined the term 'compulsory heterosexuality' to emphasise that heterosexuality is imposed on us rather than freely chosen. Rich was concerned to explain the ways in which women are kept within the boundaries of heterosexuality and kept down within it (Jackson 1999). Some of her arguments apply only to women, for example the idea that lesbianism is a form of resistance to patriarchal domination. In other respects, however, the concept of compulsory heterosexuality can be applied to the ways in which both lesbianism and male homosexuality are socially and culturally marginalised. One of the most pervasive forms this takes is through the everyday assumption that everyone is heterosexual unless we know otherwise. Heterosexuals are rarely named and identified as such. While key aspects of their identity may be related to their heterosexuality (for example as a wife or husband), they rarely adopt the identity 'heterosexual' for themselves. Lesbian and gay sexualities, on the other hand, are routinely named and made visible as 'other'.

While heterosexuality entails a great deal more than sex, homosexuality is always and everywhere sexualised, and lesbians and gays reduced to their sexualities. For example, the rationale behind the exclusion of lesbians and gays from the British armed forces was that their sexuality was in some sense threatening to others, somehow ever present and predatory, threatening to undermine morale. Until the change in the law in 2000, lesbians and gays serving in the British military were, if discovered, immediately discharged, even if they had exemplary records in all other respects. The only thing that counted was their sexuality. Elsewhere, there are signs of greater tolerance, even a certain fashionability associated with sexual dissidence, with lesbian and gay characters and images increasingly visible in the media. Yet lesbians and gays are still represented as the exception to the heterosexual norm. It may be that heterosexuality is no longer compulsory in the sense it once was (at least in those countries where liberal legislation has been passed), but it remains institutionalised (Seidman 2009).

The binary divide between heterosexuality and homosexuality has been deconstructed by what has become known as 'queer theory', a perspective developed by lesbian and gay writers influenced by post-modern theory. The main aim of queer theory is to expose the hetero/homo binary divide as a cultural artifice rather than a natural division, in such a way as to reveal its arbitrariness and instability. Hence, queer theory challenges the idea that there is such a thing as a fixed homosexual identity. Instead, queerness is constituted by its marginal location in relation to the heterosexual norm (Halperin 1995; Seidman 1997). Conversely, the normativity of heterosexuality depends on the identification of lesbians and gays as 'outsiders'. However, in shoring itself up in relation to its 'outside', it admits a destabilising potential, the possibility that lesbian and gay sexualities might disrupt its claims to be the only legitimate form of sexuality (Fuss 1991). Thus queer theorists tend to focus on the points at which heterosexual normativity can be disrupted. However, while heterosexual normativity might be unstable in theory, in everyday life it is sustained through a range of oppressive and coercive practices.

Physical violence and verbal abuse are still common experiences among lesbians and gay men (Stonewall 2008); young gay men are routinely raped by heterosexual men in prisons. While homosexual behaviour has been decriminalised in Britain since 1967, it was initially legal only within limited circumstances – in private (that is, indoors with no other person present in the house) and between 'consenting adults', which meant those over 21. The age of consent was reduced to 18 in 1994 and then, in 2001, to 16, in line with that for heterosexual sex. Sexual consent is a highly gendered concept. Applied to gay sex only after decriminalisation, it arose in a heterosexual context and rested on a construction of sex as something that men do and women consent to (McIntosh 1993; Waites 2005). This is why there was no age of consent for lesbians and indeed why lesbianism was never legally prohibited. Since the definition of the sexual act was enshrined in law as the penetration of a vagina by a penis, premised on the assumption of an active male and a passive female, women could neither initiate sex with each other nor consent to it. This absurd illogicality, while it might have made lesbians safer from prosecution, effectively erased lesbian sexuality, stigmatising it as so 'unnatural' as to be beyond definition.

Where lesbianism did come into view, it provoked punitive responses. For example, as recently as the 1980s, lesbian mothers sometimes lost custody of their children solely on the grounds of their sexuality (Harne 1984). Lesbians in the UK are now recognised as legitimate parents and can, since 2009, legally gain access to assisted conception. Lesbian sex was included in age of consent legislation as a result of the 2001 Act – which might actually be a disadvantage.

Conclusion: sexual inequality and commodity culture

Hennessy (1998: 1) has drawn attention to the contradictions of a society in which claiming a non-heterosexual identity is, on the one hand, 'a potentially lethal transgression' and, on the other, a sign of radical 'cool'. She cites the case of a young gay man brutally beaten to death in the US in October 1998, a far-from-isolated case of bigotry in a nation where, according to the FBI, lesbians and gays are twice as likely to be physically assaulted as African-Americans. Yet at the same time, lesbians and gays are being marketed as icons of style in advertising, fashion and film. The continued stigmatisation of lesbian and gay sexualities persists in a society in which those same sexualities are increasingly visible, and apparently acceptable, in the cultural mainstream. This is not merely a case of bigotry and tolerance existing side by side, but tells us something about the limits of tolerance and the place of sexuality within the commodity culture of late modernity – a culture in which consumerism is increasingly associated with the maintenance of identity.

'Tolerance' is not, of course, the same thing as equality and, even where valorised as 'cool', the radical chic that lesbians and gays embody depends on their marginal location in relation to the straight world. They are still singled out as 'other', whether damned as the perverse other or celebrated as the exciting, exotic other, and they still serve to confirm the heterosexual norm in relation to which their 'otherness' is established. Lesbians and gays have made real gains in terms of rights, but their marginality creates a barrier to further progress. As Sinfield (1994: 189) puts it: 'The trick is to have us here but disgraceful.' Non-heterosexual lifestyles continue to be tolerated, even admired, as long as gays and lesbians know their place and do not attempt to challenge heterosexual privilege. The only capacity in which lesbians and gays are regarded as full citizens is as consumers, and this may have become a substitute for, and a deterrent to pursuing, more fundamental rights (Evans 1993; Hennessy 2000; Plummer 2003). The visibility of gays and lesbians within our society and culture is in part a result of their political struggles, but it is also a result of late capitalism's relentless search for innovative advertising images and new markets. Here it should be noted that the purchasing power of the 'pink pound' is concentrated in male hands, since lesbians share with all women a disadvantaged position in the labour market relative to men.

The commodification of gay sex is also part of a wider aestheticisation of daily life, evident in the preoccupation with 'lifestyle' in the commercial sense (Hennessy 1995, 2000). In this context, it is not only gay sexuality that has been commodified, but also heterosexual sex. 'Good sex' is itself increasingly associated with other indices of taste and style, such as wearing the right jeans or drinking the right coffee (see Jackson and Scott 1997). The concern with sexual proficiency sustains, and is sustained by, a huge market in books and magazines devoted to sexual self-improvement. Meanwhile, the sociological evidence we have cited suggests that the lived reality of everyday heterosexuality is a long way from the glossy advertising. Even the apparently endless 'consumer choice' offered by the new sex manuals entails little more than variations on the conventional sequence of heterosexual sex.

Of course, commercial sex itself is nothing new. Women's sexuality, in particular, has long been commodified through prostitution and pornography. Even when it is male sexuality on sale, it is marketed largely for male consumers. Many feminists have seen pornography and prostitution as instances of the sexual exploitation, enslavement and objectification of women (see for example Jeffreys 1997). Others, however, see 'sex work' as just another occupation. Here the issue is the economic exploitation of workers and the exacerbation of that exploitation by their social exclusion (Alexander 1988; Agustín 2007). More careful research on sex workers themselves has illustrated the importance of keeping the gendering of sexuality in view, while avoiding the characterisation of sex workers as inevitable victims (see for example O'Connell Davidson 1998, 2002).

We would argue that we need to keep both gender and sexual hierarchies in view when considering these issues. That it is largely men who provide the demand for this sort of sexual service should make us think critically about the construction of male sexual desires and ask why it is the prostitutes rather than their clients who are stigmatised. With commercial sex today being transacted within a society that increasingly commodifies, sex itself is something that should also cause us to consider whether the marketing of sex opens up new possibilities for self-realisation, or imposes new constraints on us. We also need to take into account the ways in which the sexual marketplace is becoming increasingly globalised, as exemplified by sex tourism, the trafficking of women and children, and the transmission of HIV and other sexually transmitted diseases across national boundaries.

The idea that we are all free consumers able to make whatever 'lifestyle choices' we choose is clearly sociological nonsense in a world still characterised by gross economic inequalities. In the sexual realm, access to choice in our sexual practices is limited by institutionalised heterosexuality and gender hierarchy. The concern with style and aesthetics also diverts attention away from the labour entailed in producing the objects we consume and where heterosexual sex is concerned this includes sexual services performed by women for men. The commodification of sexuality glamorises and mystifies sexuality, concealing the inequality, oppression and human suffering associated with the gender inequalities and heterosexual privilege underlying everyday sexual relations and practices.

Discussion Questions

1. Spend a day collecting examples from the media and conversations which illustrate the ways in which heterosexuality is privileged over other sexual preferences.

2. Look at the Sex Education Forum's website www.ncb.org.uk/sef/ and think about your own experience of sex education. Why do you think it is so difficult for adults to talk to young people about sexuality?

FURTHER READING

Chapters in Richardson, D. (ed.) *Theorising Heterosexuality: Telling it Straight* (Buckingham: Open University Press, 1996) address aspects of feminist debates on heterosexuality. A more recent collection on heterosexuality is Ingraham, C. *Thinking Straight: The Power, Promise and Paradox of Heterosexuality* (New York: Routledge, 2005). A useful historical account is provided by Weeks, J. *Sex, Politics and Society* (Harlow: Longman, 1989), which has an introductory chapter on theories of sexuality, and deals with social regulation up to and including the so-called 'permissive' era. Seidman, S. *Queer Theory/Sociology* (Oxford: Blackwell, 1996) includes some of the classic pioneering articles on the sociology of sexuality, as well as more recent work. A collection of reading covering feminist debates on sexuality since the 1960s can be found in Jackson, S. and Scott, S. (eds) *Feminism and Sexuality: A Reader* (Edinburgh: Edinburgh University Press, 1996). A more general sociological reader is *Sexualities and Society: A Reader* edited by Weeks, J., Waites, M. and Holland, J. (Cambridge: Polity, 2002). For a more recent discussion of theoretical debates see Jackson, S. and Scott, S. *Theorizing Sexuality* (Maidenhead: Open University Press, 2010); for a more introductory overview see Rahman, M. and Jackson, S. *Gender and Sexuality: Sociological Approaches* (Cambridge: Polity, 2010).

CHAPTER 8

Disability

MARK HYDE AND RORY SHAND

This chapter will provide you with a broad critical understanding of the following issues in disability as a source of social division:

- The medical model
- Social disadvantage and the choices made by individual disabled people
- The social model
- The historical development of social disadvantage among disabled people
- Disadvantage in employment: low income and poverty
- Inadequate community care provision
- Unsatisfactory education provision
- Ineffective employment policy
- Negative stereotypes of disabled people
- The internalisation of negative experiences by disabled people
- The distinction between organisations for and of disabled people
- The decline of grassroots disability activism
- Class analysis and disability

Although they represent almost seven million of the working age population – 6.7 million or 18 per cent (Labour Force Survey 2009) – disabled people are largely excluded from satisfactory employment opportunities, experience considerably higher levels of poverty and are often dependent on state social services and benefits. Without wishing to underestimate the dimensions of inequality reviewed in other parts of this book, which of course are also relevant to the concerns of this chapter, they do not account for the unique and intense forms of deprivation that disabled people experience. Mainstream sociological approaches to the analysis of social divisions provide a necessary but insufficient basis for understanding disability. Disabled people are disadvantaged because they belong to a social group that is the object of pervasive, institutionalised discrimination. Thus, disability engenders distinct forms of social inequality which, like gender, age and social class, should be regarded as an organising principle of social inequality in its own right. Disabled people are socially divided from the rest of society.

Disability in contemporary society needs to be understood as a series of social restrictions that prevent disabled people from taking part in mainstream taken-for-granted activities, leading to profound social disadvantage. Although there is a substantial body of work on the significance of disability in contemporary society, it has largely developed outside mainstream sociology, in the specialist field of disability studies. It follows that the starting point for our analysis is to look at the concepts and perspectives used to (mis)understand disability, not least the recent ideas and arguments developed in official studies of disability and the pioneering work of disabled writers (Union of Physically Impaired Against Segregation 1976; Barnes 1990; Oliver 1990, 2004).

Competing definitions

Debates about the meaning of disability in the social science literature typically centre on two definitions. 'Official' or 'medical' definitions tend to focus on the functional limitations of people with impairments, whereas the disabled people's movement has defined disability as the social restrictions faced by disabled people in their daily lives. Official and medical definitions of disability are usefully summarised by the International Classification of Impairment, Disability and Handicap (ICIDH), developed for the World Health Organization in 1981 (see Berthoud et al. 1993). The ICIDH distinguishes four concepts and links them in a causal sequence: a complaint such as a spinal injury may lead to an impairment where a person is unable to control his or her legs, which may lead to a disability such as the inability to walk, resulting in a handicap where the individual is unable to take part in normal day-to-day activities. This approach is often referred to as the 'medical model' because of its primary focus on impairment and functional limitation. Ultimately, it treats disability as a property of individuals who, because they are physically or mentally incompetent, are unable to take advantage of the opportunities enjoyed by those without impairments. The Disability Discrimination Act 1985 (DDA) classifications follow this medical approach.

The influence of the individualistic medical model (see also Chapter 14) on official policy and government-sponsored research into disability is demonstrated by the nature of the questions in Table 8.1, taken from one of a series of Office of Population Censuses and Surveys (OPCS) surveys of disabled people in the UK (see Martin et al. 1988). The questions clearly suggest that the inability of the individual to take part in social activities can be explained in terms of an underlying impairment. Instead of promoting social rights and

Table 8.1 Selected questions from the 1985 OPCS survey of disabled adults

1. Can you tell me what is wrong with you?
2. What complaint causes your difficulty in holding, gripping or turning things?
3. Does your health problem/disability mean that you need to live with relatives or someone else who can help look after you?
4. Does your health problem/disability make it difficult for you to travel by bus?
5. Does your health problem/disability affect your work in any way at present?

Source: Adapted from Oliver (1990).

opportunities, the welfare state has attempted to compensate disabled people for the limitations allegedly imposed by their impairments, either by segregating them in specialist institutions or by exposing them to rehabilitation programmes.

In spite of its influence, the medical model has been criticised on a number of grounds. First, it takes the notion of 'normality' for granted and therefore as fixed, when what is and is not normal is socially and culturally relative. For example, the once widespread view of heterosexuality as the norm, backed by the law and sanctioned in mainstream arts, literature and especially popular culture (Chapter 7), is arguably now beginning to give way to a greater acceptance of diverse and legitimate sexual preferences. Second, the medical model fails to recognise the social constraints that prevent social participation and therefore offers only a partial explanation of social disadvantage. For example, while a focus on impairment may highlight some of the difficulties experienced by disabled people at work, it ignores discriminatory barriers, such as prejudice among employers, that impede the progress of disabled people in the labour market. Third, and following on from this, the medical model endorses policies that at best are likely to be ineffective in promoting social participation and at worst reinforce disadvantage and social exclusion. Employment policy has focused on individual rehabilitation, when an emphasis on the removal of discriminatory barriers might have been more successful (see Hyde 1996 for a fuller discussion).

Recognising these inadequacies, academics associated with the disabled people's movement have proposed a simpler classification scheme, which distinguishes two concepts, impairment and disability:

> We define impairment as lacking all or part of a limb, or having a defective limb, organ or mechanism of the body; and disability as the disadvantage or restriction of activity caused by a contemporary social organisation which takes no or little account of people with physical impairments and thus excludes them from participation in the mainstream of social activities. (Union of Physically Impaired Against Segregation 1976: 14)

Table 8.2 Survey questions informed by the social model

1. Can you tell me what is wrong with society?
2. What defects in the design of everyday equipment like jars, bottles and tins causes you difficulty in holding, gripping or turning them?
3. Are community services so poor that you need to rely on relatives or someone else to provide you with the right level of personal assistance?
4. Do poorly designed buses make it difficult for someone with your health problem/disability to use them?
5. Do you have problems at work because of the physical environment or the attitudes of others?

Source: Adapted from Oliver (1990).

Frequently referred to as the 'social model', this approach to defining disability also makes causal assumptions about the factors underlying social disadvantage. It argues that people with impairments are excluded by a social environment that is inaccessible and discriminatory. For example, disabled people are often prevented from travelling to work, not by their inability to use the buses, but because public transport has been designed for the exclusive use of people without impairments. If the social model of defining disability had been used to frame the OPCS disability survey questions, they could have been reformulated to resemble those in Table 8.2. Clearly, these questions suggest that inability to take part in social activities can be explained primarily, if not exclusively, in terms of a discriminatory and inaccessible social environment.

Although the social model provides a definition that many disabled people may prefer, it is weakened by its apparent lack of reference to the role of impairment in restricting social participation. It is possible to imagine circumstances in which impairment is a considerable influence on a person's inability to perform social activities. For example people with profoundly debilitating mental impairments may find it difficult to take part in social activities, irrespective of how these activities are defined and organised. Although the limiting effects of impairment are not always this clear-cut, they should not be dismissed lightly.

The two definitions reviewed here provide radically different interpretations of disability, each of which is endorsed by particular social constituencies. The view of disability as the inability of the individual to perform normal social activities is not only widely held by the public but has been the main influence on government-sponsored disability research and policy. In contrast, the definition of disability as social restriction is endorsed by the disabled people's movement, by its nature a much smaller and less influential minority group. Both definitions have distinct implications for the nature of social policies for disabled people.

Individualism

Any account of social inequalities would be incomplete if it did not consider the possibility that those who are socially disadvantaged are, by their own actions, responsible for their circumstances. Economic liberals, in particular, have advanced explanations of social disadvantage that focus on causation at the level of the 'individual'. This theme has two variations: one focusing on labour market inequalities, the second on welfare dependency.

Economic liberals reject the claim that occupational success reflects unfair social advantages accruing to privileged socio-economic groups, insisting that the market provides the foundation for a meritocracy in which economic opportunities are open to all. Although middle-class children have a higher statistical probability of occupational success as adults (Chapter 2), Saunders (2000) argues that this largely reflects an unequal distribution of abilities, particularly 'intelligence' but also motivation. However, occupational selection is sufficiently fluid to favour those from working-class backgrounds with demonstrable abilities, ensuring that, overall, individuals arrive at social class destinations to which they are entitled, by merit, irrespective of where they start. But if low cognitive ability leads to occupational failure, it also increases the probability of long-term, work-limiting health problems, or so we are told. Those who perform poorly on ability tests have a significantly higher probability of unemployment due to physical disability, prompting Herrnstein and Murray (1994b: 162) to speculate that 'smarter workers are typically more productive workers, and we can presume that some portion of what makes a worker productive is that he avoids needless accidents'. The authors acknowledge, however, that health problems may be cited as an 'excuse' for worklessness by a large number of non-disabled people who are merely unemployed, a notion that fits comfortably with the idea of 'welfare dependency'.

For economic liberals, welfare dependency results from a distinctive feature of contemporary society, the widespread availability of social security benefits. A particularly influential variant of this argument is reflected in the work of Charles Murray on the underclass. He argues that a 'permissive' statutory commitment to welfare has progressively removed the structure of 'natural' incentives which encourage individual responsibility, in particular, the fear of destitution (Murray 1990, 1994a, 1994b). The availability and generosity of social security benefits have encouraged voluntary unemployment, which sets a bad example for young people, who are thus socialised into a culture of dependence. Increasingly, society is characterised by polarisation between a majority of 'motivated' households, whose members are in employment, and an underclass, an expanding segment of society which is geographically isolated, workless and morally impoverished.

Because they have remarkably high levels of economic inactivity, disabled people of working age are identified as being an integral part of this under-class. Economic liberals distinguish between a negligible number of those who are in receipt of disability benefits who are 'genuinely' disabled – the 'deserving poor' – and the vast majority who are capable of working and, in effect, are fraudulently claiming benefits – the 'undeserving poor' (Marsland 1996). The problem of moral hazard has been particularly evident in the disability benefit system, where the possibility of collusion between medical practitioners and their patients has made it easier to qualify for benefits. In the 1980s and 1990s, there was a proliferation of new official disability categories, expanding the size of the population that was potentially eligible for benefits. As we shall discuss later, until the changes imposed by the ConDem Coalition Government, most disability benefits were provided on a long-term basis without sufficient assessments of work capacity. In short:

> The uptake of invalidity benefit and the prevalence of sickness absence from work is a function of the accessibility and generosity of benefits, entirely regardless of the objective condition of the population. (Marsland 1996: 124)

Welfare dependency, then, reflects the failure of the state to maintain economic conditions that promote individual responsibility.

This understanding of the causation of social disadvantage and its attendant welfare reform agenda were a clear influence on Conservative government social policies during the 1980s and early 1990s. In this view, because the overwhelming majority of those of working age who are in receipt of social security benefits, including disabled people, belong to the undeserving poor, they should be forced into self-reliance through rigorously applied means and ability tests. For this group, the route out of welfare dependency is, quite simply, the denial of social assistance (Murray 1990, 1996; Marsland 1996). For the deserving poor – those who are temporarily incapable of self-help – eligibility for social assistance should be based on needs rather than rights in order to ensure that provision goes only to those who are genuinely unable to support themselves, and it should be temporary (Marsland 1996). Time limits on benefit eligibility encourage the expectation of independence whilst obligations of the kind inherent in workfare schemes reinforce the principle that economic reward should be attached to personal effort. Ultimately, this exclusive focus on the promotion of self-reliance can be traced back to the 1834 Poor Law, which, through the incarceration of disabled people in the workhouse, sought to deter pauperism. Harsh as this may seem, however, economic liberals remind us that its modern equivalent, an efficiently administered programme of social assistance, is essential to the abolition of welfare dependency.

While the argument that perverse incentives in the social security benefit system discourage independence may have a degree of validity (Deacon
2002), the focus on causation at the level of the individual entirely ignores the
social barriers that prevent disabled people from playing a full role in society.
It is to these barriers that we now turn.

The social construction of disability

Although impairment, individual motivation and the social environment all
play a role in preventing disabled people from participating in mainstream
social activities, the last must have primary importance in any sociological explanation of social disadvantage. In western societies, from Greek civilisation
to the present day, disabled people have been socially marginalised, discriminated against and oppressed. However, social disadvantage among disabled
people takes a distinct form in western capitalist societies, involving exclusion
from economic activity and dependence on statutory social services.

In an influential contribution, Oliver (1990) relates the experiences of disabled people in contemporary society to the distinctiveness of capitalist economic relations. Before the Industrial Revolution, many disabled people were
able to take part in economic activities that were largely based in scattered
rural communities involving agriculture and small-scale industry. The development of industrial economic organisation during the eighteenth century
had profound implications for disabled people:

> The speed of factory work, the enforced discipline, the time-keeping and
> production norms – all these were a highly unfavourable change from the
> slower, more self-determined and flexible methods of work into which many
> handicapped people had been integrated. (Ryan and Thomas 1980: 101)

The subsequent development of heavy industry based on coal, iron and ship-
ping in the nineteenth century reinforced the exclusion of disabled people
from employment. Moreover, the worth of individuals came to be assessed
according to their economic value, particularly the extent and nature of their
participation in paid employment. Thus the prevailing ideology of industrial
capitalism – individualism – ensured that those among the working class who
were not in employment were assigned an inferior social status.

This economic marginality was reinforced by the distinct form of many
state welfare interventions during the nineteenth century. With the rise of capitalism, the 'total institution' was adopted as the main official response to the
needs of the non-working poor. At first, people with impairments were treated
less harshly than able-bodied paupers but, in practice, official concern about

work incentives led to many being incarcerated in the workhouse. In distinguishing between able-bodied paupers and the long-term sick, the 1834 Poor Law represented a significant milestone in the treatment of disabled people. From the early 1800s onwards, disabled people were increasingly admitted to long-stay hospitals and asylums, indicating a shift in official responsibility away from the Poor Law authorities to the expanding medical profession (Abbott and Sapsford 1988). Medical practitioners assumed growing responsibility for the assessment, treatment and care of people with impairments – a legacy that continues to this day.

Institutionalisation continued to be the main official response to the needs of people with impairments up to the 1930s. Since then, there has been a significant shift in the location of care back to the community, but disabled people continue to experience isolation, social disadvantage and dependence. Oliver describes how these problems are constructed around three organising principles. First, disabled people continue to be excluded from employment, resulting in higher levels of deprivation and social exclusion:

> Work is central to industrial societies not simply because it produces the goods to sustain life but also because it creates particular forms of social relations. Thus anyone unable to work for whatever reason is likely to experience difficulties both in acquiring the necessities to sustain life physically, and also in establishing a set of satisfactory social relationships. (Oliver 1990: 85)

Second, disabled people are largely excluded from the formal political process, meaning that they are unable to take part in public debates about the development of rights, provisions and services to meet their needs. Policy for disabled people is framed by able-bodied public servants who have a poor understanding of the needs and aspirations of disabled people, resulting in the provision of inappropriate services. Third, services for disabled people are largely delivered by able-bodied professionals who often fail to take account of the felt needs and preferences of those who use them. Taken together, these experiences result in profound levels of social disadvantage among disabled people in Britain today.

Experiencing disability: economic disadvantage

The most striking levels of social disadvantage are experienced by disabled people of working age. Work is central to social identity, personal welfare and life chances in contemporary society (see Chapter 12), but many disabled people are excluded from satisfactory employment opportunities due to a combination of their low qualification levels, difficulties with transport, problems of working hours and conditions, and direct discrimination. Among those not disabled, nearly 80 per cent are in paid employment, compared to 'typically less than 50 per cent' among the disabled (Jones 2010: 32). Fifty-six per cent of disabled people experience restrictions on the type or amount of work they can do, compared with 26 per cent of the non-disabled (Life Opportunities Survey 2010).

This can be seen in the official unemployment counts: prior to the international credit crisis in the late 2000s, disabled people in the UK had an official unemployment rate of 4.2 per cent, compared to 3.7 per cent for non-disabled people (Office for National Statistics 2003e). By 2011, this had risen to 7.3 and 6.7 per cent (Office for National Statistics 2012a). During times of very high unemployment, the difference is even greater: under the Conservative governments of 1979–97, disabled people had unemployment rates around 20 per cent compared with 7.5 per cent for non-disabled people (Hyde 2000).

However, the official figures underestimate the full scale of the problem because they exclude those who have been classified as 'economically inactive', that is, not in paid employment nor actively seeking it. Fifty-one per cent of disabled people are economically inactive compared to only 16 per cent of non-disabled people (Office for National Statistics 2012a). An earlier study based on Labour Force Survey data also provides an estimate of the proportion of those who are economically inactive who would nonetheless like to work; around 14 per cent for disabled people and 3 per cent for non-disabled people (Poverty Site 2011). For convenience, this group can be referred to as the 'hidden unemployed'. If we add this last category to the officially unemployed, we have over 21 per cent of the disabled but less than 10 per cent of those not disabled in hidden unemployment. In other words, disabled people were more than twice as likely to be unemployed, rather than the smaller difference suggested by the official unemployment figure.

A second area of labour market disadvantage is suggested by the number of hours worked by disabled people in paid employment. Again, it is widely acknowledged that part-time work is not as highly regarded or rewarded as full-time work. Part-time workers tend to be concentrated in low-status occupations, they have lower hourly earnings, fewer employment rights and little job security. On average, disabled workers are more likely to be found in part-time jobs; 28 per cent of disabled workers are in part-time work compared to only 22 per cent of non-disabled workers (Poverty Site 2011). The European Community Household Panel survey (Eurostat 2001; Zaidi and Burchardt 2003) also suggests that, as well as their higher chances of being unemployed, disabled workers are more likely to be in part-time employment, and more likely to be employed in low-status occupations in all member states of the EU.

These inequalities of employment consist both of direct effects – the social exclusion from normally accepted activities like working – and indirect effects like lower incomes even when the disabled are able to work. Evidence on the income of disabled people from employment is not as extensive as the areas that have been looked at so far, but it suggests that disabled workers are particularly disadvantaged in terms of their earnings. In 2010, the National Equality Panel study found that men who

> report a work-limited disability and are DDA-disabled have a median hourly wage 20 per cent lower than the median for non-disabled men; for women, the median is 12 per cent lower … median net individual income for men who are disabled according to both DDA and work-limiting definitions is £157, half the median for non-disabled men (£316). [For women] the corresponding figures are £131 and £198. (Hills et al. 2010: 237, 240)

In view of these figures, it is hardly surprising that disabled people have a higher risk of poverty. Berthoud et al. (1993) estimated that 45 per cent of disabled adults were living in poverty, while only 13 per cent could be classified as 'prosperous'. The poverty standard used was the long-term rate of means-tested social assistance, combined with an estimate of the additional costs that are often incurred by disabled people. Prosperity was defined as an income that was at least 200 per cent of this standard. They also showed that the chances of finding employment for disabled workers aged 45 and over have been considerably less than for younger disabled workers. Reflecting the 'ageist' values of wider society (AgeUK 2011), disabled workers tend to experience higher levels of labour market disadvantage when they reach 'middle age'. In other words, the social division of age (Chapter 5) interacts with disability in the employment field. 'Disability' and 'age' foster significant disadvantage in employment, resulting in higher levels of poverty.

However, for older people, economic disadvantage is less significant among disabled pensioners who, as a group, are less likely than non-pensioners to be living on incomes that are below the state benefit poverty threshold. The overall impact of chronological age on the welfare of disabled people is therefore ambivalent. Labour market disadvantage has implications not just for the welfare of disabled people of working age but also for disabled people in retirement. Because their employment circumstances are unfavourable, disabled people are in a weaker position to accumulate savings and adequate pension entitlements. Their economic and social well-being is thus reduced throughout the life-course.

The effects of disability are not limited solely to those who are disabled: there are consequences for those who are not themselves disabled but who care for disabled people. Recent surveys of disability and social inequality demonstrate major impacts of disadvantage in occupation and levels of salary for these carers. Carers are less likely to be in paid work than the general population: only 3 million of the 4.5 million carers of working age are in paid work, with one in five carers giving up work in order to care; many retire early for the same reason. Carers are more likely to be in low-paid and low-status professions; almost 45 per cent of men and 55 per cent of women who are in paid work but caring for more than 20 hours per week are in routine occupations (Hills et al. 2010: 237).

Public debate about the number of disabled people (and their carers) and their need for financial support from the welfare state took an abrupt turn when the Coalition Government introduced Conservative and Liberal Democrat policies to reduce the cost to the state. Adopting the view that many unemployed people during the previous governments had been incorrectly re-classified as disabled, new regulations were introduced to assess whether disabled people were in fact 'fit for work'. Despite protests that the Work Capability Assessment set the standards for disability too high (Harrington 2010), 71 per cent of those tested were treated as ineligible for the new disability benefit (BBC 2012). Instead, they were placed on the Job Seekers programme or sent to a Work Related Activity Group where they had to prepare for work under threat of sanctions for non-compliance. The full effects of this are as yet under-researched (Houston and Lindsay 2010; Patrick 2011), but commentators have drawn attention to the way this replaces 'entitlement' to disability benefits with 'conditionality'. More disadvantaged people are re-defined as the 'undeserving poor' and, among the disabled, some are treated as less deserving than others (Barnes and Smith 2010; Grover and Piggot 2010).

Experiencing disability: discriminatory social barriers

Social disadvantage among disabled people in modern industrial society reflects their experiences of discriminatory social barriers. This section explores the nature of some of these barriers, drawing on the findings of a number of studies of disabled people in the UK (Barnes 1990; Oliver and Barnes 1998; Barnes et al. 1999). Our analysis focuses on three areas of social policy: community care, education and employment practices.

While they represent a vast improvement on the institutional provision of previous decades, current arrangements for delivering community care are often unsatisfactory. Although ostensibly designed to move away from a reliance on specialist institutions, institutional care continues to be a significant component of state support for disabled people. A large proportion of health and local authority spending on community care is directed towards residential and hospital-based services and many disabled people are confined to segregated residential homes.

The response of health and local authorities to the needs of disabled people who are living in the community at large is also widely regarded as being unsatisfactory (Chapter 14). For example, although local authorities were required by the 1986 Disabled Persons Act to provide disabled people with information that is relevant to their needs, few do so. According to OPCS surveys, many disabled people fail to receive the technical aids and equipment that they need; this limits their participation in mainstream social and economic activities and reinforces their dependence on others. Where assistance from local authorities is provided, it is largely directed towards informal carers rather than disabled people. Because they fail to receive the support they require to live independently, 'disabled people are denied the right to organise their daily lives in the same way as the rest of the population' (Barnes 1990: 144).

It is widely acknowledged that there is a strong association between educational attainment and employment outcomes (see Chapter 3), but disabled people are particularly disadvantaged in the education system. In principle, education policy in the UK has endorsed 'integrated' provision but, in practice, a large number of children and young people with impairments continue to be educated in segregated special schools. If the perpetuation of special schools is the most obvious form of discrimination in the education system, children with impairments are also disadvantaged in mainstream schools. Many receive their education in separate special educational needs (SEN) classes, while others are placed in classes with younger non-disabled children, even though their impairments may be physical. The low priority assigned to SEN within mainstream schools often leads to inadequate provision for children and young people with impairments. (Few teachers are trained to work with students with special needs.) Not surprisingly, this results in lower levels of educational attainment. This is a trend which continues to have ramifications into adult life, with lower levels of educational attainment for adults: 'nearly one-third of those of working age who are classified as disabled both in terms of the Disability Discrimination Act and through reporting a work limiting condition have no qualifications at all, compared to 12 per cent of those who are not disabled' (Hills et al. 2010: 239).

Disabled people also experience considerable discrimination in tertiary education. Increasingly, young people with impairments are taking up places in further education, but the nature of the opportunities provided reflects those that are available in compulsory education and is therefore subject to the same criticisms. Disabled students are frequently segregated in special programmes in which they are invited to study courses in 'life skills' rather than academic or vocational areas. This further education experience does little to compensate for the lower levels of educational attainment from secondary education. Not surprisingly, very few disabled people become qualified for higher education. Because the education system is failing to enable disabled people to acquire the qualifications and credentials required for access to satisfactory employment, it is directly contributing to subsequent economic disadvantage among the disabled when they go on to seek paid employment (Payne 2006).

However, the primary responsibility for the unsatisfactory employment circumstances of disabled people lies with employers. Disabled applicants for jobs are six times more likely to be refused an interview than non-disabled applicants, even when they have suitable skills and qualifications. Employers are reluctant to adapt premises and equipment to the needs of disabled workers. Statutory employment policy and provision, despite any intention to the contrary, have in fact also played an important role in reinforcing labour market disadvantage among disabled people. The 1944 Disabled Persons (Employment) Act introduced the quota scheme which required employers to hire a 3 per cent quota of disabled workers. However, there were only ten prosecutions over a 50-year period for failing to comply, even though a majority of employers were 'under quota'. In 1996, the quota scheme was replaced by the employment provisions of the Disability Discrimination Act, providing disabled people with a right not to be discriminated against, but this legislation is widely regarded as being inadequate. The Equalities Act of 2010 subsequently sought to draw together several different strands of previously disparate anti-discrimination legislation.

In practice, the government continues to rely on a policy of voluntary compliance and persuasion, even though a considerable volume of research has shown that a large majority of employers are prejudiced against, and in some cases actually hostile to, disabled people. The failure of the voluntary approach has resulted in many disabled people taking jobs in segregated sheltered workshops or subsidised placements in mainstream industry. For these reasons, employment policy has failed to provide an adequate response to the vocational needs of disabled people.

Given what is happening in other social institutions, perhaps it is not surprising that employment policy has been such a failure. Research has shown that discriminatory practices also pervade the political process, social security, transport systems, the mass media and the leisure industry (Oliver and Barnes 1998; Barnes et al. 1999). Many disabled people are therefore excluded from taking part in mainstream social activities. In a variety of ways, disabled people experience pervasive discrimination resulting in profound social disadvantage.

Structure, identity and action

If the experience of disadvantage and discrimination is a certainty for many disabled people, their responses to these problems are variable. A number of sociological studies of social divisions in contemporary society have posited a causal relationship between structure, identity and action (for example Crompton 1998). The assumption is that social conditions such as structured economic inequalities are strongly associated with individual psychology and behaviour and group identity (see Chapter 1). In the context of disability, 'structure' can be defined in terms of the discrimination and social disadvantage reported in the previous section; 'identity' is defined as the psychological responses of disabled people to these experiences, particularly the persona they adopt in relation to the social world; 'action' refers to their behavioural response to social marginality and, in particular, to patterns of acquiescence and resistance.

In addition to the forms of discrimination and social disadvantage already discussed in this chapter, disabled people are frequently the object of negative stereotypes in popular media such as books, movies, theatre, magazines and national and local newspapers. In a review of research on popular disability imagery, Reiser (1995) identifies a number of negative stereotypes that are perpetuated by the mass media. One powerful image is that disabled people are pitiable and pathetic. This stereotype is particularly evident in the publicity campaigns of the disability charities which aim to maximise income from public donations.

An alternative common stereotype is that disabled people are sinister and evil. For example, people with mental health problems are often presented as frightening and dangerous when in reality they are likely to be confused and withdrawn. A third stereotype is that disabled people are incapable of taking part in everyday life. This is mainly perpetuated by the absence of images of disabled people as members of the workforce, schools and families. Other negative media stereotypes about disabled people are that they are self-pitying and non-sexual. In the absence of positive images, it is hardly surprising that the general public regards disabled people in a negative light. The preponderance of these images perpetuates and compounds economic and social disadvantage.

Oliver and Barnes (1998) identify four mechanisms through which disabled people internalise these negative experiences and images. The first concerns those who are born with impairments and grow up as members of communities in which there are few disabled people to provide positive role models. Because they experience a range of discriminatory barriers from day one, children in this situation are socialised into an early acceptance of an inferior social status. We can contrast this position of early acceptance with the experiences of those with congenital impairments who are shielded from the wider community until they reach adolescence. Children in this category may not be fully aware of the existence of discriminatory barriers until they attempt to access mainstream social activities such as leisure and work. The acquisition of a negative personal identity for this group tends to occur during their late teenage years and early twenties.

A third mechanism of internalisation of negative experience concerns those who are forced to reconsider their personal identity as a result of acquiring an impairment. The sudden realisation that disability implies discrimination and exclusion often leads to negative feelings of hopelessness and despair. Oliver and Barnes' fourth mechanism relates the experiences of those who refuse to accept their impairment and attempt to pass themselves off as 'normal'. This is easier for those with a hidden disability such as diabetes, but still requires diligence at managing information and social interaction. For those with an obvious impairment, denial is perpetually self-defeating. Many disabled people respond to their circumstances by adopting a negative self-image and, ultimately, a passive acceptance of discrimination and social marginality.

This suggests that the link between structure, identity and action is one-directional for a majority of disabled people. In spite of this, a growing number of disabled people have challenged conventional negative stereotyping, a process that has developed in the context of political self-organisation. The disabled people's movement provides a collective framework in which a minority of disabled people have been able to re-evaluate their negative experiences in the light of the social model, developing what might be described as a 'positive disabled identity'.

The disabled people's movement can best be described by distinguishing between organisations *for* and organisations *of* disabled people. Organisations for disabled people are concerned with disability issues but are largely staffed by able-bodied people working in partnership with national and local government agencies. Examples of such organisations include SCOPE, the Royal National Institute for the Blind (RNIB) and the Royal Association for Disability and Rehabilitation (RADAR). Organisations for disabled people have been criticised for adopting conventional official and medical approaches to the needs of disabled people. In contrast, organisations of disabled people are run exclusively by and on behalf of people with impairments and are informed by the social model.

Oliver (1990) develops a threefold typology of these organisations. 'Consumerist/self-help' organisations are those that provide services to meet the self-defined needs of members. A good example is Centres for Independent Living, which aims to provide appropriate support for disabled people living in the community. 'Populist/activist' organisations typically focus on consciousness-raising and political action. During the 1970s, the Union of Physically Impaired Against Segregation was established to promote political organisation among disabled people living in residential institutions. More recently, the Direct Action Network has achieved national publicity through its involvement in a campaign of civil disobedience. 'Umbrella/coordinating' organisations are those with a membership of disabled people's groups. In 1981, the British Council of Organisations of Disabled People was established to provide a national focus for the activities of its constituent organisations. Now the British Council of Disabled People, this organisation has been at the forefront of the campaign against discrimination in the UK, and is itself a member of another umbrella organisation, Disabled People's International. In addition to the three types of organisation, 'disability arts' has emerged as a form of cultural self-expression for disabled people.

The existence of these collective political and cultural activities may have a considerable impact on the psychological responses of disabled people to discrimination. The active propagation of the social model provides an alternative framework through which they are able to reinterpret their negative experiences, one that focuses on discriminatory barriers rather than personal inadequacies. The disabled people's movement also provides a focus for disabled people to become actively involved in challenging dominant negative stereotyping and discriminatory practices, an experience that can be profoundly empowering:

> Direct action is in your face. Disabled people are supposed to be invisible; they are not supposed to go out and be seen. Direct action has changed this. We are noticed! (Liz Carr, disabled activist, cited in Varo-Watson 1998: 13)

Significantly, collective organisation among disabled people can have a broader positive impact on society, as suggested by shifts towards minority programming on British television. Arguably, the Disability Discrimination Act 1995 was introduced in response to the growing public profile of discrimination, engendered by the activities of the disabled people's movement. If collective self-organisation provides an ideological and experiential framework within which disabled people develop a positive identity, it also has the potential to transform official responses to their needs, suggesting a multidirectional link between structure, identity and action.

Although the achievements of the disabled people's movement appear to be significant, it has recently been criticised by dissenting voices from within its ranks. It has been suggested, for example, that the movement is not representative of disabled people as a whole. A study by Barnes et al. (1999) observes that people with physical and sensory impairments are disproportionately involved in disability politics. While this seems to sit comfortably with

Table 8.3 Type of reported functional problem by gender, percentage

Reported functional problem	Men	Women	All
Lifting and carrying	50	68	60
Mobility	52	50	51
Physical coordination	51	47	48
Learning and understanding	40	28	33
Seeing and hearing	26	17	21
Manual dexterity	21	19	20
Continence	15	13	14
Perceptions of risk	7	5	6
Unweighted base	500	763	1263

Note: columns total more than 100 per cent as people could report having more than one functional problem. Base is all people covered by the Disability Discrimination Act.

Source: Whitfield (1997), Table 2.5.

popular stereotypes of disabled people, it may exclude a substantial number of people such as those with 'intellectual' impairments, in addition to those not registered as disabled but who have extensive literacy deficiencies (Payne 2006). Table 8.3 shows that 33 per cent of those who are defined as disabled by the Disability Discrimination Act have learning and understanding-related impairments. Similarly, Shakespeare et al. (1996) argue that disabled women, gays and lesbians are not adequately represented at an executive level within the disabled people's movement. This suggests that the 'positive disabled identity' associated with collective political action is a privilege that is enjoyed disproportionately by heterosexual disabled men with physical and sensory impairments.

Taking a different approach, Finkelstein (1996), a leading UK disability activist, identifies two recent developments which he believes have reduced the effectiveness of the disabled people's movement. First, he notes that there has been a shift away from 'grassroots' activity to parliamentary lobbying, resulting in fewer disabled people being actively involved in disability politics. Second, and perhaps more contentiously, he argues that the disabled people's movement has been 'hijacked' by disabled academics who have replaced the 'active' vision of disability rights as political action with the 'passive abstraction' of intellectual enquiry. For these reasons, Finkelstein believes the disabled people's movement has 'run out of steam'.

Disability and social divisions

These accounts of contemporary disability incidentally show how much of the source material has been only marginally 'sociological'. The basic framework for the analysis has, however, been sociological. The core idea has been a society characterised by social divisions, suggesting that social exclusion may have a variety of causes that need to be seen in terms of social processes shared with other social divisions. Nonetheless, it remains true that, while in the late 1990s sociology began to provide some welcome descriptions of the social processes of disablement, it largely failed to develop explicit and systematic theories to account for the unique and particularly intense deprivation experiences among disabled people.

Payne et al. (1996) provide a useful summary of three mainstream sociological approaches to understanding the relationship between social divisions and deprivation. Drawing on the work of Max Weber, one approach sees deprivation as resulting from people's (in)capacity to sell their labour to employers. A person's life chances, including their income, health and housing, are strongly associated with their type of employment, manifested in social divisions based on occupational status or class (see Chapter 2). In this view, deprivation is a consequence of sharply constrained ability to sell one's labour in a socially defined market, leading to unemployment or low occupational status. This approach has particular relevance for the circumstances of disabled people who, as reported above, experience considerable difficulties in selling their labour to employers. It identifies the interaction in the labour market between the sellers (both able and disabled) and the buyers (employers). However, it does not entirely explain the processes that produce the disproportionate representation of disabled people among the ranks of the semi-skilled and the unemployed, suggesting the need for a more specific and clearly defined focus on disability.

Perhaps a more fruitful approach within the Weberian sociological tradition is provided by 'consumption sector' theory, which argues that social divisions need to be understood in terms of differential access to public and private welfare. Encouraged by privatisation policies during the 1980s and 1990s, growing numbers of households opted out of the welfare state, leaving behind a minority who are entirely dependent on public sector provision, providing the basis for a new social division based on consumption. However, although disabled people are disproportionately dependent on the state, their consumption experiences are not identical to those of other groups of the poor. As reported previously, many disabled people are excluded from areas of state welfare provision such as local authority housing and mainstream education and instead are segregated in special disability programmes. While it seems to articulate the exclusion of disabled people from private welfare, consumption sector theory fails to specify their unique experiences of state welfare.

Post-Marxist formulations of the 'non-working poor' seem to be particularly relevant to understanding the experiences of disabled people in industrial society. For Wright (1993), the key to understanding this 'underclass' lies in the exclusion of the poor from satisfactory education and training, leading to long-term unemployment. Paradoxically, although the non-working poor are largely surplus to the requirements of the industrial system, they are sometimes deployed as a 'reserve army' to accommodate fluctuations in the demand for labour.

Using this approach, Hyde (1996, 1998) describes how disabled people were actively encouraged to take up paid employment during the Second World War to substitute for able-bodied men who had been conscripted into the armed forces. After the war, they were promptly expelled from the labour market and segregated into special employment programmes. During the 1980s, out-of-work disability benefits were expanded, and the disabled were reclassified as being entitled to non-work-related benefits as part of the Conservative government's massaging of the official unemployment count. More recently, disabled people of working age have, once again, been encouraged to enter the labour market, 'assisted' in no small measure by the welfare reforms of the New Labour government (see Hyde et al. 1999 for a fuller discussion) and more energetically since 2010 by the ConDem Coalition. While a focus on labour market regulation seems to account for changes in employment policy for disabled people, it fails to explain fully the disproportionate representation of the disabled among the ranks of the non-working poor, which, as we have seen, has much more to it than state policies alone.

The three approaches reviewed so far have little to say about the particular experiences of disabled women, even though they often have higher levels of social disadvantage than disabled men. For example, the LFS study reported earlier shows that the higher incidence of low-paid, low-status and part-time work among disabled women mirrors similar trends among non-disabled women, highlighting the importance of underlying gender inequalities. While feminist theories have been instrumental in promoting a growing profile for gender divisions in sociology (Chapter 3), they have neglected deprivation experiences that are specific to disabled women. For example, the failure of physically disabled women to conform to popular cultural body images leads many of them to be stereotyped as unattractive and non-sexual. Thus, in addition to the discrimination and disadvantage they experience because of their gender, disabled women are often prevented from taking up traditional female roles such as those of wife and mother.

It has also been argued that 'ethnicity' is a powerful source of social division among disabled people, although there is much less published empirical evidence on this. For Vernon (1998), black disabled people experience the 'double disadvantage' of racial discrimination (Chapter 4) and discrimination on the grounds of disability. When combined, both result in qualitatively distinct and intense forms of social disadvantage.

The interplay that we have seen between disability and other social divisions – ethnicity, gender, age and occupational class – means that there is a general framework of analysis with which to explore the isolation of disabled people. However, contemporary sociology on its own can provide a necessary, but as yet insufficient, basis for understanding disability in present-day society. Disabled people have unique and particularly intense experiences of deprivation, suggesting that there is something distinctive about their circumstances. It has been argued throughout this chapter that disabled people:

- experience profound levels of economic disadvantage, resulting in intense deprivation and, ultimately, a poor quality of life;
- are particularly dependent on state social services and benefits, which means they are frequently regarded as objects of charity;
- are often segregated by state welfare programmes, reinforcing the belief that they are unable to take part in mainstream social activities;
- experience a significant level of state regulation, a problem that may undermine individual freedom and autonomy;
- experience considerable discrimination throughout society, resulting in exclusion from a range of mainstream social activities;
- are the object of negative stereotyping in popular media; negative attitudes towards disabled people are deeply entrenched in popular culture.

The distinctiveness of these experiences suggests that disabled people are divided and separated from the able-bodied in the rest of society: disability provides the foundation for a social division in its own right. Like other disadvantaged groups in society, disabled people experience pervasive institutionalised discrimination. At the same time, their experiences of disadvantage may also be shaped by broader social divisions based on social class, consumption and gender. Ultimately, a flexible approach is required, one that recognises the specificity of disability as distinct from other social divisions but which is sufficiently sensitive to recognise differences between disabled people.

Discussion Questions

1. Can social disadvantage among disabled people be explained in terms of individual characteristics, such as impairment or work motivation?
2. Does class analysis provide an adequate foundation on which to develop an explanation of social disadvantage among disabled people?
3. How useful is the distinction between 'structure', 'identity' and 'action' in identifying the possibilities for creating a fairer and more equal society?

FURTHER READING

Barnes, C., Mercer, G. and Shakespeare, T. *Exploring Disability* (Cambridge: Polity Press, 1999) provides a comprehensive introduction to disability, while a 'classic' statement of the social model can be found in Oliver, M. *The Politics of Disablement* (London: Macmillan – now Basingstoke: Palgrave Macmillan, 1990). Barton, L. (ed.) *Disability and Society: Emerging Issues and Insights* (Harlow: Longman, 1996) is a collection of articles from the journal *Disability & Society*, which looks particularly at how sociological theories may be applied to disability research and the experiences of disabled people. The findings of the first comprehensive audit of discriminatory social barriers in the UK, Barnes, C. *Disabled People in Britain and Discrimination* (London: Hurst Calgary, 1990), still contain many relevant insights. Shah, S and Priestley, M. make use of case studies to reflect on the evolution of disability policies in *Disability and Social Change* (Cambridge: Policy Press, 2011).

Social Divisions: social, political and economic

CHAPTER 9

Religion

ALAN ALDRIDGE

This chapter will provide you with a critical understanding of the following aspects of religion as a source of social division:

- The relevance of religious divisions to the secularisation thesis
- The relationship between religion and the nation-state
- Divisions within faith communities
- Religious conflict in Northern Ireland
- Cultural bias and the legal position of different religions and faith communities
- The rights of religious minorities in multi-faith societies
- Anti-Catholic prejudice and the decline of Catholic subculture
- Islamophobia and cultural racism
- Religion and social disadvantage
- The relationship between religious and ethnic identities
- Problems with essentialist approaches to religion
- Religion as a cultural resource

The persistence of religious divisions

The place of religion in the modern world was a central concern of the great theorists who founded the discipline of sociology in the early nineteenth century. For all their theoretical, methodological and ideological differences, most of these classic founders took the view that religion was losing its place at the heart of social, cultural and political life. The modern world was, they believed, undergoing secularisation – a profound transformation captured in Wilson's (1966: xiv) concise definition: 'the process by which religious thinking, practice and institutions lose social significance'.

In a similar vein to Wilson, Berger (1967) distinguishes three different facets of the secularisation of the Christian world. The first is socio-structural: Christian churches, at least in the West, have lost functions (such as education, law-making and law enforcement) which are now performed by secular agencies. Equally important is the cultural aspect: the natural and social sciences relentlessly promote a secular perspective on the world, while the religious content of western art, music, literature and philosophy has drastically declined. This secularisation of society and culture brings a secularisation of individual consciousness: quite simply, fewer people use religious categories to understand the world and guide their own actions within it. Perhaps this last facet of secularisation has been exaggerated; thus Davie (1994) argues that 'believing without belonging' persists as a significant feature of contemporary societies, despite the decline of traditional religious institutions. Against this, Bruce (2002) contends that the secularisation of individual consciousness has been an inescapable corollary of the secularisation of society and culture. Religious belief has declined, together with religious belonging. Each succeeding generation is more secularised than its predecessors.

If the secularisation thesis is valid, then we should expect religion to become less and less important as a source of social division. That was certainly the view that Wilson took in his early work. Religion would survive and even flourish among minority religious movements ('sects' and 'cults'), but what this showed was not so much the continued vitality of religion as its consignment to the margins of society. Minority religious movements were protests against the secularisation of the wider society; their marginality and lack of impact was evidence not against but in favour of the triumph of secularity. In support of this, Wilson (1966: 81) argued that 'the marked loss of religious fervour in Northern Ireland in the decades since the end of the Second World War, and its diminished consequence in political terms, illustrates the declining relevance of religion for politics'. The pattern of events in Northern Ireland since Wilson wrote those words raises profound questions about the nature and significance of social divisions based on religion (see Chapter 10 on national identity).

Religion rarely stands alone as a cause of conflict and division, but is usually bound up with other dimensions, in particular ethnicity, 'race', language and nationality. Given that it affirms a source of meaning and authority that transcends human desires and social conventions, religion has the capacity to provide the ultimate justification for social conflict, violence, liberation struggles and war. When nation-states are created or destroyed, religion is almost invariably a focus of unity or conflict. Take the case of the Kingdom of Serbs, Croats and Slovenes, which was founded in 1918 after the end of the First World War following the fall of the Ottoman (Muslim) and Austro-Hungarian (Christian) empires. It was renamed the Kingdom of Yugoslavia in 1929, and became a Communist state in 1945. When Communism collapsed in the 1990s, Yugoslavia broke up into smaller states: Bosnia-Herzegovina, which is mainly Muslim although with a large Eastern Orthodox minority and significant Roman Catholic presence; Croatia and Slovenia, both predominantly

Roman Catholic; Macedonia, predominantly Eastern Orthodox; and the Union of Serbia and Montenegro, predominantly Serbian Orthodox. Montenegro gained its independence from Serbia in 2006, and professes itself to be a tolerant multi-faith society.

The partition of India in 1947 left its own religiously-inflected conflicts, including Hindu Nationalism, Sikh claims against Pakistan over the Punjab, and Pakistani claims against India over Kashmir and Jammu, where Muslims are in the majority. The recurring conflicts in Ireland were not solved by the partition in 1921, when the Irish Republic gained its independence from British rule, and the 'six counties' – Antrim, Armagh, Down, Fermanagh, Londonderry and Tyrone – were constituted as the UK province of Northern Ireland. Although Protestants often refer to Northern Ireland as 'Ulster', the original Ulster was made up of nine counties, including Cavan, Donegal and Monaghan. These three were predominantly Roman Catholic, which is why they were allocated to the Irish Republic, preserving a Protestant majority in the North. Within what became Northern Ireland, territorial segregation between Catholics and Protestants became more pronounced over time, particularly in the working-class areas of Belfast and Derry, where Catholics were driven out of Protestant areas and vice versa.

These examples show the potential for division not only between the world's religions but also within them. The main divide within Islam is between Sunnis and Shi'ites, the repercussions of which continue to be played out in the Middle East at the time of writing (2013), with a Shi'a minority in power in Syria and a Sunni minority in Bahrain. In Iraq, the majority Shia community had been oppressed under Saddam Hussein until 2003 when the balance of power was reversed. Christianity has a tripartite division between Catholics, Protestants and Orthodox, with numerous subdivisions in the Protestant tradition. Christianity has been more bitterly divided on doctrinal grounds than any other of the world's major religions. Clashes over doctrine and heresy have gone together with conflicts over authority: what is the correct relationship between the authority of scripture, the church, and human reason? Where is authority located (in the Pope, for example?), and who may exercise it? Contemporary divisions over the ordination of women to the priesthood or the place within the church of lesbians and gays are testimony to Christianity's continuing preoccupation with authority.

Even allowing for secularisation, the contemporary vitality of these conflicts shows that religious identity remains a powerful source of social division, not just confined to one part of the world or Britain. The UK National Census, conducted every ten years, is a useful source of information about religious affiliation. Census data on religion have been regularly gathered in Northern Ireland. The 2001 Census contained a voluntary question on religious

Table 9.1 Population of England and Wales by religion, 2011

	Numbers	Percentages
Christian	33,243,175	59.3
Muslim	2,706,066	4.8
Hindu	816,633	1.5
Sikh	423,158	0.6
Jewish	263,346	0.5
Buddhist	247,743	0.4
Other religions	240,530	0.4
No religion	14,097,229	25.1
Total	56,075,912	100

Source: Office for National Statistics (2012e), Table KS209EW.

affiliation for the rest of the UK – the first time this had been done since 1851. The exercise was repeated in 2011 and the results are shown in Table 9.1.

On these data, Britain still appears to be quite clearly a Christian country, with nearly 60 per cent of the population. Almost 80 per cent of those giving a religion stated that they were Christian. The next highest figure was the 25.1 per cent of the population who said they had no religion. Turning to other faiths, the Muslim community is markedly larger than any other. Figure 9.1 shows a broadly similar split of non-Christian religions in 2001.

In addition to the major world faiths, the 2001 Census returns show that 32,000 respondents were Spiritualists, 31,000 Pagans, 15,000 Jains, 7,000 Wiccans, 5,000 Rastafarians, 5,000 Bahá'ís and 4,000 Zoroastrians.

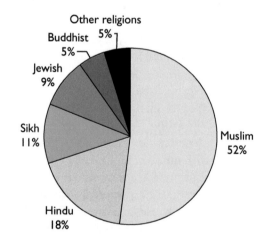

Figure 9.1 Distribution of non-Christian religions in Great Britain, 2001

Source: calculated from Office for National Statistics (2003), Census 2001.

The distribution of religious affiliation was markedly different in the various parts of Britain. By comparison with the rest of the UK, the figures for Northern Ireland show an overwhelming preponderance of Christians. The 2001 Census questions reflect this. In England and Wales, respondents were simply asked: 'What is your religion?', and were offered the following response categories:

- ☐ None
- ☐ Christian
- ☐ Buddhist
- ☐ Hindu
- ☐ Jewish
- ☐ Muslim
- ☐ Sikh
- ☐ Any other religion (please write in)

People in Northern Ireland, in contrast, were first asked a filter question: 'Do you regard yourself as belonging to any particular religion?' Those who replied 'yes' were then asked: 'What religion, religious denomination or body do you belong to?' The response categories were:

- ☐ Roman Catholic
- ☐ Presbyterian Church in Ireland
- ☐ Church of Ireland
- ☐ Methodist Church in Ireland
- ☐ Other, please write in

Perhaps the most striking difference is that, whereas in England and Wales, the major faith communities – Buddhist, Hindu, Jewish, Muslim and Sikh – were listed alongside Christianity, the census in Northern Ireland treated all religions apart from Christian denominations as falling into the category of 'other'. This differing approach reflects the patterns of religious affiliation in Northern Ireland, where, on the census figures, 86 per cent of the population identified themselves as Christian.

In Scotland, the Census asked: 'What religion, religious denomination or body do you belong to?' The results, as depicted in Figure 9.2, show that 65 per cent of Scots identified themselves as Christian, with the Church of Scotland accounting for 42 per cent of the population. Faith communities other than Christianity – including Muslims, Jews, Hindus, Sikhs and Buddhists – only total 2 per cent.

These considerable differences between England and Wales, Scotland and Northern Ireland are closely connected to the distribution of ethnicity in the UK. Ethnic minority groups account for only 2 per cent of the population of Scotland, and less than 1 per cent in Northern Ireland.

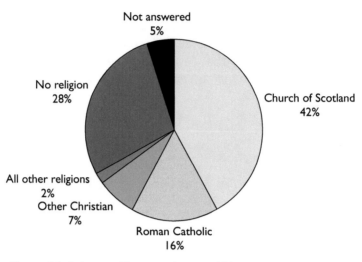

Figure 9.2 Religious affiliation in Scotland, 2001

Source: calculated from Office for National Statistics (2003), Census 2001.

Table 9.2, which relates to data on England and Wales, shows religion broken down by ethnic group (Chapter 4). The correlations are striking. Ninety-six per cent of Christians and 97 per cent of Jews are white; 84 per cent of Hindus and 91 per cent of Sikhs are Indian. Compared to the other Asian faiths, the Muslim population is more ethnically diverse: 12 per cent white, 9 per cent Indian, 43 per cent Pakistani, 17 per cent Bangladeshi and 6 per cent black African – a pattern reflecting Islam's history as a conversionist faith. As far as having no religion is concerned, it is predominantly a white affair.

When ethnicity is broken down by religion (Table 9.3), strong correlations are equally apparent. White people are predominantly Christian (76 per cent) or have no religion (15 per cent). Pakistanis are overwhelmingly Muslim

Table 9.2 Religion by ethnic group, England and Wales, 2001, row percentages

Religion	White	Indian	Pakistani	Bangladeshi	Black Caribbean	Black African	Chinese
Christian	96.3	0.1	0.0	0.0	1.11	0.9	0.1
Buddhist	38.8	1.3	0.1	0.1	0.67	0.2	23.8
Hindu	1.3	84.5	0.1	0.3	0.30	0.2	0.0
Jewish	96.8	0.3	0.1	0.1	0.21	0.1	0.0
Muslim	11.6	8.5	42.5	16.8	0.29	6.2	0.1
Sikh	2.1	91.5	0.1	0.0	0.04	0.1	0.0
No religion	94.5	0.2	0.1	0.0	0.82	0.1	1.6

Source: Office for National Statistics (2003), Census 2001.

Table 9.3 Ethnic group by religion, England and Wales, 2001, row percentages

Ethnic group	Christian	Buddhist	Hindu	Jewish	Muslim	Sikh	No religion
White	75.7	0.1	0.0	0.5	0.4	0.0	15.3
Indian	4.9	0.2	45.0	0.1	12.7	29.1	1.7
Pakistani	1.1	0.0	0.1	0.1	92.0	0.1	0.5
Bangladeshi	0.5	0.1	0.6	0.1	92.5	0.0	0.4
Black Caribbean	73.8	0.2	0.3	0.1	0.8	0.0	11.2
Black African	68.9	0.1	0.2	0.1	20.0	0.1	2.3
Chinese	21.6	15.1	0.1	0.1	0.3	0.0	52.6

Source: Office for National Statistics (2003), Census 2001.

(92 per cent), as are Bangladeshis (also 92 per cent). People giving their ethnic identification as black Caribbean are predominantly Christian, as are black Africans (with a significant Muslim minority). Indians are the most religiously diverse, with sizeable percentages of Hindus, Sikhs and Muslims, as well as a smaller percentage of Christians. Having no religion is, strikingly, a majority option only for the Chinese respondents.

Cultural bias and the law

The complexity of national identities in the UK, discussed in detail in Chapter 10, is graphically illustrated by the legal position of the Christian churches. In England, the church 'by law established' is the Church of England. It has enjoyed that privileged position since Henry VIII severed the English Church from Rome in 1534. Since then, the British monarch has been required to be a Protestant. No monarch or heir to the throne can be Roman Catholic, although they are now permitted to marry a Roman Catholic, following a change to the laws of succession in 2011.

Establishment means that the Church of England is not a voluntary society, such as a golf club or political pressure group, formed as a result of contractual agreements between its members. The Church has a unique relationship to the state. The reigning monarch is Supreme Governor of the Church of England. Its ecclesiastical laws and courts are part of the English legal system. Twenty-six senior bishops of the Church of England, including the Archbishops of Canterbury and York, sit as of right in the House of Lords, the upper chamber of the British Parliament. People living in England have a legal right to be married in their parish church and have their children baptised by a member of the parish clergy. The Anglican clergy are also required to conduct funeral services if requested to do so. These obligations were less problematic when England was a predominantly Christian culture, but the decline in church attendance and the transition to a multicultural society have put them under strain. A growing number of Anglican clergy resent these obligations, feeling themselves compelled to offer the sacraments 'cheaply' to people who have at best a 'nominal' commitment to the Christian faith.

While culturally dominant in England, the Anglican tradition was always a cultural minority in Northern Ireland and Wales, a fact reflected in the eventual disestablishment of the Church of Ireland in 1869 and the Church of Wales in 1914 (with a symbolic change of name to the Church in Wales). Scotland has an established church, but it is not the Scottish Episcopal Church, which is Anglican, but the Presbyterian Church of Scotland (known to Scots as the Kirk). Presbyterianism (the word 'presbyter' comes from the Greek *presbuteros*, meaning 'elder') has its origins in the Protestant Reformation, specifically in the teachings and forms of church governance instituted in the sixteenth century by John Calvin in Geneva and John Knox in Scotland. Presbyterians played an active part in the War of Independence of Britain's American colonies.

Upon accession to the throne, the British sovereign takes an oath to uphold the legal rights and Presbyterian government of the Church of Scotland. The monarch is Supreme Governor of the Church of England, but when the royal family visit Scotland, they are ministered to by the Church of Scotland. Occasionally, this can have unexpected benefits. The Church of England has been opposed to offering a church wedding to divorcees, on the grounds that divorce was condemned by Jesus himself. When Princess Anne remarried in 1992, the ceremony was held in Scotland, in a kirk. No controversy ensued.

To people from other countries, these peculiarities seem puzzling. In Britain, they pass almost without comment – they have become non-issues. From a historical point of view, they are the residue of once-bitter religious conflicts: the persecution of Roman Catholics under Edward VI and Elizabeth I, the persecution of Protestants under 'Bloody' Mary Tudor and the penalties suffered by members of the Free Churches who dissented from the Anglican supremacy. Arguably, what remains from the history of bigotry and oppression is a warm afterglow of quaint practices that demonstrate not conflict but mutual accommodation. Britain, on this view, has moved towards the American situation of 'denominational pluralism', in which mainstream religious institutions no longer insist on their own monopoly of the truth but instead see themselves, in Wallis' phrase (1976: 13), as 'pluralistically legitimate' – that is, simply one among many valid paths to salvation.

In contrast to this agreeable portrait of denominational pluralism, one can point to the decline of liberal Protestant denominations such as Episcopalians, Presbyterians and Methodists in the UK, and the ascendancy and political mobilisation of fundamentalist Christian groups that are hostile to tolerant liberalism, which they see as permissive, degenerate and ungodly. In the US, the political platforms of Presidents Jimmy Carter, Ronald Reagan and George W. Bush all appealed to the conservative heartlands. Although the US is a vast and culturally diverse society, many Americans live their lives encapsulated in local, homogeneous, mono-cultural milieux (Bruce 1996: 143). These stable communities are frequently breeding grounds for xenophobia, bigotry and intolerance directed against sex education, birth control, stem cell research, abortion, homosexuality, the theory of evolution, Godless Communism and selected foreign regimes that are presented as a threat to peace and liberty. Some commentators argue that *the* major social division in the United States is between religious conservatives and liberal progressives, two ideologically opposed factions fighting a 'culture war' over national identity, personal morality and the good society (Hunter 1991). Britain, too, is experiencing a confrontation between secularists and religious believers over what role, if any, religion should play in public life.

If denominational pluralism is benign, then the establishment of the Church of England, far from being a problem for other churches and faith communities, might be seen as an asset. As secularisation proceeds, the established Church of England may be uniquely positioned to represent faith in its struggle against unbelief, rationalism and secularity. Muslims, Jews, Sikhs, Hindus and others do not seem to be pressing for disestablishment, still less for a secular state on the French model. Tellingly, the most vocal advocate of disestablishment and the complete separation of Church and state is an anti-religious organisation: the National Secular Society, founded in 1866 by the atheist Charles Bradlaugh.

On the other hand, the notion that, in an increasingly multi-faith society, the Church of England can act as principal advocate for all faiths is likely to come under challenge. It may be a stage in the transition to multiculturalism, but can scarcely be the end point. A relevant case is prison chaplaincy (Beckford and Gilliat 1998; Beckford 1999). The British state expects Anglican chaplains to play a leading role in enabling prisoners of whatever religion to practise their faith while in prison. This is enshrined in the Prison Act of 1952. The Act was passed before the expansion of migration to Britain from the New Commonwealth, following which the country's Muslim, Hindu, Sikh, Jain and Buddhist communities rapidly expanded.

Their predicament is captured by Beckford (1999: 7):

In return for abandoning claims to equality of treatment or equality of opportunity to influence chaplaincy policies, minority faith communities can rely on Anglican chaplains to defend their interests and facilitate their access to prisoners. Pragmatism takes precedence over principles of equality.

Within British prisons, minority faiths may be 'tolerated', but they are scarcely accorded equal rights, as demonstrated by their dependence on the goodwill of 'the' (Anglican) chaplain.

Until relatively recently, British law presupposed a society that was Christian, with the established Church of England at the core of the worshipping life of the nation (if we forget Scotland, Wales and Northern Ireland). For example, under the Burial Laws Amendment Act 1880, it is an offence to 'bring into contempt or obloquy the Christian religion, or the belief or worship of any church or denomination of Christians, or the members or any minister of any such church or denomination, or' – the law somewhat obscurely adds – 'any other person'. Similarly, the Offences Against The Persons Act 1861 makes it an offence to

> [use] threats or force, obstruct or prevent or endeavour to obstruct or prevent, any clergyman or other minister in or from celebrating divine service or otherwise officiating in any church, chapel, meeting house, or other place of divine worship.

It would seem that, despite the use of the Anglican term 'clergyman', the phrase 'divine service' implies that the law would cover all mainstream Christian denominations. What, though, of polytheistic religions such as (arguably) Hinduism, or non-theistic religions such as (arguably) Buddhism, or religious communities such as the Quakers, who have no ministers at all?

Most contentious of all have been the laws on blasphemy and blasphemous libel. These were used twice in the twentieth century. In 1921, the secularist John William Gott published a pamphlet insinuating that Jesus's entry into Jerusalem on a donkey made him look like a circus clown. Gott was successfully prosecuted by the state and, despite public uproar, sentenced to nine months' hard labour. As the years passed, many people persuaded themselves that the last had been heard of the laws on blasphemy. However, in 1977, Mary Whitehouse, an evangelical Christian and founder of the National Viewers' and Listeners' Association, brought a successful private prosecution against the magazine *Gay News* for publishing a poem depicting a Roman centurion's homoerotic feelings for the crucified Christ. In his summing-up, the judge said:

> Blasphemous libel is committed if there is published any writing concerning God or Christ, the Christian religion, the Bible, or some sacred subject, using words which are scurrilous, abusive or offensive and which tend to vilify the Christian religion (and therefore have a tendency to lead to a breach of the peace). (quoted by Ruthven 1991: 49)

With the passage of the Human Rights Act 1998, which came into force in 2000, it was clear that these antiquated laws were no longer effective. The Human Rights Act, which makes the provisions of the European Convention on Human Rights enforceable in British courts, forbids discrimination on the grounds of religion. Any attempt to invoke laws such as blasphemy and blasphemous libel, with their protection only for Christianity in general and the Church of England in particular, would have been struck down by the court. Given this, the laws on blasphemy and blasphemous libel were quietly repealed in the Criminal Justice and Immigration Act 2008.

Until recently, British law offered scant protection to religious minorities. Some communities, notably Jews and Sikhs, had been able to secure legal protection of their rights, but only because the law recognised them as ethnic groups, which meant they were covered by legislation governing race relations. The Jewish and the Sikh faiths are not conversionist; they are the religions of people defined ethnically as a community sharing a sense of a common descent and common culture (Fenton 2003: 3). Conversionist faiths such as Christianity and Islam are not ethnic religions, and this has produced a series of legal anomalies that have caused growing resentment, particularly among Britain's Muslim community. Muslims have been left exposed as potential targets for racists, who have sought to evade prosecution by claiming that they are not unlawfully attacking an ethnic group or 'race', but are mounting an entirely lawful critique of a religion.

Membership of the EU brought about a radical shift in UK law, above all with the passage of the Human Rights Act. After years in which UK law treated religion under the heading of ethnicity, discrimination on grounds of religion is gradually being explicitly criminalised. A major development was the Racial and Religious Hatred Act 2006, which made it a criminal offence (in England and Wales) to use threatening words or behaviour, including written material, with the intention of stirring up religious hatred. The main aim of such legislation is to extend protection to communities such as Muslims, whose faith cannot be characterised as an ethnic religion. A secondary aim is to prevent extremists from claiming a platform to speak for persecuted religious minorities. Religion is firmly on the political agenda.

The erosion of Catholic subculture

Until the 1960s, Roman Catholicism in Britain formed a distinctive subculture, with its own characteristic beliefs, symbols, rituals and lifestyles. For many Catholics, their faith was experienced as an ascribed identity, similar in many ways to that of an ethnic group: a religion not simply of choice but of birth and birthright, often referred to as 'cradle' Catholicism.

At the organisational level, the Church had set itself up as a bastion – 'Fortress Rome' – defending itself against the perceived threats presented by secular culture and Protestantism. Nationally and locally, many Catholic leaders drew back from close ecumenical cooperation with other Christian churches that had 'separated' from the Catholic fold; shared communion with such churches was strictly forbidden. The Catholic Church cultivated its own organisations – schools and convents, parish clubs and Catholic associations. Catholics were encouraged to pray for the conversion of Britain to the fullness of faith embodied in the one true Church founded by Christ.

During this period, the Church was successful in inculcating traditional values and disciplines into its members. Catholics were encouraged to socialise with and marry Catholics. Catholics who married Protestants were expected to hold the wedding in a Catholic Church, to bring their children up as Catholics and to try to convert their partner. 'Marrying out' could cause family conflict, and some relatives would refuse to have anything to do with people who had formed a 'mixed' marriage.

The Catholic priesthood possessed considerable authority over parishioners. Disciplines such as Friday abstinence from meat (popularly referred to as 'fish on Friday'), regular attendance at mass, individual confession of sins and rejection of any artificial means of contraception were widely respected. Catholics were socialised into a guilt-ridden culture marked by anxiety about mortal sin and fear of eternal damnation. The Catholics' strong sense of their own distinctive identity was reinforced by anti-Catholic, anti-papal and anti-Irish prejudice in the wider society which drew on a stock of derogatory terms and negative stereotypes.

The subcultural Catholicism of Fortress Rome presented itself to the faithful as all of a piece. Hornsby-Smith (2004: 47) suggests that many Catholics probably did not draw distinctions between the various elements that made up the subculture:

- credal beliefs, such as belief in the Holy Trinity;
- non-credal beliefs, such as papal infallibility;
- moral teachings, such as marital fidelity and avoidance of artificial contraception;
- disciplinary rules, such as the obligation to attend mass and confess sins regularly to a priest.

As the 1960s progressed, this subcultural Catholicism fell apart; collective 'cradle' Catholicism gave way to a faith that had been chosen. Some critics saw the collapse of Fortress Rome as a wilful act of self-destruction perpetrated by the Church authorities through the reforms introduced by the Second Vatican Council (1962–65). Not only did the Church relax its insistence on such distinctive disciplines as Friday abstinence, it ruinously abandoned the glory of the Latin Mass (the Tridentine Mass, named after the Council of Trent, 1545–63) in favour of an insipid 'modern' version. Others would argue that the Church had to engage in this programme of 'updating' (*aggiornamento*) to secure its future in the modern world.

A wealth of evidence shows that Catholicism has been transformed socially and culturally. Instead of treating all the elements of Catholic culture as equally binding, more and more Catholics draw a distinction between the core, credal beliefs – eternal truths that cannot be challenged – and cultural symbols and practices that reflect traditional customs rather than the unchanging gospel. Priests may seek to impose the old disciplines, but their parishioners quietly disobey – an open secret being the use of contraceptives. Catholics feel less tightly bound by the Church's authority, less anxious and guilt-ridden. Their identity is more a matter of individual choice and is no longer defined in opposition to the wider culture. If the use of contraceptives stands as evidence of the weakening of the Church's once-unquestioned authority, the growth and increasing acceptance of 'mixed marriages' points unequivocally to the erosion of Catholic subculture.

We have evidence of similar processes occurring among Catholics in Northern Ireland. Boal et al.'s study (1997, cited by Mitchell 2004), which surveyed churchgoers in Belfast, showed the growth of individualism in the Catholic community. They reported an increased tendency, particularly among young people, to pick and choose among Catholic doctrines and to disobey religious disciplines, a position justified on the ground that the individual's own conscience should take priority over the formal teaching of the Church.

Cultural racism: the case of Islamophobia

'Islamophobia' was famously defined by the Runnymede Trust (1997: 4) as an 'unfounded hostility towards Islam, and therefore fear or dislike of all or most Muslims'. As with any definition of a key term, it is controversial. To speak of a phobia may suggest something irrational and beyond the control of the persons afflicted with it. Thus, arachnophobes, who have an irrational fear of spiders, are to be seen not as perpetrators of an evil but innocent victims of a mild psychopathology. People suffering from a phobia typically avoid and flee from the source of their fear; they do not aggressively attack or persecute it.

This is just one of a number of reasons why some writers have suggested alternative terms to replace Islamophobia. Halliday (1999) argues that, although its advocates are liberal and well intentioned, the concept of Islamophobia plays into the hands of extremists. It puts forward Islam as an undifferentiated abstract essence, ripe for attack by those who hate Muslims, and for defence by radical Islamists seeking to impose Islamic culture in particular nation-states or even across the globe. Islamists construct Islam as an essence. In their hands, culturally variable and invented traditions are transformed into the eternal truths of the Qur'an and the life and teaching of the Prophet Muhammad. Islamophobia lends credence to the contention that there is a deep-seated and inevitable conflict between Christian and Islamic civilisation. The concept of Islamophobia, Halliday argues, distracts attention from the enormous cultural diversity within and between Islamic communities and the social and cultural currents of change that have swept through them. Islamophobia misrepresents the target of hostility, which is not the faith that is Islam but the people who are Muslims. Halliday (1999) therefore proposes, by analogy with anti-Semitism, the term 'anti-Muslimism' – a term which has not, however, gained wide currency.

Modood (1997b) argues that the concept of 'cultural racism' captures the social realities that 'Islamophobia' allows to escape. Cultural racism must be considered a form of racism, because it uses such physical characteristics as skin colour and physiognomy as markers that indicate supposedly 'racial' groups. Cultural racists impute inferiority to these groups but do not see this as biologically determined. Instead, it is the product of the racial group's culture, as expressed in its history, traditions, values, norms of conduct and, most acutely, in its religion. In a historical perspective, Modood argues, nineteenth- and twentieth-century biological racism is the exception. Cultural racism has been far more prevalent, manifesting itself specifically in anti-Semitism and hostility towards Muslims, and more generally in ideologies based on the 'problem' of assimilating 'backward' colonial peoples into the refined civilisations of the West. Confronted with legislation forbidding incitement to racial hatred, cultural racists tend to offer spurious disavowals of racism, made superficially plausible by their focus on culture rather than biology.

Their racism may be encoded and sanitised as cultural critique, but it would be foolish to be taken in by it. The targets of racial abuse are typically Muslims from the Indian subcontinent, people who are easily identified by superficial physical characteristics (phenotypes) such as skin colour, which are falsely taken to indicate a different biological race (a genotype). For all the power of cultural racism, it is perhaps premature, as Mason points out (2000: 10; Chapter 4), to pronounce the demise of racism based on biology.

The debate about terminology is significant. It points to the intersection or overlapping of a family of key concepts – religion, ethnicity, 'race' and nation. For all the doubts raised about it, 'Islamophobia' persists as a term that is widely used, not least by Muslims who feel themselves to be the targets of it. The term has the merit of signalling that religion is a salient badge of identity and a source of social discrimination and hostility in a society that is frequently taken to be secular. While Halliday is right to say that religion is not the only thing of significance, it should not be discounted. What becomes crucial, then, is the way in which Islamophobia has been measured and assessed.

The Runnymede Trust report (1997) identified four aspects of Islamophobia:

- prejudice, institutionalised in the mass media and pervasive in everyday social interaction;
- discrimination in employment practices and the provision of services such as education and health;
- exclusion from employment, management and positions of responsibility, and from politics and government;
- violence, whether in the form of physical assaults, the vandalising of property or verbal abuse.

The report is most famous for its identification of Islamophobia as a 'closed' rather than an 'open' view of Islam. It is 'closed' in eight respects:

1. Islam is seen as monolithic and static. It is intolerant of internal diversity and debate, and unreceptive to new cultural and scientific developments.
2. Islam is perceived as entirely 'other'. It has little in common with other cultures, refuses to be affected by them and therefore exerts little influence upon them.
3. Islam is seen as inferior to Western faiths and philosophies. It is unenlightened: primitive, barbaric, oppressive, irrational and sexist. None of this is worthy of our respect.
4. Islam is seen as a violent, aggressive religion that lends comfort, support and legitimacy to terrorists. It poses a grave threat to our values and way of life. We are parties to a 'clash of civilisations', in which Islamic states are not partners but enemies.
5. Islam is not a genuine faith sincerely practised by its followers, but a political ideology manipulated by autocratic regimes for political and military advantage.
6. Islamic criticisms of the West have no validity and are dismissed as worthless.
7. Hostility towards Islam serves as justification for discrimination against Muslims and their social exclusion from mainstream society.
8. Anti-Muslim and anti-Islamic ideas and practices are accepted as natural and normal.

This closed view constructs Islam in essentialist terms and opposes it to an equally essentialised and mythologised Britishness, an indiscriminate compound of culture, history, ethnicity, 'race' and religion. The opposition constructs Islam as an enemy and Muslims as potential traitors to Britain (Ansari 2004). Muslims are said to have their primary loyalty to the umma, the worldwide Muslim community, not to the British nation-state. They are supposedly taught to see the world as divided between dar al-Islam, the house of Islam which is governed by Shari'a law, and dar al-harb, the house of war. They are allegedly bound by a sacred obligation to wage jihad or holy war in defence of Islam, irrespective of the national interests of the host society, and – a view lent colour by the attacks of 11 September 2001 – they venerate martyrdom in the cause of Islam, even if it involves carnage and self-immolation. In Ansari's words (2004: 8): 'The West has constructed and stigmatised an Islam with little resemblance to anything that is of value in ordinary Muslim lives.'

Islamophobia has deep roots in British culture. Two Gulf Wars, Western intervention in Afghanistan to oust the Taliban regime and the carnage of 9/11 in New York and 7/7 in London did not create Islamophobia, but they undoubtedly intensified it. They appear to have strengthened xenophobia and racism, creating a climate of fear and hatred, which neo-Nazi and other extremist groups have sought to exploit.

This has given a public platform to some of the most radical Islamist leaders, to the alarm of most of the Muslims for whom they claim to speak. An accumulating body of evidence shows that Britain's Muslim communities feel more vulnerable to prejudice, discrimination, exclusion and violence than any other social group. These fears have been experienced throughout Europe (Allen and Nielsen 2002). Muslims have been increasingly subjected to verbal abuse, harassment and aggression. Women wearing the hijab (covering for the head and face) have been particular targets, as have men wearing turbans, most of whom are in fact Sikhs. Mosques have suffered graffiti and vandalism, as well as arson and bomb attacks. Visual identifiers of Islamic 'otherness' are a focus of abuse. Where these are not apparent, Muslims have been relatively free from harassment. An example of this is Finland's long-established Tatar community, Muslims of Turkish descent who are well integrated into Finnish society and display few if any visual markers that they are Muslim. The Tatars have escaped abuses to which other Muslims in Finland have been subjected.

Official statistics bear out the disadvantages from which British Muslims suffer (Office for National Statistics 2004b). Almost one-third of Muslims (31 per cent) working in Great Britain have no formal qualifications at all – the highest proportion for any religious group. They are also the least likely to have university degrees. The unemployment rate among Muslims is higher than for any other religious group. This is true both of male and female unemployment.

Young Muslims aged 16–24 have the highest unemployment rate of all, 22 per cent, almost exactly twice the figure for Christians of the same age. Muslims share with Sikhs the fate of being the most under-represented faith communities in professional and managerial occupations, and the most likely to be working in poorly paid, low-skilled jobs.

The pattern of disadvantage also shows itself in housing: 32 per cent of Muslim households are officially classified as 'overcrowded', the highest figure for any religious group. This may be accounted for, in part, by cultural preferences for larger families and a strong commitment to caring for elderly family members. Such cultural factors do not, however, explain the fact that Muslim households are less likely than any other to have central heating, to offer sole use of a bathroom or to be self-contained. This pattern is replicated across the country. What is true of employment and housing is also true of health (Chapter 14). After taking account of the age structures of the various religions (the Muslim community has a relatively high proportion of children and young people), rates of disability are highest among Muslims. It is not surprising, in the light of these indices of deprivation, that Muslims report higher rates of ill health than any other faith community. Muslims may share such disadvantages with other groups – the elderly, less-skilled workers, the poor – but their identity tends to be articulated both by themselves and others in terms of their religious distinctiveness.

'Religion' as a troublesome category

'The Northern Ireland conflict is a religious conflict', as Bruce (1986: 249) pointedly reminded us. It is not purely about religion (religion in practice is never pure) nor is it mainly theological (theology is of concern to only a tiny minority of academics and clerics). In Northern Ireland, religion coincides with other bases of social division, including ethnicity, language, nationality, education and social class (Chapter10). This does not mean that religious conflict can be explained away as being 'really' class conflict, or nationalism, or tribalism. If there was any doubt that social divisions based on religion are complex, the case of Northern Ireland puts the matter beyond question.

In Bruce's interpretation, the conflict (now less openly violent) is marked by a basic asymmetry. Republicanism is nationalist and fundamentally secular. Many Catholics in the North look for the reunification of the six counties with the Irish Republic – enthusiasm for a united Ireland is notably greater among Catholics in the North than in the Republic itself. Ulster Loyalists, in contrast, do not identify straightforwardly and unequivocally with Britain. Their loyalty is to the symbol of the Crown, not the government in Westminster. They cherish a highly romanticised and nostalgic vision of Britain as it might once have been, not the social realities of the contemporary nation-state, still less its membership of the EU.

Although he describes conflict in Northern Ireland as religious, Bruce maintains that religion is not simply about humanity's relationship to the divine. People use churches and religion to signal ethnic identifications and draw boundaries around them. In doing so, religion is invoked not simply to mark ethnicity but to construct and reproduce it (Mitchell 2004: 248). This is particularly striking as far as Protestants are concerned. They regard themselves as possessing a distinctive culture, with a shared history, traditions, values, beliefs, lifestyles and symbols. The culture embodies a sense of what Max Weber called 'ethnic honour', incorporating an opposition between supposed Protestant virtues and Catholic vices – a contrast which is used to explain and justify the relative advantage enjoyed by Protestants, particularly in the field of employment.

According to Bruce (1986: 262), the evangelical Protestantism espoused by Loyalists is 'the only identity that can make sense of their history and that justifies their separation from the South'. Hostility towards Catholicism is built into this identity. In Foucauldian terms, anti-Catholicism is a discursive formation that encodes in linguistic form, through ritualised codes and slogans ('Ye must be born again', 'Remember 1690'), a sense of Protestant identity and identification with a sacred history in which 'Bible Protestants' have triumphed over 'Papists'.

Following Brewer and Higgins (1999), we can distinguish four modes of anti-Catholicism. The first two are apolitical: the passive mode, that is, a cultural backdrop of taken-for-granted stereotypes and prejudices; and the Pharisaic mode, in which Protestants, while recognising Catholics as fellow Christians, confidently assert the theological superiority of their faith and its firm biblical grounding, as a vantage point from which to critique the distortions and errors of Catholic theology.

These two modes are not without social significance. In analysing social divisions, however, we need to focus on anti-Catholicism in its politicised forms. The first of these is secular: it holds firm to the Union with Britain and rejects Irish nationalism and Republicanism. The Catholic Church is criticised as an anti-democratic conspiracy that threatens political and civil liberties and puts economic prosperity in jeopardy. Even though secular anti-Catholics are deeply suspicious of the motives of Catholic and Republican leaders, it may be politically expedient to negotiate with them.

The second mode of politicised anti-Catholicism is not secular but theological; Brewer and Higgins call it 'covenantal'. The Catholic Church is vilified as a heretical, anti-Christian organisation, a view justified by appeal to biblical prophecy and the Book of Revelation. The mission of Protestants is to save Ulster from the clutches of the evil conspiracy that is Catholicism. Not only can there be 'no surrender', there can be no political dialogue with Catholics. The covenantal mode predominates in the Free Presbyterian Church and the Democratic Unionist Party. The secular and covenantal modes are very different, but they share the capacity to legitimise social divisions that disadvantage and marginalise Catholics politically, economically and socially. They are a cultural resource through which passive anti-Catholicism can be mobilised into political action.

In Britain itself, as abroad, Northern Ireland is typically viewed as an exceptional, pathological case of abnormal politics fuelled by sectarian religion – a throwback to a pre-industrial era in which conflicts within and between societies were indeed wars of religion. Such an interpretation can lead to overlooking commonalities between Northern Ireland and the rest of the UK. The case against such a view is put sharply by Mitchell (2004: 251):

> Contemporary Britain is only beginning to face the task of formulating policies to cater for a religiously plural society. It should not ignore the experiences of religious division and change in its own backyard.

A leading example is provided by education. The question of faith-based schooling – a salient issue for Northern Ireland, during and after 'the Troubles' – remains high on the political agenda in the rest of UK, principally because of the debate about state funding of Muslim schools (Tinker 2009). A vast array of interested parties have addressed education from many angles, arguing about identity, gender, authority, multiculturalism, citizenship, social equality, social justice and human rights. Religion lies at the heart of these debates and underpins the social divisions they seek to erase or perpetuate.

Religious sects

The part played by religion in creating and perpetuating social divisions is displayed graphically in religious sects. In a sociological perspective, sects are culturally deviant religious minorities that regard themselves as having a monopoly of the truth. They have a strong sense of their own unique identity and typically have strict rules of performance which they enforce rigorously, expelling sinners in order to keep the community pure (Wilson 1970).

The Exclusive Brethren provide an instructive case. This Christian sect broke away from the wider Brethren movement in the 1840s under the leadership of John Nelson Darby. Members of the Exclusive Brethren are required to avoid worldly practices and minimise contact with non-members. So, for example, Exclusive Brethren are not permitted to watch television, listen to the radio, read newspapers, read works of fiction, attend the theatre or cinema, use computers, mobile phones or the internet, attend university, join a trade union or professional association or vote in a political election. Their places of worship have no windows through which outsiders might observe them and they live in detached houses because they are not allowed to share any facilities with outsiders. If a family member leaves the movement, they have to move out of the family home.

The Exclusive Brethren's deliberate segregation from the wider society is justified by several key biblical texts, in particular the advice given by St Paul to the fledgling Christian community at Corinth: 'Come out from among them and be ye separate'. Paul's instruction to 'remove the wicked person from amongst yourselves' justifies the practice of 'withdrawing from' – that is, completely ostracising – people who have violated the sect's strict codes of conduct.

The case of the Exclusive Brethren highlights a distinguishing feature of religion as a source of division. On the one hand, it can be argued that, in the contemporary world, religion is something that we as individuals choose for ourselves. Britain, like other First World countries, is a multicultural, multi-faith society. Unless one is the reigning monarch or heir to the throne, there is no legal impediment to joining the religion of one's preference. In apparent contrast to the other social divisions discussed in this book, religion is fundamentally something that we choose, a status that in sociological terms is achieved rather than ascribed. This point was used to question the wisdom of the Racial and Religious Hatred Act 2006, on the grounds that it would jeopardise freedom of speech. Surely, the argument runs, people's religious beliefs and practices are a legitimate target of satire; why should religion be protected as a special case in a way that secular and political philosophies are not?

Against this, it is important to see that, like ethnicity, religious affiliation involves powerful constraints as well as choices. Someone who was born into a tight-knit community such as the Exclusive Brethren but who chooses as an adult to leave them is typically forced to abandon the community and their own family. Many who leave find life outside the community unbearable. Not only do they fail to integrate into the wider society, they also feel guilty at having deserted their family and friends. The family, above all other institutions, is unique, given, irreplaceable. For all the problems of life within a sect, some who leave find they have little real choice but it rejoin.

The interplay between choice and constraint is equally acute in religions such as the Jewish, Hindu and Sikh faiths, where religion and ethnicity are inextricably linked. Ethnic identification on the basis of shared descent and common culture is overlaid with religious significance. Apostasy (renunciation of one's faith) is viewed as a serious offence, not a legitimate consumer 'choice'. With its reference to an ultimate, transcendental source of meaning and authority, religion has a unique character that sets it apart from secular belief systems.

Whether or not we subscribe to the secularisation thesis, there is a good case for Beckford's (1989: 170–2) claim that religion remains a cultural resource on which individuals and social groupings can draw for identity, motivation, mobilisation and legitimacy. As religion has lost social significance so, para-doxically, it has gained cultural significance as a powerful but increasingly volatile and unpredictable resource that can be deployed to promote social cohesion or social division.

Discussion Questions

1. How does your own religious or non-religious identity relate to your ethnic identity? Are there any conflicts between them? To what extent would you say that you have chosen your own religious or non-religious identity?

2. Why is religion given special protections under the law, when other belief systems are not? How are such protections justified? Should they all be abolished?

3. Is there a cultural bias against religious minorities? Is it typically based on hostility towards their beliefs and/or their practices? How would you distinguish between religious hostility and racism?

4. If the secularisation thesis is true, why do religious divisions persist? Are they 'really' religious?

FURTHER READING

Aldridge, A. *Religion in the Contemporary World: A Sociological Introduction* (Cambridge: Polity, 2012, 3rd edn) provides a broad overview of sociological work on religion. For a balanced account of religion in the British context, see Davie, G. *Religion in Britain since 1945: Believing Without Belonging* (Oxford: Blackwell, 1994). Among many ex-positions of the secularisation thesis, Bruce, S. *God is Dead: Secularization in the West* (Oxford: Blackwell, 2002) stands out as trenchant and thought-provoking. Beckford, J. *Social Theory and Religion* (Cambridge: Cambridge University Press, 2003) can be recommended as a sophisticated treatment of sociological theorising about religion.

CHAPTER 10

National Identity

DAVID MCCRONE

This chapter will provide you with a broad critical understanding of the following issues in national identity as a source of social division:

■ The difference between national identity and state identity in the UK
■ The variations between the different countries of the UK with regard to these forms of identity
■ How being British evolved in the context of other territorial identities in these islands
■ Why there is no single or simple way of being British
■ The relationship between national identity and citizenship
■ The problematic nature of 'nation-state' as a concept in the modern world
■ Why nationalism is an inherent ideology in modern societies
■ The strengths and the weaknesses of being British today

Who are you? If you are asked what nationality you are, what do you say? If you live in the archipelago of islands called the 'British Isles', would you say you are British? English? Scottish? Welsh? Irish? None of these? How do you decide? You may say you are British because you are a citizen of the UK, because you hold a British passport. But strictly speaking, 'British' refers to people who live on the British mainland. The state, after all, is the United Kingdom of Great Britain *and* Northern Ireland. So we are UK-people – 'Ukanians' in Tom Nairn's ironic term (1977) – who live together in the same state but who have not bothered to find a proper name for ourselves. While virtually all modern states have problems defining who their 'nationals' are, it is instructive to focus first on people in these islands where such issues are especially problematic. By focusing on these, we can begin to understand just how complex and changing national identity is in the twenty-first century, and also what we mean by 'nationality' in more general terms, together with 'citizenship, 'nation' and 'state'.

Try another question. What do you call the country you live in? The United Kingdom? Britain? Great Britain? England? Scotland? Wales? Ireland? Northern Ireland? Ulster? To many foreigners, this is England (even to some English people), but the Scots, Welsh, and Northern Irish know that it is not so. So who is right? Let us try some elementary algebra. Formally,

the United Kingdom = Great Britain (the big island) + Northern Ireland, where Great Britain = England + Scotland + Wales.

The problem with that (logically correct) formulation is that it does not correspond with sociological reality, that is, how people see themselves. The non-English peoples – the Scots and Welsh in particular – define their nationality (their 'nation-ness') primarily as Scottish and Welsh, while recognising that their citizenship – their state identity – is British. In Northern Ireland, on the other hand, being 'British' is a political statement that you wish to belong to the UK – in other words, that you are a 'unionist'.

Indeed, Northern Ireland provides us with the starkest home-grown example of why national identity is such an important principle of social division. Here, hundreds of people who were ordinary 'citizens', living in a territory that, as an accident of history and constitutionality, is part of the UK, have killed or been killed in an internal war over nationality, state and culture. Social divisions do not come much sharper than that (except in the scale and intensity of fighting elsewhere in Europe, as the Balkans showed us in the 1990s). In Northern Ireland, when about two-thirds of Protestants say they are British, it is no casual observation, just as when the significant minority (about three in five Catholics: Curtice 1990) express a powerful counter-identity by asserting that they are Irish. Catholics and Protestants do not just divide on national identity or religious grounds. They live in different areas, go to different schools, often work in separate organisations and mix with 'their own people', who share similar experiences of good or poor housing, education, occupational opportunity or exclusion (Chapters 4 and 9). Those who lead the most separate lives in this way are also the most likely to express a distinctive sense of nationalism (Breen 1998).

Although the sense of difference is not so extreme in Scotland, Scottish 'social arrangements' are not the same as in England, as has become more obvious since the Scottish Parliament was set up in 1999. Scotland has its own legal system; a less selective and subject-special education service; unique churches; separate organisation of trade associations, banks, charities and political parties; and media production systems that ensure a diet of news coverage about Scotland that even Wales with its distinctive language, and certainly no mere regional service, can match. For some sociologists, Scotland is just as suitable a 'unit of analysis' as is the more conventional, mirror-image way of thinking about the size and geographical spread of what we research – the area usually defined as 'England and Wales' (Payne 1987a; McCrone 2001).

These nuances in parts of the UK have in the past been lost on the majority people, the English, who make up 85 per cent of the state's population. The distinction between national identity and state identity in these islands is not one they usually make, although in recent times flying the English flag of St George rather than the Union Flag of the UK, appears more common than it once was, notably at sporting events. Anthony Barnett, who helped to found Charter 88, the pressure group for constitutional change, commented:

> What is the difference between being English and being British? If you ask a Scot or a Welsh person about their Britishness, the question makes sense to them. They might say that they feel Scots first and British second. Or that they enjoy a dual identity as Welsh-British, with both parts being equal. Or they might say: 'I'm definitely British first.' What they have in common is an understanding that there is a space between their nation and Britain, and they can assess the relationship between the two. The English, however, are more often baffled when asked how they relate their Englishness and Britishness to each other. They often fail to understand how the two can be contrasted at all. It seems like one of those puzzles that others can undo but you can't: Englishness and Britishness seem inseparable. They might prefer to be called one thing rather than the other – and today young people increasingly prefer English to British – but, like two sides of a coin, neither term has an independent existence from the other (Barnett 1997: 292–3).

Since Barnett wrote that, devolution has taken place in Scotland and Wales, and there is an Assembly in Northern Ireland. Some have argued that, as a result, England is 'the dog that finally barked'; that, among the English, there is an emerging sense of England as a political community driven by changes in national identity (Institute for Public Policy Research 2012). Let us review the evidence, starting with Scotland which has had a law-making parliament since 1999. Do the Scots feel more Scottish as a result? The somewhat surprising answer is 'no'. That is because Scots felt strongly Scottish to begin with. In 1999 when the parliament was set up, two-thirds of people in Scotland said they were predominantly Scottish (that is, Scottish not British, or more Scottish than British). Ten years later, that percentage had changed very little. We have here an example of a 'ceiling effect', that so many people gave priority to being Scottish at the outset that there were very few left to become so. Less than 10 per cent said they were predominantly British, and just over a quarter 'equally Scottish and British' (Bechhofer and McCrone 2009).

What about the English? Once more we find very little change in the decade since devolution. In 1999, around 30 per cent said they were predominantly English, about 25 per cent predominantly British, and the rest who had expressed an opinion, 37 per cent, equally English and British. Ten years later, virtually the same proportion – 33 per cent – were predominantly English; about 25 per cent predominantly British, and about 33 per cent equally English and British. It looks like we cannot conclude that there has been an upsurge in people saying they are English, whatever impact devolution in Scotland and Wales has had.

Put another way, while it is true that Scots are much more likely to say they are Scottish than the English are to say that they are English, things have changed very little since devolution. And what about Wales and Northern Ireland? How 'British' are they? The Welsh are more aware of their 'national' identity (being Welsh) than the English, but not as much as the Scots. So Wales is halfway between England and Scotland in terms of placing importance on 'national' identity as opposed to 'state' – British – identity. And Northern Ireland? It depends very much on which 'community' you belong to, with Catholics opting for 'Irish' and Protestants for 'British'. In Northern Ireland, issues of national identity are framed by this nexus between politics and religion in so many ways, one being a proxy for the other. In 2007 (according to the Northern Ireland Life and Times survey), 62 per cent of Catholics said they were Irish, and only 9 per cent British, while 61 per cent of Protestants said they were British, and only 4 per cent Irish – virtually a mirror image of each other. A sizeable minority of both Catholics (23 per cent) and Protestants (27 per cent) said they were Northern Irish (see also Chapter 9). These figures show relatively little change since 1988, suggesting that 'confessional' identities are more important for both communities than territorial ones.

How are sociologists to make sense of this distinction between national identity and citizenship, that is, state identity? This is, we might say, a meaningful error. There is a real puzzle about Britishness. In Cohen's helpful metaphor (1994), it is 'fuzzy', that is, blurred and opaque. (Cohen is making the analogy with 'fuzzy logic' in mathematics which allows a solution to be reached by eliminating the uncertain edges to a problem.) This fuzziness is a legacy of history and sociology in these islands and at its heart is the confusion of nationality and citizenship. At this point, you may be asking yourself whether any of this matters? After all, you may not actually think it matters much what nationality you are. Let me press you on this point. If you go abroad, do you feel yourself more or less 'national'? During the football World Cup, or for that matter most international sporting occasions, which team do you support? Well, you may reply, I do feel patriotic, but not nationalistic. That is a fairly common answer. It implies that feeling pride in one's country is not the same as hating, even killing, other people. Indeed not, but can we be sure that we are making a valid distinction between patriotism and nationalism? Most of us in the UK today are too young to remember the Second World War – you would need to be over 80 to have been an adult in 1945. However, most people in those days had little difficulty with going and fighting, and even dying, for what they felt was right. Perhaps the problem we have in thinking that we are not susceptible to feelings of patriotism and nationalism – because, in truth, they are the same thing – is that we have not been confronted by the need to do so. Those who are so confronted often feel they have no alternative.

Perhaps part of the issue here is that, for the most part, English people are not as aware of their Englishness as the Scots, the Welsh and the Irish, all of whom have historically looked to the English as the 'other' against whom they define themselves. For English people, however, there is a more fundamental confusion with being British. Let us now explore that in some depth. Where did the idea of 'Britain' come from?

Making Britain

There are two historical parts to our puzzle: how the British state was created in the eighteenth century; and how modern citizenship evolved in the twentieth. The creation of Great Britain in the early eighteenth century before the wave of modernising states transformed our world is the key. The British state managed to contain within it quite distinct self-governing 'civil societies', which coexisted within its formal boundaries more or less contentedly as long as a fairly high degree of limited autonomy was afforded them. By 'civil society' we mean that social sphere between the individual and the state: the domestic world, economic relations, cultural activities and even legal institutions which are organised by private or voluntary arrangements and largely outside the control of the state. We can now see with hindsight that, by the middle of the twentieth century, the relationship between the state and these civil societies had been radically altered in such a way that peaceful coexistence was no longer logically possible. Above all, the generic shift between the boundaries of the state and civil society in the modern world created particular difficulties for relations between the British state and its constituent civil societies.

The central relationship is the one between England and Scotland because that was the basis of the creation of the new state of Great Britain in the 1707 Treaty of Union. This relationship has always been the most problematic and intriguing one. Other civil societies, of course, existed within the state – notably those in Wales and (after 1801 when the state became the United Kingdom) Ireland, as well as local and regional ones within England itself.

However, their relationships to the political centre were different. On the one hand, the national societies of Wales and Ireland had been the subject of successful conquest by England from the thirteenth century and had elements of colonial status attached to their civil and political institutions. On the other hand, regional autonomy within England did not have to contend with competing national identities and institutional residues of historical statehood like those which existed north of the English border.

How did Scottish (or Welsh) civil society develop in the context of the unitary British state after 1707? Given that all formal political power resided in Westminster, how much (or little) autonomy did these nations continue to have? There was a consensus of political opposites on this issue. For nationalists, Scotland had ceased to exist in 1707 when it was incorporated into greater England. Their project was – and is – that Scotland should rise and be a nation again (in the sense of being an independent state). For unionists, on the other hand, the new, integrated society called Britain (or, in more formal terms, the UK) was born, and they argue that it would be disastrous if the whole were to be unscrambled into its weaker constituent parts. The problem with these two stark representations is that they play fast and loose with history as well as sociology.

Let us clarify some of our terms. The 'state' refers to the institutions of governance, and includes not simply parliament, but the legal system and the civil service. It is a 'political' concept. The 'nation' on the other hand refers to the 'cultural' realm of what people see as their shared characteristics, most usually language, religion and/or common history. In Anderson's useful term (1996), a nation is an 'imagined community' of people who believe themselves to belong to the same cultural group, and which has the right of self-determination. The important aspect to grasp is that 'state' and 'nation' belong to different spheres, even though they are frequently treated as synonyms, and linked together in the term 'nation-state'. As we shall see later in this chapter, there is nothing inevitable about linking the two together, and it is becoming increasingly problematic to do so in the modern world. How does this apply to the UK?

Scotland, while ceasing to be an independent state, did not stop being a nation or a civil society in 1707. Nor was it incorporated into greater England, but the Treaty of Union in 1707 did create something new. Great Britain was not Greater England, despite the numerical preponderance of the English. Instead, the Scots took full advantage of the opportunity that England and the Empire provided. As Colley has pointed out, a genuine sense of Britishness was 'forged' with reference to two related aspects: war with France, and Protestantism (Chapter 9). Britishness was *invented* in the long period of virtual or actual warfare with France from 1707 until 1837. These wars were religious

wars and perceived as such on both sides. The overthrow of the Catholic Stu-
arts in 1689 and their replacement with the Protestant William of Orange
reinforced the political–religious nature of the settlement. According to Colley
(1992: 5):

> [Britain] was an invention forged above all by war. Time and time again, war
> with France brought Britons, whether they hailed from Wales or Scotland or
> England, into confrontation with an obvious hostile Other and encouraged
> them to define themselves collectively against it. They defined themselves
> as Protestants struggling for survival against the world's foremost Catholic
> power. They defined themselves against the French as they imagined them
> to be, superstitious, militarist, decadent and unfree.

This struggle against the French may seem like an integrating mechanism,
a forging of a new national identity, but Colley (1992: 6) argues that 'Britishness was superimposed over an array of internal differences in response to
contact with the Other, and above all in response to conflict with the Other'.
It worked with, rather than against, the grain of older national identities that
were to persist and outlast the later British one. Britishness sat lightly on top
of the constituent nations as a kind of state identity. This is the key to understanding state–society relations in the UK. The British state was quite unlike
later state formations that sought to integrate political, cultural and economic
structures in the classical 'nation-state' outlined above. These formations demanded the lining up of state, nation, society, economy and culture in such a
way that 'national identity' ran through all these institutions. Being a citizen in
these nineteenth-century modern states demanded allegiance, and in return
the state was made accountable, and its sovereignty limited, often by means
of the doctrine of popular, rather than Crown/parliamentary, sovereignty, as
in Britain.

The British state, on the other hand, as a 'nightwatchman state' was content to concern itself with matters of defence, foreign policy and maintaining
a stable currency. It was a state externally oriented to managing its dependent
territories and arranging their defence. Above all, it left domestic civil society
to its own devices and only intervened where it perceived a threat to social and
political order. This it did most notoriously after the Jacobite Rising of 1745,
and only at the behest of, and largely by the hands of, lowland Protestant
Scots.

The point here is that the British state sat lightly on civil society, whereas
Continental European states were thoroughly interwoven with theirs. The un-
reformed quality of the British state has been commented on by many writers.

Marquand, for example, has called the UK an 'unprincipled' society. He observed:

> Thanks to the upheavals of the 17th century – thanks in particular to the victory of the English landed classes over the Stuart kings – one cannot speak of a 'British state' in the way that one speaks of a 'French state' or in modern times of a 'German state'. The UK is not a state in the continental sense. It is a bundle of islands (including such exotica as the Channel Islands and the Isle of Man which are not even represented at Westminster), acquired at different times by the English crown, and governed in different ways. Its inhabitants are not citizens of a state, with defined rights of citizenship. They are subjects of a monarch, enjoying 'liberties' which their ancestors won from previous monarchs. (1988: 152)

Marquand's point is that the British state was a minimal state with a small bureaucracy that was clearly suited to market-driven adjustment in the eighteenth century, but which failed to make the transition to full modernity in the late nineteenth century. At its root lies an ethos of market liberalism, which has survived long after the doctrine that created it has been abandoned.

Colley (1992) makes a similar point that the British state at the turn of the nineteenth century was one of the most modernised and democratic in Europe. Its Protestant 'ethic' gave it a commitment to civil and economic liberalism that helped to make it the premier power until the late nineteenth century. The problem was that, whereas the reforms of 1832 established a high degree of civil and democratic rights, by 1865 the British state had been overtaken by most Continental powers. Its political development had been arrested, possibly because its route to modernisation was more conservative than is usually made out. A thoroughgoing reform of political and constitutional structures with, for example, a written constitution and bill of rights, did not take place.

You may by now have noticed an important omission in describing who the British are. What about the Irish? Was Ireland not incorporated into the United Kingdom of Great Britain and Ireland in 1801? Constitutionally speaking, this is correct. However, if we take Colley's point that Protestantism was a prime shaper of Britishness, then, as Catholics, most of the people on the island of Ireland could not and, indeed, were not allowed to be British in this sense. To be British was to be a Protestant which in turn made one loyal to the British Crown. That is the origin of the term 'loyalist', and the reason why in Ireland over the last two centuries religion is less a matter of theology and more a matter of constitutional politics.

Making British citizens

The second piece of our puzzle about British nationality and citizenship is to be found in the second half of the twentieth century: how modern citizenship in these islands evolved. The inhabitants of the UK attained formal citizenship by a legislative sleight of hand under the 1948 Nationality Act as 'citizens of the UK and the colonies'. Prior to that date, the inhabitants of the British Isles and the British Empire were formally 'subjects' of the Crown. Hitherto, Britain was not so much a geographical entity; it was perceived in terms of those who owed allegiance to the Crown, and included those who inhabited the far-flung territories of the Empire. In other words, there was something unusual about the relationship between the British state and its inhabitants.

In essence, Britishness had grown up as an imperial identity, although a fuzzy one, defined more by an allegiance to the Crown than residence in these islands. Britain, in other words, existed as an imperial state – with colonies and dominions that came to embody its identity. Whatever else it was, Britain was not England. It evoked an imperial identity, much as in the Roman Empire. '*Civis Britannicus Sum*' ('I am a citizen of Britain') was the nineteenth-century equivalent of '*Civis Romanus Sum*'.

The post-1945 crisis arose because former parts of the Empire, such as Canada and India, wished to redefine citizenship for immigration purposes, and so a separate status was necessary for the remaining inhabitants of the UK. The preferred position of the British government was that people in Commonwealth countries were subjects of the British Crown first and citizens of individual states second, but newly-independent countries balked at this constraint on their sovereignty. The British political parties reflected the confusion. In the post-imperial age, the Labour Party sought to encourage a 'traditional', that is, non-ethnic, definition of 'Britishness' to encompass the Commonwealth, while supporting colonial peoples in their liberation struggles (Goulbourne 1991). The Conservative Party for its part developed an 'ethnic' definition – 'those groups which consider themselves to be British, and also the indigenous and/or white population' (Goulbourne 1991: 245). This was reflected in the 1962 Commonwealth Immigration Act, the 1971 Immigration Act and the 1981 Nationality Act, and an ethnic definition was reinforced ideologically under the influence of right-wing politicians like Enoch Powell and Margaret Thatcher (see Chapter 4 on ethnicity).

The politicisation of ethnic identity has helped to highlight the racial context of the debate over the last 30 years. By the 1981 Act, patriality – the right to settle in the UK if one had at least one grandparent who was born here – drew on the law of blood (*ius sanguinis*) rather than the law of territory (*ius soli*), so that ethnic definitions of Britishness were at least as important as civic ones. We will return to this important distinction between 'blood' and 'soil' later.

This overview of how 'Britishness' has come to be redefined in the post-colonial age provides a context for important shifts in national identities within the UK itself. If British identity is externally fuzzy, so too is its meaning within these islands. Until Ireland became a republic in 1948, its citizens remained formally 'subjects' of the British Crown. (Their independence was reinforced by the new republic leaving the Commonwealth a year later, largely to break finally with this colonial legacy.) A number of other key confusions remained, notably that between 'Britain' and 'England', a distinction that was rarely made in the UK's largest country as well as overseas. It was the norm to describe the UK as a 'nation-state', an extension of England. Although the Scots and the Welsh worked within a more logical model, whereby their national identities were nested in the broader British state identity, the unitary nature of that state, with a single, sovereign parliament, seemed to reinforce the equation of Britain and England, and the tendency to see the UK as 'greater England'.

We have, then, in these islands a complex set of national political identities. Following Cohen, we can identify the following 'fuzzy frontiers':

- between the English, the largest nationality, and the Scots, who were jointly responsible for founding 'Great Britain' in 1707;
- the relationship between the English/Scots and the other Celtic peoples – the Welsh on the one hand and the Irish on the other (most of whom are citizens of an independent republic, but with voting and residence rights in the UK – leaving aside the complications in Northern Ireland);
- the (white) Commonwealth or former 'Dominions' such as Australia, New Zealand and Canada, which are politically independent, but genealogically, culturally and legally linked (via 'patriality' rights of settlement);
- the (black) Commonwealth, with a history of post-war settlement (defining 'ethnicity' in the UK);
- European links (via but not exclusively with the EU), which also imply rights of settlement and residence to 'non-British' people;
- Anglophones (especially via cultural and historical links with the US).

The issues of ethnicity and nationality, in the UK are especially 'fuzzy'. Britishness is a political identity, roughly equated with citizenship, but growing out of a pre-modern prior definition of people as 'subjects' of the Crown, and even applying to those who do not live in these islands. As this older sense of Britishness declines – people retiring today were not even born when the Second World War ended – it is tempting to predict its demise.

Citizens and the nation-state

Is the United Kingdom an unusual kind of multi-national state? Let us next take a broader and comparative view of the making of modern states and nationality. It is part of our vocabulary to talk of 'nation-states'. Why does the term nation-state have such strong currency in the western world? The answer is that the term was captured by the process of state-building which has shaped Western Europe over the last two centuries. If states were not actually 'nations' too, then they could be imagined as such, either now or in the future. As we have seen, the state is a political concept, whereas the nation is a cultural one. So successful is this alignment between state and nation that it is part of our common sense, our taken-for-granted political and cultural world. Here is the orthodox view:

> All modern states are nation-states – political apparatuses, distinct from both rulers and ruled, with supreme jurisdiction over a demarcated territorial area, backed by a claim to a monopoly of coercive power, and enjoying a minimum level of support or loyalty from their citizens. (Held 1992: 87)

We might be surprised that the cultural component is downplayed and operates merely as a loyalty device for the state, but this view of the 'nation-state' is the dominant one. Sociologists like Anthony Giddens (1981: 190) reproduce this definition, but without any cultural component being mentioned. The nation-state, he comments, is:

> a set of institutional forms of governance maintaining an administrative monopoly over a territory with demarcated boundaries, its rule being sanctioned by law and direct control of the means of internal and external violence.

Giddens (1985: 120) sees the 'nation' as a 'bordered power-container', which can exist only 'when a state has a unified administrative reach over the territory over which its sovereignty is claimed'. Max Weber well understood the distinction between state and nation and defined the key characteristics of the modern state as follows: territoriality – having fixed and defensible borders; control of the means of violence – both internally and externally; an impersonal structure of power – the idea of a sovereign and impersonal political order; and legitimacy – requiring the loyalty of its citizens (Held 1992).

Does it matter that we align state and nation, the political and the cultural? Most certainly it does, because it gives a fundamental legitimacy to the modern state without which it could not function. After all, the modern state derives its legitimacy from its claim to speak on behalf of 'the people'. This is a powerful idea, and may make the United Kingdom an unusual state. However, when we look in detail at other states, it does not look so unusual.

In his study of citizenship and nationhood in France and Germany, Brubaker (1992) argued that definitions of citizenship in these states result from the fact that, whereas in France the unitary state was established before the nation, in Germany it was the other way round, the 'nation' preceded the 'state'. In France, the monarchy held sway over a fairly defined and gradually expanding territory, and promoted the concept of citizenship based on *ius soli*, the law of soil or territorial jurisdiction, in such a way that whatever their ethnic or geographical origins, all residents on French soil could in principle be subjects, later citizens, of the French state. Peasants had, in Eugene Weber's phrase, to be made into Frenchmen, but this formulation neatly expresses the prior existence of the state over the sense of nation, at least in popular terms.

In Germany, by contrast, the unitary state did not arrive until 1871, and the nation had to be defined differently. Since members of the German nation might be subjects of different kings – Bavaria, Saxony, Prussia, even Austria and Russia – national identity was based on *ius sanguinis*, the law of blood, so that anyone accepted as having German blood was German and thus after 1871 eligible to be a citizen of Germany, whether or not they actually lived on German soil.

As a result of these different routes to 'nation-statehood', the interpretation of nationality differs. In France, according to Brubaker, it is state-centred and assimilationist, so that anyone living within the territory of the French state became a French citizen. In Germany, on the other hand, it is nation-centred and differentialist. Anyone who could prove German ethnicity was counted as 'German', but the definition differentiated among those living within Germany itself so that some were counted as ethnically German and others, such as people of Turkish origin, were not, until the law was changed in 1998.

Nor is this loose association between how people identify themselves with the state in question simply confined to Germany and France (and the United Kingdom). There is a famous saying, usually attributed to the Italian politician, Massimo D'Azeglio in the 1860s: '*Fatta l'Italia; bisogna fare gli italiani*', which roughly translates as 'We have made Italy; we must now make Italians'. What is sociologically interesting about this is that it inverts the conventional wisdom that people first have a sense of themselves as a nationality and, as a result, demand their own state as a form of self-government. Here we find that it is the other way round: first, the state, and then making citizens. In other words, 'national' identity has to be actively fabricated ('forged', in Linda Colley's telling phrase) in the process of state-building. In that respect, maybe the 'British' don't look so unusual after all. And yet the assumption that nation and state are coterminous seems to be an argument many are reluctant to jettison. My argument is that it is important not to confuse the two terms, because they operate on different planes and lead us to imagine that modern states have captured political and cultural power. This is problematic because the ideal-typical process always had a more messy reality lying behind it.

Not only is the equation of nation and state historically dubious, in the twenty-first century the concepts are coming apart. The (con)fusion of nation and state is a common one, and needs to be taken seriously rather than treated as an unfortunate error of logic. What it signifies is that the cultural and the political have become so closely allied in the modern state that we usually treat their outcomes – nation and state – as synonyms. In its conventional expression – the nation-state – it is expected that the 'people' who are governed by the institutions of the state are by and large culturally homogeneous in having a strong and common linguistic, religious and symbolic identity. We see, more clearly than most, the 'impending crisis of the hyphen' (Anderson 1996: 8). Some scholars have pointed out that very few so-called nation-states are actually such. Connor (1994) claims less than ten per cent in 1971, and historical sociologists like Tilly (1992: 3) distinguish between 'nation-states' and 'national states' that are governed by common political and institutional structures. He comments that very few European states have ever qualified as nation-states (possibly Sweden and Ireland), and that 'Great Britain, Germany and France – quintessential national states – certainly have never met the test'.

Whether we use 'national' or 'nation-state' matters because it frames the world as it is meant to be, not how it is. Strictly speaking, 'nation-state' implies that all self-governing political units – states – correspond with culturally distinctive units – nations – so that the world appears as a giant jigsaw of such entities. Of course, the pieces do not fit. Not only are most states not culturally and ethnically homogeneous, but many nations are, in formal terms, 'stateless', such as Scotland and even England.

Why, we might ask, does the term nation-state have such strong currency in the West? It is one thing to fret about the inexactness of the term, but more interesting to ask why it has such hegemony in describing the contemporary world. The root of the answer lies in the process of state-building, which also shaped Western Europe over the last two centuries. If states were not actually 'nations' too, then they could be imagined as such, or at least aspired to. So successful has this alignment between state and nation been that it is part of our sociological 'common sense', our taken-for-granted political and cultural world. Does it matter? Most certainly, because it gives a fundamental legitimacy to the modern state without which it could not function.

The problem with this formulation is that, on the one hand, the covert influence of nation-state building in recent centuries dominates politics, sociology and history alike. On the other hand, societies bounded in geographical and social space are less and less likely to be unified totalities in the early twenty-first century when economic, political and cultural forces have eroded the homogeneity of states.

The key changes that impact on the relationships between state, society and nation in the twenty-first century can be characterised as follows. On the one hand, and contrary to expectations, nationalism has waxed rather than waned in importance over time. Nationalisms have arisen in regions or territories that wish to break away from existing states. When we think of nationalism in the West, we think of its rise in Scotland, Wales, Catalonia and Quebec and other formally 'stateless' nations (McCrone 2001). Nationalism has become an active basis for social divisions within states.

We need however, to recognise that there is a core form of nationalism that is frequently implicit. As the modern state became the appropriate instrument for guaranteeing the life chances of its citizens and ironing out social inequalities, governments became major actors in inter-state competition for economic growth 'in the national interest'. This is 'state nationalism' expressed in economic and political competition. Nationalism, in this form, became more, not less, common in this process of international competition. This nationalism of the 'core' – that is, existing states such as the UK, Spain and Belgium – developed alongside counter-nationalisms on the periphery among stateless nations within core states (such as Scotland, Catalonia and Flanders), which sought to redraw the limits and responsibilities of central state power and, in many cases, secede from it.

And yet, just as nationalism was growing in importance, so the 'nation-state' appeared to be losing its powers. This is one aspect of a wider process known as 'globalisation', whereby economic, cultural and political influences increasingly operate at a world or global level. We live in a world of global economic markets, with its cultural products like Coca-Cola, and supra-state institutions such as the EU, the IMF and the World Bank (Chapter 16). All these forces appear to have eroded the power of the independent state. Why then has there been an increase in national movements wanting a state of their own? How is it possible to explain this apparent contradiction?

One possibility is that the sovereignty of the nation-state was always a trick of the eye. In the words of Tamir (1993: 3):

The era of the homogeneous and viable nation-states is over (or rather the era of the illusion that homogeneous and viable nation-states are possible is over, since such states never existed) and the national vision must be redefined.

Nowhere is this more obvious than in the British Isles where, as we have seen, nationality and citizenship have evolved in an idiosyncratic way. The British are not at all like the French, in that the French civic republican tradition defines (possibly over-defines) who is to be French and how one is to behave. The British, in contrast, are under-defined. There is no common football team and no rugby team (the British Lions includes players from the whole of Ireland, most of which quit the British state over 70 years ago). Sport is a good indicator of nationality. After all, you are a 'national' if you play for the national side. In the 1980s, the Conservative politician Norman Tebbit provoked controversy when he talked about his 'cricket test'. How could people of Caribbean and Asian origins be considered English, he implied, if they opted to cheer for the West Indies, India or Pakistan against England? What he failed to notice was the 'fuzzy' nature of national identity (that England was not Britain). More recently, an important debate has started in England about whether or not black people can be 'English' rather than simply 'British'. In many ways this is a debate about ethnic (being English by lineage or 'blood') versus civic definitions (being British by residence and citizenship). Black footballers and brown cricketers playing for England help to highlight the issue.

Here we find an intriguing pattern. Non-white people living in England, including those born there, are far more likely to say they are 'British' than 'English' (Curtice and Heath 2009: 57). In truth, it is not clear why that should be so. It may be because, for their parents and grandparents, getting a British passport made them officially 'British', or because they do not feel able to say they are English, which is taken as an ethnic and racial category (being 'white'). The rise of extreme political movements like the English Defence League (note 'English', not 'British') may reinforce that point. The same does not seem to be true of Scottishness, as non-white people, notably those of Pakistani origin who are by far the largest 'ethnic minority' are prepared to call themselves 'Pakistani Scots' or 'Scottish Muslims' (Hussain and Miller 2006).

There is a related matter that is worth exploring at this point in our argument, and that is the issue of regional identity. When English people are asked to describe their nationality, it is not uncommon for many to echo the views of the person who replied: 'I'm not English. I'm from Yorkshire.' In strict terms, of course, being from Yorkshire (or Lancashire and so on) is a regional not a national identity. However, the speaker is possibly reacting to what can be perceived as the 'capture' of Englishness by a southern, 'home counties' version. (In passing, it is interesting to note the revealing terminology of English geography. The cultural core, the 'centre', is 'the home counties' (not the region called The Midlands) and the peripheries are described as 'the North' and 'the West'.) It would be difficult to argue, however, that, with few exceptions, any

English region has the cultural wherewithal – language, history, institutions – to turn regionalism into nationalism. (In 2004, voters in northeast England declined the opportunity of moving towards regional devolution.) Perhaps the only real candidate is Cornwall, where there is an embryonic 'national' movement based on precisely these cultural markers. For the rest, only their justified resentment towards the financial and political dominance of London and the South-East as an 'Other' provides a sense of difference, but not one which can unite their separate regional interests.

Being British today

What, then, does it mean to be British? We know that being British was 'forged' in the eighteenth century as a result of war with France and, relatedly, being Protestant in contradistinction to Europe's greatest Catholic power. 'Forgery' of course implies not simply something beaten into shape on the blacksmith's anvil, but a counterfeit, a subterfuge. It was nevertheless a convincing one because it created Britons (who were also Scots, English, Welsh – but only rarely Irish, most of whom were too Catholic to be British). We can measure the success of this creation by the huge number of Britons who died for their country. *Dulce et decorum est pro patria mori* (It is sweet and right to die for your country), perhaps, but the 'patria' in question was undoubtedly British and it even encompassed others in the far-flung Empire, as a visit to any war graveyard will show.

What makes people British today? By and large the same criteria that are used by other states: where you are born, your legal citizenship, being resident in the country, speaking the language, respecting the country's political institutions and the law, and generally feeling a national citizen. In these respects, the British are no different from other Western Europeans. In recent survey work we asked people in England and Scotland what they identified as the key symbols of British culture. The English and the Scots broadly agreed on the rankings. 'British democracy' was by far the most popular icon of being British, followed in England by 'the British monarchy' and in Scotland by 'British fair play'. The least chosen symbols were those of conventional iconography: the flag, anthem and sport. Even people who thought of themselves as mainly national (English or Scottish) ranked these symbols in a similar way. In other words, the importance attached by both the English and the Scots to symbols of British culture is not associated with their *own* self-identification. People are well able to identify state symbols, even though fewer than ever choose to say that they themselves are British. 'Britain' remains an important and meaningful frame of reference, even though more and more people in England and

Scotland do not define their national identity primarily as British. Agreement on the symbolic meaning of Britishness, however, only points to the strength of the concept of Britishness rather than an attachment to the reality of the British state.

Are we beginning to see an emergent proto-English nationalism? Englishness differs from Scottishness, Welshness and Irishness, in so far as it does not look to these 'Celtic' identities to provide the necessary 'other'. Instead, we would have to look to Continental Europe – France and Germany in particular, and possibly 'Europe' as a whole – for that alter ego against which being English can be constructed. We can see this most easily in the right-of-centre opinion that is hostile to the EU, held by those who commonly – and revealingly – are referred to as 'Little Englanders' (not, of course, 'little Britishers', for there is perhaps more of a 'greater England' perspective on these matters in right-wing circles). Such opinion also tends to be hostile to devolution for Scotland and Wales, and we might speculate that opposition to Europe as well as to constitutional change in these islands provides a solid platform on which a right-wing version of English nationalism might emerge onto the political stage in the next few decades. There is only a loose association between people's preferred national identity and their political views. In Scotland, those who say they are 'Scottish not British' are not necessarily making a political statement about voting nationalist or wanting Scottish Independence. The association is much looser. Similarly, in England those who prioritise being English are not demanding a separate English parliament. Indeed, the English consensus is that Westminster currently doubles up as both 'English' and 'British' (Curtice and Heath 2009).

Are we seeing the break-up of Britain, driven by resurgent Scottish, Welsh, and even English national identities? That is to look too far ahead. Instead, we might ask: how significant is national identity as a source of social division and differentiation in modern Britain? There is a strong case for saying that there is no single 'national' identity in these islands, and that, if anything, it is likely to get even weaker than it currently appears to be. The UK is a *de facto* multinational state, which is likely to grow more diverse in constitutional terms as the different nations develop their own parliaments and assemblies. Indeed, if Scotland becomes independent and leaves the United Kingdom, there will be another twist to the tale, and a redefinition of the British 'we'.

What is the prognosis for Britishness? One scenario would be that the political, religious and cultural conditions that created and sustained it – war, empire, religion and the welfare state – no longer operate to hold the British together. An alternative scenario is to say that the loose, umbrella-like identity of being British is best suited to adapt to the multicultural – ethnic as well as national – conditions that now exist in these islands. The last 50 years have

seen the growing importance of nation and ethnicity as markers of social identity. The next 50 years are likely to see an expanding sense of multi-nationality,
of layering and sharing of political identities. One key task for sociology is to
make sense of the new identity politics that this new era will bring.

Discussion Questions

1. To what extent, and why, does being English differ from being British?
2. Is national identity stronger or weaker than state identity in the countries of
   the UK?
3. Why is nationalism a taken-for-granted ideology in modern societies?

FURTHER READING

Bechhofer, F. and McCrone, D. (eds.) *National Identity, Nationalism and Constitutional
Change* (Basingstoke: Palgrave Macmillan, 2009) looks at how people in England and
Scotland 'do' national identity. McCrone, D. *Understanding Scotland: The Sociology of a
Nation* (London: Routledge, 2001) examines how Scotland has changed in the British
context, while Colley, L. *Britons: Forging the Nation* (New Haven, CT: Yale University
Press, 1992) is the key text on how 'being British' was manufactured from the eight-
eenth century onwards. A useful analysis of ethnic and national identities in the UK
can be found in Cohen, R. *Frontiers of Identity* (Harlow: Longman, 1994). Brubaker, R.
Citizenship and Nationhood in France and Germany (Cambridge, MA: Harvard University Press, 1992) is an elegant review of the different nationalisms of the two countries.

CHAPTER 11

Elites

PHILIP STANWORTH

This chapter will provide you with a broad critical understanding of the main features of elite analysis including:

- Pareto, Mosca and Michels' ideas on the origins and character of elites
- Burnham's theory of the 'managerial revolution'
- Schumpeter's thoughts on the links between leadership and democracy
- The incorporation of the concept of elites into pluralist theories of democracy
- The development of a power elite in the US as proposed by C. Wright Mills
- Djilas's theory of the 'new class'
- The Miliband/Poulantzas debate on the use of elite analysis in Marxist accounts of contemporary capitalism
- Giddens' clarification of the main dimensions of elite analysis: recruitment, structure and power
- The importance of situating elite analysis in the wider socio-economic and political context
- A comparison of the educational profiles of selected contemporary British elites
- Detailed examination of the educational profiles of the political, civil service and army elites

Even in social democracies, the sight of presidential or prime ministerial motor cavalcades, with their key players cocooned in heavy security, is a dramatic representation of the idea of elites as a separate political group, ruling over and divided from the great masses to which the rest of us belong. The commonly expressed sense of public alienation from political participation – 'my vote won't change anything: politicians are all the same' – is another testament to the gulf that is perceived to exist between rulers and the ruled. The social division between elites and masses is not only stark, but clearly demonstrates the social processes that provide the foundations of division more generally. The distinctive dimension of difference in elites is that of organisational, usually political, power.

The origins of elite theory

The concept of elites entered the sociological lexicon through the work of three major figures at the beginning of the twentieth century: Pareto, Mosca and Michels. To clarify the similarities and differences between their contributions, we need to look in more detail at each. Whereas Pareto used the term 'elite' to refer to the small group he believed dominated all complex societies, Mosca preferred the term 'political class'. However, he later also used the term 'ruling class', which should not be confused with the different meaning that Marx and Weber gave to the same expression (Chapter 2). Michels tended to use 'leadership' and 'oligarchy' rather than 'elites', although, as with Pareto and Mosca, the focus of his attention was ruling minorities.

Pareto and Mosca became embroiled in an argument about whose work had precedence in the exploration of elites, but, of the two, it was indisputably Mosca (1896) who first developed the idea of minority rule. A conservative exponent of the cause of the upper middle class, Mosca had two principal targets. On the one hand, he challenged the central claims of socialism, especially the promise of a class-free, stateless society. On the other, he opposed the over-ambitious extension of parliamentary democracy in Italy, which he believed had produced a decline of civic morality and the rise of the Left. His commitment to the idea of elite rule derived from Saint-Simon's observation (1825) that an organised minority would always hold sway over a disorganised majority, and that it was a necessary feature of any complex society. It was Mosca's hope that this minority would be a civilised, benign, patrician political elite of 'superior persons', although he recognised that this might not always be so.

All societies, he contended, consisted of two classes: the rulers and the ruled, a division expressing a universal trait in human beings – the unending struggle for power. Although this conflict resulted from the unchanging psychological structure of men, in Mosca's view dominance itself resulted from cultural, intellectual and moral attributes rather than biological superiority. Even though force was a factor in minority rule, of far more importance was the 'political formula' by which those in power legitimised their position. Such a ruling myth was constructed out of values, beliefs and habits, and rooted in the specific historical conditions and culture of a society. A feature of all stable rule was the carefully cultivated adherence to this formula by the masses in order to secure their compliance and acquiescence. A political class could maintain its position peaceably only when its rule was the expression of a unified culture and morality, which encapsulated 'real' social forces.

Pareto developed an interest in sociology after first studying engineering and later economics. He was an adherent of free-market economic theory and policies of free trade, yet found classical economic theory lacking. As he observed, in contradiction of his intellectual convictions, protectionist policies were often associated with strong economic growth. Something, Pareto concluded, must be missing from liberal economic theory, and that something was the recognition that a large proportion of human activity was 'non-logical' rather than the outcome of reasoning and rationality. Pareto's sociology was therefore an inversion of his economics, in that it analysed the irrational, rather than rational, pursuit of self-interest as the key feature in the struggle for power.

Pareto's first major book of sociological significance was a critique of socialism, *Les Systems Socialistes* (1902), which was rumoured to have given Lenin sleepless nights. Pareto's conclusion was that socialism was fundamentally flawed in its aspiration to build a classless society because all societies were, and always would be, divided between those who held power and the masses they dominated. Marxism failed to acknowledge the irredeemable inferiority of the masses and the psychological and social superiority of elites. The existence of elites reflected the differential distribution of talents amongst the population. All forms of social activity, from art, music, cooking and governing, display different levels of performance from incompetence to excellence. The elites that dominated society did so by demonstrating their force of character, capacity to command and elemental and general superiority over those they dominated.

Pareto linked the social character of elites to the 'residues' they encompassed. Most of social life, Pareto asserted, derived from relatively unchanging 'residues' – givens in human behaviour that had the quality of biologically-based building blocks of social life. These instinctual elements in behaviour were overlain by more readily observable, but less significant, 'derivations' – the varying rationales, justifications and explanations that legitimated conduct. Pareto distinguished between six types of residue. The most important distinctions were between Class 1, the 'Instinct for Combinations', which he associated with inventiveness, ingenuity, originality and progressive change, and Class 2, the 'Persistence of Aggregates', which concerned continuity, convention and the conservative tendencies in human life.

Each of these residues was dominant in different types of elite. Those elites that relied on cunning, persuasiveness and originality – 'foxes' – manifested the instinct for combination. Those characterised by force and strength of purpose – 'lions' – evidenced the persistence of aggregates. History consisted of the circulation of elites, in which the manipulative foxes would eventually concede too much to the masses, to be replaced by lions willing and able to establish their authority by means of violence. In time, their rule would stagnate and decline, only to be replaced by scheming foxes.

Michels' ([1911]1962) analysis is perhaps the most sociological of the three, yet his complex analysis of the emergence of oligarchies has a place for inherent human psychology and a conception of fixed human nature. Michels' basic idea was that all large-scale organisations, including political parties, develop bureaucratic structures that concentrate power at the top. They were, therefore, oligarchic and undemocratic. Michels argued that the increasing complexity of political organisations favoured those with the specialist knowledge and skills associated with leadership, and reduced the possibility of widespread participation in decision-making. Leaders were able to control flows of information and discipline dissidents, further strengthening their position. They became more practised in the use of power and arts of manipulation. As political organisations matured, leadership was consolidated and further alienated from the rank and file as it absorbed the lifestyle of other metropolitan elites. In contrast, subordinates for the most part, indeed the masses in general, were perennially incompetent, incapable of self-organisation and generally content to be led.

Although Michels focused on the social processes of organisational life in explaining the emergence of oligarchy, such concentrations of power were also an expression of an immutable tendency to regard power as a personal possession. The vagaries of upward and downward mobility (Chapter 2) might account for some change in the personnel comprising elites, but the tendency to manipulation and self-interest would remain the same. These were the factors that sapped the revolutionary ideas of socialist parties and produced their conservative leaderships, more concerned with furthering their own interests than those of the people they claimed to represent.

Michels maintained that the 'iron law of oligarchy' was a major problem for any political organisation that aimed to create a democratic society, especially a classless society, and which claimed to be democratic in its own procedures. This was a particular concern for Michels, a supporter of the socialist movement in Germany at the time he wrote *Political Parties* ([1911]1962). His disillusionment marked the beginning of a political journey towards the Right.

Although there were important theoretical and terminological differences between Pareto, Mosca and Michels, the object of their attention was broadly similar – the organised and self-interested minorities that, they asserted, ruled all complex societies by a combination of force and fraud. It would be going too far to claim they offer a coherent school of thought but their studies have certain elements in common. All viewed the fundamental division in society as that between a ruling minority, an elite, and the masses who were the vast majority of the population. Elites, they claimed, are driven to monopolise power whilst the masses are portrayed as typically incompetent, unorganised and inchoate. Ruling elites are characterised by the three Cs: group consciousness, internal coherence and conspiracy (common intentions).

Mosca, Pareto and Michels argued that governing minorities are composed of people of proven 'superiority', with regard to their intellects, organisational abilities, cultural attributes and capacity to rule. Such elites are required if society is not to descend into disorder. Their superiority and associated desire for power was, for Pareto, primarily innate in origin. Mosca and Michels gave more, but not exclusive, weight to social and cultural factors.

This classical conception of elites placed political manipulation and power at the centre of attention and stood in contrast with the Marxist stress on the economy and control of the means of production. For Pareto, Marx's class conflict is but a subspecies of the universal clash between elites and those who aspire to replace them. To Michels, class revolution always would end in the creation of yet another oligarchy, a view he expressed prior to the Bolshevik revolution.

These writers shared a rejection of Marxism, particularly the promise of a classless society, and opposed the ambitions of the Socialist and Communist movements in Italy, particularly after the First World War. They were also sceptical about the claims to participation and representation made on behalf of parliamentary democracy. In this case, the specific object of their criticism was the weakness, vacillation and corruption of the Italian political system in the late decades of the nineteenth century and early years of the twentieth, prior to the rise of Fascism.

Mosca, Pareto and Michels witnessed the rise to power of Mussolini, the Fascist dictator of Italy. Pareto was an enthusiastic supporter and took the rise of Fascism to be confirmation of his theories. Appointed senator by Mussolini, he died within a year of the 'March on Rome'. Mosca surveyed Fascism with the reluctant disdain of an intellectual confronted by the vulgarity of the rabble. He became a leading conservative critic of Fascism and hoped for a limited form of democratic rule under the leadership of an enlightened political class. Michels welcomed Fascism as right for Italy, in that it brought a 'forceful' clarity to a society in danger of collapse. Whilst he hoped an elitist form of democracy might eventually emerge, he accepted a chair in political science in Turin, whose purpose was the promotion of Fascism, and became a member of the Fascist Party.

The development of elite theory

Perhaps the most direct heir of classical elite theory was James Burnham, initially a supporter of Trotsky and the revolutionary Left, who moved to the political Right to become a neo-conservative of some influence. In *The*

Managerial Revolution, published in 1941, Burnham argued that managers, by virtue of their control of large-scale organisations and indispensable technical function, were taking over the world, regardless of the social, economic and political character of the societies in which they operated. For Burnham, factual control of the means of production was more important than mere legal ownership and therefore the rise of the Bolsheviks, the Nazis and indeed the so-called 'propertyless managers' in free-market democracies were all manifestations of the same phenomenon, the rise of organisational elites. This claim was quite in line with elite theory, although what Burnham purported to discern was the rise of a new class, rather than a new elite. Burnham's ideas on management had some influence on Crossman and Crosland – luminaries in the 1950s' Labour Party.

Burnham's affinity with classical elite theory was made explicit in *The Machiavellians* published in 1943. In reviewing the work of Mosca, Pareto and Michels, Burnham adapts an amalgam of their approaches to the analysis of power. Politics is portrayed as being about unceasing struggle, non-logical in character and based on instinct. Rulers always rule in their own interests by combining force, fraud and political formulations to supply the cultural foundations of power.

Schumpeter, influenced by Weber, developed the links between leadership groups, competitive elites and the prospects for democracy in his book *Capitalism, Socialism and Democracy* (1942). After a brilliant early career as an economist (three major books and finance minister in Austria in 1919 by the age of 35), Schumpeter also made a considerable impact in sociology and political science. In his ruminations on democracy, elites were regarded not as inherently at odds with representative democracy (as with Pareto and Michels) but as key elements in the modern democratic system, albeit a system in which the main political duty of the general population was to elect its leaders and little else. Thus, circulating elites and leadership groups linked to different interests competing for influence and power were conceived to be among the principal constituents of democracy. Schumpeter placed particular importance on the manipulation of symbols and the values that elites espoused. He feared that such pluralistic democratic systems would produce forms of democratic socialism and the ideal elite would be one of talent and civilised ideals able to contain such tendencies.

Schumpeter's rather conservative notion of democratic rule was an influence on the ideas of the 'pluralist' political theorists of the 1950s. Pluralists argued that the democratic systems of modern societies were characterised by the diffusion of power rather than its concentration in the hands of a dominant class or group. Picking up certain elements of Burnham's approach, they accepted that class structure was decomposing and a business elite of professionalised, propertyless managers was taking over the corporate sector. In the view of pluralists, such leadership groups and elites were linked to widely differing interests and pressure groups and competed for control of the policy-making apparatus at the local and national levels through the electoral process. In associating the concept of elites with the diffusion rather than accretion of power, pluralists were using the term in direct reversal of the ideas of the classical elite theorists.

However, the idea of elites as the locus of concentrated power re-emerged in Mills' critique of pluralism, although shorn of assumptions of inherent superiority or inevitability. Mills had reviewed Burnham's *The Managerial Revolution* and rejected its central argument, on the grounds that technical indispensability (the management function) was no guarantor of power. In his own book *The Power Elite* (1956), Mills also rejected the Marxist idea of a ruling class, arguing that it assumed too close an identity of economic and political power and the subordination of the latter to the former. The term 'power elite' was more appropriate, in that a good deal of its authority derived from the characteristics of complex organisations in modern societies rather than control of the means of production. The class society of eighteenth- and nineteenth-century America, Mills stated, was being replaced by a more concentrated, and, in some senses, less democratic configuration of power.

Mills identified three, initially distinct, components of power: the political, the military and the industrial/business sectors. He argued that a complex process of consolidation had occurred throughout the twentieth century, accelerated by the Second World War, in which a developing 'military-industrial complex' (a term used by President Eisenhower) was melding with the political sphere to produce a consolidated power elite. This elite controlled the masses in part through the manipulation of the media. Mills feared that the plurality of diverse interests that had characterised American history was increasingly unable to act as a restraint on the elite, and that the community of publics was being replaced by a mass society, with grave consequences for democracy.

Mills' *The Power Elite* was heavily criticised, especially by those of pluralist persuasion, including Talcott Parsons, who focused on Mills' insecure 'zero-sum' conception of power. However, what is notable is Mills' attempt to analyse the social origins, career paths, affiliations and connections between the occupants of elite positions. He places these sociological attributes of elite people (exclusively men, in fact) within an analysis of institutional change in the US. In so doing, he concentrates on the intersection of biography and history – the essential task of the sociologist in Mills' view.

Mills' analysis of the US, in which a class society had given way to elite domination, mirrored Milovan Djilas's analysis of Tito's Yugoslavia in the

1950s. In *The New Class* (1957), Djilas suggested that the Communist Party's power as a political elite was metamorphosing into the birth of a new class, a position that cost him years in jail. Thus, whilst Mills maintained that the US was moving from class to elite, Djilas was tracking the shift from elite to class in Yugoslavia. So, ironically, Mills, who had little sympathy with the politics of the classical elitists, used the term in some sense as they had to express the concentration of power of a minority over a manipulated mass. However, there is no suggestion that this had always been or would always be the case, was desirable or that that rule is based on inherent or civilisational superiority. Mills was indeed a vocal critic of the elite he portrayed, so much so that the FBI kept track of his activities after his defence of the Cuban Revolution.

Mills visited Britain, mixing with the emerging New Left and certainly influencing the Marxist Ralph Miliband. Yet in contrast to Mills' doubts about class analysis, Miliband linked the terms 'class' and 'elite' in his book *The State in Capitalist Society* (1969). This was intended to both extend Marxist analysis of the state and reject pluralist claims about the nature of contemporary capitalist societies. In attempting to demonstrate how the state served, defended and consolidated the interests of capital, Miliband explored, briefly, the social and educational background of those holding elite positions within the state and other organisations. He hoped, thereby, to establish the manner in which class factors influenced the recruitment and training of elites in further consolidation of the capitalist system.

For some Marxists, the use of the notions of class and elites in this way was unacceptable, not least because of the historic link between the concept of elite and Fascism. Poulantzas (1969), for instance, argued that Miliband's attempt to establish empirical links between the dominant class and the composition and operation of various institutional elites was theoretically flawed and subjectivist. It was not a matter of who occupied such positions but how the positions were arranged and functioned.

Thus, by the 1970s, there were at least four different major conceptions of elites operative in sociology:

1. Elites are leadership groups, representing different interests, competing for power and influence. They are a central feature of the democratic process and integral to a political process that ameliorates social division (pluralists such as Parsons and Dahl).
2. Elites represent necessary concentrations of power and are fundamental to social order in all complex societies. They are the key feature of the major social division between elites and masses (Pareto, Mosca, Michels, Burnham).

3. Elites reflect the interests of the dominant class but have a degree of relative autonomy. Class is the central social division of contemporary capitalist societies (Miliband).
4. The power elite has developed a complex logic of its own, serving the amalgamated interests of capital, the political establishment and the military hierarchy, and is the fundamental enemy of democratic processes however the rhetoric of democracy is deployed. The central social division in modern society (at least the US in the 1950s and 1960s) is between the elite and the masses (Mills).

Giddens' (1974) intervention in the debate aimed to remove some of the confusions patrolling elite analysis. He defined elites as holders of senior positions of formal authority in major social institutions and the state (for example, MPs, the Cabinet, senior civil servants, chairs and chief executive officers in major corporations, high-ranking military officers and so on). Giddens made a number of distinctions between three dimensions of elite analysis – recruitment, structure and power – that are still useful today.

The analysis of recruitment concerned the gender, social origins and educational experience of elites, and the avenues of occupational and professional advancement that lead to elite positions. Here the issue is the channels of entry, some highly formalised (military, judiciary), others involving a large element of custom and practice (politics). With respect to recruitment, much has been made of the high proportion of those entering British elites (the vast majority men) over the past 150 years who have been educated in public schools and attended Oxford or Cambridge universities. However, of equal significance are the professional, occupational and less formal processes of career socialisation experienced by future holders of elite positions, processes that facilitate the accumulation of the appropriate types of cultural and social capital associated with elites. For instance, army officers subscribe to the officer and gentleman ethos, regardless of their social and educational origins, due to the impact and efficacy of officer training at Sandhurst.

Giddens' notion of structure embraces two elements: patterns of organisational interaction between elites, and social linkages within an elite. The latter involves its social structure, and the values and orientations that characterise an elite – its ethos. Investigating the social structure of an elite involves attempting to discern whether there are networks of friendship, kinship, formal and informal association which embroider the formal organisational activities of elites within and between their different spheres of operation. Casual acquaintance may be as significant as strong ties in facilitating flows of information, getting things done and generally operating effectively. Some elites (the Cabinet for instance) constitute a demographic group, in that they meet and work in close proximity. Others (business leaders) never meet or act as a socially constituted group, although sharing various forms of formal and informal contact. The analysis of the values of elites incorporates questions such as whether, and to what extent, elites possess a distinctive ethos, and the extent to which different elites may share certain value orientations. Important studies of elites in the military, the police and the civil service, for instance, have noted their distinctive cultural character and elements of change and continuity in their core values.

The third and most important of Giddens' dimensions is the complex problem of power, including issues of the extent to which elites exercise power within their own institutional domains and are able to influence affairs in other areas of activity. Giddens is emphatic that formal authority should be distinguished from effective power, although it may be an important source of it. Consequently, the issue of the extent to which elites are able to transform their formal authority into decision-making and operative policy is an empirical question, not to be settled a priori by assuming that elites are, by definition, all-powerful. Nor should the examination of elite power be confined only to decision-making, for there are aspects of the powers of elites that go beyond the decisions and policies in which they are implicated and which require examination. This extended view includes control of what is publicly discussed by 'agenda-setting' and selecting personnel who will join and, in some cases, replace them.

There is an important analytical distinction to be made between 'the rich' and elites as defined by Giddens. The rich as such form part of the analysis of class structure, whereas elites belong to the realm of institutional power. Elites may include persons drawn from the upper class and holders of elite positions may accumulate enough wealth to enter the realms of the wealthy. But class structure and elite formations are distinct sociological phenomena. For instance, many of the 3000 people working in the City who were paid bonuses in excess of £1 million in 2005 were financial intermediaries, traders and bankers located in the middle echelons of their firms, and not holders of top positions. One of the points of the investigation of elites is therefore to explore the extent to which elites are drawn from different elements of the class structure.

These analytically distinct dimensions should always be placed within an analysis of broader society and global processes (Chapter 16) in order to understand the configuration of economy, state and socio-cultural structures within which elites operate and which provide the context for their formation, reproduction and operation. For instance, the structural and organisational changes characterised as the move from 'organised' to 'disorganised capitalism', the impact of globalisation and the emergence of so-called post-modern culture have significance in the general setting and context within which elites are formed and operate. Events since the financial meltdown of 2008 and its ramifications further emphasised the importance of placing national concerns within the context of global processes. Political and financial elites in Britain have never been more interested in the financial machinations of the Chinese Communist Party!

More recently, John Scott (2008) made an important contribution to the revitalisation of elite studies by reworking the theoretical bases for elite analysis. Retaining a conception of elites that focuses upon the most powerful positions in various institutional arenas, and differentiating between classes and elites, he delineates four types of elite on the basis of distinct forms of domination. He identifies coercive elites, characterised by the use of force; inducing elites, associated with manipulation; commanding elites, linked to legitimacy; and expert elites, based upon professionalised technical knowledge. Scott recognises that in practice these forms of domination overlap and thus elites will mobilise combinations of different forms of power in the practical, and often resisted, operation of control.

The kinds of questions that can be approached using these distinctions are the degree of openness of elites in socio-economic, gender or ethnic terms, the extent of their social and cultural cohesion, the range or scope of issues over which the elite has influence, the degree to which elites monopolise power within their institutional domain and the extent to which the power of an elite may extend into other spheres of activity. In this way, the study of elites throws light on the ways in which social divisions operate in contemporary society. For example, the simple observations that women and most ethnic minorities are seriously under-represented in British elites and that there is a well-defined and long-established pattern of educational selectivity are revealing of the structure of opportunity and, perhaps, ambition in the UK over the past three or four decades.

Education and elites in Britain

The tradition of investigating the educational backgrounds of holders of elite positions in the UK has been chiefly concerned with the relative importance of public schools and Oxford and Cambridge in educating elites. This type of analysis provides purchase on the question of the possible economic, political and socio-cultural consequences resulting from the historical predominance of these institutions. Attendance at certain types of school (for example independent schools, particularly the most prestigious) has often been used to infer social background. However, William Rubinstein (1993) has demonstrated that the connection between social origin and educational experience in the case of many elite position-holders has been far less straightforward than often assumed. That is, whilst it may be fair to say that children at independent schools are in general drawn from the more prosperous sections of the population, there are many cases of people from lower middle-class and even working-class backgrounds who have reached elite positions after attending such schools (perhaps on scholarships). For instance, in 1999, 17 per cent of the first-year intake at Cambridge University was drawn from the Registrar General's social classes 3B, 4 and 5 (parental background being routine, poorly paid, white-collar or manual worker), one-third of whom were educated privately. Thus, the social background of elites (which is often difficult to research) should be established independently of education. Nor will an examination of education reveal how the people comprising elites will behave or the values to which they will adhere when they achieve their position. Without recourse to other data, educational background reveals only the extent to which there are clear paths of educational achievement associated with entry to elites, how they differ between elites and the extent to which they have changed over time. Possession of a particular educational experience does not in itself cause a person to become a member of an elite, even if cultural capital is acquired in this way (Payne 1987a: 122–43).

Most of the information on the backgrounds of elites can be found in the publicly available directories, such as *Who's Who, Dod's Parliamentary Companion* and *The Whitehall Directory*. The internet is also a valuable source of information. However, given the changes in the organisation and status of many schools, especially during the 1960s and 1970s when comprehensive schools were introduced, it is important to ascertain the position of a school with regard to the state/private distinction at the time the person being investigated was attending. For instance, a number of state grammar schools moved to the independent sector rather than be transformed into comprehensive schools. Thus, persons holding elite positions today may have attended a school that is now in the private category but was a state school 35 years ago when they were there. The terms 'public', 'private' and 'independent' are used interchangeably here to refer to schools that lie outside the state sector. At the time of writing, it is too early to see the impact of the 2010 ConDem Coalition's creation of 'academies'.

During the past 30–40 years independent schools have educated approximately 5–7 per cent of the school population and 15–18 per cent of 16–18-year-olds. The vast majority of men who attended public schools and are represented in the following data attended Headmasters Conference (HMC) schools. At present, HMC schools number 247 – and 220 in the 1970s – accounting for about 6 per cent of secondary schools in Britain. Oxford and Cambridge Universities accounted for 20 per cent of UK undergraduates in the late 1930s, 4–5 per cent in the 1960s and 1970s and less than 2 per cent after

Table 11.1 Education of elite groups, 2000/01, percentages

	Judges	MPs (Con)	Military	Ambassadors	Bishops	Business chairs	Cabinet	MPs (LDs)	MPs (all)	VCs (pre-1992)	MPs (Lab)	HCS* in 1998
	158	166	105	112	105	75	26	52	659	81	412	155
Schools												
Public	77.8	65.1	67.7	64.3	50.5	49.0	34.6	32.7	30.0	28.3	16.0	56.2
HMC	75.3	62.1	61.0	58.0	49.5	45.0	26.9	32.7	26.6	23.4	11.4	49.7
Private	2.5	3.0	6.7	6.3	1.0	4.0	7.7	0.0	3.5	4.9	4.6	6.5
State	12.5	27.7	22.9	31.3	29.5	28.0	61.5	65.4	64.6	49.4	81.0	28.4
Overseas	8.2	1.8	4.8	2.7	4.1	17.0	3.8	1.9	1.7	1.1	1.7	3.9
Others	1.7	5.4	5.6	1.7	15.2	5.0	0.0	0.0	3.7	1.1	1.3	11.6
Universities												
Oxbridge	82.9	50.0	14.3	62.5	62.8	22.0	38.5	28.8	27.3	44.5	19.1	68.3
Oxford	41.0	27.1	3.8	32.1	29.5	11.0	19.2	19.2	16.4	23.5	12.6	38.1
Cambridge	42.4	24.0	10.5	30.4	33.3	11.0	19.2	9.6	10.9	21.0	6.6	30.3
Others	15.0	39.8	21.9	24.1	41.9	37.0	65.4	63.5	53.3	69.3	59.7	31.0
Overseas	5.7	10.2	2.9	6.3	8.6	22.0	7.7	7.7	7.6	4.0	6.3	9.8
Public school + Oxbridge	72.2	37.3	13.3	42.9	38.1	22.0	27.0	19.2	15.8	20.0	7.0	45.1

*HCS: Higher Civil Servants

Note

Totals exceed 100 per cent because of multiple schools and degrees.

Source: author's own research.

1992. The data in Table 11.1 refer to 1471 holders of elite positions, most of whom held post in 2000/01.

Four elites in Table 11.1 are notable for the high proportion of their membership who attended public schools (overwhelmingly HMC schools). Over three-quarters of the senior judiciary attended public schools, a figure approached by Tory MPs, the army and navy components of the military elite, and ambassadors. Approximately half of bishops, senior civil servants and the chairs of large business corporations were educated in the independent sector, whilst approximately one-third of the (Labour) Cabinet, Liberal Democrat MPs and MPs in total recorded such an education. Labour MPs were notable among these elites, in that only one-sixth had attended such schools. Put another way, amongst these elites, only vice-chancellors and certain sections of the political elite received their school education predominantly in the state sector.

Turning to university education (the lower half of Table 11.1), approximately four-fifths of senior judges, two-thirds of ambassadors, senior civil servants and bishops, and half of Tory MPs attended Oxford and Cambridge. One-third of the Cabinet and vice-chancellors and one-quarter of all MPs gained 'greybrick' (non-Oxbridge) degrees, as did one-fifth of business chairs and Labour MPs. Military leaders are trained in their own institutions (Sandhurst, Cranfield and Dartmouth) but were more likely to have attended university than in the past, with one-seventh attending Oxford or Cambridge. In the case of judges, Tory MPs, bishops, ambassadors and senior civil servants, Oxbridge outweighs the contribution of all other UK universities combined. In contrast, non-Oxbridge universities are more important in the cases of university vice-chancellors, chairs of top companies, the Cabinet, Liberal Democrat MPs, Labour MPs and MPs in total.

Since 2000 the Sutton Trust has produced a number of interesting reports on the educational background of a number of British elites. The Trust's 2010 data show the continued, though in most cases slowly diminishing, significance of independent school education – judges at 70 per cent leading barristers 68 per cent, top solicitors 55 per cent, leading journalists 54 per cent, senior medical staff 51 per cent, and prestigious scholars and scientists 42 per cent. Sixty-two per cent of the House of Lords (now mainly Life Peers, with certain Bishops, High Court Judges and a rump of hereditary peers) attended independent schools, this percentage contrasting with 35 per cent of MPs. The latter marks a small rise in public school-educated MPs from 30 to 35 per cent since 2000 (Table 11.1), deriving from the increased number of Tory and Lib/Dem MPs and decline in the number of Labour MPs as a result of the election in 2010.

The Sutton Trust figures for the Chief Executive Officers of FTSE 100 companies in 2007 mark a decline in the percentage attending public schools in the UK, from 67 per cent in 1987 to 54 per cent in 2007. These figures reflect the increasingly globalised nature of leading corporations operating in Britain, many of which are run by executives born and educated outside of the UK (10 per cent in 1987, 33 per cent in 2007: see Chapter 16). As noted above, university vice chancellors (24 per cent) were least likely to have attended an independent school, most (66 per cent) having been educated at a selective state grammar school. Only MPs at 42 per cent record a figure of more than 20 per cent for comprehensive school education with judges as low as 2 per cent.

Turning to university education, in 2010 the legal profession recorded the highest figures for attendance at Oxford or Cambridge – 82 per cent of leading barristers, 78 per cent of High Court judges, and 53 per cent of top solicitors. Fifty-six per cent of leading scholars and scientists were Oxbridge undergraduates. The comparable figure for vice chancellors was 27 per cent and that for leading doctors 15 per cent (the Edinburgh and the London Medical Schools long being pre-eminent). Journalists and CEOs record figures of 45 per cent and 39 per cent respectively. At 42 per cent, peers are far more likely to have attended one of the greybrick universities than MPs (27 per cent). Overall, and gradually, the non-Oxbridge universities (especially the leading 'Russell Group' research universities) are challenging the dominance of Oxbridge in a range of institutional elites.

It is a truism that the main route to the top in Britain has traditionally been through a public school education followed by an Oxbridge college. In the present era, only in the case of judges is this combination of private schooling and Oxbridge the overwhelming norm. However, it remains a more important route than the alternative state/Oxbridge and state/non-Oxbridge paths in the case of judges, Tory MPs, ambassadors, bishops, business leaders and the higher civil service. This illustrates one of the ways in which social division works in contemporary British society, and can be summarised in four main points:

1. Except for sections of the political elite and vice chancellors, a small percentage of the school population – that attending private schools – has provided the bulk of these elites and continues to do so, at a slightly reduced level.

2. Oxford and Cambridge Universities remain the predominant universities attended en route to the top, except for MPs as a whole, vice chancellors, the military and business leaders. (Nearly one-third of business leaders attended overseas universities.) No other individual university comes close to challenging the dominance of Oxford and Cambridge, although their importance is declining somewhat.

3. The statistics point to the importance of certain elites in bringing a greater range of educational experience to the higher circles. Among these elites it is only MPs, university vice chancellors (and chief constables: see Reiner 1991) who have educational origins that are clearly rooted in the state school sector.
4. The importance of the public school/Oxbridge route is not as important as in the past but remains well represented.

State elites: the politicians

By way of further illustration, we shall consider several of these elites in greater detail, starting with the formal political system. As the House of Commons entered the new millennium, it did so with the highest proportion of state school-educated MPs in its history. Two-thirds of MPs attended state schools, whilst just under one-third attended a public school. (The remainder were schooled overseas or their school was unknown (see Table 11.1: the numerically minor parties – Scottish Nationalists, Ulster Unionists – are included in total figures but are not accorded separate analysis).) These figures reiterate the often-observed contrast in the school experiences of Labour and Conservative MPs. Whereas two-thirds of Tories had attended a public school (nearly all HMC), only just over one-sixth of Labour members had been so educated. Similarly, 50 per cent of Conservatives had taken a degree at Oxbridge compared with 18.6 per cent of Labour MPs. The combined institutions of the University of London accounted for 86 MPs (13.1 per cent), 34 having taken degrees at the London School of Economics, 26 of whom were Labour MPs. Liberal Democrats sit in the middle, as it were, of the two main parties, with 32.7 per cent having a public school affiliation and 28.8 per cent a degree from Oxford or Cambridge. Over one-third of Tories combined a private education with Oxbridge, the other two parties recording much lower figures.

It would be wrong to look for signs of major change in the elected elite among the ranks of the Labour Party. Despite a history of representing the interests of 'ordinary people', its leadership displays a number of elite characteristics which makes it well worth studying in some detail. Labour MPs, given their connections to the labour movement throughout the history of the party, have had an educational profile that is somewhat at odds with most other British elites and closer to that of the whole population. Yet attendance at a school in the private sector (16 per cent in 2000) has always been above the percentage found in the general school population (7–8 per cent). University education has become an increasingly common experience amongst Labour MPs since 1945, when 34.2 per cent recorded a degree. By 2000 it was 75 per cent.

Since the Second World War, those attending Oxford or Cambridge have always been a minority of the university graduates in Labour's ranks. Four-fifths of Labour MPs in 2000 who had attended university studied at institutions other than Cambridge or Oxford. However, Oxford could still claim to have educated more Labour MPs in 2000 than any other institution (52), although the LSE (26) almost matched Cambridge (27). Other well-represented universities in Labour's ranks included Edinburgh (16), Manchester (13), York (12), Leeds (12), Hull (12) and Warwick (10). Seventy-five MPs had attended post-1992 universities (but, because of the time lag, mainly when they were polytechnics) and 54 attended both pre- and post-1992 universities. Naturally, the figures for university education show the general impact of the several expansions of post-war higher education. Notably, gender differences in educational background between the 317 male and 95 female Labour MPs in 2000 were small. Attendance at both public school and Oxbridge is a relatively rare occurrence among Labour MPs, the post-war high being 14.5 per cent, but halve this by 2000. In contrast, the 'public school plus Oxbridge' route accounted for about half of Tory MPs between 1945 (50.3 per cent) and 1966 (51.6 per cent), the proportion declining by approximately one-third in 1979 (37.4 per cent), where it has stabilised (37.3 per cent in 2000).

As has been the pattern throughout the twentieth century, the educational profile of the Cabinet has differed somewhat from the cohort of governing party MPs from which it is selected. It has always been the case that independent schools and Oxbridge have been better represented in the Cabinet than in the ranks of the governing party as a whole. Whereas just over 80 per cent of Labour MPs were educated in the state sector, the figure for the Labour Cabinet was lower (65.4 per cent) in 2000. Similarly, more of the Labour Cabinet attended independent schools (34.7 per cent) than did Labour MPs in general (16.0 per cent). The same kinds of regularities are repeated at university level, in that 38.5 per cent (equally divided between the two universities) of the Cabinet attended Oxbridge, whilst the figure for the Labour Party as a whole is 18.6 per cent. Whereas only 7.0 per cent of Labour MPs combined a public school and Oxbridge education, 27 per cent of the Cabinet in 2000 followed this path.

In comparison with Labour Cabinets of previous eras, the percentage of the 2000 Cabinet having a public school education evidenced a slight increase. Between 1916 and 1955, and 1955 and 1984, 26 per cent and 32 per cent respectively of Labour Cabinet members were educated in private schools, as against 34.7 per cent in 2000. Therefore, just as the percentage of Labour MPs attending public schools recorded a small rise over the figure for the 1980s, so the privately educated proportion in the Blair Cabinet also moved up slightly from the figure covering the Wilson and Callaghan Cabinets of the

1960s and 1970s. The pattern is slightly different with respect to Oxbridge representation. In 2000, 38.5 per cent of the Labour Cabinet were graduates of Oxford or Cambridge, a decline from the 1955–84 period (42.8 per cent), but both are above the figure for 1916–55 (27.6 per cent). Whilst under half of Labour Cabinets in the first period (1916–55) had attended university (44.6 per cent), nearly two-thirds (62.5 per cent) of the 1955–84 sample had done so. In 2000, all members of the Cabinet had received a university education, a number as mature students.

Following the 2010 General Election, there was a slight increase in the percentage of all MPs with a public school education, from 34 per cent in 2001 to 37 per cent, although this represented a major decline since 1981 (51 per cent). The recent rise is explained by the increase in the numbers of Conservative and Liberal Democrat MPs, with their greater propensity for independent education, and the fall in the number of Labour MPs. However, the likelihood that a Tory MP will have been privately educated is falling (73 per cent in 1973, 64 per cent in 2001, 54 per cent in 2010). Public school representation among Labour MPs has declined to 15 per cent, whilst LibDems have recorded a rise to 40 per cent since 2001 (35 per cent). The school with the highest number (20) of MPs in 2010 was Eton. Notably, however, 43 per cent of MPs attended comprehensive schools – double the figure for selective state grammar schools and the highest figure for any elite.

The proportion of MPs with an Oxbridge undergraduate education has declined since the late 1960s and stood at 28 per cent in 2010. Tory MPs not attending Oxbridge has declined from 48 per cent in 2001 to 38 per cent in 2010, whilst the Oxbridge share of Labour MPs has increased slightly to 20 per cent since 2001 (16 per cent). The main story with regard to university education is the growth of the non-Oxbridge degrees reflecting the expansion of university education in the post-war period. In 2010 46 per cent of Tory MPs, 55 per cent of Labour and 53 per cent of LibDems had taken this route. These data confirm that the electoral route into the political elite produces a more varied educational profile than the standard routes of career progression to the top in other elites.

However, there remains a contrast between the educational profile of MPs as a whole and the Cabinet and MPs holding government posts. For example, in 2010, whereas 54 per cent of Tory and 40 per cent of LibDem MPs were educated in independent schools, the figure for the Cabinet was 62 per cent. Similarly, 38 per cent of all Conservative MPs and 28 per cent of LibDems attended Oxbridge, but 69 per cent of the Coalition Cabinet graduated from Oxford or Cambridge. Although there have been small changes (Crone 2011), there is little sign of systematic or extensive reductions in the proportions of the political elite who were privately educated or attended Oxbridge.

State elites: the bureaucrats and officers

The educational backgrounds of elected politicians differ from those of the top civil servants who shape policy and remain in their positions long after the typical minister has been moved on. The highest-ranking civil servants have been subject to a number of studies and enquiries investigating their social and educational origins. In the period between the end of the Second World War and the 1990s, the broad picture was one in which private sector education, particularly the HMC schools, maintained and even increased their contributions to this Whitehall elite: 69.4 per cent between 1945 and 1964; 70.0 per cent between 1965 and 1986; and 77.0 per cent between 1979 and 1994. However, data for 34 grade 1 civil servants in 1998, a slightly more widely-drawn group than permanent secretaries alone but including them, suggests that state sector-educated civil servants are breaking through to the top ranks in greater numbers.

Thus, only half these senior administrators and half the permanent secretaries within the grade 1 group attended HMC schools, with 55.9 per cent of the former being educated in some form of independent school. If this annual sample is consistent with a more general trend, it indicates a gradually declining share for public schools at the highest levels of the civil service. State-educated grade 1 administrators stood at 26.5 per cent in 1998, broadly in line with the figures for permanent secretaries between the late 1940s and the late 1970s, but an increase on the 20 per cent recorded for the 1979–94 cohort. However, the permanent secretaries within this group recorded a higher state school representation, at 50 per cent.

Table 11.2 Permanent secretaries (1945–94) and grade 1 civil servants (1998)

	1945–64	*1965–86*	*1960–70*	*1979–94*	*1998 (G1)*
Public school	58.7	62.5	40.0	66.0	50.0
Private	10.7	7.5	n/a	11.0	5.9
State	24.0	28.8	n/a	20.0	26.5
Other	6.7	0.0	n/a	3.0	11.8
No information	0.0	1.2	60.0	0.0	5.9
Oxbridge	66.7	75.0	80.0	56.0	70.6
Oxford	40.0	45.0	35.0	30.0	35.3
Cambridge	26.7	30.0	45.0	26.0	35.3
Other university	16.0	17.5	17.5	39.0	41.2
Public school + Oxbridge					44.1

Source: Data for 1945–94 adapted from Theakston and Fry (1989) and Barberis (1996).

With regard to higher education, the position of Oxford and Cambridge remains strong, although subject to some challenge in the last decade of the twentieth century. Theakston and Fry (1989) recorded a rise in the Oxbridge component of their two post-war samples from 66.7 to 75 per cent. However, Barberis (1996: 101) reports a greybrick figure of 44 per cent for his 1979–95 permanent secretaries and observes that 'the Oxbridge presence among permanent secretaries should decline somewhat in the future'. Data for grade 1 civil servants for 1998 give a figure of 41.2 per cent having received a non-Oxbridge degree, which includes a number of civil servants who have received degrees from both Oxbridge and another UK university. Thus Oxford and Cambridge remain well represented at these levels.

As a final example of state elites, we can briefly consider senior army officers. Otley's work in the 1960s and early 1970s established the social and educational background of the army elite, work extended by von Zugbach (1988) (later with Ishaq (1999)) into the 1980s and 1990s, with further findings about the subcultural distinctions between different organisational elements within the army. Between 1965 and 1977, the proportion of major-generals attending HMC schools declined somewhat, as did the contributions of elite public schools, Eton, Harrow, Winchester and Wellington. However, amongst lieutenant generals and generals, elite public schools held their own: Eton, Harrow and Winchester increased their representation, with only Wellington's share continuing to decline. As late as 1977, 53 per cent of generals were drawn from just four public schools. (See Whitley's (1974) work demonstrating that approximately 30 per cent of directors of major merchant banks in the early 1970s attended Eton, and Bond's (2004) similar finding for business supporters of the Conservative Party.)

Von Zugbach's analysis of key-post generals demonstrates that 'those who dominate army policy and strategic thinking' were drawn overwhelmingly from a small number of schools. In 1982, 100 per cent of these officers attended HMC schools, 75 per cent attended the elite of these schools and 51 per cent were educated at Eton, Harrow, Winchester or Wellington. The most prestigious units (elite regiments within the fighting arms) were highly selective in terms of educational background, whilst units of lower status (technical and support arms) were of more diverse educational origin.

Writing with Ishaq later in the mid-1990s, von Zugbach detected a shift in the educational origins of the 'Promenente' – those senior officers who control the process of selection to the highest ranks of the army (generals) – and, employing NATO terminology, 'star'-ranked generals. In 1996, the highest ranks of the army were still occupied, overwhelmingly, by men educated in the private sector. Only among three- and two-star generals was there substantial state school representation – 30 per cent and 46 per cent respectively. However, since it is from this stratum that the highest ranks are drawn, it is likely that the trend towards increasing state school representation will continue. There was also a reduced Oxbridge share at the very top and amongst two-star generals, but a slight proportionate increase amongst three-star generals. Non-Oxbridge universities show an increasing representation amongst two- and three-star generals.

A similar profile can be detected among Royal Navy admirals in 2000 (38 in number), with 76 per cent having attended a public school and 21 per cent state schools. In contrast, in the RAF the state sector accounts for nearly half of senior officers (air vice-marshall and above). A higher proportion of the RAF hierarchy have attended university than is the case with the other services.

Overall, the military elite in 2000 remained predominantly of private school background with the state slowly gaining ground, so the balance may swing in favour of state-educated officers. Yet if public school-educated officers remain disproportionately more successful in ascending the highest ranks and securing the most influential posts, in the coming decades they may continue to occupy the most significant strategic decisions. And, as MacDonald (2004) has demonstrated, public schools continue to provide the lion's share of recruits to the officer corps of elite infantry regiments, 90 per cent having attended such schools as recently as 1999/2000.

Concluding observations

A fully rounded account of British elites would have to consider issues concerning other dimensions of recruitment as well as matters of structure and power. The disciplines of occupational socialisation and training differ among elites to produce clearly demarcated cultures (for instance, judges compared with chief constables, military officers compared with senior civil servants and so on), as well as modes of operation. These procedures induce and encourage coherence within elites, and become stronger as promotion and selection lead to top positions. However, as the structural differentiation of elites proceeds, the commonalities of social origin, gender and education – claimed in the past to be the basis for elite solidarities across institutions – are unlikely to provide the integrative element between elites they once did (or were perceived to do).

It may be that the movement of people between elite positions, what the French call 'pantoflage', may be one means by which fragmentation may be countered. In the distant past, many judges were drawn from the ranks of practising lawyers sitting as MPs, and there is some evidence of the movement of the higher ranks of the civil service into business in the present era. Perhaps the 'reformed' House of Lords will provide succour for some tired former vice chancellors, played-out Cabinet ministers and fatigued permanent secretaries. However, at the time of writing (2013), there is little systematic evidence on the current state of such inter-elite movements.

The other major issue that a more comprehensive study of elites would need to consider is the changing topography of power. For instance, there is general agreement that the House of Commons has declined in influence over the policy-making process and the power of the prime minister has been enhanced even, some argue, to the detriment of the Cabinet. The matter of whether Britain has entered a period of 'presidential' politics has been much debated, as has the role of 'special advisers' and their claimed usurpation of the role of senior civil servants in the policy-making process.

Another matter of central significance is that concerning the impact of multifaceted globalisation, particularly its economic manifestations. This restricts the capacity of governments to orchestrate the national economy and increases the constraints placed upon policy choices by the operation of financial markets. Since the financial crisis broke in 2008, the mutual incapacities of government and major banks have revealed the difficulties that national and even global elites face when dealing with systemic malfunctions of global capitalism. It is not just the masses who feel impotent in the face of worldwide processes.

Note should also be taken of the declining influence of the Church of England (Chapter 9) and the Trades Union Congress, the changing role of the diplomatic corps and the much reduced size of the military establishment and the forces they lead. The political influence of Rupert Murdoch's media empire, leading to the Leveson Inquiry in 2011/12, emphasised the need to consider the enhanced role of certain sections of media in British political and cultural life. Thus, understanding the configuration of power relations between elites, and the rise and fall of elites, has much to contribute to the wider issue of social divisions.

Who gets into elite positions is an index of the distribution of power in British society and, although there has been a restrained move to more demographically representative elites, it has been markedly slow in specific respects. Male elites are the overwhelming norm, although increasing numbers of women can now be found in the 'pools' from which elites emerge (MPs, QCs, professors, middle-rank civil servants and so on). Notably, women now make up 33 per cent of the 4900 Senior Civil Servants compared with 13 per cent in 1996. In most elites, public schools remain the most common form of education, and affiliation with Oxford and Cambridge universities the predominant form of higher education. Whilst the electoral process produces a degree of educational diversity at the top (especially when the Labour Party is well-represented), the normal patterns of career advancement in many professions produce elites that have educational profiles marked by the importance of private sector schools and the ancient universities. The extent to which this indicates that these institutions produce talented people best fitted for top positions or reflects deeply ingrained preferences for people of a certain kind remains a matter of continuing debate.

The expansion of the state grammar school system resulting from the 1944 Education Act, billed as the saviour of the bright working-class boy, made a significant impact on routes of career advancement: the vast majority of state-educated men who entered elites in the 30 years from 1975 attended such schools. It is not clear whether the graduates of comprehensive and other forms of state school or college will continue to reach elite positions to the same or an increasing extent. In an era of credentialism, when competition for places at the most prestigious universities is intense and unremitting, the independent school sector, for well-documented reasons, continues to dominate the conventional school league tables based on exam results.

It is thus possible that the representation of those with a public school education will be sustained among holders of a range of elite positions after a period when there were signs that this route of entry was loosening its hold. In this respect, education will remain of critical importance with regard to which sections of the population are drawn on in the composition of future elites. It is certain that the changing topography of social inequality and the associated structures of ambition, aspiration and educational opportunity will remain central to both the reproduction and erosion of social divisions and the composition of elites in British society.

Discussion Questions

1. What are the differences between an upper class and an elite?
2. Examine the relationship between elites and other social divisions in British society.
3. Why are the educational origins of MPs so different from those of High Court judges?
4. How does the analysis of elites aid the understanding of the relationship between education and social division?
5. Is organisation inevitably hierarchical and divisive?

FURTHER READING

The Sutton Trust has a number of interesting reports on the educational background of various elites at www.suttontrust.com/our-work. A good collection of studies which seeks to revitalise the field of elite studies can be found in Savage, M. and Williams, K. (eds) *Remembering Elites* (Blackwell: Oxford, 2008), which includes John Scott's development of his *Stratification and Power: Structures of Class, Status and Command* (Cambridge: Polity, 1996). Bottomore, T. *Elites and Society* (London: Routledge, 1993, 2nd edn) is a classic short account of the earlier development of elite theory. On particular elites there is a useful account of the impact of the new managerialism in the civil service in Dargie, C. and Locke, R. 'The British Senior Civil Service' in Page, E.C. and Wright, V. (eds) *Bureaucratic Elites in Western European States* (Oxford: Oxford University Press, 1999). Reiner, R. *Chief Constables: Bobbies, Bosses or Bureaucrats?* (Oxford: Clarendon, 1991) remains the best overall sociological account of a British elite, including some interesting material on education. Finally Adonis, A. and Pollard, S. *A Class Act* (London: Hamish Hamilton, 1997) analyses the impact of the 'financialisation' of the upper echelons of class structure in the 1980s and 1990s and contains interesting observations on how the rise of the City impacted on career choices of students studying at major universities.

Chapter 12

Work

Tim Strangleman

This chapter will provide you with a broad critical understanding of the main features of work including:

- Enlightenment and classic sociological perspectives on work: Adam Smith, Karl Marx, Emile Durkheim, Max Weber
- Industrial and post-industrial societies: the content of work and expertise
- Occupational identities as sources of social division
- Differences in employment conditions
- Paid work, unpaid work, and unemployment
- Skills and qualifications
- De-skilling and the labour market
- The gendered nature of work
- Ethnicity in the work-place
- Age in the work-place
- Three case studies: railway locomotive drivers, Campbell Soup Company, careers in the City

In many social settings when two adult strangers meet, one of the first topics of conversation will be what they both do. And by 'do' they mean what *paid* job they do. Why is this so often the case? It might indicate the importance of work to a person's identity, but it is also one of the most important, and accurate, ways of categorising a person. Whether we like it or not, what we do – or don't do – classifies us in terms of many of the social divisions discussed in this book. What employment a person is engaged in can inform us about their social class, education and training, and their skill level. It will surely tell us a great deal about how much they earn and the likelihood that they will enjoy a pension. It is an indicator of social standing, it could tell us a person's gender and in some occupations their likely ethnic status. 'So what do you do?' is both a simple and a complex way of saying 'who are you?'.

While other social divisions play into the work setting, paid employment itself creates social divisions in its own right. On the one hand, experiences inside the work-place generate feelings of belonging among co-workers, and also feelings of difference between employees and managers. On the other hand, what we work at gives us an identity that is not confined 'within the factory gates': our work identities extend into the wider society.

As a result, social divisions in the field of work are central to classical understandings of how society operates. Pre-dating classical sociology, Adam Smith, the greatest figure of enlightenment political economy, recognised the importance of the division of labour in society, not only in terms of the productivity gains that would flow from it, but also the divisive and detrimental effects of such industrial organisation. In his classic *The Wealth of Nations* of 1776 he acknowledged that greater efficiency could be achieved by the minute fragmentation of tasks so that the workers involved in one aspect could specialise and therefore speed up production. In the manufacture of pins:

> One man draws out the wire, another straights it, a third cuts it, a fourth points it, a fifth grinds it at the top for receiving the head; to make the head requires two or three distinct operations; to put it on, is a peculiar business, to whiten the pins is another; it is even a trade by itself to put them into paper; and the important business of making a pin is, in this manner, divided into about eighteen distinct operations, which in some manufactories, are all performed by distinct hands... (Smith [1776]1999, 110)

However, Smith also realised the danger for society in that the division of labour created a set of almost mindless robots with little or no interest in their jobs other than their pay. Smith's ideas were influential on Karl Marx, who combined the political economy of the Scottish enlightenment with the politics of the French revolution and German philosophy. In Marx's writing the division of labour is of central importance in understanding how societies develop. It is only by increased specialisation that greater productivity is achieved. But these divisions in terms of work allocation are also complex social relations which from the beginning create rising levels of social inequality in society. As societies advance, their industries require increasing divisions of labour and accordingly, in their wake, marked inequalities between people. Marx believed that this process would accelerate in industrial society with a polarisation between the owners and non-owners of the means of production – the bourgeoisie and the proletariat. Put simply, the way in which work was organised in each historical epoch created social divisions expressed as opposing classes, but in modern capitalist societies this division was at its most extreme. As we will see below, Marx argued that the capitalist class made use of all kinds of social divisions in order to reduce the cost of production, with employers exploiting differences in terms of skill and education, gender and ethnicity (Marx [1859]1961).

For the French classical sociologist Emile Durkheim, the division of labour was also very important: his doctoral study was concerned with the subject and was later published as *The Division of Labour in Society* ([1893]1964). Like Marx, Durkheim saw divisions at work as both technical and social. Whereas Marx saw these as divisive, Durkheim saw them as potentially cohesive because he understood the division of labour as being a necessary part of the evolution of society. As industrial society evolved it would need ever greater specialist knowledge and labour in order to function properly. If this specialisation in tasks was allocated on the basis of qualification, talent and merit would create an orderly and harmonious society as individuals would come to recognise their shared reliance on one another. Of course this idealistic portrayal of work divisions did not exist at the time Durkheim was writing. Indeed, he saw it as being at the root of what ailed modern society, namely the forced division of labour whereby individuals were compelled to carry out jobs they did not wish to do. The role of sociology was to identify how society could be made to operate in a more meritocratic manner and, therefore, where the division of labour would be seen as rational, logical and fair.

The third figure in classical sociology is, of course, Max Weber. Like Marx and Durkheim, Weber's understanding of how society operated was based on the division of labour and industrial specialisation. One of the major themes in his sociology was rationality, a trend identifiable in all aspects of modern life including work. Weber acknowledged that increasing specialisation was a necessary and unavoidable aspect of all modern societies. Like Durkheim, Weber recognised the need for jobs in this new division of labour to be allocated on the basis of rational evaluations of merit. What was distinct about Weber's analysis was that he feared the consequences of this process in that, as specialisation became more pronounced, individuals would be less rounded.

The work of the classical theorists was followed by a new concern over the changing roles of the owners of capital and the managers who ran their businesses for them, and the consequences of this for wider society. As corporations became bigger, factory owners and family-run firms were replaced by joint stock companies which hired a growing cadre of managers and directors who behaved much like owners in the authority they exercised over the workers and in their pursuit of profit. They could, however, still be fired, so that, while writers like James Burnham (1941) saw this as a 'managerial revolution', the work place – and the new powerful bureaucratic state apparatuses of Nazism and Communism – manifested a new division between workers and managers. However, they retained a further, less obvious division between those behind the scenes with real power and their more visible representatives (see Chapters 2 and 11).

Part of the same process also saw the rise of the Expert who manifested Weber's rational, knowledge-based approach to decision-making: the accountant, the company lawyer, the marketing manager, the human resources director, and also the engineers, designers and scientists more immediately involved with products. All had to be highly educated, and their fields of specialism became increasingly opaque to other specialists and to general managers. As systematic abstract knowledge grew in importance, and economic activity shifted from the production of heavy industrial goods (steel, ships, locomotives, coal) first into consumer products and then into services rather than physical goods, a new kind of 'knowledge society' began to emerge. Daniel Bell (1973) argued that this 'post-industrial society' was no longer organised around the principles of conflict over production between workers and the managers of capital. It is certainly the case that the old industrial work-forces shrunk: now increasingly doing white collar jobs, employees were located into smaller units where their reduced interaction in the work setting mitigated against a sense of common shared interests as workers. New forms of social division emerged in an economy primarily based on the provision of services, whether these were financial, commercial, or in the health, education and administrative arms of the welfare state, with additional gradations of new skills and new hierarchies.

Work as uniting, work as dividing

It has to be recognised that work (and here we are talking about paid employment) can unite as well as divide people. Marx acknowledged that industrialisation, while socially divisive on one level, was also a process that tended to unite people by bringing them together *en masse* and, in the process, creating a consciousness of their shared interests. This revolutionary potential aside, on a more modest scale we can see work and work groups as creating sets of shared interests and common identities. Increasing specialisation eroded many former occupational traditions and displaced skills, but it also produced whole new industries and with it new occupational groups. These, in turn, created rich work-place cultures which were often new sources of solidarity. The historical evolution of how we think about occupational groupings, and the consequences of how they developed, are discussed in Chapter 2.

People who spend a lot of time together tend to feel emotionally linked to one another, particularly if they are participating in shared activities, in close physical proximity where they can interact, such as in carrying out work tasks. This is all the more true when they bring common backgrounds and skill levels to the work setting. If they can take a shared pride in their productive activities, or in overcoming the physical hardships of their work – such as in dangerous, male-dominated industries like coal mining, trawling or steel making – strong bonds of mutual respect and distinctive identity can develop. These sustain a social division between co-workers and others; both other workers and others in the outside society. The strength of these feelings of shared identity has often been demonstrated most clearly in times of crisis, such as following industrial accidents, or in the form of strike action. That does not mean that there are no tensions or personal dislikes within work groups; indeed, these natural human conflicts often become expressed in terms of horseplay and banter about work performance.

As is often the case, identities which create boundaries between groups of people tend to come to the fore at certain times, especially at times of social, political or economic stress. Until the emergence of a more complex industrialised society in Britain, society was often depicted as politically and economically divided into blocks of shared material interests by *industry*. The farmers were in potential opposition to the miners, mining opposed to the textile industry, textiles to steel makers. This model saw employers, owners and employees *within* an industry group having more in common than employers had with other employers in different industries, while employees were identified with their industry group rather than being perceived as a social class of workers. It was only towards the later part of the Victorian era that the current, more political conception of occupational classes became the norm (although from 2010 the Coalition Government attempted to create new divisions among employees by re-introducing the notion of supposedly significant differences between public and private sector workers).

Thus, strong occupational solidarities both unite and divide workers as who does what, who gets access to work and who does not become important issues. This divisive side to occupational identity can be seen to operate at a number of levels. For example, groups of workers can exclude certain people – often women, minority groups or the unskilled – at the level of the shop floor (see Eldridge 1968), when certain jobs are reserved for particular types of workers. But this can also occur at levels of the organisation or even whole industries, as we will see later.

With these exclusions and reservations come differences in working conditions and employment contracts. Rates of pay, holiday entitlements, pension rights, the content of work, 'clocking in' and starting times, control over one's pace of working – even when one can take a 'comfort break' – all vary greatly. Workers in the professions and senior managers are trusted to work without close scrutiny, and to complete their work without 'clock-watching'. John Goldthorpe calls this the 'service contract', which identifies membership of the 'service class' (Chapter 2). In return, they can expect security of employment, promotion and flexible working conditions. Ordinary workers are less trusted, and have to be controlled: they are on 'employment contracts'. Indeed these differences in terms of employment now provide the rationale for the system used by the Office for National Statistics (and many sociological studies) to group occupations into socio-economic categories ('NS-SEC') or 'social classes' for analysis in the UK's official statistics.

One further major social division around work is between those who benefit from employment and those who do not. There is a straight binary divide between those in paid employment and the unemployed, and the role of unemployment and the unemployed in the labour market has long interested sociologists. The presence of a large body of people without jobs exerts powerful pressure on those in work. Marx thought of the unemployed as forming a reserve army of labour that employers could draw upon at times of high demand in the economy to stabilise or reduce wage levels. So, unemployment and under-employment are powerful divisions between workers. These themes are still with us, with some writers talking about a new set of workers who are labelled the 'Precariat' (Standing 2011) because of the insecurity of their employment. We are increasingly told that 'there is no longer any such thing as a job for life'.

Finally, there is the obvious division between paid and unpaid work. This is clearly related to the discussion of insecure work, but it highlights the issue of those engaged in work or labour for which some get paid (employed) and others don't. Context is important here: the domestic labour of caring roles within a family, for example, is usually unpaid, but child and elder care are often also undertaken as paid work. To broaden this even further, we need to consider the role of unpaid internships in all sorts of organisations. Young people's access to good jobs is often dependent on their willingness (and ability) to take unpaid internships in sectors like law, fashion, politics and media. While seemingly open to anyone, in effect these posts become the reserve of a particular, already advantaged, stratum of society (Perlin 2011).

Divisions at work: skills and qualifications

One of the clearest divisions between workers is in terms of their levels of education, skill and qualification. The ability to access particular types of employment is related to the skill and knowledge a worker possesses. In most societies, the more technically demanding the employment, the greater the rewards paid. Often reward structures for employment are expressed through market mechanisms, so those with rarer skills and greater qualifications will command higher wages. By implication, those with few or no skills will often find themselves in lower paying jobs.

In Marxian theory, the capitalist class has an interest in progressively 'de-skilling' work (Braverman 1974), so that more people can potentially do it. If labour is more substitutable in this way, it will, as a consequence, be cheaper. Therefore, labour markets dominated by the power of the employers will reward more highly skilled and qualified workers, while being able to pay lower wages to those with few or no skills. This economistic view of the labour market is highly individualistic and is based on the notion of human capital theory –that is, the more one invests in one's own human capital (such as qualifications and training), the greater the reward one can later expect in return. For example, a person who decides to continue in higher education forgoes wages at the age of 16 to 18. However, when they eventually enter the labour market at 21, the educated person will command significantly higher wages and will continue to enjoy a higher standard of living throughout their working life. The proponents of such a model argue that it represents a fair, neutral and transparent system which rewards those who invest in themselves and work hard. However, critics suggest that one's ability to access training or education, and thereby gain qualifications, is heavily dependent on social structures which may enable or constrain the exercise of choice.

We can see this in the case of a person who wants to be a lawyer. The son or daughter of a family already in the profession will have better access to the educational opportunities and experience needed to enter the profession than the child of a less well educated, working-class family. The career trajectory of a person will depend on family support and connection, the type of school they attend and even the type of university they enter. Furthermore, occupations and professions in many sectors, including law, make use of internships which effectively include some social groups and exclude others (see Perlin 2011). Divisions of opportunity due to the chances of birth then reproduce divisions in later careers.

Training and skill levels are also important in other, non-professional occupational groups. There is a long tradition of social cleavage associated with skill, and this can be between skilled and semi- or non-skilled workers, or between skilled groups. Often in traditional industries, task allocation – who was allowed to do what – was rigidly enforced by trades unions so that certain work was the preserve of skilled workers whilst unskilled workers were confined to less skilled tasks. The key qualification historically was the successful completion of a craft apprenticeship where a worker would be in formal training for a period of three to five years before they could practise their trade independently. 'Craft unions' emerged in the nineteenth century in Britain and in other industrialising countries, and have their roots in the much older craft guilds of the medieval period. Both types of organisation effectively policed entry to certain trades and enacted occupational 'closure' by restricting the number of people who could practise a trade. On a macro- and micro-level, craft or skilled unions increased the scarcity of their members' skill, and therefore maximised market pay rates. As we will see, this social division based on skill is also gendered and racialised, with skilled unions excluding others, either by accident or design.

Divisions at work: gender

Arguably, the most visible division at work is that of gender. Since the origins of human existence, there has been a gendered division of labour – in some of the earliest human societies men would hunt while women and children gathered. The gendered nature of work is complex. We could talk, for instance, about the gendering of the whole labour market, or of an organisation, or continue our discussion to the detailed division of labour in specific tasks. Sociologists think of labour markets as being horizontally and vertically segregated. Horizontal segregation is the way that, in many types of employment, women come to occupy certain tasks while men do others. Vertical segregation refers to the way in which the organisational hierarchy is often gendered, with fewer women in senior positions. Labour markets are segmented on gender grounds and certain jobs are sex-typed (see also Chapter 3).

While gendered segregation predates industrial society, modern forms of the gendered division of labour are a product of the industrial revolution and, in particular, the divide between the 'public sphere' and the 'private sphere'. It can be argued that, with the growth of modern capitalist employment, women increasingly came to occupy the private sphere where their labour – domestic unpaid work – was effectively hidden. The public sphere and the paid work that went on there, by contrast, were often dominated by men. Therefore, what counts as 'real' work becomes defined by the *employment relationship* – whether or not work is paid by an employer to an employee. This is not to say that women were excluded from the formal economy. On the contrary, women have always worked for pay, but they have often occupied particular parts of the economy and particular trades.

This was seen to be 'natural' because it arose in part from biological differences between men and women – most fundamentally the fact that women bear children. What has built up over time is a whole set of norms and values which have tended to reproduce the situation in which women are systematically likely to be disadvantaged in terms of the work they do and their ability to gain promotion. Bradley's (1989) *Men's Work, Women's Work* shows the way that industries and sectors in the UK were highly gendered from 1800 onward. This is not to say that things have not changed over time. Indeed,

Bradley shows how some jobs *became* feminised as the result of changes in the economy, often driven by technology. The classic case is that of clerical work which, in the nineteenth century before the widespread introduction of the mechanical typewriter, was often the preserve of men. By the early twentieth century this same work was increasingly the preserve of women.

One of the most influential writers on the gendering of work has been Cynthia Cockburn, most famously in her study of male domination of the printing trade. In *Brothers* (1983) Cockburn shows how male workers and their trade unions systematically opposed female labour and the introduction of new technology into their industry. In another study, co-authored with Susan Ormrod, Cockburn researched the way an item of technology – the microwave oven – was gendered in terms of the labour that surrounded its design, manufacturing, transportation, retail and eventual domestic use. Men designed the technology, female food technologists created the recipes that would be cooked in the device. Women manufactured the product while men moved them around the factory and delivered them to the shops. It was then mainly women who cooked with 'the microwave'. Cockburn and Ormrod (1993) highlight that at each stage there is a taken-for-granted gendered division of labour that creates and recreates gender roles, and by implication structures the work of men and women and, of course, inequality and divisions.

We can see the way work is gendered by examining employment and economic inactivity for men and women. Figure 12.1 shows the 2010 UK employment rate by age and gender. It is clear that at certain ages there are marked differences between the participation rates of women and men.

In order to tell a more detailed story about these patterns of labour market participation we also need to look at the reasons for economic inactivity. Figure 12.2 shows data on economic inactivity during the same period.

It is clear that there are fairly strongly gendered reasons for non-participation in work. Women, for example, are far more likely to be engaged in family or home care of some description, whereas men are more likely to be registered as long-term sick. In order to understand gender as a social division at work we need to understand, not only the labour market conditions, but also factors such as welfare policy and age (see Chapter 5).

Divisions at work: race/ethnicity

Another important social division at work is that of race and ethnicity – the way certain ethnic groups may enjoy a privileged position in the labour market or organisation whilst others are less fortunate. Organisations, labour markets and occupational groups arise from historical processes and sedimentation,

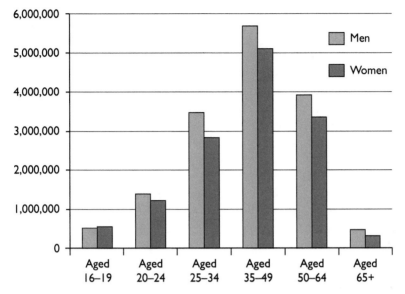

Figure 12.1 UK employment rate by age and gender, 2010

Source: Labour Force Survey, from Office for National Statistics (NOMIS 2011).
www.nomisweb.co.uk.

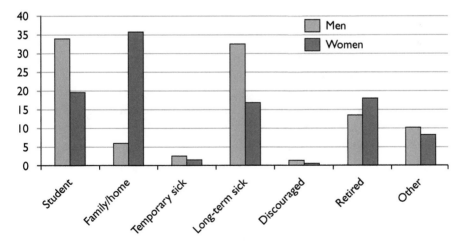

Figure 12.2 Reasons for economic inactivity by gender, UK, 2010

Source: Labour Force Survey, from Office for National Statistics (NOMIS 2011).
www.nomisweb.co.uk.

structured and reproduced as social divisions over time and space. In the case of ethnicity at work we need to recognise the way national and regional boundaries help to shape work. For example Commonwealth immigration to the UK in the 1950s and 1960s saw large numbers of black and ethnic minority people become workers in certain sectors of the economy, most notably the transport, textile and healthcare sectors. In each case, what happened to those workers is in part dependent on what occurred in the industries, whether or not they were unionised, if they were in the public or private sectors, and their international competitiveness with other countries. Often migrant labour took unattractive unskilled jobs in the larger urban conurbations where labour was scarce in the post-war period (see Chapter 4).

Another example is the United States where, until the emancipation of slaves in the 1860s, most black people in the country were subject to forced labour regimes. However, even after the abolition of the practice, African-Americans often occupied the lowest rungs of the labour market in the Deep South. By the mid-twentieth century many African-Americans migrated to the industrial north of the US to enjoy higher levels of pay and better employment prospects, continuing a process dating back a century to the American Civil War. However this upward mobility was seriously undermined by the recessions during the 1970s and the process of de-industrialisation which followed.

But divisions at work around race and ethnicity are not simply the product of long-term historical shifts in the economy. We also have to recognise overt, covert and unintentional discrimination at work which have the effect of opening up or closing down opportunities for people. A good example of this in the UK is the case of Ford Motor Company lorry drivers (almost exclusively white) who sought to protect a system of recruitment based on passing jobs from fathers to sons. This system effectively prevented ethnic minorities from ever gaining those jobs and, as a result, fewer than 2% of the 300 drivers based at the company's Dagenham Works were from ethnic minority communities. By contrast, in the local community in East London, ethnic minorities made up 40–45% of the population.

Divisions at work: age

Age in terms of a social division at work has received greater levels of attention over the last decade or so. This is for a number of reasons connected to the changing nature of work and industry and the gendered make-up of work. In a 'post-industrial society' dependent on an advanced technology and occupations requiring high levels of knowledge and expertise, many people now enter the work-force later, after a period of either further or higher education. Our interest in age is also underpinned by the increase in life expectancy enjoyed in the industrial world (see Chapter 5). Historically, in industrial economies male workers would enter employment after leaving elementary school then work into their 60s and often die soon after leaving work. Work-based pensions were rare for blue collar workers until after the First World War, marking an important division – 'blue collar'/'white collar' equated to salary/wage earners (itself an important social division within work). Since the 1980s, men, in particular, have been leaving employment at an earlier age and at a faster rate (Faggio and Nickell 2003), a trend associated with the downsizing of industries or whole sectors like manufacturing where large numbers of workers have been effectively paid off. (See Fevre 2011 for a review.)

However, the greater life expectancy most now enjoy has led governments in a number of countries to extend working life beyond the mid-60s, effectively abolishing the compulsory default retirement age of 65. One of the issues created by this move is the question of age discrimination in the workplace. Most often ageism is associated with prejudice against older people, but we have also to recognise that this can be against younger people too. In both cases – discrimination against older or younger workers – the group in question is collectively inscribed with a set of negative characteristics affecting how they perform work tasks: a lack of maturity and experience in the case of the young; a lack of flexibility in older workers.

Social divisions at work are often complex and very rarely are they based on one attribute or identity. Many of the examples used above are multi-dimensional – they are produced by the interaction of multiple forms of identity and attribute – class, gender, ethnicity, skill etc. We can illustrate this with some detailed case studies.

Case study one: railway locomotive drivers

In the era of the steam engine in the UK locomotive drivers were at the pinnacle of the working class occupational hierarchy, not only in the railway industry but also more broadly in society. They even formed part of what Eric Hobsbawm (1964) and others saw as a 'super-aristocracy of labour'. This status was underpinned by a complex set of social divisions. Perhaps most important was the relatively high levels of technical and organisational knowledge they possessed. They needed a detailed understanding of their locomotives and how they would perform in a multitude of settings and conditions. Their position was also strengthened by strong occupational closure with strict promotion and advancement agreements enforced by union rules and company policy. This occupational closure was buttressed by a system of seniority which allocated positions and work exclusively on the basis of length of service, rather than performance. This maintained the relatively privileged position of the drivers who were almost all white older men (McKenna 1980; Taillon 2009).

The drivers' position in the labour market was based on a particular historic set of social divisions which were mobilised to include and exclude certain groups. But there were also complex social divisions *within* this same work group. For example, there were two main trade unions representing these workers: a craft union and a general union. Within locomotive depots, there were disputes over which union's members could do certain duties and not others, as well as differences between depots in what was allowed. At times these disputes could resemble religious cleavages. There were also divisions within and between regions, and between the different private companies which owned Britain's railways before nationalisation in 1948. Here Frank McKenna describes the situation in one English town:

> Such intense shed loyalty also operated in the north of England. At Carlisle, when the city boasted sheds belonging to the LNWR, the Midland, the North British, the Caledonian, and the Maryport and Carlisle, it was said that engine crews would cross the street rather than recognise the men of another company and, such was the jigsaw type fragmentation of the footplate crews, that men of one company would rarely encourage romantic attachments between their own children and the offspring of men working engines for a rival company. (McKenna 1980, 179)

In one grade of workers – locomotive drivers – we can see strong pressures which enacted occupational closure and segregation, while at the same time we can witness social divisions between these same workers which could undermine solidarity.

Case study two: Campbell Soup

In his fascinating account of the business and labour policies of the Campbell Soup Company, Daniel Sidorick (2009) explores the way social divisions were exploited by an organisation in order to reduce costs. Sidorick shows how Campbell would employ the cheapest labour it could whenever possible. It made use of 'green labour', workers who were less likely to join or organise unions, at their Camden plant in New Jersey. This would often be female workers but the company also went out to recruit ethnic minority workers, particularly to fill its highly seasonal posts. This was a deliberate policy to avoid higher costs of production and unionisation. The following quote gives a flavour of this strategy in action:

> Women workers at Campbell were divided from male workers by being limited to a narrow range of jobs and locked into a wage structure significantly lower than men's. But even among male workers a myriad of divisions existed. African American, Puerto Rican, and Caribbean men, when employed at all, occupied only the lowest rungs of the employment ladder, especially before the advent of the union. The white native born and immigrant men who filled the full range of production jobs were further split into two groups: 'men' and 'boys.' Until the age of twenty-one, males were rated as 'boys,' and, though the work they performed was often as strenuous as that assigned to older workers, they were paid at a much lower rate. (Sidorick 2009: 100)

This brief paragraph highlights social divisions being manipulated in a workplace in terms of gender, ethnicity, skill and age. There were also divisions over temporary and permanent employment status. In addition, Campbell used social divisions in its external relationships with its suppliers, deliberately dividing farmers in New Jersey State who supplied vegetables and livestock, and preventing them from forming cooperatives through threat and legal contract.

Case study three: careers in the City

Linda McDowell's *Capital Culture* (1997) addresses the issue of gender within the financial sector of the City of London. In her detailed study of a number of financial institutions she examines the way jobs and organisations are gendered. Crucially, she shows that this process of gendering is dependent on, and influenced by, a number of other factors, including age, education, and class. McDowell compares a number of male and female city workers in roughly the same grades of work, and then unravels how an individual's gender shapes the type of work they do as well as their promotion prospects. One woman stated: 'There's a greater inclination on the part of people to dismiss or not take seriously someone who's both young and female' (McDowell 1997: 102).

As we have seen above, one of the crucial events shaping a person's working life is the decision over whether to have children or not. This decision is not easy and McDowell illustrates the way that, whatever choice is made, it structures future career prospects profoundly. Some women decide to give up work altogether and others choose a part-time post which is less demanding.

As the same interviewee said:

> At my level and above, this is where I think there really does start to be a difference between men and women. I feel very strongly now that women do come to a point where you've got to decide whether you want a family or career or whether you're prepared to try and juggle the two... (McDowell 1997: 102)

McDowell's study highlights the way that these decisions are made within a gendered setting, with pre-existing norms, values, and expectations which create certain dispositions towards female and male workers. Women in such settings are often highly dependent on their husbands or partners in terms of their career options in the wake of child birth. Traditionally this meant that female financial workers stepped down, or stepped off, the career ladder.

Capital Culture is a good example of the way class and education also factor into decision-making at work. Financial institutions recruit from very different pools for different roles in their organisations. Thus, traders during the period that McDowell studied the City tended to come straight from school, whilst corporate finance positions in merchant banks were the preserve of elite university-educated graduates. These banks would recruit through highly selective 'milk round' events which targeted Oxford, Cambridge, Bristol, and Durham universities. The recruitment of new employees with similar backgrounds to each other, and to senior staff overseeing the recruitment, helped to bind them together as a distinctive group, separate and closed off from the rest of society. *Capital Culture* shows the complexity of the blending of age, gender, qualifications and class. We can see that, even in one sector of the economy, short-, medium- and long-term career prospects and patterns are structured by the complex interaction of social divisions.

Work and social divisions

It is clear that work cannot be fully understood without reference to a whole range of social divisions. For classical sociologists, social division was an inevitable consequence of the ever greater division of labour in industrialising and industrialised society. For a theorist like Marx, social division was what gave society its momentum. The divisions between people were features that allowed capitalism to extract surplus value, and therefore profit, from its investment. Through work and the work-place we can witness both the impact and creation of social division. It is also apparent that, in order to fully appreciate social divisions at work, we need to understand how history, place and space construct specific work-places and their labour regimes. Social divisions in work have to be understood as complex social structures that are both inhabited by individuals and groups and strongly influence action, but at the same time they are open to change as people – workers, trade unions, managers and politicians – decide to organise work differently. As is the case with any social setting, in the work-place critical understanding is best achieved by a multidimensional approach which allows us to grasp the interactions of division, inequality and privilege.

Discussion Questions

1. Take a look at an ethnographic study of a work-place (for example, Miriam Glucksmann's ([1982]2009) *Women on the Line*, originally published under the pseudonym Ruth Cavendish). What social divisions are apparent in the study?

2. Think about the work-places in which you have been employed. What social divisions do you recognise there? Were they obvious?

3. Discuss with your parents or grandparents the careers that they have followed. What sorts of work did they do, what sorts of people did they work with, and what kinds of choices did they enjoy over what work they did?

FURTHER READING

Bradley, H. *Men's Work, Women's Work* (Cambridge: Polity, 1989) is a very useful, if a little dated, introduction to historical and sociological gendered divisions at work. Ray Pahl's (1984) classic study of economic life on the Isle of Sheppey in Kent, *Divisions of Labour* (Oxford: Blackwell) is an excellent illustration of social, gendered and welfare divisions in an intensely local and isolated labour market. Linkon, S. and Russo, J. *Steeltown U.S.A: Work and Memory in Youngstown* (Lawrence, KS: Kansas University Press, 2002) is a great study of the processes of industrialisation and de-industrialisation, drawing on themes of race and ethnicity, class, gender and religion in the US. Also from the US is Cowie, J. *Capital Moves: RCA's 70-Year Quest for Cheap Labor* (Ithaca: Cornell University Press, 1999). Cowie examines the way the RCA Company sought to draw on social difference in their factory moves between different parts of the US and then Mexico, and illustrates gender, class and ethnic differences at work. Toynbee, P. *Hard Work: Life in Low Paid Britain* (London: Bloomsbury, 2003) is a popular ethnographic account of life on the minimum wage in Britain in the new millennium. Issues of skill, gender, class and ethnicity come to the fore in this fascinating study. Finally, Strangleman, T. and Warren, T. *Work and Society: Sociological Approaches, Themes and Methods* (London: Routledge, 2008) has a useful chapter on social divisions at work.

The Interplay of Social Divisions

CHAPTER 13

Poverty

LUCINDA PLATT

This chapter will provide you with a broad critical understanding of the following issues in defining, measuring and evaluating poverty as a source of social division:

- Why poverty is a social division
- Poverty definitions
- Poverty as lack of income
- Poverty as lack of necessities
- Poverty as material deprivation or social deprivation
- The capability framework for understanding poverty
- Relative versus absolute poverty
- Poverty as a fixed amount of income or goods
- Poverty conceived relative to a socially endorsed standard
- Poverty relative to changing incomes or income at a fixed point in time
- Changes in poverty over time
- Experience of long-term versus short-term poverty
- Poverty as a social division: ethnicity, gender, childhood

Poverty may seem like a self-evident concept synonymous with lack of income. Lack of income, however, implies other 'lacks': it is often felt that poverty can only be understood explicitly through its consequences. Poverty has therefore been defined as a level of income which renders it impossible or unlikely that certain material goods can be obtained or certain activities can be engaged in, or, alternatively, as the direct lack of those goods and activities. It can sometimes also be defined (a little problematically) as the poorer outcomes themselves in terms of health, educational achievement and so on that are more likely for those on a low income. For example, the UN Report of the World Summit (1995) talked about:

> [poverty's] various manifestations, including lack of income and productive resources to ensure sustainable livelihoods; hunger and malnutrition; ill-health; limited or lack of access to education and other basic services;

increased morbidity and mortality from illness; homelessness and inadequate housing; unsafe environments and social discrimination and exclusion. It is also characterised by lack of participation in decision making and in civil, social and cultural life. It occurs in all countries: as mass poverty in many developing countries, pockets of poverty amid wealth in developed countries, loss of livelihood as a result of economic recession, sudden poverty as a result of disaster or conflict, the poverty of low-wage workers, and the utter destitution of people who fall outside family support systems, institutions and safety nets. (quoted in Howard et al. 2001: 21)

This wider perspective shows that poverty is also closely associated with other social divisions – such as class, ethnicity and gender. It is both produced by those divisions and contributes to their character. For example, certain ethnic minorities are over-represented among the poor, leading to poorer average outcomes. Equally, their over-representation is in part a consequence of differential treatment by wider society (Chapter 4). In addition, it is often argued that there is a cyclical aspect to poverty, such that poverty results in poorer outcomes which lead to a greater risk of subsequent poverty. The relationship between poverty and health, whereby poverty leads to poorer health outcomes, but those who are ill are also more likely to be poor, is one illustration of the intertwined nature of cause and effect in relation to poverty (Chapter 14). In order to understand these connections, we need as a first step to give further consideration to the different ways in which poverty has been defined.

What is poverty?

Poverty can be defined as a state in which lack of resources leads to an unacceptably low standard of living. However, what is meant by 'resources' and what is deemed acceptable is clearly open to debate, resulting in a plethora of approaches and measurements, from living on less than a dollar a day, to specifying a particular 'basket of goods and services' which people need in order to avoid poverty.

In Britain, much of the debate has focused around distinguishing a supposedly absolute level of poverty from a *relative* standard. According to this distinction, 'absolute poverty' is regarded as being concerned with minimum human needs for survival, such as implied in the following quotation:

a condition characterised by severe deprivation of basic human needs, including food, safe drinking water, sanitation facilities, health, shelter, education and information. It depends not only on income but also on access to services. (UN 1995, quoted in Gordon et al. 2000: 9)

The levels of deprivation that existed in nineteenth-century Britain or currently exist in other parts of the world (Townsend and Gordon 2002) do not encompass the experience of the modern British population. This recognition has on occasions led people to deny that poverty is an issue in Britain at all. For example, in the 1970s, a Conservative minister, Sir Keith Joseph said that: 'A family is poor if it cannot afford to eat. By any absolute standards there is very little poverty in Britain today' (quoted in Oppenheim and Harker 1996: 8).

In contrast, 'relative poverty' is concerned with specifying people's lack of welfare relative to acceptable standards within the society in which they live. For example, this is the understanding in the following EU definition:

> the poor shall be taken to mean persons, families and groups of persons whose resources (material, cultural and social) are so limited as to exclude them from the minimum acceptable way of life in the Member State in which they live. (European Commission 1984, quoted in Gordon et al. 2000: 12)

This approach, with its emphasis on exclusion, fits more comfortably with the concept of 'social division'.

The definition of poverty as a relative concept owes much to the work of Peter Townsend, who, with colleagues including Brian Abel-Smith, was responsible for the 'rediscovery of poverty' in the late 1950s and 1960s. Their investigations demonstrated that the post-war welfare state had not succeeded in eliminating poverty, as had previously been assumed (Abel-Smith and Townsend 1965).

In developing his understanding of poverty, which he presented most comprehensively in his major 1979 study entitled *Poverty in the United Kingdom*, Townsend set his approach in opposition to what he saw as the absolute definition of poverty. He located this 'absolute' perspective as originating in Rowntree's 1899 study of poverty in York in which Rowntree first articulated an income-based threshold as a measure of poverty, through his conception of the 'primary poverty line' (Rowntree 1902). This approach to poverty was repeated and re-used by both Rowntree and other social investigators subsequently (Rowntree 1918, 1937, 1942; Rowntree and Lavers 1951). In fact, however, as Veit-Wilson (1986) has pointed out, Townsend's take on Rowntree's primary poverty line as an absolute definition of poverty against which to contrast his own approach derived from a misreading of Rowntree (see also Hennock 1991).

Townsend was, then, effectively establishing a 'straw man' of absolute poverty to emphasise those aspects of his own conception of 'relative poverty' that stressed the importance of the ability to participate in everyday life according to contemporary standards:

> Poverty can be defined objectively and applied consistently only in terms of the concept of relative deprivation. The term is understood objectively rather than subjectively. Individuals, families and groups in the population can be said to be in poverty when they lack the resources to obtain the types of diet, participate in the activities and have the living conditions and amenities which are customary, or are at least widely encouraged or approved, in the societies to which they belong. Their resources are so seriously below those commanded by the average individual or family that they are, in effect, excluded from ordinary living patterns, customs and activities (Townsend 1979: 31).

'Luxuries' and the bare 'necessities' of life

The absolute/relative dichotomy was also pursued in the work of Amartya Sen, who returned to the work of Adam Smith, the eighteenth-century political economist. Sen argued that, while the understanding of what constitutes deprivation or excludes people from participation may be contextually specific, there are underlying elements or capabilities which everyone requires, although they may be differentially interpreted or mean different things in different circumstances. As long ago as 1776, Adam Smith had argued that undergarments were essential for acceptability within contemporary society, even if they may not have been in Roman times. In a much-cited passage, Smith said that:

> By necessaries I understand, not only the commodities which are indispensably necessary for the support of life, but whatever the custom of the country renders it indecent for creditable people, even of the lowest order, to be without. A linen shirt, for example, is, strictly speaking, not a necessary of life. The Greeks and Romans lived, I suppose, very comfortably, though they had not linen. But in the present times, through the greater part of Europe, a creditable day-labourer would be ashamed to appear in public without a linen shirt, the want of which would be supposed to denote that disgraceful degree of poverty, which, it is presumed, no body can well fall into without extreme bad conduct. (Smith 1976: 399)

Sen (1983) took off from this position to argue that freedom from shame constitutes a capability or essential which is necessary for someone not to be deprived. What goods or attributes will allow such freedom are contextually specific – in Smith's day a linen shirt, in other times and contexts something else. Sen thus maintained that it was important to retain the absoluteness of needs in the conception of poverty. He argued for seeing needs in terms of absolute minimum capabilities, which:

> translates into a relative approach in the space of commodities, resources and incomes in dealing with some important capabilities such as avoiding shame from failure to meet social conventions, participating in social activities, and retaining self-respect. (Sen 1983: 167–8)

Or, as he expressed it in a lecture given in 1985:

> Some capabilities, such as being well nourished, may have more or less similar demands on commodities (such as food and health services) irrespective of the average opulence of the community in which the person lives. Other capabilities, such as the ones with which Adam Smith was particularly concerned, have commodity demands that vary a good deal with average opulence. To lead a life without shame, to be able to visit and entertain one's friends, to keep track of what is going on and what others are talking about, and so on, requires a more expensive bundle of goods and services in a society that is generally richer, and in which most people have, say, means of transport, affluent clothing, radios or television sets, and so on. Thus, some of the same capabilities (relevant for a 'minimum' level of living) require more real income and opulence in the form of commodity possession in a richer society than in poorer ones. The same absolute levels of capabilities may thus have a greater relative need for incomes (and commodities). There is thus no mystery in the necessity of having a 'relativist' view on the space of incomes even when poverty is defined in terms of the same absolute levels of basic capabilities. (Sen 1987: 18)

Sen's attachment to retaining an absolute element in defining poverty resulted in a somewhat unedifying print disagreement between himself and Peter Townsend. Townsend rejected the idea that any 'absolute' understandings of poverty should have a role in its definition, while Sen objected to being misrepresented (Sen 1985; Townsend 1985). Nevertheless, substantively, the distance between them does not seem to be that wide. In fact, despite Townsend's major contribution to ways of thinking about poverty that incorporate understandings of participation and social activity rather than simply material needs, the absolute/relative distinction, even as it retains wide currency is a somewhat spurious one, as Ringen (1988) has noted.

This soon becomes apparent at the level of measurement. As soon as researchers are faced with the business of attempting to identify what constitutes poverty in order to count those in poverty or distinguish the poor from the non-poor, it is impossible to escape consideration of what is normative practice and what is local convention. Adam Smith had recognised this in the eighteenth century, not only in his famous discussion of the linen shirt, which recognised the relevance of temporal context, but also in his discussion of shoes, which, he observed, could vary geographically and with gender at the same point in time:

> Custom, in the same manner, has rendered leather shoes a necessary of life in England. The poorest creditable person of either sex would be ashamed to appear in public without them. In Scotland, custom has rendered them a necessary of life to the lowest order of men; but not to the same order of women, who may, without any discredit, walk about bare-footed. In France, they are necessaries neither to men nor to women; the lowest rank of both sexes appearing there publicly, without any discredit, sometimes in wooden shoes, and sometimes bare-footed. Under necessaries therefore, I comprehend, not only those things which nature, but those things which the established rules of decency have rendered necessary to the lowest rank of people. (Smith 1976: 399–400)

Moreover, when trying to consider what normatively defined practices or goods could actually be seen as necessary, he was found to waver in his consideration of beer from one edition of *The Wealth of Nations* to the next. Such indeterminacy illustrates both the salience of the researcher's judgement (on the relevance of explicit judgements in poverty measurement, see Atkinson 1987), and the recognition of the significance of actual behaviour patterns, regardless of what is formally recognised as necessary for life. Smith states categorically:

> All other things I call luxuries; without meaning by this appellation, to throw the smallest degree of reproach upon the temperate use of them. Beer and ale, for example, in Great Britain, and wine, even in the wine countries, I call luxuries. A man of any rank may, without any reproach, abstain totally from tasting such liquors. Nature does not render them necessary for the support of life; and custom nowhere renders it indecent to live without them. (Smith 1976: vol II, 400)

Yet the 1976 editor points out that in the original version of the list of necessities in volume I, malt beer was listed first, before 'soap, salt, leather, candles etc.' (Smith 1976: vol I, 488).

A similar difficulty with separating custom or habit from even socially-defined needs can be found in Rowntree's development of his supposedly 'absolute' poverty measure. First, Rowntree took pains to show that his 'primary poverty' line was actually an inconceivable measure in terms of people's actual or expected behaviour:

> And let us clearly understand what 'merely physical efficiency' means. A family living upon the scale allowed for in this estimate must never spend a penny on railway fare or omnibus. They must never go into the country unless they walk. They must never purchase a halfpenny newspaper or spend a penny to buy a ticket for a popular concert. They must write no letters to absent children, for they cannot afford to pay the postage. They must never contribute anything to their church or chapel, or give any help to a neighbour which costs them money. They cannot save, nor can they join sick club or Trade Union, because they cannot pay the necessary subscriptions. The children must have no pocket money for dolls, marbles, or sweets. The father must smoke no tobacco, and must drink no beer. The mother must never buy any pretty clothes for herself or for her children, the character of the family wardrobe as for the family diet being governed by the regulation, 'Nothing must be bought but that which is absolutely necessary for the maintenance of physical health, and what is bought must be of the plainest and most economical description.' Should a child fall ill, it must be attended by the parish doctor; should it die, it must be buried by the parish. Finally, the wage-earner must never be absent from his work for a single day. (Rowntree 1902: 134)

In addition, even his 'primary poverty' line used relative elements: it took the actual cost of housing, and involved a discussion with his subjects over the minimum cost of adequate and respectable dress. In Rowntree's attempt to develop his poverty line into a more realistic measure of poverty (*The Human Needs of Labour*, 1918), he engaged in deliberations comparable to those of Adam Smith over beer, when considering whether meat and tea – and even alcohol – should be included in a basic diet:

> In this country almost everyone takes a mixed diet – even the poorest try to get a certain amount of meat; and though undoubtedly health can be maintained without it, we cannot, in selecting our dietary, ignore the fact that meat-eating is an almost universal custom. So is the drinking of tea and coffee, and though these do not actually supply any nutriment, a certain amount must be included in the dietary. I think we may reasonably exclude alcoholic beverages, but should bear in mind possible expenditure upon them when considering the amount to be allowed for personal sundries. (Rowntree 1937: 78–9)

Absolute or relative?

The measurement of 'absolute' poverty was clearly always a lot more relative than the proponents of a relative line have made out. And the suggestion that specifying a minimum set of goods in itself presupposes an absolute approach to poverty is similarly misleading. Baskets of goods (and services) representing the selection of items necessary to avoid poverty do not in themselves constitute absolute measures, and are not necessarily open to the criticism that they do not reflect normative standards and expectations. Indeed, Townsend's own poverty measure in his major (1979) study was constituted from a selection of goods and activities deemed to represent an appropriate standard of living at the time. It is the failure to adjust such baskets of goods to changing circumstances that leads to their appearing inappropriate or inadequate.

Thus, despite its currency and use as a reference point, the absolute/relative dichotomy tends to dissolve as soon as we move to operationalisation and measurement. Whatever the chosen operationalisation, it will occur along a continuum rather than involving a dichotomous distinction. And, in all measurement, both judgement (about what actually constitutes necessities or a poverty line) and context (a relationship to what occurs and/or is acceptable in the surrounding society) necessarily have a bearing.

Before moving on to consider the current measurement of poverty in more detail, it is important to mention another context in which the absolute/relative contrast is used. This is in relation to the common practice of measuring poverty or low income by means of proportions of average income. The numbers or percentages of the population who are below a proportion of average income, such as 50 per cent of the mean or 60 per cent of the median, can be compared over time. In such comparisons, the proportion in poverty can be measured in relation to contemporary average income which is allowed to vary year by year (the 'relative line'). Alternatively, the value of the proportion at a particular point in time can be held constant, and the proportions below that fixed value can be compared over time (the 'absolute line'). (We shall see examples of these two lines over a comparable period in Figure 13.2.) While it is appropriate to make a distinction between these two approaches to an income line, the terminology in terms of absolute versus relative has very little connection with the debate on defining low income in absolute or relative terms. This is because the choice of year at which to set and fix the absolute line is arbitrary and the choice of goods is not supposed to represent a fixed set of necessities. Indeed, it is a relative measure in the year in which it is set. Representing the distinction as one between relative and absolute low income, while a widespread practice, can thus potentially lead to confusion.

Measuring poverty

There are two primary ways in which to measure poverty among the population or among sub-populations. The first of these is by income, representing the resources available to achieve a particular standard of living. The basis for setting the income level is the moot question. The alternative is to attempt to measure standard of living directly. Again, what indicators should be used for measures of standard of living, and at what point to designate an individual or household in poverty or suffering material deprivation, are vexed questions.

Using income as a means of measuring poverty has a number of advantages. It is transparent and easy to understand and is available as a measurement in a wide range of sources from which we might wish to estimate poverty. While assumptions about necessities and reasonable expenditure might go into setting the amount of income that constitutes the poverty line, it also does not require that people actually spend their money in particular ways, and therefore allows for people getting welfare out of a set income in diverse ways. It also enables direct comparison with incomes provided by subsistence benefits which are intended to meet minimum needs. Moreover, income lines allow comparison over time much more straightforwardly than measures of consumption, which may either become out of date or, if adjusted over time, result in difficulties in claiming that they are strictly comparable.

On the other hand, a number of criticisms can be made of income as a poverty measure. First, it is only a proxy for standard of living (Ringen 1988). That is, it does not necessarily measure standard of living or consumption. These may be related to future expectations and ability to incur debt, the length of time that poverty has been experienced or the differential costs of goods and services for those in different circumstances, for example the extra costs that disabled people are liable to incur, for transport, heat and so on (Chapter 8). In fact, the development of longitudinal measures of income poverty that evaluate the period over which poverty is experienced, as well as extra costs measures and different adjustments for households of different composition, have made some of these criticisms less salient.

When setting an income poverty line, there have been two main approaches. The 'basket of goods' or 'budget standards' approach is based on estimating the cost of a set of goods necessary to avoid poverty (or to ensure participation). The more arbitrary, but simpler, approach is to select a fixed proportion of average income. Additional approaches have been to use the actual value of subsistence benefits or some multiple of them (for example Abel-Smith and Townsend 1965), or to select some essential components of standard of living (such as food) and increase these by a factor deemed to take account of expenditure on other essentials (for example Orshansky 1965).

The first main method, the budget standards approach, was developed by Rowntree in setting his 'primary poverty line' in his first study of York (Rowntree 1902). It was subsequently adopted in a range of poverty surveys, as well as in Rowntree's own *Human Needs of Labour* (1918). More recently, a number of studies have adopted this approach. Piachaud (1979) estimated an income line for children, to enable direct comparison with allowances in supplementary benefit allowances; Bradshaw and colleagues developed a set of budgets for a selection of families of different sizes and compositions (Bradshaw 1993); and Parker, with others, developed income levels for both families with children and older people (Parker 1998, 2000). Since 2008, the Joseph Rowntree Foundation has developed and updated annually a minimum income standard that is intended to reflect the costs (or the income needed to support) socially accepted necessities (see www.jrf.org.uk). These minimum income thresholds could be explicitly compared with subsistence benefit rates for families with the same composition as those estimated, thus illustrating the adequacy (or inadequacy) of state benefits which have never explicitly used estimates of needs in their rates, even though implicitly such benefits constitute a poverty line (Veit-Wilson 1992, 1994; Platt 2005). Bradshaw explained this potential:

> Policy makers who have responsibility for making decisions about the level of benefits can be faced through budget standards with the consequence of those decisions. If the low cost budget is more than the income support scales then they can indicate which items in the budget claimants should expect to go without. (Bradshaw 1993: 238)

Although budget standards are not intended to be prescriptive, but instead to act as reference points, they at least imply that if incomes based on them are not spent roughly as indicated, the family will suffer hardship. Piachaud, on the other hand, has argued that it might be more appropriate to take as an income measure the level of income at which the vast majority of the population (he suggests 95 per cent) can be guaranteed to spend the prescribed amounts on the different necessities, even if their priorities are not those specified by the 'ideal' budget (Piachaud 1987: 159–60). This would leave just 5 per cent who would perhaps never allocate income to identified necessities.

Given the difficulties that budget standards measures have in providing methods of estimating poverty in the population, it is perhaps unsurprising to find that the income poverty measures which have gained the greatest currency among both researchers and governments are those which enable a straightforward estimation of proportions and composition of those in poverty at a point in time and over time. The establishment of the Households Below Average Income (HBAI) series in the mid-1980s provided an annual series of measures of low income in relation to various proportions of household income adjusted for household size and composition. It also demonstrates the relative risks of different forms of household of falling below particular proportions of income, and the rates of different household types falling across fifths of the income distribution. Currently, the most common cut-off for low income is 60 per cent of median income by 'equivalised household' (see below). Trends over time and differential risks of different family types using the 60 per cent of median cut-off are shown in Figures 13.2 to 13.4 later in this chapter.

These relative income lines of poverty have been criticised on the grounds that they are informative about inequality but not about poverty per se (Sen 1983). Others would argue that inequality is in itself significant (Hills et al. 2010; see also the discussion of this point in Atkinson 1987). In fact, a highly unequal distribution of resources is likely to exclude those near the bottom. Wilkinson (1996; Wilkinson and Pickett 2009) has repeatedly argued that in developed countries it is inequality rather than income which results in health divides, and that greater equality of income, even at a lower average level (once a certain minimum has been achieved), results in better social outcomes – or fewer 'social ills'.

While the poverty or low income lines used in this approach are, in a sense, arbitrary, they represent an acceptance of the notion that poverty is related to general living standards. In so far as average income is a proxy for such living standards, participation in or attainment of normative standards of living are hard to achieve at incomes that fall far short of the average. It has also been recommended that to verify the picture of poverty and who it affects, particularly for comparative purposes, a range of lines can (and should) be used (Atkinson 1987, 1998). Relative poverty lines, by being comparable over time and over populations, also enable evaluation of the extent to which policy is influencing the extent of poverty in a population. For example, the government's aim of reducing child poverty is evaluated against the proportions of children in child poverty according to such a measure, although other measures of child poverty are also employed in the Child Poverty Act 2010.

The extent to which poverty lines are appropriate for measuring risks of low income across individuals living in different sizes of household will depend to a certain extent on the way that household incomes are adjusted to take account of the number (and ages) of the people living in them. Equivalence scales are typically employed to adjust incomes of households to be comparable regardless of size. Thus, single-person households with a given real income are accorded a higher 'equivalised' income than households with two adults and children. Individuals' consumption or standard of living may not be fully represented by the household income adjusted for size, as distributions may not be equitable within the household. In so far as children are prioritised for expenditure by their parents, they may be better off than their household income implies. There may also be variations in the experienced standard of living according to sex, to the extent that actual distributions of household income are gendered, an issue taken up in the discussion of differential risks of poverty, below.

Temporal issues in measuring material disadvantage and consumption

Income-based poverty lines, then, represent the most appropriate measure of poverty, even more so when they are able to take the issue of time into account (Jenkins 2011). There are two aspects of time that are important in the measurement of poverty: life-course and poverty duration. Life-course issues refer to the fact that there are times when people are more vulnerable to poverty, which also might have knock-on effects on their subsequent experiences. One example might be students, who may have very low incomes – and high levels of debt – but whose future income is likely to be above average, and their current consumption patterns may in part reflect their anticipated income. Another example would be lone parents, who are on average more vulnerable to poverty, even though some will move out of poverty faster than others. Those who become poor, for example through divorce or separation, may also be at greater risk of poverty later in life through missed pensions contributions (Ginn et al. 2001; Ginn 2003; Jenkins 2008). Being able to recognise poverty risks and their implications at different points in the life-course is obviously important for understanding well-being in the population and appropriate policy intervention. Given the changing relationships between income and consumption throughout the life-course, expenditure rather than income provides a better and more direct measure of well-being and poverty, although it brings its own issues of complexity of measurement and reliability.

The second issue is the duration of poverty. Poverty for ten years is more serious in terms of its impact on both standards of living and life chances than poverty for one month. While this aspect of poverty duration has been recognised as significant for a long time – and has been one of the criticisms of the appropriateness of cross-sectional income measures as representations of poverty risks – it is only relatively recently that it has been possible to measure durations of poverty in Britain. The measurement of poverty as a temporal phenomenon and a state that people can enter and leave (and return to) has also tended to emphasise the conceptualisation of poverty as a general risk rather than an inherent characteristic of certain individuals (Walker and Ashworth 1994; Jenkins 2011). The inception of the British Household Panel Survey (BHPS) in 1991, in which members of a representative sample of households are re-interviewed annually and their experience over time charted, has been a core element in the ability to track poverty (Taylor et al. 2003; Jenkins 2011).

Consideration of poverty duration has also illustrated that there is a connection between the duration of low income and the inability to participate or have particular consumer goods, which is the alternative way of measuring poverty. The two types of current poverty research thus tend to come together here. Nevertheless, there is ongoing development of measures of material disadvantage and commitment to them as direct rather than proxy measures of poverty.

In his 1979 survey, Townsend measured poverty using a range of indicators without which people were deemed to be disadvantaged. Nevertheless, he attempted to use these to identify a point of income at which a steep decline in participation in everyday life occurred. Despite criticism of his method and his indicators (Piachaud 1981), a number of other studies building on his work have tried to use direct measures of poverty to ascertain the levels of disadvantage in this country (see Payne et al. 1996). Some, which argued that they were producing a consensual measure of poverty (Mack and Lansley 1985; Gordon and Pantazis 1997; Gordon et al. 2000), used a sample of respondents to validate which of the listed items and activities were necessities. Those items which were regarded as necessities by 50 per cent of the population were considered to reflect a consensus about what represented an adequate standard of living. Deprivation or poverty was deemed to be present among those who did not have – because they could not afford – two or more of the necessities.

There has been much subsequent discussion of the desirability and practicality of a consensual measurement of poverty (Veit-Wilson 1986; Piachaud 1987; Walker 1987), including criticism of deeming a bare majority to represent consensus. Re-examination of Gordon et al.'s 2000 survey data showed that there was substantial heterogeneity in the rating of necessities by different subgroups (McKay 2004). Equally it may be inappropriate for measuring deprivation across different population subgroups (Platt 2002). Moreover, the combination of deprivation measures with a confirmatory low income measure is clearly problematic for the claims of a direct measurement of poverty through deprivation indicators, as is the arbitrary choice of a cut-off of deprivation at two or more items.

A series of studies by Nolan, Whelan and others has also been influential in developing the role of deprivation measures in poverty research. The initial studies were conducted in Ireland (Callan et al. 1993; Nolan and Whelan 1996); while subsequent studies incorporated European comparisons (Whelan et al. 2001; Layte et al. 2001). This body of research has partly been driven by the observation that deprivation and low income do not necessarily correlate, although the combination of material deprivation and low income is held to represent a truer understanding of poverty. There has also been criticism of the meaningfulness – and the susceptibility to policy intervention – of an index of deprivation that is supposed, through indicators, to represent an underlying continuum of poverty. In addition, it could be pointed out that the measures of deprivation are market-based and can therefore be removed through expenditure – thus a conceptualisation in relation to income levels is already implicit. Moreover, in the Nolan and Whelan study (1996), it transpires perhaps unsurprisingly, that it is the element of time which explains the difference between those suffering deprivation as a result of current low income and those not. Those who were not suffering deprivation had only been on a low income for a short time, and the longer the duration of low income, the greater the levels of deprivation.

Berthoud et al. (2004) took this insight a stage further by looking at the trends over time in the relationship between income and material deprivation. They found that changes in income were important for changes in material deprivation, but that the long-run effects of poverty implied much greater levels of deprivation than implied by the cross-sectional relationships. The authors also observed that material deprivation measures lost their purchase over time because general social conditions and expectations change. That is, simply the passage of time reduced levels of deprivation as measured earlier. To remain an effective measure in the long term, material deprivation measures need to be adjusted upwards rather than held constant.

Despite some of the problems around the use of measurements of material deprivation to represent poverty, they have been incorporated into official assessments of child poverty targets, and are reported in annual updates on progress towards the aim of reducing child poverty (Department for Work and Pensions 2011a). High deprivation scores are combined with a particular income threshold (70 per cent of median) to create a combined low income and deprivation measure of poverty. In addition, similar sets of questions on participation and necessities, which check both for their lack through any reason and their lack through unaffordability (to avoid conflation with lifestyle choices), is regularly asked in many national surveys.

Following the Independent Review of Poverty and Life Chances, Frank Field's (2010) recommendation for the introduction of a measure of 'severe child poverty' was realised in the form of combining the deprivation measure with incomes below 50 per cent of median. This is intended to focus attention on the very worst off, given the high number of children in poverty according to the standard measure. It also complements the measure of the worst off through length of time in poverty (three years out of four), according to the official longitudinal measure.

Figure 13.1 summarises some of these different ways that poverty has been conceived and measured, and the intersections between them. Three general approaches are identified, which then lead via the solid lines to different measures and definitions. These illustrate the multiple ways in which poverty has been realised. However, as the dotted lines make clear, there are points of correspondence across the measures stemming from the different approaches

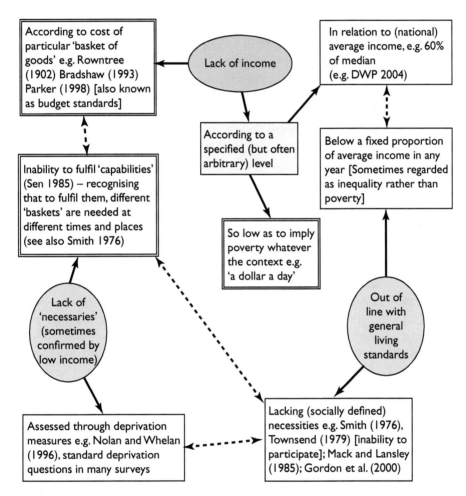

Figure 13.1 What is poverty?

Notes: Solid lines show the ways different conceptions of poverty have been defined or measured. Dashed lines illustrate the overlaps or correspondences between different approaches, even though the correspondences are sometimes denied by proponents of particular approaches. The boxes in double borders are those measures sometimes regarded as 'absolute'.

Source: Author's own research.

(even if their proponents would dispute them). What is taken to be poverty becomes more a matter of emphasis than seeing approaches as being inherently contradictory.

A more recent development has taken consideration of poverty beyond both income and material deprivation to emphasise overall well-being. In this approach, demonstrated in the Organisation for Economic Co-operation and Development's (2011a) *How's Life?*, material living conditions and income, earnings and housing position are considered key components of the framework for evaluating well-being, but are set alongside quality of life measures and informed by sustainability issues. The quality of life measures include subjective measures of well-being or 'life satisfaction' but the OECD does not attempt to subsume well-being within life satisfaction or subjective well-being in a way that has marked UK policy pronouncements. In the OECD approach a focus on both meeting basic needs and fulfilling capabilities are incorporated into an overall framework which can be used to measure well-being, both comparatively across countries and its progress over time. Nevertheless, there is no attempt to incorporate all the indicators of well-being into a unified whole. Instead, they are considered separately and alongside the variation or inequalities within particular domains, which can be informative about differential access to aspects of well-being within societies.

Poverty in Britain today

This section reviews patterns of poverty over the last couple of decades according to official measures, and explores the groups and circumstances with which higher rates of poverty are associated. Figure 13.2 shows a poverty line held constant at 60 per cent of the 1998/9 median as well as the proportions below 60 per cent of contemporary income. This enables us to see that, while relative poverty rates remained more or less constant over the period from 1998/9 to 2009/10, there was a distinct decline in the number of people with incomes below the 1998/9 median. The poverty rate in 2009/10 was 17 per cent for all individuals, but it varied such that 16 per cent of men, 17 per cent of women and 20 per cent of children were in poverty.

Moving on to look at trends measured in terms of material deprivation, Figure 13.3 compares those deprived of certain activities/necessities because of their unaffordability. The indication is that, over the seven-year period measured, there was a substantial decline in deprivation across households on all measures. Given the assumption about the relative and contextual nature of poverty, it might be possible to ask whether the questions asked in 1996 were

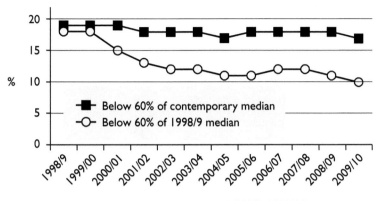

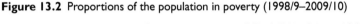

Figure 13.2 Proportions of the population in poverty (1998/9–2009/10)

Source: Derived from Department for Work and Pensions (2011a), Tables 3.1tr and 3.2tr.

still pertinent in 2002 (as Berthoud et al. (2004) do). However, the relatively short period between the two time points would suggest that they should have still been reasonably salient in 2002 if they were in 1996.

Similarly, looking at the number of indicators on which households are deprived (Figure 13.4), we see that a reduction at all levels of deprivation would appear to hold across the seven-year period.

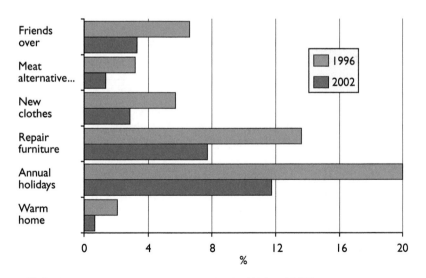

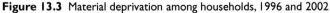

Figure 13.3 Material deprivation among households, 1996 and 2002

Source: Author's analysis of British Household Panel Survey, main sample households (n = 4978 in 1996, n = 4574 in 2002) with cross-sectional weights.

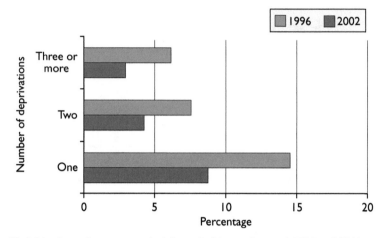

Figure 13.4 Number of counts on which households are deprived, 1996 and 2002

Source: Author's analysis of British Household Panel Survey, main sample households (*n* = 4978 in 1996, *n* = 4574 in 2002) with cross-sectional weights.

Another way to judge how well people are doing is to consider their own subjective views of their situation. There has been growing momentum to measure, in the words of the UK's National Statistician 'what matters' (Office for National Statistics 2011c). This has resulted in a programme concerned with the measurement of national well-being which, in 2012, published a set of statistics on subjective well-being. When adults over-16 were asked to rate their overall satisfaction on a scale of 0–10, the average score was 7.4. Women had slightly higher scores (more satisfaction) then men, and younger and older people had slightly higher scores than those in their middle years. Across ethnic groups, people of mixed or multiple ethnicity, and from one of the Black ethnic categories (Black African, or Caribbean or Black British) reported significantly lower satisfaction than the overall average (at 6.9 and 6.6 respectively).

From the general rates of poverty, we now turn to look in more detail at who is likely to be poor. Table 13.1 shows the risks of falling below the 60 per cent of the median low-income threshold for those in a range of differently characterised families, or with different characteristics, that is the proportion of the group in poverty, for each individual according to their circumstances. These rates can be compared to the overall poverty risk of 17 per cent.

We can see that living in a workless family, particularly a non-pensioner workless family, is associated with high risks of poverty, as is coming from a minority ethnic group household. An alternative view is given in Table 13.2,

Table 13.1 Individuals in poverty by characteristics of household/household head, 2009/10

Characteristics of household/household head	Percentage below 60% median before housing costs
Workless, head or spouse aged 60 or over	22
Workless, head or spouse unemployed	61
Workless, other inactive	42
White	16
Mixed	23
Indian	24
Pakistani/Bangladeshi	49
Black Caribbean	24
Black non-Caribbean	30
Chinese or other ethnic group	27
Disabled children	18
Disabled working age adults	25
Disabled pensioners	18
Lone parents	27
Couple with children	16
Couple without children	10
All individuals	17

Notes

Household characteristics are not mutually exclusive – risks on one characteristic may be associated with risks in another (e.g. high rates of worklessness among certain minority groups; higher risks of disability among those who are retired) or may be compounded (e.g. the risks of poverty among those from particular ethnic groups who are also living with a disabled adult may be particularly high).

Ethnic group is the ethnic group of the household head and is a three-year average to ensure robust estimates.

Source: Department for Work and Pensions (2011a), Table 3.5db.

which shows the *share* of these high-risk groups who fall below the 60 per cent median line. This analysis shows how poverty rates and numerical representation in the population intersect, so that most of the poor are not from the highest-risk groups. Thus, for example, those in households workless through unemployment, and Pakistanis and Bangladeshis, have very high poverty risks, but they make up only 13 per cent and 6 per cent respectively of those poor. However, couples with children have slightly below average poverty risks, but they make up 34 per cent of the poor.

Both approaches are important from a policy point of view. Impacting on the high-risk groups will do most to meet the demands of social justice and avoid the exclusion from society of certain groups, while focusing on those who make up the biggest share of the poor is likely to do more to bring down overall poverty rates.

Table 13.2 Contribution of individuals in households at risk of poverty to all those below 60 per cent of median income by household characteristics, 2002/3

Characteristics of household/household head	Percentage of all below 60% median before housing costs
Workless, head or spouse aged 60 or over	22
Workless, head or spouse unemployed	13
Workless, other inactive	23
White	83
Mixed	1
Indian	3
Pakistani/Bangladeshi	6
Black Caribbean	1
Black non-Caribbean	3
Chinese or other ethnic group	2
Disabled children	1
Disabled working age adults	12
Disabled pensioners	9
Lone parents	13
Couples with children	34
Couples without children	10

Note: Proportions are not additive as they neither include those without high risks of poverty (for example non-disabled adults) nor are they mutually exclusive (many of those living with a disabled adult may also be living in a workless household).

Source: Department for Work and Pensions (2011a), Table 3.3db.

As discussed, income poverty over a period could offer a preferable way of considering people's resulting levels of deprivation. Jenkins (2011) explored the persistence of poverty among individuals over the period between 1991 and 2004. He examined how it differed by individual and family characteristics, as well as identifying moves into and out of poverty and 'trigger' events associated with them. Using four-year and nine-year windows of observation, he showed that, while in any given year around one-fifth of the population were poor, around one-third were poor for at least one year in four across the period. Around one in seven were poor for three out of the four years towards the beginning of the 1990s, falling to around one in nine by the mid-2000s. Thus, while cross-sectional estimates show little difference in poverty rates over the last decade or so (see Figure 13.2), there has been a decline in those who remain in poverty for successive years.

This finding becomes more marked when explored for particular sub-groups. Thus, the persistent poverty rate of around 20 per cent of children who were poor for three out of four years at the beginning of the 1990s, falls to around 11 per cent of children who were persistently poor by the mid-2000s. This trend was found for both those living in couple-parent and lone-parent families; but among couple-parent families the change was from 9 per cent to 6 per cent persistently poor, while among lone-parent families the risks of persistent poverty reduced from around 42 per cent in the early 1990s to around 26 per cent in the mid-2000s.

Differential risks of poverty: ethnicity, gender, children

There is extensive evidence that minority group members have higher risks of poverty than the majority population and also that there are great differences between different minority groups in relation to the proportions in poverty. This is particularly true of minority ethnic groups (Berthoud 1997, 1998; Platt 2007, 2009). While all minorities appear to experience excess poverty – that is, higher rates than those for the population as a whole – for some, in particular Bangladeshis and Pakistanis, the levels of poverty are extremely high. And even here, although these two groups are commonly aggregated in available statistics, there are differences between the groups, with Bangladeshis having substantially higher rates of poverty than Pakistanis.

Table 13.3 shows the differences in poverty rates between the different groups. The striking rates of poverty among Bangladeshis and Pakistanis and the excess rates of poverty for both adults and children from all minority groups are clearly evident. While factors such as concentration in deprived areas, demographic profile and differential rates of educational achievement play some part in explaining the differences in poverty between different minorities and the majority, all the evidence suggests that there remains an 'ethnic penalty' in incomes, as in earnings and employment, which cannot be accounted for by the characteristics of group members (see for example Heath and McMahon 1997; Blackaby et al. 2002; Longhi and Platt 2008; Platt 2007, 2009).

Table 13.3 Proportions of children, working age adults, and all individuals below 60 per cent of median income by household characteristics, by ethnic group, 2003/4–2005/6

Ethnic group	Children	Working age adults	All individuals
White	19	13	16
Indian	30	20	24
Pakistani	53	48	49
Bangladeshi	64	54	57
Black Caribbean	30	22	25
Black African	37	27	29

Source: Author's analysis of Households Below Average Income data, combined 2003/4–2005/6 rolling averages.

These patterns are also replicated when we look at deprivation measures across ethnic groups, with higher scores than the White majority for all minority groups, with the exception of Indian families. When looking at the combination of low income and material deprivation, minority ethnic groups (again with the exception of Indian families) have higher scores than the White group, even among those who are all below the poverty threshold (Platt 2009). They are also more likely to face risks on the official measure of combined material deprivation and low income. For example, 15 per cent of White children but 24 per cent of Black Caribbean children and 39 per cent of Pakistani or Bangladeshi children were at risk of combined low income and material deprivation in 2009/10 (Department for Work and Pensions 2011a; Table 5.4db). Moreover for both poverty risks and material deprivation, differences remain for most minority groups, even if attenuated, when holding constant other factors associated with higher poverty risks, such as family type (e.g. couple- or lone-parent), household work status, region and family disability.

Women have a higher risk of poverty than men. Yet the relatively small gap in the proportions in poverty disguises the fact that certain groups in which women are over-represented have much higher risks of poverty (Rake 2000). The two most striking such groups are lone parents (of whom 90 per cent are women) and older single people, among whom women are over-represented (Chapter 5) and for whom poverty risks are much greater than for male single pensioners (Ginn 2003). Figure 13.5 provides the most recent estimates of poverty risks for male and female pensioners and for lone parents. It also indicates the scale of the issue, by supplying the contribution to the population poor of each group.

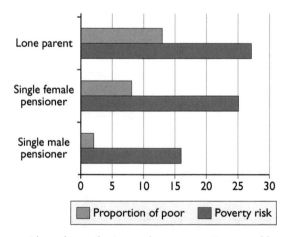

Figure 13.5 Poverty risks and contribution to the poor: pensioners and lone parents, 2009/10
Source: Derived from Department for Work and Pensions (2011a), Tables 3.3db and 3.5db.

Marriage or living in a partnership would appear to protect women against poverty to a degree. However, the situation is not as clear-cut as that because the way these poverty proportions are calculated assumes that there will be certain economies of scale within households and that the aggregate income of all household members will result in the same standards of living for all household members. To a certain extent this is a valid assumption, in that housing, amenities and common goods such as refrigerators are likely to benefit all household members fairly equally. Similarly, evidence from deprivation measures suggests that lone parents suffer greater hardship than their poverty risks reveal. However, the assumption that net household income is equally shared has long been problematised, particularly in relation to women's command over resources.

There are also substantial differences between women. The National Equality Panel report of 2010 highlighted how 'groups' categorised by characteristics such as gender or ethnicity experienced substantial *within group* inequalities that typically outweighed the inequalities between groups (Hills et al. 2010). Moreover, women's experience (and their inequalities, both between them and men, and among women) also vary substantially by ethnic group (Nandi and Platt 2010). Thus Bangladeshi women, with high poverty risks and lower-than-average within-group inequalities, arguably share more (in terms of disadvantage and poverty risks) with Bangladeshi men than they do with women from other ethnic groups.

Children as a group have tended to suffer higher rates of poverty in Britain than the population as a whole. They have historically borne much of the burden of total poverty, which has been shown to have the potential for lasting impacts into their later lives. Nevertheless, despite strong campaigning interest over an extended period, it was really only at the end of the 1990s that their poverty was acknowledged as a priority within government (Walker 1999; Platt 2005). In a lecture in 1999, Tony Blair famously announced that:

> Poverty should not be a birthright. Being poor should not be a life sentence ... Our historic aim will be for ours to be the first generation to end child poverty, and it will take a generation. It is a 20-year mission but I believe it can be done. (Blair, 1999: 17)

Children are recognised as being a particular concern because of their perceived vulnerability (Chapter 6), the fact that they are the future of the nation and fears that disadvantage can repeat itself across generations in a cyclical form. The concern with child poverty has continued, with the establishment of an apparatus for monitoring progress towards the elimination of child poverty, and legislation to embed it in policy, the Child Poverty Act 2010. This was supplemented by the recommendation in the Independent Review on Poverty and Life Chances, conducted by Frank Field, and published at the end of 2010, that a measure of severe child poverty also needed to be monitored, alongside a much greater emphasis on parenting and concern with non-economic aspects of disadvantage.

Children's individual risks of poverty are not just a function of their status as children but also vary with other household characteristics, such as ethnicity, disability and economic activity. Table 13.4 illustrates the poverty risks for children according to the household characteristics associated with higher-than-average poverty. It also shows the contribution of the children in families with different sorts of risk to total child poverty. Again, we see that the highest risks are not necessarily associated with major contributions to total child poverty, given the relatively low prevalence of those with some of the highest risks, for example, workless couple-parent families or Pakistani and Bangladeshi families. The exceptions are workless households and lone-parent households, where very high risks combine with substantial prevalence to result in either of them (and there will be substantial overlap between the two) contributing almost half of child poverty.

Children not only face higher risks of poverty but they are particularly vulnerable to its negative consequences, particularly when these persist over time. Effects are both long-term (into adulthood) and have been shown to emerge early in life. Analysis of children's early life outcomes has shown how these are influenced by family poverty and that the impact is particularly stark when that poverty is enduring (Dickerson and Popli 2012).

Table 13.4 Children's poverty risks

Risk characteristic	Poverty risk	Share of poor children
Lone parent	38	32
Couple not in work	62	20
All workless households	53	42
Three plus children	26	34
Disability within the household	25	31
White	19	73
Mixed	28	2
Indian	27	3
Pakistani/Bangladeshi	54	10
Black Caribbean	24	1
Black non-Caribbean	36	4
Chinese or other ethnic group	33	2
All children	20	100

Source: Department for Work and Pensions (2011), Tables 4.3db and 4.5db.

Conclusion

This chapter has shown that, while poverty and what it means to be poor is intuitively straightforward, the concept can prove complex in terms of both definition and measurement and has been much contested. Nevertheless, it has been argued that there are clear points of contact between the various approaches and that the reality of poverty – a state of disadvantage which impacts on life chances, divorces people from connections with the surrounding society, finds expression in a lack of the basic goods with which normal life can be pursued and is cumulative in effect – is a characteristic of modern Britain.

Moreover, poverty disproportionately affects particular groups in the population: it is both an illustration and a consequence of social divisions. Thus, the recognition of the different poverty rates – between different ethnic groups, between different age groups, between disabled and able-bodied, between men and women – serves to give such distinctions continuing salience. While the reasons for these different poverty rates may not rest in the characteristics themselves (why should disability per se increase the risks of poverty?), it reveals the ways in which society is structured so that it impacts disproportionately on those from particular groups or with particular characteristics. Thus an analysis of poverty and poverty rates is a crucial element in understanding the operation of social divisions within society.

This chapter has stressed the importance of a temporal understanding of poverty. In order to be fully meaningful, assessments of poverty need to be located within a specific temporal context and measured over time. A further issue concerns these temporal patterns and whether we should be optimistic or pessimistic in relation to the future. Tony Blair's commitment in 1999 to abolish poverty introduced a much greater policy focus on monitoring and addressing poverty – or at least child poverty. This was accompanied by a raft of policy measures to lift the incomes of poor families. This moment thus marked both an explicit recognition at government level of the existence of poverty and made a commitment towards doing something about it. However, despite some reductions, poverty did not decline as swiftly as anticipated; partly because, in the context of rising living standards, the increases in incomes at the bottom were related to higher-middle incomes through a poverty measure adjusted to changing living standards. The recession which began in 2008 had not brought a marked increase in poverty or income inequality by 2013. However, with an ongoing rise in unemployment rates and major changes to the 'safety net' of the welfare state, that was anticipated to change at the time of writing. The Institute for Fiscal Studies predicted that Coalition Government policies will result in child poverty rising from 2.6 million in 2010/11 to 2.9 million in 2013/14 (Jin et al. 2011).

To the extent that those who suffer from widening income inequalities and the predicted increase in poverty have particular characteristics, social division – or particular social divisions – may be enhanced. While current debate has challenged a focus on income-related measures of 'well-being' with an emphasis on subjective measures and a focus on social mobility rather than inequality, it is critical that analysis continues to focus on poverty to assess whether changes in poverty mark growing or narrowing divides between social groups. Without differences in poverty risks, or economic inequalities to sustain them, social divisions are more likely to lose salience as indicators of structures determining life chances and shift towards focusing on the fluid aspects of culture and identity as the main elements of differences between groups.

Discussion Questions

1. Why does it not make sense to contrast relative and absolute definitions of poverty? Think of the different ways in which relative and absolute are used and those writers associated with the different uses.

2. Why is it important to take account of time when measuring poverty? You can think here of time as a point in time/history, time as duration or time as change over time.

3. Who is poorer: a person with a high income who doesn't spend it and lacks 'essentials'; a person who lives well but spends more than their income and lives in debt; or a person who has a low income but lives within it and spends only on essentials? Perhaps you can think of examples of each from your own experience, as well as thinking who would be shown to be poor on different measures.

4. How useful is the current focus on well-being, compared to an earlier focus on poverty, for tackling social divisions?

5. How and why does poverty intersect with other social divisions – including those not covered in this chapter? You can think about cause and effect: is it the other division which results in the poverty or is it differences in poverty which cause us to notice the other divisions?

FURTHER READING

Alcock, P. *Understanding Poverty* (Basingstoke: Palgrave Macmillan, 2006, 3rd edn) and Lister, R. *Poverty* (Cambridge: Polity Press, 2004) provide accessible and informed takes on the topic. A justification for the material deprivation approach to poverty, alongside an understanding of poverty as social exclusion can be found in Pantazis, C, Gordon, D and Levitas, RA (eds). *Poverty and Social Exclusion in Britain:*

The Millennium Survey (Bristol: The Policy Press, 2006). A more detailed, and international survey of key developments in poverty measurement and analysis and of the relationship between poverty and inequality can be found in Jenkins, S.P. and Micklewright, J. *Inequality and Poverty Re-examined* (Oxford: Oxford University Press, 2007). UK trends and projections for child poverty can be found in Jin, W., Joyce, R., Phillips, D. and Sibieta, L. *Poverty and Inequality in the UK* (London: IFS Commentary C118, 2011), while the OECD's 2011 publication, *How's Life?* explores a wide range of aspects of 'well-being' across 40 countries.

CHAPTER 14

Health

RUTH GRAHAM

WITH JUDY PAYNE, GEOFF PAYNE AND MATTHEW BOND

This chapter will provide you with a broad critical understanding of the following issues in social class as a source of social division:

- Health as a social division: distinct but connected to other divisions
- Definitions of health and illness
- Patients' own views of being 'ill'
- Causes of illness: genetics, biology, responsible behaviour, social factors
- Health and other social divisions
- Social class and illnesses
- Gender, age and health
- Ethnic differences
- Geographical variations in public health

Health is a different kind of social division from the others discussed in this book. In some of its manifestations, it does not even fully meet all the defining criteria as set out in Chapter 1 or the start of Chapter 18. For example, people can often move quickly from one side of the divide to the other, from the category of being healthy to that of being ill (and back again). Health is also the only social division in which one category, being 'well', is conceptualised widely as desirable. In contrast, being 'ill' has its own major institutions – like Britain's NHS – initially at least dedicated to its eradication. Similar to disability perspectives (Chapter 8), sociological understandings of chronic illness challenge the idea that illness is a purely negative experience, but the tendency to see wellness as self-evidently good remains dominant.

Despite these peculiarities, there is still a strong case for treating health and illness as a social division. At its most basic, the sense of difference that comes from even small losses of health (minor changes that would otherwise hardly warrant calling a social division) is arguably among the most intense of all divisions. The misery and social isolation that may result from catching the common cold, or having a serious illness, can feel overwhelming, while serious illness can lead to death, arguably the most absolute of all 'social divisions'. Death cannot be avoided forever, but the risks of an early death or being ill are not the same for everybody in society. These variations in health, illness and death are strongly related to other social divisions, so health cannot be treated separately from them.

It follows that we need to approach health in a somewhat different way from that used in Chapters 2 to 12. Each of these take one social division and explore its meaning and significance in contemporary life, analytically separate from all the others. While we shall look at the categories of 'healthy' and 'ill' as comprising a division, this chapter (like those on poverty, community and identity) will also reflect on the ways other social divisions can be seen to interact with and, indeed, produce this particular one. Health can be thought of as an 'arena' in which various social divisions compete to influence a particular outcome. Gender and age are self-evidently related to certain kinds of physical conditions, and therefore the ways that gender and age are socially constructed (Chapters 3 and 5) are relevant to the social construction of what we think of as being 'well', 'healthy' or 'ill'. Class and ethnicity have also routinely been shown to have statistical associations with variations in health. However, it is important to see that we cannot simply 'add' class to ethnicity, or age to gender. Social divisions *interact* when they combine, producing new outcomes. It follows that, in incorporating the divisions that are discussed in other chapters and in emphasising social construction rather than a 'biomedical model' (challenged in the chapters on childhood, sexuality and disability), this chapter is a natural development of our overall approach.

Although the consequences of lack of health are fundamental to our feelings, opportunities to lead a full life and our sense of identity, this chapter is more concerned with the social explanations of health and illness. This focus involves an exploration of how combinations of social divisions interconnect to produce health (or interact more generally, as we see in Chapter 15, in the context of producing a sense of community). The starting point for this is to consider what is really meant by the terms 'health' and 'illness'.

Defining health and illness

'Health', 'illness', 'well', 'fit' and 'unfit' are all terms that we use to describe our perceptions of bodily states. Because contemporary society is characterised, inter alia, by having specialist medical services, knowledge and personnel operating in permanent organisations, there is an administrative system to measure and record illness, but no comparable social apparatus to record health systematically. The existence of social institutions to combat illness – being 'ill' is an undesirable problem whereas being 'fit' is not – means that there is a strong normative tendency to talk more about illness, leaving health to be a residual category implicitly defined as a lack of illness. One notable exception is the positive view of health as well-being, which was central to the definition put forward in the Constitution of the World Health Organization in 1946, and still prominent on its web pages. Here, health is defined as 'a state of complete physical, mental and social well-being and not merely the absence of disease or infirmity' (World Health Organization 1948, 2012). In contrast, medical definitions are primarily based on the process of diagnosis of the biomedical pathology that constitutes 'disease' (or its absence). This disease-focused approach remains dominant, despite the inclusion of various syndrome-based illnesses or conditions (such as ME or obesity) that are de-fined with reference to criteria that are more visibly constructed (Whitehead 2006; Monaghan 2007).

But even a disease-based approach can lead to quite different ways of iden-tifying ill health. What counts as disease is not a given biological fact, but is in part socially constructed. When does mental illness become, or cease to be, an illness? Do the symptoms and medical care received during pregnancy render it an illness? When we say someone is ill, that categorisation arises out of a social process, in which human beings decide what is going to be called sickness or health. More detailed studies of the social construction of these medical definitions by clinicians are reported by Brown (1995) and by Conrad and Barker (2010).

Social construction means not only that our general perceptions of what is health arise out of social processes, but also that some things are counted as lack of health while others are not, and this in turn feeds back into our per-ceptions. To take the most obvious example, we could define 'illness' as cases recorded by GPs and hospitals. Such morbidity records are used to describe social and geographical variations in health within and between countries. Morbidity data (together with death rates) have played an important part in influencing the development of welfare policies. Information about rates of ill-ness has been collected in most countries as they industrialised and so encoun-tered the need for welfare programmes to deal with the public health problems of overcrowding and lack of sanitation (Strong 1990). However, morbidity measures depend first on what experiences people conceptualise as problem-atic and so report as 'illnesses' to doctors, and how that comes about (Ding-wall 1976; Blaxter and Paterson 1982); then on how doctors and paramedical professions perceive, process, medically diagnose and decide on treatment for them (White 2009: 109–10); and finally on how administrators register them as cases of particular diseases in the population. Some registers (for example, mortality registration) are organised via the state to provide universal coverage in the UK. Others have developed in a more patchwork manner, and do not provide coverage in all regions, such as the umbrella organisation British Isles Network of Congenital Anomaly Registers (BINOCAR) (British Isles Network of Congenital Anomaly Registers 2010).

Thus on the one hand, there are apparent 'facts' about illness, such as cancer registrations, outbreaks of communicable diseases (for example, various types of food poisoning, measles, hepatitis, tuberculosis and meningitis) and cases of congenital malformations such as spina bifida and Down's syndrome. Similarly, the medical process produces data on low birth weight, teenage pregnancies and obesity, which then become the 'truths' around which public policy is debated. Concepts that start out as descriptors can evolve into something more normative, such as the concept of 'overweight' (Jutel 2006) in relation to obesity debates. On the other hand, even in the examples of serious illness, 'cases' only occur if, first, the 'patients' see themselves as sufficiently 'ill' to consult a doctor and, second, when doctors decide on medical diagnoses. As we shall see below, attendance at surgeries and self-descriptions of being ill vary between men and women, old and young, and middle and working classes. Similarly, the ways in which doctors react to and treat their patients have for many years been identified by social scientists as socially patterned and socially produced (Bloor 1976; Cartwright and O'Brien 1976; Doyal 1994, 1995; Bury 2004). This suggests that the 'facts' about illness are more dependent on processes of social construction than is commonly recognised.

A clearer and less disputable measurement is death (as noted above, certification of death is one of the more complete administrative records), but mortality rates imply a somewhat extreme level of illness, shifting the focus from the living to the dead. Despite this, the Black Report (Townsend et al. 1992) – 'which remains one of the most influential documents on health inequalities' (Bury 1997: 48) – chose mortality rates and causes of death as its key measurements. These convey the powerful notion of life chances, fairness of expectations and the penalty some groups pay through early death. Death rates have also been well documented over a long period and do not normally suffer from short-term fluctuations, so that comparisons between periods, locations and groups are relatively secure.

It has long been recognised that rates of death vary: for example, higher mortality rates are found among older age groups and, within this, men tend to die at an earlier age than women. Obviously populations with high proportions of older people (and men) would be expected to have higher mortality rates than those with lower proportions. To control for this, mortality rates can be statistically standardised to allow for variations in age and gender distributions between sub-populations. The most widely-used standardised morality measure is known as the Standard Mortality Ratio (SMR). However, even when age and gender distributions between specific populations are controlled for, differences in mortality still remain. Other commonly used mortality rates include infant mortality rates and deaths from specific causes (for example, different types of cancer, heart disease, asthma and suicide).

These individual rates have normally been used as separate variables. However, they can also be combined to produce composite indices of health status, such as that developed by Townsend et al. (1986) to study the relationship between health and poverty. Administrative health data for census wards, consisting of premature SMRs (deaths below the age of 65), long-term sick and disabled persons (aged over 16 years) and low birth weights (under 2500 grams) were used to calculate a single health status score for each ward. The rationale for choosing these particular variables was that they reflected different aspects of health status: past health experience (premature deaths); future child development and past maternal health (low birth weight); and past and current health status (long-term sick and disabled). These index scores were then used with other variables and indices to investigate the association between health status and other socio-economic factors. High correlations were found between poor health status and material deprivation in urban areas, but less clearly so in rural areas. The composite indices used to measure deprivation have changed since Townsend et al.'s (1986) study, but health remains one of the key domains used (McLennan et al. 2011, Ch3). However, even within the UK, different indices are used in the four constituent countries, which can make comparisons within the UK more difficult but not impossible (see Payne and Abel 2012).

The example of mortality rates shows that, while medical records and official statistics need to be treated with caution because they are socially constructed, they should not be dismissed out of hand. Often they are the only available data and, as the Black and Townsend studies demonstrate, can still be used effectively to explore social aspects of health. If anything, there is too much data on specific illnesses, so that researchers have to select which items to explore, so opening the door to further confusion.

Asking the 'patient'

The only realistic alternative to starting from the use of medical records, collected for purposes other than social research, is to ask ordinary people directly how well they feel, how they define health and how they experience health issues. The interest in lay perspectives has also been encouraged by changes in the doctor–patient relationship, as shared decision-making and patient-centred care become increasingly important in medical work (Morgan 2008). More experiential perspectives of health and illness have been forcibly advocated as a corrective to the medical standpoint and a way of increasing and improving understandings of health among sub-populations such as ethnic minorities and local communities (Williams and Popay 1994; Popay et al. 1998; Payne 1999). Studies that have examined such lay definitions have found that people think about health in several different ways, according to who they are. One of the most influential of these studies identified three different elements of health:

- health as absence of illness or vacuum;
- health as reserve or capital (for example, a 'strong constitution' that is resistant to illness);
- health as equilibrium or well-being. (Herzlich 1973)

Despite differences in the terminology used, later studies found similar distinctions (Blaxter and Paterson 1982; Pill and Stott 1982; Williams 1983; d'Houtard and Field 1984; Calnan 1987; Blaxter 1990). A fourth element – functional capacity (the ability to do things) – is also identified by Blaxter.

These elements are not discrete, and individual accounts are often found to contain aspects of each. This is clear from our comments added to the following extract:

> I feel alert [well-being] and can always think of lots of things to do. No aches and pains – nothing wrong with me [absence of illness] – and I can go out and jog [functional capacity]. I suppose I have more energy [reserve], I can get up and do such a lot. (Blaxter 1990:19)

Although the different elements are found in combination, accounts are socially patterned. Many studies have found that 'health as well-being' was more likely to be expressed by the middle class or those with higher levels of education, with working-class respondents and those with lower educational levels expressing health as 'absence of illness' (for example, d'Houtard and Field 1984). However this pattern was not repeated in the Health and Lifestyles Survey (Blaxter 1990). Here, the greatest distinction was between those of different age groups, with the young more likely to see health as well-being and older respondents drawing on ideas of functional capacity. Gender differences were found among the younger age group: young men often expressing ideas of physical fitness, while young women emphasised health as vitality. Howlett et al. (1992) and Hughes and Kleine (2004) also report differences in health beliefs between ethnic groups.

Health status questionnaires have also been designed to quantify health in general populations, those with specific diseases and disabilities, and measure 'quality for life'. These questionnaires attempt to measure the multi-dimensional aspects (social, psychological and physical) of health and illness through self-rating scales. Thus, the Nottingham Health Profile (Hunt et al. 1986) includes the following 'yes/no' statements, to which we have added comments:

- I'm in pain when I walk [physical]
- I lose my temper easily these days [psychological]
- I feel there is nobody I am close to [social]

The widely-used Short Forms-36 and -12 (Ware 1993) concentrate on the self-assessment of physical and psychological health alone, while others focus on behavioural/lifestyle factors (for example Berkman and Breslow 1983; Pill et al. 1993). Although not often employed by sociologists, these approaches have been important in health policy. These attempts to quantify health status and/or quality of life can also be used to determine eligibility for certain kinds of treatment. Such evaluations of individuals tend to involve using scales based on an assumption of full capacity. Those with existing or chronic conditions are in a position where feelings of wellness or suitability for treatment may render them ineligible to become top scorers on such scales (see, for example, Graham 2004). A full discussion of these and other health status scaling techniques can be found in Bowling (1997). In addition to mortality and morbidity, a third key category in contemporary discourses is the 'risk' of morbidity (and/or mortality). Although risk has generally been a regular feature of debates on public health, the concept of risk has taken on a particularly prominent role more recently (Baggott 2000). This is perhaps to be expected, given the theoretical attention that understandings of risk have received in the social sciences since the emergence of Beck's (1992) *Risk Society*. Certainly, understandings of risk of morbidity and mortality have been highly influential in arguments for resource allocation to areas in public health such as obesity and tobacco use. However, as Baggott (2000) notes, these types of interventions have been interpreted by some as a form of social control. If the perceived risk of morbidity and mortality are associated with particular groups in society, then so too are the interventions (or surveillance) that seek to prevent those risks.

Explaining patterns of health

The previous section showed that the study of health variations involves dealing with a complex phenomenon. They can be studied from the perspectives of several disciplines, not least sociology, social policy and epidemiology (the branch of medicine concerned with the distribution of disease in human populations) and, indeed, from alternative positions within disciplines. Differences between these approaches are made all the more acute by the political nature of how social problems emerge, and how policies develop accordingly. Rubington and Weinberg's (2011) definition of a social problem highlights the interconnectedness of defining a problem and whether it will be considered a viable target for social intervention. And if intervention is deemed viable – in the case of health – each particular conception of health and illness implies that one kind of intervention would be 'more effective' than others. If ill health is thought of mainly as symptoms, viruses or genetics, this points towards solutions in medical technology, whereas if ill health is defined in terms of loss of well-being, then intervention might mean tackling pollution, poverty, unemployment, loneliness or institutionalised racism. Those accounts that have drawn on lay definitions and focused on health status have been associated mainly with identifying inequalities in health and have sought explanations of them based in social processes. But even here there are disagreements about the most important causes of differences in health. These disagreements have sometimes been intense (Macintyre 1997).

Dahlgren and Whitehead's (1991) 'rainbow' account of health inequalities has been one of the most influential explanatory models. It maps the complex array of factors into five related clusters:

1. biological models of illness;
2. lifestyles;
3. social and community influences;
4. living and working conditions;
5. general socio-economic, cultural and environmental conditions.

Dahlgren and Whitehead's starting point is the cluster of studies using physical or straightforward *biological* models of illness. These take age, sex, genetic inheritance and in utero (pre-birth) experiences, which predispose to being at risk of certain illnesses later in life, as producing differences in health. Individuals have no control over these factors.

In contrast, a second cluster of factors are sometimes seen (not least by health educators, moralisers and right-wing politicians) as things that people can and should control as matters of personal responsibility. These are the individual *lifestyles* of diet, consumption of alcohol, nicotine and other drugs, and exercise that differentially predispose to health.

Any objection that unhealthy lifestyles are mainly associated with people living in poverty and therefore that intervention should be addressed to the alleviation of poverty, found little favour with government in the 1980s and 1990s. The 'official line' was reflected in the Conservative Minister of Health's 1986 observations about the connection between health and poverty:

> I honestly don't think that is has anything to do with poverty. The problem very often for many people is just ignorance ... and failing to realise that they do have some control over their own lives. (quoted in Bury 1997: 64)

Whilst the Labour Government elected in 1997 seemed more willing to accept the concept of health inequalities as a legitimate social problem, health policy and the public health agenda have remained heavily influenced by the concept of individual choice and lifestyles. As Baggott (2004: 365) notes, practical steps to resolve the tensions between choice and equity are less evident.

Dahlgren and Whitehead's next two clusters are more sociological: *social and community influences*, and *living and working conditions*. Although these might be considered by some as individual features, in practice most refer to life experiences that no single person can control. For instance, social circumstances involving a lack of supportive personal relationships, community processes such as risk of crime and the occupational experiences of stress or accidents at work are not simply there for individuals to experience or avoid at will.

In this sense, the distinction between the two categories, social/community and living/working, is not particularly helpful, nor should they be regarded as equally important: for example, the 'Whitehall studies' have demonstrated how working conditions have a major impact on health (Cabinet Office 2004). There is also overlap with Dahlgren and Whitehead's final category, *general socio-economic, cultural and environmental conditions*, which is meant to identify factors that are even more susceptible to international market forces and therefore even less within individual control. In practice, this category is similar to the previous two – are poor housing, low income, and unemployment 'general socio-economic' or 'living and working' conditions?

While the Dahlgren and Whitehead typology is less than perfect (Syme 1996; Shy 1997), it has been widely adopted. The model has been challenged by some who wish to amend it to remedy perceived problems, such as Jinks et al.'s (2010) use of the model in exploring prevention of knee pain in older adults. Their research was informed by the model, but their approach attempted to compensate for a perceived neglect of the structure/agency debates that are now well established within the social sciences. Despite its weaknesses, the model nevertheless offers a way of identifying where particular research contributions stand. Developments of the model have been influential in the Acheson Report (Department of Health 1998a) and the subsequent public health Green and White Papers (Department of Health 1998b, 1999). These government documents placed greater emphasis on the social nature and interactions of the clusters and the need for improvements in access to services.

Similarly, whilst the White Paper *Choosing Health* (Department of Health 2004) places greater emphasis on 'individual responsibility', it also stresses that it is harder for disadvantaged sections of the population to make healthy choices. Health inequalities remain a strand of public health policy as inequality indicators continue to be monitored, and sometimes trigger further policy initiatives – such as the Strategic Review of Health Inequalities in England (2010). However, as Baggott (2012: 396) notes, policy success has tended to be 'precarious' at best. Although the net effect of public health policy was to reduce the infant mortality rate gap between rich and poor, the level of reduction (4%) fell far short of the 10% target reduction set in 2001.

It would be wrong to think that this change in government policy reflects unanimity among those who have studied health inequalities. A number of writers have identified four major points of disagreement about the explanations of inequalities (see Armstrong 1994; Benzeval et al. 1995; Bury 1997; Macintyre 1997; Scambler 1997; Taylor and Field 1997; and, with a more medical emphasis, British Medical Association 1995). On the one hand, there are two arguments in which health inequalities are not seen as a product of socio-economic processes, and in particular, social class. The first of these argues that it is poor health that leads to social disadvantage, rather than the other way round, thus standing the conventional sociological wisdom on its head. The second view proposes that the apparent connection does not even exist in reality, being no more than an artificial product of unreliable statistics and incorrect reasoning. Against these two positions are those who argue that there are health/deprivation connections, but this camp is split into two. One group attributes unequal health outcomes to socially structured differences in people's financial and resource (material) circumstances, while the other sees the key issue as being what people know, believe and think (their 'culture') and how this makes them act. Each of these four positions is given fuller consideration in the next section.

Health inequalities and their explanations

The 'cultural' or 'behavioural' theory school of thought is the basis for the 'lifestyle' approach already discussed in terms of the Dahlgren/Whitehead typology and Conservative reactions to the Black Report. It focuses on what people believe, suggesting that, because different groups perceive health and its causes in different ways, their health-related behaviours are going to vary.

As well as being specifically concerned with 'good' practice in healthy living behaviour, this approach also takes account of basic orientations to life. For instance, compared with less-advantaged groups, well-educated people in jobs where they have personal autonomy, and can control others, are more likely to be knowledgeable about good health practice, have higher expectations of the effectiveness of taking action against illness and expect faster and better medical treatment to protect their health. This cultural 'mindset' can be seen as contributing to their lower levels of illness, translating any material advantage into attitudes conducive to good health. From this perspective, variations in health status do not result from the differences in access to material resources, but rather, to the way people think and act.

As well as offering this general mode of explanation, the cultural perspective has particular resonance of ethnic group variations in health. While it is true that variation within each ethnic group tends to be greater than between groups (Nazroo 1997: 240), there are substantial differences in folkways (traditional and customary ways of living) and traditional remedies, ideas about health, religious beliefs and morally and socially acceptable ways of life. For example, Howlett et al. (1992) report that Indians tend to see health as a matter of luck and regard smoking and alcohol as major causes of illness, whereas the white group see ill health as the 'fault of the individual' and more often caused by stress. Thorogood's (1990) description of the home remedies used by women of Caribbean origin raises the question of when and why African-Caribbean families use medical services and so become part of medical statistics. American research has suggested that psychiatric misdiagnosis of African-Caribbeans may be attributable to cultural misunderstandings, such as the way language is used and social behaviour is sanctioned. These cultural and behavioural factors are not easily reducible to the material circumstances of class or employment. Such cultural explanations remain a regular feature of health research (see for example, Redshaw and Heikkila's (2012) interpretation of the higher rate of worries about embarrassment during labour amongst ethnic minority women).

Critics of this view argue that mindsets come from social locations such as class position and, rather than intervening to try to change ideas, it is the structural systems that must first be tackled. The freedom of choice, which is otherwise open to the better off, is constrained among the poor by unsatisfactory housing, physical environments, working conditions and income. This argument from a 'materialistic perspective', the second of the four points of contention (and exemplified by the discussion of class differences in Chapter 2), tends to treat cultural variations as a product of social class or wider socio-economic systems. Emphasis may be placed either on the constraints and workings of the economic system, or on actual poverty that it produces.

The Black Report and Townsend's work on deprivation argued that the kinds of relative poverty experienced within advanced industrialised nations is a significant cause of ill health. Living in poverty brings direct problems (Chapter 13) as well as the stress of dealing with them. In a 1991 survey of low-income families, one-fifth of parents and one-tenth of children had gone without food for at least once in a previous month (National Children's Home 1991). Low-income interviewees had to do without proper food and heating:

> I don't cut down, as I say, with the kids. I try to make sure they get, but like I cook a meal and as long as there's enough for them, I make do with a piece of toast ... Many a Sunday afternoon our electric has gone. We've just waited 'til Monday. (Kempson et al. 1994)

Access to healthy food when on a low income became a more prominent issue after the 2008 Credit Crunch, with research highlighting the financial implications of shopping for food. For example, Bowyer et al. (2009) argue that individual agency alone cannot solve the problems of limited choice they found in their study of food shopping in an inner-London borough.

It is hardly surprising that people exposed to low levels of living tend to suffer ill health. Among families living on income support, over two-thirds report ill health, with asthma, bronchitis and eczema the commonest complaints (Cohen et al. 1992). They have no 'spare' money to meet the extra costs of the illness or to pay for the heating needed to relieve symptoms. Not only do poor housing conditions contribute to poor child health, but their parents suffer from depression and stress-related disorders as a result of their financial difficulties (Morris and Ritchie 1994).

However, this view of health inequalities as the product of deprivation is rejected by the third of the four schools of thought. While not denying an association between ill health and disadvantaged economic positions in society, it has been claimed the people are 'socially selected' by their health to occupy distinctive social locations (Illsley 1955, 1986; Klein 1988). The healthy get better jobs, the unhealthy descend into unemployment or low-paid jobs. Illness causes their poverty, rather than the other way round.

While at the margins (extreme physical or mental disability), bodily conditions may limit occupational achievement (although the research base to support this view is limited), extensive social mobility research has shown that by far the biggest factors in movements up and down the class scale have been the changing availability of types of occupation and class differences in access to qualifications and desirable jobs (Payne 1987b). Those advocating 'social selection' have not properly understood the dynamics of social mobility. Nor is their underlying logic clear. If we take the case of infant mortality rates (deaths within one year of birth) we need to explain why very young children die and

Table 14.1 Infant mortality[1] by social class[2], UK

NS-SEC	1994–6	2010
Large employers and higher managerial	–	3.9
Higher professional	–	2.9
Lower managerial and professional	–	3.0
Managerial and professional	4.4	–
Intermediate	6.1	4.6
Small employers and own account workers	4.9	3.8
Lower supervisory and technical	5.3	3.1
Semi-routine and routine	7.5	5.8
Routine	–	5.1
Sole registration	7.9	–

Notes

1 Deaths within one year of birth per 1000 live births.

2 Classified by occupation of father – births 'inside marriage'.

Source: adapted from Table 7, Office for National Statistics (2010b), and Figure 6.4, Office for National Statistics (2004b).

why infant mortality rates are worse the lower down the class scale one goes – a pattern that holds even though rates of infant mortality have improved (Table 14.1).

This child health problem, coming after the parents became members of a lower class, could not directly have caused the parents' social class location. The social selection argument actually implies either a three-part logical chain – parents' previous poor health leads to low social class, which leads to poor infant health (that is, class does have a direct effect in the middle of the chain) – or that parents' previous poor health directly causes poor infant health (which misses out the class element, and does not explain the observed class differentials). Similarly, if we examine the class differentials in the use of dental services, we see sharp contrasts (Table 14.2). Propensity to take up medical services, or prevalence of tooth decay, are implausible explanations of why people are in their particular occupations or classes, whereas class differences (either knowledge and good health practice or having the resources to gain access to treatment) are a more convincing explanation of propensity to visit the dentist. Other data on social class differentials in health can be found in Chapter 2.

The last of the four arguments, that class and health are not actually connected in the way the Black Report suggests, is largely based on the premise that 'class' is not a real phenomenon, but rather an intellectual construct. Two things follow from this: first, 'class', because it is only an idea represented by categories of occupations, cannot cause poor 'health'; and second, the way in which class is constructed becomes crucial. In connection with health

Table 14.2 Adults who visit dentists for regular check-ups, UK, 2003

Socio-economic group	Percentage
Large employers and higher managerial	71
Higher professional	71
Lower managerial and professional	66
Intermediate	63
Small employers and own account	63
Lower supervisory and technical	58
Semi-routine	54
Routine	50
Never worked and long-term unemployed	45
All	61

Source: adapted from Office for National Statistics (2003a), Table 7.35.

inequalities, Illsley (1986, 1990), Klein (1988) and Carr-Hill (1990) have argued that classes have changed in definition and size (see Chapter 2), so that comparison over time is invalid. Because classes represent large aggregates of people in a range of occupations, there must also inevitably be a range of variation within each class (not least because social mobility moves people between classes). A parallel debate in mainstream sociology has been stimulated by Pahl's doubts about using occupation to define class categories (Pahl 1993; Crompton 2008).

The case that class is an artefact and its association with health is 'artefactual' is in part correct. It is true that definitions and classification schemes have evolved over time, while the classes they identify have shown major changes – the manual classes decreasing, the middle classes expanding (Chapter 2). This does make time-based comparisons more difficult, and the replacement of the old Registrar General's Social Class schema in the 2001 Census was a long overdue recognition of the need to change. It is also the case that the present members of a class may well have moved into it and so brought previous health-related characteristics from their former class.

However, some of the difficulties that Illsley identifies are due precisely to the limitations of the old Registrar General's classification (which had been extensively used in medical records). Other schema offer more flexible alternatives. If there is 'excessive' variation within classes, the answer lies in devising better representations of the class structure, not in abandoning class as a variable. It is insufficient to claim that the nature of social class has changed or that people are socially mobile: that does not render all association between class and health irrelevant.

The main problem with the artefactual critique is that it misrepresents what research based on social class is actually trying to do. The purpose of a class schema is to provide a framework for analysis, not a complete answer. As Chapter 2 showed, class is the connection between the fundamental economic and power structures of society and the lives people lead. Except for a few, unrepresentative purists, most researchers implicitly assume that class is not directly associated with every outcome, but works through a complex of other 'intervening variables' to shape the social patterns under investigation. Class is associated for instance, with work conditions, education, income, housing and beliefs; each of these factors interacts and is in turn associated with health and illness. Class is only the starting point for the construction of a 'narrative' that explores how the end point of health or illness can be traced back to the deep structures of the social order. To complain that any one class schema does not explain everything perfectly is to miss the point entirely. Tables 14.1 and 14.2 show clear 'class gradients' in two aspects of health: the challenge is how to explain them, not to try to explain them away.

Health inequalities and other social divisions

Infant mortality and visits to the dentist are only two examples from a strikingly large range of class/health associations. It would be possible to present a series of individual factors, each with a class-based association, but this would be to misrepresent what researchers actually do. (It could also create the impression that class is the only important social division.) Researchers tend to analyse combinations of social factors that impact on health. For example, Table 14.3 shows visits to GP surgeries by gender (here, strictly speaking 'sex') and age, as well as household heads' class (and the unemployed). GP consultations are important because, as we saw earlier, cases of 'illness' cannot become part of the health record without them.

Table 14.3 GP consultations[1] by age, sex and economic activity status, GB, 2009

	Male (%)				Female(%)			
	16–44	45–64	65+	Total	16–44	45–64	65+	Total
Working	9	12	17	11	17	16	13	17
Unemployed	6	11	24[2]	8	16	18	26[2]	16
Economically inactive	11	26	24	21	20	24	23	22
All	9	15	23	13	18	19	23	19

Notes
1 Consultations in previous 14 days.
2 The values for unemployed men aged 65 and over are 'deemed unreliable'.

Source: adapted from Office for National Statistics (2011b), Table 7.21.

Although age and gender are separate social divisions, they also interact, for example, women live longer and young men are more prone to die from injuries and poisoning (Office for National Statistics 1998a). Men are more liable to die of circulatory disease in late working life and cancer in old age. Gender differences alone do not bring this out: it requires the inclusion of age to obtain a fuller picture. Attitudes towards illness, in terms of propensity to say in interview that one has health problems, are also gendered. Table 14.4 shows that men are less likely to define themselves as having health problems, again, most notably among the very old. As Chapter 5 showed, these data are likely to be subject to change, as 'early old age' is progressively socially redefined as a life stage of greater activity and vitality, and 'late old age' expands, with more people living longer.

The differences between men and women in these health data are particularly interesting in the context of debates about gender. Feminist writers have drawn attention to the distinctive features of women's health (for example Arber 1990; Doyal 1994). On the one hand, medical records indicate that women suffer more from acute and chronic illnesses, are more likely to be treated for mental illness and obviously have distinctive health needs concerning pregnancy and childbirth. On the other hand, they are less likely to work in hazardous occupations, or engage in 'high-risk', macho lifestyle behaviour such as excessive consumption of alcohol, dangerous sports or violence. Women are more likely to consult their doctors and admit to illness, although their willingness to adopt the 'sick role' seems to be related in a complex way to child care and their continuing role in domestic labour (Chapter 3). The prevalence of male doctors (and female nurses) is seen as gendering healthcare (for an interesting analysis of how this can impact on use of space and identity at work, see Halford and Leonard 2003). The modern tendency to define social issues as medical problems has resulted in a 'medicalisation' of women's bodies.

Table 14.4 EuroQol[1] assessment for age and gender groups, GB, 1996, percentages

	16–44		45–64		65–74		75+		Total	
	M	*F*	*M*	*F*	*M*	*F*	*M*	*F*	*M*	*F*
No problems	74	70	54	50	38	38	30	21	60	55
Mild problems	15	16	18	20	23	19	19	19	17	18
Moderate problems	5	6	9	11	16	16	21	16	9	10
Substantial problems	6	8	18	18	23	27	30	44	14	17

Note
1 A self-assessed health status questionnaire.

Source: Office for National Statistics (1998b), Table 8.38.

Similarly, although more recently, others have argued that it is time to consider 'men's health for a change' (Cameron and Bernardes 1998: 115). Men die younger, do not use health services properly and engage in more life-threatening activities. These basic social facts will not be properly investigated if women are seen as the only category having 'interesting' health research problems. Furthermore, work by Macintyre et al. (1996) has questioned whether women actually are more ill than men. In a study in which men and women were carefully matched for the grade of their jobs and perceived working conditions, there were no gender differences in health. Overall, women reported more colds, eye strain, aches, nerves and sleeping problems, but no more than men in the equivalent jobs. The higher female totals were a product of their concentration into certain jobs. Men as well as women were also found to encounter difficulties with balancing domestic and employment commitments. These findings suggest that the relationship between gender, health and other social divisions is a more complex one than hitherto recognised. As narrative approaches to health and illness have become more important to the social sciences, so too have men's experiences of illness been evaluated more explicitly (for example, see Ridge et al. 2011, on research into men's experiences of mental distress).

The complexity of interacting factors can also be seen in health and illness patterns among ethnic groups. While overall there are relatively few health differences between the ethnic groups, some do exist. For example, African-Caribbeans tend to be more prone to strokes, as well as the more commonly mentioned sickle cell anaemia. Several Asian groups suffer more from eye problems, high blood pressure and diabetes. Established social divisions such as class, gender and age are by no means a complete list of explanatory factors in ethnic health inequalities. If we consider the psycho-social stress of being subjected to racism, the facts that some illnesses, such as sickle cell anaemia. have a genetic component, and that many ethnic groups live in inner-city locations with poorer health services, we must only anticipate ethnic health differences, but we must also expect to use a variety of explanations (see Senior and Viveash 1998: 158–86).

Geographical variations in health status are also an important theme that runs through the health inequalities literature. England has the lowest standard mortality rates, and the difference between nations is greater than between men and women. Scotland, in particular, has poorer health, which, taken together with the political and cultural characteristics discussed in Chapter 10, might suggest that a characteristic way of life exists in Scotland (see Table 14.5). Some caution is, however, needed in making statements about large aggregates of data like countries: this chapter's earlier analysis suggests that a number of social divisions could be explored in order to account for national

Table 14.5 Age standardised mortality for UK countries and gender, 2007

Country	All	Male	Female
UK	831	759	880
England	809	734	861
Wales	872	807	914
Scotland	981	926	1021
Northern Ireland	877	829	907

Note: Rates per 100,000 population

Source: Office for National Statistics (2009b).

Table 14.6 Self-reported health status indicators for the ONS classification of English areas, 1994–96, average percentage standardised for age

	Poor/bad health	Long-standing illness	Acute sickness	Prescribed medication
England	22.6	39.6	15.0	40.3
Mining and industrial	28.0	42.7	16.7	42.7
Inner London	27.9	42.2	18.2	40.7
Urban	25.7	40.3	15.4	40.0
Rural	21.6	38.5	14.4	39.7
Mature	21.5	39.7	14.7	40.2
Prosperous	18.7	38.2	14.2	39.6

Source: adapted from Social and Community Planning Research (1999).

patterns. There are nonetheless substantial differences in health in geographically distinct areas, as Table 14.6 shows.

The demographics, occupational opportunities, physical environment and health services in inner London, and areas marked by the run-down of heavy industry, are clearly reflected in these figures (see also Joshi et al. 2000; MacIntyre et al. 2002). Residents of mature areas (long-established towns) are relatively advantaged, while prosperous areas – dormitory suburbs for the prosperous middle classes, mainly in the southeast – show quite different health patterns from those in urban or rural areas (and indeed in other aspects of social life, as we see in Chapter 15 on communities). Rural areas contain a wider range of lifestyles, and a distinctive problem of service delivery for remote locations. As Joshi et al. argue:

Area difference in self-reported ill-health, long term or current, are mainly, but not simply, attributable to the socio-economic characteristics, occupational and migration histories of individual residents. But where people live also matters. (Joshi et al. 2000: 152)

Conclusion

In this chapter we have attempted to balance the two broad views of health. Despite advocating here a sociological rather than an individual or biological approach, we wish to maintain that no single perspective offers a complete answer. Social explanations for health and illness have developed in critical dialogue with more medical, individualised explanations. Both have been enriched by this dialogue and both are needed to conceptualise adequately health inequalities in the UK. While it is easy to show that health is associated with social divisions, there is more work to be done on why there are such associations. What precisely are the causal connections between social factors and health? How do people experience and make sense of the health inequalities that characterise contemporary society?

Health does have a social as well as a physical basis. Risk of illness and premature death are socially patterned: health inequalities divide people in a range of ways. The consideration of social divisions – in particular class, gender, ethnicity and age – help at one level of analysis to explain health inequalities. In return, other social divisions, like national differences, childhood, sexuality, disability and community life, are affected by health and access to health services. Health and illness are not simply products of one or other of these other divisions: being sick, particularly chronically sick, is a deep divisive experience which makes health a social division in its own right, as well as one whose interactions with other social divisions provide a key to unlock the complexity of contemporary society.

Discussion Questions

    1. Is health a distinct social division?

    2. What factors do Dahlgren and Whitehead identify as causes of illness?

    3. What is the relationship between health and social class?

    4. Which is the more important for understanding and preventing illness: biological or social factors?

FURTHER READING

An introductory but clear account of this field can be found in Senior, M. and Viveash, B. *Health and Illness* (London: Macmillan – now Basingstoke: Palgrave Macmillan, 1998). Among a number of very good textbooks, Bury, M. *Health and Illness in a Changing Society* (London: Routledge, 1997) is particularly well written, while

Taylor, S. and Field, D. *Sociology of Health and Health Care* (Oxford: Blackwell, 2003, 3rd edn) gives systematic coverage. Bury, M. *Health and Illness* (Cambridge: Polity Press, 2005) provides a 'short introduction' which emphasises the dynamics of health and illness. Townsend, P., Davidson, N. and Whitehead, M. (eds) *Inequalities in Health: The Black Report and The Health Divide* (Harmondsworth: Penguin, 1992, rev. edn) remains a classic on health and poverty. For those with a more theoretically driven interest in health and illness, White, K. *An Introduction to the Sociology of Health and Illness* (Sage: London, 2009, 2nd edn) is a very accessible overview of the theoretical perspectives on health that inform many of the explanations in this field. For those with more interest in how health inequalities operate in policy, Rob Baggott's work on public health is insightful. See either *Public Health: Policy and politics* (Basingstoke: Palgrave, 2000) or his 2012 article 'Policy success and public health: the case of public health in England', *Journal of Social Policy*, **41**(2): 391–408.

CHAPTER 15

Community

GRAHAM CROW AND CATHERINE MACLEAN

This chapter will provide you with a broad critical understanding of the following aspects of community as a source of social division:

- The relevance of community to the analysis of social divisions
- The distinction between communities of place, interest and identity
- The bases of distinctions between community insiders and outsiders
- The dynamic nature of community relationships and solidarities
- The tradition of regarding community as being in decline: Ferdinand Tönnies
- The impact of geographical and social mobility on community relationships
- The importance of kinship networks in community ties and support
- The potential of new means of communication to facilitate alternative community links
- The mechanisms by which control is exercised in informal social life
- Community as an arena in which rival groups compete to secure access to scarce resources
- The dangers of idealising community as a sphere of harmonious social relationships
- The potential of community to be defined in a variety of ways
- The challenges that face researchers who seek to gain access to communities
- The rhetorical appeal of community as a sphere in which diverse individuals can come together

The inclusion of a chapter on 'community' in a book about social divisions is not as odd as it might appear at first sight. There is nothing automatic about people coming together as communities, even though the most effective community bonds may be those that members believe to be 'natural'. The unity of any community is always vulnerable to disputes among the individuals and social groups who make it up, and the achievement of community solidarity requires members to be mindful of the collective good alongside their own more immediate agendas. Communities frequently encompass divisive social identities. In many villages, for example, a distinction is made between those who 'belong' and those who are viewed as 'outsiders', while in urban areas, neighbourhoods often have distinctive population profiles and reputations into which some people fit more readily than others. In addition, community is often the arena in which the social divisions discussed in other chapters are played out. It is here that the various dimensions of social division manifest themselves and come together in making up people's everyday lives, rather than existing as separate ideas, principles or variables in the realm of sociological 'macro' analysis.

Sociological interest in community matters has revived in recent years. In both theoretical and methodological terms, sociologists working in the field have become more sophisticated than earlier generations of researchers, whose work frequently suffered from uncritical conceptions of 'community' and unreflexive techniques of investigation. This chapter examines the nature of 'community' and the ways in which social divisions figure in community life. In so doing, it raises the issue of social cohesion: if we are all so divided from one another, how do we collaborate in social life? In particular it discusses the various bases of community, the factors influencing the ease with which an individual can join or leave a community and the question of the desirability of community as an ideal. The analysis first outlines the development of sociological analysis in this field, and then considers recent conceptual trends.

The nature of community

Communities place a requirement on members to limit their individualism and acknowledge their dependence on a wider network of relationships. The same sort of point can be made about community solidarity as Durkheim ([1893]1984) famously made about social solidarity more generally: people who are motivated by narrow self-interest do not have a sufficient basis for sustainable social relationships. Just as sociologists from Durkheim onwards have sought to answer the fundamental question of what makes 'society' possible, so too has the issue of the basis of 'community' been the subject of extensive discussion. If communities are defined as groups of people who have something in common, then the thing that they share may be identified as geographical location, position in the wider social structure or sense of identity. On this basis, Willmott (1986) makes the useful analytical distinction between 'place community', 'interest community' and 'community of attachment', although he notes that in practice particular communities probably will have more than one of these elements in common.

The fact that they are constructed around members having something in common makes it appropriate to treat communities as phenomena of social cohesion rather than social division. However, even if potential social divisions between community members can be overcome, communities will still have associations with rivalry and conflict because communities are exclusive as well as inclusive. People who do not share the common characteristic(s) by which a community is defined are necessarily 'outsiders'. Individuals who do not 'belong' to a community pose a threat because affiliations to other places, interests and/or identities make them potential rivals for the scarce material resources and social status to which communities lay claim. The sense of solidarity among community members may even be strengthened where divisions between 'insiders' and 'outsiders' are highlighted. Often it turns out to be harder to specify who we are than who we are not, and in this way a strong and positive sense of 'us' will be enhanced by a clear and correspondingly negative sense of 'them', the 'other' against which we define ourselves (Bauman 1990). Putnam's (2000: 350) reference to intolerance as the 'dark side' of community is relevant here.

This conflict is perhaps most obvious in 'place communities', but also applies to 'imagined communities' of all types (see Chapters 4, 9 and 10). In Chapter 1, the discussion of separateness and identity stressed that people's sense of being *different* is not just an individual matter but involves beliefs, feelings and attitudes about who 'we' are. What appears to be a sense of community is often a way of expressing other underlying social divisions, which are perceived to mark off our community from the rest of the world, and *our part* of the community from their part of the community. The distinction between us and them that arises from this is an important one.

This has commonly been expressed through concerns about respectability. Traditional working-class communities frequently operated with a distinction between 'respectable' and 'rough' groupings (see Chapter 2), the difference being defined in terms of standards of appearance, type of employment, patterns of money management, religious observance, leisure activities and sexual behaviour. The judgemental language in which the respectable/rough distinction is framed could be contested by the alternative portrayal of people as either 'stuck up' or 'ordinary', but the underlying social division could not be denied. Similar distinctions operate in contemporary communities, as the continued use of vocabulary such as 'good neighbourhoods' and 'rough areas' demonstrates (Rogaly and Taylor 2011). Friction and rivalry between parts of communities identified in this way have also persisted, so that, in so far as community is a social division, it could be said to operate in a fragmented, localised way, involving discursive 'turf wars' (Modan 2007). Nonetheless, it is one that is nationally replicated, and which has been well established over a long period of time (Chapter 17).

On the other hand, the dynamic nature of relations within communities and the competitive nature of links between communities mean that people's sense of the communities to which they belong is not fixed. Despite the appeal of the common-sense notion that communities have enduring qualities, with a fixed character that is so desirable that we should all aspire to attain it, change is inherent in communities because of the inevitability that community membership is altered with the passage of time (Crow et al. 2001). Geographical mobility, social mobility and individuals' progression through the life-course all necessitate adjustment in community relationships (see Chapter 5). In consequence, the continuity of community phenomena is just as difficult to explain sociologically as the process of change in community attachments.

The main focus of sociological writing on community has been on change. From Tönnies' classic *Community and Association* ([1887]1955) onwards, a powerful body of literature has argued that the Industrial Revolution, the development of capitalism and, more generally, 'modernity' brought with them loss of community. Although it remains influential, this conclusion can be challenged. Many writers have identified important continuities in community relationships, thereby casting doubt on the claim that community is a declining phenomenon (Crow and Allan 1994; Payne 1996; Day 2006). Others have argued that vigorous new forms of community are emerging in response to major social trends such as globalisation and the rise of internet communities (Castells 1997). Globalisation may have the effect of generating new solidarities, some of which are constructed defensively around places or values that are felt to be threatened, while others involve people taking advantage of opportunities to communicate in the different ways that developments in information technology have made possible (Chapter 16). Both perspectives suggest that the significance of community relationships in societies like contemporary Britain extends well beyond bemoaning the passing of how things used to be.

It has been noted already that communities are diverse phenomena that may be based on people having place, interests and/or identities in common. The association of community with place is an established tradition within the sociology of community, epitomised by community studies being given place names as their titles (sometimes substituting pseudonyms in order to protect anonymity). Whalsay, one of the smaller Shetland Isles (Cohen 1987), provides one example of how easily community can be read into place. However, community is not just a sense of division between 'us in this locality' and the rest of the world.

People who share common interests are less readily identified in everyday language as 'communities'. One example would be certain kinds of elite group (Chapter 7). Another common example is people with the same employer, who may constitute an 'occupational community'. Most studies of occupational communities have been of male-dominated heavy industries, such as Warwick and Littlejohn's (1992) study of coal miners and their families, but other groups of workers besides these (such as police officers) are also usefully regarded as occupational communities (Salaman 1986). Of course, where members of occupational communities live in a single, physically identifiable location, the two senses of community reinforce each other, and strengthen the sense of separate identity.

Communities of the third type, 'communities of attachment' are built around common identities and are more free-floating than either place or interest communities, because they are not tightly bounded by geography or social structural features such as social class. People in these communities come together through their shared culture, uniting around symbols that emphasise, for instance, common ethnicity (Baumann 1996; Chapter 4), shared difference from able-bodied norms (Gregory and Hartley 1991; Chapter 9), shared political visions (Lichterman 1996) or aspects of lifestyle such as taste in music (Finnegan 1989).

Willmott's point that, in practice, communities do not always fall neatly into one of the three analytical types that he distinguishes is evident in the above examples. The people of Cohen's (1987) Whalsay are less a place community than a community of attachment, in which place is drawn on in the symbolic construction of boundaries around 'insiders' and 'outsiders'. Likewise, Roberts (1993) notes that the occupational community of Wearside shipbuilders has been weakened by their dispersal through patterns of residential migration, while Baumann's (1996) analysis of ethnic communities in Southall locates them in relation to common interests as well as shared cultural affinities.

As several of the chapters in this book show, particular social divisions operate across society as a whole, that is, at the macro-level. In practice, where individuals find that they share a position with other people on the same side of a social divide, those others are likely in the first place to be found close to hand. If we can see and talk to others 'in the same boat' as ourselves in respect of social divisions, namely those who live and work nearby, our interaction has the potential to grow into a sense of shared social identity with regard to that division. Where residential areas are largely homogeneous, for example in terms of the social class or ethnicity of the residents, the social divisions discussed earlier in the book take on a sharp new focus. Middle-class suburbs and inner-city areas in which poorer ethnic minority populations are concentrated are exclusive in a way that more mixed areas are not. Proximity does not necessarily entail common identity but community of place in practice often overlaps with community of interest. The less concrete community of attachment also depends on mechanisms for sharing symbolic meanings, a cultural sharing, and such non-located attachments cut across the simplistic idea of homogeneous, unified 'communities' without social divisions.

Communities and change

It is important to consider the temporal dimension of community relationships (Crow and Allan 1995). By constantly moving into and out of communities, people's arrival or departure highlights the fundamental question of what it is that community members share. Place communities may be constructed to include former residents who have migrated elsewhere but retain some attachment to the location (so-called 'diaspora communities'), while excluding those local residents whose recent arrival or temporary residence disqualifies them from being considered 'real locals' (Cohen 1982). Mewett (1982: 230) has reported how people who have left the Scottish island of Lewis are referred to as 'exiles', a term which implies that 'though physically absent, the migrant retains a social presence'. Conversely, physical presence does not grant a person 'local' status, although the distinction between 'old incomers' and 'new incomers' that Phillips (1986) found in a Yorkshire parish indicates that the exclusion of 'in-migrants' can diminish over time. Similarly, new recruits are frequently accepted as full members of interest and attachment communities only once they have been appropriately socialised and established the trust of existing members by demonstrating their loyalty to the group, as Hornsby's (2011) analysis of virtual communities shows.

The question of how community relationships are affected by changing membership has particular significance in contemporary societies that are characterised by high rates of geographical and social mobility. In-migrants have to start from scratch when they enter a new community: their learning process and initial absence or lower levels of personal relationship will be complicated if the incomers are socially different, for example in class or attitudes to the locality (Payne 1973). Inward geographical mobility can be disruptive of existing arrangements where newcomers enter into competition with established community members for scarce resources such as housing. It is certainly the case that conflicts have been associated with much geographical relocation, including the migration of middle-class ex-urbanites into the countryside (Newby 1980), ethnic minority populations in urban areas (Rex and Moore 1967), and, more recently, middle-class gentrifiers into favoured inner-city locations (Butler and Robson 2003).

There are well-known problems associated with the arrival of more affluent newcomers. These new middle classes (with their easier access to finance)
can afford to pay much larger sums for the kinds of properties local (often
working-class) young couples would otherwise occupy. This process prices existing local people out of the local housing market, producing social antagonisms far removed from the idealised notions of community that attracted the
in-migrants in the first place.

In more extreme cases, the new middle-class residents own other houses
elsewhere and have less need of a local school, shop, library, public transport
or other welfare or commercial services. Such part-time presence does not
offer much to community life. Having contributed to the displacement of the
next generation by buying up the available houses, their lack of involvement
tends to weaken what is left. Even in localities in which this tendency is less
pronounced, the potential for conflict between in-migrants' ways and those of
the locals, often expressed through competition for control of policy in clubs,
committees and councils, remains high (Maclean 2003).

However, there is no simple causal connection between in-migration and
conflict, since many of these patterns of in-migration were preceded by population exoduses. In such cases, as one local resident put it:

> You can't blame them (incomers) for wanting their own place to live. If they
> get a house then it's our own fault for selling it to them or letting them build
> it in the first place. Once they're in there's nothing you can do about it, so
> there's no point complaining. (Macleod 1992: 198)

Rural areas often have a history of migration to the towns that long pre-dates
the more recent pattern of middle-class settlement – which is connected to the
numerical expansion of the middle classes (Chapter 2) – and a similar point
can be made about 'white flight' from inner-city areas preceding the settlement there of much of Britain's black population. Inner-city areas were losing
population for most of the twentieth century, and it was only once this process
was under way that they became major centres for settlement by ethnic minorities who are better understood as a 'replacement population' (Sarre 1989:
139) than as a group whose arrival displaced others.

Migration affects social divisions in two ways. It may weaken the common
sense of identity among the 'original' members of a category by the loss of
some of their number who gain new identities through migration. Additionally, migration may strengthen division through new encounters with non-
members across categories and the conflicts that frequently arise as a result
between locals and incomers. One particularly interesting case study of migration and community is O'Reilly's (2000) *The British on the Costa Del Sol*,
an analysis of a group which constitutes a transnational community whose

members' identities are neither straightforwardly British nor Spanish, but something in between.

The conventional view of in-migration as a cause of social problems has had to be modified further in the light of the recognition that newcomers may well generate additional resources for the benefit of established residents, not least by stimulating economic activity. In Gilligan's (1990) study of Padstow, for example, local people were often dependent on newcomers for employment, making it difficult to characterise conflicts there as straightforward contests between 'insiders' and 'outsiders'. Without the development of new industries to replace declining ones that had previously been major employers (such as the development of tourism to replace fishing in the case of Padstow), communities are likely to shrink as people move elsewhere in search of work. Despite extravagant claims by its proponents, individual 'teleworkers' can contribute little to shore up collapsing local economies. This story is currently being played out in the former coal-mining areas of Britain. Even in the context of economic decline, however, Wight's (1993) study of the Scottish village of 'Cauldmoss' found people reluctant to move away permanently, and those who did move were careful to keep open the possibility of return.

Less research has been undertaken into the impact of out-migration but what studies there are tend to emphasise the loss of community vitality (and ultimately viability) that follows from people moving elsewhere. Out-migration can result in residual communities being highly unbalanced in terms of several of the social divisions dealt with in earlier chapters – age, gender, ethnicity and social class. Out-migrants tend to be younger, more affluent and better linked into non-local networks than are their less mobile counterparts, and their relocation can contribute to the social isolation of older relatives who have stayed put (Phillipson et al. 2001). In the extreme, sustained out-migration can lead to the 'death' of communities (Porteus 1989), but it is more common for migration patterns to be made up of a mixture of out-migration, in-migration and return migration.

The common assumption that the dynamism of contemporary communities contrasts with static communities in the past does not bear closer examination, as Maclean (2003) found in her research into the changing population composition of the parish of 'Beulach' in the Scottish Highlands. The recent trend for people from the south of Scotland and beyond to make their homes in 'Beulach' is merely one more twist in a long and complicated story, in which population losses and gains have contributed to a situation of constant flux. Maclean found that many of the elderly 'real locals' had forebears from outside the parish. In another study, Macleod and Payne (1994) similarly found that, of 105 locally born residents, only 60 had one locally born parent, and fewer than one in ten could boast that both parents had been born locally.

The dynamics of community living

People's sense of 'belonging' is indisputably important to understanding the attachment that underlies their reluctance to leave and desire to return to place communities. It would be wrong to attach too much significance to place in this context, however, because the attraction is to the social networks of kin and friends that are centred on these places as well as to the familiar geographical location. The association of community with social support reflects the repeated finding that many people live in close proximity to relatives (beyond those in their immediate household). The 'traditional' working-class communities that have entered folklore for their mutual supportiveness frequently revolved around extensive kinship networks.

While this type of arrangement has generally been superseded by decades of social change, the geographical link with kin has not disappeared. Rather it is the case that people's migration strategies often maintain closeness to relatives because of the social support that they provide (Charles et al. 2008). Kin ties had been re-established to a significant degree even among the affluent workers of Luton when they were restudied by Devine (1992a) some two decades after Goldthorpe et al. (1969) had identified them as pioneers of more 'privatised' lifestyles.

In communities characterised by geographical immobility, kinship can be a particularly prominent feature, as Wight (1993) reports regarding 'Cauldmoss', where as many as two-thirds of the population were linked together by kin networks and strong kinship loyalties persisted. However, it should also be acknowledged that the other side of the coin of a kinship system linking people together is that it also defines who are not kin, and thereby divided off from the category of people who are entitled to support. An offence against one person becomes a potential offence against all other members of the kin group. In some cultures, this is institutionalised into the inter-group conflict involving the prolonged 'settling of scores', namely the 'feud'. Kinship in Britain is, for many people, a much weaker principle of division and attachment, which is why it has not been treated as a full-scale social division in this book. Nonetheless, identity with both immediate family and the wider kinship group is not uniform across the country, having significant social class, gender, age and ethnic variations, as other chapters have shown.

The reinforcement of people's attachment to communities by ties of kinship is supplemented by other associations such as those with neighbours, friends and co-workers. Of course, kin, friends and colleagues are not limited to persons living in close proximity, and social network analysis shows that 'personal communities' have the capacity to develop well beyond the confines of an individual's neighbourhood (Spencer and Pahl 2006). The extent to which communities have been 'de-territorialised' has been a topic of considerable interest in recent years since, on the face of it, powerful social trends have given individuals greater freedom of choice over those with whom they interact socially. Improvements in transport and communications technology allow people to be more mobile geographically and maintain contact with others over an expanded area. Rising living standards make it possible to take up opportunities to socialise beyond the locality and also make unnecessary the interdependence with neighbours that was forced on members of traditional working-class communities by their shared poverty. In the extreme, Beck (1992) sees participation in community relationships as increasingly a matter of individual choice. Post-modern theorists have argued that personal identities can now be changed and manipulated, because they are no longer class-based. While there is undoubtedly more individual choice in contemporary society (and this must weaken place community identity), place communities can still exert strong influences, and choosing a 'new' social identity may in practice be only to exchange membership of a local community for membership of an 'imagined community'.

It is, of course, important not to exaggerate the impact of broad trends towards geographical mobility and rising affluence. In societies characterised by widening inequalities, the easy mobility enjoyed by those in more advantaged situations is closed off to marginal groups (such as lone parents), whose poverty and social exclusion effectively deny them the same opportunities to overcome the constraints of place (Duncan and Edwards 1997: also Chapter 12). In a society increasingly dependent on the car as the means of transport that gives access to all aspects of life outside the home, we should also recognise that car use is uneven both across the population and within households, with the result that women and children may be more closely tied to place communities (see Chapter 9).

Additionally, it is necessary to keep in mind the peculiar character of face-to-face interaction to which theorists such as Goffman (1972) have drawn our attention. Communities are not confined to people who have face-to-face contact, as the extensive usage of Anderson's (1991) concept of 'imagined communities' demonstrates, but at some level community relationships need to be sustained by people coming together to reaffirm their shared membership (Weeks 1995). Family gatherings, conferences, political meetings and local carnivals all serve to bring people together in one place periodically for face-to-face interaction, which revitalises their sense of community in a way that impersonal contacts maintained at a distance cannot. On the more mundane level of everyday life, the significance of routine encounters and conversations for reproducing social solidarity among community members also deserves to be acknowledged. The young Punjabis living in Southall in Gillespie's

(1995) research were aware of the relevance of such everyday interactions, even though they were acknowledged to be more prosaic than the community scenarios portrayed in the television soap operas with which they compared them. These processes help to forge the strength of category membership on either side of any social division.

Researchers in this area have examined the ways in which gossip operated in traditional working-class communities, not just to reinforce what, by today's standards, appear to be highly restrictive and oppressive codes of behaviour, but also to promote social support. Gossip helps to build and maintain collective identities. Information passed on through gossip has often been vital to the well-being of poor households where it has concerned employment and benefit opportunities (Allatt and Yeandle 1992). While people now are generally less constrained financially and socially than their ancestors were, gossip networks continue to thrive and to be effective in a variety of settings (Dempsey 1990; Gill and Maclean 2002). Analyses framed in terms of economic necessity are clearly inadequate to account for people's acquiescence to such social control, so explanations of the continuing effectiveness of gossip within communities have to be sought elsewhere. What accounts of gossip emphasise is the role it plays in maintaining people's sense of place in and belonging to communities alongside the influence over the behaviour of others that it gives.

One feature of community life that the analysis of gossip highlights is the persistently unequal nature of community relationships. Patterns of gossip reveal that established community members, affluent groups and men are more powerful than newcomers, poorer people and women and children. What is revealed, in other words, is that, while gossip may serve to reinforce existing norms of behaviour by negative assessments of acts that transgress those norms, it also reinforces hierarchies and divisions whose existence is written into the heart of community arrangements. The very language in which everyday conversations are conducted reproduces the marginality of certain groups, such as when in-migrants are referred to pejoratively as 'emmets', 'blow-ins', 'bongleys', 'white settlers', 'outsiders' and 'foreigners', or when poorer people are labelled 'rough' and 'no-hopers'. In addition, the exchange of information that is a vital part of gossip is conducted selectively within communities, and exclusion from such exchanges reinforces the powerlessness of groups which are negatively labelled.

Against this background, it is unsurprising to find that 'leadership' of communities is generally monopolised by more 'respectable' figures, although the processes determining precisely who becomes a community leader are often convoluted. Baumann's (1996) Southall study and Eade's (1989) study of Tower Hamlets both found political processes underlain by competition between the different ethnic groups living in the two areas of London, and

Farrar's (2002) research in the Chapeltown area of Leeds comes to similar conclusions. Among these groups, there were widely divergent views about which individuals would be best placed to represent the community within formal political structures that define 'community' in territorial terms as the local ward or constituency population. Disputes over who should act as leaders to represent communities in turn reveal the contested nature of community definition.

Baumann (1996), Eade (1989) and Farrar (2002) all show that notions of place community sit uneasily alongside conceptions of ethnic community rooted in the common culture of a linguistic or religious group (Chapters 4 and 5), and the same could be said about tensions existing within conceptions of 'community' that are constructed around common interests. Competing community leaders operate with different understandings of community, with boundaries drawn more or less inclusively or exclusively, and with different conceptions of how actively community members can be mobilised. When faced with powerful challenges, such as the redevelopment of the Isle of Dogs into part of 'Docklands', the competition between leaders, between local council organisations and between the two groups threatened to incapacitate local involvement or resistance to change even among strongly-based communities (Foster 1999; Dench et al. 2006). Having said that, 'community' does have the potential to be used as a basis for different groups to come together to exert an influence on local regeneration (Mumford and Power 2003).

In the context of the long-term decline in allegiance to traditional (class-based) party politics and the growing heterogeneity of the population, not least in terms of changing class structures (Chapter 2), community politics has increased dramatically in recent decades. The growth of community action is one of the most striking features of the contemporary political scene, and legitimation through appeals to 'community' has become a vital part of mainstream political discourses. This is partly a reflection of the flexibility with which such appeals can be deployed, although this flexibility is double-edged. The proliferation of phenomena treated as communities carries with it the danger that the effectiveness of appeals to community will be undermined by the meaning of the concept becoming ever more imprecise and contested. There are signs that 'community' is no longer automatically assumed to have only positive connotations. For some critics of discourses built around community, the problem is that they serve to mask particular sectional interests, while others detect in them the agenda of state agencies attempting to withdraw from publicly funded service provision (Craig et al. 2011). One result of these unfolding debates is that the meaning of 'community' is becoming further politicised.

Recent conceptual developments and trends

The general tendency to associate community with supportiveness and social cohesion has been widely noted, but the word 'community' may be used negatively as well as positively. Recognition has grown that community relationships have the potential to constrain individuals as well as empower them and to be exclusive as well as inclusive. Social divisions are as much based on unifying the membership of each particular category as in mutual opposition across social divides. This reassessment has been prompted by policy initiatives in which community has figured prominently (such as 'community care' policies) as well as being the outcome of more theoretically and methodologically informed analyses. The assumptions made by policy-makers about the caring capacities of communities have been confronted by some fairly harsh realities. Numerous research projects have shown that there are definite limits to the extent to which community members are able and willing to provide informal care for dependent people and the bulk of the caring that is provided informally is performed by female relatives (Dalley 1996).

The dangers of operating with idealised conceptions of 'community' have also been revealed in other areas of social policy such as housing. Manipulation of the 'built environment', with the aim of creating 'balanced communities' in the New Towns experiment, was a notably ambitious venture in this respect (Crow and Allan 1994). Its history reveals the disjunction that exists between the image of communities as social phenomena that supposedly have a natural capacity to unite diverse individuals and the tendency in practice for communities to be less than universally inclusive. The persistence of community exclusivity is a common theme in the literature on geographical segregation. A principal lesson of the New Towns experiment is that there is likely to be considerable resistance to plans that mix people from different social classes in the same residential area.

The expectation that people from different ethnic backgrounds would become progressively less spatially segregated with the passage of time (Chapter 4) has also not been fulfilled in practice, and there is evidence of spatial segregation along other lines of social cleavage such as those of occupation and age (Crow and Allan 1994; Chapters 2 and 8). Of course, there are limits to how far residential areas can be monopolised by particular groups, but the emergence of the phenomenon of 'gated communities', with definite boundaries and restricted access, is a sign of the times in which we live. Understood alternatively as 'fortress communities', such settlements illustrate the general point that the boundaries of communities will be jealously guarded by members who feel themselves to be under threat from outsiders. Sometimes these boundaries will have the physical expression of 'keep out' notices, surveillance cameras, fences, or walls, as in the early example of the Cutteslowe Walls built between two housing estates (Collison 1963). On the other hand, exclusion of outsiders can be effected by more informal social means, for example by requiring that members express their commitment or loyalty to some symbol of the community (Cohen 1985).

Such exclusion or residential segregation necessarily limits the opportunities that people have to gain direct experience of 'how the other half lives'. Indeed, this may be one important reason why there is not more enthusiasm for the 'mixed communities' that planners aspire to create. One of the ways that we can tolerate differences in other people's lives – the ways of people on the opposite side of social divisions – is that we may not have to mix with them. If we do not meet, if they remain invisible, we can ignore them: we need not feel upset by encountering their differences. How can we feel human concern for other people's poverty, loneliness or disadvantage if we never engage with them except in the most superficial ways? This may be considered a powerful impetus behind people's frequently expressed desire to live among 'people like us' (Butler and Robson 2003).

This is not to say that, if we somehow all lived in neat communities, everything would be fine. The assumptions embodied in inherited notions of community have led to extensive theoretical reflection about the desirability of community. Feminists have been prominent among those who have questioned the meaning of community, prompted in part by the need to re-examine the gender orders written into traditional conceptions of community relationships. As has been noted already, policy-makers' views about the caring capacity of communities turn out to assume women's availability and preparedness to undertake care work, and such ideas reflect broader, male-dominated, taken-for-granted understandings of the allotted places of men and women in public and private spheres (Chapter 3). It is for these reasons that feminists and others have been wary of the communitarian agenda, developed by writers like Etzioni (1993), in which the value of community is promoted as an alternative to both unbridled individualism and excessive state involvement in welfare provision. Young (1986), for example, regards as problematic the way in which community is constructed to deny scope for difference and heterogeneity. In like fashion, Dalley (1996) has challenged the way in which the language of community is used as a cover for policies that shift the responsibility for care from state agencies to families (and, within families, to women).

The pursuit of community is open to criticism for introducing a conservative bias into the political agenda, because of its associations with idealised social arrangements in which people of different classes, genders and ages come together in pre-set, traditional ways where everyone 'knows their place'. In addition, critics point to the parochialism of community's negative evaluation not only of change but of all things different, captured in a mistrust of 'strangers' or 'outsiders'. It is undoubtedly true that there are established sociological understandings of community which are conservative, in that they look backwards to supposedly golden ages of authentic communal relationships that have subsequently been lost (Nisbet 1970). Arensberg and Kimball's (1940) classic account of rural Ireland, with its overtones of permanence, integration, cosy neighbouring and the slow turn of the seasons, contrasts sharply with Brody's (1973) later focus on famine, poverty, social dysfunction and clinical depression. Scheper-Hughes' (2001) more recent study of another Irish village further confirms the dangers of romantic images of community.

As was remarked above, however, the notion of a loss of community perspective does not stand up to scrutiny once it is recognised that various forms of community relationships are present in contemporary societies. Some of these are modified versions of what went before while others are more innovative. Put another way, the concept of community is most useful sociologically when it is treated as having the potential to capture the essence of a variety of different social arrangements rather than being tied to one particular type, such as village communities of the pre-industrial era (Crow and Allan 1995). There is no compelling theoretical reason to restrict the definition of community to people who have place in common, a point established in Hillery's celebrated review of the many sociological definitions of the term 'community' (Bell and Newby 1971). Once this is acknowledged, then the charge that the concept of community has a built-in conservative bias loses much of its force.

Broadening out the definition of community to include groups of people who have something other than place in common is important if many of the more innovative forms of collective endeavour are to be acknowledged. New social movements such as the groups of environmentalists that have grown in prominence in recent decades may be understood as radical and alternative communities, built as they are around cultural ideas at odds with the dominant ideology of consumer capitalism. A similar point can be made about the emergence of community identities among groups whose shared disability, sexual orientation or ethnicity (Chapters 11, 10 and 4, respectively) marks them as distinct from the 'normal' culture of the majority population (Weeks 1995). At the same time, it should be noted that place continues to figure in the operation of many such alternative communities, even if their members are held together principally by common political, religious or other cultural values. As Castells (1997) notes, most of these new community movements are essentially defensive in character, forged in the attempt to limit the impact of global forces on their lives. The defence of place is a powerful element in the construction of what he calls the 'communal havens' that offer to provide anchor points for an individual's identity in an uncertain world. In similar fashion, Bauman (2001a) portrays community as offering safety to people who feel insecure in the modern world.

The 'threat' to community life of the uncertainty of a global economy can be dramatic. Communities based on single occupations – or, more precisely, on a few employers – are potentially vulnerable to the effects of international competition. Agriculture, fishing, coal mining, shipbuilding, dock work and metal manufacture, industries that tended to have specific, relatively isolated, geographical locations in Britain, have already experienced major decline with the growth of alternative suppliers in other parts of the world. Decisions about people's lives become even more removed from their own hands.

Similarly, the rise of international media, largely funded by advertising, has spread knowledge of consumer behaviour and alternative lifestyles. To the extent that local community cultures depend on a sense of valued collective difference, this new awareness can be seen as undermining traditional ways of life. Nevertheless, it would be wrong to place too much emphasis on these broad statements of general tendencies. In practice, life 'on the ground' is far more complex, with people and organisations engaging in a variety of strategies to sustain and change their social and physical environments. Even Foster's (1999: 344) account of major social innovation, which stresses the power of external and global forces to change the local community, notes that connecting macro-economics 'with the alarming predictions about globalisation, and an individual development programme and its impact on local residents is very problematic'.

The growth of different sorts of communities is understandable as the expression of people's dissatisfaction with individualism and their consequent desire to feel part of a collectivity. Where conventional community organisations are exclusive of newcomers and other 'outsider' groups, alternative communities provide rival bases for community identities, quite possibly within the same spatial reference points. Patrick Wright's (1985) study of how Stoke Newington is home to middle-class, white working-class and various ethnic minority communities provides an excellent illustration of competing claims to place among groups who live alongside each other but do not constitute an integrated whole. Ethnic minority in-migrants and middle-class gentrifiers occupy the same space as the members of the white working class who have lived there for longer, but they live in different social worlds, leading Wright to conclude that they constitute more than one community. There is no necessary contradiction in noting how the definition of community has been broadened, while recognising that place continues to matter to how interest communities and communities of attachment are constructed.

The need to broaden the definition of community beyond people having place in common has been highlighted by the debate over the difference between 'community' and 'locality'. According to Day and Murdoch (1993), 'locality' fails to capture the subjective dimension of how place is experienced, and people's frequent use of the language of community to convey their sense of identity, belonging and common endeavour indicates that they are referring to more than just locality. Yet if a broad definition of community has the potential to capture a wider spectrum of social phenomena than do more restrictive definitions, at the same time it compounds the methodological difficulties of studying communities empirically. The problem confronting researchers of how to gain access to a study population is obviously easier if people's location is known than it is when the people being investigated are 'hidden' by their not being fixed to particular places, as was the case with Finnegan's (1989) amateur musicians.

Of course, even place communities are not straightforwardly open to inspection. Frankenberg (1957) famously found himself physically present in the village in which his research was being conducted, but excluded from many aspects of the social life of the place until he found his point of entry through involvement in the football team. The problem of research findings being influenced by the researcher's point of access to the social phenomena being studied is common in investigations of community relationships. Indeed, Payne (1996) has suggested that selectivity in terms of the community members consulted by researchers has led to a systematic distortion in which communities are typically represented as being full of nice people and devoid of undesirable characters. When combined with romanticised notions of 'community', research methods that screen out people with whom the researcher has little sympathy produce community studies that are seriously one-sided and incomplete. Recognition of the fact that having something in common does not entail community members being alike in all respects has sharpened awareness that research in the field of community needs to be methodologically sound if it is to be credible, and community researchers have responded to this challenge in careful but imaginative ways (Brunt 2001).

Conclusion

The unity of 'community' cannot be taken for granted once the contested nature of communities is recognised (Hoggett 1997). Central importance is now attached to studying the processes by which unity is created and maintained over time. Equally important is the analysis of how community conflicts are generated and work themselves out. Sociologists of community have shown how appeals to community have the potential to transcend particular social divisions along the lines of gender, social class and ethnicity, through (for example) community relationships being likened to family relationships (Crow and

Maclean 2004). An illustration of this point is provided by Dempsey's (1990: Ch. 4) Australian 'Smalltown' study in which he records how the community is represented by many of its members as 'one big happy family'. Such appeals are effective in securing the unity of community members to the extent that ensuing loyalty to the wider group overrides narrower sectional interests and perspectives. We can contrast this with the social situation in Northern Ireland (Chapters 5 and 6).

Where identification with and loyalties to a community are secondary to narrower and more particular interests and perspectives, community solidarity will be correspondingly unstable. Just as contemporary societies are subject to disunity as the power of dominant groups is challenged from a range of other positions, so too are contemporary communities vulnerable to fragmentation. The challenge mounted by women to their subordination within conventional understandings of community has already been mentioned. Neutral-sounding social policies constructed around notions of community can in practice have gender-biased outcomes, and feminists have been prominent among those asking of community discourses, 'who is this "we"?' (Godway and Finn 1994).

Just as challenges to conventional conceptions of 'community' have problematised women's allocation to inferior positions, it is also the case that the place of other subordinate groups been problematised by developments in community politics. Parry et al.'s (1987) research in inner-city Manchester found extensive consciousness of ethnic minority groups constituting a black community distinct from the white population and also subject to division into various 'sub-communities'. Taylor et al.'s (1996) comparison of Manchester and Sheffield identifies further cleavages besides gender and ethnicity, along the lines of social class, sexuality and age, which also problematise speaking of local people as if they constitute a simple community.

The conventional understanding of community as a sphere of harmonious social relationships does not stand up to scrutiny, and in many ways it is more appropriate to regard community as an 'arena' in which social divisions are given expression. Social divisions are encountered and expressed in specific concrete social situations: the place community in particular acts as a locus for personal life experiences. 'Community' is often in fact an expression of one or more social divisions of the kind explored in this book. This is not to say that the idea of community is reducible to one or more of the other social divisions. The appeal to community is a powerful rhetorical device by which groups can seek to reinforce their solidarity (Crow 2002), although as we have seen, this is often achievable only by the exclusion of others. It follows that the more 'community' is interpreted differently according to people's social class, gender, ethnicity, sexuality, age and health status, the greater the potential will be for it to be the focus of social conflicts.

Paraphrasing Marx's formulation, community can be treated as one of the ideological battlegrounds onto which people, who have become conscious of conflicts of interest, venture in order to 'fight it out' (Marx and Engels [1859]1969: 504). This ties in with Barnes' (1995) point that people are often motivated to act as members of communities rather than as members of more abstract entities such as social classes. Especially in place communities, there can be real and often visible splits, not least between newcomers and longer-term residents, as we have seen earlier in this chapter. These patterns are repeated throughout the country, each conflict independent and localised, but echoing those going on elsewhere. Thus, while the idea of community identity may not offer the same purchase on social division as a macro-principle of categorisation as, say, class or ethnicity, it does show how such things may appear 'on the ground'. The interconnection between social divisions means that we cannot think of any one division in isolation: it is only superficially a paradox that bonds of attachment are part of social division. Attachments to more than one category blur our perception of the sharpness of social divisions.

Currently fashionable analytical moves to deconstruct communities into their various component parts correspond to broader post-modernist concerns in sociology. People's consciousness of being members of communities is of growing significance in the context of the rise of identity politics, which has seen the rejection of overarching theories of what it is that determines who we are and an emphasis instead on the multifaceted nature of individuals and the communities of which they are a part. Yet the operation of forces that fragment communities is only part of the story, because alongside them there are opposite forces that bring people together. Homans (1951) refers to these as 'centrifugal' and 'centripetal forces', and this idea of social forces pushing people to either the margins or the centre of community relationships has been employed by Warwick and Littlejohn (1992) in their analysis of change in Yorkshire mining villages.

The notion is interesting for several reasons. First of all, it suggests that people may be thrown together or pushed apart despite their personal wishes; a person's position within a community is governed by more than simply individual choice. Second, the notion of centrifugal and centripetal forces directs our attention to the dynamic nature of community relationships and the importance of 'community time' (Crow and Allan 1995). Third, the imagery focuses attention on the question of what constitutes the 'centre' of 'community'. Shared place, shared interests and shared identities are all possible answers to this question, as is some combination of these. Whether such communities can come together on a larger scale as coherent and united societies, in the face of so many powerful social divisions, is one of the most pressing issues of our time.

Discussion Questions

1. What is community?
2. Peter Willmott (1986) distinguishes between 'place community', 'interest community' and 'community of attachment', arguing that people's community relationships connect them to others with whom they share common residence (for example, a neighbourhood), common interests (for example, an occupation), and common identities (for example, a religion). How important is each of these types of community in the modern world?

FURTHER READING

A useful introduction to the sociology of British communities is Crow, G. and Allan G. *Community Life* (London: Harvester Wheatsheaf, 1994). The potential of community studies to capture the complexity of local social life is well illustrated by Foster, J. *Docklands* (London: UCL Press, 1999). Methodological issues relating to community research are considered thoughtfully in Payne, G. 'Imagining the Community' in Lyon, E.S. and. Busfield, J. (eds) *Methodological Imaginations* (Basingstoke: Palgrave Macmillan, 1996), while an interesting collection of papers on the policy-relevance of community research can be found in Craig, G. et al. (eds) *The Community Development Reader* (Bristol: Policy Press, 2011). Bauman, Z. *Community: Seeking Safety in an Insecure World* (London: Polity, 2001) is a very readable introduction to contemporary meanings of community.

Expanding the Idea of Social Division

CHAPTER 16

Global Social Divisions

ROBERT HOLTON

This chapter will provide you with a critical understanding of the following issues in the study of globalisation and social divisions:

- Why a purely national approach to social divisions is inadequate
- What globalisation means and how it might best be defined in the study of social divisions
- How social divisions within nations are influenced by processes in the world beyond
- How a historical approach to global social division contributes to an understanding of social inequality
- The scale of inequality in the contemporary world, and main trends in between-country and within-country inequality
- Intersections between class, gender, and ethnicity within global inequality
- Global network society and social division
- Global cities and social inequality

Introduction: beyond national boundaries

Social division has typically been thought of as a feature of nation-states, including the regions and communities which comprise them. Sociologists have asked how unequal are nations like Britain, France, or Australia, and what are the main social divisions or cleavages within them. This 'national' focus assumes that the nation-state is the predominant power-container and point of reference for social identity and division. But is this focus adequate in an age of globalisation where capital, technology, people, cultural influences and power flow across national borders, creating cross-national connections in an increasingly interdependent world? This chapter provides global perspectives on social divisions.

Thinking of inequality and social division in national terms makes greatest sense where labour and capital markets, democratic politics, public policy-making, and cultural identity take a predominantly national form. Social divisions, in such circumstances, appear to be constituted by national processes, and become the subject of debate and conflict within national parliaments, industrial relations, and communities.

Yet the internal worlds of nations are not, and never have been, separated from the world beyond. This was evident to Marx and Engels writing in the middle of the nineteenth century when they identified capitalist production for a world market as key to radical social changes that they believed would overwhelm national differences and create similar conditions of life between nations. Processes largely external to particular nation-states have played an important and growing role in the making of social divisions during the long-term development of capitalism, industrialisation, cross-border migration and urbanisation. Global social divisions between North and South, or West and East, matter just as much as national patterns of division according to class, gender and ethnicity.

In addition to this global social geography, there is a long global history to the patterns of social division that we now see about us. Racial division in contemporary Europe can only be fully understood in terms of western encounters with Africa and Asia, linked with the history of slavery and doctrines of racial supremacy. The decline of manufacturing employment in Britain, meanwhile, is part of a long-standing global division of labour that exports jobs to low-wage centres overseas, although some jobs may yet be repatriated back to the UK if rising Chinese production costs begin to exceed low-wage employment in depressed parts of the UK. Gender inequalities also connect with this situation, in terms of the feminisation of much low-wage employment, whether in China or the UK. To understand social divisions in the present, therefore, it is important not only to think globally, but also to think historically.

Key concepts

To think globally means coming to terms with the widely-used but controversial idea of globalisation. This has been defined in a variety of ways, some of them restricted to economic processes like the global division of labour, free trade, capital export and economic de-regulation. From this perspective, social divisions follow from a global division of labour, in which nations and regions participate in unequal ways. In Wallerstein's influential world system theory (1976, 1979), the unequal social geography of the global economy is divided between a more powerful 'core' of capitalist nations in North America and Europe, and a relatively powerless 'periphery' of poorer nations, akin to the idea of a Third World. Between the two ends of this hierarchy are 'semi-peripheral' countries like Australia. As the system is dynamic, some movement over time between categories is possible, whether this be moving up or moving down.

While not reliant on the concept of globalisation, Wallerstein's approach has been influential in freeing up sociologists from a purely national focus on social divisions in favour of world- or global-level processes. Since 1990, however, much globally focused literature, in the hands of writers like Robertson (1992), Held (1995), Beck (2002), Held and McGrew (2007) or Holton (2011), has operated with an explicit concept of globalisation. This body of work also conceives of globalisation in multi-dimensional terms, including autonomous political and cultural, as much as economic, processes. In addition to multinational corporations, and international markets for capital and labour, globalisation also includes the development of trans-national institutions like the World Bank; global cultural phenomena like world music; trans-national ideas like human rights; and social movements around global civil society.

While not discounting the merits of an economic approach, this chapter uses a more multi-dimensional conception of globalisation to capture cross-border relationships that are not simply economic in form. These include cross-border movements of political and cultural influence, and new information and communications technologies. Such processes have helped to create a wider social consciousness of the world as a single space. It is however one that remains torn by suffering, social division and enduring inequality, issues which threaten ideals of a secure, sustainable future based on cosmopolitan harmony. Cosmopolitanism, in this context, refers to ways of life and public policies that seek to overcome the conflicts involved in social division, through inclusive cooperative relationships (for further elaboration, see Holton 2009).

While economic globalisation is connected with many of these broader aspects of globalisation, it does not necessarily dominate them, instead facing periodic resistance and challenge. There are, in other words, multiple or alternative globalisations. This wider approach is thus open-ended, allowing the possibility of global complexity rather than monolithic global domination. Thinking globally may then alert us both to global causes of social division, but equally to global movements that challenge division.

It is one thing to define globalisation in this manner and another to deal successfully with the barrage of criticism that this idea engenders. Foremost amongst the criticisms is the argument that national, rather than global, processes and institutions matter most. Much of what is called globalisation really amounts to 'inter-national' transactions between national societies, rather than 'trans-national' processes that somehow transcend nation-states. Whereas much of the earliest thinking about globalisation claimed it would create a new borderless world and lead to the end of nation-states and national societies, this simply has not happened.

Nation-states persist both as centres of political life and sources of identity. First, on issues such as economic policy, immigration, education and social expenditure, state roles have, if anything, expanded (Holton 2011). Second, democratic politics remains nation-focused to a considerable degree. Survey evidence indicates that national identity also remains the predominant form of cultural identity (Norris 2000). So nation-states still matter, even in a world characterised by intensified cross-border linkages and dependencies. National patterns of inequality and social divisions within nations remain issues for political debate and policy formation. The idea of globalisation, according to this argument, is mainly hype.

This argument is persuasive – but only up to a point. Nation-states remain intact, yet they have been profoundly affected by global or trans-national processes. We see this in the global financial crisis since 2008. Here, globally mobile financial sectors operating beyond state regulation created massive losses for powerful nations like the US and the UK, with negative effects on employment, savings and pensions. National sovereignty was conspicuous by its absence, and was further compromised by sovereign debt crises in Europe that were partly caused by state bail-outs to global banking institutions at public expense. Borders may still matter for purposes of national democratic politics and cultural identity, but in no way do they protect nation-states from destabilising external influences and the negative social consequences that arise.

There is, therefore, a balance to be struck between the impact of global forces on nation-states, and the capacity of nation-states to retain at least some autonomy, if not full sovereignty, in responding to economic change and social crisis. The policies adopted by nation-states, especially the wealthier and more powerful ones, influence national patterns of inequality, even in an age of globalisation. A key example here is welfare policy. No single standardised policy is evident if we compare European, North American, and Australasian countries. Economic globalisation has not produced a uniform hollowing-out of social welfare provision. State policy, as Esping-Anderson (1990) has shown, has varied between stronger forms of welfare on the Scandinavian Social-Democratic model, Continental social paternalism, and US-style minimalism. Such variations inevitably have consequences for inequality, irrespective of external global influences

Clearly global and national processes and institutions coexist and interrelate. Both are therefore important for any study of social division and social inequality. There are three broad reasons why this is the case.

First, social divisions within nations are profoundly influenced by factors external to them. These may include political and cultural domination by other nations or empires; economic domination by externally imposed rules and forms of market power; and processes of migration and settlement of people from other places. Second, patterns of social division have global dimensions. Just as there may be inequality within countries, so there may be inequality between populations living in different countries. Similarly social divisions may be constituted, experienced, and understood as global in form. This may occur where groups in different countries feel common interests and bonds with similar groups elsewhere, whether these are based on social class (for example, working-class solidarity), race (for example, pan-Africanism), or religion (for example, the world of Islam). Third, however, patterns of national inequality may stem from domestic causes, including public policies towards economic growth and social welfare. It makes a good deal of difference to national patterns of inequality how far governments choose to support or dismantle social policies that redistribute resources to the poorest and most disadvantaged. Such 'national' effects are independent of specifically 'global' causes of inequality and division.

A short historical sociology of social divisions

Much commentary on global inequality plunges straight into contemporary questions of income, poverty, and unequal life-chances across the world. A snapshot of this kind is vital. But it is equally important to put today's situation in some kind of perspective. Where we are now can only be fully understood by appreciating how we arrived at the current state of affairs. In the next two sections of this chapter, I look first at a wider historical sociology of globalisation and social division. This allows us to see how many of the roots of social division and inequality are connected with historical trends and transformation, rather than being the product of very recent economic events and political decisions. Attention then turns to a survey of inequality and social division today.

Globalisation has a long history that pre-dates the world of nation-states which emerged between 1700 and 1900. Cross-border trade, imperial conquest, long-distance migration, and religious expansion have been around for several millennia. They did not create the intensified and rapidly moving globalisation of today's world society, tied together by virtually instantaneous communications technology. Early globalisations were at best patchy and uneven: trans-continental connections were forged that fell short of a truly global scope. But these have left influences and residues behind that strongly influence the present (Hopkins 2002).

One example is the institution of empire which has created powerful territorial cores, as in ancient Greece or Rome, seventeenth-century Spain, or nineteenth-century Britain. These empires sought to control or hold sway over wider areas, extracting wealth and resources and dominating, sometimes enslaving, populations. All this was justified by some sense of enhanced or superior cultural mission.

Empires usually create both economic inequality and politico-cultural domination, sometimes in extreme form as in the attempted genocide of indigenous populations. They also create demographic change through the settlement of colonisers, the co-option of compliant local populations in administration, and the importation of labour, whether into new colonies or the core imperial heartland. The relevance of all this to contemporary life is that the legacy of empire remains a global influence in the minds and lives of today's populations. This applies whether they live in old imperial 'cores' such as the UK, France, and the Netherlands or in de-colonised regions in Africa, Asia or the Caribbean.

In the old imperial cores, such as Britain, the immigration of post-colonial populations from, for example, former Caribbean, Asian, and African colonies runs up against a cultural baggage of racial perception and exclusion (Chapter 4). Legacies of racial superiority persist among segments of indigenous populations. They typically surface when immigration is seen as creating competition for jobs or where cultural tensions within localities are interpreted in racial terms. Recent examples in Britain include conflicts within the older industrial towns of Lancashire. Imperial legacies are also evident in countries of colonial settlement such as South Africa or Australia, where relations between white settlers and indigenous peoples continue to reflect historical experiences of exclusion and abuse.

The legacy of past colonial occupation continues in newly-independent nations, and may take a variety of forms. The idea of a major global social division between North and South is, at least in part, connected with inequalities of wealth and power that are associated with empire, and with continuing inequalities experienced in the post-imperial epoch. In symbolic terms, the rich and powerful North continues to dominate the poor and less powerful South, though the mechanisms may have changed from territorial control to market-based exchanges skewed in favour of multinational corporations.

Empires may magnify social divisions based on evaluations of cultural difference, (whether associated with race, religion or ethnicity: see Chapters 4, 9 and 10), but they may equally create some of the conditions for more positive inter-cultural engagement. This may be expressed within intermarriage and inter-faith dialogue. Imperial and post-colonial cities may often have been segregated by inequalities of race as much as income, but in the aftermath of de-colonisation they have created opportunities for forms of cooperation that seek to transcend race, whether in politics, education or leisure pursuits.

Moving beyond empire as such, further long-term historical influences stem from patterns of long-distance migration, whether voluntary or coerced in some manner. Humankind, according to the anthropologist James Clifford (1992), has always been a travelling species. People migrate to find land and food, to secure ways of making a better living, to free themselves from political control and domination, and to enhance their way of life. Empires have sometimes been instigators of migration, as have processes of economic development based on foreign investment. Each requires additional sources of labour, whether to work as slaves on plantations producing crops like cotton or sugar, to be employed in the military, or in factory work. The number of migrants has continued to expand, doubling since 1980 and reaching a world total of over 200 million by 2010 (International Organization for Migration 2010).

Migration has also generally taken place within cultural groups rather than through isolated individual actions. Such cultural groups, often defined by a mix of ethnicity and religion, have a particular history and social characteristics which may contrast in real or imagined ways with other groups living in places to which they migrate. This creates a possible basis, not simply for social tension, but also for social division and inequality. This occurred historically with processes of Jewish migration and settlement, which sometimes occurred relatively peacefully but in other contexts created bitter social divisions and anti-Semitism. As in all cases of social division based on cultural characteristics, the attribution of difference and division is based on evaluative rather than objective criteria. This often takes the form of derogatory cultural stereotypes invented by dominant groups as ways of demeaning and dominating migrants. This has led in extreme cases to genocide such as the Nazi genocide of the Jews and 'ethnic cleansing' in both central Africa and Balkan Europe during the 1990s.

Global migration, both through history and in the present, has created ethnic diaspora, a term literally meaning dispersed populations of people with common or shared origins. The presence of ethnic diaspora populations within many regions of the world, however, has often been in tension with the political and cultural ideals of nineteenth-century nationalism. The ideas claimed not merely national self-determination for each and every people, but determined that each nation-state should correspond with a singular ethnic or cultural group. The difficulties here are threefold. First, populations prior to the epoch of nation-states were often culturally mixed, especially in cities and along trade routes. Second, patterns of continuing migration have complicated the cultural homogeneity of many nations. Third, many of the post-colonial nations in places like West Africa combined culturally mixed populations within boundaries that were arbitrarily imposed by previous colonial rulers.

The net effect of all this is to provide both internal and external reasons for social division within many nation-states. And yet cultural mixture does not necessarily produce conflict and, under certain conditions, may produce its opposite. Historical examples include largely successful inter-cultural moments under Moorish rule in Andalusia in the twelfth century, and under Akbar in India in the sixteenth century (Holton 2009). It may, therefore, be the insistence of cultural nationalists on homogeneity that turns division into conflict rather than cultural mixing. Put another way, some historical legacies lead to inter-culturalism or cosmopolitanism rather than enduring social division.

Religion is also relevant to patterns of global social division across history. One of the most fundamental ways of describing social division is through the contrast within the West and the world beyond, sometimes referred to as the East or Orient. This has its origins not so much in economic or political developments as in medieval and early modern religious conflict and division between Christendom and Islam. This occurred in the 'Christian' Crusades, and resistance to the Moorish occupation of Spain and the expansion of the Ottoman Empire into south-east Europe. Subsequently the contrast between the West and its 'Others' extended after 1700, through economic and political as much religious processes, with the global expansion of both western empires and capitalism into Asia and Africa.

This earlier religious sense of 'civilisational contrast' has nonetheless come to the fore again since the 1990s with the rise of radical Islam, the impact of 9/11, and the so-called 'war on terror'. One symbolic way of conceiving the contemporary position is through Benjamin Barber's (1995) vivid contrast between what he calls Jihad and McWorld. Jihad, the Arabic word for holy struggle, encapsulates the broader Islamic challenge to what is perceived as western materialism and spiritual emptiness, as much as it expresses a call to take up arms. McWorld, by contrast, stands for western consumer capitalism, an amalgam of McDonald's fast foods, Apple Mac computers, and MTV entertainment. This social division between Jihad and McWorld has geo-political as much as cultural dimensions.

A final dimension to the historical sociology of globalisation and social division – long-distance trade – re-introduces the strong economic thread that runs through the history of globalisation. A trans-continental trade zone, linking Asia, the Middle East, North Africa, and Europe, has been in existence for several millennia, and was linked with trade in luxury goods. This may be seen as a mini-globalisation rather than a comprehensive new global system, since it did not transform participating economic sectors into self-sustaining expansive modes of cross-border exchange. Put more vividly, the medieval

Silk Road that brought Asian luxury goods to Europe did not generate an Industrial Revolution.

Transformation of this more fundamental kind depended on further phases of globalisation, associated not simply with trade, but with plantation agriculture, industrialisation using new technology, improved communications, and, by the nineteenth century, export of capital as well as commodities. A fundamental aspect of transformation was inequalities of class, which by the mid- to late-nineteenth century, had become the leading social division (Chapter 2). Nonetheless, new instruments of transformation, such as factory employment, perpetuated older gender divisions of labour, with women continuing to occupy lower-paid and insecure positions in the new setting (see Chapters 3 and 13).

In the long history of globalisation, the periods from 1850 to 1914, and again from 1950 to the present day have seen an intensification of global economic expansion. It is within this period of time that integrated global markets for commodities and capital have been established, and the welfare and life-chances of individuals and households have been profoundly affected by global capitalism. Set within this historical background, we now turn to examine global inequality.

How unequal is economic inequality in today's world?

Global economic inequality is a huge topic. In the first place, there are different units of comparison. Inequality can be compared between countries or within countries, and the units in question can be households or individuals. Different answers to questions about the scale and trends in inequality may apply, as we see below, depending on the basis of comparison. Secondly there are different dimensions to inequality, including not simply income, but also health status, food security, housing, literacy and access to education, together with gender and ethnicity.

All these comparative global data are difficult to assemble quickly and accurately, especially for the poorest countries which lack the resources to survey and measure economic and social characteristics. This often means a time lag of four or five years before the latest data become available. A larger methodological problem is that of comparing the purchasing power of incomes in different regions and countries, where typical consumption patterns may vary considerably.

At first sight, there seems little doubt that the period of greatest global economic expansion experienced a very significant increase in inequality. In 1820 the richest country was around three times better off than the poorest. Yet by the 1990s the ratio of the richest to the poorest had already increased to around 70 to 1 (Milanovic 2005: 46). Another way of grasping the sheer magnitude of global inequality is that 80 per cent of the inequality among households across the world depends on the country (Milanovic 2011: 112).

In the contemporary world the gap between the richest and poorest, whether measured in terms of income, health or literacy is vast. According to the United Nations (2011a), the number of people subject to malnutrition increased from 818 to 837 million (16 per cent of the worlds' population) in the first seven years of this century. Equally disturbing is an increase in the number of countries in which per capita income levels are one-third or less than those of the wealthiest group of countries. This now stands at around 70, mostly countries in Africa or Asia. More are joining this group and few, if any, are moving upward and out of it. The existence of a global poverty trap is further indicated by the difficulty poor countries face in moving out of the category of those most indebted to foreign lenders.

Such inequalities are often linked with inequalities of economic power between multinational corporations, on the one hand, and the poorest nations on the other, compounded by the fact that the poorest countries have the weakest governments. Corporations, in this argument, have enormous autonomy, both in terms of whether to invest in such locations, what terms are agreed in relation to tax rates and royalties, whether to pay any more than subsistence wages, and whether to pull out and walk away. Examples of low-wage labour integrated into global corporate manufacturing regimes include Nike's footwear operations in Vietnam (*China Times* 2011) and the production of iPhones in China (CNN 2012).

These, then, are general features of the pessimistic interpretation of global economic inequality. However if we look more closely at a wider range of data, the situation turns out to be less straightforward, allowing at least some grounds for limited optimism. Looking first at global inequality, economists disagree about its scale and about changes over time. There is also dispute over whether there is necessarily any connection between inequality and economic globalisation. One argument is that globalisation in the form of free trade, together with mobility of capital and labour, leads to greater opportunity and rises in real wages compared with what is available elsewhere in subsistence agriculture (Dinopoulos et al. 2008). From this optimistic perspective, it may be lack of integration into global capitalism, as is the case in much of sub-Saharan Africa, which perpetuates poverty rather than participation within it. Against this, pessimists point to the destabilising effects involved in the contraction of agricultural employment, and uncertain transfers of labour into manufacturing and services. These undermine the food security of poorer nations, while expanding insecure low-wage employment. Much of this continues to be feminised (Mills, 2003).

Evidence on long-term trends in patterns of inequality provides some interesting insights into the complexity of the issues involved. Inequality between countries can be measured in two ways: in terms of inequalities in the per capita income of individual countries, or in terms of inequalities between countries, taking account of the size of their populations and their share in the world's total population. For example, O'Rourke (2001), taking the latter approach, argues that there are divergent patterns of between-country and within-country inequality. Since 1820, patterns of inequality in per capita income *between* countries increased up until the late twentieth century, very much as the pessimists have suggested. In the same period, by contrast, *within-country* income inequality reduced, largely it seems as a result of welfare states and possibly trade unions. Since the 1980s, by contrast, the position seems to have reversed with between-country inequality decreasing and within-country inequality increasing (Therborn 2012).

The pattern of decreasing inequality between countries may be linked with the expansion of the so-called 'BRIC' nations of Brazil, Russia, India, and China since 1990. The rise of China as a global economic power is especially important here, given that its population of around 2 billion inevitably skews measures of per capita incomes across the globe. If average wages in China double, there will be a significant upward effect on global statistics of between-country inequality, despite the continued existence of major areas of gross poverty among the far smaller populations of many of the poorest African and Asian nations.

What explains the increase in within-country income inequality in recent decades? Is this perhaps a result of a widening gap between skilled and unskilled labour, that is, between those who have marketable skills in an open global economy and those who do not? It is certainly true that elite managers and professionals, even within developing nations, have done very well out of globalisation. For example, the International Monetary Fund calculated that it was only the top 20 per cent of the world's population whose income improved during the 1990s (International Monetary Fund 2007). For other groups, economic openness may have more mixed outcomes.

The economics of foreign trade predict that unskilled workers in the poorest countries should benefit from openness because opportunities for employment will increase. Exposure to foreign trade should not, therefore, cause inequality. This proposition is supported by Babones and Vonada (2009) in their analysis of trade globalisation and inequality in 90 countries between 1975 and 1995. They find no correlation between increased openness to trade globalisation and inequality within nations. They go on to argue that, where inequality is worsening, this is less to do with globalisation and more to do with national policies. Some evidence, however, points in the opposite direction.

In Latin America, for example, growing inequality in the 1990s seems to have been correlated with economic openness, and only reversed after 2000 by national policies of income redistribution (Therborn 2012).

It may, nonetheless, be too simplistic to see entire nations as open to world markets and globalisation. Rather, openness varies between different parts of the economy and across different regions. In the case of the BRIC countries, economists such as Lindert and Williamson (2003) also argue that the problem of inequality is not due to globalisation, but rather to incomplete and uneven integration into global markets. Their evidence suggests that workers in open sectors of the economy do better than those in local or subsistence sectors. In the case of China, for example, inequalities have not grown amongst those in globally open sectors, but they have increased between such sectors, located largely in the coastal regions, and those in the more closed areas of the interior. All this indicates that it is dangerous to generalise about inequality and globalisation across all nations.

Gender and globalisation

Income inequality is only one of a number of ways to examine within-country inequality. The Global Gender Gap project on gender-based inequality within nations looks at a wider set of issues, including health status and political participation, as well as income and employment (Hausmann et al. 2008). Their report argues that on some dimensions, such as health status and educational attainment, the gap between men and women has been closed to around five per cent in aggregate for the 130 countries surveyed. On other dimensions, the gap remains wider. These include economic outcomes, where the aggregate gap stands at 38 per cent and political participation, where it stands at a lamentable 82 per cent.

These data are of course a snapshot at one point in time. They need to be supplemented with evidence of trends over time. In the case of global gender inequality, the gender gap remains wide. Nonetheless there is some evidence that trade globalisation has helped to narrow gender-based labour market segmentation for developing countries as well as reducing the gender gap for incomes (Meyer 2003).

These data are of course aggregates, and the story for individual nations varies. Some of the most economically open countries, such as those in Western Europe, have the lowest gender gaps, while the gap is widest for societies like the Yemen, Chad, and Pakistan, with lesser levels of openness (Hausmann et al. 2008). This raises the question of how far the mixed patterns of inequality depend on historic practices of patriarchy (for example, in relation to political participation), and how far improvements may be linked with beneficial aspects of national policies or global influences (for example, in relation to education and health indicators).

Notwithstanding such recent changes within nations, it remains the case that most global inequality is the product of between-country inequality. This brings us back to the issue of whether it is globalisation that drives most of the inequality we see. Unfortunately the answer is still not straightforward.

There are two reasons for this. One is that some poorer countries – such as the BRICs – have managed to integrate themselves into the global economy and done well out of it. The other is that global inequality pre-dated modern globalisation, and thus has historical causes, including legacies of empire, ethnicity and religious division that are not solely the product of capitalist development.

Taken overall, the world is an incredibly unequal place. This has created despair, suffering, misery, and anger, as well as policy responses aimed at poverty reduction, and a range of campaigning global non-governmental organisations (NGOs) pursuing a sub-politics of resistance. What is less clear-cut is the precise part that globalisation plays in global inequality: whether it is the primary cause, and how it contributes to both the creation and the reduction of inequality.

This sounds paradoxical, but it is in line with the argument advanced by the maverick Austrian economist, Joseph Schumpeter. He claimed that capitalism represented a force for creative destruction. Put another way, capitalism is a dynamic force both for innovation in technology and organisation, which sees periodic crises that destroy economic value and people's livelihoods. Schumpeter owed this idea in part to Marx, but also to his historical research into cycles of boom and bust, like those experienced in the 2008 global financial crisis. Recent global economic inequality has certainly generated crisis, but not the political dynamic for revolution that Marx associated with social divisions between capital and labour.

We can, however, explore the theme of global social divisions further, moving from quantitative indicators of inequality to look at qualitative changes in social structure.

Globalisation and network society

One of the most important contributions to the analysis of global social change has been provided by Castells' theory of network society (1996). Globalisation, in this argument, is linked with the growth of an information economy organised through networks. New communications technology associated with the internet and the world wide web allow the virtually instantaneous transmission of huge volumes of digitised data. Networks, rather than markets or business corporations, take over as the dominant principle of social organisation. This allows global capitalism to become more flexible than in the days of bureaucratic corporations, but also creates an anchorage for social structures in a world of highly atomised markets and economic individualism. Yet it also brings with it new inequalities and social divisions.

In a very general sense, the information age has alerted analysts to divisions between the information-rich and the information-poor. The former are networked, the latter are not. Castells' argument is more subtle and precise than this. Information inequalities are seen as profoundly spatial, based on a dichotomy between the 'space of flows' and the 'space of place'. The former comprises flows of electronic impulses, and flows of capital organised through networked businesses. It is also very much the preserve of global elites, managers, and professionals, whose lives are conducted within the context of mobile information and mobile employment. Elites within this 'space of flows' typically have cosmopolitan perspectives attuned to a culture that permeates territorial boundaries.

All this contrasts with the 'space of place'. This is the local milieu in which the mass of people live, centred on local employment and locally-focused lifestyles. It is far less networked than the space of flows, and disadvantaged in terms of the material rewards and benefits of the global economy. There is also increasing residential segregation between the gated communities in which elites reside and the broader place-centred context in which most others live (Chapter 15). Zygmunt Bauman sums up the inequalities involved with the phrase 'Globalization for some, localization for some Others' (Bauman 1998: 37).

Where the 'space of flows' dominates the 'space of place', Castells diagnoses a threat to political democracy based on bounded territories. This was borne out in the 2008 global financial crisis, in which the mobile world of capital markets conducted electronically in an instantaneous manner across the globe clashed with the far slower bounded territorial world of democratic politics.

The idea of the 'space of place' should not, however, be seen as completely static, in that it may generate social movements of resistance. Castells argues that exclusion from the space of flows is very largely responsible for the contemporary explosion of identity politics, including the revival of nationalism and ethnicity. What is less clear is how far resistance in this context can take a global form. Marx, over 150 years ago, saw working-class revolution as the political basis for overturning capitalism. What, if any, is an equivalent social force that may be able to resolve the discontents of global capitalism based on the space of flow?

Castells identifies environmentalism as one such possibility. Environmental justice is of relevance to everyone, and offers a way of linking struggles against wealth, power, and technology. Local place-based movements may then be transformed into a more general political strategy, which can be enhanced by using information technology for global resistance.

I have dwelt on Castells at some length because he offers a way of broadening accounts of social inequality with more general theories of social change. There are, to be sure, a number of criticisms that can be levelled against these arguments (see Holton 2008: 21–9). One is that the distinction between the space of place and space of flows is drawn far too sharply. The worlds of ethnic diaspora and trans-border religious community suggest there are many spaces of place beyond specific territorially-bounded locations. Many people, not simply global elites, are involved in processes of global migration, and these tend to foster cross-border allegiances. This is not to deny the inequalities associated with contrasting special worlds. The connections between global spaces and inequality are nonetheless more complicated than Castells suggests.

Global cities

One way of exploring the connections between global spaces and inequality is by examining the social structure of global cities, like London, New York or Paris. Much analysis of global social divisions looks, as we have seen, at national differences. Sassen (1994, 2006), however, argues that it is not so much nations as major cities that are at the centre of global economic power, and that powerful interests within cities create and reproduce both new patterns of opportunity and also growing inequality within them.

Global cities, connected with global finance, business services and corporate headquarters, have certainly grown to offer a considerable number of jobs in financial services and information technology that are relatively highly-paid. Yet this expansion has also been accompanied by a growth in far lower-paid service work in occupations like cleaning, hospitality, and routine maintenance work. Empirical evidence also indicates a growth of inequalities within such locations (Fainstein 2001). All this connects with global migration, in that many positions within social structures of this kind bring in new migrants.

Discussions of global migration rightly point to the low-wage and casual positions that many migrants occupy within global cities. Cleaners, janitors, or snack bar employees in the City of London or Wall Street are rarely white but far more likely to be Asian, African, or Caribbean in origin, and they are often female. This does not however mean that higher-paid positions within finance and associated professions like accountancy or law systematically exclude those of migrant background. Tertiary-educated migrants have done well in such settings. Nonetheless, gender inequalities in access to certain higher-level positions, especially traders, persist, as high-profile legal cases in New York attest (Law360 2012). The general implication, then, is that global cities remain highly unequal spaces, and that much inward global migration is located in some of the worst-paid and most insecure jobs. Whether this is experienced in more positive terms does, however, depend on what conditions migrants have left, and what comparisons are made between past and present.

Conclusion

Social divisions have a strong global dimension. It is no longer sufficient to discuss issues of social inequality at a purely national level. This is not because globalisation has destroyed the nation-state. It hasn't. What globalisation, more especially global capitalism, has done is re-shape national economies within a constantly shifting global division of labour. This profoundly affects patterns of opportunity, and levels of inequality. The world remains a very unequal place, even though between-country inequality has started to decrease.

Much global inequality is of an economic kind, suggesting the continuing salience of social class divisions. These may be sharpening because within-country inequality is on the increase. Conducting class politics on a national basis is, however, very vulnerable to global capitalism, especially where capital markets are concerned. This was evident in Greece in 2013 when radical forces of the Left faced major challenges in redressing the widening inequalities created by fiscal austerity, in the teeth of hostility from the international financial system. Economic inequality is not then simply a matter of structural inequalities engendered by the global division of labour, but also of periodic crisis tendencies within global finance, which undermine the redistributive politics of welfare.

Class inequalities are also simultaneously entangled with social divisions of gender, race and ethnicity. This is partly because global migration creates new sources of low-cost labour involving women and the unskilled. Migration also generates cross-cultural engagements which may generate conflict over real or perceived competition for jobs. Racial divides are not founded on any real distinctions of biology or nature, but represented cultural evaluations of groups of individuals, which may then be used for purposes of cultural and economic domination (see Chapters 4 and 10).

Although class, gender and ethnicity may be entangled, this should not lead to a reductionist explanation in which global capitalism is ultimately responsible for all global social divisions. Patriarchy and cultural divisions have a long history that largely pre-dates that of economic globalisation. Empire and cross-border religion are also important elements in the making of social divisions. While each may on occasion be linked with economic domination, the connection is not a necessary one. Sometimes geo-political or religious power has an autonomy of its own. The contemporary social division between Jihad and McWorld, for example, pits radical Islam against global capitalism (Chapter 9).

Finally, it is important to reaffirm that global social division is multi-centred in origin and effect. This is best captured in Castells' idea of network society in an information age. The hubs in the networked world are elites located in global cities rather than in national parliaments, with new hubs like Shanghai joining London and New York as financial and corporate centres. Markets for capital and labour also work through networks, creating multiple nodes of social life alongside the multiple nodes of cultural life and global civil society. The intense pace of social change is likely to multiply, as well as complicate, this arrangement of hubs and nodes. It remains vital that the mapping of global social division remains alert to this.

Discussion Questions

1. Why is a historical approach to global social divisions useful?
2. Is globalisation the main cause of global inequality? Identify the aspects of globalisation which are most relevant to answering this question.
3. Can between-country inequality and within-country inequality point in different directions?
4. Critically assess the significance of Castells' theory of network society for an understanding of contemporary social divisions.

FURTHER READING

There is no comprehensive study of global social division. A useful introduction to methodological and substantive issues involved is Mills, M. 'Globalization and Inequality', *European Sociological Review*, **25**(1) (2009): 1–8. A survey of theories of globalisation and historical themes can be found in Holton, R. *Globalization and the Nation-State* (Basingstoke: Palgrave Macmillan, 2011, 2nd edn). The most comprehensive accounts of global economic inequality are in Milanovic, B. *Worlds Apart, Measuring Global and International Inequality* (Princeton: Princeton University Press, 2005), and the same author's *The Haves and the Have Nots* (New York: Basic Books, 2011). Important sociological contributions to the study of global social divisions are Castells, M. *The Rise of Network Society* (Oxford: Blackwell, 2006), and Sassen, S. *Cities in a World Economy* (Thousand Oaks: Pine Forge Press, 1994).

CHAPTER 17

Identities and Social Divisions

STEPH LAWLER

This chapter will provide you with a broad critical understanding of the following issues in the relationship between identities and social divisions:

- Issues involved in defining 'identity'
- Processes of identification and dis-identification
- One identity or many identities
- Marked and unmarked identities
- The operation of power through identity categories
- The relationship between distribution (of resources) and recognition (of identities)
- The naturalisation of identities

Introduction

Social divisions do not simply divide up the world or act upon us as persons: they circumscribe what kind of persons we are and can be. They affect what kinds of identities are understood as normal and desirable, and what kinds of identities are seen as abnormal and pathological. Identities, then, are intrinsically linked with social divisions; they are produced within the crucible of social division and social inequality and carry their traces. Social divisions do not *only* exist 'out there', in social structures and social organisation, but also within the person, determining how people see and understand us, and, equally, our own sense of who we are. Nira Yuval-Davis argues that, as well as existing in social institutions and organisations,

> Social divisions also exist in the ways people experience subjectively their daily lives in terms of inclusion and exclusion, discrimination and disadvantage, specific aspirations and specific identities. Importantly, this includes not only what they think about themselves and their communities but also their attitudes and prejudices towards others. (Yuval-Davis 2006: 198)

Furthermore, the ways in which identities are understood in any given social formation has important implications for the ways in which that social formation itself takes shape. As Zygmunt Bauman (2009) has argued, not only is identity socially produced, but the kind of world we live in depends on the ways in which identities are framed and socially understood.

Identity troubles

The precise character and definition of the term 'identity' proves evasive. In the West, it hinges on a paradoxical combination of sameness and difference (Jackson 2002). As Jackson argues, Westerners believe that people are both absolutely unique and also the same as some wider group. This wider group may be as capacious as 'humanity' or as narrow as 'White English men', and in practice it is likely to involve some combination of different groups. It is immediately clear that there is a relationship between social divisions and identities. The social divisions operating in any time and space will affect the range of identities 'on offer', and social divisions themselves can be said to be formulated in the complex interplay between large-scale processes and categories of person. Yet, to see identities as entirely *reducible* to specific axes or categories of social division (gender, 'race', nation, sexuality, and so on) would be to miss some of their crucial characteristics. Such a categorical approach, as Craig Calhoun (1994) says, obscures the tensions within and between identities, and tends to see identities as 'finished' products, rather than as active, processual engagements with the social world:

> To see identities only as reflections of 'objective' social positions or circumstances is to see them always retrospectively. It does not make sense of the dynamic potential implicit – for better or worse – in the tensions within persons and among the contending cultural discourses that locate persons. Identities are often personal and political projects in which we participate, empowered to great or lesser extents by resources of experience and ability, culture and social organisation (Calhoun, 1994: 28).

Indeed, for some, the very term 'identity' comes laden with too much intellectual baggage, suggesting a whole, complete and undivided identity that is at odds with the complex negotiation and identifications (and dis-identifications) that people make in living identities (see below). Partly to address this issue, in some accounts identity has been separated from 'subjectivity' (or selfhood) where identity stands for an association with social categories (race, gender, class, nation and so on) – categories that are normative and ideological – and subjectivity refers to the more conflictual, complex and cross-category processes by which a person or a self gets to be produced (see, for example, Venn 2006). As Margaret Wetherell puts it, commenting on Couze Venn's work, within this formulation 'it is "subjectivity" that makes it possible for any particular social identity to be lived either thoroughly or ambivalently, while "identity" helps specify what there is to be lived' (Wetherell 2008: 75).

However, Wetherell, while acknowledging the productive work achieved by an investigation of both identity and subjectivity, is critical of the split itself, noting that it potentially leaves us with a de-contextualised, overly individualised model of the person. We could also point to the complementary danger of seeing the social world as being stripped of its personal, affective and subjective elements. Equally, we could be led to an understanding of the person as entirely passive, 'acted upon' by the social world, which 'injects' its norms and precepts 'into' the person, in a hypodermic model. As Wetherell herself also notes, this spilt brings with it a suggestion that the 'real', authentic person can be found in their subjectivity, while 'identity' is manufactured, inauthentic (even fraudulent) and, unlike subjectivity, can be changed by 'seeing through' its falsity.

At its most fundamental, then, such a split can lead to a suggestion that one part of the person (identity) is a social product, while there is another part (subjectivity, selfhood) that is an expression of a real, 'inner' person, untainted by the social. It is not that contemporary theorists of identity are arguing that this *is* so; it is rather that the terms carry unhelpful suggestions – compatible with powerful normative understandings of identity – of such a divide.

Others have also pointed to the inadequacy of 'identity talk' with Skeggs (2011), for example, eschewing both identity and subjectivity in favour of 'personhood'. However, throughout this chapter, I shall continue to use the term 'identities' but will use it as a wide-ranging term to refer to *both* public, 'categorical' expressions, *and* the more complicated, personal and ambivalent ways in which people take up and negotiate these public forms. I do this to avoid the split between 'outer' (social) identity and 'inner' (psychological) subjectivity criticised by Wetherell, and, above all, to mark all aspects of identity – whether understood as interior or exterior states – as profoundly and intrinsically socially produced.

Producing identities

This emphasis on personhood as socially produced is one that has been important in recent social theorisations about the self, subjectivity, personhood and identity. While sociology has always had an interest in people's personal lives, 'identity' as such was barely investigated within the discipline until the late twentieth century. While it was used as a term, few theorists asked what it meant to have an identity, or how identity was possible as such.

There have, of course, been important exceptions to this trend, most notably Norbert Elias and Erving Goffman, both of whose work opened up issues of identity and personhood to sociological investigation. In the main, though, when identity was considered, it was in terms of the conditions of entry into adult social life (Calhoun 1994), as, for example, in Parsonian socialisation theory. The legacy of this perspective has been enduring, despite notions of 'socialisation' as an explanation for identities being beset with problems (Stanley and Wise 2002). It is clear that everyone is in some ways 'socialised' throughout life – as Goffman shows, we tend to obey rather than disobey social rules and the obedience to rules can act as moments of collective bonding. However, Parsons' perspective and similar versions tend to conceptualise the person as innately possessing the characteristics that would enable them to be socialised into the norms of the group. The child, it is assumed, is born pre-disposed to being socialised within their specific local norms. As Stanley and Wise (2002) point out, this model is both over-socialised – it assumes that the individual is completely malleable – and psychologistic – it assumes that the individual is always already essentially and innately receptive to such manipulation. This contradiction is built into socialisation theories. Identity is apparently determined by social structures, but it is *also* endowed with an agency that predisposes it to being moulded by those structures. More generally, socialisation theories rest on assumptions that the status quo will (and, for some, must) more or less reproduce itself through the development of 'appropriate' forms of identity (or personality) in each generation. Identity itself, and in particular the processes by which it might come about, is not considered. It remains a 'black box'.

Against such a 'black box' view, the more recent 'turn to identity' has been associated with other intellectual concerns within sociology (and beyond) such as Marxism, psychoanalysis, feminism, and an increasing attention to language as making – not simply carrying – meaning. There is not space in this chapter to explore the various developments in identity-theorising that have come out of these recent concerns. But it is important to note that all of these developments, as Hall et al. (1992) suggest, have turned 'identity' into a question: they have made it a problem to be thought about rather than a self-explanatory category to be applied to other concerns.

The more recent development of Queer Theory – a set of theoretical perspectives which highlight the instability of *all* identities – has added impetus to the study of identities. This work has highlighted how apparently stable, unproblematic forms of identity – assumed to be given at birth and often also assumed to be visible on the body – are not as stable as they might appear. So the sex/gender identity, for example, which is usually assumed to be marked on the body, contained in psychology, and ordinarily unchangeable, is generally understood as a 'natural' form of identity, in that it is assumed to come from nature (however defined) rather than from social arrangements. Yet recent perspectives have shown the various ways in which gender must be repeatedly performed in order to come into being – through work on the body and the mind, clothing, appearance, association and so on. This perspective goes beyond a conventional sex/gender spilt, and indeed is intrinsically critical of such a dichotomy because the dichotomy suggests a 'real' identity (sex) overlaid with an artificial one (gender). Instead, queer theory has highlighted the intrinsically social character of *all* aspects of sex/gender (see, for example, Butler 1993). The claim here is that, rather than social relations acting on already-formed identities, those identities have to be *produced* – and produced in relation to other identities. So, staying with the example of gender, small differences between men and women are made into defining characteristics, such that two sexes become 'opposites'. Gayle Rubin puts it well:

> In fact, from the standpoint of nature, men and women are closer to each other than either is to anything else – for instance, mountains, kangaroos or coconut palms … though there is an average difference between males and females in a variety of traits, the range of variation of those traits shows a considerable overlap … [E]xclusive gender identity … requires repression, in men, of whatever is the local version of 'feminine' traits; in women of the local version of 'masculine' traits. (Rubin 1975: 179–80)

Such social constructionist approaches – not only to gender but to all forms of identity – have been formulated in contrast to, and as critiques of, an alternative formulation: essentialism. Essentialism has a long intellectual legacy in the West, such that it could be said to structure the 'common sense' of identity. It posits identity – or some part of identity – as stemming from some aspect of the person's nature, rather than from social relations. That is, identity is understood as an *essence*. In this context, an essence refers to something fundamental and integral to the person, which is not alterable (it is not possible to 'be' contrary to one's essence) and is held to persist throughout time and despite other social changes. This essence may be understood as coming from some aspect of the body (biological essentialism), or the mind (psychological essentialism), or existing in a 'soul' (religious essentialism). Whatever the form, an essence of identity is understood as being 'internal' and divided from the 'external' world of others (the social world) (Fuss 1989).

Although not necessarily spelled out as such, the essentialist understanding of the person is one that has held sway in the West for several centuries, and can be said to form an important part of the Western tradition for thinking about issues of identity, selfhood and personhood. The entrenchment of such normative understandings is no doubt one reason why conceptualising identity as a social product can seem counter-intuitive. But in addition, we are not dealing with knowledge about a world 'out there', but knowledge about *what one is*. In this respect, our most dearly-held assumptions about our selves can be difficult to question. We are all subject to what Hacking (1995) has called 'looping effects', or 'interactions'. That is, in knowing something of the group to which we belong, we know ourselves through that knowledge. People are aware that they are classified in the way they are – as members of groups such as 'men', 'women', 'children', 'British people', and so on. While, as I noted above, such classifications cannot sum up or contain the person, people may nevertheless use such classifications, and their behaviour and responses may well have effects on how the classifications change in the future. Thus, for Hacking, a matrix of socially constructed categorisations is produced:

> [People] can make tacit or even explicit choices, adapt or adopt ways of living so as to fit or get away from the very classifications that have been applied to them. These very choices, adaptations or adoptions have consequences for the very group, for the kind of people that is invoked. What was known about people of a kind may become false because people of that kind have changed in what they believe about themselves. (Hacking, 1999: 34)

Hacking's argument here raises two important issues: first, that people take up notions of 'identity' (for example) and view themselves through the lens of what is socially said and thought about 'identity'. Hence, if identity is socially constituted as a natural or essential state, that is how people themselves will see themselves. Second, this is not static: socially constructed understandings are not fixed forever but are changed by people's own take-up and understandings of them. What it means to be a woman in the early twenty-first century, for example, is not what it meant to be a woman in the seventeenth century. However, this does not mean that we can simply change social and cultural understandings at will. It is not a question of 'attitudes'; to see the situation so would be a voluntarism and would suggest we could change the world simply by changing our minds. To claim that identities are socially produced is not to claim they can easily be changed.

Sameness and difference

If categorical approaches fail to do justice to the complexity of identities, they nevertheless provide some of the raw materials for it. In this respect, most people identify to a greater or lesser degree with available identity categories. Indeed, for some categories, such an identification is compulsory. In most countries it would be legally impossible and socially extremely difficult not to identify with one or other gender category (male/female). Every ticking of either the 'M' or the 'F' box on official forms represents a re-statement of a much earlier form of identification that is reiterated throughout life (Butler 1993). Similarly, nationality, while a more open category – it is possible, if relatively uncommon, to have more than one legal nationality – involves compulsory forms of identification, at least as far as legal and official discourses are concerned.

However, not all identity categories operate in the same way: they do not all obey the same logic. Some forms of identity (paradigmatically, childhood) are assumed to be 'grown out of' and others (like old age) grown into. Some are seen as more fixed than others (gender and race are generally understood to be more fixed than class). Nevertheless, every claiming of an identity rests on processes of *identification*. Of course, such identificatory processes may not be straightforward. I might identify myself as 'British' (as a factual account) while dissociating myself from certain aspects of Britishness, or more strongly, dissociating from the category itself – for example by claiming that I am not like other British people (Chapter 10). Yet even such partial and ambivalent identifications are significant, not only for giving an account of oneself to others, but, very often, for one's sense of oneself.

However, every identification also involves a *dis-identification*. All identities are relational in this sense: all rely on *not* being something else. This 'something else' is what Stuart Hall calls the 'constitutive outside' to identity. For Hall, identification is made possible by a simultaneous dis-identification from other possibilities. For example, an identification with 'woman', at its most basic, involves dis-identification from 'man'. Hall and du Gay (1996: 5) argue that every identity '[names] as its necessary, even if silenced and unspoken other, that which it "lacks"'. If this is so, then processes of identification can be seen as active – even if non-conscious – processes which spring from social relations, rather than from some 'natural and inevitable or primordial totality' springing from within the person themselves.

In stressing the fundamental relatedness – and indebtedness – of all forms of identity, Hall's work undermines the myth of identity as being a coherent entity belonging to an isolated, autonomous individual. All identities are in some sense indebted to what they are not. And identities can *only* be made in social relations. For Erving Goffman, for example, it is only through interaction that we 'become persons'. Arguing against the 'vulgar tendency' to see the self when alone as the 'real self', and the self in interaction as always susceptible to falsity, he suggests that it is only through the performance of the self – in an ensemble cast of others – that we can, in any meaningful sense, have any identity at all (Goffman [1959]1990). It is not, as commonly assumed, that identity performances are 'false', but that identities – and social reality – are brought into play through performance (Hacking 2004).

If the recognition of the significance of others in forming identity is one challenge to the notion of an internally coherent identity, another challenge comes from the recognition that all identities must work *across*, as well as *within*, categories. In other words, no identity category can contain the person it (partially) describes. One of the most fundamental features of identity as it is lived is that it always and necessarily *combines* social categories. This insight has been especially developed in discussions of the category 'woman' in feminist theorising, expressed as the question of '*which* women was feminism talking about?' (e.g. Anthias and Yuval-Davis 1983; Fuss 1989; Walkerdine and Lucey 1989; Spelman 1990).

Not only does no-one have only one categorical identity, but also – and against theories of 'double' or 'triple' oppression – identities are not 'additive'. That is, identities do not work as though one has a gender, and in addition to that, a 'race', and in addition to that, a class, and so on. Instead, all categories are marked, inflected and informed by others. To be a black woman is not to be a white woman with the addition of 'race' disadvantage; rather the category 'woman' itself is raced, classed, and the rest. And so, too, with all categories. Nira Yuval-Davis, commenting on her early intervention in these debates with Floya Anthias (Anthias and Yuval-Davis 1983) states that:

> Our argument against the 'triple oppression' approach was that there is no such thing as suffering from oppression 'as Black', 'as a woman', 'as a working-class person'. We argued that each social division has a different ontological basis, which is irreducible to other social divisions … However, this does not make it less important to acknowledge that, in concrete experiences of oppression, being oppressed, for example, as 'a Black person' is always constructed and intermeshed in other social divisions (for example, gender, social class, disability status, sexuality, age, nationality, immigration status, geography, etc.). Any attempt to essentialise 'Blackness' or 'womanhood' or 'working classness' as specific forms of concrete oppression in additive ways inevitably conflates narratives of identity politics with descriptions of positionality as well as constructing identities within the terms of specific political projects. (Yuval-Davis 2006: 195).

This emphasis on differences within identities and the intermeshing of social divisions has been glossed in terms of 'intersectionality', although the arguments themselves pre-date the coining of the term. However, intersectionality, while becoming something of a 'buzzword' (Davis 2008), is frequently used to refer to different kinds of phenomena (social structures, social processes, identities, relations) and often lacks analytic precision. In some versions, it returns us to the additive models of identity that Anthias and Yuval-Davis's work critiqued in the first place (Yuval-Davis 2006) and is rarely used to consider privileged identities, or indeed the complex interplay of privilege and its lack that characterises many identities. That is, it is possible to be privileged along one axis of identity, while un-privileged along another. Nevertheless, the insight that identities are multiple, complex and interrelating is an important one, reminding the analyst that identity must necessarily exceed the categories assigned to it. It might most usefully be seen as a way of approaching issues of identity and inequality, a reminder of the need for a careful attention to the complexities of lived identities rather than as a blueprint for analysis.

Recognition and redistribution

Within social theory, debates have raged about the relationship between social divisions and social identities. In some discussions, issues of identity have effectively been ruled out of analyses of social divisions, which have instead been theorised as entirely an issue of the distribution of resources: a matter of who gets what, rather than 'who is the who?' (Starr 1992). In turn, questions of the distribution of resources have, in some cases, been seen as entirely separate from issues of identity. The contention in these cases has tended to hinge on the explicit or implicit claim that *some* social divisions are bound up with identity matters while others are definitely not. So, for example, with the possible exception of debates about 'class consciousness' (see Savage 2000), class divisions have conventionally been discussed in terms of the distribution of resources, while divisions around sexuality, for instance, have often been regarded as primarily or even solely matters of identity.

Yet theorists have challenged such a clear demarcation between identities and resource allocation. This can be seen in the work of Nancy Fraser on 'recognition and redistribution', and the debate it engendered (Fraser 1989, 1997, 2001; Butler 1997). In brief, Fraser's argument centres on a divide she identifies in social and political thought between perspectives which stress *redistribution* of material resources and those that stress *recognition* of identities. Fraser's point throughout is that social justice demands *both* recognition and redistribution. It demands both an equitable distribution of resources, and an end to the normative marking of identities as in some way faulty, inadequate or pathological. In early work Fraser (1997) characterises class divisions as properly dealt with through redistribution, and 'despised sexualities' through recognition of their bearers' identities as valuable. Gender and 'race', she argued, were 'bivalent', that is, tackling their damage (and the possible reparation) involved both recognition and redistribution. The damage inflicted by gender and 'race' results from both a lack of resources and a lack of value attached to those whose gendered and raced identities were understood as differing from a (male, white) norm.

This characterisation prompted Judith Butler (1997) to comment that Fraser ignored the material inequalities inherent in being marked with a 'despised sexuality' (such as those stemming from the denial of citizenship rights, the exclusion from a normatively-defined 'family', the workings of property and tax law and so on) and regarded inequalities around sexuality as 'merely cultural'. In her 2001 work, however, Fraser seems to have subtly shifted her argument so that she holds open the possibility that all forms of inequality could be characterised in terms of *both* misrecognition *and* unequal distribution.

Fraser's work makes an important contribution to debates about identities and social divisions in a number of ways. First, she outlines the ways in which social inequalities do not only work through redistributive issues of 'who gets what', but also through the rendering of identities pathological, abnormal or without value. She argues that:

> [M]isrecogntion arises when institutions structure interaction according to cultural norms that impede parity of participation. Examples include marriage laws that exclude same-sex partnerships as illegitimate and perverse, social-welfare policies that stigmatise single mothers as sexually-irresponsible scroungers, and policing practices such as 'racial profiling' that associate racialised persons with criminality. (Fraser 2001: 24–5)

As she notes, all of these cases rest on a tacit comparison between 'right' and 'wrong', 'good' and bad' categories:

> straight is normal, gay is perverse; 'male-headed households' are proper, female-headed households are not; 'whites' are law-abiding, 'blacks' are dangerous. In each case, the result is to deny some members of society the status of full partners in interaction, capable of participating on a par with the rest. (Fraser 2001: 25)

Second, Fraser stresses that the issue here is justice, rather than a simple recognition of all forms of identity. Misrecognition, she argues, is '*social subordination* in the sense of being *prevented from participating as a peer* in social life' (2001: 24, emphasis in original). Since not all groups are socially subordinated, not all demands for recognition are equivalent. For example, racist claims that white people in the UK or US are now disadvantaged by the presence of minority ethnic groups are not demands to right an unjust balance, but demands to further entrench injustice in the form of white privilege. This insight is absolutely central to a discussion of identities and social divisions and reminds us of the significance of privilege, discussed more fully below.

Third, Fraser points to the ways in which unequal distribution may be bound up with issues of misrecognition (although she does not develop her thinking). If to be misrecognised is to be denied the status of full actors in demands for justice, then misrecognised groups are unlikely to be heard when they make their own demands for both recognition *and* redistribution. As I discuss in more detail below, groups like that now cast as 'the underclass' are not generally vilified for being poor, but for having faulty ideals, psychologies and practices. Having been cast in this way, how can their demands – which may include demands not to be stigmatised as well as demands for more resources – be listened to?

Power, privilege and identity

Identities are forged in the play of power and privilege, so that they do not exist in happy relativism – a universe of 'equal but different' – but in hierarchical relations. In this respect, the link with social divisions perhaps becomes most clear. In this section, I will outline some of the ways in which power can be seen to be at work in processes of identity-making.

Some forms of identity are so normalised they are hardly seen as identities at all. They are *unmarked* categories in that they are not usually considered to need to be named. So, for example, heterosexual couples tend to simply be described as 'couples', while gay couples are rarely just 'couples' but are marked as 'gay couples'. Heterosexual people rarely 'come out' as heterosexual because everyone is assumed to be heterosexual unless there is compelling evidence to the contrary. 'Gender' is often seen as referring to something peculiar to women, as though men have no gender. When class is invoked, it tends to be used to refer to working-class identity/existence, so that middle classness remains the silent norm. When race or ethnicity are invoked they rarely refer to whiteness. It is still possible to read 'ethnic' as *meaning* 'non-white', as though 'ethnicity' were somehow confined to non-white people (Chapter 4). Furthermore, whiteness, in many contexts, operates as a background assumption: 'whiteness as ordinary' (Dyer 1997); 'if no one looks black, everyone is [assumed to be] white' (Phelan 1993: 98). Do white people even have an identity *as* white? And if not, why not?

These questions are, of course, concerned with social arrangements and, specifically, with the workings of power. To be the bearer of an 'unmarked' identity is to experience privilege. As Michael Kimmel notes:

> The very processes that confer privilege to one group and not another group are often invisible to those on whom that privilege is conferred ... Invisibility is a privilege in a double sense – describing both the power relations that are kept in place by the dynamics of invisibility, and in the sense of privilege as a luxury. It is a luxury that only white people have in our society not to think about race every day of their lives. It is a luxury that only men have in our society to pretend that gender does not matter. (Kimmel 2000: 7)

Identities can only be unmarked because social relations render some positions, practices and identities as 'normal' and others as deviating from this norm. This is why identities cannot be treated in a relativist way – 'difference' presupposes difference from a norm (Walkerdine and Lucey 1989; Calhoun 1994). Yet this is not because of something intrinsic to the identities themselves; rather, it is an effect of the unequal social relations in which identities, and the value (or lack) attached to them, are forged and reproduced.

On the other hand, while some forms of identity go silently unmarked, others get conferred on people whether they accept them or not. One example is 'underclass identity'. The term 'underclass' entered mainstream UK discourse after being popularised by the US journalist Charles Murray in a series of articles on British life (Murray 1990, 1994a, 1994b, 1996). It was a term used to designate a group that might previously have been called 'the undeserving poor'. Murray devised this categorisation on the basis of place (the so-called underclass tended to live in deprived areas), but also, he alleged, welfare-dependency, petty criminality, bad parenting, idleness, sexual excess, and general lack of 'respectability'.

As Nikolas Rose (1989) has shown, this term has been conceptualised in such a way as to bring together quite disparate groups of people – single mothers, the long-term unemployed, the sick and disabled, petty criminals – who would otherwise have little in common except, in some cases, poverty. In this way, a new identity category is formed, unchosen by the bearers of that identity, yet used to mark them in pathological terms. Zygmunt Bauman notes that people identified as 'underclass' are denied 'the right to *claim* an identity as distinct from an ascribed and enforced classification' (Bauman 2004: 39, emphasis in original). In other words, an identity is imposed and there is no 'official' space allowed to contest this or to affirm a different identity. Bauman argues:

> The meaning of 'underclass identity' is an *absence of identity*; the effacement or denial of individuality, of 'face' – that object of ethical duty and moral care. You are cast outside the social space in which identities are sought, chosen, constructed, evaluated, confirmed or refuted. (Bauman 2004: 39, emphasis in original)

This absence of identity can be seen in other forms of identification, such as 'the socially excluded', the 'socially immobile', 'illegal immigrants' or 'economic migrants', as well as in more hateful forms such as 'chavs' (in the UK) or 'white trash' in the US. None of these forms of identification depend on those designated as such choosing or claiming these identities. Those with the power to name can *identify* both themselves and those without such power. Further, those who are denied any chance to name and define themselves tend to be defined in terms of a 'mass' or a 'mob' and to be contrasted with an 'us' who are defined as individuals.

This ascription of stigmatised identities is frequently bound up with a marking of the group in terms of faulty psychological traits. The language of inequality and disadvantage is, increasingly, replaced by the language of an individual pathology (Walkerdine 2003). In this way, the identity ascribed to them is assumed to come from some common (and pathological) feature of the group itself, who can, moreover, be blamed for their own misfortune. Loic Wacquant (1994) argues that the concept of 'underclass' in the US characterises people assigned to this category as fundamentally 'other' to the rest of society. But, he argues, this is an effect, not of the people themselves, but of the 'preconceptions, fears and fantasies' (Wacquant 1994: 236) of the observers who would mark them as 'underclass' in the first place. Writing of ghettos in the US, he adds:

> '[T]he grave mistake of theories on the urban slum has been to transform socio-logical conditions into psychological traits and to impute to the victims the distorted characteristics of their victimisers'. This is an apt description of the recent scholarly and public policy debate on the ghetto in the United States. By focusing narrowly on the presumed behavior and cultural deficiencies of inner-city residents ... recent discussions of the so-called underclass have hidden the political roots of the predicament of the ghetto and contributed to the further stigmatization and political isolation of its residents. (Wacquant 1994: 264–5, citing Portes. Emphasis is Wacquant's)

It is important to note that these formulations of disparagement and stigmatisation rest on a naturalisation of social issues. In other words, part of the slippage from social relations to personal pathology involves a marking of the problem as inhering in the 'nature' of the stigmatised group. This essentialism means that when people are talking about class – a manifestly artificial, 'made' set of social relations – what they *seem* to be talking about is a set of innate characteristics (Lawler 2008). For Pierre Bourdieu, this slippage from the social to the natural becomes a justification for inequality – what he calls 'a sociodicy':

> Max Weber said that dominant groups always need a 'theodicy of their own privilege', or more precisely a sociodicy, in other words a theoretical justification of the fact that they are privileged. Competence is nowadays at the heart of that sociodicy, which is accepted, naturally, by the dominant – it is in their interest – but also by the others. In the suffering of those excluded from work, in the wretchedness of the long-term unemployed, there is something more than there was in the past. The Anglo-American ideology, always somewhat sanctimonious, distinguished the 'undeserving poor' from the 'deserving poor', who were judged worthy of charity. Alongside or in place of this ethical justification there is now an intellectual justification. The poor are not just immoral, alcoholic, and degenerate, they are stupid, they lack intelligence. (Bourdieu 2010: 119)

The naturalisation of social characteristics is one very powerful form that such a sociodicy can take. The 'correct' (middle-class) social competences, tastes, distinctions, and dispositions are always learned, but that learning is eclipsed in a kind of 'social magic' that turns them into natural characteristics.

If this is so for class, it is equally or even more so for other forms of identity, which tend to be more closely associated with 'nature' in the first place. Essentialising moves, which make social inequalities into problems with identities, remain. Across numerous axes, they are powerful ways of legitimating those very inequalities.

Conclusion

In this chapter, I have discussed some of the ways in which recent work on identity has highlighted its social production. If, as I have argued, identities are socially produced, then they are linked to social divisions in important ways; not because social divisions *work on* already-unequal identities, but because social divisions, and social inequality, *work on and through identity*, conferring value on some and stripping it from others (Skeggs 2004). The normative association of identities with 'nature' means that inequalities attached to identities can appear to be natural – arising out of something in those identities themselves. Yet the work discussed here suggests that the ascribing of faulty identities to dominated groups is a justification of, and not an explanation for, social inequality.

Discussion Questions

1. Thinking about identities depends on having a classificatory system. What classifications of identities exist in the contemporary West? Could this be different?

2. What does it mean to see identities as socially constructed? How does this perspective challenge 'common-sense' assumptions about identity?

3. To what extent are identities defined for us and to what extent can we ourselves make them? What are the limits to making identities?

4. Are some forms of identity seen as more valuable than others? If so, how would you explain this?

5. Taking one form of social division, consider:
   (a) some ways in which it can be made to seem natural, rather than social;
   (b) some consequences of this naturalisation.

FURTHER READING

For a general overview of sociological/cultural discussions of identity, see Burkitt, I. *Social Selves: Theories of the Social Formation of Personality* (London: Sage, 1991); du Gay, P., Evans, J. and Redman, P. (eds) *Identity: A Reader* (London: Sage, 2000); Elliott, A. and du Gay, P. (eds) *Identity in Question* (London: Sage, 2009); Lawler, S. *Identity: Sociological Perspectives* (Cambridge: Polity, 2009); Williams, R. *Making Identity Matter* (Durham: Sociology Press, 2000); Woodward, K. *Identity and Difference* (London: Sage, 2002). A good introductory text on this topic is Elliott, A. *Concepts of the Self* (Cambridge: Polity, 2007). For discussions of the interrelationships of various forms of identity, see Fuss, D. *Essentially Speaking* (New York: Routledge, 1989); Spelman, E. *Inessential Woman* (London: The Women's Press, 1990); Reay, D. et al. (2007) '"A darker shade of pale?" Whiteness, the middle classes and multi-ethnic inner city schooling', *Sociology*, 41(6): 1041–60. Mariam Fraser considers the operation of different kinds of identity and social divisions in Fraser, M. (1999) 'Classing queer: politics in competition', *Theory, Culture and Society* 16(2): 107–32.

CHAPTER 18

Social Divisions as a Sociological Perspective

GEOFF PAYNE

This chapter will provide you with a broad critical understanding of the following issues in social division:

- The formal definition of a social division
- Social divisions as socially embedded forms of social inequality
- Social difference, social inequality and social division
- Temporal and 'essential' characteristics of social divisions
- Social division and social cohesion: overlapping memberships, cross-cutting ties and social conformity
- The complexity of multiple memberships and identities
- Social division and sociological theory: structural-functionalism, Marxism and post-modernism
- Alternative perspectives: the number of social divisions
- Hierarchy and inequality versus 'others' and personal identity

Each of the other chapters has been deliberately written in a way that 'defines' social divisions indirectly by talking about key examples. This approach, if enough chapters are sampled, gives a good feel of what social division is all about through an exploration of cases and details. The advantage of this approach is not only that we have dealt with concrete examples which are relatively easy to understand, rather than getting tangled in the precision of abstract deliberations. It has also enabled us to demonstrate the advantage of using our perspective in terms of displaying and analysing the major structural processes in our society. We could also have taken the alternative approach of starting with a formal definition expressed as a set of precise principles, but that would have distracted from the details of how contemporary society operates. Of course, in the end, a satisfactory definition needs both examples and a

407

more abstract formal statement, distinguishing between what we are defining and other similar concepts. This chapter provides the second part of the fuller definition, which will also enable us to reflect on what social divisions in the plural might mean as a distinctive way of 'seeing' society.

A definition of 'social division'

A 'social division' of the kind explored in the preceding chapters conforms to ten core characteristics:

- Social division is a form of social organisation resulting in a series of society-wide distinctions, each of which consists of two or more logically inter-related categories of people.
- Social divisions are expressed through, and sustained by, dominant cultural beliefs, the organisation of social institutions and the situational interaction of individuals: members of related categories within any division are socially sanctioned as substantially different in material and cultural ways from those in other categories.
- Membership of a category in a social division confers unequal opportunities of access to desirable 'resources' of all kinds: hierarchically different life chances and lifestyles are therefore associated with membership of each category.
- Social divisions are socially constructed, in the sense that they are not a simple manifestation of 'natural' or 'inevitable' laws of existence, but this does not mean that social divisions can be ignored or completely revised by the moment-to-moment social interactions, interpretations, decisions or social acts of individuals.
- However much specific social divisions are opposed by those disadvantaged by them, the principle of social division is a universal systematic feature of human society.
- Although not permanently established in any given form, a social division tends to be long-lasting.
- The extent of differentiation between categories varies from social division to social division, but movement across a divide is either rare or relatively slow to be achieved.
- The experience of being socially divided tends to produce shared social identities for people in the same category, often expressed by reference to their perceived difference from those in an alternative category of the same division.

- Each social division encompasses all members of society in one or other of its categories, but individuals seldom have matching 'profiles' of category membership across the whole range of social divisions.
- An examination of life chances and lifestyles is an empirical method of identifying social divisions and categories.

This definition means that rather than concentrating on just two or three social divisions, we need to include a larger number in our sociological perspective (Payne 2004).

While each division can consist of two, three, or more categories, these form an interrelated whole that includes all members of a society: paradoxically the *distinction* between the categories expresses the logical *connection* between them. These distinctions are marked by clear-cut – rather than small-scale – differences in material circumstances or cultural advantages (although 'clear-cut' and 'small-scale' are terms which at the margin involve subjective judgements by the researcher and the reader). The differences between categories are maintained by a normative order which supports those who accept the division and constrains those who seek to alter it.

As we saw in Chapter 1, the idea of social division entails both extensive differences and a continuity of existence over time, which stems from its integration in the social order through values, institutions and day-by-day interactions. On the one hand, there is a sense, if not of permanence, then of massive inertia: it is not easy to challenge and change the boundaries. On the other hand, all the chapters have shown how things have changed over longer periods of time and stressed that social divisions are not immutable. The key to understanding this is the embedded nature of the social practices that sustain each division. It follows that, while not being based on 'natural' laws, divisions are typically encountered as constraining (particularly so for those in the less advantaged categories) or sustaining (for the advantaged). In some cases, social divisions appear to be caused by physical or biological principles, but even here we have seen that in fact it is the divisions which utilise such differences as legitimation, rather than the division which arises from some essential human difference.

It might be tempting – and indeed not unfair – to read this emphasis on constraint, disadvantage and differential life chances as meaning that to some extent each of the contributors to this book perceives social division as inherently undesirable. Some commentators, like Marsland and Saunders, have commented on the general tendency of sociologists to side with the underdog, or indeed to be ideologically biased. While it will be apparent from the style and content of the chapters that the authors have varying degrees of personal commitment to this aspect of their topics, they are also all concerned with its sociological analysis. The fact that the divisions can reasonably be identified as social injustice – a potential source of unhappiness and even civil strife – should lend purpose, rather than bias, to the analysis. All social arrangements entail settlements that bring relative advantage: those who gain most from present circumstances are likely to wish them to continue, not to have them challenged and to present the current outcome as a consensus supported by all parties, rather than one that yields advantages for some, to the disadvantage of others. One task of sociology is to question things that would otherwise be taken for granted, even if there are those who would rather not have such questions raised.

The strength of social division

A social analyst's unhappiness with the current patterns of a particular social division does not automatically lead to biased research or a simplistic belief that all social divisions can somehow be removed. One may take comfort that divisions may take different forms in some societies, as described by anthropologists or historians, but there is no evidence of societies – even the simplest hunter-gatherer societies – operating without divisions. However, the universality of division is no justification for the continuation of all divisions in exactly their current form, or of extremes of differentiation.

Nonetheless, it is a feature of social divisions that they persist. As has been seen, one class system may give way to another, or the role of one group may be enhanced, such as that of women through emancipation or entry into the workplace, but the core division survives. It may be possible for cracks in the glass ceiling to be exploited, for some of us to be socially mobile between classes, or for us all to move through the life-course, but these are opportunities for individuals who need to devote many years to achieving the transition from one category to the other or moving the boundaries. Divisions are not absolute or invariable, but they do a pretty good job of seeming to be.

In part, this appearance of substance comes from the nature of the categories. These are 'oppositional', both in the sense of the opposing interests of the members of different categories (advantaged/disadvantaged) and in terms of defining one category in terms of another, as its mirror image. Inside each division, we perceive the members of the oppositional categories as being different, as being 'others'. Although it is possible to make more of these notions of comparison, difference and 'otherness' (for example, see Hetherington and Munro 1997), there is little to be gained from straying into the arcane world of the more extreme forms of post-structuralism and post-modernism. Contrary to any impression given by the often wordy elaborations of such writings, the core issue is fairly straightforward.

Identity is not only shared with others, but expressed as not sharing or belonging with others. Normally, when the members of a disadvantaged category identify the long-term existence of a more advantaged group to which they do not belong, this recognition makes the probability of change seem less likely. The more that membership of a category is marked by characteristic lifestyles and life chances, the more prominently the category boundaries are marked off. If social divisions overlap, and their category memberships and identities coincide, the maintenance of the differences is reinforced.

However, we have been at pains to stress that individuals hold dual (or multi-) memberships in a range of social divisions. As Chapter 1 observed, people take their identities from a mixture of categories and therefore have some choice of identity. The 'profile of membership' differs from person to person, and is one of the reasons why simple explanations of social behaviour being 'caused' by membership of a single category do not work. Social life is not completely determined by social class (or gender, or race and so on), whatever may have seemed to be the case with sociological analysis in former times. Our sense of distinctiveness or difference is a complex one.

Definitions as differentiation

The advantage of formalising and elaborating a definition is that it provides a means of marking off a boundary between social divisions and other similar, but subtly different, ideas. This removes a source of potential confusion, as the lack of a clear distinction in some of the literature shows (e.g. in *Social Differences and Divisions*, Braham and Janes (2002) offer no detailed definition of division, or explanation for their selection of material). Not all separations of people into opposing categories are of a scale to merit inclusion as social divisions. For example, the many 'rages' and 'hells' popular in contemporary media representations – 'road rage', 'trolley rage', 'neighbours from hell', holidays from hell' and so on – may involve disagreements and conflicts, but they hardly constitute a social division. They certainly are not society-wide, all-inclusive, permanent divisions, nor are they socially sanctioned as 'natural'. To be counted as a social division requires that all ten of the criteria in our formal definition (above) should be in place. This latter requirement also helps to distinguish between the idea of a social division and other concepts such as social inequality, 'difference', and the 'social division of labour' and social differentiation.

'Social inequality' is a condition of disproportionate access to 'resources' – not just financial resources but any human or cultural resources. Statements about social inequalities tend to deal, at their most simple, with 'facts'. Thus one can talk about specific social inequalities in, say, housing, educational qualifications, risk of being a victim of crime or access to political influence. It is certainly interesting to learn that 7 per cent of the population own 84 per cent of the land in Scotland, that 1 per cent of adults own over 40 per cent of personal net capital in England and Wales, or that the worst-off 20 per cent of our society have incomes lower than half the national average. But what is 'interesting' lies in discovering why and how such patterns of inequality come about, are maintained by power relationships, and what the consequences are for those experiencing them.

Patterns of inequality may be seen either as resulting from social divisions or as the visible markers of division. However, as Roberts (2001: 4) has suggested, social division is an all-embracing term. Even when it is used to refer only to class, gender and ethnicity, it places the interaction of the divisions at the centre of research and debate rather than presupposing a simple hierarchy or set of social strata. The idea of social divisions brings greater meaning and structure to the simple patterns of differences. It attempts to include the way in which some core features cover the whole population, contributing to their various senses of identity and working as an interrelated set, without prioritising one division above all others. The way we discuss health in Chapter 14 illustrates this point very clearly.

Thus, while it follows that social identity and our sense of our own distinctiveness are important, this has to be seen in terms of material differences and hierarchies of power, and not simply our 'difference' from a generalised 'other'. This position is incompatible with that of Best (2005) who, drawing heavily on the work of Foucault, is over-concerned with the sense of 'other' in divisions. He argues that social divisions are not material or social realities but exist only as defined by the ideas of the time – the cultural discourses by which we make sense of them. This leads to a rather confused and all-inclusive treatment of a great many social differences as if they were full-scale social divisions.

A less extreme version of the emphasis on difference can be found in the work of O'Brien and Howard (1998: xiii), who argue that the call for inclusion of race, class, gender and other 'differences':

has served to point out the weaknesses in attempts to compare sexism with racism or classism (and other 'isms'). Additive approaches to incorporating race, class and gender fail to comprehend how experiences are qualitatively different from others rather than being simply an additional component.

As ethnographers, they favour the study of how social inequalities and difference are 'performed' in everyday life or, in our terms, how systems of social division are manifested 'on the ground' in social interaction. This places sociological research into situational encounters, rather than at the more macro level adopted by most of the contributors here. While O'Brien and Howard start from this different methodological stance, much of their basic view of divisions, as about hierarchy, has a lot in common with the authors'.

On the other hand, their approach has a quite separate origin, in concerns with affirmative action and the 'celebration of difference' – the attempt to promote acceptance of cultural differences between (mainly) ethnic groups. They find a simplistic reliance on difference unhelpful because it leaves unproblematised the 'what' from which things differ, that is, the normative structures of white middle class male America. Gender, for example, is not just a statement of difference, but one of hierarchy. The celebration of difference, which resonates so directly and strongly in the lives of American students, nonetheless makes those who have 'difference' carry the responsibility for it. This is like blaming the victim for the crime.

The third sociological term which can be confused with social division is the social division of labour, sometimes referred to as 'social differentiation'. 'Social differentiation' is a more specific term, often used to deal with a key difference between 'simple' tribal or agrarian societies and more complex, industrial and contemporary societies. With greater social division of labour in the latter societies, in particular around production and occupations, specialisation and variety of tasks demarcate people from each other and groups from other groups. This formulation, drawing on Durkheim's concerns with social cohesion and his ideas of mechanical and organic solidarity, was particularly attractive among sociologists who were attempting to deal with evident and extensive social inequalities without recourse to class analysis, for example in a US context where 'class' carried the politically charged association of Marxism and anti-American ways.

Social divisions and social cohesion

The account of social life presented in this volume is characterised on the one hand by division, disadvantage, hierarchy, inequality and resistance, and on the other by group or category identity as the basic unit, shaped by a sense of difference from others. The question this poses, and which was noted in passing in Chapter 1, is that, if social life is so fragmented, does it make much sense to think in terms of such a vast conglomeration as 'society'? Indeed, even the extensive divisions like class, gender or ethnicity, that create the categories on which identity is based, could be said to be too complex to form single divisions. If people lead their lives in terms of divisions and categories, each remarkably different from the next, how is collective life possible (Crow 2002)? Why does everything not fly apart and collapse in chaos? On the whole, despite divisions, things do hold together (as the discussion of community in Chapter 15 showed). The simple answer to understanding this conundrum lies in seeing how social divisions interconnect and institutional processes constrain.

In the first place, while human behaviour is not totally determined by structures of relationships and normative assumptions, individuals conduct their unique lives within frameworks of accepted actions. Social divisions are 'sustained by dominant cultural beliefs', so that they are carried in our heads, 'embodied', and become taken for granted. Social divisions also operate through complex, powerful and extensive institutions, that is, through systems of ways of acting in recognised, appropriate ways backed by positive and negative social sanctions.

Our capacity to modify these systems through situational interactions is constrained, not just by what is in our heads or the promise/threat of sanctions, but by the willingness of others to engage on their part in that modification. If they are members of the same category, they are also part of a constraining system that encourages group identification and solidarity, not non-conformity. If they are members of a more advantaged oppositional category, they have a vested interest in preventing the individual from modifying the relationships that give them advantages. The scope for adapting meanings and beliefs, initiating innovatory action and creating change is limited by the willingness of other actors to tolerate and support non-conforming behaviour.

In that sense, social structuration is a process which never starts with a clean sheet of uncommitted other actors. The normative order that is inherited and recreated is certainly not monolithic or uniform, but its component elements and segments are undoubtedly powerful. It is usually easier to go on doing the same thing – not to 'rock the boat'; acceptance of one's lot in a given category is usually the easiest solution.

This does not provide a complete answer, however, because if people are all in fragmented categories, how do the cultural/institutional/interactional processes hold the disparate categories together? Social cohesion is more common than social disorder or total disintegration of a society. Lower-level conflicts of interest are largely kept within bounds, mainly because individuals have multiple memberships of categories. It follows that, unless memberships (or the lines of division) coincide across the social divisions, they do not reinforce one another. For instance, being working class may offer one source of identity and motivation for action, but the members of the working class are also variously black or white, male or female, fit or ill, old or young. These other identities fragment the class identity and they in turn are fragmented by class and all the other identities.

It is also the case that divisions do not manifest themselves either in consistent form (each always the same), or in a uniform 'mixture' (in the same combination of equal importance). For a start, they are not equally 'socially visible'. They may be embodied to varying degrees in physical differences (age, ethnicity, gender or disability) or in less obvious ways (national identity or religion). Small minorities within a division may be excluded from public consciousness by media selectivity or physical isolation. These differences feed back into our senses of identity.

They may manifest themselves in more or less dramatic forms: a social division which takes the main form of a dichotomy is likely to be more obvious than a division with a multiplicity of categories. Taking the main divisions covered in this book and treating each as if it consisted of a dichotomy would offer about 30 possible categories to which individuals could belong. Those categories can logically be combined into a profile that an individual might manifest as a result of their various memberships, giving many thousands of possible profiles. Of course, some profiles are unlikely: to a considerable extent, disadvantage on one division tends to be associated with disadvantage on others, as Anthias (1998: 531) argues with reference to gender, ethnicity and class. However, this is more than balanced numerically by the fact that most of the social divisions exist with more than two categories in each (see, for example, the number of classes in Chapter 2).

Complex multiple memberships blur differences in two ways. First, their complexity reduces the chances of a 'single issue' identity or cause for action emerging. Even when individuals consciously define themselves in specific terms – feminist, black, class warrior, grey panther – their own other memberships still have a part to play. The same is true of those who attempt a dual identity, for example 'black feminist'. The multiplicity of memberships of people in a group mitigates against them all 'moving in the same direction' at once. Whatever the individual may intend, the views of others have to be taken into account and their membership-based agendas contribute to a confusion of perspectives. Complex profiles disguise the underlying divisions.

Multiple memberships bring together individuals in one social context who are disparate in other contexts. Employees may define themselves in class terms, but share national identity with their employers. Conversely, they may use gender or ethnicity as grounds for not acting in class terms, by seeking to exclude or discriminate against women or minority ethnic groups despite their shared membership of the working class. Employers and managers are then able to exploit such differences for their own ends (see, for example, the

Chapter 12 case studies). Major 'fault lines' in society are likely to develop only when social divisions coincide.

These 'overlapping ties' were sharply demonstrated in Gluckman's (1960) classic account of feuding between clans among the Nuer and other African peoples. Drawing on several anthropological studies, he shows first that, even in open conflict, what today we would call 'rules of engagement' apply. Among close kin, fighting with sticks was tolerated, but not the use of spears or knives. The ultimate weapon of burning the granaries and killing the livestock of other tribes was acceptable, but never practised within one's own people. By extension, the capacity for society to fall apart is always reduced by constraints on how conflict is to be managed. Social cohesion is protected by virtue of the continuing recognition that other shared memberships remain valid, even when relationships concerning one division break down.

Second, Gluckman argues that, in practice, this is not a simple matter of cultural norms but an outcome of situational processes. Because people belong to several groups, they have a vested interest in constraining and resolving conflict in any one group. In a simple society based largely on kinship, marriage partners may be chosen from outside the immediate kin group: clans intermarry. If there is a feud between two clans, both those who have 'married in', and their immediate marriage partners have a strong interest in achieving a resolution. This is worked out, in part, in the relationships between partners and the interpersonal pressures that can be brought into play. In this sense, the multiple memberships bind. Individuals become the glue that helps to hold the institutions together, rather than the untidy and uncooperative components that threaten to break them apart.

Even the process of challenging division is in itself a means of releasing tensions. A number of other safety valves – humour, symbolic public events, role-reversal festivals and so on – operate to promote accommodation. At another level, institutional frameworks, such as citizens' rights in law, can offer a means of limiting the full impact of division, exploitation and discrimination. This is not to say that conflict is always contained. Societies do sometimes collapse into open warfare: Northern Ireland in the 1970s, the Balkans twenty years later and Syria at the time of writing (2013) are painful reminders of what happens when the lines of division do coincide, and the urge to compromise is weaker than the pressure to dispute.

Social divisions as a distinctive perspective

It was earlier suggested that a social divisions approach represents a distinctive perspective on society. In part this is evident in its systematic concern with division, inequality and social injustice. However, to appreciate the extent to which this does constitute a particular perspective, it is necessary to reflect briefly on alternative theoretical stances.

Without wishing to engage in a detailed analysis, it can be claimed that sociological theories operate with underlying domain assumptions about the nature of the social world. This point can be illustrated by contrasting the core metaphors that seem to operate in three well-known theoretical perspectives. In the first, that of structural-functionalism (and in particular in the earlier work of Parsons), the image of society is one of coherence, order and integration: humans operate willingly within institutions, whose forms follow naturally from the socially sustaining functions fulfilled by those institutions. Any apparent inequalities or divisions (for example occupational classes or gender) are seen as positively contributing in some way to social cohesion and maintenance. Only those who are psychologically disturbed will disrupt this precise system. The metaphor is Newtonian clockwork, its cogwheels accurately machined and neatly interlocking: a place for each part and each part in its place in a tidy, integrated system.

In contrast, the conception advocated by Marx and Marxian accounts of society presents conflict as endemic, periodically breaking out as revolutionary change. The parts of the system are held in place by the power of the ruling classes, who are able to enforce their wishes on the working class by virtue of their ownership of the means of production and promoting their own ideological interpretations to create false consciousness among the other classes. The routine experience is exploitation, and the 'social' is essentially the 'economic'. Social order, indeed, all social forms can be derived from the economic 'base' of production, and in that sense are a superficial 'superstructure'. The one essential social division of class renders other social divisions mere super-structural inconveniences. The image that can stand for this view of society is a heavy weight, balanced precariously on a coiled spring, or perhaps two animals fighting inside a large but frail bag. Both images convey the idea of two forces in mutual opposition.

We can compare the clock and the struggling bag with the view from the wilder shores of post-modernist social constuctionism. Here the emphasis is on individuals, reflectively selecting a personal identity from a host of possible choices and reconstituting the world through the thoughts and words used to understand experience. The idea of large-scale social processes or structures is an illusion, a product of social science's fevered imagination, of no more value than any other person's opinion. There is no need for 'logical consistency' or 'evidence', since these, too, are artificial constructions. Our social image might be taken either from a New Wave film, with the self-absorbed inmates of an upmarket asylum drifting past each other on a sunlit lawn, or alternatively, particles of dust which float randomly in a beam of light.

A social divisions perspective does not start from the assumption that society depends on neatly integrated and accepted social practices, or an 'over-socialised' view of humanity. Rather it seeks to question the assumptions and normative beliefs that veil division, in contrast to structural-functionalism's acceptance of the status quo. The multiplicity of social divisions which is an essential part of the idea of social division equally contrasts with the narrow Marxian focus on class. On the other hand, in displaying systematic undesirable social inequalities and injustices, the constraining power of institutions and the ordered way in which identities are socially created, social division rejects the hyper-individualism and relativism of post-modernist social constructionism.

One advantage of this perspective is that the components (or subsystems of division) of 'society' do not need to be neatly or tightly connected, or held in some specific relationship to each other. Social order is achieved through the operation of one or more social divisions in specific social settings, rather than through all of them, all of the time, in a fixed relationship to each other (called 'society'). This fluidity is one reason for not adopting the otherwise helpful metaphor of the 'vertical mosaic', so tellingly employed in Porter's (1965) analysis of Canadian society. In taking a more fluid or flexible view of society, the key point is that flexibility operates through divisions as social processes rather than just through individuals. This means the social processes make up a series of constraining practices that do not apply equally or consistently in every context to every individual. Not all aspects of multiple divisions impinge directly on our day-to-day interactions at the same time. Social division as the social injustice suffered by others is easier to accept when much of its multifaceted visibility is largely hidden from us. The metaphor might be a young child's very inexpert attempt to construct a complex multicoloured assemblage of Lego blocks.

Furthermore, as the chapters show, there is a tension within each division between its capacity to constrain social action and the mutability of its assumptions and forms. In terms of how institutions operate at any given point, their constituent roles are not rigid blueprints that precisely, minutely and exactly define social action, but rather rough sketches that can be altered. There is a great deal of 'play', in the engineering sense, in role play. In social situations, we exploit the room to manoeuvre that this 'play' allows us. Social divisions, however well-defined each may seem to be at one level, are part of a conception of society as more messy, untidy and hard to see than in most other accounts. It is *normal* for there to be a conflict of expectations between social divisions.

Nor is there a uniformity of approach in the sociology of social divisions. Among those who have adopted a social divisions perspective or terminology, there are considerable differences in stance: sociologists, like other people, bring to their work their own intellectual and personal baggage. This variety of stances does not however make it impossible to work within a social divisions framework, because there is no need to commit to a single narrow perspective, or to assert that one position is so inherently superior that all others must be worthless. For example, while we prefer not to become as fixated on social class as Reid , there is much of value in his work. Indeed, while he operates 'on the assumption that social class is the most fundamental form of social stratification' (1998: 238) he accepts that other divisions have to be included.

> Put as boldly as possible, being Black, female or elderly and middle class is different from being Black, female or elderly and working class ... This is not to deny the importance of gender, ethnicity and age either objectively or subjectively, or to suggest that changes in class would necessarily end the differences between them.

A similar view can be found in Carling (1991), although he advocates an even narrower Marxian concentration on class.

Conversely, Anthias' (2001) treatment of social division prioritises gender and ethnicity, but nonetheless lists class as the third division. Her highlighting of class, gender and ethnicity (echoed in our Chapters 2, 3, and 4) does reflect our recognition of how these predominate in sociology, but our inclusion of the other divisions lays the emphasis on the advantages of taking a broader view. It is not the intention of this book to claim that one or other division is the most important (although some of our contributors might well wish to make such a case!).

This leaves us with choices about which divisions to select, and how to explain the way they work together in any given social setting, an issue which has come to the fore since the turn of the millennium, particularly in feminist writing. We can see this as a parallel to how the Higher Education curriculum has shifted away from a core focus and single topic modules, like social class, to cover a wider range of subjects, and how sociological interest has moved towards a level of analysis that tries to take account of detail, complexity and variation, rather than major structural issues. Much of the recent literature which has tried to integrate gender, race and class (and other factors) has drawn extensively on the idea that divisions intersect. Although this perspective shares several features with a social divisions approach, 'intersectionality' is in practice a more limited perspective, despite its current popularity in some fields of sociology.

Intersectionality: an evolutionary or a metaphorical dead end?

Intersectionality started life as a simple analogy for how two legal principles could be in conflict when deciding a legal case. The image conjured up was a road junction (or 'intersection' in American parlance) at which traffic converged from two different directions, each legitimate in its own right. It was necessary to take account of both traffic flows, and to have rules to decide which had right of way (Crenshaw 1989: 149). Each stream of traffic represented one legal principle. In an accident between the two streams at the intersection, blame could potentially be attributed to drivers from one or other direction, or both. Applying the analogy to the case of discrimination law, a black woman (accident victim at the intersection) might be found to be subject to gender discrimination (traffic from one direction) or to race discrimination (traffic from the other direction) or both.

In her original formulation, Crenshaw was writing about how the law deals with legal rights and two types of inequality, not about the complexity of a complete society. As often happens, the analogy has got out of hand as attempts were made to develop it. The metaphor now prompts awkward questions about how many roads can lead into the intersection (as when later commentators have introduced new factors into the equation, such as class or sexuality), or what types of vehicle are involved, and if the traffic lights are working, and so on. The way social institutions intersect is obviously a more complicated question than the way two legal principles may be in conflict.

Crenshaw in part recognises this in another analogy, expanding the grounds for discrimination from the original two of race and gender to five, by including class, age and disability visualised as a pyramid in which those on the bottom suffer five discriminations while those at the top are discriminated against in only a single way (ibid.: 151). Her second analogy extends to the five factors, because these feature in legal cases, not because they are the most significant divisions in society or in every social setting. She assumes that each of the variables is discrete: when they intersect, one is added to the other; a model that is sufficient for discussion of legal statutes and how they might work. In law, court decisions are made by deciding which of conflicting positions take precedence in each case. In society, life is not that simple.

Crenshaw's original model was popularised by feminist writers concerned with the way the position of black women – doubly discriminated against – had not been properly addressed by the feminist literature's focus on white women (e.g. Brah and Phoenix 2004). However this concern with the interplay of gender and race inevitably raised several issues. For a start, if we need more than a single factor to explain social inequalities, is there any reason to limit ourselves to introducing only one other? How many factors can be said to interact, and are there any guidelines for including or excluding factors from our account of the intersection? The list of factors present at the intersection has been progressively expanded: for example in addition to race, gender, class, sexuality, and age, Richardson and Monro (2012, 46) talk about 'faith'; 'ability'; and social 'space'. There seems to be no limit to the variables that are said to 'intersect'.

It follows that if a number of factors are intersecting, we also need to decide if they all carry equal weight – are some factors always more important? Should gender and race continue to be treated as the most significant, or should, say, class be given priority, as we saw both Carling and Reid advocate (albeit not from an intersectionist perspective). If some forms of inequality are to be given priority, does that mean that other forms can be explained by, or 'reduced' to, a single factor, or a small set of core factors?

Even if we can agree on how many factors should be included, and whether some are more important, this does not solve the question of how the various dimensions relate to one another. Do they reinforce or add to each other as Crenshaw's pyramid model seems to suggest, are they in conflict as the core intersection analogy implies, or do they create a variety of contradictory combinations? Are the dimensions actually separate or do aspects of one feed into others, so that, when they interact, they produce entirely new situations and identities?

In turn this raises a fourth issue. Do intersection studies compare like with like, or are the comparisons between different types of social phenomena? At one level one may address the situation of individuals, while at another (and more commonly for sociologists) it is groups, social institutions or social processes that are the focus. In the thriving literature on intersection there has been relatively little debate about exactly which level of social phenomenon should be considered. Instead, the literature combines different kinds of social phenomena: identity politics; 'difference'; groups, processes and systems (Choo and Ferree 2010) with little agreement or discussion about which phenomena are most appropriate.

This lack of coherence or clarity has prompted Davis (2008) to note how the ambiguities and imprecisions of intersectionality enabled it to be all things to all people. Despite its inconsistencies, it has become common to describe intersectionality as a 'theory' or a theoretical approach. Indeed, intersectionality has become such a fashionable way of writing not only about gender and race, but also other concerns, that it has been described as the outstanding analytical perspective produced by feminism, and has acquired the status of a 'buzzword' (McCall 2005; Nash 2008; Davis 2008).

Social division and intersectionality

The question of how many intersections there can be is of course not unique to an intersectional approach. The same question may be asked about social divisions. Both approaches (a term to be preferred to the over-ambitious claim that intersectionality is a 'social theory') do share the defect that there are no absolute grounds for limiting the number of factors or divisions that can be brought into play. In this book we report on a range of divisions, but that does not entirely exhaust possibilities: we might have included chapters on education, kinship or geographical/regional locations. There are no absolute rules to determine how many make up any study. For example, Gibbon (2000) explores health by examining gender, class, ethnicity and place community while Callaghan (1998) illuminates women's experiences by showing how gender, class and neighbourhood interact. Ifekwunigwe (1999) focuses on the capacity of divisions to offer alternative statuses and identities, but concentrates on gender, sexuality and nationality, whereas Marcus and Manicom (2000) combine class, ethnicity and gender with location and wealth in researching children's experiences in a new education system.

A social division perspective does not entirely escape these criticisms of intersectionality. However, rather than adding divisions in an ad hoc way, depending on the particular problem of individual pieces of research, it starts with an open mind on the total number of divisions and no assumptions about which will be most evident in a given situation. Social division is therefore a more adaptable perspective because, by offering a formal definition of what the interacting factors (i.e. social divisions) actually are, it has at least an outline framework for thinking about the problem of what is involved in intersection. By specifying community and health in earlier chapters as divisions in their own right, as well as arenas in which other social divisions interplay, we see the possibility of this more flexible, but still structured alternative approach.

Second, despite assuming a legitimate multiplicity of divisions, a social division approach does not assume a priori any greater salience for any division in any given social situation. It does not insist on prioritising gender and race, nor does it arbitrarily omit factors that happen to interest the writers' own topic of preoccupation. It is true that as we have acknowledged, class, gender and ethnicity do occupy a de facto long-term centrality in sociological analysis. However, that is neither to commit to a simple reproduction of mainstream traditions, nor to evaluate the 'big three' as distinctive in kind or to guarantee them a position of intellectual or moral primacy.

If we do not assert a priori that one division/factor is going to be dominant, we need techniques for deciding between possible effects. For example Bonney (2007), in commenting on an earlier version of *Social Division*, poses the question of how we are to distinguish between divisions when they interplay. He argues for quantitative methods: multivariate analysis provides a means of discriminating between class and gender as effects in employment. Iganski and Payne (1996, 1999) report how their data on occupational class differences among ethnic groups actually led them to see that, contrary to their expectations, gender had a stronger predictive power than ethnic group affiliation. Because the social divisions perspective does not commit to prior assumptions about dominance, it offers the researcher more freedom for inductive analysis.

We can contrast this with the original formulation of intersectionality which neither offered a general framework nor gave consideration to what might be the other factors beyond gender and race. Its initial contribution was to provide feminists with an explanation which would help them escape from the trap of a mono-causal analysis based narrowly on gender, and it is in that context that many of its adherents have operated. It therefore pointed its followers in the direction of prioritising gender and race over other divisions (although see Anthias and Yuval-Davis 1983 for the inclusion of social class) for pragmatic and ideological, as much as sociological, reasons. Consequently, many empirical studies of intersection have concentrated on race and gender (Valentine et al. 2010). This focus has tended to produce a deceptively attractive picture of inequalities cumulating and reinforcing each other, inequalities which can then be rejected by a consensus of 'progressive' commentators because naturally 'we are all against racism, sexism, ageism, and so on'.

Again, while a social divisions perspective is also antagonistic to inequality, it does not start from the belief that dividing factors necessarily all coincide, with all the Good Guys on one side of the barricade, and the Bad Guys on the other. Our core counter-assumption is that cross-cutting memberships of divisional categories also normally prevent fission along a common fault line. Situations of disadvantage do not all line up neatly in one underlying meta-structure. This in turn allows social divisions to come together in a variety of different combinations, rather than always operating in unison.

Crenshaw's image of a pyramid suggests that inequalities can be added together, but while two variables do sometimes work in this way, their interaction may produce dissonance or indeed create something new. In quantitative sociology, this is referred to as the difference between main, additive and multiplicative effects, and helps to keep the original variables in play along with the interactions. Because we are talking about complex and extensive social processes, we need both to see the factors on their own (because we find it easiest to write or think about only one issue at a time) as well as how these processes work in conjunction. They may just add together, but equally their institutional and cultural forms may be structured in similar ways and work more systematically in a combined fashion, as Anthias and Yuval-Davis (1983) argue. Anthias (1998: 531–2) suggests two possible outcomes: cross-cutting systems of domination may articulate by being 'mutually reinforcing' – 'social divisions articulate to produce a coherent set of practices of subordination' – or may give rise to 'contradictory locations', where individuals dominate within one division but are subordinate in another.

Alternatively, combinations of divisions may take entirely new forms of social inequality. Thus while we can analytically perceive class, race, gender and so on as separate and discrete, in ordinary social life each is directly involved with the others, helping to formulate and shape them. We are not talking here about boundary lines coinciding, but rather that the mechanics of categorisation and identification result in a 'fuzzy' overlap of dividing processes. Each factor contributes to how we construct and construe the others, although this does not extend to meaning that all divisions can be reduced to a single dominant division which 'explains everything else'. Thus as noted earlier, we do not share the view of Carling, or Reid, that class ultimately and always takes precedence.

Finally we can ask if social division studies are any improvement on intersectionality in terms of identifying what types of phenomena can be drawn into the analysis. Here the answer is less clear. The social division approach leaves open the question of exactly which social phenomena make up a division, although by using a formal definition as earlier in this chapter, it imposes some limitation on what can be included. By examining life chances and lifestyles, we can build empirical descriptions of social divisions. This takes us into consideration of the form and operation of social institutions, the cultural beliefs that sustain them, and how this plays out in our social existence. In turn, to understand these we need to include the dynamics of social interactions and group relationships, and the social processes that reproduce them. This breadth of treatment means that there is no simple answer to the question of what we should study: nothing is ruled out.

Of course, at one level neither an intersectional nor a social divisions approach is world-shattering. To argue that we should get away from monocausal explanations is a fairly mundane observation. Equally, it is obvious that we cannot study all divisions in one take. In practice we can only discuss complexity in a serial way (for example, as in Chapters 14 and 15) and normally limit ourselves to discussing a sub-set of all possible divisions, which still leaves analysts able to concentrate on their own preferred main topic of interest, rather taking the broader view.

The significance of social division

The study of divisions is not simply a means of examining a random selection of segments of society. Its coherence lies in the notions of hierarchy, social inequality and social injustice that such a study entails. The way the divisions come together is a difficult sociological problem that we may not have entirely resolved, but we have tried to show that worse errors are likely if one takes the crude perspective that prioritises a single social division. This latter approach may help to simplify but it is unlikely to generate an adequate analysis. If we want an adequate analysis of specific social situations, it is the range of social divisions which provides perspective and structure.

Social divisions are not just about the intellectual problems of how sociology conceives of society, but also about how we research and make sense of more concrete events and local processes. Equally, because they share the idea of social inequality, they connect academic considerations with our ordinary concerns as citizens about the way the world we live in operates. Because divisions are persistent, the social injustices they entail are a constant source of frustration and anger for ordinary people. Division is not itself pathological; divisions are the normal state of society. It is the *persistence* of their associated disadvantages that is the problem, with extremely unequal access to the desirable things in life continually impinging on the same categories of people. Only by the integrated analysis of social divisions can we understand, let alone change, the nature of contemporary society and the lives of our fellow citizens.

Discussion Questions

1. Are some social divisions more important than others?
2. Locate your own position on each of the social divisions described in this book: are there any other divisions that you think might be usefully included?
3. Contrast the meanings of 'social inequality', 'social differentiation' and 'social division'.
4. Are social divisions 'pathological'?
5. What is the importance of cross-cutting ties and overlapping memberships?
6. Is social division just another term for what post-modernists call 'difference' and 'other'?
7. Can social divisions be changed?

Bibliography

Abbott, P. and Ackers, L. (1997) 'Women and Employment'. In Spybey, T. (ed.) *Britain in Europe*. London: Routledge.

Abbott, P. and Sapsford, R. (1987) *Women and Social Class*. London: Tavistock.

Abbott, P. and Sapsford, R. (1988) *Community Care for Mentally Handicapped Children*. Milton Keynes: Open University Press.

Abbott, P. and Tyler, M. (1995) 'Ethnic variations in the female labour force: a research note'. *British Journal of Sociology*, **46**, 3: 339–53.

Abbott, P. and Wallace, C. (1992) *The Family and the New Right*. London: Pluto.

Abbott, P. and Wallace, C. (2011) *Work and Care: Key Findings and Policy Recommendations from European Research on Reconciling Work and Care for Parents with Dependent Children*. Aberdeen: University of Aberdeen http://workcaresynergies.eu/ (accessed 7 April 2012).

Abbott, P., Wallace, C. and Tyler M (2005) *An Introduction to Sociology: Feminist Perspectives* (3rd edn). London: Routledge.

Abel-Smith, B. and Townsend, P. (1965) *The Poor and the Poorest*, Occasional Papers on Social Administration, 17. London: G. Bell & Sons.

Adonis, A. and Pollard, S. (1997) *A Class Act*. London: Hamish Hamilton.

AgeUK (2009) *One Voice: Shaping Our Aging Society*. www.ageuk.org.uk/documents/en-gb/for-professionals/research/one%20voice%20%282009%29_pro.pdf?dtrk=true (accessed 13 March 2012).

AgeUK (2011) *A Snapshot of Ageism in the UK and across Europe*. www.ageuk.org.uk/Documents/EN-GB/ID10180%20Snapshot%20of%20Ageism%20in%20Europe.pdf?dtrk=true (accessed 08 March 2012).

Agustín, L. (2007) *Sex at the Margins: Migration, Labour Markets and the Rescue Industry*. London: Zed Books.

Albrow, M. (1994) 'Skills and capacities in the sociology curriculum'. In Payne, G. and Cross, M. (eds) *Sociology in Action*. London: Macmillan.

Alcock, P. (2006) *Understanding Poverty* (3rd edn). Basingstoke: Palgrave Macmillan.

Aldridge, A. (2012) *Religion in the Contemporary World: A Sociological Introduction* (3rd edn). Cambridge: Polity Press.

Alexander, P. (1988) 'Prostitution: a difficult issue for feminists'. In Delacoste, F. and Alexander, P. (eds) *Sex Work*. London: Virago.

Allatt, P. and Yeandle, S. (1992) *Youth Unemployment and the Family*. London: Routledge.

Allen, C. and Nielsen, J.S. (2002) *Summary Report on Islamophobia in the EU after 11 September 2001*. Vienna: European Monitoring Centre on Racism and Xenophobia.

Allen, L. (2005) *Sexual Subjects: Young People, Sexuality and Education*. Basingstoke: Palgrave Macmillan.

Allen, L. (2011) *Young People and Sexuality Education: Rethinking Key Debates*. Basingstoke: Palgrave Macmillan.

American Psychological Association (APA) (2007) *Report of the APA Task Force on the Sexualization of Girls*. www.apa.org/pi/wpo/sexualization.html (accessed 29 April 2012).

Anderson, B. (1996) 'Introduction'. In Balakrishnan, G. (ed.) *Mapping the Nation*. London: Verso Books.

Anderson, G. (1976) *Victorian Clerks*. Manchester: Manchester University Press.

Anderson, P. (1991) *Imagined Communities*. London: Verso.

Ansari, H. (2004) *'The Infidel Within': Muslims in Britain since 1800*. London: Hurst.

Anthias, F. (1998) 'Rethinking Social Divisions'. *Sociological Review*, **46**, 3: 505–35.

Anthias, F. (2001) 'The concept of "social divisions" and theorising social stratification'. *Sociology*, **35**, 4: 835-54.

Anthias, F. andYuval-Davis, N. *(*1983*)* 'Contextualizing feminism: gender, ethnic and class divisions'. *Feminist Review*, **15**: 62–75.

Anthias, F. and Yuval-Davis, N. (1992) *Racialized Boundaries: Race, Nation, Gender, Colour and Class and the Anti-racist Struggle*. London: Routledge.

Arber, S. (1990) 'Opening the '"black box": inequalities in women's health'. In Abbott, P. and Payne, G. (eds) *New Directions in the Sociology of Health*. London: Falmer Press.

Arber, S. (2006) 'Gender and later life: change, choice and constraints', in Vincent, J.A., Phillipson, C.R. and Downs, M. (eds) *The Futures of Old Age*. London: Sage.

Arber, S. and Ginn, J. (1991) *Gender and Later Life: A Sociological Analysis of Resources and Constraints*. London: Sage.

Arber, S. and Ginn, J. (1995) *Connecting Gender and Ageing*. Buckingham: Open University Press.

Arber S. and Ginn, J. (2004) 'Ageing and gender: diversity and change'. In Summerfield, C. and Baab, P. (eds) *Social Trends 2004 Edition, No.34*, ONS, London: The Stationery Office.

Archard, D. (1993) *Children, Rights and Childhood*. London: Routledge.

Arensberg, C. and Kimball, S. (1940) *Family and Community in Ireland*. Gloucester, MA: Peter Smith.

Ariès, P. (1962) *Centuries of Childhood*. London: Jonathan Cape.

Armstrong, D. (1994) *Outline of Sociology as Applied to Medicine*. London: Butterworth-Heinemann.

Askham, J., Henshaw, L. and Tarpey, M. (1993) 'Policies and perceptions of identity: service needs of elderly people from black and minority ethnic backgrounds'. In Arber, S. and Evandrou, M. (eds) *Ageing, Independence and the Life Course*. London: Jessica Kingsley.

Atkinson, A. (1987) 'On the measurement of poverty'. *Econometrica* **55**(4): 749–64.

Atkinson, A. (1998) *Poverty in Europe*. Oxford: Blackwell.

Babones, S. and Vonada, D. (2009), 'Trade globalization and national income inequality. Are they related? *Journal of Sociology*, **45**, 5: 5–30.

Baggott, R. (2000). *Public Health: Policy and Politics*. Basingstoke: Palgrave Macmillan.

Baggott, R. (2004). *Health and Health Care in Britain* (3rd edn). Basingstoke: Palgrave Macmillan

Baggott, R. (2012). 'Policy success and public health: the case of public health in England'. *Journal of Social Policy*, **41**, 2: 391–408.

Bailey, J. (1998) 'In front of the Arras: some new introductions'. *Sociology*, **31**(1): 203–9

Bailey, R. (2011) *Letting Children be Children – Report of an Independent Review of the Commercialisation and Sexualisation of Childhood*. London: Department for Education. https://www.education.gov.uk/publications/standard/publicationDetail/Page1/CM%208078 (accessed 29 April 2012).

Banks, J. and Smith, S. (2006) 'Retirement in the UK', *Oxford Review of Economic Policy*, **22** (1): 40–56

Banton, M. (1967) *Race Relations*, London: Tavistock.

Banton, M. (1977) *The Idea of Race*, London: Tavistock.

Banton, M. (1987) *Racial Theories*, Cambridge: Cambridge University Press.

Banton, M. (1988) *Racial Consciousness*, London: Longman.

Banton, M. and Harwood, J. (1975) *The Race Concept*, Newton Abbot: David & Charles.

Barber, B. (1995) *Jihad vs McWorld*. New York: Ballantine.

Barberis, P. (1996) *The Elite of the Elite: Permanent Secretaries in the British Higher Civil Service*. Aldershot: Dartmouth.

Barnes, B. (1995) *The Elements of Social Theory*. London: UCL Press.

Barnes, C. (1990) *Disabled People in Britain and Discrimination: A Case for Anti-Discrimination Legislation*. London: Hurst & Company.

Barnes, C. and Smith, K. (2010) 'No longer deserving?'. *Critical Public Health*, **20**(1): 71–83

Barnes, C., Mercer, G. and Shakespeare, T. (1999) *Exploring Disability: A Sociological Introduction*. Cambridge: Polity.

Barnett, A. (1997) *This Time: Our Constitutional Revolution*. London: Vintage.

Barrett, M. and Phillips, A. (1992) *Destabilizing Theory: Contemporary Feminist Debates*. Cambridge: Polity.

Barth, F. (ed.) (1969) *Ethnic Groups and Boundaries*. Bergen: Universitetsforlaget.

Bartkey, S.L. (1990) *Femininity and Domination: Studies in the Phenomenology of Oppression*. London: Routledge.

Barton, L. (ed.) (1996) *Disability and Society*. Harlow: Longman.

Bauman, Z. (1990) *Thinking Sociologically*. Oxford: Basil Blackwell.

Bauman, Z. (1998) 'On glocalization. Or globalization for some, localization for some others.' *Thesis Eleven*, **54**(1): 37–49.

Bauman, Z. (2001a) *Community: Seeking Safety in an Insecure World*. Cambridge: Polity.

Bauman, Z. (2001b) *The Individualized Society*. Cambridge: Polity Press.

Bauman, Z. (2004) *Identity*. Cambridge: Polity.

Bauman, Z. (2009) 'Identity in a globalizing world'. In Elliott, A. and du Gay, P. (eds) *Identity in Question*. London: Sage.

Baumann, G. (1996) *Contesting Culture*. Cambridge: Cambridge University Press.

BBC (2012) *Incapacity Tests reject 71% of Claimants*, www.bbc.co.uk/news/business-17379564 (accessed 30 April 2012).

Bechhofer, F. and McCrone, D. (eds) (2009) *National Identity, Nationalism and Constitutional Change*. Basingstoke: Palgrave Macmillan.

Beck, U. (1992) *Risk Society: Towards a New Modernity.* London: Sage.

Beck, U. (1998) 'Politics of risk society'. In Franklin, J. (ed.) *The Politics of Risk Society.* Cambridge: Polity Press.

Beck, U. (2002) *What is Globalization?* Cambridge: Polity Press.

Beck, U. and Beck-Gernsheim, E. (1995) *The Normal Chaos of Love.* Cambridge: Polity Press.

Beck, U. and Beck-Gernsheim, E. (2002) *Individualization: Institutionalized Individualism and its Social and Political Consequences.* London: Sage.

Beckford, J.A. (1989) *Religion and Advanced Industrial Society.* London: Unwin Hyman.

Beckford, J.A. (1999) 'The management of religious diversity in England and Wales with special reference to prison chaplaincy'. *MOST Journal on Multicultural Societies,* 1(2).

Beckford, J.A. (2003) *Social Theory and Religion.* Cambridge: Cambridge University Press.

Beckford, J.A. and Gilliat, S. (1998) *Religion in Prison: Equal Rites in a Multi-Faith Society.* Cambridge: Cambridge University Press.

Beck-Gernsheim, E. (1996) 'Life as a planning project'. In Lash, S., Szerszynski, B. and Wynne, B. (eds) *Risk, Environment and Modernity: Towards a New Ecology.* London: Sage.

Bell, C. and Newby, H. (1971) *Community Studies.* London: George Allen & Unwin.

Bell, D. (1973) *The Coming of Post-Industrial Society.* New York: Basic Books.

Bengston, V. (1996) 'Continuities and discontinuities in intergenerational relationships over time'. In Bengston, V. (ed.) *Adulthood and Aging: Research on Continuities and Discontinuities.* New York: Springer Publishing Company.

Benzeval, M., Judge, K. and Whitehead, M. (eds) (1995) *Tackling Inequalities in Health.* London: Kings Fund.

Berger, P.L. (1967) *The Sacred Canopy: Elements of a Sociological Theory of Religion.* New York: Doubleday.

Berkman, L. and Breslow, L. (1983) *Health and Ways of Living: the Almeda County Study.* Oxford: Oxford University Press.

Berlin, G., Furstenberg, F. Jr. and Waters, M. (2010) 'Introducing the issue'. *The Future of Children,* **20**(1):.3–18.

Bernardi, B. (1985) *Age Class Systems: Social Institutions and Polities Based on Age.* Cambridge: Cambridge University Press.

Berthoud, R. (1997) 'Income and living standards'. In Modood, T. and Berthoud, R. et al. (eds) *Ethnic Minorities in Britain.* London: Policy Studies Institute.

Berthoud, R. (1998) *The Incomes of Ethnic Minorities.* ISER Report 98-1, Colchester: University of Essex, Institute for Social and Economic Research.

Berthoud, R. (2000) 'Ethnic employment penalties in Britain'. *Journal of Ethnic and Migration Studies,* **26**(3): 389–416.

Berthoud, R., Bryan, M. and Bardasi, E. (2004) *The Dynamics of Deprivation: The Relationship between Income and Material Deprivation over Time.* DWP Research Report No. 219. Leeds: Corporate Document Services.

Berthoud, R., Lakey, J. and McKay, S. (1993) *The Economic Problems of Disabled People.* London: Policy Studies Institute.

Best, S. (2005) *Understanding Social Divisions.* London: Sage.

Blackaby, D., Leslie, D., Murphy, P. and O'Leary, N. (2002) 'White/ethnic minority earnings and employment differentials in Britain: evidence from the LFS'. *Oxford Economic Papers* **54**.

Blackburn, R. (2002) *Banking on Death.* London: Verso.

Blackburn, R. and Prandy, K. (1997) 'The reproduction of social inequality'. *Sociology,* **31**(3): 491–509.

Blaikie, A. (1999) *Ageing and Popular Culture.* Cambridge: Cambridge University Press.

Blair, T. (1999) 'Beveridge revisited: A welfare state for the 21st century'. In Walker. R. (ed.) *Ending Child Poverty: Popular Welfare for the 21st Century?* Bristol: The Policy Press.

Blakemore, K. and Boneham, M. (1994) *Age, Race and Ethnicity.* Oxford: Oxford University Press.

Blaxter, M. (1990) *Health and Lifestyles.* London: Routledge.

Blaxter, M and Paterson, E. (1982) *Mothers and Daughters.* London: Heinemann.

Bloch, A. and Solomos, J. (eds.) (2009) *Race and Ethnicity in the 21st Century,* Basingstoke: Palgrave Macmillan.

Bloor, M. (1976) 'Professional autonomy and client exclusion'. In Wadsworth, M. and Robinson, D. (eds) *Studies in Everyday Medical Life.* London: Martin Robertson.

Boal, F., Keane, M. and Livingstone, D. (1997) *Them and Us: Attitudinal Variation among Churchgoers in Belfast.* Belfast: Institute of Irish Studies.

Bond, M. (2004) 'Social influences on corporate political donations in Britain'. *British Journal of Sociology,* **55**(1): 33–78.

Bonney, N. (2007) 'Gender, employment and social class'. *Work, Employment and Society,* **21**(1): 143–55.

Booth, C. (1901–2) *Life and Labour of the People of London,* 17 volumes. London: Macmillan.

Bottomore, T. (1993) *Elites and Society* (2nd edn). London: Penguin.

Bourdelais, P. (1998) 'The ageing of the population: relevant question or obsolete notion?'. In Johnson, P. and Thane, P. (eds) *Old Age from Antiquity to Post-modernity.* London: Routledge.

Bourdieu, P. (1984) *Distinction: a Social Critique of the Judgement of Taste.* Trans. R. Nice. London: Routledge & Kegan Paul.

Bourdieu, P. ([1996]2010). 'The myth of "globalization" and the European welfare state'. In Bourdieu, P., *Sociology is a Martial Art: Political Writings by Pierre Bourdieu.* New York: The New Press.

Bourdillon, M., Levison, D., Myers, W. and White, B. (2010) *Rights and Wrongs of Children's Work.* Piscataway NJ: Rutgers University Press.

Bowling, A. (1997) *Measuring Health* (2nd edin). Buckingham: Open University Press.

Bowyer, S. et al. (2009). 'Shopping for food: lessons from a London borough'. *British Food Journal,* **111**(4–5): 452–74.

Bradley, H. (1989) *Men's Work, Women's Work.* Cambridge: Polity.

Bradley, H. (1996) *Fractured Identities: Changing Patterns of Inequality.* Cambridge: Polity.

Bradshaw, J. (ed.) (1993) *Budget Standards for the United Kingdom*. Aldershot: Avebury.

Brah, A. and Phoenix, A. (2004) 'Aint I a woman? Revisiting intersectionality'. *Journal of International Women's Studies*, 5(3): 75–86.

Braham, P. and Janes, L. (2002) *Social Differences and Divisions*. Oxford: Blackwell.

Brannen, J. (1995) 'Young people and their contribution to household work'. *Sociology*, 29(2): 317–38.

Braungart, R. and Braungart, M. (1986) 'Life-course and generational politics'. *Annual Review of Sociology*, 12: 205–31.

Braverman, H. (1974) *Labor and Monopoly Capitalism*. New York: Monthly Review Press.

Breen, R. (1998) *Self Interest, Group Interest and Ethnic Identity*. Florence: Department of Political and Social Sciences, European University Institute (unpublished paper).

Brewer, J. and Higgins, G. (1999) 'Understanding anti-Catholicism in Northern Ireland'. *Sociology* 33(2): 235–55.

British Isles Network of Congenital Anomaly Registers (BINOCAR) (2010). *Congenital Anomaly Statistics 2009*: England and Wales. London: BINOCAR.

British Medical Association (BMA) (1995) *Inequalities in Health*. BMA Occasional Paper. London: BMA.

Brody, H. (1973) *Inishkillane*. London: Allen Lane.

Brown, B., Burman, M. and Jamieson, L. (1993) *Sex Crimes on Trial: The Use of Sexual Evidence in Scottish Courts*. Edinburgh: Edinburgh University Press.

Brown, C. (1984) *Black and White Britain: The Third PSI Survey*. Aldershot: Gower.

Brown, C. and Gay, P. (1985) *Racial Discrimination: 17 Years After the Act*. London: Policy Studies Institute.

Brown, M. (1995) 'Naming and framing: the social construction of diagnosis and illness'. *Journal of Health and Social Behaviour*, 36 (extra issue): 34–52.

Brubaker, R. (1992) *Citizenship and Nationhood in France and Germany*. Cambridge, MA: Harvard University Press.

Bruce, S. (1986) *God Save Ulster: The Religion and Politics of Paisleyism*. Oxford: Clarendon Press.

Bruce, S. (1996) *Religion in the Modern World: From Cathedrals to Cults*. Oxford: Oxford University Press.

Bruce, S. (2002) *God is Dead: Secularization in the West*. Oxford: Blackwell.

Brunt, L. (2001) 'Into the community'. In Atkinson, P., Coffey, A., Delamont, S., Lofland, J. and Lofland, L. (eds) *Handbook Of Ethnography*. London: Sage.

Buckingham, D. (2000) *After the Death of Childhood: Growing up in the Age of Electronic Media*. Cambridge: Polity

Bühlmann, F. (2010) 'Routes into the British service class: feeder logics according to gender and occupational groups'. *Sociology*, 44(2): 195–212.

Bulmer, M. (ed.) (1975) *Working Class Images of Society*. London: Routledge & Kegan Paul.

Burgess, A. (1990) 'Co-education – the disadvantage for schoolgirls'. *Gender and Education*, 2: 91–6.

Burkitt, I. (1991) *Social Selves: Theories of the Social Formation of Personality*. London: Sage.

Burnham, J. (1941) *The Managerial Revolution: What is Happening in the World.* New York: John Day.

Burnham, J. (1943) *The Machiavellians: Defenders of Freedom.* Chicago: Henry Regnery.

Bury, M. (1997) *Health and Illness in a Changing Society.* London: Routledge.

Bury, M. (2004) 'Researching patient/professional interactions'. *Journal of Health Services Research and Policy,* **9**(1): 48–54.

Bury, M. (2005) *Health and Illness.* Cambridge: Polity Press.

Business in the Community (2010) *Race and the Professions: Aspiration and Frustration,* www.bitc.org.uk/workplace/diversity_and_inclusion/race/aspfrust.html (accessed 7 October 2010)

Buston, K., Wight, D. and Scott, S. (2001) 'Difficulty and diversity: the context and practice of sex education'. *British Journal of Sociology of Education,* **22**(3): 353–68.

Butler, J. (1990) *Gender Trouble: Feminism and the Subversion of Identity.* New York: Routledge.

Butler, J. (1993) *Bodies That Matter: On The Discursive Limits of 'Sex'.* London: Routledge.

Butler, J. (1997) 'Merely cultural'. *Social Text,* **52/53**: 265–77.

Butler, T. and Robson, G. (2003) *London Calling: The Middle Classes and the Re-Making of Inner London.* Oxford: Berg.

Bytheway, W. (1995) *Ageism.* Buckingham: Open University Press.

Cabinet Office (2004) *Work, Stress Health: the Whitehall II study.* London: Cabinet Office, Corporate Development Division/Council of Civil Service Unions.

Caine, N. (1997) 'Give Wives a Stake in Pensions'. *Sunday Times,* 17 October.

Calhoun, C. (1994) 'Social theory and the politics of identity'. In Calhoun, C. (ed.) *Social Theory and the Politics of Identity.* Maldon, MA: Blackwell.

Callaghan, G. (2000) 'The Interaction of Gender, Class and Place in Women's Experience'. *Sociological Research Online,* **3**(3). www.socresonline.org.uk/3/3/8.html

Callan, T., Nolan, B. and Whelan, C. (1993) 'Resources, deprivation and the measurement of poverty'. *Journal of Social Policy,* **22**: 141–72.

Calnan, M. (1987) *Health and Illness: The Lay Perspective.* London: Tavistock.

Cameron, E. and Bernardes, J. (1998) 'Gender and disadvantage in health: men's health for a change'. In Bartley, M., Blane, D. and Davey Smith, G. (eds) *The Sociology of Health Inequalities.* Oxford: Blackwell.

Cannadine, D. (1998) *Class In Britain.* New Haven: Yale University Press.

Carling, A. (1991) *Social Division.* London: Verso.

Carr-Hill, R. (1990) 'The measurement of inequalities in health'. *Social Science and Medicine,* **31**(3): 393–404.

Cartwright, A. and O'Brien, J. (1976) 'Social class, variations in health care and the nature of general practitioner consultations'. In Stacey, M. (ed.) *The Sociology of the NHS.* Sociological Review Monograph No. 22. Keele: University of Keele.

Castells, M. (1996) *The Rise of Network Society.* Oxford: Blackwell.

Castells, M. (1997) *The Power of Identity.* Oxford: Blackwell.

Chaney, J. (1981) *Social Networks and Job Information: The situation of Women who Return to Work.* Report presented to the Equal Opportunities Commission. London: Equal Opportunities Commission.

Charles, N., Davies, C. and Harris, C. (2008) *Families in Transition: Social Change, Family Formation and Kin Relations*. Bristol: Policy Press.

Chauvel, L. (1999) 'Classes et générations: l'insuffisance des hypothèses de la théorie de la fin des classes sociales'. *Actuel Marx*, **26**: 37–52.

China Times (2011) 'Vietnam takes China's place as top Nike producer'. *China Times*, 1 July 2011. www.wantchinatimes.com/news-subclass-cnt. aspx?id=20110701000011&cid=1102 (accessed 9 July 2013).

Choo, H. and Ferree, M. (2010) 'Practicing intersectionality is sociological research'. *Sociological Theory*, **28**(2): 129–49.

Clark, C. (1940) *The Conditions of Economic Progress*. London: Macmillan.

Clifford, J. (1992) 'Travelling cultures'. In Grossberg, L., Nelson, C. and Treichler, P. (eds) *Cultural Studies*. London: Routledge.

Clift, D. and Fielding, D. (1991) *A Survey of Management Morale in the 90s*. London: Institute of Management.

CNN (2012) 'Why Apple will never bring manufacturing jobs back to the US', 18 October 2012. http://edition.cnn.com/2012/10/18/opinion/prestowitz-debate-apple (accessed 9 July 2013).

Cockburn, C. (1983) *Brothers: Male Dominance and Technological Change*. London: Pluto Press.

Cockburn, C. (1991) *In the Way of Women: Men's Resistance to Sex Equality in Organisations*. London: Macmillan.

Cockburn, C. and Ormrod, S. (1993) *Gender and Technology in the Making*. London: Sage.

Cohen, A. (1985) *The Symbolic Construction of Community*. London: Tavistock.

Cohen, A. (1987) *Whalsay*. Manchester: Manchester University Press.

Cohen, A. (ed.) (1982) *Belonging*. Manchester: Manchester University Press.

Cohen, M. (1998) 'A habit of healthy idleness: boys' underachievement in historical perception?'. In Epstein, D., Elwood, J., Hey, V. and Maw, J. (eds) *Failing Boys: Issues in Gender and Achievement*. Milton Keynes: Open University Press.

Cohen, R. (1994) *Frontiers of Identity: the British and Others*. London: Longman.

Cohen, R., Coxall, J., Craig, G. and Sadiq-Sangster, A. (1992) *Hardship Britain*. London: CPAG/FSU.

Cole, T. (1992) *The Journey of Life: A Cultural History of Ageing in America*. Cambridge: Cambridge University Press.

Colley, L. (1992) *Britons: Forging the Nation, 1707–1837*. New Haven: Yale University Press.

Collison, P. (1963) *The Cutteslowe Walls*. London: Faber & Faber.

Comfort, A. (1977) A *Good Age*. London: Mitchell Beazley Publishers Ltd.

Connor, W. (1994) *Ethnonationalism: the Quest for Understanding*. New Jersey: Princeton University Press.

Conrad, P. and Barker, K. (2010). 'The social construction of illness'. *Journal of Health and Social Behaviour* **51**(1), suppl.: 567–79.

Cook, D. (2000a) 'The rise of "the toddler" as subject and as merchandising category in the 1930s'. In Gottdiener, M. (ed.) *New Forms of Consumption: Consumers, Culture and Commodification*. Oxford: Rowman & Littlefield.

Cook, D. (2000b) 'The other "child study": figuring children as consumers in market research 1910s–1990s'. *Sociological Quarterly* **41**(3): 487–507.

Cooper, D. (1995) *Power in Struggle: Feminism, Sexuality and the State.* Buckingham: Open University Press.

Cowie, J. (1999) *Capital Moves: RCA's 70-Year Quest for Cheap Labor.* Ithaca, Cornell University Press.

Cracknell, R. (2012) *Women in Public Life, the Professions and the Boardroom.* SN/SG/5170 House of Commons Library.

Craig, G., Mayo, M., Popple, K., Shaw, M. and Taylor, M. (eds) (2011) *The Community Development Reader: History, Themes and Issues.* Bristol: Policy Press.

Crenshaw, K. (1989) 'Demarginalizing the intersection of race and sex: a black feminist critique of antidiscrimination doctrine, feminist theory and antiracist politics'. *University of Chicago Legal Forum* 139–67. Reprinted in Kairys, D. (ed.) (1990) *The Politics of Law: A Progressive Critique* (2nd edn). New York: Pantheon: 195-217.

Crompton, R. (1998/2008) *Class and Stratification: An Introduction to Current Debates* (2nd /3rd edn). Cambridge: Polity.

Crompton, R. and Le Feuvre, N. (1996) 'Paid employment and the changing system of gender relations: a cross national comparison'. *Sociology,* **50**(3): 427–45.

Crompton, R. and Mann, M. (1986) *Gender and Stratification.* Cambridge: Polity Press.

Crone, S. (2011) '*Are public school boys still running Britain?*'. Democratic Audit. www.democraticaudit.com/are-public-school-boys-still-running-britain (accessed 5 May 2012).

Crossick, G. (1977) 'The emergence of the lower middle class in Britain'. In Crossick, G.(ed.) *The Lower Middle Class in Britain, 1870–1914.* London: Croom Helm.

Crow, G. (2002) *Social Solidarities: Theories, Identities And Social Change.* Buckingham: Open University Press.

Crow, G. and Allan, G. (1994) *Community Life.* Hemel Hempstead: Harvester Wheatsheaf.

Crow, G. and Allan, G. (1995) 'Community types, community typologies and community time'. *Time and Society,* **4**(2): 147–66.

Crow, G. and Maclean, C. (2004) 'Families and local communities'. In Scott, J., Treas, J. and Richards, M. (eds) *The Blackwell Companion to the Sociology Of Families.* Oxford: Blackwell.

Crow, G., Allan, G. and Summers, M. (2001) 'Changing perspectives on the insider/outsider distinction in community sociology'. *Community, Work and Family,* **4**: 29–48.

Curtice, J. (1990) 'The Northern Irish dimension'. In Jowell, R., Witherspoon, S., Brook, L. and Taylor, B. (eds) *British Social Attitudes: the 7th Report.* Aldershot: Gower.

Curtice, J. and Heath, A. (2009) 'England Awakes? Trends in National Identity in England'. In Becchofer and McCrone, q.v.

d'Houtard, A. and Field, M. (1984) 'The image of health: variations in perceptions by social class in a French population'. *Sociology of Health and Illness,* **6**: 30–60.

Dahlgren, G. and Whitehead, M. (1991) *Policies and Strategies to Promote Social Equity in Health.* Stockholm: Institute for Future Studies.

Dalley, G. (1996) *Ideologies of Caring* (2nd edn). Basingstoke: Macmillan.

Daniel, W. (1968) *Racial Discrimination in England*. Harmondsworth: Penguin.

Dargie, C. and Locke, R. (1999) 'The British Senior Civil Service'. In Page E.C. and Wright V. (eds) *Bureaucratic Elites in Western European States*. Oxford: Oxford University Press.

Davidson, K. (1998) *Doing Good Offices*. Sheffield: Paper presented to the British Society of Gerontology Conference, 'Ageing: All Our Tomorrows', September.

Davidson, K. (2001) 'Late life widowhood, selfishness and new partnership choices: a gendered perspective'. *Ageing and Society* 21(3): 297–317

Davie, G. (1994) *Religion in Britain since 1945: Believing Without Belonging*. Oxford: Blackwell.

Davis, D. (1984) *Slavery and Human Progress*. New York: Oxford University Press.

Davis, K. (2008) 'Intersectionality as buzzword: a sociology of science perspective on what makes a feminist theory successful'. *Feminist Theory,* 9(1): 67–85.

Davis, M. (2009) *Comrade or Brother? A History of the British Labour Movement* (2nd edn). London: Pluto Press.

Day, G. (2006) *Community and Everyday Life*. London: Routledge.

Day, G. and Murdoch, J. (1993) 'Locality and community'. *Sociological Review,* 41(1): 82–111.

de Beauvoir, S. ([1949]1972) *The Second Sex*. Trans. Purskley, H. Harmondsworth: Penguin.

de Jong Gierveld, J. (2003) 'Social networks and social well-being of older men and women living alone'. In Arber, S., Davidson, K. and Ginn, J. (eds) *Ageing and Gender: Changing Roles and Relationship*, Maidenhead: Open University Press.

Deacon, A. (2002) *Perspectives on Welfare: Ideas, Ideologies and Policy Debates*. Buckingham: Open University Press.

Delphy, C. (1984) *Close to Home: A Materialist Analysis of Women's Oppression*. London: Hutchinson.

Delphy, C. (1993) 'Rethinking sex and gender'. *Women's Studies International Forum,* 16(1): 1–9.

Delphy, C. and Leonard, D. (1992) *Familiar Exploitation: A New Analysis of Marriage in Contemporary Western Societies*. Cambridge: Polity Press in association with Blackwell.

Dempsey, K. (1990) *Smalltown*. Melbourne: Oxford University Press.

Dench, G., Gavron, K. and Young, M. (2006) *The New East End: Kinship, Race and Conflict*. London: Profile Books.

Dennis, N., Henriques, F. and Slaughter, C. (1956) *Coal Is Our Life*. London: Eyre & Spottiswoode..

Department for Business, Skills & Innovation (BIS) (2011) *Default Retirement Age to End this Year*. Available at www.bis.gov.uk/news/topstories/2011/Jan/default-retirement-age-to-end (accessed 14 March 2012).

Department of Communities and Local Government (DCLG) (2011) *Indices of Deprivation 2010*. www.gov.uk/government/publications/English-indices-of-deprivation-2010 (accessed 15 August 2013).

Department for Education (2012) *National Curriculum Assessments*. www.education.gov.uk/researchandstatistics/statistics/allstatistics/a00196102/ (accessed 7 April 2012).

Department for Education and Science (2007) *Gender and Education: the Evidence on Policies in England*. London: Department for Education and Science.

Department for Education and Skills (2004) *Education and Training Statistics*, www.ddfes.gov.gov.uk/resgateway/DB/SFR

Department of Health (DoH) (1998a) *Independent Inquiry into Inequalities in Health*. London: The Stationery Office.

Department of Health (DoH) (1998b) *Our Healthier Nation*. London: The Stationery Office. Cmd 3852.

Department of Health (DoH) (1999) *Saving Lives: Our Healthier Nation*. London: The Stationery Office. Cmd 4386.

Department of Health (DoH) (2004) *Choosing Health*. London: The Stationery Office.

Department for Work and Pensions (DWP) (2004) *Households Below Average Income 2002/03*. London: Department for Work and Pensions.

Department for Work and Pensions (DWP) (2011a) *Households Below Average Income 1994/5–2009/10*. London: Department for Work and Pensions.

Department for Work and Pensions (DWP) (2011b) *The Pensioners Income Series 2009–10*, available at: research.dwp.gov.uk/asd/asd6/2009_10/pi_series_0910.pdf (accessed: 13 March 2012)

Department for Work and Pensions (DWP)/ONS (2012) *Households Below Average Income* www.dwp.gov.uk/asd/hbai/hbai2011/pdf_files/full_hbai12.pdf (accessed 1 November 2012)

Devine, F. (1992a) *Affluent Workers Revisited*. Edinburgh: Edinburgh University Press.

Devine, F. (1992b) 'Gender segregation in the engineering and science professions: a case of continuity and change'. *Work, Employment and Society*, **6**(4): 557–95.

Dickerson, A. and Popli, G. (2012) *Persistent Poverty and Children's Cognitive Development: Evidence from the UK Millennium Cohort Study*. Centre for Longitudinal Studies Working Paper 2012/2. London: Institute of Education.

Dingwall, R. (1976) *Aspects of Illness*. London: Martin Robertson.

Dinopoulos, E., Krishna, P., Panagariya, A. and Wong, K.-Y. (eds) (2008) *Trade, Globalization and Poverty*. London: Routledge.

DirectGov (2012a) *Employment: Age Discrimination*. www.direct.gov.uk/en/Employment/ResolvingWorkplaceDisputes/DiscriminationAtWork/DG_10026429 (accessed: 14 March 2012).

DirectGov (2012b) *Pensions and Retirement Planning: Calculating your State Pension Age*. www.direct.gov.uk/en/Pensionsandretirementplanning/StatePension/DG_4017919 (accessed: 14 March 2012).

Dixon, C. (1996) 'Having a laugh, having a fight. Masculinity and the conflicting needs of the self in Design and Technology', *International Studies in Sociology of Education*, **6**(2).

Djilas, M. (1957) *The New Class: An Analysis of the Communist System*. London: Thames & Hudson.

Donzelot, J. (1978) *The Policing of Families: Welfare versus the State*. London: Hutchinson.

Doyal, L. (1994) 'Changing medicine? Gender and the politics of health care'. In Gabe, J., Kelleher, D. and Williams, G. (eds) (1994) *Challenging Medicine*. London: Routledge.

Doyal, L. (1995) *What Makes Women Sick*. London: Macmillan.

Draper, P. (1976) 'Social and economic constraints on childlife among the !Kung'. In Lee, R. and DeVore, I. (eds) *Kalahari Hunter-Gatherers*. Cambridge, MA: Harvard University Press.

du Gay, P., Evans, J. and Redman, P. (2000) (eds) *Identity: A Reader*. London: Sage.

Duffield, M. (1985) 'Rationalization and the politics of segregation: Indian workers in Britain's foundry industry, 1945–62'. In Lunn, K. (ed.) *Race and Labour in Twentieth Century Britain*. London: Frank Cass.

Duncan, G., Brooks-Gunn, J., Yeung, W. and Smith, J. (1998) 'How much does childhood poverty affect the life chances of children?'. *American Sociological Review* **63**: 406–23.

Duncan, S. and Edwards, R. (eds) (1997) *Single Mothers in an International Context*. London: UCL Press.

Duncombe, J. and Marsden, D. (1996) 'Whose orgasm is this anyway? "Sex work" in long-term heterosexual couple relationships'. In Weeks, J. and Holland, J. (eds) *Sexual Cultures*. Basingstoke: Macmillan.

Dunleavy, P. (1980) *Urban Political Analysis*. London: Macmillan.

Durkheim, E. ([1893]1984) *The Division of Labour in Society*. London: Macmillan.

Dychtwald, K., Erickson, T. and Morison, B. (2004) 'It's time to retire retirement'. *Harvard Business Review*, March: 2–11.

Dyer, R. (1997) *White*. New York: Routledge.

Eade, J. (1989) *The Politics of Community*. Aldershot: Avebury.

Edmunds, J. and Turner, B (2002) *Generations, Culture and Society*. Buckingham: Open University Press.

Eldridge, J.E.T. (1968) *Industrial Disputes: Essays in the Sociology of Industrial Relations*. London: Routledge & Kegan Paul.

Elliott, A. (2007) *Concepts of the Self*. Cambridge: Polity.

Elliott, A. and du Gay, P. (eds) (2009) *Identity in Question*. London: Sage.

Epstein, D., Elwood, J., Hey, V. and Maw, J. (eds) (1998) *Failing Boys: Issues in Gender and Achievement*. Buckingham: Open University Press.

Equal Opportunities Commission (2003) *Pay and Income*. Manchester: EOC.

Equal Opportunities Commission (2004) *Facts about Women and Men in Great Britain*. Manchester: EOC.

Erikson, R. and Goldthorpe, J. (1993) *The Constant Flux*. Oxford: Clarendon Press.

Esping-Anderson, G. (1990) *The Three Worlds of Welfare Capitalism*. Cambridge: Cambridge University Press.

Estes, C., Biggs, S and Phillipson, C. (2003) *Social Theory, Social Policy and Ageing: A Critical Introduction*, Maidenhead: Open University Press.

Etzioni, A. (1993) *The Spirit of Community*. New York: Touchstone.

Eurobarometer (1997) 'Women and men in Europe: equality of opportunity summary report'. *Equal Opportunities Magazine*, 2 July 1997.

European Commission (2010) *Report on Equality Between Women and Men 2010* Luxembourg: Office for Official Publications of the European Communities.

Eurostat (2001) *Disability and Social Participation in Europe*. Luxembourg: Office of Official Publications of the European communities.

Eurostat (2011) *Youth in Europe*: available at http://epp.eurostat.ec.europa.eu/cache/ ITY_OFFPUB/KS-78-09-920/EN/KS-78-09-920-EN.PDF (accessed: 15 March 2012).

Evans, D. (1993) *Sexual Citizenship: The Material Construction of Sexualities*. London: Routledge.

Evetts, J. (1994) *Women and Career*. Harlow: Longmans.

Faggio, G. and Nickell, S. (2003) 'The rise in inactivity among adult men'. In Dickens, R., Gregg, P. and Wadsworth, J. (eds) *The Labour Market Under New Labour: The State of Working Britain*. Basingstoke: Palgrave.

Fainstein, S. (2001) 'Inequality in global-city regions'. In Scott, A. (ed.) *Global-City Regions: Trends, Theory, Policy*. Oxford: Oxford University Press.

Fairclough, C. (ed.) *Ageing Bodies*, Walnut Creek, CA: AltaMira Press.

Farrar, M. (2002) *The Struggle For 'Community' in a British Multi-Ethnic Inner-City Area: Paradise in the Making*. Lampeter: Edwin Mellen.

Featherstone, M. and Hepworth, M. (1989) 'Ageing and old age: reflections on the postmodern life course'. In Bytheway, W. (ed.) *Becoming and Being Old: Sociological Approaches to Later Life*. London: Sage.

Fenton, S. (2003) *Ethnicity*. Cambridge: Polity.

Ferrant, J. (2009) *A New Way to Measure Gender inequalities in Developing Countries: The Gender Inequalities Index*. Paris: University of Sorbonne

Fevre, R. (1984) *Cheap Labour and Racial Discrimination*. Aldershot: Gower.

Fevre, R. (2011) 'Still on the scrapheap?: The meaning and characteristics of unemployment in prosperous welfare states'. *Work, Employment and Society*, **25**(1): 1–9.

Field, F. (2010) *The Foundation Years: Preventing Poor Children Becoming Poor Adults*. Independent Review on Poverty and Life Chances, December 2010.

Field, S. (1987) 'The changing nature of racial discrimination'. *New Community*, **14**(1/2): 118–22.

Fieldhouse, E. and Gould, M.I. (1998) 'Ethnic minority unemployment and local labour market conditions in Great Britain', *Environment and Planning*: A **30**: 833–53.

Fine, M. and McClelland, S. (2006) 'Sexuality education and desire: still missing after all these years'. *Harvard Educational Review*, **76**(3): 297–338.

Finkelstein, V. (1996) 'The disability movement has run out of steam'. *Disability NOW*. February: 11.

Finnegan, R. (1989) *The Hidden Musicians*. Cambridge: Cambridge University Press.

Finney, N. and Simpson, L. (2009) *'Sleepwalking to Segregation'?*. Bristol: Policy Press

Firestone, S. (1974) *The Dialectic of Sex: The Case for Feminist Revolution*. New York: Morrow.

Ford, C. and Beach, F. (1952) *Patterns of Sexual Behaviour*. London: Eyre & Spottiswoode.

Fortes, M. (1970) 'Social and psychological aspects of education in Taleland'. In Middleton, J. (ed.) *From Child to Adult: Studies in the Anthropology of Education*. Austin: University of Texas Press.

Foster, J. (1974) *Class Struggle and the Industrial Revolution*. London: Methuen.

Foster, J. (1999) *Docklands*. London: UCL Press.

Foucault, M. (1981) *The History of Sexuality Volume I*. London: Allen Lane.

Frankenberg, R. (1957) *Village on the Border*. London: Cohen & West.

Fraser, M. (1999) 'Classing queer: politics in competition'. *Theory, Culture and Society* **16**(2): 107–32.

Fraser, N. (1989) *Unruly Practices: Power, Discourse and Gender in Contemporary Social Theory*. Cambridge: Polity Press.

Fraser, N. (1997) 'Heterosexism, misrecognition, and capitalism: a response to Judith Butler', *Social Text*, 52/53: 279–89.

Fraser, N. (2001) 'Recognition without ethics?'. *Theory, Culture and Society*, **18**(2-3): 21–42.

Freud, S. (1977) *The Penguin Freud Library Volume 7: Sexuality*. Harmondsworth: Penguin.

Friedan, B. (1993) *The Fountain of Age*. London: Simon & Schuster.

Fulcher, J. and Scott, J. (2012) *Sociology* (4th edn). Oxford: Oxford University Press.

Furstenberg, F. Jr (2010) 'On a new schedule: transitions to adulthood and family change'. *The Future of Children*, **20**(1): 67–87.

Fuss, D. (1989) *Essentially Speaking: Feminism, Nature and Difference*. New York: Routledge.

Fuss, D. (1991) *Inside/Out: Lesbian Theories, Gay Theories*. New York: Routledge.

Gabriel, J. (1998) *Whitewash: Racialized Politics and the Media*. London: Routledge.

Gagnon, J. (2004) *An Interpretation of Desire*, Chicago: University of Chicago Press.

Gagnon, J. and Simon, W. (1974) *Sexual Conduct*. London: Hutchinson.

Gavey, N. (2005) *Just Sex?: The Cultural Scaffolding of Rape*. Hove: Routledge.

Giannelli, G., Mangiavacchi, L. and Piccoli, L. (2010) *GDP and the Value of Family Caretaking. How much does Europe Care*. Bonn: Institute for the Study of Labour.

Giarchi, G. (1996) *Caring for Older Europeans*. Aldershot: Ashgate.

Gibbon, M. (2000) 'The Health Analysis and Action Cycle: an empowering approach to women's health'. *Sociological Research Online*, **4**(4) www.socresonline.org.uk/4/4/gibbon.html

Giddens, A. (1974) 'Elites in the British class structure'. In Stanworth, P. and Giddens, A. (eds) *Elites and Power in British Society*. Cambridge: Cambridge University Press.

Giddens, A. (1981) *A Contemporary Critique of Historical Materialism, vol. I: Power, Property and the State*. London: Macmillan.

Giddens, A. (1985) *A Contemporary Critique of Historical Materialism, vol. II: The Nation-State and Violence*. London: Polity Press.

Giddens, A. (1990) *The Consequences of Modernity*. Cambridge: Polity Press.

Giddens, A. (1991) *Modernity and Self-Identity: Self and Society in the Late Modern Age*. Cambridge: Polity Press.

Giddens, A. (1992) *The Transformation of Intimacy: Sexuality, Love and Eroticism in Modern Societies*. Cambridge: Polity Press.

Gierveld, J., de Valk, H. and Blommesteijn, M. (2001) 'Living arrangements of older persons and family support in more developed countries'. In *Population Ageing and Living Arrangements of Older Persons: Critical Issues and Policy Response*. United Nations Population Bulletin, Special Issue Nos. 42/43.

Gill, F. and Maclean, C. (2002) 'Knowing your place: gender and reflexivity in two ethnographies'. *Sociological Research Online* 7(2). www.socresonline.org.uk/7/2/gill.html.

Gilleard, C. and Higgs, P. (2000) *Cultures of Ageing.* Harlow: Prentice Hall.

Gillespie, M. (1995) *Television, Ethnicity and Cultural Change.* London: Routledge.

Gilligan, H. (1990) 'Padstow'. In Harris, C (ed.) *Family, Economy and Community.* Cardiff: University of Wales Press.

Gillis, J.R. (1974) *Youth in History.* London: Academic Press.

Ginn, J. (2003) *Gender, Pensions and the Lifecourse: How Pensions Need to Adapt to Changing Family Forms.* Bristol: The Policy Press.

Ginn, J. and Arber, S. (2001) 'A colder pension climate for British women'. In Ginn, J., Street, D. and Arber, S. (eds) *Women, Work and Pensions.* Buckingham: Open University Press.

Ginn, J., Street, D. and Arber, S. (eds) (2001) *Women, Work, and Pensions: International Issues and Prospects.* Buckingham: Open University Press.

Glendinning, C. and Miller, J. (1992) *Women and Poverty in Britain in the 1990's.* London: Harvester Wheatsheaf.

Gluckman, M. (1960) *Custom and Conflict in Africa.* Oxford: Blackwell.

Glucksmann, M. (aka Ruth Cavendish) ([1982]2009) *Women on the Line.* London: Routledge.

Glucksmann, M. (1995) 'Why work?'. *Gender Work and Organisation.* 2: 67–9.

Godway, E. and Finn, G. (eds) (1994) *Who is This 'We'?* Montreal: Black Rose Books.

Goffman, E. (1961) *Asylums.* New York: Anchor.

Goffman, E. (1972) *Encounters.* Harmondsworth: Penguin.

Goffman, E ([1959]1990) *The Presentation of Self in Everyday Life.* Harmondsworth: Penguin.

Goldthorpe, J. (1964) 'Social stratification in industrial society'. In Halmos, P. (ed.) *The Development of Industrial Societies.* Sociological Review Monograph, 8. Keele: University of Keele.

Goldthorpe, J. (1980) *Social Mobility and Class Structure in Modern Britain.* Oxford: Clarendon Press.

Goldthorpe, J. (1983) 'Women and class analysis: in defence of the conventional view'. *Sociology*, 17(4): 465–88.

Goldthorpe, J. and Lockwood, D. (1963) 'Affluence and the British class structure'. *Sociological Review*, 11(1): 133–63.

Goldthorpe, J., Lockwood, D., Bechhofer, F. and Platt, J. (1969) *The Affluent Worker in the Class Structure.* Cambridge: Cambridge University Press.

Gordon, D. and Pantazis, C. (1997) *Breadline Britain in the 1990s.* Aldershot: Ashgate.

Gordon, D., Adelman, L., Ashworth, K., Bradshaw, J., Levitas, R., Middleton, S., Pantazis, C., Patsios, D., Payne, S., Townsend, P. and Williams, J. (2000) *Poverty and Social Exclusion in Britain.* York: Joseph Rowntree Foundation.

Goulbourne, H. (1991) *Ethnicity and Nationalism in Post-Imperial Britain.* Cambridge: Polity Press.

Government Actuary's Department (2013) *Period and Cohort Life Expectancy Tables at Age 65, UK.* www.gad.gov.uk/Demography Data/Life Tables/Period EOL/ 2004/2004UKe65.html (accessed 4 July 2013).

Graham, H. (1987) 'Women's poverty in caring'. In Glendenning, C. and Miller, J. (eds) *Women and Poverty*. Hemel Hempstead: Harvester/Wheatsheaf.

Graham, R. (2004). 'Cognitive citizenship: access to hip surgery for people with dementia', *Health* **8**(3): 295–310.

Gray, P., Elgar, J. and Bally, S. (1993) *Access to Training and Employment for Asian Women in Coventry*. Coventry: Coventry City Council, Economic Development Unit, Research Paper

Gray, R. (1981) *The Aristocracy of Labour in Nineteenth Century Britain*. London: Macmillan.

Green, J. (1997) *Risk and Misfortune: The Social Construction of Accidents*. London: University College London Press.

Gregory, S. and Hartley, G. (eds) (1991) *Constructing Deafness*. London: Pinter.

Grillis, J. (1987) 'The case against chronologization: changes in the Anglo-American life cycle 1600 to the present'. *Ethnologia Europaea*, **17**(2): 97–106.

Grover, C. and Piggot, L. (2010) 'From Incapacity Benefit to Employment and Support Allowance'. *Policy Studies* **32**(2): 265–82.

Grubium, J. and Holstein, J. (2000) *Ageing and Everyday Life*, Oxford: Blackwell.

Guardian, The (2004a) 'Census shows Muslims' plight'. 12 October 2004 (accessed 8 October 2010). www.guardian.co.uk/religion/Story/0,2763,1325094,00.html,

Guardian, The (2004b) 'Poll shows Muslims do not feel respected'. 22 November 2004. www.guardian.co.uk/religion/Story/0,2763,1356581,00.html (accessed 8 October 2010).

Guardian, The (2011) *Datablog* www.guardian.co.uk/news/datablog/2011/aug/18/a-levels-analysis-subject-school (accessed 11 May 2012)

Guardian, The (2012) 'Household incomes: how do you compare?' www.guardian.co.uk/society/datablog/2012/jun/22/household-incomes-compare

Guillaumin, C. (1995) *Racism, Sexism, Power and Ideology*. London: Routledge.

Guillemard, A. (1989) 'The trend towards early labour force withdrawal and reorganisation of the life course: a cross-national analysis'. In Johnson, P., Conrad, C. and Thomson, D. (eds) *Workers versus Pensioners*. Manchester: Manchester University Press.

Guillemard, A. (1990) 'Re-organising the transition from work to retirement in an international perspective: Is chronological age still the major criterion determining the definitive exit?'. Paper presented to the International Sociological Association Conference, Madrid.

Guttsman, W. (1963) *The British Political Elite*. London: MacGibbon & Kee.

Hacking, I. (1995) 'The looping effect of human kinds'. in Sperber, D. et al. (eds) *Causal Cognition: An Interdisciplinary Approach*. Oxford: Oxford University Press:

Hacking, I. (1999) *The Social Construction of What?* Cambridge, MA: Harvard University Press

Hacking, I. (2004) 'Between Michel Foucault and Erving Goffman: between discourse in the abstract and face-to-face interaction', *Economy and Society*, **33**(3): 277–302.

Hakim, C. (1991) 'Grateful slaves and self-made women: fact and fantasy in women's work orientations'. *European Sociological Review*, 7: 101–21.

Hakim, C. (1995) 'Five feminist myths about women's employment'. *British Journal of Sociology*, **46**(4): 424–55.

Hakim, C. (2003) 'Public morality versus personal choice'. *British Journal of Sociology*, **54**(3): 339–45.

Halford, S. and Leonard, P. (2003) 'Space and place in the construction and performance of gendered nursing identities'. *Journal of Advanced Nursing* **42**(2): 201–8.

Hall, S., Held, D. and McLennan, G. (eds) (1992) *Modernity and its Futures*. Cambridge: Polity Press.

Hall, S. and du Gay, P. (1996) *Questions of Cultural Identity*. London: Sage.

Halliday, F. (1999) '"Islamophobia" reconsidered', *Ethnic and Racial Studies*, **22**(5): 892–902.

Halperin, D.M. (1995) *Saint Foucault: Towards a Gay Hagiography*. Oxford: Oxford University Press.

Halson, J. (1991) 'Young women: sexual harassment and mixed-sex schooling'. In Abbott, P. and Wallace, C. (eds) *Gender, Power and Sexuality*. London: Macmillan.

Hardy, M. (ed.) (1997) *Studying Ageing and Social Change: Conceptual and Methodological Issues*. London: Sage.

Hardy, T. ([1886]1902) *The Mayor of Casterbridge*. London: Macmillan.

Hardy, T. ([1895]1975) *Jude the Obscure*. London: Macmillan.

Hareven, T. (1994) 'Ageing and generational relations: a historical and life-course perspective'. *Annual Review of Sociology*, **20**: 437–61.

Harne, L. (1984) 'Lesbian custody and the new myth of the father'. *Trouble and Strife*, 3: 12–14.

Harrington, M. (2010) *An Independent Review of Work Capability Assessment*. London: The Stationery Office.

Harrison, M. (2003) 'Housing black and minority ethnic communities: diversity and constraint', in Mason 2003c, q.v.

Hartman, H. (1978) 'The unhappy marriage of Marxism and feminism: towards a more progressive union'. *Capital and Class*, **8**: 1–33.

Hausmann, R., Tyson, L. and Zahidi, S. (2008) *The Global Gender Gap Report 2008*. Geneva: World Economic Forum.

Hawkes, G. (1996) *A Sociology of Sex and Sexuality*. Buckingham: Open University Press.

Heath, A. and McMahon, D. (1997) 'Education and occupational attainment: the impact of ethnic origins'. In Karn, V. *Ethnicity in the 1991 Census, Vol 4*. London: HMSO.

Heath, A. and Yi Cheung, S. (2006) *Ethnic Penalties in the Labour Market: Employers and Discrimination*, Department for Work and Pensions Research Report No. 341, Crown Copyright.

Heath, S. (1982) *The Sexual Fix*. London: Macmillan.

Held, D. (1992) 'The development of the modern state'. In Hall, S. and Gieben, B. (eds) *Formations of Modernity*. London: Polity Press.

Held, D. (1995), *Globalization and the Global Order*. Cambridge: Polity Press.

Held, D. and McGrew, A. (2007) *Globalization/Anti-Globalization* (2nd edn). Cambridge: Polity Press.

Help Age International (1999) *The Ageing and Development Report: Poverty, Independence and the World's Older People.* London: Earthscan.

Hennessy, R. (1995) 'Queer visibility and commodity culture'. In Nicholson, L. and Seidman, S. (eds) *Social Postmodernism.* Cambridge: Cambridge University Press.

Hennessy, R. (1998) 'Disappearing capital: the queer material of sexual identity'. Paper presented at the Centre for Interdisciplinary Gender Studies, Leeds.

Hennessy, R. (2000) *Profit and Pleasure.* London: Routledge.

Hennock, E. (1991) 'Concepts of poverty in the British social surveys from Charles Booth to Arthur Bowley'. In Bulmer, M., Bales, K. and Kish Sklar, K. (eds) *The Social Survey in Historical Perspective.* Cambridge: Cambridge University Press.

Herdt, G. (1981) *Guardians of the Flutes.* New York: McGraw Hill.

Herrnstein, R. and Murray, C. (1994) *The Bell Curve: Intelligence and Class Structure in American Life.* New York: The Free Press.

Herzlich, C. (1973) *Health and Illness: A Social Psychological Analysis.* London: Academic Press.

Hetherington, K. and Munro, R. (1997) *Ideas of Difference.* Oxford: Blackwell.

Heywood, C. (2001) *A History of Childhood.* Cambridge: Polity.

Hicks, S. and Thomas, J. (2009) *Presentation of the Gender Pay Gap.* ONS Position Paper www.ons.gov.uk (accessed 7 April 2012).

Hill, M. and Jenkins, S. (2001) 'Poverty amongst British children: chronic or transitory?'. In Bradbury, B., Jenkins, S. and Micklewright, J. (eds) *The Dynamics of Child Poverty in Industrialised Countries.* Cambridge: Cambridge University Press.

Hillman, M., Adams, J. and Whitlegg, J. (1990) *One False Move: A Study of Children's Independent Mobility.* London: Policy Studies Institute.

Hills, J. and Stewart, K. (eds) (2005) *A More Equal Society? New Labour, Poverty, Inequality and Exclusion.* Bristol: Polity Press.

Hills, J., Brewer, M., Jenkins, S., Lister, R., Lupton, R., Machin, S., Mills, C., Modood, T., Rees, T., and Riddell, S. (2010) *An Anatomy of Economic Inequality in the UK: Report of the National Equality Panel.* Government Equalities Office and Centre for Analysis of Social Exclusion London: London School of Economics and Political Science.

Hobsbawm, E. (1964) *Labouring Men: Studies in the History of Labour.* London: Weidenfeld & Nicolson.

Hockey, J. and James, A. (1993) *Growing Up and Growing Old.* London: Sage.

Hoggett, P. (ed.) (1997) *Contested Communities.* Bristol: Policy Press.

Holcombe, L. (1973) *Victorian Ladies At Work.* Newton Abbott: David & Charles.

Holland, J., Ramazanoglu, C., Sharpe, S. and Thomson, R. (1990) *Don't Die of Ignorance – I Nearly Died of Embarrassment: Condoms in Context.* London: Tufnell Press.

Holland, J., Ramazanoglu, C., Sharpe, S. and Thomson, R. (1991) *Pressure, Resistance, Empowerment: Young Women and the Negotiation of Safer Sex.* London: Tufnell Press.

Holland, J., Ramazanoglu, C., Sharpe, S. and Thomson, R. (1994) 'Power and desire: the embodiment of female sexuality'. *Feminist Review,* **46**: 21–38.

Holland, J., Ramazanoglu, C., Sharpe, S. and Thomson, R. (1998) *The Male in the Head: Young People, Heterosexuality and Power.* London: Tufnell Press.

Holton, R. (2008) *Global Networks.* Basingstoke: Palgrave Macmillan.

Holton, R. (2009) *Cosmopolitanisms: New Thinking, New Directions*. Basingstoke: Palgrave Macmillan.

Holton, R. (2011) *Globalization and the Nation-State* (2nd edn). Basingstoke: Palgrave Macmillan.

Homans, G. (1951) *The Human Group*. London: Routledge & Kegan Paul.

Home Office (1998) *Statistics on Race and the Criminal Justice*. London: The Stationery Office.

Home Office (2012) *Homicides, Firearm Offences and Intimate Violence 2010/11: Supplementary Volume 2 to Crime in England and Wales 2010/11*. Available at www.homeoffice.gov.uk/publications/science-research-statistics/research-statistics/crime-research/hosb0212 .(accessed 29 April 2012).

Hood-Williams, J. (1990) 'Patriarchy for children: on the stability of power relations in children's lives'. In Chisholm, L., Büchner, P., Krüger, H.-H. and Brown, P. (eds) *Children, Youth and Social Change: A Comparative Perspective*. London: Falmer.

Hopkins, A. (ed.) (2002) *Globalization in World History*. London: Pimlico.

Hornsby, A. (2011) 'Surfing the net for community: a Durkheimian analysis of electronic gatherings'. In P. Kivisto (ed.) *Illuminating Social Life: Classical and Contemporary Theory Revisited*. London: Sage.

Hornsby-Smith, M. (2004) 'The changing identity of Catholics in England'. In Coleman, S. and Collins, P. (eds) *Religious Identity and Change: Perspectives on Global Transformations*. London: Ashgate.

Houston, D and Lindsay, C. (2010) 'Fit for Work?'. *Policy Studies* **31**(2): 133–42.

Howard, M., Garnham, A., Fimister, G. and Veit-Wilson, J. (2001) *Poverty: The Facts* (4th edn). London: CPAG.

Howlett, B., Ahmad, W. and Murray, R. (1992) 'An exploration of White, Asian and Afro Caribbean peoples' concepts of health and illness causation'. *New Community*, 18: 281–92.

Hubbock, J. and Carter, S. (1980) *Half a Chance? A Report on Job Discrimination Against Young Blacks in Nottingham*. London: CRE.

Hughes, R. and Kleine, S. (2004). 'Views of health in the lay sector'. *Health*, **8**(4): 395–422.

Hugman, R. (1994) *Ageing and the Care of Older People in Europe*. Basingstoke: Macmillan.

Hunt, S., McEwen, J. and McKenna, S. (1986) *Measuring Health Status*. London: Croom Helm.

Hunter, J. (1991) *Culture Wars: The Struggle to Define America*. New York: Basic Books.

Hussain, A. and Miller, W. (2006) *Multicultural Nationalism: Islamophobia, Anglophobia and Devolution*. Oxford: Oxford University Press.

Hyde, M. (1996), 'Fifty years of failure: employment services for disabled people in the UK'. *Work, Employment and Society*, **10**(4): 683–700.

Hyde, M. (1998) 'Sheltered and supported employment in the 1990s: the experiences of disabled workers in the UK'. *Disability and Society*, **13**(2): 199–215.

Hyde, M. (2000) 'Disability'. In Payne, G. (ed.) *Social Divisions*. Basingstoke: Macmillan.

Hyde, M., Dixon, J. and Joyner, M. (1999) 'Work for those that can, security for those that cannot: the new United Kingdom social security reform agenda'. *International Social Security Review*, **52**(4): 69–86.

Ifekwunigwe, J. (1999) *Scattered Be-*Longings. London: Routledge.

Iganski, P. and Payne, G. (1996) 'Declining racial disadvantage in the British labour market'. *Ethnic and Racial Studies*, **19**(1): 113–34.

Iganski, P. and Payne, G. (1999) 'Socio-economic re-structuring and employment: the case of minority ethnic groups'. *British Journal of Sociology*, **50**(2): 195–216

Iganski, P., Payne, G. and Roberts, J. (2001) 'Inclusion or exclusion? Reflections on the evidence of declining racial disadvantage in the British labour market'. *International Journal of Sociology and Social Policy*, **21**(4–6): 184–211.

Illsley, R. (1955) 'Social class selection and class differences in relation to still births and infant deaths'. *British Medical Journal*, **ii**: 1520–4.

Illsley, R. (1986) 'Occupational class, selection and the production of inequalities in health'. *Quarterly Journal of Social Affairs*, **2**: 151–65.

Illsley, R. (1990) 'Comparative review of sources, methodology and knowledge'. *Social Science and Medicine*, **31**(3): 229–36.

International Monetary Fund (IMF) (2007) *World Economic Outlook: Globalization and Inequality*. Washington DC: IMF.

Ingraham, C. (1996) 'The heterosexual imaginary'. In Seidman, S. (ed.) *Queer Theory/Sociology*. Oxford: Blackwell.

Ingraham, C. (2005) *Thinking Straight: The Power Promise and Paradox of Heterosexuality*. New York: Routledge.

International Organization of Migration (2010) *International Migration Report, 2010*. www.publications.iom.int (accessed 7 June 2012).

Institute for Public Policy Research (IPPR) (2010) *Youth Unemployment and the Recession*, London: IPPR. www.ippr.org.uk/uploadedFiles/events/Youth%20unemployment%20and%20recession%20technical%20briefing.pdf (accessed 6 October 2010).

Institute for Public Policy Research (IPPR) (2012) *The Dog Which Finally Barked*. London: IPPR.

Isin, E. and Wood, P. (1999) *Citizenship and Identity*. London: Sage.

Jackson, B. (1968) *Working Class Community*. London: Routledge & Kegan Paul.

Jackson, M. (2002) 'The exterminating angel: reflections on violence and intersubjective reason', *Focaal – European Journal of Anthropology* **39**: 137–48.

Jackson, P. and Salisbury, J. (1996) 'Why should secondary schools take working with boys seriously?' *Gender and Education*, **8**: 103–16.

Jackson, S. (1982) *Childhood and Sexuality*. Oxford: Blackwell.

Jackson, S. (1990) 'Demons and innocents: western ideas on children's sexuality in historical perspective'. In Money, J. and Musaph, H. (eds) *Handbook of Sociology*. Vol. VII. Amsterdam: Elsevier.

Jackson, S. (1998) *Britain's Population: Demographic Issues in Contemporary Society*. London: Routledge.

Jackson, S. (1999) *Heterosexuality in Question*. London: Sage.

Jackson, S. (2005) 'Gender, sexuality and heterosexuality: re-thinking the intersections'. In Casey, M., McLaughlin, J. and Richardson, D. (eds) *Queer Intersection.* Basingstoke: Palgrave.

Jackson, S. and Scott, S. (eds) (1996) *Feminism and Sexuality: A Reader.* Edinburgh: Edinburgh University Press.

Jackson, S. and Scott, S. (1997) 'Gut reactions to matters of the heart: reflections on rationality, irrationality and sexuality'. *Sociological Review,* 45(4): 551–75.

Jackson, S. and Scott, S. (2004) 'Sexual antinomies in late modernity'. *Sexualities* 7(2): 233–48.

Jackson, S. and Scott, S. (2010) *Theorizing Sexuality.* Maidenhead: Open University Press.

James, A. and Prout, A. (1990) *Constructing and Reconstructing Childhood.* London: Falmer.

James, A., Jenks, C. and Prout, A. (1998) *Theorizing Childhood.* Cambridge: Polity Press.

Jeffreys, S. (1997) *The Idea of Prostitution.* Melbourne: Spiniflex.

Jenkins, R. (1986a) *Racism and Recruitment,* Cambridge: Cambridge University Press.

Jenkins, R. (1986b) 'Social anthropological models in inter-ethnic relations'. In Rex, J. and Mason, D. (eds) *Theories of Race and Ethnic Relations.* Cambridge: Cambridge University Press.

Jenkins, R. (1997) *Rethinking Ethnicity.* London: Sage Publications.

Jenkins, S. (2008) *'Marital splits and income changes over the longer term'.* In Brynin, M. and Ermisch, J. (eds) *Changing Relationships.* London: Routledge.

Jenkins, S. (2011) *Changing Fortunes.* Oxford: Oxford University Press

Jenkins, S. and Micklewright, J. (2007) *Inequality and Poverty Re-examined.* Oxford: Oxford University Press.

Jenks, C. (1996) *Childhood.* London: Routledge.

Jewson, N., Mason, D., Waters, S. and Harvey, J. (1990) *Ethnic Minorities and Employment Practice, A Study of Six Employers.* London: Department of Employment Research Paper, No. 76

Jin, W., Joyce, R., Phillips, D. and Sibieta, L. (2011) *Poverty and Inequality in the UK.* London: IFS Commentary C118.

Jinks, C., Ong, B. and O'Neill, T. (2010). '"Well, it's nobody's responsibility but my own." A qualitative study to explore views about the determinants of health and prevention of knee pain in older adults'. *BMC Public Health* **10,** 148:1–9. http://repository.keele.ac.uk:8080/intralibrary/open_virtual_file_path/i9688n459009t/Jinks1.pdf (accessed 11 May 2012).

Johnson, A., Mercer, C., Erens, B. et al. (2001) 'Sexual behaviour in Britain'. *Lancet,* **358**(9296): 1835–42.

Johnson, M. (1995) 'Interdependency and the Generational Compact'. *Ageing and Society,* 15: 234–65.

Johnson, P. (1985) *The Economics of Old Age in Britain: A Long-Run View 1881–1981.* London: Discussion paper no. 47. Centre for Economic Policy Research.

Johnson, P. (1994) 'The employment and retirement of older men in England and Wales, 1881–1981', *Economic History Review,* 47: 106–28.

Johnson, P., Conrad, C. and Thomson, D. (eds) (1989) *Workers Versus Pensioners*. Manchester: Manchester University Press.

Johnson, T. (1972) *Professions and Power*. London: Macmillan.

Jones, M. (2010) 'Disability, education and training'. *Economic and Labour Market Review* (ONS) 4(4): 32–7.

Jones, T. (1993) *Britain's Ethnic Minorities*. London: PSI.

Joseph, J. ([1974]1987) 'Warning'. In Adcock, F. (ed.) (1987) *The Faber Book of 20th Century Women's Poetry*. London: Faber & Faber. (Originally published in Joseph, J. (1974) *Rose in the Afternoon*. London: Dent).

Joshi, H. (1990) 'The cash opportunity costs of child bearing: an approach to estimation using British data'. *Population Studies*, 44: 52–3.

Joshi, H., Wiggins, D., Bartley, M., Mitchell, R., Gleave, S. and Lynch, K. (2000) 'Putting health inequalities on the map'. In Graham, H. (ed.) *Understanding Health Inequalities*. Buckingham: Open University Press.

Jutel, A. (2006). 'The emergence of overweight as a disease entity: measuring up normality'. *Social Science and Medicine* 63(9): 2268–76.

Kelly, L. (1988) *Surviving Sexual Violence*. Cambridge: Polity Press.

Kelly, L., Lovett, J. and L. Reagan, L. (2005) *A Gap or a Chasm: Attrition in Reported Rape Cases*. London: Home Office. http://webarchive.nationalarchives.gov. uk/20110218135832/http://rds.homeoffice.gov.uk/rds/pdfs05/hors293.pdf (accessed 29 April 2012).

Kempson, E., Bryson, A. and Rowlingson, K. (1994) *Hard Times*. London: Policy Studies Institute.

Kimmel, M. (2000) *The Gendered Society*. Oxford: Oxford University Press.

Kimmel, M. (2009) *Guyland: The Perilous World Where Boys Become Men*. New York: Harper.

Kingston, P. (2000) *The Classless Society*. Stanford: Stanford University Press.

Klein, J. (1965) *Samples From English Culture*. London: Routledge & Kegan Paul.

Klein, R. (1988) 'Acceptable inequalities'. In Green, D. (ed.) *Acceptable Inequalities? Essays on the Pursuit of Equality*. London: Institute of Economic Affairs.

Kohli, M. (1986) 'The world we forgot: a historical review of the life course'. In Marshall, W. (ed.) *Later Life: The Social Psychology of Ageing*. London: Sage.

Kohli, M., Rein , M., Guillemard, A. and Van Gunstern, H. (eds) (1992) *Time for Retirement: Comparative Studies on Early Exit for the Labour Force*. Cambridge: Cambridge University Press.

Kuhn, T. (1970) *The Structure of Scientific Revolutions* (2nd edn). Chicago: Chicago University Press.

Kumar, K. (1978) *Prophecy and Progress*. Harmondsworth: Penguin.

Labour Force Survey (2009) www.esds.ac.uk/government/lfs/ (accessed 30 April 2012).

Labour Force Survey (2011) www.esds.ac.uk/government/lfs/ (accessed 30April 2012).

Lacan, J. (1977) *Écrits*. London: Tavistock.

Laczko, F. and Phillipson, C. (1991) *Changing Work and Retirement*. Milton Keynes: Open University Press.

Lancy, D. (2008) *The Anthropology of Childhood: Cherubs, Chattels, Changelings*. Cambridge: Cambridge University Press.

Langford, W. (1999) *Revolutions of the Heart: Gender, Power and the Delusions of Love*. London: Routledge.

Laslett, P. ([1987]1991) *A Fresh Map of Life: The Emergence of the Third Age*, Cambridge, MA: Harvard University Press.

Law360 (2012) *Ex-Barclays Trader Says She Was Fired For Sex Bias Complaints*. www.law360.com/articles/367363/ex-barclays-trader-says-she-was-fired-for-sex-bias-complaints (accessed 9 July 2013).

Lawler, S. (1999) 'Why difference (still) makes a difference: sociology's obligations'. Paper presented to the British Sociological Association Annual Conference, Glasgow.

Lawler, S. (2008) 'The middle classes and their aristocratic others: culture as nature in classification struggles'. *Journal of Cultural Economy* **1**(3): 245–61.

Lawler, S. (2009) *Identity: Sociological Perspectives*. Cambridge: Polity.

Layte, R., Whelan, C., Maître, B. and Nolan B. (2001) 'Explaining levels of deprivation in the European Union'. *Acta Sociologica* **44**: 105–21.

Layton-Henry, Z. (1992) *The Politics of Immigration: Immigration, Race and Race Relations in Post-war Britain*. Oxford: Blackwell.

Lee, R. and De Vore, I. (1968) *Man the Hunter.* Chicago: Aldine.

Lees, S. (1993) *Sugar and Spice: Sexuality and Adolescent Girls*. Harmondsworth: Penguin.

Lees, S. (1997) *Carnal Knowledge*. London: Penguin.

Lengermann, P.M. and Niebragge-Brantley, J. (1998) *The Women Founders: Sociology and Social Theory 1830–1930*. Boston and London: McGraw Hill.

Leonard, D. (1990) 'In their own right: children and sociology in the UK'. In Chisholm, L., Büchner, P., Krüger, H-H. and Brown, P. (eds) *Children, Youth and Social Change: A Comparative Perspective*. London: Falmer.

Leslie, D., Drinkwater, S. and O'Leary, N. (1998) 'Unemployment and earnings among Britain's ethnic minorities'. *Journal of Ethnic and Migration Studies*, **24**(4): 489–506.

Levitas, R. (1998) *The Inclusive Society?* Basingstoke: Macmillan.

Lewis, J. (2009). *Work-Family Balance, Gender and Policy*. Cheltenham: Edward Elgar.

Li, Y. and Devine, F. (2011) 'Is social mobility really declining? Intergenerational class mobility in Britain in the 1990s and the 2000s'. *Sociological Research Online*, **16**(3): 4. www.socresonline.org.uk/16/3/4.html.

Liberty (1994) *Sexuality and the State: Human Rights Violations Against Lesbians, Gays, Bisexuals and Transgendered People*. London: National Council for Civil Liberties.

Lichterman, P. (1996) *The Search for Political Community*. Cambridge: Cambridge University Press.

Life Opportunities Survey (LOS) (2010) *Life Opportunities Survey – Bulletin, 2009/10*. Newport: Office for National Statistics. www.ons.gov.uk/ons/rel/los/life-opportunities-survey/life-opportunities-survey/index.html (accessed 30 April 2012).

Lindert, P. and Williamson, J. (2003) 'Does globalization make the world more unequal?'. In Bordo, M., Taylor, J. and Williamson, J. (eds) *Globalization in Historical*

Perspective. National Bureau of Economic Research Conference Report, Chicago: University of Chicago Press.

Linkon, S. and Russo, J. (2002) *Steeltown U.S.A: Work and Memory in Youngstown.* Lawrence, KS: Kansas University Press.

Lister, R. (2004) *Poverty.* Cambridge: Polity Press.

Locke, J. ([1693]1989) *Some Thoughts Concerning Education.* Edited by Yolton, J. and Walton, J. Oxford: Clarendon Press.

Lockwood, D. (1958/1989) *The Black-coated Worker.* London/Oxford: Allen & Unwin/ Clarendon Press.

Lockwood, D. (1960) 'The new working class'. *European Journal of Sociology,* 1(3): 248–59.

Lockwood, D. (1975) 'Sources of variation in working class images of society'. In Bulmer, M. (ed.) *Working Class Images of Society.* London: Routledge & Kegan Paul.

Longhi, S. and Platt, L. (2008) *Pay Gaps Across Equalities Areas.* EHRC Research Report 9. Manchester: Equalities and Human Rights Commission.

Luthra, M. (1997) *Britain's Black Population.* Aldershot: Ashgate.

Mac an Ghail, M. (1994) *The Making of Men: Masculinities and Schooling.* Buckingham: Open University Press.

MacDonald, K. (2004) 'Black Mafia, loggies and going for the stars: the military elite revisited'. *The Sociological Review,* 52(1): 106–28.

Macintyre, S. (1997) 'The Black Report and beyond: what are the issues?' *Social Science and Medicine,* 44(6): 723–45.

Macintyre, S., Ellaway, A. and Cumins, S. (2002) 'Place effects on health'. *Social Science and Medicine,* 55: 125–39.

Macintyre, S., Hunt, K. and Sweeting, H. (1996) 'Gender differences in health'. *Social Science and Medicine,* 42(5): 617–42.

Mack, J. and Lansley, S. (1985) *Poor Britain.* London: Allen & Unwin.

Maclean, C. (2003) '"Making it their home": in-migration, time, social change and belonging in a rural community'. In Allan, G. and Jones, G. (eds) *Social Relations and the Life Course.* Basingstoke: Palgrave.

Macleod, A. (1992) *Social Identity, Social Change and the Construction of Symbolic Boundaries in a West Highland Settlement.* PhD thesis, Plymouth: University of Plymouth.

Macleod, A. and Payne, G. (1994) 'Locals and Incomers'. In Baldwin, J. (ed.) *Peoples and Settlements.* Edinburgh: SSNS.

Malinowski, B. (1929) *The Sexual Life of Savages in North-Western Melanesia.* London: Routledge & Kegan Paul.

Mannheim, K. (1997) 'The problem of generations'. In Hardy, M. (ed.) *Studying Aging and Social Change: Conceptual and Methodological Issues.* London: Sage.

Marcus, T. and Manicom, D. (2000) 'Consciousness in transition'. *Sociological Research Online,* 4(4). www.socresonline.org.uk/4/4/marcus.html

Marcuse, H. (1964) *One Dimensional Man.* London: Routledge & Kegan Paul.

Marcuse, H. (1972) *Eros and Civilization.* London: Abacus.

Marquand, D. (1988) *The Unprincipled Society.* London: Fontana.

Marshall, G., Rose, D., Vogler, C. and Newby, H. (1988) *Social Class in Modern Britain.* London: Hutchinson.

Marsland, D. (1996) *Welfare or Welfare State? Contradictions and Dilemmas in Social Policy*. London: Macmillan.

Martens, L., Southerton, D. and Scott, S. (2004) 'Bringing children and parents into the sociology of consumption: towards a theoretical and empirical agenda'. *Journal of Consumer Culture*, 4(2): 155–92.

Martin, J. and Roberts, C. (1984) *Women and Employment: A Life time Perspective*. London: HMSO.

Martin, J., Meltzer, H. and Elliot, D. (1988) *The Prevalence of Disability Among Adults*. London: HMSO.

Marx, K. ([1867]1961) *Capital, Volume 1*. London: Penguin.

Marx, K. and Engels, F. ([1859]1969) *Selected Works, Vol. 1*. Moscow: Progress Publishers.

Mason, D. (1986) 'Controversies and continuities in race and ethnic relations theory'. In Rex, J. and Mason, D. (eds) *Theories of Race and Ethnic Relations*. Cambridge: Cambridge University Press.

Mason, D. (1994) 'On the dangers of disconnecting race and racism'. *Sociology*, 28(4): 845–58.

Mason, D. (1996) 'Themes and issues in the teaching of race and ethnicity in sociology'. *Ethnic and Racial Studies*, 19(4): 789–806.

Mason, D. (2000) *Race and Ethnicity in Modern Britain* (2nd edn). Oxford: Oxford University Press.

Mason, D. (2003a) 'Changing ethnic disadvantage: an overview'. In Mason, D. (ed.) (2003c) q.v.

Mason, D. (2003b) 'Changing patterns of ethnic disadvantage in employment'. In Mason, D. (ed) (2003c) q.v.

Mason, D. (ed.) (2003c) *Explaining Ethnic Differences: Changing Patterns of Disadvantage in Britain*, Bristol: Policy Press.

Masters, W. and Johnson, V. (1966) *Human Sexual Response*. Boston: Little, Brown.

Mayall, B. (ed.) (1994) *Children's Childhoods: Observed and Experienced*. London: Falmer.

Mayall, B. (2002) *Towards a Sociology for Childhood*. Buckingham: Open University Press.

McCall, L. (2005) 'The complexity of intersectionality'. *Signs* 30(3): 1771–800.

McCormick, B. (1986) 'Evidence about the comparative earnings of Asian and West Indian workers in Britain'. *Scottish Journal of Political Economy*, 33(2).

McCrone, D. (2001) *Understanding Scotland: The Sociology of a Nation*. London: Routledge.

McCrone, D. and Kiely, R. (2000) 'Nationalism and citizenship', *Sociology*, 34(1): 19–34.

McDowell, L. (1997) *Capital Culture: Gender at Work in the City*. Oxford: Blackwell.

McIntosh, M. (1993) 'Queer theory and the war of the sexes'. In Bristow, J. and Wilson, A.R. (eds) (1993) *Activating Theory*. London: Lawrence & Wishart.

McKay, S. (2004) 'Poverty or preference? What do "consensual deprivation indicators" really measure?'. *Fiscal Studies* 25(2): 201–23.

McKenna, F. (1980) *The Railway Workers 1840–1979*. London: Faber.

McKibbin, R. (1998) *Class and Cultures: England, 1918–1951.* Oxford: Oxford University Press.

McKnight, A., Elias, P. and Wilson, R. (1998) *Low Pay and the National Insurance System: A Statistical Picture.* Manchester: Equal Opportunities Commission.

McLennan, D., Barnes, M., Noble, M., Davies, J. and Garratt, E. (2011) *The English Indices of Deprivation 2010.* London: Department for Communities and Local Government.

McMillan, L. (2007) *Feminist Organising Against Gendered Violence.* Basingstoke: Palgrave.

McRae, S. (2003a) 'Constraints and choices on mothers' employment'. *British Journal of Sociology,* 54(3): 317–38.

McRae, S. (2003b) 'Constraints and choices on mothers' employment: McRae replies to Hakim'. *British Journal of Sociology,* 54(4): 585–92.

Meade, K. (1995) 'Promoting Age Equality'. *Generations Review.* 5(3): 7–10.

Meigs, A. (1990) 'Multiple gender ideologies and statuses'. In Sanday, P. and Goodenough, C. (eds) *Beyond the Second Sex: New Directions in the Anthropology of Gender.* Philadelphia: University of Pennsylvania Press.

Mewett, P. (1982) 'Exiles, nicknames, social identities and the production of local consciousness in a Lewis crofting community'. In Cohen, A. (ed.) *Belonging.* Manchester: Manchester University Press.

Meyer, L. (2003) 'Economic globalization and women's status in the labour market: a cross-national investigation of occupational sex segregation and inequality'. *Sociological Quarterly,* 44: 351–83.

Michels, R. ([1911]1962) *Political Parties: A Sociological Study of the Oligarchical Tendencies of Modern Democracy.* New York: Free Press (first published as *Zur Soziologie der Partiewesens in der Modernen Demokratie* 1911).

Middleton, S., Ashworth, K. and Braithwaite, I. (1997) *Small Fortunes: Spending on Children, Childhood Poverty and Parental Sacrifice.* York: Joseph Rowntree Foundation.

Milanovic, B. (2005) *Worlds Apart: Measuring Global and International Inequality.* Princeton: Princeton University Press.

Milanovic, B. (2011) *The Haves and the Have Nots.* New York: Basic Books.

Miles, R. (1982) *Racism and Migrant Labour.* London: Routledge & Kegan Paul.

Miles, R. (1993) *Racism after Race Relations.* London: Routledge.

Miliband, R. (1969) *The State in Capitalist Society: An Analysis of the Western System of Power.* London: Quartet

Mills, C.W. (1956) *The Power Elite.* New York: Oxford University Press.

Mills, C.W. (1959/1970) *The Sociological Imagination.* London: Oxford University Press.

Mills, M. (2003) 'Gender inequality in the global labor force'. *Annual Review of Anthropology,* 32: 41–62.

Mills, M. (2009) 'Globalization and inequality'. *European Sociological Review,* 25(1):1–8.

Minns, R. (2006) 'The future of Stock Market pensions'. In Vincent, J.A., Phillipson, C.R. and Downs, M. (eds) *The Futures of Old Age.* London: Sage.

Mirza, H. (2003) '"All the women are white, all the blacks are men – but some of us are brave": mapping the consequences of invisibility for black and minority ethnic women'. In Mason (2003c), q.v.

Mitchell, C. (2004) 'Is Northern Ireland abnormal? An extension of the sociological debate on religion in modern Britain', *Sociology* **38**(2): 237–54 .

Modan, G. (2007) *Turf Wars: Discourse, Diversity and the Politics of Place*. Oxford: Blackwell.

Modood, T. (1988) 'Black, racial equality and Asian identity', *New Community*, **14**(3): 397–404.

Modood, T. (1990) 'Catching up with Jesse Jackson: on being oppressed and on being somebody', *New Community*, **17**(1): 85–96.

Modood, T. (1992) *Not Easy Being British*. Stoke-on-Trent: Trentham Books.

Modood, T. (1997a) 'Culture and identity' in Modood, T. and Berthoud, R. (eds) *Ethnic Minorities in Britain*. London: Policy Studies Institute.

Modood, T. (1997b) '"Difference", cultural racism and anti-racism'. In Werbner, P. and Modood, T. (eds) *Debating Cultural Hybridity*. London: Zed Books.

Modood, T. (1997c) 'Employment' in Modood, T. and Berthoud, R. (eds) *Ethnic Minorities in Britain*. London: Policy Studies Institute.

Modood, T. (2003) 'Ethnic differentials in educational performance'. In Mason, (ed.) (2003c) q.v.

Modood, T., Berthoud, R. et al. (eds) (1997) *Ethnic Minorities in Britain*. London: Policy Studies Institute.

Monaghan, L. (2007) 'Body Mass Index, masculinities and moral worth: men's critical understandings of "appropriate" weight-for-height'. *Sociology of Health and Illness* **29**(4): 584–609.

Montague, A. (1964) *The Concept of Race*. New York: Free Press.

Montague, A. (1974) *Man's Most Dangerous Myth: The Fallacy of Race*. New York: Oxford University Press.

Morgan, M. (2008) 'The doctor–patient relationship'. In Scambler, G. (ed.) *Sociology as Applied to Medicine* (6th edn). London: Saunders Elsevier.

Morris, J. (1974) *Conundrum*. Oxford: Oxford University Press.

Morris, L. (1995) *Social Divisions*. London: UCL Press.

Morris, L. and Ritchie, J. (1994) *Income Maintenance and Living Standards*. York: Joseph Rowntree Foundation/SCPR.

Morris, L. and Scott, J. (1996) 'The attenuation of class analysis'. *British Journal of Sociology*, **47**(1): 45–55.

Morris, R. (1990) *Class, Sect and Party: The Making of the British Middle Class, Leeds 1820–1850*. Manchester: Manchester University Press.

Morrow, V. (1994) 'Responsible children? Aspects of children's work and employment outside school in contemporary UK'. In Mayall, B. (ed.) *Children's Childhoods: Observed and Experienced*. London: Falmer.

Mosca, G. (1896/1939) *Elementi di Scienza Politica*. Trans. and reprinted as Mosca, G. (ed. Arthur Livingston) (1939) *The Ruling Class*. New York: McGraw Hill.

Mosca, G. (1923) *Elementi di Scienza Politica* (2nd edn). Trans and reprinted as Mosca, G. (ed.) (1932) *The Ruling Class*. New York: McGraw Hill.

Mumford, K. And Power, A. (2003) *East Enders: Family and Community in East London.* Bristol: Policy Press.

Murgatroyd, L. and Neuburger, H. (1997) 'A household satellite account for the UK'. *Economic Trends,* **527**(October): 63–71.

Murray, C. (1984) *Losing Ground: American Social Policy 1950–1980.* New York: Basic Books.

Murray, C. (1990) *The Emerging British Underclass.* London: Institute of Economic Affairs.

Murray, C. (1994a) 'The new Victorians and the new rabble', *Sunday Times,* 29 May 1994.

Murray, C. (1994b) *Underclass: The Crisis Deepens.* London: Institute of Economic Affairs.

Murray, C. (1996) *Charles Murray and the Underclass: the Developing Debate.* London: IEA.

Naipul, V.S. (1964) *A House for Mr Biswas.* London: Deutsch.

Nairn, T. (1977) *The Break-Up of Britain.* London: New Left Books.

Nandi, A. and Platt, L. (2010) *Ethnic Minority Women's Poverty and Economic Well Being.* London: Government Equalities Office.

Nash, J. (2008) 'Re-thinking intersectionality'. *Feminist Review* **89**: 1–15.

National Association of Head Teachers (2008) *Women in Headships.* www.naht.org.uk/welcome/news-and-media/magazines/features/womeninheadships.

National Association of Citizens Advice Bureaux (1984) *Unequal Opportunities: CAB Evidence on Racial Discrimination.* London: NACAB.

National Children's Home (1991) *Poverty and Nutrition Survey.* London: National Children's Home.

National Society for the Prevention of Cruelty to Children (2010) *Keeping Your Child Safe.* www.nspcc.org.uk/help-and-advice/for-parents/for-parents-hub_wda96726.html.

Nazroo, J. (1997) 'Health and health services'. In Modood, T. and Berthoud, R. (eds) *Ethnic Minorities in Britain.* London: Policy Studies Institute.

Newby, H. (1975) 'The deferential dialectic'. *Comparative Studies in Society and History,* **17**(2): 139–64.

Newby, H. (1980) *Green and Pleasant Land?* Harmondsworth: Penguin.

Nisbet, R. (1970) *The Sociological Tradition.* London: Heinemann.

Nolan, B. and Whelan, C. (1996) *Resources, Deprivation and Poverty.* Oxford: Clarendon Press.

Noon, M. (1993) 'Racial discrimination in speculative applications: evidence from the UK's top one hundred firms', *Human Resource Management Journal,* **3**(4): 35–47.

Norris, P. (2000) 'Global governance and cosmopolitan citizens'. In Nye, J. and Donaghue, J. (eds) *Governance in a Globalizing World,* Washington DC: Brookings Institute.

Northern Ireland Life and Times Survey (2007) www.ark.ac.uk/nilt/2007/ (accessed 20 May 2012).

O'Brien, J. and Howard, J. (eds) (1998) *Everyday Inequalities.* Oxford: Blackwell.

O'Connell Davidson, J. (1998) *Prostitution, Power and Freedom.* Cambridge: Polity.

O'Connell Davidson, J. (2002) 'The rights and wrongs of prostitution', *Hypatia* **12**(2): 84–98.

O'Reilly, K. (2000) *The British on the Costa Del Sol: Transnational Identities and Local Communities*. London: Routledge.

O'Rourke, K. (2001) 'Globalization and inequality: historical trends'. Centre for Economic Policy Research, *CEPR Discussion Paper no 2865*. www.srn.com/abstract=277292 (accessed 7 June 2012).

Oakley, A. (1972) *Sex, Gender and Society*. Oxford: Martin Robertson.

Office for National Statistics (ONS) (1997) *Social Trends 27*. London: The Stationery Office.

Office for National Statistics (ONS) (1998a) *Social Trends 28*. London: The Stationery Office.

Office for National Statistics (ONS) (1998b) *General Household Survey 1996*. London: The Stationery Office.

Office for National Statistics (ONS) (1999) *Annual Abstract of Statistics 1999*, No. 135. London: The Stationery Office.

Office for National Statistics (ONS) (2001–2) *General Household Survey 2001–2002*. London: The Stationery Office/(computer file) 2nd edn. Colchester: UK Data Archive (distributor) 14 July 2003 SN: 4646.

Office for National Statistics (ONS) (2002) *Living in Britain*. London: The Stationery Office. www.statistics.gov.uk/downloads/theme_social/Family_Spending_2000–01/Family Spending_2000–01.pdf

Office for National Statistics (ONS) (2003e) *Social Trends 34*. London: The Stationery Office.

Office for National Statistics (ONS) (2003a) *General Household Survey 2003*. London: The Stationery Office.

Office for National Statistics (2003c) *Population of the United Kingdom: By Ethnic Group, April 2001*, National Statistics Online www.statistics.gov.uk/cci/nugget.asp?id=273 (accessed 29 September 2010).

Office for National Statistics (2003d) *Regional Distribution of the Minority Ethnic Population, April 2001*, National Statistics Online www.statistics.gov.uk/cci/nugget.asp?id=263 (accessed 29 September 2010).

Office for National Statistics (ONS) (2003b), *Labour Force Survey 2007*, London.

Office for National Statistics (ONS) (2004a) *Focus on Ethnicity: Employment Patterns*, Office for National Statistics, National Statistics Online. 8 January 2004. www.statistics.gov.uk/cci/nugget.asp?id=463 (accessed 1 March 2005).

Office for National Statistics (ONS) (2004b) *Focus on Inequalities*. London: The Stationery Office.

Office for National Statistics (ONS) (2004c) *Focus on People and Migration: Overseas Born*, Office for National Statistics, National Statistics Online, 24 June 2004 www.statistics.gov.uk/CCI/nugget.asp?ID=767&Pos=3&ColRank=2&Rank=176, (accessed 1 March 2005).

Office for National Statistics (ONS) (2004d) *Focus on Religion*. London: The Stationery Office. http//www.statistics.gov.uk/focuson/religion/.

Office for National Statistics (ONS) (2004e) *Social Trends 35*. London: The Stationery Office.

Office for National Statistics (2006a) *Ethnicity and Identity, Employment Patterns 2004,* National Statistics Online. www.statistics.gov.uk/cci/nugget.asp?id=463 (accessed 6 October 2010).

Office for National Statistics (2006b) *Unemployment Rates by Ethnic Group and Sex, 2004,* National Statistics Online. www.statistics.gov.uk/cci/nugget.asp?id=462 (accessed 29 September 2010).

Office for National Statistics (ONS) (2007) *Labour Force Survey 2007,* A77–222531 London.

Office for National Statistics (ONS) (2009a) *The Changing Living Arrangements of Young Adults in the UK.* www.ons.gov.uk/ons/rel/population-trends-rd/population-trends/no--138--winter-2009/the-changing-living-arrangements-of-young-adults-in-the-uk-.pdf (accessed 15 March 2012).

Office for National Statistics (ONS) (2009b) *Regional Trends No 41* (online tables for regional portraits). www.ons.gov.uk/ons/search/index.html?content-type=Reference+table&pubdateRangeType=allDates&newquery=regional+trends+online+tables+2007&pageSize=50&applyFilters=true (accessed 14 May 2012).

Office for National Statistics (ONS) (2009c) *Social Trends 39, Full Report.* www.ons.gov.uk/ons/rel/social-trends-rd/social-trends/social-trends-39/social-trends-full-report.pdf (accessed 15 March 2012).

Office for National Statistics (ONS) (2010a) *Divorces in England and Wales 2010 Release.* www.ons.gov.uk/ons/rel/vsob1/divorces-in-england-and-wales/2010/stb-divorces-2010.html#tab-Age-at-divorce (accessed 28 April 2012).

Office for National Statistics (ONS) (2010b) *General Lifestyle Survey 2010.* www.ons.gov.uk/ons/rel/ghs/general-lifestyle-survey/2010/index.html (accessed 12 March 2012).

Office for National Statistics (ONS) (2010c) *Pension Trends, Chapter 11: Pensioner Income and Expenditure.*

Office for National Statistics (ONS) (2010d) *Social Trends,* 40. London: Office for National Statistics.

Office for National Statistics (ONS) (2011a) *Family Spending: A Report on the 2010 Living Costs and Food Survey,* London: Stationery Office.

Office for National Statistics (ONS (2011b) *General Lifestyle Survey Health Tables.* www.ons.gov.uk/ons/search/index.html?pageSize=50&newquery=Health glf09chapter-7healt_tcm77–237966 (accessed 11 May 2012).

Office for National Statistics [ONS] (2011c) *Measuring what Matters: National Statistician's Reflections on the National Debate on Measuring National Well-being.* London: HMSO.

Office for National Statistics (ONS) (2011d) *Population Trends* **145.**Cardiff: ONS.

Office for National Statistics (ONS) (2012a) *Labour Market Status of Disabled People.* A08feb2012_tcm77–260611xls (accessed 30 April 2012).

Office for National Statistics (ONS) (2012b) *Pension Trends: The Labour Market and Retirement.* www.ons.gov.uk/ons/about-ons/our-statistics/publications/pension-trends/index.html (accessed 13 March 2012).

Office for National Statistics (ONS) (2012c) *Region and Country Profiles, Key Statistics Tables – February 2012.*www.ons.gov.uk/ons/publications/re-reference-tables.html?edition=tcm%3A77–242593 (accessed 8 March 2012).

Office for National Statistics (ONS) (2012d) Table EMP09UK Oct-Dec 2011 www. ons.gov.uk (accessed 7 April 2012).

Office for National Statistics (ONS) (2012e) *2011 Census: Religion and Local Authorities England and Wales.*

Office for National Statistics (ONS) (2013) *Labour Market Statistics by Ethnic Group.* www.ons.gov.uk/ons/publications/re-reference-tables.html?edition=tcm%3 (accessed 10 January 2013).

Office of Population Censuses and Surveys (OPCS) (1993) *Census 1991: Historical Tables, Great Britain.* London: HMSO.

Office of Population Censuses and Surveys (OPCS) (2003) *Census 2001 Great Britain.* London: ONS.

Oliver, M. (1990) *The Politics of Disablement.* London: Macmillan.

Oliver, M. (2004) 'The social model in action: if I had a hammer?'. In Barnes, C. and Mercer, G. (eds) *Implementing the Social Model of Disability: Theory and Research.* Leeds: Disability Press.

Oliver, M. and Barnes, C. (1998) *Disabled People and Social Policy: From Exclusion to Inclusion.* Harlow: Longman.

Oppenheim, C. and Harker, L. (1996) *Poverty: The Facts* (3rd edn). London: CPAG.

Organisation for Economic Co-operation and Development (OECD) (2004) 'Ageing and financial markets', *Financial Market Trends*, **86**: 85–117.

Organisation for Economic Co-operation and Development (OECD) (2009) *Pensions and the Crisis.* www.oecd.org/dataoecd/10/26/43060101.pdf (accessed 12 March 2012)

Organisation for Economic Co-operation and Development (OECD) (2011a) *How's Life?* Paris: OECD.

Organisation for Economic Co-operation and Development (OECD) (2011b) *Pensions at a Glance 2011: Retirement-Income Systems in OECD and G20 Countries.* www. oecd-ilibrary.org/finance-and-investment/pensions-at-a-glance-2011_pension_ glance-2011–en (accessed 16 March 2012)

Orshansky, M. (1965) 'Counting the poor: another look at the poverty profile'. *Social Security Bulletin*, **28**(1): 3–29.

Osgood, D.W and Siennick, S.E. (2012) 'Young adults' "need": in the eye of the beholder?'. In Booth, A., Brown, S.L., Landale, N.S., Manning, W.D. and McHale, S.M. (eds) *Early Adulthood in a Family Context, National Symposium on Family Issues,* **2**(2). New York: Springer.

Owen, D. (1992) *Ethnic Minorities in Britain: Settlement Patterns.* Coventry: University of Warwick, Centre for Research in Ethnic Relations, National Ethnic Minority Data Archive, 1991 Census Statistical Paper No. 1.

Owen, D. (1993) *Ethnic Minorities in Britain: Economic Characteristics.* Coventry: University of Warwick, Centre for Research in Ethnic Relations, National Ethnic Minority Data Archive, 1991 Census Statistical Paper No. 3.

Owen, D. (2003) 'The demographic characteristics of people from minority ethnic groups in Great Britain', in Mason, D. (ed) (2003c) q.v.

Page, E. and Wright, V. (eds) (1999) *Bureaucratic Elites in Western European States* (Oxford: Oxford University Press, 1999).

Pahl, J. (1983) 'The allocation of money and the structuring of inequality within marriage'. *Sociological Review* **21**(2): 237–62.

Pahl, J. (ed.) (1985) *Private Violence and Public Policy*. London: Routledge & Kegan Paul.

Pahl, R. (1984) *Divisions of Labour*. Oxford: Blackwell.

Pahl, R. (1993) 'Does class analysis without class theory have a promising future?'. *Sociology*, **27**(2): 253–8.

Pantazis, C., Gordon, D. and Levitas, R.A. (eds) (2006) *Poverty and Social Exclusion in Britain: The Millennium Survey*. Bristol: Policy Press.

Papadopoulos, L. (2010) *Sexualisation of Young People Review*. webarchive.national-archives.gov.uk/20100418065544/homeoffice.gov.uk/documents/sexualisation-young-people.html (accessed 29 April 2012).

Pareto, V. (1902) *Les Systems Socialistes*. Paris: Giard et Briere.

Pareto, V. ([1916]1963) *A Treatise on General Sociology*. In Livingstone, A. (ed.) (1963) New York: Dover (four volumes bound as two).

Park, A. et al (2002) *British Social Attitudes: The 19th Report*. London: Sage.

Parker, H. (1998) *Low Cost but Acceptable: A Minimum Income Standard for the UK*. Bristol: The Policy Press.

Parker, H. (ed.) (2000) *Low Cost but Acceptable Incomes for Older People: A Minimum Income Standard for Households aged 65–74 Years in the UK*. Bristol: The Policy Press.

Parkin, F. (1971) *Class Inequality and Political Order*. London: McGibbon & Kee.

Parry, G., Moyser, G. and Wagstaffe, M. (1987) 'The crowd and the community'. In Gaskell, G. and Benewick, R. (eds) (1987) *The Crowd in Contemporary Britain*. London: Sage.

Patrick, R. (2011) *Deserving or Undeserving?* UK Social Policy Association. www.social-policy.org.uk/lincoln2011/Patrick%20symposium%20P4.pdf (accesssed 15 August 2013).

Paxman, J. (1999) *The English: A Portrait of a People*. London: Penguin.

Payne, G. (1973) 'Typologies of middle class mobility'. *Sociology*, 7(3): 417–28.

Payne, G. (1987a) *Employment and Opportunity*. London: Macmillan.

Payne, G. (1987b) *Mobility and Change in Modern Society*. London: Macmillan.

Payne, G. (1989) 'Social mobility'. In Burgess, R. (ed.) *Investigating Society*. London: Longmans.

Payne, G. (1992) 'Competing views of contemporary social mobility and social divisions'. In Burrows, R. and Marsh, C. (eds) *Consumption and Class*. London: Macmillan.

Payne, G. (1996) 'Imagining the community'. In Lyon, S. and Busfield, J. (eds) *Methodological Imaginations*. Basingstoke: Palgrave Macmillan.

Payne, G. (2004) *Social Dividing*. Paper presented to the British Sociological Association Annual Conference, York.

Payne, G. (2006) 'Re-counting 'illiteracy': literacy skills in the sociology of social inequality'. *British Journal of Sociology*, 57(2): 219–40.

Payne, G. and Grew, C. (2005) 'Unpacking class ambivalence'. *Sociology*, **39**(5): 893–910.

Payne, G. and Roberts, J. (2002) 'Opening and closing the gates: recent developments in male social mobility in Britain', *Sociological Review Online*, **6**(4). www.socresonline.org.wks/6/4/payne.html.

Payne, G., Payne, J. and Hyde, M. (1996) 'Refuse of all classes? Social indicators and social deprivation'. *Sociological Research Online*, **1**(1). www.socresonline.org.uk/socresonline/1/1/3.html (accessed 15 August 2013).

Payne, J. (1999) *Researching Health Needs: A Community-based Approach*. London: Sage.

Payne, R. and Abel, G. (2012) 'UK indices of multiple deprivation – a way to make comparisons across constituent countries easier'. *Health Statistics Quarterly* **53** (Spring). London: ONS.

Pensions Commission (2004) *Pensions: Challenges and Choices: The First Report of the Pensions Commission*. London: The Stationery Office

Pensions Commission (2006) *Implementing an Integrated Package of Pension Reforms: The Final Report of the Pensions Commission*. London: The Stationery Office

Perlin, R. (2011) *Intern Nation: How to Earn Nothing and Learn Little in the New Economy*. London: Verso.

Perrons, D (2009) *Women and Gender Equity in Employment: Patterns, Progress and Challenges*. IES Working Paper: WP23.

Perry, E. and Francis, B. (2010) *The Social Class Gap for Educational Achievement: A Review of the Literature*. London: RSA.

Phelan, P. (1993) *Unmarked: the Politics of Performance*. London: Routledge.

Phillips, A. and Taylor, B. (1980) 'Sex and skill: moves towards a feminist economics'. *Feminist Review*(6): 79–88.

Phillips, S. (1986) 'Natives and Incomers: the symbolism of belonging in Muker parish, North Yorkshire'. In Cohen, A. (ed.) *Symbolising Boundaries*. Manchester: Manchester University Press.

Phillipson, C. (1998) *Reconstructing Old Age*. London: Sage.

Phillipson, C., Bernard, M., Phillips, J. and Ogg, J. (2001) *The Family and Community Life of Older People*. London: Routledge.

Phizacklea, A. (1983) *One Way Ticket: Migration and Female Labour*. London: Routledge.

Piachaud, D. (1979) *The Cost of a Child*. London: Child Poverty Action Group.

Piachaud, D. (1981) 'Peter Townsend and the Holy Grail'. *New Society*, 57: 419–21.

Piachaud, D. (1987) 'Problems in the definition and measurement of poverty'. *Journal of Social Policy*, 16(2): 147–64.

Pickard, S. (1995) *Living on the Front Line*. Aldershot: Avebury.

Pilcher, J. (2005) 'School sex education: policy and practice in England 1970 to 2000', *Sex Education*, **5**(2): 153–70,

Pill, R. and Stott, N. (1982) 'Concepts of illness causation and responsibility: some preliminary data from a sample of working class mothers'. *Social Science and Medicine*, **16**(1): 43–52.

Pill, R., Peters, T. and Robling, M. (1993) 'Factors associated with health behaviour among mothers of lower socio-economic status: a British example'. *Social Science and Medicine*, **36**, 9: 1137–44.

Pinchbeck, I. and Hewitt, M. (1969) *Children in English Society Volume I*. London: Routledge & Kegan Paul.

Platt, L. (2002) *Parallel Lives? Poverty among Ethnic Minority Groups in Britain*. London: CPAG.

Platt, L. (2003) *The Intergenerational Social Mobility of Minority Ethnic Groups*. Working Paper of the Institute for Social and Economic Research Paper 2033–04. Colchester: University of Essex.

Platt, L. (2005) *Discovering Child Poverty: The Creation of a Policy Agenda from 1800 to the Present*. Bristol: Policy Press.

Platt, L. (2007) *Poverty and Ethnicity in the UK*. Bristol: Policy Press.

Platt, L. (2009) *Ethnicity and Child Poverty*. Department for Work and Pensions Research Report No 576. Leeds: Corporate Document Services.

Plummer, K. (2003) *Intimate Citizenship*. Seattle: University of Washington Press.

Popay, J., Williams, G. Thomas, C. and Gatrell, A. (1998) 'Theorising inequalities in health: the place of lay knowledge'. In Bartley, M., Blane, D. and Davey Smith, G. (eds) *The Sociology of Health Inequalities*. Oxford: Blackwell.

Porter, J. (1965) *The Vertical Mosaic*. Toronto: University of Toronto Press.

Porteus, J. (1989) *Planned to Death*. Manchester: Manchester University Press.

Postman, N. (1994) *The Disappearance of Childhood*. New York: Vintage Books.

Potts, A., Gavey, N., Grace, V. and Vares, T. (2003) 'The downside of Viagra: women's experiences and concerns'. *Sociology of Health and Illness*, **25**, 7:697–719.

Poulantzas, N. (1969) 'The problem of the capitalist state'. *New Left Review*, **59**: 67–78.

Poverty Site (2011) www.poverty.org.uk/45/index.shtml (accessed 5 July 2013).

Powell, A. (2010) *Sex, Power and Consent: Youth Culture and the Unwritten Rules*. Cambridge: Cambridge University Press.

Power, S., Whitty, C. and Edwards, T. (1998) 'School boys and school work: gender, identification and academic achievement'. In Epstein, D., Maw, J., Elwood, J. and Hey, V. (eds) *International Journal of Inclusive Education* (special edition on boys' under-achievement)(2): 135–53.

Prandy, K. (1991) 'The evised Cambridge Scale of Occupations'. *Sociology*, **24**(4): 629–56

(3):1–Price, D. and Ginn, J. (2006) 'The future of inequalities in retirement income'. In Vincent, J.A., Phillipson, C.R. and Downs, M. (eds) *The Futures of Old Age*. London: Sage.

Pringle, R. (1988) *Secretaries Talk: Sexuality, Power and Work*. London: Verso.

Punch, S. (1998) 'Negotiating independence: children and young people growing up in rural Bolivia'. Unpublished paper, School of Geography, University of Leeds.

Putnam, R. (2000) *Bowling Alone: The Collapse And Revival Of American Community*. New York: Simon & Schuster.

Rake, K. (2000) *Women's Incomes over the Lifetime*. London: Stationery Office.

Rahman, M. and Jackson, S. (2010) *Gender and Sexuality: Sociological Approaches*. Cambridge: Polity.

Raphael M. (1964) *Pensions and Public Servants: A Study in the Origins of the British System*, Paris: Mouton.

Rattansi, A. and Westwood, S. (1994) *Racism, Modernity and Identity on the Western Front,* Oxford: Polity Press.

Reay, D., Hollingworth, S., Williams, K, Crozier, G., Jamieson, F., James, D. and Beedell, P. (2007) '"A darker shade of pale?" Whiteness, the middle classes and multiethnic inner city schooling'. *Sociology,* **41**(6): 1041–60.

Redshaw, M. and Heikkila, K. (2011) 'Ethnic differences in women's worries about labour and birth'. *Ethnicity and Health* **16**(3): 213–23.

Rees, T. (1992) *Women and the Labour Market.* London: Routledge.

Reich, W. (1951) *The Sexual Revolution.* London: Vision Books.

Reid, I. (1998) *Class in Britain.* London: Polity.

Reiner, R. (1991) *Chief Constables: Bobbies, Bosses or Bureaucrats?* Oxford: Clarendon.

Reiser, R. (1995) 'Stereotypes of disabled people'. In Reiser, R. (ed.) *Invisible Children.* London: Save the Children.

Renold, E. (2005) *Girls, Boys and Junior Sexualities.* London: Routledge.

Rex, J. and Mason, D. (eds) (1986) *Theories of Race and Ethnic Relations.* Cambridge: Cambridge University Press.

Rex, J. and Moore, R. (1967) *Race, Community and Conflict.* London: Oxford University Press.

Rich, A. (1980) 'Compulsory heterosexuality and lesbian existence'. *Signs,* **5**(4): 630–60.

Richardson, D. (ed.) (1996) *Theorising Heterosexuality: Telling it Straight.* Buckingham: Open University Press.

Richardson, D. and Monro, S. (2012) *Sexuality, Equality and Diversity.* Basingstoke: Palgrave Macmillan.

Ridge, D., Emslie, C. and White, A. (2011) 'Understanding how men experience, express and cope with mental distress: where next?'. *Sociology of Health and Illness* **33**(1): 145–59.

Ringen, S. (1988) 'Direct and indirect measures of poverty', *Journal of Social Policy* **17**(3): 351–65.

Roberts, I. (1993) *Craft, Class and Control.* Edinburgh: Edinburgh University Press.

Roberts, K. (2001) *Class in Modern Britain,* London, Palgrave.

Robertson, R. (1992) *Globalization: Social Theory and Global Culture.* London: Sage.

Rogaly, B. and Taylor, B. (2011) *Moving Histories of Class and Community: Identity, Place and Belonging in Contemporary England.* Basingstoke: Palgrave Macmillan.

Roscigno, V.J. (2007) 'Age discrimination, social closure and employment'. *Social Forces,* **86**(1): 313–34.

Rose, D. and O' Reilly, K. (1998) *The ESRC Review of Government Social Classifications.* London: Office for National Statistics and ESRC.

Rose, N. (1989) *Governing the Soul: The Shaping of the Private Self.* London: Routledge.

Rose, N. (1991) *Governing the Soul: The Shaping of the Private Self.* London: Routledge.

Rowntree, B. (1901) *Poverty: A Study of Town Life.* London: Longmans Green.

Rowntree, B. (1902) *Poverty: A Study of Town Life* (2nd edn). London: Macmillan.

Rowntree, B. (1918) *The Human Needs of Labour.* London: Thomas Nelson & Sons.

Rowntree, B. (1937) *The Human Needs of Labour* (2nd edn). London: Longmans, Green & Co.

Rowntree, B. (1942) *Poverty and Progress: A Second Social Survey of York*. London: Longmans, Green & Co.

Rowntree, B. and Lavers, G. (1951) *Poverty and the Welfare State: A Third Social Survey of York Dealing only with Economic Questions*. London: Longmans, Green & Co.

Rubin, G. (1975) 'The traffic in women: notes on the 'political economy' of sex'. In Reiter, R. (ed.) *Toward an Anthropology of Women*. New York: Monthly Review Press.

Rubin, G. (1984) 'Thinking sex: notes for a radical theory of the politics of sexuality'. In Vance, C. (ed.) *Pleasure and Danger: Exploring Female Sexuality*. London: Routledge & Kegan Paul.

Rubington, E. and Weinberg, M. (2011). *The Study of Social Problems: Seven Perspectives* (7th edn). New York: Oxford University Press.

Rubinstein, W. (1981) *Men of Property*. London: Croom Helm.

Rubinstein W. (1993) *Capitalism, Culture and Decline in Britain 1750–1990*. London: Routledge.

Runnymede Trust (1997) *Islamophobia: A Challenge for Us All*. London: Runnymede Trust.

Ruthven, M. (1991) *A Satanic Affair: Salman Rushdie and the Wrath of Islam*. London: Hogarth Press.

Ryan, J. and Thomas, F. (1980) *The Politics of Mental Handicap*. Harmondsworth: Penguin.

Ryder, N.B. (1965) 'The cohort as a concept in the study of social change'. *American Sociological Review*, **30**: 843–61

Saint-Simon, H. (1825) *De L'Organisation Sociale*. For relevant material see Saint-Simon (1975) *Selected Writings On Science, Industry and Social Organisation* (ed. K. Taylor). London: Croom Helm.

Salaman, G. (1986) *Working*. London: Tavistock.

Sarre, P. (1989) 'Race and the class structure'. In Hamnett, C., McDowell, L. and Sarre, P. (eds) *The Changing Social Structure*. London: Sage.

Sassen, S. (1994) *Cities in a World Economy*. Thousand Oaks: Pine Forge Press.

Sassen, S. (2006) *Territory, Authority, and Rights. From Medieval to Global Assemblages*. Princeton: Princeton University Press.

Saunders, P. (1990) *A Nation of Home Owners*. London: Unwin Hyman.

Saunders, P. (2000) *Unequal But Fair? A Study of Class Barriers in Britain*. London: Institute of Economic Affairs.

Savage, M. (1992) 'Women's expertise, men's authority: gendered organisation in the contemporary middle classes'. In Savage, M. and Witz, A. (eds) *Gender and Bureaucracy*. Oxford: Blackwell.

Savage, M. (2000) *Class Analysis and Social Transformation*. Buckingham: Open University Press.

Savage, M. and Miles, A. (1994) *The Remaking of the British Working Class, 1840–1940*. London: Routledge.

Savage, M. and Williams, K. (eds) (2008) *Remembering Elites*. Oxford: Blackwell.

Savage, M., Bagnall, G. and Longhurst, B. (2001) 'Ordinary, ambivalent and defensive: class identities in Northwest England', *Sociology*, **35**(4):875–92.

Savage, M., Barlow, J., Dickens, P. and Fielding, T. (1992) *Property, Bureaucracy and Culture: Middle Class Formation in Contemporary Britain*. London: Routledge.

Savage, M., Devine, F., Cunningham, N., Taylor, M., Li, Y., Hjellbrekke, J., Le Roux, B., Friedman, S. and Miles, A. (2013) 'A New Model of Social Class: Findings from the BBC's Great British Class Survey Experiment', *Sociology*, 47(2): 219–50.

Scambler, G. (ed.) (1997) *Sociology as Applied to Medicine* (4th edn). London: W.B. Saunders.

Scase, D. and Goffee, L. (1982) *The Entrepreneurial Middle Class*. London: Croom Helm.

Scheper-Hughes, N. (2001) *Saints, Scholars And Schizophrenics: Mental Illness In Rural Ireland*. Berkeley: University of California Press.

Schumpeter, J. (1942) *Capitalism, Socialism and Democracy*. New York: Harper Row.

Scott, J. (1991) *Who Rules Britain?* Cambridge: Polity Press.

Scott, J. (1994a) 'Class analysis: back to the future'. *Sociology*, 28(4): 933–42.

Scott, J. (1994b) *Poverty and Wealth: Citizenship, Deprivation and Privilege*. Harlow: Longman.

Scott, J. (1996) *Stratification and Power: Structures of Class, Status and Command*. Cambridge: Polity Press.

Scott, J. (1997) *Corporate Business and Capitalist Classes*. Oxford: Oxford University Press.

Scott, J. (2008) 'Modes of power and the re-conceptualization of elites'. In

Savage, M. and Williams, K. (eds) *Remembering Elites*. Oxford: Blackwell.

Scott, S. and Freeman, R. (1995) 'Prevention as a problem of modernity: the example of HIV and AIDS'. In Gabe, J. (ed.) (1995) *Medicine, Health and Risk*. Oxford: Blackwell.

Scott, S. and Watson-Brown, L. (1997) 'The beast, the family and the little children'. *Trouble and Strife*, 36: 12–19.

Scully, D. (1990) *Understanding Sexual Violence: A Study of Convicted Rapists*. London: Unwin & Hyman.

Seager, J. (1997) *The State of Women in the World Atlas* (rev. edn). Harmondsworth, Penguin.

Seidman, S. (1996) *Queer Theory/Sociology*. Oxford: Blackwell.

Seidman, S. (1997) *Difference Troubles: Queering Social Theory and Sexual Politics*. Cambridge: Cambridge University Press.

Seidman, S. (2009) 'Critique of compulsory heterosexuality'. *Sexuality Research and Social Policy, Journal of NSRC*, 6(1): 18–28.

Sen, A. (1983) 'Poor, relatively speaking'. *Oxford Economic Papers*, 35:153–69.

Sen, A. (1985) 'A sociological approach to the measurement of poverty: a reply to Professor Peter Townsend'. *Oxford Economic Papers*, 37: 669–76.

Sen, A. (1987) *The Standard of Living: The Tanner Lectures, Clare Hall, Cambridge, 1985* (ed. by G. Hawthorn). Cambridge: Cambridge University Press.

Sen, K. (1994) *Ageing: Debates on Demographic Transition and Social Policy*. London: Zed Books.

Senior, M. and Viveash, B. (1998) *Health and Illness*. London: Macmillan.

Shah, P. and Kleiner B. (2005) 'New developments concerning age discrimination in the workplace', *Equal Opportunities International*, **24**(5): 15–23.

Shah, S. and Priestley, M. (2011) *Disability and Social Change*. Cambridge: Policy Press.

Shahar, S. (1990) *Childhood in the Middle Ages*. London: Routledge.

Shakespeare, T., Gillespie-Sells, K. and Davies, D. (1996) *The Sexual Politics of Disability: Untold Desires*. London: Cassell.

Shy, C. (1997) 'The failure of academic epidemiology'. *American Journal of Epidemiology*, **145**: 479–87.

Sidorick, D (2009) *Condensed Capitalism: Campbell Soup and the Pursuit of Cheap Production in the Twentieth Century*. Ithaca: Cornell University Press.

Simon, W. (1996) *Postmodern Sexualities*. New York: Routledge.

Simpson, B. (2011) 'Sexualizing the child: The strange case of Bill Henson, his "absolutely revolting" images and the law of childhood innocence', *Sexualities*, **14**(3): 290–311.

Sinfield, A. (1994) *The Wilde Century*. London: Cassell.

Skeggs, B. (2004) *Class, Self, Culture*. London: Routledge.

Skeggs, B. (2011) 'Imagining personhood differently: person value and autonomist working-class value practices', *The Sociological Review*, **59**(3): 496–513.

Skelton, C. (1993) 'Women and education'. In Richardson, D. and Robinson, V. (eds) *Introducing Women's Studies: Feminist Theory and Practice*. London: Macmillan.

Skolnick, A. (1973) *The Intimate Environment: Exploring Marriage and the Family*. Boston: Little, Brown.

Skolnick, A. (1980) 'Children's rights, children's development'. In Empey, L.T. (ed.) *Children's Rights and Juvenile Justice*. Charlottesville: University of Virginia Press.

Smith, A. (1776/1999) *The Wealth of Nations, books I-III*. London: Penguin.

Smith, A. (1976) *An Inquiry into the Nature and Causes of the Wealth of Nations* (ed. by E. Cannan). Chicago: University of Chicago Press.

Smith, D. (1974) *The Facts of Racial Disadvantage*, London: Political and Economic Planning.

Smith, D. (1979) 'A peculiar eclipse: women's exclusion from men's culture'. *Women's Studies International Quarterly*(1): 281–95.

Smith, D. (1981) *Unemployment and Racial Minorities*. London: Policy Studies Institute.

Smith, J. and Gerstorf, D. (2004) 'Ageing differently: potential and limits'. In Daatland, S. and Biggs, S. (eds) *Ageing and Diversity: Multiple Pathways and Cultural Migrations*, Bristol: Policy Press.

Smith, M. (1986) 'Pluralism, race and ethnicity in selected African countries'. In Rex, J. and Mason, D. (eds) *Theories of Race and Ethnic Relations*. Cambridge: Cambridge University Press.

Social and Community Planning Research (1999) *Geographical Variations in Health Indicators by Health Authority, 1994–1996*. London: Department of Health.

Solomos, J. and Back, L. (1996) *Racism in Society*. Basingstoke: Macmillan.

Song, M. (1996) '"Helping out": children's participation in Chinese take-away businesses in Britain'. In Brannen, J. and O'Brien, M. (eds) *Children in Families*. London: Falmer.

Spelman, E. (1990) *Inessential Woman: Problems of Exclusion in Feminist Thought*. London: The Women's Press.

Spencer, L. and Pahl, R. (2006) *Rethinking Friendship: Hidden Solidarities Today*. Princeton NJ: Princeton University Press.

Stacey, M. (1960) *Tradition and Change: A Study of Banbury*. Oxford: Oxford University Press.

Stacey, M., Batstone, E., Bell, C. and Murcott, A. (1975) *Power, Persistence and Change*. London: Routledge & Kegan Paul.

Stanley, L., and Wise, S. (2002) 'What's wrong with socialization?'. In Jackson, S. (ed.) *Gender: A Sociological Reader*. Abingdon: Routledge.

Standing, G. (2011) *The Precariat: The New Dangerous Class*. London: Bloomsbury.

Stanworth, M. (1984) 'Women and class analysis: a reply to Goldthorpe'. *Sociology*, 18(2): 159–70.

Starr, P. (1992) 'Social categories and claims in the liberal state'. In Douglas, M. and Hull, D. (eds) *How Classification Works: Nelson Goodman Among the Social Sciences*. Edinburgh: Edinburgh University Press.

Stepan, N. (1982) *The Idea of Race in Science*. London: Macmillan.

Stone, L. and Stone, J. (1984) *An Open Elite?* Oxford: Oxford University Press.

Stonewall (2008) *The Gay British Crime Survey*. London: Stonewall.

Strangleman, T. and Warren, T. (2008) *Work and Society: Sociological Approaches, Themes and Methods*. London: Routledge.

Strategic Review of Health Inequalities in England (2010) *Fair Society, Healthy Lives* (The Marmot Review). London: Department of Health.

Strong, P. (1980) 'Black on class and mortality'. *Journal of Public Health Medicine*, 12: 168–80.

Summerfield, C. and Babb, P. (eds) (2004) *Social Trends 34: A Portrait of British Society*, London: The Stationery Office. Sydie, R. (1994) *Natural Women, Cultured Men*. Vancouver: University of British Columbia Press.

Syme, S. (1996) 'To prevent disease: the need for a new approach'. In Blane, D., Brunner, E. and Wilkinson, R. (eds) *Health and Social Organisation*. London: Routledge.

Synge, J.M. (1911) *The Playboy Of The Western World*. Dublin: Maunsel.

Taillon, P. (2009) *Good, Reliable, White Men: Railroad Brotherhoods, 1877–1917*. Chicago: Illinois University Press.

Tam, M. (1997) *Part-time Employment: A Bridge or a Trap*. Aldershot: Avebury.

Tamir, Y. (1993) *Liberal Nationalism*. New Jersey: Princeton University Press.

Taunton Commission (1868) *Commissioners School Inquiry Report*. 23 volumes. London: Taunton Commission.

Taylor, I., Evans, K. and Fraser, P. (1996) *A Tale of Two Cities*. London: Routledge.

Taylor, M. (ed.) with Brice, J., Buck, N. and Prentice-Lane, E. (2003) *British Household Panel Survey User Manual Volume A: Introduction, Technical Report and Appendices*. Colchester: University of Essex.

Taylor, S. and Field, D. (1997/2003) *Sociology of Health and Health Care* (2nd/3rd edn). Oxford: Blackwell.

Telegraph, The (2011) 'David Willetts warns over "striking" university gender gap'. www. telegraph.co.uk/education/universityeducation/8873031/David-Willetts-warns-over-striking-university-gender-gap.html (accessed 11 May 2012).

Thane, P. (2002) *Old Age in English History: Past Experiences, Present Issues*, Oxford: Oxford University Press.

Thane, P. (2003) 'Social histories of old age and aging', *Journal of Social History*, 37(1): 93–111

Theakston, K. and Fry, G. (1989) 'Britain's administrative elite: permanent secretaries 1900–1986'. *Public Administration*, 67: 129–47.

Therborn, G. (2012) 'Global inequality: the return of class'. *Global Dialogue*, 2(1): www.isa-sociology.org/global-dialogue/2011/09/global-inequality-the-return-of-class/ (accessed 7 June 2012).

Thompson, E.P. (1968) *The Making of the English Working Class*. Harmondsworth: Penguin.

Thompson, F. (1963) *English Landed Society in the Nineteenth Century*. London: Routledge & Kegan Paul.

Thomson, R. and Scott, S. (1991) *Learning About Sex: Young Women and the Social Construction of Sexual Identity*. London: Tufnell Press.

Thorne, B. (1987) 'Re-visioning women and social change: where are the children?'. *Gender and Society*, 1(1): 85–109.

Thorne, B. (1993) *Gender Play: Girls and Boys in School*. Buckingham: Open University Press.

Thorogood, N. (1990) 'Caribbean home remedies and their importance for black women's health care in Britain'. In Abbott, P. and Payne, G. *New Directions in the Sociology of Health*. London: Falmer Press.

Tilly, C. (1992) *Coercion, Capital and European States, AD 990–1992*. Oxford: Blackwell.

Times, The (1997) 18 October – Ch. 3

Tinker, C. (2009) 'Rights, social cohesion and identity: arguments for and against state-funded Muslim schools in Britain'. *Race Ethnicity and Education* 12(4): 539–53.

Tolman, D. (2002). *Dilemmas of Desire: Teenage Girls Talk about Sexuality*. Cambridge, MA: Harvard University Press.

Tönnies, F. ([1887]1955) *Community and Association*. London: Routledge & Kegan Paul.

Townsend, P. (1979) *Poverty in the United Kingdom, A Survey of Household Resources and Standards of Living*. Harmondsworth: Penguin.

Townsend, P. (1985) 'A sociological approach to the measurement of poverty: a rejoinder to Professor Amartya Sen'. *Oxford Economic Papers*, 37:659–68.

Townsend, P. and Gordon, D. (2002) *World Poverty: New Policies to Defeat an Old Enemy*. Bristol: The Policy Press.

Townsend, P., Davidson, N. and Whitehead, M. (1992) *Inequalities in Health: The Black Report and the Health Divide* (rev. rdn). Harmondsworth: Penguin.

Townsend, P., Phillimore, P. and Beattie, A. (1986) *Poverty and the London Labour Market: An Interim Report*. London: Low Pay Unit.

Toynbee, P. (2003) *Hard Work: Life in Low Paid Britain*. London: Bloomsbury.

Trudell, B.N. (1993) *Doing Sex Education: Gender, Politics and Schooling.* New York: Routledge.

Trades Union Congress (TUC) (2012) *Women's Pay and Employment Update: a Public/private Sector Comparison. A Report for Women's Conference 2012.* London: Trades Union Council.

Trades Union Congress and Young Women's Christian Association (TUC and YWCA) (2010) *Apprenticeships and Gender.* www.tuc.org.uk/extras/Apprenticeships_and_gender.pdf (accessed 7 April 2012).

Turnball, C. (1984) *The Forest People.* London: Triad/Paladin.

Turnbull, C. (1966) *Wayward Servants: The Two Worlds of the African Pygmies.* London: Eyre & Spottiswoode.

Tyler, M. (1997) *Women's Work as the Labour of Sexual Difference: Female Employment in the Airline Industry.* PhD Thesis. Derby: University of Derby.

Union of Physically Impaired Against Segregation (1976) *Fundamental Principles of Disability.* London: Union of Physically Impaired Against Segregation.

UNICEF (2013) *United Nations Convention on the Rights of the Child.* www.unicef.org. uk/Documents/Publication-pdfs/UNCRC_PRESS200910web.pdf (accessed 5 July 2013).

United Nations (UN) (2002) *World Population Ageing: 1950–2050.* New York: Population Division, Department of Economic and Social Affairs, United Nations. www.un.org/esa/population/publications/worldageing19502050/index.htm

United Nations (UN) (2011a) *The Millennium Development Goals Report 2011.* New York: UN.

United Nations (UN) (2011b) *World Population Prospects: The 2010 Revision, Volume II: Demographic Profiles,* New York: Population Division, Department of Economic and Social Affairs, United nations. http://esa.un.org/unpd/wpp/Documentation/pdf/WPP2010_Volume-II_Demographic-Profiles.pdf (accessed 12 March 2012).

Valentine, G. (1996) 'Angels and devils: moral landscapes of childhood'. *Society and Space,* **14**: 581–99.

Valentine, G., Vanderbeck, R., Andersson, J., Sadgrove, J. and Ward, K. (2010) 'Emplacements: the event as a prism for exploring intersectionality'. *Sociology* **44**(5): 925–43.

Van den Berghe, P. (1967) *Race and Racism,* New York: Wiley.

Van Every, J. (1996) 'Heterosexuality and domestic life'. In Richardson, D. (ed.) *Theorising Heterosexuality: Telling it Straight.* Buckingham: Open University Press.

Varo-Watson, D. (1998) 'Does it work?', *Disability NOW.* April: 13.

Veit-Wilson, J. (1986) 'Paradigms of poverty: a rehabilitation of B.S. Rowntree', *Journal of Social Policy,* **15**: 69–99.

Veit-Wilson, J. (1992) 'Muddle or mendacity? The Beveridge Committee and the poverty line'. *Journal of Social Policy,* **21**: 269–301.

Veit-Wilson, J. (1994) 'Condemned to deprivation? Beveridge's responsibility for the invisibility of poverty'. In Hills, J., Ditch, J. and Glennerster, H. (eds) *Beveridge and Social Security.* Oxford: Clarendon Press.

Venn, C. (2006) *The Postcolonial Challenge: Towards Alternative Worlds.* London: Sage.

Vernon, A. (1998) 'Multiple oppression and the Disabled People's Movement'. In Shakespeare, T. (ed.) (1998) *The Disability Reader: Social Science Perspectives.* London: Cassell.

Victor, C. (1991) *Health and Health Care in Later Life.* Milton Keynes: Open University Press.

Vincent, J. (1995) *Inequality and Old Age.* London: UCL Press.

Vincent, J. (1996) 'Who's afraid of an ageing population?' *Critical Social Policy,* **16**(1): 3–26.

Vincent, J. (2001) *Politics and Old Age: Older Citizens and Political Processes in Britain.* Basingstoke: Ashgate.

Vincent. J. (2003) *Old Age.* London: Routledge.

Vincent, J. Phillipson, C. and Downs, M. (2006) *The Future of Old Age.* London: Sage.

von Zugbach, R. (1988) *Power and Prestige in the British Army.* Aldershot: Avebury

von Zugbach, R. and, Ishaq, M. (1999) 'The decline in social eliteness in the senior ranks of the British Army'. In Strachan, H. (ed.) *British Army, Manpower and Society: Towards 2000.* Abingdon: Frank Cass

Wacquant, L. (1994) 'The new urban color line: the state and fate of the ghetto in PostFordist America'. In Calhoun, C. (ed.) *Social Theory and the Politics of Identity.* Maldon, MA: Blackwell.

Waites, M. (2005) *The Age of Consent: Young People, Sexuality and Citizenship.* Basingstoke: Palgrave Macmillan.

Walby, S. (1986) *Patriarchy at Work.* Cambridge: Polity.

Walby, S. (1990) *Theorising Patriarchy.* Oxford: Blackwell.

Walker, A. and Foster, L. (2006) 'Ageing and social class: an enduring relationship', in Vincent, J.A., Phillipson, C.R. and Downs, M. (eds) *The Futures of Old Age.* London: Sage.

Walker, R. (1987) 'Consensual approaches to the definition of poverty: towards an alternative methodology'. *Journal of Social Policy,* **16**(2): 213–26.

Walker, R. (ed.) (1999) *Ending Child Poverty: Popular Welfare for the 21st Century?* Bristol: Policy Press.

Walker, R. and Ashworth, K. (1994) *Poverty Dynamics: Issues and Examples.* Aldershot: Avebury.

Walkerdine, V. (2003) 'Reclassifying upward mobility: femininity and the neo-liberal subject'. *Gender and Education,* 15(3): 238–48.

Walkerdine, V. and Lucey, H. (1989) *Democracy in the Kitchen: Regulating Mothers and Socialising Daughters.* London: Virago.

Wallace, C. (2010) *Social Quality and the Changing Relationship between Work and Care in Europe. Final Report to European Union.* www.abdn.ac.socsci/research/nec/workcare (accessed 7 April 2012).

Wallace, C. and Abbott, P. (2011) *Flexible working or Flexible Fatherhood.* Aberdeen: University of Aberdeen http://workcaresynergies.eu/ (accessed 7 April 2012).

Wallace, C., Mateeva, L. and Abbott, P. (2004) *Women and Enlargement. Report to the European Parliament.* Vienna: Institute for Advanced Studies.

Wallerstein, I. (1976) 'A world system perspective on the social sciences'. *British Journal of Sociology,* **27**,2: 343–52.

Wallerstein, I. (1979) *The Capitalist World Economy*. Cambridge: Cambridge University Press.

Wallis, R. (1976) *The Road to Total Freedom: A Sociological Analysis of Scientology*. London: Heinemann.

Wallman, S. (1979) 'Introduction'. In Wallman, S. (ed.) *Ethnicity at Work*. London: Macmillan.

Wallman, S. (1986) 'Ethnicity and the boundary process in context'. In Rex, J. and Mason, D. (eds) *Theories of Race and Ethnic Relations*. Cambridge: Cambridge University Press.

Walsh, J. (1999) 'Myths and counter-myths: an analysis of part-time female employees and their orientations to work and working hours'. *Work, Employment and Society*, **13**(2): 179–203.

Ware, J. (1993) 'Measuring patients' views: the optimum outcome measure'. *British Medical Journal*, **306**: 1429–30.

Warwick, D. and Littlejohn, G. (1992) *Coal, Capital and Culture*. London: Routledge.

Waskler, F. (ed.) (1991) *Studying the Social Worlds of Children*. London: Falmer.

Weber, M. (1914/1968) 'The distribution of power within the political community: class, status, party'. In Roth, G. and Wittich, C. (eds) (1968) *Economy and Society*. New York: Bedminster Press.

Weber, M. (1920/1968). 'Status groups and classes'. In Roth, G. and Wittich, C. (eds) (1968) *Economy and Society*. New York: Bedminster Press.

Weeks, J. (1989) *Sex, Politics and Society*. Harlow: Longmans.

Weeks, J. (1991) 'Pretended family relationships'. In Clark, D. (ed.) *Marriage, Domestic Life and Social Change*. London: Routledge.

Weeks, J. (1995) *Invented Moralities*. Cambridge: Polity.

Weeks, J., Waites, M. and Holland, J. (eds) (2002) *Sexualities and Society: A Reader*. Cambridge: Polity.

Weiner, M. (1981) *English Culture and the Decline of the Entrepreneurial Spirit*. London: Heinemann.

Wellings, K., Field, J., Johnson, A. and Wadsworth, J. (1994) *Sexual Behaviour in Britain*. London: Penguin.

Wells, K. (2009) *Childhood in a Global Perspective*. Cambridge: Polity.

Westergaard, J. (1995) *Who Gets What? The Hardening of Class Inequality in the Late Twentieth Century*. Cambridge: Polity Press.

Wetherell, M. (2008) 'Subjectivity or psycho-discursive practices? Investigating complex intersectional identities', *Subjectivity*, **22**: 73–81.

Whelan, C., Layte, R., Maître, B. and Nolan, B. (2001) 'Income, deprivation and economic strain: an analysis of the European Community Household Panel'. *European Sociological Review* **17**(4): 357–72.

White, K. (2009). *An Introduction to the Sociology of Health and Illness* (2nd edn). Sage: London.

Whitehead, L. (2006) 'Quest, chaos and restitution: living with chronic fatigue syndrome/myalgic encephalomyelitis', *Social Science and Medicine* **62**, 9: 2236–45.

Whitfield, G. (1997) *The Disability Discrimination Act: Analysis of Data from an Omnibus Survey*. London: Department of Social Security.

Whitley, R. (1974) 'The City and Industry'. In Stanworth, P. and Giddens, A. (eds) *Elites and Power in British Society.* Cambridge: Cambridge University Press.

Wight, D. (1993) *Workers not Wasters.* Edinburgh: Edinburgh University Press.

Wilkinson, R. (1996) *Unhealthy Societies: The Afflictions of Inequality.* London: Routledge.

Wilkinson, R. and Pickett, K. (2009) *The Spirit Level: Why Equality is Better for Everyone.* London: Allen Lane.

Williams, G. and Popay, J. (1994) 'Lay knowledge and the privilege of experience'. In Gabe, J., Kelleher, D. and Williams, G. (eds) *Challenging Medicine.* London: Routledge.

Williams, R. (1983) 'Concepts of health: an analysis of lay logic'. *Sociology,* **17**(1): 185–204.

Williams, R. (2000) *Making Identity Matter.* Durham: Sociology Press.

Willis, P. (1977) *Learning to Labour.* Farnborough: Saxon House.

Willmott, P. (1986) *Social Networks, Informal Care and Public Policy.* London: Policy Studies Institute.

Wilson, B.R. (1966) *Religion in Secular Society: A Sociological Comment.* London: Watts.

Wilson, B.R. (1970) *Religious Sects: A Sociological Study.* London: Weidenfeld & Nicolson.

Wilson, G. (2000) *Understanding Old Age.* London: Sage.

Wilton, T. (1996) 'Which one's the man? The heterosexualisation of lesbian sex'. In Richardson, D. (ed.) (1996) *Theorising Heterosexuality: Telling it Straight.* Buckingham: Open University Press.

Winquist, K. (2002) *Women and Men Beyond Retirement.* Brussels: European Commission.

Wood, M., Hales, J., Purdon, S., Sejersen, T. and Hayllar, O. (2009) *A Test for Racial Discrimination in Recruitment Practice in British Cities.* London: Department for Work and Pensions, Research Report No 607.

Woodward, K. (2002) *Identity and Difference.* London: Sage.

World Bank (1994) *Averting the Old Age Crisis: Policies to Protect the Old and Promote Growth,* Oxford: Oxford University Press.

World Health Organization (WHO) (1948). *Preamble to the Constitution of the World Health Organisation, April 1948.* www.who.int/about/definition/en/print.html (accessed 7 May 2012).

World Health Organization (WHO) (2012) www.unbrussels.org/agencies/who.html (accessed 8 May 2012).

Wright, E.O. (1985) *Classes.* London: Verso.

Wright, E.O. (1989) *The Debate on Classes.* London: Verso.

Wright, E.O. (1993) *Interrogating Inequality: Essays on Class Analysis, Socialism and Marxism.* London: Verso.

Wright, E.O. (1997) *Class Counts.* Cambridge: Cambridge University Press.

Wright, P. (1985) *Living in an Old Country.* London: Verso.

Wyness, B. (2005) *The Sociology of Childhood.* Basingstoke: Palgrave Macmillan.

Yeandle, S. (1984) *Women's Working Lives: Patterns and Strategies.* London: Tavistock.

Yinger, J.M. (1986) 'Intersecting strands in the theorisation of race and ethnic relations'. In Rex, J. and Mason, D. (eds), *Theories of Race and Ethnic Relations. Cambridge:* Cambridge University Press.

Yinger, J.M. (1994) *Ethnicity: Source of Strength? Source of Conflict?* Albany: State University of New York.

Young, I. (1986) 'The ideal of community and the politics of difference'. *Social Theory
and Practice* **12**(1): 1–26.

Young, M. and Willmott, P. (1957) *Family and Kinship in East London.* London: Routledge & Kegan Paul.

Yuval-Davis, N. (2006) 'Intersectionality and feminist politics'. *European Journal of
Women's Studies* **13**(3): 193–209.

Yuval-Davis, N. (2010) 'Theorizing identity: beyond the "us" and "them" dichotomy',
Patterns of Prejudice, **44**(3): 261–80.

Yuval-Davis, N. and Anthias, F. (eds) (1989) *Woman-Nation-State.* London: Macmillan.

Zaidi, A. and Burchardt, T. (2003) *Comparing Incomes when Needs Differ: Equivalisation
for the Extra Costs of Disability in the UK.* Centre for Analysis of Social Exclusion.
London: London School of Economics.

Zweig, F. (1961) *The Worker in an Affluent Society.* London: Heinemann.

Index